CHILDREN'S WRITER'S & ILLUSTRATOR'S MARKET
2017

includes a one-year online subscription to **Children's Writer's & Illustrator's Market** on

Where & How to Sell What You Write

THE ULTIMATE MARKET RESEARCH TOOL FOR WRITERS

To register your *Children's Writer's & Illustrator's Market 2017* book and **start your one-year online genre-only subscription**, scratch off the block below to reveal your activation code, then go to www.WritersMarket.com. Find the box that says "Purchased a Deluxe Edition?" then click on "Activate Your Account" and enter the activation code. It's that easy!

UPDATED MARKET LISTINGS FOR YOUR INTEREST AREA

EASY-TO-USE SEARCHABLE DATABASE • RECORD-KEEPING TOOLS

PROFESSIONAL TIPS & ADVICE • INDUSTRY NEWS

Your purchase of *Children's Writer's & Illustrator's Market* gives you access to updated listings related to this genre of writing (valid through 12/31/17). For just $9.99, you can upgrade your subscription and get access to listings from all of our best-selling Market Books. Visit **www.WritersMarket.com** for more information.

WritersMarket.com
Where & How to Sell What You Write

Activate your WritersMarket.com subscription to get instant access to:

- **UPDATED LISTINGS IN YOUR WRITING GENRE:** Find additional listings that didn't make it into the book, updated contact information, and more. WritersMarket.com provides the most comprehensive database of verified markets available anywhere.

- **EASY-TO-USE SEARCHABLE DATABASE:** Looking for a specific magazine or book publisher? Just type in its name. Or widen your prospects with the Advanced Search. You can also search for listings that have been recently updated!

- **PERSONALIZED TOOLS:** Store your best-bet markets, and use our popular recording-keeping tools to track your submissions. Plus, get new and updated market listings, query reminders, and more every time you log in!

- **PROFESSIONAL TIPS & ADVICE:** From pay-rate charts to sample query letters, and from how-to articles to Q&As with literary agents, we have the resources writers need.

YOU'LL GET ALL OF THIS WITH YOUR INCLUDED SUBSCRIPTION TO

WritersMarket.com
Where & How to Sell What You Write

CWIM17

CHILDREN'S WRITER'S & ILLUSTRATOR'S MARKET

◀ 29ᵀᴴ ANNUAL EDITION ▶

CHILDREN'S WRITER'S & ILLUSTRATOR'S MARKET

2017

Chuck Sambuchino, Editor
Nancy Parish, Contributing Editor

WD
WRITER'S DIGEST
BOOKS

WritersDigest.com
Cincinnati, Ohio

Children's Writer's & Illustrator's Market 2017. Copyright © 2016 F+W Media. Published by Writer's Digest Books, an imprint of F+W, 10151 Carver Road, Suite 200, Blue Ash, Ohio 45242. Printed and bound in the United States of America. All rights reserved. No part of this book may be reproduced in any form or by any electronic or mechanical means, including information storage and retrieval systems, without permission in writing from the publisher, except by a reviewer, who may quote brief passages in a review.

Publisher: Phil Sexton

Writer's Market website: www.writersmarket.com
Writer's Digest website: www.writersdigest.com

Distributed in Canada by Fraser Direct
100 Armstrong Avenue
Georgetown, Ontario, Canada L7G 5S4
Tel: (905) 877-4411

Distributed in the U.K. and Europe by F&W Media International
Brunel House, Newton Abbot, Devon, TQ12 4PU, England
Tel: (+44) 1626-323200, Fax: (+44) 1626-323319
E-mail: postmaster@davidandcharles.co.uk

ISSN: 0897-9790
ISBN-13: 978-1-4403-4777-1
ISBN-10: 1-4403-4777-8

Attention Booksellers: This is an annual directory of F+W Media.
Return deadline for this edition is December 31, 2017.

Edited by: Chuck Sambuchino
Designed by: Claudean Wheeler
Production coordinated by: Debbie Thomas

CONTENTS

FROM THE EDITOR

I'm pumped, and you should be, too. Why? Because we have a fantastic roundup of author (and illustrator) interviews in this edition of *Children's Writer's & Illustrator's Market*. There's Rainbow Rowell, whose young adult novels are amazing and touching; Salina Yoon, whose heartfelt picture books I read to my own three-year-old every week; Victoria Aveyard, whose breakout young adult novel *Red Queen* will be a major motion picture one day, I'm convinced; and many more. Read these great interviews and soak in successful author advice. Learn from their journeys.

Thank you for picking up the 29th annual edition of *CWIM*. We've got oodles of kidlit markets for you to check out. In these pages, you'll find plenty of newly added publishers (based in the U.S., Canada, and elsewhere) seeking submissions, up-and-coming literary agents actively building their client lists, and lots more. But before you review this guide's many listings, check out our instructional articles on topics such as creating a compelling fantasy novel, understanding the differences between middle-grade and young adult, and avoiding query letter pitfalls and pet peeves. These articles will strengthen your chances of success.

Please stay in touch with me at www.guidetoliteraryagents.com/blog and on Twitter (@chucksambuchino). I love hearing feedback and success stories. And don't forget to download your free supplemental webinar at www.writersmarket.com/cwim17-webinar.

Chuck Sambuchino
literaryagent@fwmedia.com; chucksambuchino.com
Editor, *Guide to Literary Agents/Children's Writer's & Illustrator's Market*
Author, *Get a Literary Agent* (2015)/*Create Your Writer Platform* (2012)

HOW TO USE *CWIM*

Maximize your education.

//

As a writer, illustrator, or photographer first picking up *Children's Writer's & Illustrator's Market*, you may not know quite how to start using the book. Your impulse may be to flip through the book and quickly make a mailing list, then submit to everyone in hopes that someone will take interest in your work. Well, there's more to it. Finding the right market takes research. The more you know about a market that interests you, the better chance you have of getting work accepted. We've made your job a little easier by putting a wealth of information at your fingertips. Besides providing listings, this directory has a number of tools to help you determine which markets are the best ones for your work. By using these tools, as well as researching on your own, you raise your odds of being published.

USING THE INDEXES

This book lists hundreds of potential buyers of material. To learn which companies want the type of material you're interested in submitting, start with the indexes.

Editor and agent names index

This index lists book editors, magazine editors, art directors, agents, and art reps—indicating the companies they work for. Use this specific index to find company and contact information for individual publishing professionals.

Age-level index

Age groups are broken down into these categories in the Age-Level Index:

- **PICTURE BOOKS OR PICTURE-ORIENTED MATERIAL** are written and illustrated for preschoolers to eight-year-olds.
- **YOUNG READERS** are for five- to eight-year-olds.
- **MIDDLE READERS** are for nine- to eleven-year-olds.

- **YOUNG ADULT** is for ages twelve and up.

Age breakdowns may vary slightly from publisher to publisher, but using them as general guidelines will help you target appropriate markets. For example, if you've written an article about trends in teen fashion, check the Magazines Age-Level Index under the Young Adult subheading.

Subject index

But let's narrow the search further. Take your list of young adult magazines, turn to the Subject Index, and find the Fashion subheading. Then highlight the names that appear on both lists (Young Adult and Fashion). Now you have a smaller list of all the magazines that would be interested in your teen fashion article. Read through those listings and decide which seem (or look) best for your work.

Illustrators and photographers can use the Subject Index as well. If you specialize in painting animals, for instance, consider sending samples to book and magazine publishers listed under Animals and, perhaps, Nature/Environment. Because illustrators can simply send general examples of their style to art directors to keep on file, the indexes may be more helpful to artists sending manuscript/illustration packages who need to search for a specific subject. Always read the listings for the potential markets to see the type of work art directors prefer and what type of samples they'll keep on file, and obtain art or photo guidelines if they're available online.

Photography index

In this index, you'll find lists of book and magazine publishers that buy photos from freelancers. Refer to the list and read the listings for companies' specific photography needs. Obtain photo guidelines if they're offered online.

USING THE LISTINGS

Some listings begin with symbols. Many listings indicate whether submission guidelines are indeed available. If a publisher you're interested in offers guidelines, get them and read them. The same is true with catalogs. Sending for and reading catalogs or browsing them online gives you a better idea of whether your work would fit in with the books a publisher produces. (You should also look at a few of the books in the catalog at a library or bookstore to get a feel for the publisher's material.)

A note for artists & photographers

Along with information for writers, listings provide information for illustrators and photographers. Illustrators will find numerous markets that maintain files of samples for possible future assignments. If you're both a writer and an illustrator, look for markets that accept manuscript/illustration packages and read the information offered under the **Illustration** subhead within the listings.

If you're a photographer, after consulting the Photography Index, read the information under the **Photography** subhead within listings to see what format buyers prefer. For example, some want the highest resolution .JPG available of an image. Note the type of photos a buyer wants to purchase and the procedures for submitting. It's not uncommon for a market to want a résumé and promotional literature, as well as sample URLs linking to previous work. Listings also note whether model releases and/or captions are required.

QUICK TIPS FOR WRITERS & ILLUSTRATORS

If you're new to the world of children's publishing, reviewing this edition of *Children's Writer's & Illustrator's Market* may have been one of the first steps in your journey to publication. What follows is a list of suggestions and resources that can help make that journey a smooth and swift one:

1. MAKE THE MOST OF *CHILDREN'S WRITER'S & ILLUSTRATOR'S MARKET*. Be sure to take advantage of the articles and interviews in the book. The insights of the authors, illustrators, editors, and agents we've interviewed will inform and inspire you.

2. JOIN THE SOCIETY OF CHILDREN'S BOOK WRITERS AND ILLUSTRATORS. SCBWI, more than 22,000 members strong, is an organization for both beginners and professionals interested in writing and illustrating for children, with more than seventy active regional chapters worldwide. It offers members a slew of information and support through publications, a website, and a host of Regional Advisors overseeing chapters in almost every state in the US and a growing number of locations around the globe. SCBWI puts on a number of conferences, workshops, and events on the regional and national levels (many listed in the Conferences & Workshops section of this book). For more information, visit www.scbwi.org.

3. READ NEWSLETTERS. Newsletters, such as *Children's Book Insider*, *Children's Writer* and the *SCBWI Bulletin*, offer updates and new information about publishers on a timely basis and are relatively inexpensive. Many local chapters of SCBWI offer regional newsletters as well.

4. READ TRADE AND REVIEW PUBLICATIONS. Magazines such as *Publishers Weekly* (which offers two special issues each year devoted to children's publishing and is available on newsstands as well as through a digital subscription) offer news, articles, reviews of newly published titles, and ads featuring upcoming and current releases. Referring to them will help you get a feel for what's happening in children's publishing.

5. READ GUIDELINES. Most publishers and magazines offer writers' and artists' guidelines that provide detailed information on needs and submission requirements, and some magazines offer theme lists for upcoming issues. Many publishers and magazines state the availability of guidelines within their listings. You'll often find submission information on publishers' and magazines' websites.

6. LOOK AT PUBLISHERS' CATALOGS. Perusing publishers' catalogs can give you a feel for their line of books and help you decide where your work might fit in. If catalogs are available (often stated within listings), visit publishers' websites, which often contain their full catalogs. You can also ask librarians to look at catalogs they have on hand. You can even search Amazon.com by publisher and year. (Click on "book search" then "publisher, date" and plug in, for example, "Lee & Low" under *publisher* and "2016" under *year*. You'll get a list of Lee & Low titles published in 2016, which you can peruse.)

7. VISIT BOOKSTORES. It's not only informative to spend time in bookstores—it's fun, too! Frequently visit the children's section of your local bookstore (whether a chain or an independent) to see the latest from a variety of publishers and the most current issues of children's magazines. Look for books in the genre you're writing or with illustrations similar in style to yours, and spend some time studying them. It's also wise to get to know your local booksellers; they can tell you what's new in the store and provide insight into what kids and adults are buying.

8. READ, READ, READ! While you're at that bookstore, pick up a few things, or keep a list of the books that interest you and check them out of your library. Read and study the latest releases, the award winners and the classics. You'll learn from other writers, get ideas, and get a feel for what's being published. Think about what works and doesn't work in a story. Pay attention to how plots are constructed and how characters are developed, or the rhythm and pacing of picture book text. It's certainly enjoyable research!

9. TAKE ADVANTAGE OF INTERNET RESOURCES. There are innumerable sources of information available online about writing for children (and anything else you could possibly think of). It's also a great resource for getting (and staying) in touch with other writers and illustrators through listservs, blogs, social networking sites, and e-mail, and it can serve as a vehicle for self-promotion.

10. CONSIDER ATTENDING A CONFERENCE. If time and finances allow, attending a writers conference is a great way to meet peers and network with professionals in the field of children's publishing. As mentioned earlier, SCBWI offers conferences in various locations year round. (See scbwi.org and click on "Events" for a full conference calendar.) General writers' conferences often offer specialized sessions just for those interested in children's writing. Many conferences offer optional manuscript and portfolio critiques as well, giving you feedback from seasoned professionals. See the Conferences section of this book for information on conferences.

11. NETWORK, NETWORK, NETWORK! Don't work in a vacuum. You can meet other writers and illustrators through a number of the things listed earlier—SCBWI, conferences, online. Attend local meetings for writers and illustrators whenever you can. Befriend other writers in your area (SCBWI offers members a roster broken down by state)—share guidelines, share subscriptions, be conference buddies and roommates, join a critique group or writing group, exchange information, and offer support. Get online—sign on to listservs, post on message boards and blogs, visit social networking sites and chatrooms. Exchange addresses, phone numbers, and e-mail addresses with writers or illustrators you meet at events. And at conferences, don't be afraid to talk to people, ask strangers to join you for lunch, approach speakers and introduce yourself, or chat in elevators and hallways.

12. PERFECT YOUR CRAFT AND DON'T SUBMIT UNTIL YOUR WORK IS AT ITS BEST. It's often been said that a writer should try to write every day. Great manuscripts don't happen overnight; there's time, research, and revision involved. As you visit bookstores and study what others have written and illustrated, really step back and look at your own work and ask yourself, *How does my work measure up? Is it ready for editors or art directors to see?* If it's not, keep working. Join a critique group or get a professional manuscript or portfolio critique.

13. BE PATIENT, LEARN FROM REJECTION, AND DON'T GIVE UP! Thousands of manuscripts land on editors' desks; thousands of illustration samples line art directors' file drawers. There are so many factors that come into play when evaluating submissions. Keep in mind that you might not hear back from publishers promptly. Persistence and patience are important qualities in writers and illustrators working toward publication. Keep at it—it will come. It can take a while, but when you get that first book contract or first assignment, you'll know it was worth the wait. (For proof, read the "First Books / Debut Authors" article later in this book!)

BEFORE YOUR
FIRST SALE

If you're just beginning to pursue your career as a children's book writer or illustrator, it's important to learn the proper procedures, formats, and protocol for the publishing industry. This article outlines the basics you need to know before you submit your work to a market.

FINDING THE BEST MARKETS FOR YOUR WORK

Researching markets thoroughly is a basic element of submitting your work successfully. Editors and art directors hate to receive inappropriate submissions; handling them wastes a lot of their time, not to mention your time and money, and they are the main reason some publishers have chosen not to accept material over the transom. By randomly sending out material without knowing a company's needs, you're sure to meet with rejection.

If you're interested in submitting to a particular magazine, see if it's available in your local library or bookstore, or read past articles online. For a book publisher, obtain a book catalog and check a library or bookstore for titles produced by that publisher. Most publishers and magazines have websites that include catalogs or sample articles (websites are given within the listings). Studying such materials carefully will better acquaint you with a publisher's or magazine's writing, illustration, and photography styles and formats.

Many of the book publishers and magazines listed in this book offer some sort of writers', artists', or photographers' guidelines on their websites. It's important to read and study guidelines before submitting work. You'll get a better understanding of what a particular publisher wants. You may even decide, after reading the submission guidelines, that your work isn't right for a company you considered.

SUBMITTING YOUR WORK

Throughout the listings, you'll read requests for particular elements to include when contacting markets. Here are explanations of some of these important submission components.

Queries, cover letters, & proposals

A query is a no-more-than-one-page, well-written letter meant to arouse an editor's interest in your work. Query letters briefly outline the work you're proposing and include facts, anecdotes, interviews, or other pertinent information that give the editor a feel for the manuscript's premise—enticing her to want to know more. End your letter with a straight-forward request to submit the work, and include information on its approximate length, date it could be completed, and whether accompanying photos or artwork are available.

In a query letter, think about presenting your book as a publisher's catalog would present it. Read through a good catalog and examine how the publishers give enticing summaries of their books in a spare amount of words. It's also important that query letters give editors a taste of your writing style. For good advice and samples of queries, cover letters, and other correspondence, consult the article "Crafting a Query" in this book, as well as *Formatting & Submitting Your Manuscript, 3rd Ed.* and *The Writer's Digest Guide to Query Letters* (both Writer's Digest Books).

- **QUERY LETTERS FOR NONFICTION.** Queries are usually required when submitting nonfiction material to a publisher. The goal of a nonfiction query is to convince the editor your idea is perfect for her readership and that you're qualified to do the job. Note any previous writing experience and include published samples to prove your credentials, especially samples related to the subject matter you're querying about.
- **QUERY LETTERS FOR FICTION.** For a fiction query, explain the story's plot, main characters, conflict, and resolution. Just as in nonfiction queries, make the editor eager to see more.
- **COVER LETTERS FOR WRITERS.** Some editors prefer to review complete manuscripts, especially for picture books or fiction. In such cases, the cover letter (which should be no longer than one page) serves as your introduction, establishes your credentials as a writer, and gives the editor an overview of the manuscript. If the editor asked for the manuscript because of a query, note this in your cover letter.
- **COVER LETTERS FOR ILLUSTRATORS AND PHOTOGRAPHERS.** For an illustrator or photographer, the cover letter serves as an introduction to the art director and es-tablishes professional credentials when submitting samples. Explain what services you can provide as well as what type of follow-up contact you plan to make, if any. Be sure to include the URL of your online portfolio if you have one.
- **RÉSUMÉS.** Often writers, illustrators, and photographers submit résumés with cover letters and samples. They can be created in a variety of formats, from a single-page listing information to color brochures featuring your work. Keep your résumé brief, and focus on your achievements, including your clients and the work you've done for them, as well as your educational background and any awards you've received. Do not use the same résumé you'd use for a typical job application.

- **BOOK PROPOSALS.** Throughout the listings in the Book Publishers section, listings refer to submitting a synopsis, outline, and sample chapters. Depending on an editor's preference, some or all of these components, along with a cover letter, make up a book proposal.

A *synopsis* summarizes the book, covering the basic plot (including the ending). It should be easy to read and flow well. The gold standard for synopsis length is one page, single-spaced.

An *outline* covers your book chapter by chapter and provides highlights of each. If you're developing an outline for fiction, include major characters, plots, and subplots, and book length. Requesting an outline is uncommon, and the word is somewhat interchangeable with *synopsis*.

Sample chapters give a more comprehensive idea of your writing skill. Some editors may request the first two or three chapters to determine if they're interested in seeing the whole book. Some may request a set number of pages.

Manuscript formats

When submitting a complete manuscript, follow some basic guidelines. In the upper-left corner of your title page, type your legal name (not pseudonym), address, and phone number. In the upper-right corner, type the approximate word count. All material in the upper corners should be single-spaced. Then type the title (centered) almost halfway down that page, the word "by" two lines under that, and your name or pseudonym two lines under "by."

The first page should also include the title (centered) one-third of the way down. Two lines under that, type "by" and your name or pseudonym. To begin the body of your manuscript, drop down two double spaces and indent five spaces for each new paragraph. There should be one-inch margins around all sides of a full page. (Manuscripts with wide margins are more readable and easier to edit.)

Set your computer to double-space the manuscript body. From page two to the end of the manuscript, include your last name followed by a comma and the title (or key words of the title) in the upper-left corner. The page number should go in the top right corner. Drop down two double spaces to begin the body of each page. If you're submitting a novel, type each chapter title one-third of the way down the page. For more information on manuscript formats, read *Formatting & Submitting Your Manuscript, 3rd Ed.* (Writer's Digest Books).

Picture book formats

The majority of editors prefer to see complete manuscripts for picture books. When typing the text of a picture book, don't indicate page breaks and don't type each page of text on a new sheet of paper. And unless you are an illustrator, don't worry about supplying art. Editors will find their own illustrators for picture books. Most of the time, a writer and an illustrator who work on the same book never meet or interact. The editor acts as a go-between who works with the writer and illustrator throughout the publishing process. *How to Write and Sell Children's Picture Books* by Jean E. Karl (Writer's Digest Books) offers advice on preparing text and marketing your work.

If you're an illustrator who has written your own book, consider creating a dummy or storyboard containing both art and text, and then submit it along with your complete manuscript and sample pieces of final art (hi-res PDFs or .JPGs—never originals). Publishers interested in picture books specify in their listings what should be submitted. For tips on creating a dummy, refer to *How to Write and Illustrate Children's Books and Get Them Published*, edited by Treld Pelkey Bicknell and Felicity Trotman (North Light Books), or Frieda Gates' book, *How to Write, Illustrate, and Design Children's Books* (Lloyd-Simone Publishing Company).

Writers may also want to learn the art of dummy-making to help them through the writing process with things like pacing, rhythm, and length. For a great explanation and helpful hints, see *You Can Write Children's Books*, by Tracey E. Dils (Writer's Digest Books).

Mailing submissions

Your main concern when packaging material is to be sure it arrives undamaged. If your manuscript is fewer than six pages, simply fold it in thirds and send it in a #10 (business-size) envelope. For a SASE, either fold another #10 envelope in thirds or insert a #9 (reply) envelope, which fits in a #10 neatly without folding.

Another option is folding your manuscript in half in a 6x9 envelope, with a #9 or #10 SASE enclosed. For larger manuscripts, use a 9x12 envelope both for mailing the submission and as a SASE (which can be folded in half). Book manuscripts require sturdy packaging for mailing. Include a self-addressed mailing label and return postage. If asked to send artwork and photographs, remember they require a bit more care in packaging to guarantee they arrive in good condition. Sandwich illustrations and photos between heavy cardboard that is slightly larger than the work. The cardboard can be secured by rubber bands or with tape. If you tape the cardboard together, check that the artwork doesn't stick to the tape. Be sure your name and address appear on the back of each piece of art or each photo in case the material becomes separated. For the packaging, use either a manila envelope, a foam-padded envelope, or a mailer lined with plastic air bubbles. Bind nonjoined edges with reinforced mailing tape and affix a typed mailing label or clearly write your address.

Mailing material first class ensures quick delivery. Also, first-class mail is forwarded for one year if the addressee has moved, and it can be returned if undeliverable. If you're concerned about your original material reaching its destination, consider other mailing options such as UPS. No matter which way you send material, never send it in a way that requires a signature for receipt. Agents and editors are too busy to sign for packages.

Remember, companies outside your own country can't use your country's postage when returning a manuscript to you. When mailing a submission to another country, include a self-addressed envelope and International Reply Coupons, or IRCs. (You'll see this term in many listings in the Canadian & International Book Publishers section.) Your postmaster can tell you, based on a package's weight, the correct number of IRCs to include to ensure its return. If it's not necessary for an editor to return your work (such as with photocopies), don't include return postage.

Unless requested, it's never a good idea to use a company's fax number to send manuscript submissions. This can disrupt a company's internal business. Study the listings for specifics and visit publisher and market websites for more information.

E-mailing submissions

Most correspondence with editors today is handled over e-mail. This type of communication is usually preferred by publishing professionals because it is easier to deal with as well as free. When sending an e-mailed submission, make sure to follow submission guidelines. Double-check the recipient's e-mail address. Make sure your subject line has the proper wording, if specific wording is requested. Keep your introduction letter short and sweet. Also, editors and agents usually do not like opening unsolicited attachments, which makes for an awkward situation for illustrators who want to attach .jpgs. One easy way around this is to post some sample illustrations on your website. That way, you can simply paste URL hyperlinks to your work. Editors can click through to look over your illustration samples, and there is no way your submission will be deleted because of attachments. That said, if editors are asking for illustration samples, they are most likely used to receiving unsolicited attachments.

Keeping submission records

It's important to keep track of the material you submit. When recording each submission, include the date it was sent, the business and contact name, and any enclosures (such as samples of writing, artwork or photography). You can create a record-keeping system of your own or look for record-keeping software in your area computer store.

Keep copies of articles or manuscripts you send together with related correspondence to make follow-up easier. When you sell rights to a manuscript, artwork, or photos, you can "close" your file on a particular submission by noting the date the material was accepted, what rights were purchased, the publication date, and payment.

Often writers, illustrators, and photographers fail to follow up on overdue responses. If you don't hear from a publisher within their stated response time, wait another month or so and follow up with an e-mail asking about the status of your submission. Include the title or description, date sent, and a SASE (if applicable) for response. Ask the contact person when she anticipates making a decision. You may refresh the memory of a buyer who temporarily forgot about your submission. At the very least, you will receive a definite "no" and free yourself to send the material to another publisher.

Simultaneous submissions

Writers and illustrators are encouraged to simultaneously submit—sending the same material to several markets at the same time. Almost all markets are open to this type of communication; those that do not take simultaneous submissions will directly say so in their submission guidelines.

It's especially important to keep track of simultaneous submissions, so if you get an offer on a manuscript sent to more than one publisher, you can instruct other publishers to withdraw your work from consideration. (Or, you can always use the initial offer as a way to ignite interest from other agents and editors. It's very possible to procure multiple offers on your book using this technique.)

AGENTS & ART REPS

Most children's writers, illustrators, and photographers, especially those just beginning, are confused about whether to enlist the services of an agent or representative. The decision is strictly one that each writer, illustrator, or photographer must make for herself. Some are confident with their own negotiation skills and believe acquiring an agent or rep is not in their best interest. Others feel uncomfortable in the business arena or are not willing to sacrifice valuable creative time for marketing.

About half of children's publishers accept unagented work, so it's possible to break into children's publishing without an agent. Writers targeting magazine markets don't need the services of an agent. In fact, it's practically impossible to find an agent interested in marketing articles and short stories—there simply isn't enough financial incentive.

One benefit of having an agent, though, is it may speed up the process of getting your work reviewed, especially by publishers who don't accept unagented submissions. If an agent has a good reputation and submits your manuscript to an editor, that manuscript will likely bypass the first-read stage (which is generally done by editorial assistants and junior editors) and end up on the editor's desk sooner.

When agreeing to have a reputable agent represent you, remember that she should be familiar with the needs of the current market and evaluate your manuscript/artwork/ photos accordingly. She should also determine the quality of your piece and whether it is salable. When your manuscript sells, your agent should negotiate a favorable contract and clear up any questions you have about payments.

Keep in mind that no matter how reputable the agent or rep is, she has limitations. Representation does not guarantee sale of your work. It just means an agent or rep sees potential in your writing, art, or photos. Though an agent or rep may offer criticism or advice on how to improve your work, she cannot make you a better writer, artist, or photographer.

Literary agents typically charge a fifteen percent commission from the sale of writing; art and photo representatives usually charge a twenty five or thirty percent commission. Such fees are taken from advances and royalty earnings. If your agent sells foreign rights or film rights to your work, she will deduct a higher percentage because she will most likely be dealing with an overseas agent with whom she must split the fee.

Be advised that not every agent is open to representing a writer, artist, or photographer who lacks an established track record. Just as when approaching a publisher, the manuscript, artwork, or photos, and query or cover letter you submit to a potential agent must be attractive and professional looking. Your first impression must be as an organized, articulate person. For listings of agents and reps, turn to the Agents & Art Reps section.

For additional listings of art reps, consult *Artist's & Graphic Designer's Market*; for photo reps, see *Photographer's Market*; for more information and additional listings of literary agents, see *Guide to Literary Agents* (all Writer's Digest Books).

BE YOUR OWN LITERARY AGENT

A roundtable on bypassing representation.

by JoAnn Early Macken

Plenty of authors—either by choice or by default—submit their work directly to children's book editors without the assistance of a literary agent. Since unagented writers act as their own advocates, knowing the market is critical to their success; thus, these writers must go out of their way to educate themselves and organize their submission process.

Because many publishers don't accept unsolicited submissions, unagented writers are limited in the number of markets they can target. One way around the restriction is to attend conferences where editors from closed houses speak. Usually, these editors allow attendees to personally pitch them their projects, and if an agent is interested, he will request that the author submit the manuscript. Of my five published picture books, three offers resulted from critiques or meetings with editors at SCBWI regional events. Another followed after I met an editor at a small group retreat.

I've never worked with an agent, although I've queried several. Most of those who responded do not love rhyming picture books, nonfiction, and poetry as much as I do, so I handle my own submissions. And I'm not alone. I spoke with four other children's book authors who have successfully marketed their own manuscripts without the help of an agent.

JANET HALFMANN (www.janethalfmann.com), who grew up on a farm in Michigan and now lives with her husband in South Milwaukee, is an award-winning author of forty fiction and nonfiction children's books. Halfmann writes picture books about nature and animals, including *Grandma Is a Slowpoke* (2016, Star Bright Books), which was inspired by walks with her grandchildren. She also writes about little-known historical figures who have accomplished amazing feats, such as Robert Smalls in *Seven Miles to Freedom: The Robert Smalls Story* (2012, Lee & Low Books). When Halfmann isn't writing, she enjoys gardening, exploring nature, visiting museums, and spending time with her family.

LISA MOSER (www.lisamoserbooks.com) is the author of nine picture books and easy readers. She was a Picture Book Mentor for SCBWI in 2012 and 2014. Before becoming a children's book author, Moser was a fifth-grade teacher who taught reading, writing, and other required subjects. Moser's newest book is *Stories from Bug Garden* (2016, Candlewick).

MARY ANN RODMAN (www.facebook.com/mary.ann.rodman) writes picture books and middle-grade and young adult historical fiction. For her first picture book, *My Best Friend*, she received the Ezra Jack Keats New Writer Award and the Charlotte Zolotow Award for the best picture book text published in the US. Her first middle-grade novel, *Yankee Girl*, was nominated for twelve state book awards. The Georgia Center for the Book named it one of "25 Books All Young Georgians Should Read." A former public, high school, and university librarian, Rodman conducts young author workshops in the Metro Atlanta area. She is a graduate of the Vermont College, with an MFA in writing for children and young adults.

GRETCHEN WOELFLE (www.gretchenwoelfle.com) is the award-winning author of fiction and nonfiction books for young readers, including *All the World's A Stage: A Novel in Five Acts*; *Write On, Mercy! The Secret Life of Mercy Otis Warren*; and *Mumbet's Declaration of Independence*. Her latest book is a group biography, *Answering the Cry for Freedom: Stories of African Americans and the American Revolution*. When she is not traveling the world hunting for stories, she lives in Los Angeles.

As writers, we're well-versed in research. When researching the submission process, which do you look for first, a publisher or an editor?

HALFMANN: I look for a publisher first. I keep a list of publishers that publish the kinds of books I write, with brief notes about what they or their editors are looking for. I've found publishers through *Children's Writer's & Illustrator's Market* (CWIM), SCBWI's Market Surveys, *Book Markets for Children's Writers*, the market news features of the *SCBWI Bulletin* and *Children's Book Insider*, and other online lists. Every time I see a new publisher mentioned anywhere, I check out its website to see if it's one that I would want to submit to.

If a publisher says to submit to its acquisitions editor or someone similar rather than to [a specific] individual, I usually do that. If a contact is not specified, I research the editors listed in the SCBWI Market Survey. I search online and in the SCBWI "Edited by" listing to find out what kinds of books each editor likes.

MOSER: I've had the blessing to work with some really wonderful editors. Like friends, I've met them in all sorts of different ways. I met one editor at a writing retreat, and she ended up publishing the story I submitted for critique and two others. I met another editor at an SCBWI conference, and she published a story I submitted through the conference guidelines. A dear friend put me in touch with another editor who was a great mentor to me in the beginning years. The editor has retired, but I now work with another incredible editor at that house.

RODMAN: Step one: Submit to editors who have bought my work in the past. (I am obligated by two publishers to give them the right of first refusal.)

Step two: If rejected, I turn to my "bible," *CWIM*. I know the market well, so I know which publishers would like my style and genre. I check to see if the publisher still takes unsolicited manuscripts. Then I go to my "master list" of books and writers whose style and genre are similar to mine. My list includes the name of the acquiring editor, which I find in a book's acknowledgments (and also the [name of the] agent, just in case I need it someday). Because the publishing world is so fluid, I check *CWIM* to make sure that editor is still with the house. My final step is to search *Publishers Weekly* (PW) for the editor. PW's official website, www.publishersweekly.com, updates job changes almost daily. This is how I found out that one of my favorite editors had not only changed houses but had gotten married and changed her name.

I sold my picture book *First Grade Stinks* to an editor who critiqued my work at a regional SCBWI conference. I went all the way to Wisconsin to sell a book to a publisher twenty miles from my home in Atlanta.

WOELFLE: Networking is huge for me. I've been in this business since 1994 and have met a lot of writers and editors along the way. I've sold several books to editors recommended to me by other authors. I look for publishers who publish the sort of books I write—picture book biographies, environmental nonfiction, middle-grade biographies, and fiction. I've worked with many editors, including Carolyn Yoder at Calkins Creek/Boyds Mills Press, for three books.

Once you've found an appropriate editor or publisher, how do you submit your work?

HALFMANN: Before submitting a manuscript, I always read the publisher's most recent guidelines online and follow them. When submitting to houses with which I have a relationship, I do what they prefer—some by e-mail and some by snail mail.

MOSER: If I know the editor, I usually submit via e-mail as they have requested. If I'm submitting to a new editor from a conference I attended, I follow the guidelines supplied.

RODMAN: First, I check *CWIM* [for how] to format. Some publishers want a query letter. Some want sample chapters. Some still insist on snail-mail submissions. Unless stipulated in CWIM that it is permissible, I would never make a first contact with an editor by e-mail. For the past five years, editors I have a working relationship with have been taking my work electronically. However, I made a point of asking them first.

WOELFLE: I submit a manuscript first to editors I've worked with in the past. To expand my list of contacts, I attend American Library Association conferences whenever they are within a few hundred miles of Los Angeles. I cruise the aisles looking at new books and chat up the staff if I've got something they might like. We exchange business cards, and I follow up before they even arrive home.

For record keeping, I'm a fan of Excel workbooks. I list editors in the first column and manuscripts across the top row. I enter the date submitted at the intersection and cross it out for a rejection.

How do you track your submissions?

HALFMANN: I keep a log in a folder for each of my manuscripts. It lists every publisher or editor to which that manuscript has been submitted and the outcome, along with dates and notes. The log also lists possible future publishers for that manuscript.

I also keep a list of all the publishers I have found that are matches for my work. For each publisher, I include a brief description of what the house and its editors are looking for, the names of editors I have submitted to, and brief guidelines. Under each publisher, I list submissions, with dates, outcomes, and notes. I also list other manuscripts suitable for the publisher. I also keep a file of all rejections/comments so I can look back at them for anything important to include in my next cover letter.

MOSER: I have a list of editors that I know, and I try very hard to fit the story I wrote with what the editor likes and may be looking for.

RODMAN: In my "master list," I keep track of which editor has what manuscript and the date sent. I am not so prolific that I have lots of different manuscripts out at any one time, but I do submit the same manuscript to three or four publishers at a time.

WOELFLE: I've got two spreadsheets. One contains every manuscript I send out with names, dates, etc. When I get an acceptance or rejection, I delete the entry. The second spreadsheet is dedicated to one story with a column for replies. This is a permanent document that tells me how many rejections I've received and how long I've been flogging the same story. It also suggests to me when to quit.

We've all seen contracts grow more complex over the years. Do you negotiate your own, or do you have help?

HALFMANN: I negotiate my own contracts. I research what to look for on the SCBWI website and other online writer sources.

MOSER: I do not have an agent, but I do have a fabulous literary lawyer. When the editor and I have worked through revisions and are at the point of signing a contract, I turn the negotiations over to my literary lawyer. We discuss the contract, what points we would like to negotiate, and our end goals. I pay my lawyer to negotiate the contract as I think it's best to remove myself from this portion of the process. She's the expert, after all. I get to skip the part I find the most difficult—negotiating—and it makes sense from a business standpoint.

RODMAN: With my first book, I became a member of the Authors Guild (www.authorsguild.org) because they offer free legal contract vetting. Four months after I sent them my contract, I received thirty-five suggestions for improving it. I narrowed the list to three or four important items. I talked to the contracts department by phone and came away with one major and one minor change. I was pretty pleased with myself as a first-time author.

However, I am not a terribly aggressive person. I also hate doing business by phone. So for the next book, I contacted a literary attorney. For a reasonable fee, she not only picked out the "bugs" in the contract, but negotiated the changes with the contracts department.

WOELFLE: I negotiate my own contracts with the help of the fabulous Authors Guild, which reviews members' contracts for free. I can never get all the changes they suggest, but there are some that I will fight for: additional free copies, a royalty escalation clause, rights to approve abridgements, a clear out-of-print definition, and maybe more.

One thing I love about submitting on my own is that I can send what I want when my writing group and I decide it's ready. I still agonize over the submission process, though, so I try to set aside time regularly to submit manuscripts and follow up on submissions. What do you find are the biggest obstacles and rewards of being your own agent?

HALFMANN: The biggest obstacle is that more and more publishers are becoming closed houses. I was lucky to get my foot in the door of some houses before they closed, so now I have a relationship with them. One of the biggest rewards of being my own agent is being able to work at my own pace and to write about exactly what I want.

MOSER: I'm a shy person, so it can be uncomfortable doing the "business" part of being my own agent—following up on stories, deciding when to submit elsewhere, etc. However, I had the chance to learn from the wonderful author Dori Chaconas, who is in my writing group. For many years, she sold a lot of books acting as her own agent. She found the same situations uncomfortable as I did, but she'd say, "Today I'm putting on my agent hat." Then she'd forge ahead and get things done. There are days when I just have to put on my agent hat and be a businessperson.

RODMAN: The biggest plus of representing myself is that I am in control. I am free to make my contacts with editors and submit to them. I also like knowing where a manuscript is at any time. I like getting my advances and royalties straight from the publisher.

Yes, I would love to find my Prince/Princess Charming Agent. I am still looking. Meanwhile, I am a one-woman operation.

WOELFLE: I've tried a couple of times to get an agent and find that they are not interested in nonfiction—there's so little money in it. Don't I know it! So I soldier on alone. I'm in charge of what goes out to whom, which is not a bad thing. More and more publishers only accept submissions from agents, but that hasn't bothered me. Most of the houses I prefer are smaller and open to all submissions. I probably wouldn't turn down an offer if an agent I respect came begging, but I'm content with my agentless writer's life.

JOANN EARLY MACKEN (www.joannmacken.com) is the author of five picture books, including *Baby Says "Moo!"*; *Waiting Out the Storm*; and *Flip, Float, Fly: Seeds on the Move*. She is also the author of the poetry guide *Write a Poem Step by Step* and more than 130 educational books for young readers. Her poems appear in many children's magazines and anthologies. JoAnn earned her MFA in writing for children and young adults from Vermont College of Fine Arts. She has taught writing at four Wisconsin colleges, contributes to TeachingAuthors (www.teachingauthors.com), and regularly speaks at schools, libraries, and conferences.

10 PICTURE BOOK PITFALLS

Learn common mistakes—and how to fix them.

....

by Marie Lamba

///

Picture books seem easy enough to write. They're short, have simple plots, and star a small cast of characters. So how difficult could it possibly be to write one that will capture the attention of a publisher?

More difficult than you think.

Picture books, being printed in full color and often in hardcover, are expensive to produce. Publishers will sink money only into stories they feel are exceptional enough to become profitable. As a literary agent, I get many picture book submissions from hopeful writers, yet few of these are what I'd call "book worthy" in the eyes of a publisher. It's not just new writers who miss the mark, but established authors as well. Writing an exceptional picture book is an art, and art does not come easy. Trust me, I know: I also write picture books myself.

Here are the ten picture book pitfalls I most often see in my submissions inbox. If you recognize your own work here, don't despair. I've also suggested fixes to help you transform your story into one that will be embraced by publishers and readers alike.

PITFALL NO. 1: THE SHTICK

Picture books suffering from The Shtick revolve around a zany idea or phrase, but don't go anywhere. They may lure you in by seeming "quirky"—a quality plenty of editors say they are seeking—but ultimately they lack substance.

Let's examine an unpublished manuscript titled *Monkey Feet and Peanut Butter Sandwiches*. The story hinges on a kid putting rubber gloves on her feet and pretending she's queen of the monkeys—and only on that. Basically, the author had a silly idea, but didn't take the next step to develop an interesting tale. Confession: I was the author! It was an early attempt, but fortunately, I learned from the fact that it never sold.

THE FIX: To combat The Shtick, describe your story in one sentence. Does it have a true arc—with a beginning, middle and end? It should. In revisiting my shticky manuscript, forcing myself to craft a one-liner with an actual plot might have yielded something like this: *A girl puts rubber gloves on her feet to become monkey queen, but when the monkeys discover the truth, she must find another way to fit in—even with the tiniest toes of all.* Hint: Try including "but when" in your one-liner. It will point you to a conflict to be worked out in your plot.

PITFALL NO. 2: GREAT CONCEPT, POOR EXECUTION

Sometimes a picture book's concept is something of high interest that could resonate with readers—so much so that the writer figures the concept alone is enough and drops the ball. Great concepts can deceive their creators into thinking, *It practically writes itself!* But no matter how strong the concept, it works only if it's carried out effectively.

I don't want to embarrass anyone from my query pile, so I'll use a made-up example: "A disabled girl who longs to be a ballerina realizes her dream." This has true heart, and represents a diverse character in a positive way. Plus, many girls love ballet. How could you go wrong?

Here's how: The writing could be dull without any interesting action. The tale could be told from the wrong point of view (say, an adult's). It could focus too much on the girl's disability and not enough on her dream. It could also be handled insensitively, with a condescending tone. Don't expect a great concept to sell itself. You still have work to do.

THE FIX: Ask yourself what aspect of your concept is most appealing to children, and make sure that is what you spotlight as central to the story—but, as with The Shtick, that it isn't the *whole* story. Support your concept with actions, characters, dialogue, and tone that honors its spirit.

PITFALL NO. 3: PREACHY TEACHY

I frequently get queries that say, "I want to teach kids it's important to do homework," or, "… to listen to their parents," or "… to give to charity." A lesson is not a picture book, and as soon as you try to cram a lesson down a kid's throat, your story will fail. But wait! Isn't the *point* to convey lessons to children?

That's a common misconception. Actually, the point is to write an entertaining story that resonates. If, through that story, readers get a gentle reinforcement about something that transcends the page, that's great.

The challenge, therefore, is to craft a book that'll be both meaningful *and* widely loved. Take one of my favorites, *The Hallo-Wiener* by Dav Pilkey. In it, Oscar the dachshund is teased and called "Wiener Dog" by the other dogs. Things don't improve when he's forced to wear a hotdog costume for Halloween, and his mother calls out, "Farewell, my little Vienna sausage!" But when those same dogs who teased him end up in trouble, Oscar saves the day, and gets a new nickname: "Hero Sandwich." Instead of harping on a "bullying is bad" lesson, this book humorously shows what being a true friend is all about.

What about nonfiction picture books? Aren't they *supposed* to teach something? Sure—but they still should have an entertaining story. *To the Stars*, co-authored by Dr. Kathy Sullivan and my client Carmella Van Vleet, shows how Dr. Sullivan became the first American woman to walk in space. The authors wisely pulled technical facts and details out of the main text, and instead included this info as interesting supplementary material in the back of the book (known as "back matter"). The end result, which *Kirkus* called "informative and inspiring," is a story focusing on how a little girl who wanted to see the entire world grew up to see it from space.

THE FIX: If your picture book's one-line description consists of a moral or lesson (e.g., "bullying is bad," "Indian culture is fascinating") then massage your concept to make sure a story with an entertaining and complete arc takes center stage. If there is a lesson, make it secondary and reveal it in a fresh way. If your story has an educational tie-in, consider whether pulling facts and figures out of your story and including those as back matter would help things flow better.

PITFALL NO. 4: NOT FOR KIDS

Picture books are for young children, right? Yet I get submissions about adult topics, such as financing an education, as well as those featuring inappropriate levels of romance or violence. Those obvious examples aside, sometimes a story that might otherwise be suitable for kids is ruined by having an adult point of view. These types of stories feel sentimental and nostalgic, and depict kids as precious and adorable. Picture books must tap into the way kids view themselves and the world. These stories should also relate to their emotional development.

There's a Nightmare in My Closet by Mercer Mayer does just that. A boy finds a monster in his closet, but the monster is just a big baby, and the child must tuck it into his own bed to stop it from crying. No precious adult point of view here. The book acknowledges a child's fear as big and ugly, then reduces it into something silly and easily handled. Note that the child is the one who saves the day; kids want to be the heroes of their own stories.

THE FIX: Really get to know your audience. Read up on the physical and emotional development stages of childhood. Spend time around children in your target group, and talk with teachers and children's librarians for further perspective. You might also volunteer to read picture books to kids at your local library, or attend a scheduled reading. You'll soon get a sense of what draws them in and what turns them off.

PITFALL NO. 5: RHYME WITHOUT REASON

Lots of writers feel compelled to force their story into rhyme. But in most cases, rhyme really doesn't belong there at all. The beat is off. Or if it isn't, it's because weird phrasing and meaningless filler words are used just to keep things bouncing along. It might look something like this:

> She stayed awake all through the night
>> She didn't see one single light
>> That is what happened all right
>> The day, by then, was really bright!

Rhyme works *only* when it adds something to the story. It should feel necessary and be pitch perfect. Take a look at this passage from Leah Komaiko's *Annie Bananie*, which features a best friend moving away and a girl talking about their unusual friendship:

> Made me brush my teeth with mud,
>> Sign my name in cockroach blood,
>> Tie my brother to the trees,
>> Made me tickle bumblebees,
>> Promised we would always play.
>> Now Annie Bananie's going away.

The words are unexpected yet fitting, funny yet touching. This is rhyming done well. When it does work, rhyme adds a fun element to read-alouds. But when it doesn't work, it's painful to the ear.

THE FIX: If you're writing in rhyme, ask someone else to read it aloud to you. Listen for moments when the beat is off or the reader stumbles over clunky phrasing. Then, re-evaluate your text. Is it filled with meaningless words just to keep the rhyme? Try telling the story without any rhyme at all—do you see an improvement? An in-between option is to ditch the poetry except for a brief rhyming refrain, which becomes a fun pattern throughout your tale.

PITFALL NO. 6: CAN'T PICTURE THAT

In picture books, illustrations are integral to the story, and something visually interesting must happen on every page. Sometimes manuscripts are filled only with abstract ideas, or with little action from scene to scene. And sometimes they're loaded with page after page of dry dialogue. Even if an agent or editor likes the story, she'll still be thinking: *How can anyone illustrate that?*

THE FIX: Imagine the story told only in pictures. Storyboard it in standard thirty-two-page picture book format by doodling each separate scene within your book onto large sticky notes. You don't need to be an artist to do this—stick figures work just fine. Now look at your images. Could an artist easily make them interesting? Do the pictures change enough from scene to scene? Is it hard to imagine what could possibly illustrate certain sections? Edit your story for better visual results, moving and changing your sticky notes. If a more visually engaging story emerges, see how you might revise your manuscript accordingly.

PITFALL NO. 7: WAY TOO MUCH

Picture books are trending shorter, ideally fewer than 500 words. Sometimes manuscripts much longer than that are absolutely perfect just the way they are—but more often, they suffer from Way-Too-Much-itis. This isn't the genre for a large cast of characters, frequent scene changes, or more than one main plot problem.

THE FIX: Cut, cut, cut! Anything that deviates from your central story must go. Ask: Is every character needed? Can one friend take the place of three? Can the story occur in one setting versus five? Can the story happen within a shorter time frame? Your job is to create one simple story line, elegantly told.

PITFALL NO. 8: BAIT AND SWITCH

These stories start off with a nice premise, and then suddenly shift characters, setting, plot, and even voice.

For example, say we begin with a young prince in need of his first haircut, but he doesn't want to go. Then the prince comes across trolls mining the countryside. Next thing you know, a giant stomps through and scares away the trolls. *Um, what?* In this case, the writer seems to have let his imagination take him on a wild ride, but lost the reader along the way.

THE FIX: Even if your creative mind wanders, your story shouldn't. Look at the start of your book and ask: *What is the story you are setting the reader up for? Who is the main character and what is the main problem?* That is the tale you are promising the reader. Be sure you deliver *that* story.

PITFALL NO. 9: CHARACTER CRAZE

In this type of manuscript, there's an adorable character. She's funny, she's cranky, she's mischievous. Oh, look at her eat! Look at her dance! My goodness, just look at what she's wearing now!

I don't care if this is the cutest little bunny or the sassiest bulldog or the funkiest four-year-old ever—this isn't a book. It's a *character*. Illustrators who want to write their own stories often fall into this trap. They can create a fun and engaging hero and plug her into different settings, but a picture book needs much more.

THE FIX: A character isn't a story, but a character *reacting to a conflict* is. If your starting point is a fussy elephant named Meg, you might turn that into a plot by brainstorming what might truly challenge her fussy nature. What if she must work with someone who's even fussier? Think of the different reactions she might have to the problem, and how the experience might change her. You'll soon see a story emerge.

PITFALL NO. 10: BEEN DONE BEFORE

A boy wants a pet. A mother so loves her baby. A sibling is jealous. Someone is afraid of the first day of school. All of these stories have already been written. And many get rejected because nothing new is shown.

But hasn't *every* story been done before? You can certainly argue that. There are archetypal experiences we all share, and we do keep coming back to certain tales again and again. The trick, though, is to be sure your picture book is original and told in a fresh way.

THE FIX: If you're starting from a been-done trope, try asking, "What if ...?". *What if a dog wanted a pet boy? What if a Cinderella story was told from the glass shoe salesman's point of view?* Study up on similar books, reading as many as you can. Also, for $25 a month you can subscribe to www.publishersmarketplace.com and browse the recent deals. This will show what books like yours may be coming out within the next couple of years. Armed with this info, you can better craft your story with a unique angle.

Ultimately, these fixes should help you do what you set out to do: Zero in on the heart of your story, and connect with what's really important to children. That's how you capture the interest of publishers—and the hearts of young readers.

MARIE LAMBA (www.marielamba.com) is author of the young adult novels *What I Meant ...*, *Over My Head*, and *Drawn*, as well as the upcoming picture book *Green, Green*. She's also an associate literary agent at The Jennifer De Chiara Literary Agency (www.jdlit.com).

PITCH AGENTS THROUGH TWITTER

Agents love online pitch parties.

....

by Lisa Katzenberger

The publishing industry has embraced Twitter with open arms, and it's time for you to join the party. If you're an aspiring writer looking to secure an agent, Twitter is absolutely the easiest, quickest, and most impactful way to connect with the gatekeepers of the publishing industry.

Twitter is not just for tech-savvy professionals, young adults, extroverts, or folks with too much to say. It's a free, easy-to-use communication platform accessible to—and welcoming of—everyone. And while Twitter is a viable tool for getting a literary agent, that doesn't mean it can't also be fun.

The key to a successful Twitter experience is who you follow; in other words, whose status updates you will be able to read in your Twitter feed. To get started, create your profile and Twitter handle, and then determine who to follow. Start with your favorite writers, and then search for agents, editors, publishing houses, and bookstores. The publishing industry is very active on Twitter, and you can learn so much just by reading the posts of those you follow. The great thing about Twitter is that you don't actually have to post anything to reap the benefits. At first you can just sit back and read what others have to say.

HOW TO USE TWITTER TO PITCH YOUR BOOK

Once you're comfortable with the basics of Twitter, it's time to use it to your advantage. The *pitch party* is an emerging trend on Twitter that can prove a valuable strategy for snagging an agent's attention. During a pitch party, writers pitch their completed, submission-ready, unpublished manuscript to an agent within a specified time frame. They create 140-character pitches of their manuscripts and post them to Twitter with a hashtag to make them searchable. A group of invited agents and editors attend the party (i.e., read the hashtagged Twitter feed) and review as many pitches as they can. If an agent enjoys your pitch, she will like (or "heart") your tweet by clicking the heart icon. This is an invitation for the writer to submit a query or manuscript to the agent—she is interested in your story and wants to know more!

While the pitch party is an up-and-coming method for securing representation, it already boasts its share of success stories. If you're ready to join them, follow these simple steps.

1. Craft your Twitter pitch.

A stellar pitch requires a few key ingredients. Here is a great formula I came across (on Twitter, of course):

> When [Main Character] encounters [Obstacle], he/she must [Reaction] or else [Stakes.] #MG #PitMad

Aside from the actual pitch, you also need to include the name of the pitch party, which in this example is "#PitMad." (The hashtag symbol is used to group posts together. In this example, adding the "#PitMad" hashtag would group your pitch with other writers' pitches for this particular party.) You should also include the genre or category, such as #HF for historical fiction or #MG for middle-grade. (Lists of genre shortcut names are typically provided with the contest rules online.) You must convey your pitch in 140 characters, which includes spaces, punctuation, and the content of the hashtags. Think about what you can abbreviate without sacrificing proper grammar.

"Focus on what makes your story readable—mainly stakes," says agent Heather Flaherty of The Bent Agency (@HeddaFlaherty). "If the plot stakes are high, they need to be in the pitch. If the emotional (character development) stakes are high, that needs to go in. Think about what in your story keeps people turning the page, and make sure that gets in the pitch."

If you've dreaded whittling down your story to a 250-word synopsis—much less a 140-character pitch—fear not. I personally think that crafting a Twitter pitch is easier. First, if you cannot summarize the essence of your story in one sentence, it might simply not be ready to submit—so keep writing and revising. I'm not saying you will come up with a perfect pitch on your first attempt; it absolutely takes time and practice. But pitch writing is an important exercise to ensure your story is clear and complete.

Author Brenda Drake (@brendadrake), who runs the #PitMad pitch party, believes that pitch parties can be an opportunity for writers to test the attractiveness of their hooks and pitches. "Sometimes it's successful, sometimes not, but it's great practice," Drake says. "It teaches a writer how to focus on the main plot and how to pitch it."

Just as you would for your manuscript, enlist some beta readers or critique partners to help you refine your tweet before you send it out. Also, because Twitter doesn't like spam any more than you do, it will not let you tweet the same text twice in a row. To get around this rule, you can tweet different pitches (as the rules of the party allow), or change the placement of the hashtag.

2. Plan ahead.

While I'm sure we all wish we could devote the entire day to writing and tweeting, we writers often have other responsibilities like day jobs, school, or children to keep us busy. The good news is that you do not have to be active on Twitter the day of the party in order to participate. Many free scheduling tools, such as TweetDeck and Hootsuite, allow you to write your tweets in advance and set specific times to post them.

3. Grab an agent's attention.

Agents who participate in parties scan through hundreds of tweets in a row, and they are looking for something to jump out and grab their attention. Thao Le (@ThaoLe8) of Sandra Dijkstra & Associates Literary Agency, offers her advice on building a great pitch: "I want to know what the conflict is! Too often people are vague in their pitches, and it comes off as cliché or generic. Know what your hook is, and present it concisely."

Bear in mind that the agent isn't just considering your pitch party tweet; she's also looking at your Twitter presence as a whole. "What also grabs me is the person's Twitter picture and profile," Flaherty says. "Can I see that they've thought through how they wish to be seen by the industry and the world? Have they considered their profile pic or just thrown something random up from last year's barbecue?"

4. Follow the rules.

Even though it's a party, you're still making a business pitch. "Read the rules carefully for each pitch party—they can be different," Le says. "Follow those rules for the best results. Be polite. Be professional."

Be sure to check the pitch party website for specific instructions. For example, pitch parties often start and end at specific times, and some limit the number of times you can post your pitch within that time frame. To prevent the feed from becoming too cluttered, many parties ask that you not retweet any pitch party posts (in which you share someone else's post on your own feed).

Make sure you do not like or heart someone else's pitch—let the agents do that! Also, be prepared to get a few likes from well-meaning strangers who enjoy your topic. These likes from strangers are encouraging, but don't really help you in the pitch party and should be ignored.

5. Submit requested materials.

So an agent expressed interest in your work and has asked you to submit your manuscript—congratulations! Each agent has his own submission process. If an agent likes your tweet, it is your responsibility to go to his website, research the agency guidelines, and then follow him. Sometimes an agent will tweet a tip about additional information

FROM THE AGENT'S VIEWPOINT

With their extremely busy schedules and overflowing slush piles of queries, many agents still choose to join Twitter pitch parties. Agent Thao Le of Sandra Dijkstra Literary Agency finds that writers who are active on Twitter are typically more industry savvy. "They've done their research, and they know how to pitch in 140 characters or less," she says. "Also, they usually have mentors and/or critique partners, so I know that their work is polished. Twitter pitch party participants tend to be an active part of the writing community, which is great because the relationships they build will support them later down the road ([in soliciting] blurbs and reviews, or generating buzz), and social media is so important to readers today."

Heather Flaherty of The Bent Agency thinks Twitter is having an impact on the writing community: "I feel we're getting to know authors more through Twitter, and bonds are made as we're considering their queries. If the Twitter parties do anything for querying, I think and hope they're teaching writers how to create a dynamic, pithy, and perfectly brief pitch, and that this skill will transfer into their queries."

you should provide with your submission. For example, he may ask you to include the name of the pitch party in the subject of your e-mail.

SUCCESS STORIES

Rena Olsen, author of *The Girl Before*, secured her agent, Sharon Pelletier of Dystel & Goderich Literary Management, through the #PitMad pitch party. Pelletier actually liked a pitch from Olsen:

> Clara raised them as her own daughters. She didn't know her husband kidnapped them to be sold to the highest bidder. #PitMad

"Sharon tweeted on the day of #PitMad that if she favorited the tweet, you should send the query and manuscript," Olsen says. "I thought she couldn't possibly want the full [manuscript] right away, so I went on the agency website to double-check her submission guidelines and followed those. The same day, she e-mailed back and requested the full manuscript. #PitMad was September 9, I sent the initial request in the wee hours of the morning on September 10, and her request came at a more reasonable hour later on September 10."

Now, things don't always happen this quickly. Remember that getting published is a process that requires lots of patience. Pitch parties are just one avenue to agent representation. Olsen emphasizes: "My biggest advice is to not stress if you don't get requests from a Twitter pitch contest. I did many where I got only a couple of favorites, and several more

PARTY HOPPING

Twitter is an evolving tool that changes over time. Keep in mind that what is true today might be slightly different a few months down the road. Here is a list of popular Twitter pitch parties, with more popping up all the time:

- #DVPit (marginalized and diverse voices) www.bethphelan.com/dvpit
- #PBPitch (picture books) no website
- #PitMad (open to all kinds of books, but usually novels) www.brenda-drake.com/pitmad/
- #AdPit (adult and new adult novels) www.heidinorrod.webs.com/
- #PitchMAS (general and open) www.pitchmas.blogspot.com/
- #PitMatch (general and open) www.manuscriptwishlist.com
- #PitchCB (special for pitching the agency Curtis Brown): www.curtisbrowncreative.co.uk/blog/pitchcb
- #SFFPit (science fiction and fantasy): www.dankoboldt.com/sffpit

where I got none at all. It's a wonderful opportunity, and obviously it can turn out really well, but it's not the only path."

Le has a success story, too: "I discovered the amazingly talented Jessie Sima via #Pit-Mad last June. She tweeted the most darling picture of a baby unicorn in a clamshell with the caption 'Kelp always thought he was a narwhal. Turns out he was wrong. He's a unicorn. KELP, THE NOT-QUITE NARWHAL #PitMad #pb.' I immediately fell head-over-heels in love and requested her full picture book. We went on to sell that picture book, *Not Quite Narwhal*, to Simon and Schuster, with publication coming in spring 2017."

Any opportunity to pitch your work to agents is worth looking into—from sending a query letter to meeting them in person at a writers conference. Pitch parties are a hot and growing opportunity, so engage with agents on Twitter right now and give yourself another avenue to find a rep who loves your work.

LISA KATZENBERGER (www.lisakatzenberger.com) is an Illinois-based freelance writer.

CRAFTING A QUERY

How to write a great letter that gets agent and editor attention.

···

by Kara Gebhart Uhl

So you've written a book. And now you want an agent. If you're new to publishing, you probably assume that the next step is to send your finished, fabulous book out to agents, right? Wrong. Agents don't want your finished, fabulous book. In fact, they probably don't even want *part* of your finished, fabulous book—at least, not yet. First, they want your query.

A query is a short, professional way of introducing yourself to an agent. If you're frustrated by the idea of this step, imagine yourself at a cocktail party. Upon meeting someone new, you don't greet them with a boisterous hug and kiss and, in three minutes, reveal your entire life story including the fact that you were late to the party because of some gastrointestinal problems. Rather, you extend your hand. You state your name. You comment on the hors d'oeuvres, the weather, the lovely shade of someone's dress. Perhaps, after this introduction, the person you're talking to politely excuses himself. Or, perhaps, you become best of friends. It's basic etiquette, formality, professionalism—it's simply how it's done.

Agents receive hundreds of submissions every month. Often they read these submissions on their own time—evenings, weekends, on their lunch break. Given the number of writers submitting, and the number of agents reading, it would simply be impossible for agents to ask for and read entire book manuscripts off the bat. Instead, a query is a quick way for you to, first and foremost, pitch your book. But it's also a way to pitch yourself. If an agent is intrigued by your query, she may ask for a partial (say, the first three chapters of your manuscript). Or she may ask for the entire thing.

As troublesome as it may first seem, try not to be frustrated by this process. Because, honestly, a query is a really great way to help speed up what is already a monumentally slow-paced industry. Have you ever seen pictures of slush piles—those piles of unread queries on many well-known agents' desks? Imagine the size of those slush piles if they held full manuscripts instead of one-page query letters. Thinking of it this way, query letters begin to make more sense.

Here we share with you the basics of a query, including its three parts and a detailed list of dos and don'ts.

PART I: THE INTRODUCTION

Whether you're submitting a 100-word picture book or a 90,000-word novel, you must be able to sum up the most basic aspects of it in one sentence. Agents are busy. And they constantly receive submissions for types of work they don't represent. So upfront they need to know that, after reading your first paragraph, the rest of your query is going to be worth their time.

An opening sentence designed to "hook" an agent is fine—if it's good and if it works. But this is the time to tune your right brain down and your left brain up—agents desire professionalism and queries that are short and to the point. Remember the cocktail party and always err on the side of formality. Tell the agent, in as few words as possible, what you've written, including the title, genre, and length.

In the intro, you also must try to connect with the agent. Simply sending one hundred identical query letters out to "Dear Agent" won't get you published. Instead, your letter should be addressed not only to a specific agency, but to a specific agent within that agency. (And double, triple, quadruple check that the agent's name is spelled correctly.) In addition, you need to let the agent know why you chose her specifically. A good author-agent relationship is like a good marriage. It's important that both sides invest the time to find a good fit that meets their needs. So how do you connect with an agent you don't know personally? Research.

1. Make a connection based on an author or book the agent already represents.

Most agencies have websites that list who and what they represent. Research those sites. Find a book similar to yours and explain that, because such-and-such book has a similar theme or tone or whatever, you think your book would be a great fit. In addition, many agents will list specific genres/categories they're looking for, either on their websites or in interviews. If your book is a match, state that.

2. Make a connection based on an interview you read.

Search agents' names online and read any and all interviews they've given. Perhaps they mentioned a love for X and your book is all about X. Perhaps they mentioned that they're looking for Y and your book is all about Y. Mention the specific interview. Prove that you've invested as much time researching them as they're about to spend researching you.

3. Make a connection based on a conference you both attended.

Was the agent you're querying the keynote speaker at a writing conference you were recently at? If so, mention it, and comment on an aspect of his speech you liked. Even better, did you meet the agent in person? Mention it, and if there's something you can say to jog her memory about the meeting, say it. Better yet, did the agent specifically ask you to send your manuscript? Mention it.

Finally, if you're being referred to a particular agent by an author the agent represents—that's your opening sentence. That referral is guaranteed to get your query placed at the top of the stack.

PART II: THE PITCH

Here's where you really get to sell your book—but in only three to ten sentences. Consider a book's jacket flap and its role in convincing readers to plunk down $24.95 to buy what's in between those flaps. Like a jacket flap, you need to hook an agent in the confines of very limited space. What makes your story interesting and unique? Is your story about a woman going through a mid-life crisis? Fine, but there are hundreds of stories about women going through mid-life crises. Is your story about a woman who, because of a mid-life crisis, leaves her life and family behind to spend three months in India? Again, fine, but this story, too, already exists—in many forms. Is your story about a woman who, because of a mid-life crisis, leaves her life and family behind to spend three months in India, falls in love with someone new while there and starts a new life—and family? And then has to deal with everything she left behind upon her return? *Now* you have a hook.

Practice your pitch. Read it out loud, not only to family and friends, but to people willing to give you honest, intelligent criticism. If you belong to a writing group, workshop your pitch. Share it with members of an online writing forum. Know anyone in the publishing industry? Share it with them. Many writers spend years writing their books. We're not talking about querying magazines here; we're talking about querying an agent who could become a lifelong partner. Spend time on your pitch. Perfect it. Turn it into jacket-flap material so detailed, exciting, and clear that it would be near impossible to read your pitch and not want to read more. Use active verbs. Write your pitch, put it aside for a week, then look at it again. Don't send a query simply because you finished a book. Send a query because you finished your pitch and are ready to take the next steps.

PART III: THE BIO

If you write fiction for adults or children, unless you're a household name or you've recently been a guest on some very big TV or radio shows, an agent is much more interested in your pitch than in who you are. If you write nonfiction, who you are and what you've done—more specifically, your platform and promotional ability (such as social media)—is very important. Regardless, these are key elements that must be present in every bio:

1. Publishing credits
If you're submitting fiction, focus on your fiction credits—previously published works and short stories. That said, if you're submitting fiction and all your previously published work is nonfiction—articles, essays, etc.—that's still fine and good to mention. Don't be overly long about it. Mention your publications in bigger magazines or well-known literary journals. If you've never had anything published, don't say you lack official credits. Simply skip this altogether and thank the agent for his time.

2. Contests and awards
If you've won many, focus on the most impressive ones and those that most directly relate to your work. Don't mention contests you entered and weren't named in. Also, feel free to leave titles and years out of it. If you took first place at the Delaware Writers Conference for your fiction manuscript, that's good enough. Mentioning details isn't necessary.

3. MFAs
If you've earned or are working toward a Master of Fine Arts in writing, say so and state the program. Don't mention English degrees or online writing courses.

4. Large, recognized writing organizations
Agents don't want to hear about your book club and the fact that there's always great food, or the small critique group you meet with once a week. And they really don't want to hear about the online writing forum you belong to. But if you're a member of something like the Romance Writers of America (RWA), the Mystery Writers of America (MWA), the Society of Children's Book Writers and Illustrators (SCBWI), the Society of Professional Journalists (SPJ), the American Medical Writers, etc., say so. This shows you're serious about what you do and you're involved in groups that can aid with publicity and networking.

5. Platform and publicity
If you write nonfiction, who you are and how you're going to help sell the book once it's published become very important. Why are you the best person to write it and what do you have now—public speaking engagements, an active website or blog, substantial cred in your industry—that will help you sell this book?

DOS AND DON'TS FOR QUERYING AGENTS

DO:

- Keep the tone professional.
- Query a specific agent at a specific agency.
- Proofread. Double-check the spelling of the agency and the agent's name.
- Keep the query concise, limiting the overall length to one page (single-spaced, 12-point type in a commonly used font).
- Focus on the plot, not your bio, when pitching fiction.
- Pitch agents who represent the type of material you write.
- Check an agency's submission guidelines to see how to query—for example, via e-mail or mail—and whether or not to include a SASE.
- Keep pitching, despite rejections.

DON'T:

- Include personal info not directly related to the book. For example, stating that you're a parent to three children doesn't make you more qualified than someone else to write a children's book.
- Say how long it took you to write your manuscript. Some best-selling books took ten years to write—others, six weeks. An agent doesn't care how long it took—an agent only cares if it's good. Same thing goes with drafts—an agent doesn't care how many drafts it took you to reach the final product.
- Mention that this is your first novel or, worse, the first thing you've ever written aside from grocery lists. If you have no other publishing credits, don't advertise that fact. Don't mention it at all.
- State that your book has been edited by peers or professionals. Agents expect manuscripts to be edited, no matter how the editing was done.
- Bring up scripts or film adaptations—you're querying an agent about publishing a book, not making a movie.
- Mention any previous rejections.
- State that the story is copyrighted with the U.S. Copyright Office or that you own all rights. Of course you own all rights. You wrote it.
- Rave about how much your family and friends loved it. What matters is that the agent loves it.
- Send flowers or anything else except a self-addressed stamped envelope (and only if the SASE is required), if sending through snail mail.
- Follow up with a phone call. After the appropriate time has passed (many agencies say how long it will take to receive a response), follow up in the manner you queried—via e-mail or mail.

Finally, be cordial. Thank the agent for taking the time to read your query and consider your manuscript. Ask if you may send more, in the format she desires (partial, full, etc.).

Think of the time you spent writing your book. Unfortunately, you can't send your book to an agent for a first impression. Your query *is* that first impression. Give it the time it deserves. Keep it professional. Keep it formal. Let it be a firm handshake—not a sloppy kiss. Let it be a first meeting that evolves into a lifelong relationship—not a rejection slip. But expect those slips. Just like you don't become best friends with everyone you meet at a cocktail party, you can't expect every agent you pitch to sign you. Be patient. Keep pitching. And in the meantime, start writing that next book.

KARA GEBHART UHL, formerly a managing editor at *Writer's Digest* magazine, now freelance writes and edits in Fort Thomas, Kentucky. She also blogs about parenting at pleiadesbee.com. Her essays have appeared on The Huffington Post, *The New York Times'* Motherlode and *TIME: Healthland*. Her parenting essay, "Apologies to the Parents I Judged Four Years Ago" was named one of *TIME*'s "Top 10 Opinions of 2012."

① SAMPLE QUERY 1: LITERARY FICTION
Agent's Comments: Jeff Kleinman (Folio Literary Management)

From: Garth Stein
To: Jeff Kleinman
Subject: Query: "The Art of Racing in the Rain" ①

Dear Mr. Kleinman:

② Saturday night I was participating in a fundraiser for the King County Library System out here in the Pacific Northwest, and I met your client Layne Maheu. He spoke very highly of you and suggested that I contact you.

③ I am a Seattle writer with two published novels. I have recently completed my third novel, *The Art of Racing in the Rain*, and I find myself in a difficult situation: My new book is narrated by a dog, and my current agent ④ told me that he cannot (or will not) sell it for that very reason. Thus, I am seeking new representation.

⑤ *The Art of Racing in the Rain* is the story of Denny Swift, a race car driver who faces profound obstacles in his life, and ultimately overcomes them by applying the same techniques that have made him successful on the track. His story is narrated by his "philosopher dog," Enzo, who, having a nearly human soul (and an obsession with opposable thumbs), believes he will return as a man in his next lifetime.

⑥ My last novel, *How Evan Broke His Head and Other Secrets*, won a 2006 Pacific Northwest Booksellers Association Book Award, and since the award ceremony a year ago, I have given many readings, workshops, and lectures promoting the book. When time has permitted, I've read the first chapter from *The Art of Racing in the Rain*. Audience members have been universally enthusiastic and vocal in their response, and the first question asked is always: "When can I buy the book about the dog?" Also very positive.

⑦ I'm inserting, below, a short synopsis of *The Art of Racing in the Rain*, and my biography. Please let me know if the novel interests you; I would be happy to send you the manuscript.

Sincerely,
Garth Stein

① Putting the word "Query" and the title of the book on the subject line of an e-mail often keeps your e-mail from falling into the spam folder. ② One of the best ways of starting out correspondence is figuring out a connection to the agent. ③ The author has some kind of track record. Who's the publisher, though? Were these books both self-published novels, or were there reputable publishers involved? (I'll read on, and hope I find out.) ④ This seems promising, but also know this kind of approach can backfire, because we agents tend to be like sheep—what one doesn't like, the rest of us are wary of, too (or, conversely, what one likes, we all like). But in this case getting in the "two published novels" early is definitely helpful. ⑤ The third paragraph is the key pitch paragraph and Garth gives a great description of the book—he sums it up, gives us a feel for what we're going to get. This is the most important part of your letter. ⑥ Obviously it's nice to see the author's winning awards. Also good: The author's not afraid of promoting the book. ⑦ The end is simple and easy—it doesn't speak of desperation, or doubt, or anything other than polite willingness to help.

② SAMPLE QUERY 2: YOUNG ADULT
Agent's Comments: Ted Malawer (Upstart Crow Literary)

Dear Mr. Malawer:

I would like you to represent my 65,000-word contemporary teen novel, *My Big Nose & Other Natural Disasters*.

① Seventeen-year-old Jory Michaels wakes up on the first day of summer vacation with her same old big nose, no passion in her life (in the creative sense of the word), and all signs still pointing to her dying a virgin. Plus, her mother is busy roasting a chicken for Day #6 of the Dinner For Breakfast Diet.

② In spite of her driving record (it was an accident!), Jory gets a job delivering flowers and cakes to Reno's casinos and wedding chapels. She also comes up with a new summer goal: saving for a life-altering nose job. She and her new nose will attract a fabulous boyfriend. Nothing like the shameless flirt Tyler Briggs, or Tom who's always nice but never calls. Maybe she'll find someone kind of like Gideon at the Jewel Café, except better looking and not quite so different. Jory survives various summer disasters like doing yoga after sampling Mom's Cabbage Soup Diet, Enforced Mother Bonding With Crazy Nose-Obsessed Daughter Night, and discovering Tyler's big secret. But will she learn to accept herself and maybe even find her passion, in the creative (AND romantic!) sense of the word?

③ I have written for *APPLESEEDS, Confetti, Hopscotch, Story Friends, Wee Ones Magazine*, the *Deseret News, Children's Playmate* and Blooming Tree Press' *Summer Shorts* anthology. I won the Utah Arts Council prize for *Not-A-Dr. Logan's Divorce Book*. My novels *Jungle Crossing* and *Going Native!* each won first prize in the League of Utah Writers contest. I currently serve as an SCBWI Regional Advisor.

④ I submitted *My Big Nose & Other Natural Disasters* to Krista Marino at Delacorte because she requested it during our critique at the summer SCBWI conference (no response yet).

Thank you for your time and attention. I look forward to hearing from you.

Sincerely,
Sydney Salter Husseman

① With hundreds and hundreds of queries each month, it's tough to stand out. Sydney, however, did just that. First, she has a great title that totally made me laugh. Second, she sets up her main character's dilemma in a succinct and very interesting way. In one simple paragraph, I have a great idea of who Jory is and what her life is about—the interesting tidbits about her mother help show the novel's sense of humor, too. **②** Sydney's largest paragraph sets up the plot and the conflict, and introduces some exciting potential love interests and misadventures that I was excited to read about. Again, Sydney really shows off her fantastic sense of humor, and she leaves me hanging with a question that I needed an answer to. **③** She has writing experience and has completed other manuscripts that were prize-worthy. Her SCBWI involvement—while not a necessity—shows me that she has an understanding of and an interest in the children's publishing world. **④** The fact that an editor requested the manuscript is always a good sign. That I knew Krista personally and highly valued her opinion was, as Sydney's main character Jory would say, "The icing on the cake."

③ SAMPLE QUERY 3: NONFICTION (SELF-HELP)
Agent's Comments: Michelle Wolfson (Wolfson Literary Agency)

Dear Ms. Wolfson:

① Have you ever wanted to know the best day of the week to buy groceries or go out to dinner? Have you ever wondered about the best time of day to send an e-mail or ask for a raise? What about the best time of day to schedule a surgery or a haircut? What's the best day of the week to avoid lines at the Louvre? What's the best day of the month to make an offer on a house? What's the best time of day to ask someone out on a date? ②

My book, *Buy Ketchup in May and Fly at Noon: A Guide to the Best Time to Buy This, Do That, and Go There*, has the answers to these questions and hundreds more.

③ As a longtime print journalist, I've been privy to readership surveys that show people can't get enough of newspaper and magazine stories about the best time to buy or do things. This book puts several hundreds of questions and answers in one place—a succinct, large-print reference book that readers will feel like they need to own. Why? Because it will save them time and money, and it will give them valuable information about issues related to health, education, travel, the workplace, and more. In short, it will make them smarter, so they can make better decisions. ④

Best of all, the information in this book is relevant to anyone, whether they live in Virginia or the Virgin Islands, Portland, Oregon, or Portland, Maine. In fact, much of the book will find an audience in Europe and Australia.

⑤ I've worked as a journalist since 1984. In 1999, the Virginia Press Association created an award for the best news writing portfolio in the state—the closest thing Virginia had to a reporter-of-the-year award. I won it that year and then again in 2000. During the summer of 2007, I left newspapering to pursue book projects and long-form journalism.

⑥ I saw your name on a list of top literary agents for self-help books, and I read on your website that you're interested in books that offer practical advice. *Buy Ketchup in May and Fly at Noon* offers plenty of that. Please let me know if you'd like to read my proposal.

Sincerely,
Mark Di Vincenzo

① I tend to prefer it when authors jump right into the heart of their book, the exception being if we've met at a conference or have some other personal connection. Mark chose clever questions for the opening of the query. All of those questions are, in fact, relevant to my life—with groceries, dinner, e-mail, and a raise—and yet I don't have a definitive answer to them. ② He gets a little more offbeat with questions regarding surgery, the Louvre, buying a house, and dating. This shows a quirkier side to the book and also the range of topics it is going to cover, so I know right away there is going to be a mix of useful and quirky information on a broad range of topics. ③ By starting with "As a longtime print journalist," Mark immediately establishes his credibility for writing on this topic. ④ This helps show that there is a market for this book, and establishes the need for such a book. ⑤ Mark's bio paragraph offers a lot of good information. ⑥ It's nice when I feel like an author has sought me out specifically and thinks we would be a good fit.

4 **SAMPLE QUERY 4:** WOMEN'S FICTION
Agent's Comments: Elisabeth Weed (Weed Literary)

Dear Ms. Weed:

1 Natalie Miller had a plan. She had a goddamn plan. Top of her class at Dartmouth. Even better at Yale Law. Youngest aide ever to the powerful Senator Claire Dupris. Higher, faster, stronger. This? Was all part of the plan. True, she was so busy ascending the political ladder that she rarely had time to sniff around her mediocre relationship with Ned, who fit the three Bs to the max: basic, blond, and boring, and she definitely didn't have time to mourn her mangled relationship with Jake, her budding rock star ex-boyfriend.

The lump in her right breast that Ned discovers during brain-numbingly bland morning sex? That? Was most definitely not part of the plan. And Stage IIIA breast cancer? Never once had Natalie jotted this down on her to-do list for conquering the world. When her (tiny-penised) boyfriend has the audacity to dump her on the day after her diagnosis, Natalie's entire world dissolves into a tornado of upheaval, and she's left with nothing but her diary to her ex-boyfriends, her mornings lingering over "The Price is Right," her burnt-out stubs of pot that carry her past the chemo pain, and finally, the weight of her life choices—the ones in which she might drown if she doesn't find a buoy.

2 *The Department of Lost and Found* is a story of hope, of resolve, of digging deeper than you thought possible until you find the strength not to crumble, and ultimately, of making your own luck, even when you've been dealt an unsteady hand.

3 I'm a freelance writer and have contributed to, among others, *American Baby, American Way, Arthritis Today, Bride's, Cooking Light, Fitness, Glamour, InStyle Weddings, Men's Edge, Men's Fitness, Men's Health, Parenting, Parents, Prevention, Redbook, Self, Shape, Sly, Stuff, USA Weekend, Weight Watchers, Woman's Day, Women's Health*, and ivillage.com, msn.com and women.com. I also ghostwrote *The Knot Book of Wedding Flowers*.

If you are interested, I'd love to send you the completed manuscript. Thanks so much! Looking forward to speaking with you soon.

Allison Winn Scotch

1 The opening sentence reads like great jacket copy, and I immediately know who our protagonist is and what the conflict for her will be. (And it's funny, without being silly.) **2** The third paragraph tells me where this book will land: upmarket women's fiction. (A great place to be these days!) **3** This paragraph highlights impressive credentials. While being able to write nonfiction does not necessarily translate over to fiction, it shows me that she is someone worth paying more attention to. And her magazine contacts will help when it comes time to promote the book.

⑤ SAMPLE QUERY 5: MAINSTREAM/COMEDIC FICTION
Agent's Comments: Michelle Brower (Folio Literary Management)

Dear Michelle Brower:

① "I spent two days in a cage at the SPCA until my parents finally came to pick me up. The stigma of bringing your undead son home to live with you can wreak havoc on your social status, so I can't exactly blame my parents for not rushing out to claim me. But one more day and I would have been donated to a research facility."

Andy Warner is a zombie.

After reanimating from a car accident that killed his wife, Andy is resented by his parents, abandoned by his friends, and vilified by society. Seeking comfort and camaraderie in Undead Anonymous, a support group for zombies, Andy finds kindred souls in Rita, a recent suicide who has a taste for consuming formaldehyde in cosmetic products, and Jerry, a 21-year-old car crash victim with an artistic flair for Renaissance pornography.

② With the help of his new friends and a rogue zombie named Ray, Andy embarks on a journey of personal freedom and self-discovery that will take him from his own casket to the SPCA to a media-driven, class-action lawsuit for the civil rights of all zombies. And along the way, he'll even devour a few Breathers.

Breathers is a contemporary dark comedy about life, or undeath, through the eyes of an ordinary zombie. In addition to *Breathers*, I've written three other novels and more than four dozen short stories—a dozen of which have appeared in small press publications. Currently, I'm working on my fifth novel, also a dark comedy, about fate.

Enclosed is a two-page synopsis and the first chapter of *Breathers*, with additional sample chapters or the entire manuscript available upon request. I appreciate your time and interest in considering my query and I look forward to your response.

Sincerely,
Scott G. Browne

① What really draws me to this query is the fact that it has exactly what I'm looking for in my commercial fiction—story and style. Scott includes a brief quote from the book that manages to capture his sense of humor as an author and his uniquely relatable main character (hard to do with someone who's recently reanimated). I think this is a great example of how query letters can break the rules and still stand out in the slush pile. I normally don't like quotes as the first line, because I don't have a context for them, but this quote both sets up the main concept of the book *and* gives me a sense of the character's voice. This method won't necessarily work for most fiction, but it absolutely is successful here. **②** The letter quickly conveys that this is an unusual book about zombies, and being a fan of zombie literature, I'm aware that it seems to be taking things in a new direction. I also appreciate how Scott conveys the main conflict of his plot and his supporting cast of characters—we know there is an issue for Andy beyond coming back to life as a zombie, and that provides great momentum for the story.

5 REASON QUERIES GET REJECTED

Don't make these query mistakes.

....

by Holly Jennings

//

In the summer of 2014, I set out on an epic quest: to draft a query letter that would not only garner the attention of literary agents, but would have them drooling over my book.

I spent every spare minute I had hunched over the computer, reading blog post after blog post on query-writing advice. At first, I could only find basic information about writing a three-part book summary for a query letter. This essentially boiled down to listing the character, conflict, and stakes of my novel. I wondered: Is that really all it took to impress an agent?

In a word: No.

Former agent Nathan Bransford once mentioned on his blog that he had received one hundred queries in a single holiday weekend. Of that one hundred, he requested material from two—which is a pretty abysmal rate for a hopeful author. Of course, some of those queries probably failed to follow the submission guidelines and were automatically rejected, and others probably weren't considered because they said nothing about the actual book. But a lot of queries do follow the agency's guidelines and faithfully follow the "character, conflict, and stakes" formula recommended by so many online resources. So of the dozens, if not hundreds, of queries that make it past the auto-reject stage, how can you make yours stand out from the slush pile?

Instead of sending you on the same virtual expedition I underwent, I'm going to share some commonly overlooked mistakes that can cripple your query letter—and your chances of securing representation. I'm no expert, but when I fixed these problems within my own query, something magical happened: I got requests.

Here's the breakdown. Between querying and pitching contests, I sent out fourteen letters. Six agents requested material, three passed, and five hadn't responded before I was offered representation.

That's a 42 percent request rate.

Wondering how you can achieve the same results? Examine your query letter for the following problems.

PROBLEM ONE: YOU'RE NOT HOOKING THE AGENT FAST ENOUGH

When yours is one letter in a pile of a thousand queries, you don't have much time to grab an agent's attention. The hard truth is that most agents don't read every query all the way through. Frankly, they don't have time. Sometimes they skim. Sometimes they stop reading after the first few lines.

Pretend you only have one line to get the agent's attention. What is the most interesting thing you could say about your story or its main character?

Here are the opening lines to the query that landed me an agent:

> The warrior. It's a title twenty-year-old Kali Ling earned bringing men to their knees ... inside video games.

Is it perfect? No. But it does the job. It's short, simple, and ends in a twist. As the reader, you're left wondering: How is she bringing men to their knees inside video games? Is she literally inside a game? What's going on here? The only way anyone can find out—including the agent—is to continue reading the query.

With that first line, you need to catch the agent's attention—hook, line, and sinker. Here are some other ways to hook an agent within the first one to two sentences.

Include an unexpected twist:

> When Cate Benson was twelve, her sister died. Two hours after the funeral, they picked up Violet's replacement, and the family made it home in time for dinner and a game of cards.
> —*Falls the Shadow* by Stefanie Gaither

Include humor:

> You'd have to be drunk or crazy to hire Dahlia Moss as a detective, and her client was conveniently both.
> —*The Unfortunate Decisions of Dahlia Moss* by Max Wirestone, the New Adult Query Champion of the Query Kombat Contest 2014

Include something shocking:

> Shawn knows he's going to die on his eighteenth birthday.
> —Query #260 on QueryShark.com

Pull at the heartstrings:

> She had the talent, she had the drive, and she had the opportunity. Only one thing stood between Penelope Sparrow and the dance career of her dreams: her imperfect body.
> —*The Art of Falling* by Kathryn Craft

Remember to take your genre into consideration. A mysterious and unexpected detail might work well for science fiction, while a line with an emotional edge might bode better for contemporary fiction. Don't bore the agent with a bland opening line. Instead, toss the biggest bait you can into the querying ocean, and wait for an agent to bite.

PROBLEM TWO: YOUR CONCEPT ISN'T UNIQUE

Don't panic. This doesn't mean your book isn't unique enough. But your query letter summary paragraphs could probably use some work. The majority of queries agents receive are generic and boring, and don't describe the plot of the story. Instead, they contain trite phrases and clichés that could be used to describe every B-rated movie ever made. As Agent Moe Ferrara of BookEnds recently said on Twitter: "Authors! Don't be vague in your queries ('unfortunate events' or 'bad things happen to her'). Tell me what happened! I want plots!"

The key to having a memorable query is specifics, specifics, specifics. Here are two examples. (For the sake of simplicity, I've reduced these summaries to two sentences; yours will likely be longer.) The first example below is bland and generic. The second is specific and engaging.

> 1. Mandy loves scuba diving. But when someone mysterious starts killing those who love the water, she must uncover the killer's identity before it's too late.

> 2. Sixteen-year-old scuba diver Mandy lives for the water. But when a psychopath starts killing members of the local marina, she must uncover the murderer's identity before more than her tank runs out of oxygen.

Calling the killer a "psychopath" is much more chilling than saying "someone mysterious." And "before her tank runs out of oxygen" is much more distinct than "before it's too late." See how the specific details add more emotion, create concrete imagery, and make the story memorable?

Look at every line of your query and ask yourself: Could this line apply to other queries from other authors? If so, can you describe the plot, the characters, and other summary components in a way that applies to only your story?

As you revise your summary, avoid using these generic, overused phrases:

- "Things will never be the same again."
- "Things have changed forever."
- "Everyone will die if …"
- "… before time runs out."
- "Something unexpected happens."
- "All of a sudden …"

- "He is the chosen one."
- "It's the end of the world as she knows it."
- "She discovers she has superpowers!"
- "Someone mysterious starts at his school."
- "A stranger moves to town."

Your story is unique to you and only you. Make sure your individuality is reflected in your query paragraphs.

PROBLEM THREE: YOUR COMPARATIVE TITLES AREN'T UP TO PAR

A standard query letter should contain a few comparative titles that are similar to your own book. This helps the agent understand the tone and potential audience for your novel, while reassuring her that you understand the market you're writing in. Get your comp titles wrong and your query could be toast.

Agents are looking for a reason to say no. Don't make it easy for them by choosing poorly. Okay, if an agent was over-the-moon in love with your summary paragraphs, maybe they'd overlook this mistake. But if they're on the fence about requesting material, the wrong comp title can send you to Camp Rejection.

So how do you pick the right comp titles?

- Choose book titles within the upper-mid range of popularity. People who read the genre should be familiar with them, even if the general reading public is not.
- Make sure at least one of your titles was published in the last five years. Better yet, choose titles published in the last three years if you can.
- If applicable, try a mash-up of two titles that wouldn't naturally be paired together. Writing a comedy horror? Try: "It's Monster Island meets The Hangover."
- If you feel your writing is similar to another author's, mention that. (For example, "My book should appeal to fans of Author X.") Just make sure you don't compare yourself to Shakespeare or Mark Twain.

A FEW ADDITIONAL TIPS:

- Limit yourself to listing two to three titles. Including more makes you seem amateurish. Listing only one implies you don't know your genre or market.
- Strive for examples that match the tone of your novel. For example, if your writing is more upbeat and humorous, don't list a comp title with a dark and depressing tone.
- You can list movies, television shows, or comic books, but limit yourself to one nonbook title per query.
- Avoid listing mega-bestsellers like the Harry Potter or Twilight series books.

- Conversely, avoid listing superobscure titles that no one—not even an agent—has ever heard of.

PROBLEM FOUR: YOUR STAKES AREN'T HIGH ENOUGH

Stakes represent conflict and danger. They make the reader care about and root for your character. What happens if your protagonist wins? What happens if he loses?

Let's look at the stakes from my debut novel, *Arena*. The main character, Kali Ling, is stuck between becoming the first female captain to win a gaming tournament and honoring her fallen teammate by exposing the corruption within virtual sports.

If she exposes the corruption, she risks losing her spot as captain, and thousands of young girl gamers are counting on her to be the first woman to claim the title. But if she pursues becoming captain, then corruption in virtual sports lives on, and her friend will have died in vain.

Does she become a role model or a rebel? Notice how the plot presents no clear choice. Worst of all, what if she can't decide and accomplishes nothing? Or what if she picks one of the two options and fails miserably? OMG! The drama! Agents love this.

Even when superheroes have to save the entire world, their thoughts aren't about all of humanity. They think about those closest to them. Iron Man thinks of Pepper Potts. Superman thinks of Lois Lane, Jimmy Olsen, and his parents. Neo thinks of Trinity. Thor thinks of Jane Foster and his newfound friends on Earth.

Stakes are defined by what is most important to your character and how she could lose it. So ask yourself: *What choices does my character make, and how will this affect her?*

PROBLEM FIVE: YOUR LETTER IS DEVOID OF VOICE

Ah, voice. This element is quite possibly the hardest thing to include in your query. But if your query is constructed properly and oozes with voice, chances are high that an agent will request your full manuscript.

Here's a perfect example of a voice-laden query:

> In fourteen-year-old Anne's opinion, there are two kinds of quests: the kind that lead to unicorns and lollipops, and the kind that get you and everyone you love killed, horribly and painfully (possibly by zombie sharks). She knows this because her budding magick abilities have accidentally entangled her in a quest, and so far she hasn't encountered any lollipops.
>
> She could opt out, but then, as per Paragraph 5 Subparagraph 3 of the Official Questing Regulations, she'd be exiled forever, and all of her friends would be tossed into a dungeon. She'd rather kiss a Steam Troll than let that happen …
>
> —*The Adventurer's Guide to Successful Escapes* by Wade Albert White, the Middle-Grade Query Champion of the Query Kombat Contest 2014

I'll be honest here: I don't even enjoy reading middle-grade fiction, but I need to read this novel now. And if you're wondering, White's book had multiple offers.

Notice how White names the prizes of the quest as "unicorns and lollipops." Maybe this isn't what you or I would want to find at the end of a quest, but these examples are completely in line with the tone of an middle-grade novel. And as adults, we know there are far worse things in life than kissing a troll, but from the perspective of a middle-grade girl? Ew, yuck.

Does voice really have that much impact on a query? Editor Jordan Wright of Jolly Fish Press had this to say on Twitter: "I know it's a good query when the synopsis alone convinces me the [manuscript] is worth reading. Great voice!"

Voice comes from knowing your point-of-view character intimately and funneling the world through their perspective. A ten-year-old boy wouldn't looks at things in the same way as an eighty-year-old woman. Use voice to your advantage in your query. Does your character have a favorite catchphrase? Put it in. Is he happy and optimistic, or does he have a dark, snarky sense of humor? His personality should be reflected in the words he chooses to describe his world.

This is *voice*.

If all the other parts of your query are solid, voice becomes the whipped cream on a hot fudge sundae. And you can never have too much whipped cream.

If you send your query out unedited, you allow an agent to find reasons to reject your work. Pay attention to these five common mistakes and aim for a 42 percent rate (or better!) for your work.

HOLLY JENNINGS writes from her home in Tecumseh, Ontario. Her short fiction has appeared in *Daily Science Fiction*, and *AE: The Canadian Science Fiction Review*, among others. *Arena*, her debut novel, released in April 2016. Described as *"Ready Player One* meets *The Hunger Games,"* it stars a female cyber-athlete inside a corrupt world of fame, venality, and gaming. Follow Jennings on Twitter: @HollyN_Jennings.

MIDDLE-GRADE VS. YOUNG ADULT

Different audiences, different styles.

by Marie Lamba

OK, class. What sets a middle-grade (MG) novel apart from a young adult (YA) novel? If you said MG is for readers ages eight to twelve, and YA is for readers ages thirteen through eighteen, then give yourself a check plus. But if you're writing for the juvenile market and that's *all* you know about these two categories, then I'm afraid you still need to stick around for the rest of this class. A book that doesn't fit within the parameters of either age category is a book you won't be able to sell.

In my work with The Jennifer De Chiara Literary Agency, I see my inbox flooded every day with queries for manuscripts that suffer from an MG/YA identity crisis. Like when a query says, "I've written a 100,000-word MG novel about a seventh-grader who falls in love and has sex for the first time." Or when one states, "In my 20,000-word YA novel, a fourteen-year-old holds her first sleepover and learns the meaning of true friendship." Both queries would earn a swift rejection, based on both inappropriate manuscript lengths and on content that's either too mature or too young for the audience they're targeting. Sadly, by not understanding what makes a book a true MG or a solid YA, these writers have hamstrung their chances for success, regardless of how well written their stories may be. It's like they showed up to a final exam without ever cracking a book.

On the bright side, writers who study up on the many key differences between MG and YA will be able to craft the kind of well-targeted manuscript that will make both agents and editors take notice. Pay attention, because someday your manuscript *will* be tested.

MG AT A GLANCE

AGE OF READERS: eight through twelve. **LENGTH:** Generally 30,000–50,000 words (although fantasy can run longer to allow for more complex world-building). **CONTENT RESTRICTIONS:** No profanity, graphic violence or sexuality (romance, if any, is limited to a crush or a first kiss). **AGE OF PROTAGONIST:** Typically age ten for a younger MG novel, and up to age thirteen for older, more complex books. **MIND-SET:** Focus on friends, family, and the character's immediate world and relationship to it; characters react to what happens to them, with minimal self-reflection. **VOICE:** Often third person.

YA AT A GLANCE

AGE OF READERS: thirteen through eighteen. **LENGTH:** Generally 50,000–75,000 words (although there's also a length allowance for fantasy). **CONTENT RESTRICTIONS:** Profanity, graphic violence, romance, and sexuality (except for eroticism) are all allowable (though not required). **AGE OF PROTAGONIST:** Ages fourteen-fifteen for a younger YA with cleaner content aimed at the middle-school crowd; for older and more edgy YA, characters can be up to eighteen (but not in college). **MIND-SET:** YA heroes discover how they fit in the world beyond their friends and family; they spend more time reflecting on what happens and analyzing the meaning of things. **VOICE:** Often first person.

MG VS. YA CHARACTERS

When picking your hero's age, remember that kids "read up," which means they want to read about characters who are older than they are. So an eight-year-old protagonist won't fly for the MG category, though it'd be OK for a younger chapter book or easy reader. For the widest audience, you'll generally want your protagonist to be on the oldest side of your readership that your plot will allow. That means a twelve- or even thirteen-year-old hero for MG, and a seventeen- or eighteen-year-old for YA (just remember your hero can't be in college yet—that would push it into the "new adult" category).

MG VS. YA READERS

Middle-grade is *not* synonymous with middle school. Books for the middle-school audience tend to be divided between the MG and YA shelves. So which shelf do those readers go to? While there is no such thing as a 'tween category in bookstores, there are degrees of maturity in both MG and YA novels that'll appeal to the younger and older sides of the middle-school crowd. A longer, more complex MG novel with characters who are thirteen could take place in middle school and be considered an "upper-MG novel." But the material can't be too mature. It's still an MG novel, after all, and most readers will be younger. Writing a sweeter, more innocent YA? Then it's pretty likely that your readers will be 'tweens, that your characters should be around fifteen years old, and that your book will be marketed as a "young YA."

While it's useful for you to understand these nuances as you craft your story and relate to your true audience, when it comes time to submit, don't go so far as to define your novel as upper MG or younger YA in your query. That's already pointing to a more limited readership. Instead, just stick to calling it either MG or YA when you submit, and let an interested agent draw conclusions about nuances from there.

MG VS. YA CONTENT AND VOICE

What's cool to a fourth-grader differs from what a tenth-grader will idolize. Same goes for the way they speak and the way they view the world. Which is why if romance appears in an MG novel, it's limited to a crush and maybe an innocent kiss, as it is in *Shug* by Jenny Han. A YA could involve deep, true love as well as sexuality, as in *The Fault in Our Stars* by John Green. Another key difference? Overall, MG novels end on a hopeful note, while YA novels could have less optimistic endings, as in Green's tearful story. You could say that that's youth vs. experience coming into play.

When it comes to content, here's another important thing to keep in mind: There are gatekeepers between your book and your targeted audience. MG readers typically don't have direct access to their novels. To get a book, kids first go through a parent, a teacher, or a librarian. While you might want to have that gritty character in your upper-MG novel drop a few four-letter words, doing so *will* hurt book sales, so choose your language wisely.

Also, think *carefully* about your content. MG is not the place for graphic or persistent violence, but can it be scary and dark? Sure—look at *Holes* by Louis Sachar, where boys are threatened by a crazy warden and nearly killed by poisonous lizards. (Note, however, that book *does* have a happy ending.)

If you're writing a YA, you don't have to worry about those gatekeepers as much. But while YA authors cover just about anything in their novels, keep in mind that *gratuitous* sex, excessive foul language, or graphic violence can be tough sells, as school and library support are often what catapult a YA title to success. While dropping a ton of F-bombs is OK if it fits with your characters and setting, be prepared for your book to be perhaps on fewer school shelves as a result, and make sure it's worth that risk.

EXCEPTIONS TO EVERY RULE

Like any rebellious teen can tell you, rules are made to be broken. Word counts often vary from the suggested norms. Just don't deviate too low or too high, especially for a debut. True, *Harry Potter and the Deathly Hallows* came close to a whopping 200,000 words, but her debut novel, *Harry Potter and the Sorcerer's Stone*, was roughly 77,000 words—which is still long for the genre, but not outrageously so for an MG fantasy. Hey, once you get as popular as Rowling, you can write doorstopper-sized tomes, too.

Content can also stray from the stated guidelines, *with good reason*. You might, say, choose to have an MG with a swear word, or with a more edgy storyline. Whatever norm you do stray from, just make sure you do so for a specific and valid purpose, that your book still fits your audience's point of view, and that you understand what deviating from the norm might mean for your book's marketability.

Whether you aim to write a YA or an MG novel, there is one thing you absolutely *must* do: Tell a story that is meaningful to your intended reader. And to do that, you must first know *who* that reader is.

So which shelf does your book belong on? Know *that* and your book will surely graduate with full honors, moving on to a long and happy future in your readers' appreciative hands.

A WHOLE NEW WORLD

An agent shares advice on writing fantasy.

....

by Ammi-Joan Paquette

How clearly I remember my childhood experiences of being catapulted into a book world so much bigger than my own narrow reality. Most of us do, I'm guessing; maybe that's even why we aspire to for children and teens. That first tumble into Wonderland is not easily forgotten, and it's also something that can't quite be replicated in adult life with the same intensity. The worlds you inhabit in childhood are stitched into the fabric of who you will grow to be. How lucky we are, then, and how big a responsibility rests on our shoulders, to be the ones shaping these worlds for the next generation of readers!

Speculative fiction, in particular, hinges almost fully on the strength of its story world. (I say *almost* because, of course, the critical elements of character, plot, and voice can't be discounted.) But even if you don't write fantasy or science fiction (or for young readers), the right approach to world-building can be gold. Make setting your superpower, whatever your story, and readers will line up for more.

In writing about this subject, my perspective is threefold: as a voracious reader, as an author of books for young people, and as a literary agent with a strong presence in the genre. Each of these lenses shapes my view a little differently, but the result never varies: I'm forever seeking a world I can get truly lost in, one that brings me as close to that lose-track-of-everything-else sense I felt curled up in that armchair when I was nine.

That's the feeling we're chasing. Now let's go find it.

MASTERING YOUR UNIVERSE: THE BIG BANG

What comes first, the chicken or the egg? The world or its story? I like the analogy of a (modern) photographer planning a shoot. First, you have to figure out the composition, content, and focal point of your image. Only then are you ready to zero in on details of lighting, aperture and depth of field.

When I began writing *Princess Juniper of the Hourglass*, I was not unfamiliar with the writing process—it would be my fourth published novel—but this *was* my first time creating an entirely new world for my characters to populate. So, how to begin?

"Don't do a lot of worldbuilding before you start writing," *The Wicked and the Just* author J. Anderson Coats advises. "Do just enough to get the basics clear in your mind, then let the characters reveal things to you as you work. This keeps you from boxing yourself in mentally and lets discovery drive the build." Blocking out the first draft is key: You need to know where you're going before you can figure out the nuance of how to get there.

As you get to know your characters and charge pell-mell along with them into their tale, make careful notes of the holes in their backstory and world. Here, for example, were some of mine:

- *Why* is the country of Monsia attacking the country of Torr?
- Juniper's mother comes from a little-known tribe. *Who* are they, and *what* has caused them to be so withdrawn?

Once you know the questions, then the fun begins: You get to go panning for answers.

MAPPING YOUR QUEST—LITERALLY

I still get a little thrill when I open a book and find that it begins with a map. This is a *real* world! Luckily, the tool works both ways. Like many other writers (and readers), I'm a visual person. There's only so much detail I can hold in my head without succumbing to the inevitable blank spots in my mental canvas. And that's where a map can be invaluable. With *Princess Juniper of the Hourglass*, the act of sketching out the Lower Continent early on—in extremely rough format, I might add, as I'm no artist—let me more clearly envision where each country was located, how its size and geographical features would impact its inhabitants, and the distances spanned in the various journeys in the book.

"Maps are one tool to keep me grounded in a world that feels real," says Jennifer A. Nielsen, *The New York Times* best-selling author of *The False Prince*. "Although I change a lot of details in the worlds I create, having an actual map is a reliable way to build places that seem new, and yet also a little familiar, to my readers."

Your goal here isn't artistry: This is a visionary work, pure and simple. You might be pleasantly surprised at the country you create and the unexpected places it takes you.

BUILDING FROM THE GROUND UP

Ask any god anywhere: Building a world is a *lot* of work. That's why it can help to take a few shortcuts. Your fantasy realm will be an amalgamation, but using real places as a springboard can help you frame elements consistently and with a more grounded result.

Princess Juniper of the Hourglass was loosely modeled on medieval Europe. I saw my invented country of Torr as a mashup of Belgium and France, with a dash of British influence thrown in. Flora and fauna, general customs, weather patterns, and even things like distance were all made easier by the use of this shortcut. Having a bedrock allowed me to sift through the elements I wanted to use and those I wanted to discard in favor of invented details that would make my world unique.

And being unique is key. Write what you know, sure—but then go beyond it. A predictable world is a dull world.

"Ask *What if?* about just one element of the real world," suggests Megan Morrison, author of *Grounded: The Adventures of Rapunzel.* "Let everything else stay as is, but try: *What if cats could talk? What if children could fly once they turned 12? What if all curly-haired people were psychic?* Then apply logic to build the necessary systems and laws that would have to be in place in such a world, prejudices and fears that would arise, and workarounds that characters would have to use."

If you hit a roadblock—whether in world, plot, or character, try this trick:

- Write down your problem.
- Quickly brainstorm three distinct and unique solutions to this problem.
- Cross out those three solutions. Then dig deeper to find *another* answer. Once you dispose of the easy, quick fixes, you're putting your deepest creative mind to work.

LETTING IT ALL HANG OUT

So you have your draft. You have your map. Your world is starting to take shape. It's time for the nitty-gritty. Your goal now is to learn as much as you can about this world you're putting together. I find it best if this happens in a document apart from the story. Create a place where you give yourself permission to info-dump, loud and proud. Remember, always, your young readers: What will they find most fascinating about this imagined place?

Sarah Aronson, author of *Believe* and *Head Case*, offers this list of further questions to help you get started:

- What is the most wonderful part of your world?
- What always stays the same?
- What makes this world different?
- Are there vices in this world?
- Special events in this world?
- What about controlling beliefs?
- What is the history of the world? How did it get to this point?

Aronson's list makes for a great starting point, but don't stop there. Write a historical treatise, a precise geographic and zoological description, a chronicle of culture and customs and mores in as much detail as the mood strikes. Write whatever you need to write to fill the gaps in your writer-consciousness. For me, this was where I discovered what Princess Juniper *really* knows, and what drives the cultures of the Torrean people and their neighbors: the historical enmities that would lead one country to invade another, the type of ruler who has kept such a threat at bay for so long, and why things are suddenly falling apart. Edge yourself—detail by description by nuance by fact—into the center of your imagined world.

Once this is done, you can return to your draft with that blinding spotlight behind you to illuminate every dark spot. Most of it may—and dare I say, *should*—never make it into the final manuscript. But behind the scenes, you'll benefit from having it there, ready to inform the main story text where needed.

AGE MATTERS

It's worth noting that there's a big difference in tolerance for world-building and back-story between kidlit (middle grade and young adult) and adult speculative fiction. Adult science fiction and fantasy stories have a larger margin for copious exposition, as can be seen in such recent hits as Andy Weir's *The Martian* and Neal Stephenson's tome *Seveneves*. Those of us who write for young people are kept to a much stricter confine. Build your world, but keep it close to your vest. Dole it out like it's a secret, and readers will receive it like the prize it is.

WRITING IN LIVING COLOR

As you set the bones of your world just below the surface, remember that the best worlds extend outward, too. They give a clear sense of living beyond the page. They drop hints of past and future events. They tease and whisper and, through this, they linger. Teasing out the ends of your story counteracts the feeling of a box-shaped book quivering in blank space. It blurs those edges and extends vine-like tendrils to anchor it into the world—*your* world.

The first paragraph of Holly Black's magnificent *The Darkest Part of the Forest* plunges us headfirst into the world of her making:

> Down a path worn into the woods, past a stream and a hollowed-out log full of pill bugs and termites, was a glass coffin. It rested right on the ground, and in it slept a boy with horns on his head and ears as pointed as knives.

Can you see that path, how it beckons? Who *wouldn't* follow her down it?

As you work your way through your second draft, info-dump in hand, trying to decide which bits really belong in your story, you might find yourself in what feels like an all-out war with words. Here are some quick techniques for hand-to-hand combat:

- **SEE THROUGH YOUR CHARACTER'S EYES.** "Don't try to show the reader the world you've created. Instead, show the reader how your *character* sees their world," *Icefall* author Matthew Kirby says. Linking the information you dispense directly to the character's actions and emotions will make it feel authentic, vital and earned. For a strong example of this technique in action, look to Marie Rutkoski's *The Winner's Curse*: a fully layered, intensely political young adult fantasy in which the main characters never leave the helm.
- **FIND A BETTER WAY.** Some books *need* heavy worldbuilding for the story to work. Trent Reedy's *Divided We Fall,* which describes a modern American civil war, could have been filled with easy tropes of the characters watching TV news or the like to give context. Instead, Reedy layered his first-person narrative with "media noise" segments in line with what young readers might catch glimpses of in their own, real worlds: presidential speeches, social media posts, radio broadcasts, and more. This omniscient overview of the broader events occurs outside of the main character's purview, preserving the authenticity of the reading experience, but still giving a full big-picture view. What creative format might help give your readers a better view of your world's narrative context?
- **OWN YOUR LEVEL OF DETAIL.** In some books, the world *is* the story. These are rare, and rarer still for a debut author, so choose this path with care. But in reading a story such as Angie Sage's *Magyk*, you can see that it thrives on what could be seen as extraneous detail. The result is a live, pulsating world, the success of which can be handily summed up in the catchphrase printed on my battered paperback: "The bestselling series: over 1 million copies sold." Know the rules, respect them—but also know when to follow your muse, wherever she might lead.

CHECKING YOURSELF

I can't count the times I've been sailing along reading a book, only to be yanked out cold by some illogical contradiction. However peripheral the element, if it doesn't make sense you've lost me as a reader. This is where getting feedback is invaluable: It's humanly impossible for any one person to think of all angles and views on a situation. Swapping manuscripts with a few trusted writing friends can illuminate different sides to issues you haven't thought of before—and can save much embarrassment, or even loss of readership, down the road.

Building a world is hard work. Once you get to the final stage of your manuscript, you might find it helpful, as I do, to create a "world bible." This is especially vital if you are writing a series, but even for a stand-alone: Who knows when you might want to revisit this world, or use it as a point of reference in crafting another universe? (Note: Assemble this document as late in the process as possible—preferably at the copyediting stage or later. Small things often change very late in the game, and the last thing you want is an inaccurate map guiding your way to later books.) List each character (descriptions, traits, mannerisms, etc.), specifics of each setting, and details of history, geography and culture throughout the series. It can be grueling work, but when you start the next book and your memories of this one have faded, you'll be glad to have it.

AMMI-JOAN PAQUETTE (www.ajpaquette.com) is a senior literary agent with Erin Murphy Literary Agency, the author of *Princess Juniper of the Hourglass*, as well as several other books for young readers..

PLOT & TENSION

Write with rhythm and thrills.

....

by Steven James

You're stuck.

Your story has a great hook, a killer opening, and an unforgettable climax, but you can already tell that the pace of the journey from beginning to end is too slow.

No. That's not going to work. So you decide to build in a climactic sequence right there in the middle. However, then you face a new problem: How do you keep readers flipping pages past the resolution of the mid-book climax and through to the even-more-climactic final climax in the last act?

Is there a way to balance all this out? Is there a way to keep readers enthralled through the buildup and resolution of multiple plot points as they move on to the finale? Can you really continue to escalate a story even after you've closed up some of its threads?

The answer is yes. And it all has to do with the interplay of subplots, narrative promises, structure, pace, and reader expectations. Here's how to pull it off.

1. UNDERSTAND THE DYNAMICS OF ENGAGEMENT

Readers want to wonder, worry, anticipate, and hope. They'll set a book down if they (1) don't know what's going on, (2) don't understand why it's going on, or (3) don't care that it's going on.

So give them what they want: an excuse to keep turning pages.

First, keep them oriented to the central struggles of the story. Nothing is as confusing as action without intention. Readers need to know why a character is doing what she is doing. So give her a goal rather than simply an activity. Don't let her just go through the motions. Make it clear why your characters are acting in specific ways, make the stakes high enough for readers to care, and always keep the action believable.

Second, remember that there is nothing as boring as relentless action.

What? Action can be *boring*?

Yes. Unwavering, sustained conflict ends up having the same effect as no conflict at all—it wears readers out and causes them to lose interest. That's why stories that draw readers in and strike them as honest about life have moments between the action sequences—just as real life does. At the climax of each of your escalating acts, there'll be a moment of calm as the characters process what just happened and make decisions that lead to the next scene.

The greater the buildup to the climax, the more important that interlude is. But during those interludes you can lose readers. Too many stories stall out and languish in the mire of reorientation after exciting sequences.

So when you look again to your story, don't just add more problems. Add more *promises*. Keep readers guessing, caring, and worrying.

How?

1. Keep them guessing through twists, plot turns, mysteries, secrets, and revelations.
2. Keep them caring by creating characters worthy of their attention, emotion, and time.
3. Keep them worrying by having danger crouch in the background or hover on the horizon.
4. And even more important, keep readers *longing for things to be different.*

To create longing you'll need to induce both empathy with and concern for your characters. In real life when we care about someone who's in a crisis, we long for things to be resolved, for the situation to be different. This is just as true of our relationship to fictional characters.

Strive to do more than convince readers to care about your characters. Take it deeper. Skewer readers on the longing they have for those characters to achieve their unmet desires. Let that lead them through the story.

2. REEVALUATE THE STRUCTURE OF YOUR STORY

If you take a textbook approach to structure, the number of acts you're trying to use might be counter-intuitive to the type of story you're trying to tell.

Some stories work well in three acts. Others need two. Or four. Or more. Stories move from origination into tension, then through escalating cycles of conflict until they reach a satisfying conclusion. Don't get trapped into thinking that this has to happen in a certain number of acts.

In the traditional three-act paradigm, stories often falter in the long second act. Even those who teach this approach talk about the story sagging in the middle.

If you find that's the case with your story, consider (1) moving the second act's climax forward, (2) breaking the story up into four (or more) acts rather than three, or (3) adding subplots to enrich your story and to provide staggered moments of resolution.

Every story is unique, and the pace of your story's movement toward the climax needs to be unique as well. Be wary of anyone who suggests you fix your narrative by recasting it so that it fits into his formula—whatever that might be. Instead, look carefully at the pace of your story based on how it *reads* rather than how well it meshes with a certain predetermined theoretical framework.

Trust your instinct over your outline.

Start thinking beyond the conventions of two-, three- or four-act structure and instead view your story as a dynamic whole with interlaced promises that build and pulse and inform each other on the way to the climax.

3. OVERLAP PROMISES THAT MATTER

Stories have rhythms, beats. They pause and regroup; they rocket forward into unforgettable sequences of action and resolution.

This naturally happens as the ever-escalating heartbeat of tension/release takes readers on a journey deeper into emotion, deeper into themselves.

Stories are about more than just what's happening on the page at any given moment. They're about promises, anticipation, fulfillment, and satisfaction.

Promises come in two forms: overt and implied. Overt promises often originate from the characters themselves:

> "I'll meet you at five o'clock for our meeting. Don't be late."
> "I'm not going to rest until I catch Ben's killer."
> "He's got a twist waiting for you at the end that you wouldnever expect."

These promises tell readers straight-out what's coming and create either anticipation or apprehension, depending on the specific promise being made.

Implied promises, on the other hand, come from subtext, backstory, or from readers' implicit understanding of story.

For example, if the killer is caught on page 250 of a 500-page novel, readers are thinking, *OK, he's either going to escape or get set free on some sort of technicality.*

They know this not because you told them it was going to happen, but because they already instinctively understand narrative principles. Note that foreshadowing differs from promise-making. Foreshadowing is used to eliminate coincidences. Promises are made to elicit interest.

Dead spots in a storyline happen when a promise isn't being made or kept—but a story that's rich in promises is a story that's hard to put down.

So, layer in, overlap, and intertwine the overt and implied narrative promises, and you'll move readers up to and then past moments of resolution in your story.

EVERY SUBPLOT WILL:
- Have its own narrative arc—that is, its own movement from origination to escalation to resolution.
- Add tension to (rather than distract from or drag down) the main plot.
- Relate to and inform (at least peripherally) the protagonist's journey as he strives to fulfill his unmet desire.
- Have an essential and meaningful connection to the other storylines.
- Resolve at different times or in different ways to provide a progression of moments of resolution.

4. STAGGER THE RESOLUTION OF PLOT THREADS

Closure is the enemy of tension, but tension is the lifeblood of your story. So if you include too much resolution too early you'll undermine your reader's engagement with the story. What about a mid-book climax, then?

Well, we sustain tension when we have different levels of struggles relating to the protagonist's journey. These struggles revolve around how your character deals with himself, with others, and with the world around him.

So, your detective might be struggling with depression (inner turmoil), trying to catch the killer (external quest) and also attempting to salvage her marriage after her husband's affair (interpersonal crisis).

Make the most of the interplay of these three facets of your plot. The tension will increase as she faces setbacks in each area—and if closure occurs on one level (for example, she reconciles with her husband), there's still underlying tension to keep readers engaged.

Bring that to the forefront of their attention.

And remember that these struggles might originate, escalate, and resolve at different times.

As you stagger the moments of resolution, remember to keep readers oriented to the characters' intentions and the stakes. Use reversals, in which the things that appear to be good are actually devastatingly bad. Keep questions alive—not necessarily *if* a character will find closure, but *how*. And sustain the narrative momentum as the strands of the story escalate in tension.

5. USE SUSPENSE TO YOUR ADVANTAGE

In a mystery, the crime has occurred and must be solved. In suspense, it's going to occur and must be stopped.

Unanswered questions (mysteries) keep readers flipping pages because of *curiosity*, whereas impending peril (suspense) keeps them reading because of *concern*.

And the event in question doesn't have to be a crime. Any event in the character's past (or backstory) could have deeply impacted him. You can provide a slow reveal that also keeps readers on the edge of their seats as they look forward to (or fear) the consequences of the secret coming to light.

Curiosity appeals to intellect and creates intrigue: Readers wonder what will happen or why it has.

Concern appeals to emotion and creates apprehension: Readers worry about what will happen and what the consequences will be when it does.

Use the interplay of curiosity and concern to keep readers engaged. Alternate between letting them desire what's coming (closure, a happy ending, etc.) and dreading that it will (pain, suffering, dramatic plunges, etc.).

And here's the secret: Always keep either curiosity or concern alive until the final climax of your story. For example, if you resolve suspense in one area (the crime is thwarted) keep the mystery alive in another (they still don't know who the perpetrator is).

Conversely, if a mystery is solved (they discover the villain's identity), keep the suspense alive (they must now stop him before he strikes again). At the end of every act, accentuate the mystery or suspense that has become primary at that point in the story.

6. CAPITALIZE ON MULTIPLE PLOTLINES

Every relationship your protagonist has will provide you with an opportunity for a subplot. This doesn't mean you'll pursue all of these potential story threads, but it does mean that you can capitalize on the most important ones to keep readers engaged.

Think of subplots as layers of unmet desire that intertwine with, rather than simply parallel, the main plot. If a subplot has nothing to do with the main character's journey toward her unmet desire (or object of desire), then it can probably be cut.

Effective subplots do more than add texture to stories; they provide opportunities for you to spread out mini climaxes and resolutions throughout the novel.

In my novels featuring FBI criminologist Patrick Bowers, I often give him two apparently unrelated cases to solve. Readers rightly expect that the two plotlines will eventually intertwine. Making it seem as if there are parallel plots can be a way of drawing readers in as they wonder, "What do these story lines possibly have to do with each other?"

Multifaceted plots like this provide a strong underlying layer of conflict: Even as Agent Bowers moves forward with one case, the other one is there in the background. While one of the storylines might rise to the forefront at any given moment, both are essentially facets of the same plot rather than either one being subordinate to the other.

In multifaceted plots, there needs to be more than just a coincidental or tangential connection between the story lines. The more central the connection is in retrospect late in the story—and the more invisible it is at first—the more satisfying it'll be when it's revealed.

Using multifaceted story lines broadens the story's appeal, helps it span genres, deepens readers' engagement and ratchets up the tension.

7. REMIND READERS OF THE RIPTIDES

An ocean might appear calm, but there are always undercurrents lurking just beneath the surface. And even when the waves you can see are flowing in one direction, undertows might be flowing in an entirely different direction.

As it is in the ocean, so it is in your story.

When things start to appear calm, you need to catch your readers in the riptides and draw them deeper into the currents of tension running through the sea of your story.

How?

- Point out the overt promises, mysteries, and unanswered questions.
- Slowly reveal clues that uncover a long-hidden skeleton in the closet or explain a unique character trait that has been present throughout the story.
- Emphasize the time crunches or introduce a countdown to the climax.
- Use multiple point-of-view characters to layer in conflict, accentuate storylines, or build subplots.
- Have characters discuss the difficulty of the quest (or the task at hand) or the devastating consequences of failure.
- Pivot the narrative so the central struggles of the story are at the forefront by calling back to mind what the protagonist wants, or the dueling desires that are vying for her attention or allegiance.

As you escalate the middle of your story, or keep things rolling after a mid-book climax, remind readers of the promises, the plans and the stakes. Work to make sure there's always escalating tension and unresolved conflict, as well as unanswered questions, overlapping subplots, underlying promises, or unrevealed secrets.

The resolution will come in the final act, but until then, entice readers to fly through the book toward that satisfying climax where you've saved the best revelations, secrets and twists for last.

STEVEN JAMES is a contributing editor to *Writer's Digest* magazine. He is the critically acclaimed, best-selling author of 10 novels as well as the craft book *Story Trumps Structure* (WD Books). When he's not writing, trail running, or watching science fiction movies, he teaches creative storytelling around the world.

AGENTS EVALUATE KIDLIT FIRST PAGES

Why agents stop reading MG & YA submissions.

by MacKenzie Fraser-Bub, Carly Watters, Kirsten Carleton, and Kate McKean

Writing a compelling first page is difficult. No matter what genre or category you write in, combining the right degree of action, description, dialogue, and voice is a delicate balancing act. Agents and editors want to get pulled in on page one. And when they don't, writers wonder: Where did I go wrong? At what point did the agent give up?

So to help you understand exactly what goes through an agent's mind, we've asked four literary agents to participate in a brand-new *CWIM* feature: the "First Pages Read," which documents exactly when an agent stops reading your submission and why. Here you'll find nine real, unpublished first pages of manuscripts, accompanied by notes from four literary agents. (The authors of these pages are anonymous and have given their consent to be included in this article.) Pay attention to where and why the agents stopped to issue a rejection—or where they *didn't* stop—and note the advice they have to share. But before we begin, meet the four participating literary agents:

MACKENZIE FRASER-BUB is the founder of Fraser-Bub Literary (www.fraserbubliterary. com). Fraser-Bub began her career in publishing at the Crown Publishing Group, a division of Penguin Random House. She's a veteran of the Columbia Publishing Course, having taught and worked there. She also spent several years at Simon and Schuster (Touchstone Books), in one of the industry's finest marketing departments, before becoming an agent at the venerable Trident Media Group. While at Trident, she quickly built a diverse list that included multiple *New York Times* and *USA Today* best-selling titles, including romance, new adult, women's fiction, and science fiction. The number ❶ on the following manuscript pages indicates where Fraser-Bub stopped reading.

CARLY WATTERS is a senior agent with P.S. Literary (www.psliterary.com). Watters began her publishing career in London at the Darley Anderson Literary Agency. She has a bachelor of arts degree in English literature from Queen's University and a master of arts degree in publishing studies from City University London. Since joining P.S. Literary in 2010, she has had great success launching new authors both domestically and abroad. Representing debut novels and bestsellers, Watters is drawn to emotional, well-paced fiction with a great voice and characters that readers can get invested in, as well as platform-driven nonfiction. The number ❷ on the following manuscript pages indicates where Watters stopped reading.

KIRSTEN CARLETON is a literary agent with Prospect Agency (www.prospectagency.com). Before joining Prospect in 2015, she agented at Sobel Weber Associates and the Waxman Leavell Agency. Carleton fell in love with working with writers while getting her bachelor's degree in English with a creative writing concentration from Amherst College, and she cemented her fascination with publishing with a graduate certificate in publishing from the Columbia Publishing Course and internships at Charlesbridge and Liza Dawson Associates. The number ❸ on the following manuscript pages indicates where Carleton stopped reading.

KATE MCKEAN is a literary agent with Howard Morhaim Literary (www.morhaimliterary. com). She earned her master's degree in fiction writing at the University of Southern Mississippi and began her publishing career at the University Press of Florida. She is proud to work with *New York Times* best-selling authors in a wide variety of genres. In addition to working with clients, she is an adjunct professor at New York University. The number ❹ on the following manuscript pages indicates where McKean stopped reading.

While the manuscript pages below show agents' specific reasons for why they rejected a submission, they also reveal the extremely subjective nature of the business. After all, one agent could review a scene and say it has "too much description," while another could be entranced by the same passage. Such subjective contradiction is nothing new, but it does prove that, when submitting fiction, you should cast a wide net and contact many agents. You never know which rep will completely fall in love with your storytelling ability, plot, and voice.

Also, it's important to note that just because an agent says no to one of the following submissions doesn't mean that the writer in question has written a poor book or is a poor writer. It simply means that the book fails to start in the right place, or that the submission doesn't pull the agent in with immediate story conflict or writing prowess.

Before we begin, remember that the numbers you see in each submission represent the exact point where the literary agent stopped reading and would issue a rejection. If agents' numbers appear at the bottom of the first page of the manuscript, this indicates that the agent read the entire first page.

MIDDLE-GRADE

As a recent graduate of the sixth grade, Michael Chapman knew a thing or two about how the world worked and felt more than qualified to say that this was the most boring summer in the history of the universe.

Michael was short for his age with straight blonde hair and ears that stuck out a little more than he would have liked. He lived with his father in a cabin on a river in the town of Beaver Creek, Alaska. Beavers were extinct, of course, and had been for centuries, but no one had bothered to change the name. In fact, no one on Earth had bothered to change much of anything in over three hundred years. It just took too much effort.

Beaver Creek was never an exciting place to live, but Michael didn't think it was too bad. There was great fishing right outside of his house, and his best friend, Tom Quinn, lived just down the road. Each summer the two of them would spend a month at Uncle Bunyan's Camp for Kids where they rode horses, practiced archery, and hiked in the mountains. While their town may not have had a zoo or a movie theater or enough kids for a baseball team, Michael didn't mind. It was his home, and he was happy.

But that was before this summer.

The trouble all started a month ago when the entire Quinn family disappeared. Mr. Quinn left a note on their front door that said they'd be vacationing in Borneo until August. Michael had no idea where Borneo was, but his father told him it was about as far from Alaska as somebody could get. This wasn't like them at all. Michael had known the Quinns his whole life, and they'd never even thought about traveling beyond Anchorage before. And Tom didn't even bother to say goodbye. **❶ ❷ ❸ ❹**

1. FRASER-BUB: I read to the end because this had some intriguing threads, but this is way too much information; I feel thoroughly confused about a lot of details, including: Was it a boring summer, or did a family go missing?

2. WATTERS: I enjoyed this. It has the most crucial feature of MG fiction: voice. I liked that on the first page we were introduced to important information, but it never felt like an "information dump" overload. We had a strong voice, interesting setting, and great sense of what the problem or conflict was going to be.

3. CARLETON: I enjoyed it. The first sentence has humor and personality, and I like the way the author slid the futuristic setting into the second paragraph. I think it could be clearer that the third paragraph is the way things *used* to be, not the way it is currently, but correcting the tense throughout would do the trick.

4. MCKEAN: I read the whole sample, but mainly to get to the part where the central problem of the novel is revealed. I was much less interested in what Tom and Michael normally did in the summer than what's different about this summer.

YOUNG ADULT NO. 1

The rafters stretch across the ceiling of the Zoo Chamber like honeycomb. I sit high in the metal branches, my legs thrown over one of the beams. It's a thirty meter drop into the sea of trees below. Not real trees, of course. The Zoo Chamber is filled with rubber trunks and plastic leaves, a fake forest that stretches beyond the horizon. I call it the horizon only because I have no better word. The so-called trees disappear where the curve of our ship takes a mighty turn. I haven't seen a real horizon since I was six. Normally I'm good at forgetting all of this isn't real, but today is different. Today I can't forget anything. I guess that's why they call it Remembrance Day. **❶**

"Here it comes," Sybil whispers. My sister leans forward, as close as she can get to the glass wall that surrounds the Zoo Chamber.

Outside the glass, the moon slips from view.

Earth appears.

The colors always take me by surprise. Earth is color. A thousand shades of blue. A hundred tints of green. Ribbons of white, circling everything like a cage. It looks just like the pictures they used to show us in school, except for all the red light. That's new. The glow covers the planet like a second skin. If you watch carefully, you can almost see it pulse. I was born down there, somewhere in the green mountains of a country called the United Northern Republics. The red light is why I left. It's why we all left, while we still could.

Sybil holds up two fingers and closes an eye, extending her arm toward our old planet.

"What are you doing?"

"Picking a point."

I've had enough of this. **❷ ❸ ❹**

1. FRASER-BUB: I'm already exhausted. I need to feel immediately immersed in another world; the artificial forest is an interesting concept, but I want to be able to feel and see it, and I thought this description was needlessly convoluted.

2. WATTERS: I read to the end. What I think this page did really well was set the scene, which is absolutely paramount in a fantasy novel's success.

3. CARLETON: I read the full page and would read more, warily. I like the writing and the imagery, but the setup feels a bit familiar, especially the trope of the young adult story opening on an "Official Day" of some sort.

4. MCKEAN: This does a great job of world-building and establishing mystery. I would keep reading to learn more about the story.

YOUNG ADULT NO. 2

Macon, Ga., 1962

I'm in French when "Squinty" Swinfield, our principal, pokes his head in the classroom door and whispers to Miss Tewksbury, aka The Queen of Kankakee, to send me to his office.

My Dad's on the phone. He tells me to meet him at the front of the school in fifteen minutes.

It's Mom! ❷ ❸

My heart starts beating hard. Crazies dart through my brain like a flock of caffeinated bats. After I cram my books into my book bag, I rush down the school steps outside. The front of the school is massive, one of those institutions built in the roaring twenties, dear old Timrod High or Dimrod Sty. These days the glory's a little faded with the integrationists going at the segregationists and Marilyn Monroe dead from pills. It's a chilly October day here in the old burg. The sweet gum balls are dropping from the tree across the street, and I'm pounding my feet when Dad pulls up. I slide into the warm, smell coming from his aftershave and his coffee mug steaming in the console.

He doesn't look at me. I don't speak. We've both been expecting this day to come.

He wheels away from the curb fast.

"Mom threw up for three hours," he says. "She was at home alone, so there was no one to help. Mrs. Schwartz looked in and found her crawling around in her puke." ❶ ❹

1. FRASER-BUB: I was reading the tone as spontaneous and whimsical, and then ... not. I read to the end, but I feel conflicted; there was something endearing about the oddness of the kid, but I feel deceived by his mother's condition.

2. WATTERS: I didn't feel that the voice and writing style matched the intended YA audience. The YA issues are usually more within the kids and their drama-filled teen lives, with perhaps a mention here and there of teachers and parents, but not typically as a central conflict. I was surprised to see this on the first page.

3. CARLETON: I love the oddball nicknames in the first sentence, but this awkward exclamation took me out of the narrative.

4. MCKEAN: I found myself reading on to figure out what was happening, more so than because I was particularly drawn in to the story. Historical YA can be very hard. I felt there was more attention paid to nicknames and setting than to the possibly tense situation happening with Mom. Her health seems more important than a description of the school. That scene setting can come later.

YOUNG ADULT NO. 3

The girl was gone and had been for years. Holding on to the hope of seeing her again after so long seemed more foolish each trip Ahrielle made to the village of Phoenecia and the Lowlands beyond. But no matter how hard she tried, she couldn't banish the thought that her friend was out there somewhere and she would see Khari again—someday. ❸

Ahrielle tugged at the hood of her cloak, making sure her fiery red hair was completely concealed. She kept her head lowered as she walked through Phoenecia, hoping no one would recognize her. The village was a rushing sea of golden-skinned faces hurrying in all directions, tending to their daily business as usual. Shops lined either side of the street that sold anything a person could ever desire. The smell of freshly baked bread perfumed the section of street right outside Kato's Bakery and the bell on the door tinkled as a woman pushed it open and led her two small children inside who were already asking if they could buy a couple of sun-berry muffins. Next door to the bakery, a woman stood in the window and worked diligently at setting up a display of a beautiful sapphire gown that dripped in shimmering crystal.

Ahrielle turned a corner and stepped out of the warmth of the golden yellow sky, trading the happy chatter and pleasant smells of Phoenecia for a cool, dark alleyway that reeked of mud and garbage that had sat far too long underneath the rays of the photosphere sky 222. Although she'd made this trip more times than she could count, her heart still thumped hard against her ribcage like it was the first. The sound of hooves clopping against cobblestone followed by the voices of two men talking and laughing sent a nervous jolt through Ahrielle's body. She turned her back to the main street and moved to run but the men were at the alley before she could escape. One of the men called out to her, stopping her in her tracks. ❶ ❷ ❹

1. FRASER-BUB: There's some nice imagery here. However, I would certainly be looking for some creativity and freshness very quickly as this feels familiar.

2. WATTERS: I read the whole page, but I didn't feel like I got a good sense of who the character was here. I understand the need to set the scene, but this was a very placid first page for me.

3. CARLETON: I like the first sentence a lot, but the writing quickly starts to feel cliché and overblown. It seems like the author is imitating some kind of fantasy writing she's read rather than forging her own style.

4. MCKEAN: I read the whole sample, but I felt like there was more of an emphasis on flowery adjectives than substantive world-building. Why is Ahrielle so nervous? Why does she travel so much? That feels more important than the physical details here.

YOUNG ADULT NO. 4

"My father was a doughnut man. Many times in life we declare a profession, but that one claimed him. Ever since I can remember, I associated the smell of fried dough with Dad. Some smokers could never wash the cigarette stench off their clothing. My father couldn't rub the saturated browned cake smell out of his. It was total pandemonium if the man ever took a day off—a reason I speculate my mother adored him for." ❶

"It was love at first whiff, if you like that sort of thing. Hard work and low income can wear on any man, especially with a family to support. It seemed the long hours had taken a toll on his body. If only dreams paid what they were worth."

"I never missed a morning without my dad until that day. It was raining. Because it always rains when I go camping, and of course it would rain on the day he died. Life had an odd way of foreshadowing misfortune. With so very little in your control, it only leaves you clues to look for, if you're present enough to notice. By my guess, the signs were probably right in front of us, but we never managed to look up. Some say ignorance is bliss; I say ignorance is mundane. We all do it, clinging so tightly to our daily routines like a warm security blanket." I paused, glancing away from the paper, ready to be done with this whole charade. "It is what it is and there is nothing we can do about it." ❷

I felt confident enough about what I had written. It was a lot of effort on my part, surely she knew that. The last time Ms. Leamer asked me to write a short paragraph in regards to my feelings, I choked, turned in a blank sheet of paper after sitting on my hands all week. She thought it was a joke. I just didn't know what to write. ❸ ❹

1. FRASER-BUB: This first sentence is great, but it's a rapid downhill. The sentence structure is flawed and this part about the "pandemonium" doesn't doesn't make any sense.

2. WATTERS: I'm on the fence about the opening—it made me pause and feel unsure, which is never what a writer wants the reader to feel. My issue was that I didn't know what I was reading. I thought it was a monologue or the quotation marks were misplaced.

3. CARLETON: I like the writing, so I read to the end of the page, but I have to admit that I was thrown by the revelation that these first paragraphs were an essay within the story. I wish the author had let me know sooner, either by shortening the quoted portion or by hinting at the structure earlier. There's an interesting contrast between the tone of the essay and the character's impatience, and I'd read more to see how it plays out.

4. MCKEAN: I am curious why Ms. Leamer is asking this student to write about his/her feelings, but I felt using this as an opening felt like an info dump and convenient way for the character to *tell* the reader his/her feelings, instead of *showing* it in action or dialogue.

YOUNG ADULT NO. 5

To the trees, leaves and birds, Michael Torrent was a blur. He ran through the woods like mad, his eyes focused but his heart racing. *He was going to miss it, he just knew he was going miss it!* The spilled contents of his book bag were clutched in his arms as he flew down the forest path, as well as the signed permission slip grasped tightly in his hand. *It was the permission slip's fault*, Michael thought as he ran, *that stupid pink permission slip!* ❸

Of course, Michael could have had it signed the week before when his social studies teacher, Mrs Gradleman, handed them out to everyone in class; but, as thoughts have a way of doing, it left his mind nearly as soon as it entered. Instead, Michael shoved it into his bag and somehow managed to think about anything but the folded pink half-sheet for a week until he was halfway to the bus stop with his friends the day of the field trip.

The realization jolted him like a starter pistol. He immediately turned heel and sprinted back along the path through the woods to his house. Luckily his father happened to be running late as well and Michael caught him as he was getting into his car. He hastily procured the required signature before starting out at a run again the other way. His father called out after him, "You're not gonna be late, are ya?" to which Michael shouted back over his shoulder, "Plenty of time!" *Famous last words*, Michael thought now. ❶ ❷

Not a minute after he'd run back into the woods the bottom of his book bag busted a seam, dropping spiral notebooks and school supplies at his heels. ❹ He hastily scooped his soiled things into his arms and continued running, only with a renewed sense of urgency. He passed where he'd had his epiphany and was beginning to relax, when he heard his friends' voices faintly through the trees. They were yelling his name over and over which Michael astutely recognized could only mean one thing: the bus was coming.

1. FRASER-BUB: I wish this moved forward linearly. This entire section could be one paragraph; we're just reiterating the same information the entire four paragraphs.

2. WATTERS: I found this scattered opening unsettling. It's one thing to start with some action, but it's another to give the reader confusion. I think this first page would have benefited from more setting. In doing that, you'd slow down the pace a tad, which would be helpful in this case. It would still be suspenseful, but we would be more grounded in where we are and able to root for him.

3. CARLETON: The double repetition of the internal monologue feels forced, like the author is trying to convince me of an urgency that's not really there. Also, if the italicized sentences are Michael's thoughts, then they should be in first person.

4. MCKEAN: What is this permission slip for? In the first paragraph, we know he is late and his book bag broke, so the next two paragraphs don't need to reiterate that. *Why* he is late is less interesting than what he is late *for*.

YOUNG ADULT NO. 6

The Doctor approached the clock and stopped it right at three fifteen A.M. Then not even looking back swiftly left the room just as the body of Margaret Wilshire took its last breath. After all, a running clock in a room of death would certainly bring even more bad luck to three children now stricken with the loss of not one but both parents. The now silent timepiece's gears and bells allowed the pounding of the rain on the shutters to echo even louder. ❸ Ronnie, the eldest daughter at seventeen, whose given name was Sophronia, continued to hold onto her mother's hand as the warmth slowly faded away. The bright streaks of light which illuminated and then dissipated followed by a crash of thunder so loud it shook the brick mansion only added to the emptiness and despair of the grieve stricken boudoir. The fever had come on quick, and Doctor Chauncey had tried everything imaginable. It was as if the will to live was plucked from her in the same instant the dark red lines appeared on her face, down her arms, and along her back. The same affliction had taken her father not even three weeks prior. Janie the youngest had fallen asleep at the foot of the bed. Dallas, the middle child, had tried desperately to maintain his alertness. He had however lost his fight with the night some two hours ago and sunk in the far corner of the room with his arms still crossed in defiance. Tears fell from Ronnie's eyes as she struggled to maintain her posture beside the bed. "You must not even for an instance lose your composure in public, young Lady, they feed off weakness" her mother had told her in the final moments between gasps as she struggled to fill her lungs. "If you must be sad, do it only in private and never let your guard down. You are now the keeper and the protector." ❶ ❷

"Mother! No! Please do not leave me." She exclaimed. "Shh child do not wake your brother and sister I have much to tell you and my time draws short. The broken medallion and key around my neck quickly removed it and put it on" the Lady Wilshire struggled to continue. ❹ "You must promise me you will always wear it. Promise me now."

1. FRASER-BUB: I think with some reorganization this would work better. I think we should open with the mother's last words before the doctor lets us know she's dead.

2. WATTERS: (Watters did not review this submission.)

3. CARLETON: Where are the commas? Once I mentally inserted them, the sentences in this first paragraph were readable, but the prospect of doing that throughout the rest of the novel is exhausting.

4. MCKEAN: These seem like long sentences to be uttered by a dying woman struggling to breathe. I also couldn't get a sense of the point of view of this story. It feels like it might be from the doctor's point of view, which would seem out of place for YA. The prose here does not create an authoritative narrative to me.

SALINA YOON

On novelty books, picture books, and the key to "smart" publishing.

·····································

by Kara Gebhart Uhl

Born in Korea, 1972, Salina Yoon came to the United States in 1976. Like many immigrant children, Yoon's parents didn't read, write, or speak English. As a young child with no one to read books to her, Yoon studied the images and illustrations. "As I would pore over the art, my love of drawing grew and grew," she says. "I connected with the illustrations more than the words. I knew that my future would involve art, even from a very young age."

While Yoon loved to draw as a teenager at Los Angeles County High School for the Arts, she also enjoyed graphic design. Album covers, book covers, and signs on billboards fascinated her, and she went on to study graphic design at California State University, Northridge. Little did Yoon know that she was building the foundation to a book career in which graphic design will be critical.

But upon graduation, Yoon realized she missed drawing and illustrating. So she enrolled in the illustration program at the ArtCenter College of Design. While between terms at ArtCenter, she cold-called a small publishing house and book packager that specialized in novelty and pop-up books, to ask about an internship at their office. After an interview, she was accepted, and that led to a full-time position as a book designer, then art director.

Yoon eventually left that job to freelance as a book creator. "I played with paper to see what I can make happen," she says. "More than 130 of my published books are novelty board books, so I did a lot of playing. To submit a novelty board book, I designed the book in its entirety, including the physical format, created the illustrations, and wrote the text. I used every skillset I had up to that point to create these books."

Today Yoon says she's more focused on writing stories for picture books and illustrating them. Here Yoon talks about the process of creating a novelty book, how she's managed to publish more than 160 books since 2001, and why she chose to seek representation after having published more than 100 books on her own.

"How I Broke In" stories are favorites with aspiring author/illustrators. Please share yours.

I published with Intervisual Books (Piggy Toes Press imprint), though I don't consider these titles as my breakout books since they were acquired by the company I worked for in-house for three years. I aspired to publish with a major New York house, specifically Simon & Schuster, Penguin, and Scholastic at the time. After creating a dummy that I felt was ready, I used the *Children's Writer's & Illustrator's Market* (*CWIM*) to find the submission guidelines for Price, Stern, and Sloan (PSS!), an imprint of Penguin at the time (now Penguin Random). I always targeted my submissions to a specific imprint based on the publisher's current list.

The *CWIM* was an excellent resource in helping to navigate the trials of book submission without having an agent. My first authored/illustrated submission to PSS! was a big success. I received a phone call from an intern to express great interest in the project. This turned into an eight-book deal, but even better was building a long-lasting relationship with the Penguin group. We went on to publish more than forty books together, including a massive twenty-two-book deal just a few years after my first deal with them.

You are prolific. As a mother of two sons and someone who is actively involved in talks, signings, and appearances, how do you manage your time?

I have published mostly novelty and board books, and these are much shorter in length and smaller in size than a picture book. Typically, I could complete the art, design, and illustrations for one book within a few weeks.

The nice thing about novelty books is that, usually, they are sold as a series. By selling two formats, this may mean four to six books, or more down the line. They add up quickly! But now, my focus is on the longer and larger forty-page picture book series or my sixty-four-page early reader series, which take me a few months to complete. I have help from my husband when I travel, but mostly, I work at home or at a nearby library or café. My work schedule is highly unstructured and flexible.

As for events, I am very selective with what I participate in (they are mostly vetted by my PR team or agent), and I limit school visits to about just a dozen a year. Contrary to what most may think, I don't actually work every day. Sometimes, I don't accomplish much in even a week or two. Unscheduled downtime is so important to me, and while I may not be productive every day, the work happens quickly when I begin.

You are represented by Jamie Weiss Chilton of the Andrea Brown Literary Agency. Has Chilton been your agent from the beginning? What is the key to a successful relationship between an author and agent?

I published more than one hundred books before seeking an agent. For me, I wasn't seeking an agent for publishing contacts or to sell books since I had many contacts, and was selling on my own quite well. I was seeking one to help me publish in a new genre (picture books), and do it in the most effective way possible. I was ready to go to the next level in my publishing career, and I knew a knowledgeable partner would be the best thing to make that happen.

Our first book submission together was an all-ages upmarket novelty book titled *Kaleidoscope*. Due to the interest of multiple imprints, it went to auction, a great benefit in working with an agent. Our third submission, *Penguin and Pinecone*, also went to auction, which launched my picture book career in a big way.

My agent is also an editorial agent, so she will advise me on my manuscripts and tighten them up before submission. We work together in building our editorial submission list, and draft the query letter together as well. Some like to be hands off, but I actually like to develop work with my agent since I had been doing it all on my own for the first ten years of my career.

I think the keys to a successful client/agent relationship are trust, great communication, mutual respect for one another, and having a shared vision with realistic goals. She does not work for me, and I do not work for her. We truly are partners in all aspects of my publishing career, though she always gives me the power of final say in all matters. She is remarkably supportive, both professionally and personally, and she's just such a good person. We've been together since 2010.

I would have likely published another hundred books without my agent, but by having Jamie in my corner, I don't have to. I now publish smarter, not simply "more." She helped me grow as a businesswoman as well as an author/illustrator. I only wish I had sought her out earlier in my career.

Your early work was made up of interactive books for young children featuring tabs, die-cuts, and flaps. They had, as you've said, "play-appeal." Tell us about the process that goes into creating such books, and how that process differs from creating a traditional picture book.

The process of creating a novelty book is multifaceted. I am thinking about format first, which means the physical design of the book. The size, the shape, and the interactive elements all make up the novelty format (the physical design). I have to make sure that the cost to produce such a format is not cost prohibitive to the publisher. This means that one should not add bells and whistles to a format simply to make it more interesting. If they are not absolutely needed or adding value in an effective way, it is simply adding cost, which kills a novelty project before it even gets considered at an acquisitions meeting.

Then I start thinking about the concept for the book, and how effective that concept works with the physical format. Typically, there is no story line for a novelty book. They are mostly concept or themed books. A bath-time theme, a colors or shapes theme, or a book about animal sounds are all concept books. Then I think about the art style that would be most appropriate to the target audience as well as fitting with the publisher's list.

The last thing I think about when creating my novelty books is the text. I add in the text to work with the concept. So one can say that novelty books are format- or art-driven and, typically, less text-driven.

But for a picture book, it's the opposite! Story is key in a picture book, so the words are essential. Picture books are typically story- or character-driven, and the physical format is inconsequential. The format of a picture book is typically a standard size, and it need not be unique. In fact, it may hurt the submission if the format does not follow a standard thirty-two- or forty-page picture book format with traditional trim sizes, though there are always exceptions to the rule.

What inspired the more character-driven Penguin series? How does the writing and illustrating process differ?

I wrote *Penguin and Pinecone*, the first book in the Penguin series, when my sons were in kindergarten and first grade. At the time, I was reading more picture books to them than board books. This grew an interest in picture books for me, but the character of Penguin was actually inspired by my older son, Max, who holds similar personality traits to Penguin, like his curiosity for the world and his compassionate heart.

I draw more than I write when drafting a picture book manuscript. It is in the pictures that I discover important plotting points and page turns. The words often come after, when the illustrations have done their work. I use text to support the illustrations, rather than the other way around.

How did the Penguin series transition into the Bear series? What special considerations have to be made when writing a series compared to stand-alone work?

I wrote the first book in the Bear series (titled *Found*) after finishing Penguin's second book. But in both cases, I did not intend to write a series. *Penguin and Pinecone* was actually submitted as a standalone title, but it was the publisher who offered on a two-book deal, which forced me to consider a second title. I had to learn quickly as I had to write the second book as soon as I finished the first. With *Found*, I knew that there was potential for a second book because the character was so lovable and relatable.

Any standalone book may have the potential of being a series if the character is appealing with unique quirks, and sells well enough. And all series titles must be as strong as a standalone even without the support of the series.

What inspired *Be a Friend* (Bloomsbury, January 2015)? It seems to be a departure from your interactive and picture books, which often feature animals?

Be a Friend was certainly a departure from my ongoing Penguin and Bear series of picture books in many ways. The main characters are human here, which I admit to avoiding whenever humanly possible. Humans are just harder to draw, while my animal characters are often very stylized to make them easier to illustrate over and over again. But when the story began to develop in my mind, the character had to be human, so I was forced to explore this visually.

The inspiration behind the character was very personal. While I was never a mime, I was a child that felt different and unable to communicate with others because I was a non-English speaker in kindergarten. I stayed silent until I found a friend that spoke Korean. But when we connected, my world opened up and I was able to laugh and play like all of the other children. *Be a Friend* is a book that is close to my heart because it celebrates differences, individuality, and the power of friendship.

What are some of the unique ways you've connected with your readers and what has resulted from those interactions?

My books are published all over the world, and I am pretty easy to access via my website. I had one parent who e-mailed me from vacation in Croatia and sent a photo of her son standing next to a pine tree where she had placed rocks around it in the shape of a heart. This image comes straight out of my book, *Penguin and Pinecone*, but hers was in real life! Not only did I write them back, but I created a special piece of artwork to send to her children all the way in the UK. I then received a book that her older child made with my Penguin character. We are still very much in touch today, and remain friends.

How do you manage working on several different projects at once with various publishers? Do you ever worry about your different projects being too similar to one another and competing?

When I was working with various publishers, I often chose an art style to use with one publisher and [would] change it for the next. It was important to me *and* the publisher to have non-competing works in any given year, and I enjoyed this challenge of having to consistently create new series with new art styles.

What three tips would you give to an aspiring author/illustrator?

(1) Read as many books in your genre as possible. If you want a number, at least one hundred books before writing your first. (2) Power through your insecurity—and grow as an author/illustrator. Remember that rejections are necessary stepping stones to publishing. The more you have, the more likely you'll get published. (3) Don't fall in love with your work. Be ready to let go, move on, and create new work if one [project] isn't getting the attention you desire. There is never a wasted project. Each one helps us grow and improve our craft.

What tips would you give to someone pitching their work?

Know why your work matters, know why your work is unique, and know why your work should be published. If you can effectively communicate these three things in a pitch letter, then you'll grab the attention of an editor or agent.

How involved are you in the products (such as the Found Floppy Bunny Doll) that accompany your books?

It depends with each company. In the case of the Floppy doll from *Found* (made by MerryMakers, Inc.), they will send a plush prototype and ask for specific comments from the creator to make sure it is exactly how they envision the work. But I am not always asked for input on licensed material.

What's on the horizon?

There will definitely be more in all three of my series: Penguin, Bear, and Duck Duck Porcupine. But look out for something unexpected, because this is what makes it interesting for me, and I don't even know what that is yet!

VICTORIA AVEYARD

On writing the story you want to read.

···

by Hannah Haney

Victoria Aveyard may be newer to the writing scene than other scribes, but you'd never know it based on her impressive résumé and accomplishments thus far. After Aveyard earned her bachelor of fine arts in screenwriting at the University of Southern California, she realized that the story she wanted to read wasn't available—so she started writing it herself. That story became her debut young adult novel, *Red Queen* (HarperTeen, 2015), which released at the top of *The New York Times* bestseller list and stayed there for weeks.

    Red Queen received rave reviews from *Kirkus* and *USA Today*, and is now optioned to be a major motion picture with Universal Studios. *Glass Sword*, the second book in the Red Queen trilogy, was released in February 2016, and Aveyard is currently hard at work on the final book. She also penned the digital novella *Cruel Crown*, set in the same world.

Despite her success, the twenty-six-year-old seems just like the girl next door. She shares fan art and answers questions on her Tumblr page, and takes to Twitter to share intense feelings about the television shows she's currently binge-watching. Her desktop computer background is a still shot from *Star Wars*, her bookshelves are overflowing, and her success continues to fill her with awe and wonder. (For more on Aveyard, visit her at www.victoriaaveyard.com.) *CWIM* sat down with Aveyard to discuss her rise to success, and what she did right along her journey.

What does your typical writing day look like? Do you set specific goals or just see what happens? Do you write from home?

    On a usual day, I wake up and spend an hour or so checking up on social media. I answer reader questions and posts on Tumblr, screw around on Twitter, make any

updates I need to make—and then grab some coffee. Sometimes I catch up on a TV show, depending on what I missed. By 10 A.M., I'm hopefully starting work and writing. Depending on what kind of groove I get into, I break for a walk in the afternoon and usually wrap up by 6 A.M. I like to keep evenings and weekends to myself. (Sometimes I'll work on other projects.) It helps keep my momentum and makes me excited to work. As awesome as this job is, it is a job, and treating it like one helps me work HARDER and better.

Tell us about how you acquired your agent, and what your publishing journey was like with *Red Queen*.

My path to publishing was a bit unorthodox. After graduating college in May 2012, I had management for my screenwriting deal, and after I [mentioned to them that I had an idea for] a YA novel, they encouraged me to pursue it. I moved home to Massachusetts from Los Angeles and finished the first draft of *Red Queen* in January 2013. My script management passed the draft to Pouya Shahbazian and Suzie Townsend at New Leaf Literary, and the latter offered representation after some much-needed edits. We went on submission in April 2013 and sold to HarperCollins two weeks in. It was a wild ride!

You blend a lot of genres here: dystopia, fantasy, science fiction, and so on. What was it like to write a novel like this?

My basic approach to writing is crafting a story I would like to read or see. I love all these genres, so naturally they wormed into what I was working on. I went for broke and wrote a story I loved. Writing is difficult, but letting my natural instincts take over, as well as the characters, was really fun to experience. The first draft took about seven months, from June 2012 to January 2013, with many edits afterward to get to the version currently on bookshelves.

Did you plan for *Red Queen* to be part of a trilogy, or did that evolve as you wrote?

I knew it would be a series from the start (because I'm greedy), but I had no idea where the ending was or how long it would take me to get there. Luckily, the ending is taking form, and I know where I want everyone to be. But I'm still working on getting them there.

You earned your B.F.A. in screenwriting. Did that help you in writing a novel or cause difficulties?

Oh, it was nothing but help. Every writing trick I know comes from my own screenwriting education. I structure my plot, flesh out my characters, and write scenes and dialogue all with the visual in mind.

What drew you to the YA category?

I have always wanted to write novels, but I never believed I could finish one until I had several screenplays under my belt. When I finally thought it was possible to finish a book, I didn't set out to write YA, but naturally gravitated toward the genre because of my age (I was twenty-one when I started) and my personal tastes.

According to New Leaf Literary's website, *Red Queen* is in the process of being adapted into a movie—with Gennifer Hutchison of "Breaking Bad" fame writing the first draft of a screenplay. Tell us about this process.

We're still very, very early in the journey from book to screen, but so far everything is going swimmingly. Fingers crossed for more news soon!

When creating your main character, Mare, how did you make her stand out?

The way I approached Mare—and most of my characters—was to understand their background and let that set the parameters of their personalities. From there, it was easy to understand what they would do in the face of the story. It's kind of like putting a mouse in a maze; all of them find their own way through, and I just have to write the twists and turns they take.

You've created an incredibly detailed world in *Red Queen*. Do you have any world-building advice for writers trying to do the same?

The rule I learned in screenwriting—and that I try to stick to—is that you can get your audience to believe one unbelievable thing. Everything else must realistically spread from this [detail] and make sense based on this divergence. I built *Red Queen* out of the idea that superhumans became real.

What was your reaction to debuting as a No. 1 *New York Times* bestseller?

I was in Chicago, about to do my very first tour stop ever, and I did not believe my editor when she called. But then I heard the rest of the HarperTeen [staff] screaming on the end of the phone, and I knew she wouldn't lie to that many people. Honestly, it didn't make sense then, and it doesn't make sense now. I still can't believe it.

Because *Red Queen* was so successful, does that create added pressure for the rest of the series?

Of course, but it's exciting to know so many people want to see what happens! The pressure is on, and I hope everyone enjoys other installments.

What should readers anticipate from the rest of the series?

Downward spirals. At the end of the day, my characters are teenagers. They don't know who they are or where they're going, and they are going to struggle with every step of the journey. The obstacles they face and the steps they take to overcome them have dire consequences, both inside and out.

What are some of your favorite moments interacting with fans online and in person?

I love Tumblr. Seeing fan art, fancasts, favorite quotes, and just plain old reader reactions to parts of the story makes my day. And, of course, in-person events can't be beat. Meeting readers is so much fun, and I adore doing it!

HANNAH HANEY (@hannah_haney) is a writer, editor, and frequent contributor to www.writersdigest.com.

RAINBOW ROWELL

On depicting the lives (and loves) of teenagers.

....

by Tyler Moss

Rainbow Rowell believes every story "is driven by relationships—whether we tell it that way or not."

This will come as no surprise to readers of her five novels, as Rowell's ability to depict deep, genuine connections between diverse characters is her hallmark. Her first novel, *Attachments* (about an Internet security officer who falls in love with an employee through monitoring her e-mail), was dubbed one of Kirkus' "Outstanding Debuts of 2011." But it was in early 2013 that Rowell was vaulted into the literary spotlight, as her runaway crossover *Eleanor & Park* took its place among such hits as *The Fault in Our Stars* and *The Perks of Being a Wallflower* as a title equally recognizable in high school halls and at adult book club meetings.

A tale of first love between teens with disparate backgrounds at an Omaha high school in the 1980s, what makes the story stand out is the viscerally real—and, at times, heartbreaking—portrayal of youthful romance between the two title characters. It's *Romeo & Juliet* with less melodrama and more comic books. In addition to being a No. 1 *New York Times* bestseller, *Eleanor & Park* won the Michael L. Printz Honor for Excellence in Young Adult Literature, and was named one of the best books of 2013 by *Publishers Weekly*, NPR, and *The New York Times Book Review*.

Rowell's follow-ups, the adult novel *Landline* (in which a thirty-something Los Angeles TV writer attempts to mend her marriage through a magical telephone) and YA smash *Fangirl* did not disappoint, either. And her October 2015 release *Carry On* was named one of the best books of 2015 by *TIME* magazine, *School Library Journal*, NPR and *The Millions*. It quickly joined *Fangirl* on *The New York Times* bestseller list, where both books sat together for fourteen weeks.

"If you're building relationships," Rowell says, "and those relationships make sense to people, that'll take you most of the way."

Always one to challenge herself creatively, Rowell is now taking a crack at writing graphic novels, as well as translating *Eleanor & Park* into a screenplay for DreamWorks. Here she chats with us about bringing life—and love—into your characters.

What appeals to you about tackling an archetype like "The Chosen One"—a la Harry Potter or Lord of the Rings—and making it your own?

I'd had a steady diet of those stories since I was aware of myself, even before I was reading. I'm drawn to the certainty of them. I like it when a character's path is pretty clear, that this is who they are: They're going to save the world. When you're "The Chosen One," there's not a lot of *choosing* [left] for you. You do what you have to do. I've always been drawn to that clarity, and I've always been drawn to the idea of having a mission or a calling—which is also about clarity. You know exactly why you're on Earth. Which is something I don't know about myself, and I don't often feel. It was probably inevitable that some of that was going to come out of me someday, because I've taken in so much of it.

For a novel about a magical war, *Carry On* is fundamentally about relationships. How did the dynamic of the love story drive the plot forward?

Every real thing that happens in our lives, even if it's a war, is driven by the relationships of the people involved—where they are in their lives. It isn't as if war is this external force that is visited upon us from another galaxy. War comes out of us. Our problems come out of where we are and who we are. For the people at the heart of the war, their personalities and relationships are a huge part of this event. It seems to me like a very realistic way to tell stories—to talk about the relationships of the people involved.

In *Carry On*, did you approach the relationship between Simon and Baz—two male wizards—any differently than you approached love in your prior novels?

At the beginning, I was more thoughtful. Their experience is not my experience—[though] you can say that for any book, any time you cross into someone else's identity. I asked myself if it should affect how I write them. I was very conscious of it not being written in a way that fetishized their relationship, or turned them into props. I didn't want the focus to be on their sexuality, because I think sometimes we, as a culture, see gay people as hypersexualized—we see their identity as their sex. I didn't want that.

When you're writing a love story, you want it to be really rare and magical and special. I thought, *What's the difference between that and something that would fetishize them?* So I was thoughtful at the beginning, then realized I should write them like I write my other characters—which is just to disappear into them. They don't fall in love differently than a straight couple. They're human beings and this is their love story.

Carry On is your first pure fantasy novel. What's the key to building a believable magical world?

Follow your own rules. Readers *want* to believe—we *want* to suspend our disbelief. If you love fantasy, you don't walk into a fantasy book cynical and critical. You really just accept. The author has to screw it up for you. You want to be taken on a trip. Readers want to go there with you—you just don't want to shock them out of it. More important is writing with a consistent tone.

I think relationships are probably more important than world-building. I mean, I buy into some really silly worlds. When I watch Star Wars, I'm not thinking, *Why are there human beings here and not there?* I'm not taking apart the world-building. I'm more like, *Oh, these characters are wonderful, and I'm feeling swept away by them and the story.*

Your books include diverse characters without making their diversity a defining characteristic. Do you think that attitudes about diversity in publishing have shifted, or that the industry still has a ways to go?

I'm not actually inside publishing, so from where I am and where I work, I can't say, "Here's my [opinion on publishing now] now versus publishing ten years ago"— I don't know. I would say there's probably still a long way to go, because I still think that our books are dominated by white authors writing white characters. Even from my distant perspective, I would say, clearly, there's a long way to go.

I [do] think perspectives have changed a lot. People are more aware. Before, white people especially weren't even thinking about it. My perspective in writing my own books is that I'm writing about the real world. The world I live in is not all white. I do live in Omaha, so it's whiter than most places, but even then, that becomes part of the book. In *Eleanor & Park*, you get Park talking about being one of the only Asian people in a white school. In *Fangirl*, you get Cath moving from the least white part of the state to the university, which is very white. Race is a part of our lives, and diversity is just a part of our lives. So it feels like a very *realistic* way to write, to me. I'd feel so ashamed of myself if my books were less diverse than my life.

What was your experience like selling your first novel, *Attachments*?

I just had really no idea what was happening. And I didn't know to what extent it would change my life.

I worked on *Attachments* for many years—I set it aside for two years at one point—and would come back to it. It took somewhere between five to seven years. I did most of the writing in a year and half at the end. Then I thought, *OK, maybe I'm done. Maybe I just needed to write it, and now I'm just going to set it aside and do something else.* I think I was afraid of rejection. I've always been afraid to try anything big—my fear has always been greater than my ambition in that way. So the idea of querying an agent or penetrating the world of publishing seemed unlikely or impossible. But my husband was like, "Well, you wrote this thing. Why *wouldn't* you try? You have nothing to lose."

When I started pitching agents, it was incredibly difficult for me. Everyone wants something different, or has a different opinion about what sells or what works. I found it so confusing. So I did it very slowly—I'd pitch one or two agents at a time and wait for them to get back to me. It took me 13 months to get an agent. When the book sold, it sold at auction. And I didn't know what to expect. During that publishing process, I didn't know, "Are they doing a good job? Is this a good publisher?" I didn't trust my instincts necessarily, because I'd always think, *I'm the person here who doesn't know anything, so I should just listen.*

So you put aside *Attachments* for two years. What's your advice for aspiring writers who are constantly shuffling their priorities?

I got pregnant and my husband opened a business—it was a laser tag business—and I would work there every day after work. So I was a newspaper columnist [at the *Omaha World-Herald*], and would go work at the laser tag business at night and on the weekends, and I was pregnant. And honestly, being pregnant at that point kind of felt like … the book was not a goal for me, if that makes sense. It was more of a hobby. It was something I'd do to spend time with my friends—we'd write together. It was something I did to distance my brain from my day job. It was an escape—writing *Attachments*.

I got pregnant and I thought, *Maybe this is my new thing. I'll escape into this—take my extra energy and think about having a baby.* Going into my son's birth and his first few months, I didn't write. I was feeling depressed. My sister said, "Weren't you writing a book? I want to see it." So I showed her what I had. She thought it was really funny. That was what I needed to get back into it, because I hadn't let anyone see

it, but the first person who read it really liked it. She left little notes in the margins—
"Funny! Funny!"

**Setting is such an important part of your books, from specific time periods (the
1980s in *Eleanor & Park*) to Nebraska itself (*Attachments, E&P, Fangirl*). What
role do place and time play in shaping your stories?**

With *Attachments* and *Eleanor & Park*, I really wanted to capture how Omaha felt at
those times. How it felt to be in that neighborhood—because I can. I can *maybe* write
about what it was like to live in East Omaha in 1986 better than anyone else currently
writing. I was there and I saw it and know what it smells like. So part of it is just trying to capture that.

It's a question I get asked a lot, and I find it's difficult for me—because I'm trying to capture something, but I'm not doing it in a journalistic way. It's not for a time
capsule or for history. I'm more trying to make it feel very specific, so you can get a
specific feeling from it.

I've ventured outside of it in the last two books. When I started, I think I felt very
safe writing about Omaha and Nebraska, because it's where I'm from, and these are the
people I know best. I wonder if the fact that I've traveled so much in the past two years
is the reason I felt confident enough to [set] *Landline* and *Carry On* somewhere else. By
the time I'd written *Carry On*, I'd been to the UK three times. That doesn't make me an
expert or anything, but I felt like I could hear the rhythms a little bit better.

**You've said *Eleanor & Park* was a very personal story for you, and in *Fangirl*,
Cath's professor tells her that strong writing is derived from personal experience. How do you translate that onto the page?**

It's mostly subconscious, I think. I do it without realizing it. It's like all of the things
that I've experienced or witnessed or heard are inside of me. And sometimes I can't
access them any other way. Sometimes I couldn't recall a memory if you asked me to,
but then if I'm writing, it comes out of me.

With *Eleanor & Park*, I intentionally set that book in the time and place that was
the most turbulent in my life. It was that neighborhood, that time, that situation. The
characters then went on and had their own things happen. So all of those memories
sort of rose up.

It's like you're turning on a tap—you're writing and all this stuff is coming out.
You're not actively seeking or digging, but you've turned on the tap, so lots of things are
moving inside of you. You've introduced movement into your brain and your heart.

TYLER MOSS is the managing editor of *Writer's Digest*.

JUDY SCHACHNER

On character bibles, creating a series, and the importance of reading.

....

by Jenna Glatzer

Judith Schachner can trace her success as a author and illustrator to her youth. She started drawing as an escape from a difficult childhood marked by financial difficulty and her mother's illness and death. She was no superstar at school, either, and was shy to boot. So she created a happier world in illustrations, "where mothers were healthy and teachers were kind."

Her first job as an artist was with a greeting card company, and she spent five years designing cards—fairly miserably. It wasn't until she met her husband, Bob, that she was able to take the time to figure out what she really wanted to do and put herself on the course to accomplish it. In 1995, she wrote and illustrated her first picture book, *Willy and May* (Dutton Books for Young Readers), and has been on a rocket ship ride through bestseller lists in the decades since—most notably with her Skippyjon Jones series.

Her latest hero is Dewey Bob Crockett, a raccoon who likes to turn trash into treasure. The lead series title, *Dewey Bob*, was released by Dial Books in September 2015.

You set out to be an illustrator, but the writing came accidentally. Can you tell us how your career trajectory changed course?

It was two editors who changed my course over twenty-five years ago—they both wanted to know if I could write. I lied and said yes. It really was that simple.

You've said that reading taught you everything you know about writing. Do you read with an analytical mind?

Ha! There is nothing analytical about me. My editor, the wonderful Lucia Monfried, whom I've had the great fortune of working with for over twenty-five years, calls me an organic bookmaker. I think that is her lovely way of implying that I go about the creating of a book in a convoluted, weedy way.

Reading picture books to my daughters during my thirties is what really taught me how to write. I absorb more than analyze. And to be specific, *A Visit to William Blake's Inn*, [written] by Nancy Willard and illustrated by the great Alice and Martin Provensen, is the book that inspired me to write. The imagery in both art and words tricked me into thinking that I could actually do something like that, too. So far that has not happened—but it's always good to set goals.

Art served as an escape for you during your childhood. When you began working as an illustrator-for-hire and were no longer just drawing whatever you wanted, did it still feel therapeutic and creative? Did you find it challenging to receive notes, approval, or criticism for your work?

The anxiety that came with the signing of my first contract was like going to confession and lying about your sins to a priest (which, by the way, I was really good at doing, but didn't exactly enjoy, because what eight-year-old ever enjoys choosing hell over telling the truth?). I knew it would be only a matter of weeks before [my publisher] discovered that I was a fake. I knew nothing about making books. I knew nothing about writing. So to answer your question, working for hire is always creative but never, ever, ever therapeutic. At least not for me. It wasn't then, and it's not now. But I love my job.

Tell us about how you work with Lucia: Do you still have to get approval for your new books, or do you have mostly free reign?

Lucia and I have been a team for a long time. Back in the day, an editor could discover an unknown talent with the idea of bringing her along—teaching her things—watching her ripen. That rarely happens now, if ever.

Lucia allows me a great deal of freedom. I pitch an idea and work out something (God knows what) before I show her anything. Sometimes I show her my character bibles and story-talk the idea. We have such a quirky and trusting way of working that I can't imagine working with an editor who demands more structure. I'd be sunk.

Talk to us about what it means to create a character bible.

Oh, my character bibles are where I have the most fun! No pressure.

Since most of my books are character driven, I explore a personality and a possible story route through collage. Character bibles are a safe place to experiment with illustration styles, too. I solve so many problems with these journals. And I discover things about my characters that I might never have otherwise … such as a raccoon being born in the pocket of an old pair of pants. Most artists keep sketchbooks, so

there is really nothing unusual or special about them—it's just a process that really works for me.

Well, after I've finished one of these bibles, I usually have a clear idea of where I want to go with the story. I begin sifting through the pages; certain images have bubbled to the top, and I begin the process of writing and laying out the book. It's kind of like parallel play. It's very hard for me to describe my process from the bible point on because it's never the same—it actually makes me kind of crazy to explain it.

Was Skippyjon Jones pitched as with series potential? Did you and your editor feel strongly that this was going to be a big hit from the start?

No, it was not pitched as a series … and we had no idea.

Once the first book gained traction, did you feel any pressure to make the next book live up to it?

Yes, I remember feeling some pressure as to where I would go with his character, but Lucia made it easy. He had to go back into his closet. I wasn't planning on that—I had Skippy sneaking into the apartment building next door to play with a bunch of bobble heads.

It's been great fun developing his character and the characters of his family. The hardest part has been painting him. I always say it took Walt Disney a lifetime to develop the look of Mickey Mouse, and it's taken me almost as long to be satisfied with the look of Skip. The funny thing is, I hate to repeat myself, and that's exactly what you have to do in a series.

How much of your job now focuses on writing and illustrating, and how much involves visiting schools, teaching workshops, speaking at conferences, promoting your work, and so on?

It's mostly about the work. I do a lot of traveling and speaking at conferences, workshops, and [completing] goodwill requests on behalf of my publisher. Book tours can take you away from home for weeks at a time, and if you are in the middle of illustrating a book, that can be difficult. I don't do many school [visits] anymore—I just don't have the time. In the beginning, schools helped to pay the bills, and it's a great way to get your name out there. It takes a few years to make a living wage from doing children's books.

People assume that your books are pure fiction, but you've drawn elements from your real-life family and pets for every book you've written. Do you have any tricks for mining your life for these fantastic storylines?

Real life is just full of story possibilities—the trick is not to tell a story in an absolutely linear or literal fashion. For instance, did my Aunt May have a canary named Willy? Yes, she did. Did she sleep with a nest tied to her head? No, she did not.

What's the best and worst part of your job?

The best part is seeing the unexpected ways in which your books affect children, families, teachers, and librarians. I have been moved to tears more than once. The worst part is a bad review.

For twenty years, you've been a member of the Society of Children's Book Writers and Illustrators (SCBWI). Why would you recommend it to aspiring writers?

I learned how to give a good presentation from watching Elvira Woodruff speak many years ago. She showed slides of her home, children, and travels. It was a game changer for me. And nowadays it's all about making connections, and there is no better place to do that than at an SCBWI conference.

....

JENNA GLATZER (www.jennaglatzer.com) is the author or ghostwriter of twenty-seven books for adults and kids, including Celine Dion's authorized biography. She is working on a book about heroes of the Underground Railroad.

....

KIKI THORPE

On working with licensed content and creating growth within her characters.

....

by Hannah Haney

The name *Tinkerbell* has been synonymous with magic since the release of Disney's film *Peter Pan*, inspired by the story of the same name by J.M. Barrie. Thanks to chapter book author Kiki Thorpe, girls all over the world continue to travel to Neverland and go on adventures with Tinkerbell and her friends.

Thorpe is originally from Guam and spent her childhood in Idaho, chasing imaginary fairies—a game that would benefit her later. She began her career as a children's book editor writing kidlit for licensed series and content, and has penned a Bob the Builder board book, a Spy Kids junior novel, a Toy Story chapter book, and dozens more.

Nowadays, Thorpe is a critically acclaimed children's book writer who's established herself with some enduring series. She has written two series under the name Mimi McCoy (Candy Apple and Poison Apple) and three under Kiki Thorpe (Disney Fairies, Meet the Kreeps, and her latest series hit, The Never Girls).

Thorpe is still going strong. The first book in The Never Girls series, *In a Blink*, was published in 2013 by Disney-Hyperion. The series is now a *New York Times* bestseller and has made the *Publishers Weekly* Children's Frontlist Fiction bestseller list. Four more of her Never Girls titles will be published throughout 2016, the most recent of which dropped in July 2016. (For more on Thorpe, visit her at www.kikithorpe.com or on Twitter @kiki_thorpe.)

We caught up with Thorpe to talk about how she sits down to write different series, and the lessons she's learned as an author.

Tell us about how you got your agent and started publishing children's books.

My trajectory was a bit backwards—I was published before I got an agent. I started out as a children's book editor working in licensed publishing. I started out as an editorial assistant at The Jim Henson Company, back when they had a publishing department. I also worked as an editor at Simon and Schuster and Disney Publishing Worldwide. I did some freelance writing on the side—first with tie-in books, then original stories based on licensed characters. Then I started writing my own characters and stories. Along the way, I realized I really wanted to be writing full time. While I never had that one big, exciting book that started my whole career, it was a great path for me. As an editor I learned a lot about storytelling, not to mention a lot about publishing. I also had good contacts, so when I finally realized I needed an agent, the editors I knew gave me referrals. I had a few conversations with Steven Malk [of Writers House], who represents me now, and we agreed to work together. He's the agent I most wanted to work with, so I feel very lucky!

Tell us about how The Never Girls series got started. Did Disney approach you, or did you pitch to them?

The editor at Disney-Hyperion came to me with the idea. She liked the work I had done on the Disney Fairies series. That series was wrapping up, but they wanted to look at other ways of extending the world, and they had the idea of bringing kids to Pixie Hollow. I created the characters Kate, Mia, Lainey, and Gabby and went from there. We didn't have any idea how well it would do. My original contract for the Never Girls series was for two books.

The Never Girls series has several similarities to the Disney Fairies series you started in 2007. After writing four books in that original series, was it difficult to continue your new writing in that world?

Not at all. I think one of the reasons Disney approached me to write the Never Girls series was because I was familiar with the fairies' world. It was easy to slip right into it.

Disney owns the world of Tinkerbell and Neverland. How much leeway did you get in world-building for the Never Girls series? Were you given strict parameters, or could you create new fairies and so on?

Disney owns the world of Pixie Hollow [the setting of the Disney fairies franchise], but Neverland and Tinkerbell are in the public domain, which is why so many different authors have been able to use it as a setting. Of course, The Never Girls is a Disney series, so I'm working with that version of the world. I have a good deal of leeway, though. I've been able to create new fairies, new locations on the island, and even new phenomena (like the mist horses). That's one of the great things about working with a setting like Never Land. There are established places like Skull Rock and the Mermaid Lagoon, but I've approached it with the idea that there's much more on the island to explore. So there's always something new for the girls to discover. [Editor's note: The two spellings of *Neverland* and *Never Land* in this paragraph are intentional. *Neverland* is J.M. Barrie's original spelling, and *Never Land* is how Disney has chosen to spell it in the series.]

You published four books in the Never Girls series in 2015. What is this publishing process like?

It's a little different from other books in that I have two editors, one at Disney and one at Random House, the series publisher. I work more closely with the Random House editor—we discuss concepts, and she reviews all the drafts. But the Disney editor also steps in at key points.

The schedules are very tight. We have roughly three months between books, including review time. I always do a chapter-by-chapter outline. I've found that when you're writing a book in a matter of weeks, you need to have a pretty good idea of where you're going, even if you end up changing things along the way. It's also a good chance for the editors to weigh in on a plot or concept early on.

All of the books in the Never Girls series revolve around the main characters experiencing emotional growth—learning about responsibility, empathy, selflessness, and so on. What advice do you have for other writers trying to do the same thing?

I'd say you should never set out to *try* to tell a story about characters experiencing emotional growth. I still remember reading this story as a kid that was set up as a mystery. It was very spooky and exciting, but the end was so preachy. I felt snookered! I dislike being lectured to, and I believe most people feel this way, kids especially.

With any Never Girls book, my main goal is to come up with a fun adventure. But there still needs to be some kind of emotional arc, otherwise the story has no heart. The main characters are all good kids, but they have their flaws and weak moments, and ideally this helps feed the storyline. Also, one of the main themes of the series is friendship, so I tend to come back to that a lot.

How has having children influenced your writing? Are they beta-testers for your manuscripts?

My kids are still pretty young—they were both born after I began working on the Never Girls—so we're not quite ready for chapter book manuscripts. But I think having children has taught me to economize, especially when it comes to language. Nothing drives home the importance of choosing your words carefully like reading a book over and over again. I can't stand reading some of the picture books I wrote before I had kids. Too many words! I've even hidden some of the really long ones so my kids won't pick them off the shelf.

What does an average writing day look like for you?

Well, I tend to procrastinate, and the Internet is very bad for people like me. I usually fiddle around for an hour checking e-mail, reading articles, etc. Then I turn the Internet off completely (I use an app called Freedom) and get some real work done. I sometimes rough out scenes or chapters in longhand before I write them. I write two to four pages on a good working day, sometimes more if I'm very close to a deadline. Then I rough out the next scene or chapter so I have a place to start the next day.

You wrote the Candy Apple and Poison Apple series under the pen name Mimi McCoy. What led to that decision?

Those books were for a slightly older audience than ones I'd written in the past, and I wanted to distinguish them from previous work. Like the Never Girls, though, I didn't expect to write so many. Once I put the pen name Mimi McCoy on the first book, I had to use it on the other four.

Do you have advice for authors trying to break into children's book writing?

All writers have moments of doubt about their work—sometimes several in one day. Find a trusted reader, someone who's willing to give you notes and can help you see your story more clearly. Every piece of writing needs revision, and it's difficult to edit your own work. Often you need someone else to help you figure out how to make it better.

Also, be nice. By "nice," I mean friendly, reasonable, and respectful. It sounds trite, but it's not. Remember, editors and agents get to decide who they work with.

What's been the biggest lesson you've learned throughout your writing career?

When you're stuck, you have to learn to figure out what's stopping you. Is it fear that the story, idea, or writing isn't good enough? If that's the case, then tell yourself that it's just a draft. You can always make it better. But if you're plodding along on a story every day and you just can't move it forward, maybe that story isn't working. Then you need to scrap it and start over. Sometimes it can be hard to distinguish between the two.

Also, have faith. Writing is an uncertain way to make a living. It can be tempting to take every gig that comes your way. But sometimes it's okay to say no.

What was your reaction when the Never Girls book *The Trouble with Tink* became a *New York Times* best-selling series?

Thrilled—and very surprised.

What has been the most rewarding part of being an author?

I've had parents come up at readings and say, "I had a hard time getting my kid interested in reading until we found this series." That has been the biggest reward and the most unexpected one. I never sit down to write thinking, *This book is really going to matter to somebody*, so it's astonishing and wonderful to find out that it does. The other day I got an e-mail from a mom who told me that her daughters' playtime had become "more imaginative" since they'd started reading my books. I can't think of a higher compliment.

JENNIFER MASCHARI

On teaching and school visits.

....

by Kara Gebhart Uhl

Cincinnati-based children's book author Jennifer Maschari grew up in a family that valued books and reading. Her literary-rich childhood, coupled with her former profession—teaching—greatly impacted her ability to connect with her audience: middle-grade readers. The result? A debut book that *School Library Journal* describes thusly: "Beautifully crafted sentences read almost as if they were poetry … Fans of both fantasy and realistic fiction will appreciate this painful, but ultimately triumphant, multilayered novel."

Maschari taught for nine years, including stints as a fifth-grade science and language arts teacher and a junior high literacy specialist. "I have always written, but I started getting serious about writing with the goal of publication in 2010," she says. "I found it made me a better writing teacher. I was better able to understand what I was asking the students to do." She says that difficult tasks like revision became clearer to her after teaching them.

Maschari left teaching two years ago to pursue writing full time, with the initial thought of devoting just one year to her craft. As fate would have it, shortly after making that decision she landed both an agent and a book deal. *The Remarkable Journey of Charlie Price* was published in February 2016 to rave reviews.

Here Maschari talks about the challenges of writing while holding a full-time job, what she's learned as a debut author, and the keys to a successful school presentation.

How did your childhood experience impact your decision to write?

My father was an avid reader, and my mother was an elementary school teacher. I was always surrounded by books. I loved participating in the summer library reading

program and took great satisfaction in writing down all of the titles I read. This love of stories definitely impacted my decision to write. I loved meeting characters, going different places, and experiencing new things all through the pages of a book. I wrote a lot of poetry when I was younger—fun, rhyming poetry in the style of Shel Silverstein. I wrote short stories, too, and I always enjoyed writing in school. One of my favorite parts of being a teacher was getting to share my love of reading and of books with young people. I also was able to work with and encourage young writers, as I was encouraged in my childhood by my family and teachers. As an author, I still get to do that, which is amazing.

You taught the same age group of children you now write for, correct? How did the years you spent teaching influence the language, style, and tone of your current works?

Yes—I taught fifth grade for many years. This age group is the greatest. These kids are funny, kind, and smart. They're capable of thinking about big things and are starting to think about where they fit in the world. They're growing up and learning who they are. Also, just seeing how the kids interact with each other, what's important to them and what they value, and their relationships with their friends and family has influenced my writing in so many ways. Kids are complex. They're tackling big and small things in their lives. I want my writing to honor that.

What was it like maintaining a full-time job while also dedicating time to the craft?

Writing while teaching is difficult. You are teaching during the day and then grading and planning at night as well as on the weekends. I wrote on snow days, during snatches of time when I could get them, and over the summer (in between professional development courses and tutoring jobs). Writing while maintaining a full-time job is all about scheduling and setting time aside. I took several online writing courses taught by established writers where we could submit a certain number of pages for feedback each week. This helped me because it allowed me to set deadlines for myself and encouraged me to carve out the time for writing.

What inspired you to quit teaching and write full time?

Right before our school's spring break, about two years ago, I decided after much soul-searching that I would take a year off to just write. I was working several jobs—teaching, tutoring, and creating teaching units to sell online—as well as writing. I had burned myself out. In a strange twist of fate, I actually ended up signing with my agent, Victoria Marini [of Gelfman Schneider/ICM Partners], over that spring break, and then she sold my book to Balzer + Bray, an imprint of HarperCollins, in May. I still do have several flexible part-time jobs and am working to expand the school visit side of my career. The circumstances were right for me at the time to make the move from teaching, but I don't know if that will be a forever decision. I do miss the classroom and the kids!

How long did it take to write *The Remarkable Journey of Charlie Price*?

The first half of the initial draft of *Charlie Price* took a little over a year. The second half took three months.

Once Balzer + Bray bought *Charlie Price*, what was the publishing process like? What makes for a good author/editor relationship?

The publishing process has been a complete whirlwind and such a learning process for me. I've heard that some people describe the publishing process as slow. I view it as fast with some waiting periods in between. The most daunting aspect of the process was the developmental edits. I think there is an element of doubt that creeps in when you're making big changes. *Will I be able to do this story justice? Will everything come together?* I enjoyed the copyediting process. Copyeditors are wonderful, detail-oriented people. I loved looking at the very nitty-gritty details of my work (continuity, time frame, etc.). Receiving my cover was also a very memorable part of the process. To see the story captured so beautifully was such a wonderful moment. It's like the story had come to life.

The relationship with my editor, Alessandra Balzer, has been incredible. I value her excellent insight, her knowledge of what makes a story great, and the respect with which she views my work. I see us as a team, working together to make the story the very best it can be, and I am so lucky to be working with her. She sees the heart of the book. I think for a good author/editor relationship, communication, respect, and a shared vision is crucial. As an author in the author/editor relationship, I think it's important to be open and receptive to change.

As a debut author, what has surprised you the most?

I always knew that there would be author jobs to do—school visits, sending out marketing materials, creating workshops, etc.—but I severely underestimated how much time these things can take if you let them! I constantly remind myself to go back to the writing and make that a priority.

What's your current writing day like? Do you have a routine or a schedule?

My writing schedule changes from day to day. I'm working to put myself on a more consistent schedule—I get a lot more accomplished that way. Typically, I'll start with reading a chapter or so of a book I really love. This helps me get in the right frame of mind for my writing day. Then I read over my notes or pages I had written the day before. I'll jot down some more ideas about what I need to do in terms of scene or character work. I'll do a quick outline; I find having this road map is important for me.

After I write in the morning, I'll take a break to answer some e-mails and have lunch. Then I return to writing in the afternoon until I leave to work with students as a tutor. On some days, though, I might have … a school visit. I also might have other things I need to accomplish like mailing out postcards to libraries or putting together materials for a workshop. It was definitely a big transition (and continues to be) coming from working as a teacher, where you have a very structured day, to being able to set your own schedule.

Speaking of which, in terms of publicity, it looks like you do a lot of school visits and bookstore signings. Why is that important? And what tips do you have for authors embarking on such events for the first time?

I love doing school visits and bookstore signings. I miss teaching and interactions with kids … so school visits work to fill that gap in my life. Also, there is nothing better than talking with enthusiastic readers about books and writing. I think school visits help keep you connected to your reader, and they can be especially important when writing middle-grade [because they] connect you with hardworking teachers and librarians who are often making book-buying decisions. As a middle-grade writer, you are slowly building your audience, book by book. School visits are a great way to get the word out.

I also love connecting with readers via Skype. Technology has allowed me to connect with classrooms all across the country.

I believe that independent bookstores are the heart of a community. There is nothing better than going into a bookstore and connecting with the seller who has a wide knowledge of books and is ready to match the right reader to the right book. … I think doing bookstore signings helps you connect to the greater literary community at large and support the arts. All of the booksellers I have met have been wonderful, passionate advocates for books. …

For authors embarking on school visits for the first time, I recommend planning out your programs. They should leave kids feeling excited about reading and writing. I try to include a technology component with each of mine, but I know authors who have also been successful without it. Find what works best for you and your presentation style.

Think about writing activities or workshops you could give that involve students in the process, and have them flex their writing muscles. Interactive programs that require active participation are always great. Also, remember that building up the school visit side of your career can be slow. People need to discover your book and who you are as an author. I do recommend sending information (a postcard, professional packet, or brochure) to local schools about what you can offer [as a potential speaker].

How have your years of teaching influenced your school visits? Tell me more about these interactive presentations and workshops.

I think my years in the classroom have given me a good sense of what schools and students need from an author visit. Mainly, I think they are looking for authors who bring enthusiasm for books and writing. … I made sure to have some [presentations and workshops] that could be done for large groups, and others that would work best with a smaller group of students. For the large group presentations, I've still tried to make them interactive. It can be very hard for students to sit and listen for an extended period of time, even in the best of circumstances. Getting them involved in the presentation was critical for me. In one of my favorite workshops, the students and I talk about the elements of a story. Then I bring three "mystery items" in a brown paper bag, and the students have to incorporate them into their own piece. It is always fun to see what they come up with. It is a lot of fun to work with them, and it inspires me in my own work as well.

What three tips would you give to an aspiring author/illustrator?

The first thing I would suggest is to read—a lot. Read in the area or genre you're trying to write—both the age group and genre. Read … for the enjoyment of it. Read as a writer—study the work, figure out how it's done. I always read before I start a writing session. Immersing yourself in great writing is a must!

Second, always be willing to write the next thing. Whether you are querying or on submission or writing the next book, you always need to return to the page. That doesn't necessarily mean giving up on a concept you love, but sometimes it might be necessary to set a piece aside for a while and work on something new. You can come back to it with fresh eyes and perspective.

Third, cultivate patience. So many aspects of publishing require patience. Practicing patience (and returning to the page) early on will definitely benefit you as you begin to build a career in writing books.

Tell me more about your next book.

The next book, coming out in 2017, is a [middle-grade novel about] sixth-grader Emily Murphy, who is dealing with friend and family issues that are difficult for her to handle. She turns to self-help CDs she's purchased from an infomercial on TV to help her navigate her problems. It's a story about sisters, friendship, and figuring out who you are.

4 QUESTIONS FOR 4 KIDLIT AGENTS

A quartet of agents talk kidlit submissions.

by Jessica Strawser

OUR 4 AGENTS

1. SARAH DAVIES The Greenhouse Literary Agency, www.greenhouseliterary.com

2. SARA MEGIBOW KT Literary, www.ktliterary.com

3. JOHN RUDOLPH Dystel & Goderich Literary Management, www.dystel.com

4. TINA WEXLER ICM Partners, www.icmtalent.com

1. What do you see as the most important difference between middle-grade (MG) and young adult (YA) books?

TINA WEXLER: "The most important difference is how the author shapes the elements of the story—the narrative voice, the way the subject matter is presented, the protagonist's evolution—for the intended readership, typically eight to twelve for MG and twelve-plus or fourteen-plus for YA. Everything falls out of that, in a sense."

SARA MEGIBOW: "The major conflict in a YA novel centers around the question of, *Who will I be when I grow up?* A YA novel is a coming-of-age story, whether the book is contemporary, fantastical, historical, dystopian, etc. In MG fiction, the major conflict is a bit different, as it's about firsts—first fight with parents, first questions of independence, first time friends are more important than family, etc.

"In addition, an important difference between MG and YA is the age of the protagonist(s). MG narrators are younger than YA narrators. I want to see MG protagonists at ten to thirteen years old and YA protagonists at fourteen to nineteen years old (generally)."

JOHN RUDOLPH: "For me, it's age of the protagonist … I know, that's totally arbitrary, but as MG keeps creeping into YA territory, other traditional markers like content and outward/inward perspective are starting to blur, so age seems like one clear and easy way to differentiate."

SARAH DAVIES: "MG fiction will revolve around a younger protagonist(s), which means the concerns and rites of passage will be preteen rather than older. But if we 'unpack' that difference, it will necessitate a different voice and character arc. It's not just baldly a question of characters' ages; for any age group, it's about a story that sees and explores the world through the lens of a particular stage in life. Teen fiction will inevitably have a touch more introspection and sophistication in the interpretation of relationships, the wider world and the self."

2. What makes standout writing for MG readers?

RUDOLPH "Showing [rather than telling], naturally, and sophistication of both vocabulary and sentence structure. I've been reading Harry Potter to my son lately, and I'm repeatedly blown away by [J.K.] Rowling's use of big words, virtually all of which can be understood in context without running to the dictionary. There's absolutely no need to dumb it down for MG!"

DAVIES: "In all fiction I look for a strong and unique hook, a voice that stands out and conveys the world and personalities of the characters, and an author's ability to craft that story so it becomes compelling on the page. With MG fiction, I'm also, of course, looking for a story with appeal and resonance to readers of that age, whether it be in the vein of classic, heartfelt fiction or a more adventurous and action-packed story."

MEGIBOW: "*Voice!* The most common mistake I see (by far) in MG submissions is writing that sounds too much like it's written by an adult for an adult. An authentic MG voice that matches the age, conflict, tone, and story makes for standout writing for MG readers."

WEXLER: "The strongest MG writing captures the experience of that particular age without being nostalgic; it feels lived and not remembered."

3. What do you want to see more of in young adult novel submissions?

DAVIES: "Unique ideas, diverse characters, and settings. I enjoy stories that make me think but also move me emotionally. I don't like being super-definite on genre—I'm just open to anything that feels fresh, vivid, and compelling."

WEXLER: "I'm always looking for stories with unreliable narrators, unconventional story structures, magical realism, and ambitious ideas fully realized. I'd love to see a sweeping, epic fantasy novel that is done and complete in one book—not a trilogy but a truly stand-alone epic fantasy.

MEGIBOW: "I'm always looking for more diversity—whether that's in fantasy YA or contemporary YA or historical YA or … anything. I'd like to see more protagonists of color, more religious diversity, cultural diversity, diversity of gender and sexual orientation, diversity of ability, socio-economic status, geography, etc. Diversity!"

RUDOLPH: "I would love to see more writers go Gonzo. Plots, characters, voice, whatever they can do to push the envelope in realistic or magical-realistic fiction. And humor—boy, would I love to find a funny YA."

4. What common story mistakes do you see in the MG and YA manuscripts you consider?

MEGIBOW: "Some common mistakes I see in MG and YA submissions include: incorrect voice (a narrator who sounds like an adult), data dump (too much telling, especially in the first thirty pages of the manuscript) and uneven dialogue (frequently too much or too stiff)."

RUDOLPH: "It's not so much mistakes as just the same tired clichés: dead parents, spunky redheaded heroines, superheroes in MG, dystopias in YA. But one thing I do see a lot is the opening chapter where everything is crammed in—plot, central problem, character, etc. I understand why writers do it, especially when submission guidelines ask for only a partial, but I'd much rather have a slower introduction and let the author's voice convince me that I want to read more. Or, to put it a different way, *show* us what you can do, don't *tell* us everything up front."

WEXLER: "The author has been too kind to the protagonist, where the worst thing that could happen isn't truly the worst, where bad things happen to the protagonist but never because the protagonist made a bad choice. Like a helicopter parent, the author is afraid to let the protagonist fail or fall. But fail and fall they must, or there is no story, no growth."

DAVIES: "Most commonly, I see ideas that are already out there in the marketplace and don't feel unique. I also see a lot of stiff writing where characters feel distant and unrelatable. Also, quite a bit of overwriting—by which I mean that the author is using tons of adjectives and adverbs in an attempt to convey emotion. Sometimes, less can be more, and spare writing can be very effective."

JESSICA STRAWSER (www.jessicastrawser.com) is the editor of *Writer's Digest* magazine. Her debut novel, *Almost Missed You*, comes out from St. Martin's Press in April 2017.

DIVERSE BOOKS

Why inclusion and diversity generate discussion and excitement.

by Suzanne Morgan Williams

Do you want to capture a child's attention? Bring a voter to your way of thinking? Pass along religious beliefs or family traditions? Tell a story. Stories engage, teach, and reinforce our world views. The books and stories we share help our children develop social attitudes, personal passions, and self-esteem. Recognizing themselves in books helps children feel part of the greater world and seeing unfamiliar characters helps them step into other people's shoes. The children's book community has a big responsibility—to create and share books for all our children.

Which is why the current conversation about diversity in children's books is so important. If you think "diversity" is a trend—like dystopian or mystery—think again. Today in the US, ethnic demographics are changing, yet in 2015, according to the Cooperative Children's Book Center Study (see this article's sidebar), eighty-five percent of children's books featured white characters.

While book professionals have been talking about the lack of diversity in books for many years, the discussion was given a huge boost in 2014 by the We Need Diverse Books movement. Following some tweets between Ellen Oh and Malinda Lo about the all-white, all-male panel of children's authors at BookCon's 2014 reader event in New York City, the social media campaign took off. Today, We Need Diverse Books is a nonprofit group with a variety of programs aimed at education, internships, mentorships, and book promotion.

Their partners include American Booksellers Association, SCBWI, and the National Education Assocation to name a few.

The We Need Diverse Books website (www.diversebooks.org) defines diversity as "including (but not limited to) LGBTQIA, people of color, gender diversity, people with disabilities, and ethnic, cultural, and religious minorities." I was honored to interview five well-respected authors and illustrators who are African American, American Indian, Asian American, and Latino American. Among them they have been awarded Pura Belpré, Coretta Scott King, Caldecott, and Newbery medals and honors.

Please remember that no one person speaks for all of his or her community any more than one book can represent the experiences of an entire racial or ethnic group.

1 JOSEPH BRUCHAC (www.josephbruchac.com) is a storyteller, educator, and author of more than one hundred books. His ancestry includes Abenaki Indian and Slovakian. He received the Native Writers' Circle of the Americas Lifetime Achievement Award and the New York Library Association's Knickerbocker Award for Juvenile Literature. His best-known credit is possibly *Code Talker: A Novel About the Navajo Marines of World War Two* (Speak, 2006).

2 NIKKI GRIMES (www.nikkigrimes.com), an African-American writer, was born in Harlem and is the recipient of the 2016 Virginia Hamilton Literary Award and the 2006 NCTE Award for Excellence in Poetry for Children. Her works include *Bronx Masquerade*, which won the Coretta Scott King Award, and Coretta Scott King Author Honor books *Jazmin's Notebook, Talkin' About Bessie, Dark Sons, The Road to Paris*, and *Words with Wings*.

3 MEG MEDINA (www.megmedina.com) is a Cuban-American author who is the 2016 recipient of the Pura Belpré Honor for her picture book, *Mango, Abuela and Me*, and the 2014 Pura Belpré Award winner for her young adult novel, *Yaqui Delgado Wants to Kick Your Ass*.

4 YUYI MORALES (www.yuyimorales.com) has won multiple Pura Belpré Awards and Honors for both illustration and narrative, and a Caldecott Honor in 2015 for *Viva Frida!* Morales grew up in Mexico and immigrated to the US at age twenty-four before returning to Mexico, where she currently lives and writes. She writes books in both Spanish and English, and has authored many titles, including the picture book *Nino Wrestles the World*.

5 LINDA SUE PARK (www.lindasuepark.com), the daughter of Korean immigrants, grew up outside of Chicago. In 2002 she won the Newbery Medal for *A Single Shard*. She also received the New York Library Association's Knickerbocker award. Her *New York Times* best-selling *A Long Walk to Water* won the Jane Addams Children's Book Award in 2012.

Why is it important to create and publish diverse books?

GRIMES: It is a miraculous thing to see the joy on the face of a child when he opens a book and sees himself on those pages! But it is equally important for readers to encounter characters from cultures other than their own. This is an important step toward planting the seeds of empathy.

MORALES: I know how diverse books have provoked a powerful change in my own life! I began to recognize my own value as a human as I found that people like me—brown skin, Spanish speaker, immigrant—were represented and celebrated inside children's books. I was in awe at finding that here in the US, where I had felt I didn't belong, there were children's books that told stories where people who looked and lived like I did could also be heroes.

BRUCHAC: To identify with a main character does not depend on that character being exactly like you. Books can take us into other lives, places we have never been. However, if the only books available are ones that never reflect your own community, your cultural or ethnic background, then you may feel excluded by literature as a whole.

One reason I chose, long ago, to write for young readers is that I wanted them to have the books I did not have when I was their age. I wanted such books to be there for my own sons, who now have children of their own. As far as my own life goes, what I saw in books and in the media did not, by and large, represent Native American culture in an accurate or positive way. The depiction of Abenakis—what little there was—was horrible. In the book by Kenneth Roberts that was turned into the classic movie *Northwest Passage* (1940) we are portrayed as bloody vicious savages who are wiped out by the noble Rangers led by Robert Rogers. My novel *The Winter People* (Dial 2002) tells the story from the Abenaki perspective. Many Abenaki young people have told me how important that book of mine has been to them.

MEDINA: The best way to reach diverse readers is by writing stories that resonate with their experiences. These are the stories that capture their families, their personal relationships, and how it is to move through the world behind their eyes.

Mostly I focus on the experience of growing up—boils, beauty, and all. I do my best to tell stories through the unique lens of a Latino child. For me, that is the best way to have my stories read by all children.

Historically artists have taken on the role of examining culture, creating change, and speaking out even when it may be discouraged or uncomfortable. As an author and artist, what do you consider your role and responsibility to be?

GRIMES: We reach diverse readers by creating books in which all readers see themselves reflected. That's the job of the artists and every artist has her part. I urge writers to look around the world in which they live and to reflect the diversity they find in the stories they create.

MORALES: As book creators, I believe that it is our duty to be as truthful as we can (and this has nothing to do with whether we write fiction or nonfiction). Such a truth tells us that we live in a world where some voices and experiences are muffled by the always-heard voices of the ones in power. If we intend to diversify readers, then we are going to have to create room for a body of literature that reflects the experiences of as many different humans as we are. Does this mean

BOOKS BY AND ABOUT PEOPLE OF COLOR

As of 2014, 38 percent of the US population was non-white/non-Hispanic; more than half the children under age five in the US were from minority populations. These children are the new audience for our children's books. So what books are being produced that reflect our neighborhoods and communities?

Cooperative Children's Book Center, part of the College of Education at the University of Wisconsin, reports:

Books about main characters of color

- 2015: 15 percent
- 2005: 12 percent
- 1994: 9 percent (by *and* about—the first year or reporting)

Books by people of color

- 2015: 10 percent
- 2012: 6 percent
- 2005: 6 percent

Some members of the publishing community are taking a hard look at these numbers, creating committees, articles, programs, and new strategies. But there is much more progress to be made and change will need to come from buyers—parents, teachers, librarians, and older readers, as well as gatekeepers, booksellers, reviewers and bloggers, and publishing companies, writers, and illustrators themselves.

we should attempt to reproduce the voices of others? I believe that there is no one book creator whose role is to represent all the voices around. We need to give access to diverse creators.

We can always recognize the world we live in —we are part of a multicultural universe—and be ready to reflect and celebrate such diversity in our work. But using power and privilege to appropriate other people's voices is not diversity. True diversity will only be reached when we listen to the voices of those who are most vulnerable, of those we seldom hear.

MEDINA: It's absolutely possible to write outside your culture and your gender, but it's a very delicate task. You have to acknowledge that you are writing against the complicated and tender backdrop of race relations in the US. That act requires your fullest respect, including the courage to admit that in some cases, that, no, you are not the right person to tell the story.

PARK: Those of us who work in the field of children's books have a particular responsibility. We all need to examine how race has affected our lives. By that I mean in every way: historically, culturally, personally. We have all have either benefitted from or been harmed by systemic racism. Sometimes both. Accepting and then examining this concept as it applies to ourselves and our communities gives us the opportunity to begin making different choices. If you are a creator of books for young people, what are the different choices you can begin to make in your stories? Making the same choices means making the same mistakes.

BRUCHAC: Our cultures are not like the flies caught in blocks of amber, unchanging since the nineteenth century or earlier. We are part of the modern world and our cultures are vital, dynamic, complex.

Far too many writers and illustrators fall into not just using the past tense, but presenting us (and other ethnic minorities) as victims. Yes we have problems, but so do all human beings. Deadly serious depictions of our cultures fail to understand how important a sense of humor is—how much laughter is a part of every American Indian community.

Few writers and illustrators want their subject matter limited or to be told how to create their work. This goes for diverse artists and members of the white majority culture, as well. So if you decide that the story you need to write is outside of your own experience, how can you best proceed?

BRUCHAC: There is a saying found in many of our Native American cultures here in the US and Canada that "you need to humble yourself." Accepting what you do not know and then being humble enough to ask for and then *accept* help—that is crucial. Be aware of how important it is to seek help and how eager people often are to help you.

Put aside your preconceptions. Be prepared to find out that you are wrong. Open your ears and eyes. Open your heart. Turn to those who truly know and belong to the culture you'd like to focus on. Do not just do it through books and online research. There is a lot of bad information in both places.

Be sure those who advise you are legit. Just because someone is, for example, Lakota, it does not mean they know everything about their own culture.

Also remember it takes time to learn things. Do not make deadlines more important than integrity.

MEDINA: The biggest landmine is writing reductive characters. Well-intentioned authors often say, I've worked with X group for years, or I have good friends from X group ... but that doesn't mean you can understand and write the deep truths of that experience. You run the risk of constructing an archetype rather than a fully developed character. Worse, you may be reinforcing a reductive stereotype that you don't even recognize as hurtful. So extensive research and vetting is vital. Be open to their input and reactions.

MORALES: When creating books outside one's own culture, we better be prepared to be analyzed, criticized, proved wrong, to recognize there was much we didn't know and to make it right as needed. We'd better be ready to truly learn about what we failed to know. Be respectful. Be curious. Be delighted. But don't stand in the way of people from that culture to tell their truth.

GRIMES: We must require editors to do their due diligence, especially when it comes to historical material, no matter who's writing and illustrating it. For my book *Chasing Freedom* (Orchard Books, 2015) my editor drove me to distraction with three full rounds of fact checking, which was then sent to a panel of experts in the field who all came back with questions, comments, critique, and in a couple of instances, corrections. I was forced to review and re-do my research several times to make certain I got everything right.

How do you get diverse work into the hands of readers? Who can help?

GRIMES: We have to take a multi-pronged approach to reaching diverse readers and marketing is part of that. Take self-promotion seriously. Readers won't look for books they don't even know exist. One hopes the publisher will take up this charge, and some do. But until they step up in the marketing of diverse books in a big way, book creators have to do what we can by planning book launches, talking up our work at conferences, handing out promotional material and teachers guides, etc.

DIVERSE RESOURCES

There are many lists, blogs, teacher guides, and other resources devoted to diverse books. Here is a sampling. Be sure to check for more comprehensive links within these listings.

- Children's Book Council: www.cbcbooks.org
- Diversity Blog: www.cbcdiversity.com
- Suggestions and Resources for Teachers and Librarians: hwww.cbcbooks.orgwp-content/uploads/2013/02/7-Steps-to-Representative-Reads-Librarians.pdf
- Cooperative Children's Book Center: https://ccbc.education.wisc.edu
- Books by and about People of Color Statistics: https://ccbc.education.wisc.edu/books/pcstats.asp
- Multicultural Page: https://ccbc.education.wisc.edu/books/multicultural.asp
- Awards and Best of the Year Lists including many diverse awards: https://ccbc.education.wisc.edu/links/links.asp?idLinksCategory=2
- First Book (free and discounted books for low-income institutions): www.firstbook.org
- Open e-Books link: http://fbmarketplace.org/openebooks
- Lee and Low (multicultural publisher): www.leeandlow.com
- Diversity Gap Blog: http://blog.leeandlow.com/category/diversity-race-and-representation/the-diversity-gap
- School Library Journal: www.slj.com
- List of Blogs and Collection Development Resources: www.slj.com/resources/slj-resources-for-diversity-in-kid-and-ya-lit/#_
- General diversity resources: www.scbwi.org/diversity-resources
- Emerging Voices Award and Multicultural Work-In-Progress Grant: www.scbwi.org/awards/grants/grants-to-promote-diversity-in-childrens-books
- SCBWI's ideas for everyone on supporting diversity: www.scbwi.org/diversity-what-can-we-do-about-it/
- We Need Diverse Books: www.weneeddiversebooks.org
- "The Windows and Mirrors of Your Child's Bookshelf" (TedX talk by Grace Lin): www.youtube.com/watch?v=_wQ8wiV3FVo
- "Can A Children's Book Change the World?" (TedX talk by Linda Sue Park): www.youtube.com/watch?v=40xz0afCjnM

PARK: How do we reach readers? Through teachers, librarians, and booksellers. These superheroes have always been the ones who urge readers to pick up books they might not choose on their own. Teacher and librarians are the *only* way we have to reach readers who come from homes that lack a reading culture.

MEDINA: I believe strongly in the need to make bilingual and dual language editions of books available to families. We (Latinos) often have families living under the same roof where people speak different languages. Stories can help bind and strengthen families, but we have to make the materials available. We should encourage the addition of English rather than its substitution of the language spoken at home.

Then there are the mechanics of marketing. What are the price points and formats that make sense? What are the best channels of distribution to match buying habits? Not everyone buys a book at a bookstore. Not everyone hears about books in *The New York Times*.

Imagine the impact of engaging hundreds of thousands of readers with diverse books—created by people of many voices and backgrounds—that celebrate our common humanity. What would be the end result?

BRUCHAC: While I was at a conference a few years ago, another Native author stated publicly that he became an author "because of Joe Bruchac." He then went on to explain that while in college, his teacher, the Japanese-American poet Alex Kuo, gave him a copy of an anthology of Native American poetry I edited called *Songs From This Earth On Turtle's Back* (1983). He said that reading it showed him that there were other Native Americans writing authentically about being Indian, about present day things and it inspired him to do the same. That Native writer who was so moved by a single book in which he recognized himself was Sherman Alexie, author of many acclaimed books of poetry and fiction including *The Absolutely True Diary of a Part-Time Indian* (Little Brown, 2009).

GRIMES: One of the best letters I ever received came from a seventh grader in Holland, Pennsylvania. If this letter doesn't express why it's so important we get diverse books into the hands of all readers, I don't know what will. It read:

> Dear Ms. Grimes,
>
> I'm currently reading your book, *Bronx Masquerade* ... I am very happy I read this book ... You made me realize that even though we look different on the outside, we are pretty much the same on the inside. Everybody should read this book to help them change the way they think about other people they make fun of. I know it changed the way I think of people.

SUZANNE MORGAN WILLIAMS (www.suzannemorganwilliams.com) has written several picture books, including *Library Lil, Mommy Doesn't Know My Name,* and *My Dog Never Says Please.* She lives in Washington state.

DEBUT AUTHORS TELL ALL

Learn how first-time kidlit writers got published.

compiled by Donna Kuzma and Chuck Sambuchino

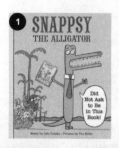

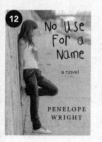

As some inevitable rejections begin to come during the querying process, the regularly imagined "big break" scenarios begin to lose a bit of their glimmer. But big breaks do happen, and those stories serve as inspirational reminders to keep submitting. It's with that in mind that we collected seventeen successful debuts from the past year and sat down to ask the authors questions about how they broke in, what they did right, and what advice they have for scribes who are trying to follow in their footsteps. These are writers of picture books, middle-grade stories, and young adult novels—same as you—who saw their work come to life through hard work and determination. Read on to learn more about their individual journeys.

PICTURE BOOKS

① Julie Falatko

WWW.JULIEFALATKO.COM

Snappsy the Alligator (Did Not Ask to Be in This Book) (February 2016, Viking Books for Young Readers, illustrations by Tim Miller)

QUICK TAKE: "Snappsy the alligator is having an ordinary day until a pesky narrator steps in to spice up the story with slanderous claims." **WRITES FROM**: Maine. **PRE-SNAPPSY**: I wrote a lot of stories that I pray no one will ever see. They were all part of the process. I did picture book reviews for the Brain Burps About Books podcast from 2011 to 2015, which allowed me to fuel my book-reading habit while also talking into a cool-looking microphone. **TIME FRAME:** The idea for *Snappsy* came out of Picture Book Idea Month in November 2012. I had been diligently writing ideas all month, and the idea for this book inserted itself wholesale into my brain then. *Snappsy* is the only time a book has come to me all at once. **ENTER THE AGENT:** My agent is Danielle Smith of Red Fox Literary. When I read her blog it was easy to see that we had very similar taste in books. **WHAT I LEARNED**: There are so many people who work on making a book. There are dozens of people in marketing, publicity, media, and sales. It is boggling to think of how many people whose names I don't even know are talking about my book. **WHAT I DID RIGHT**: I took my time. I had heard that picture book authors should have three polished manuscripts before they start querying agents, and I spent two years writing and revising to get to those three manuscripts. **PLATFORM**: I got my name out through the Brain Burps About Books podcast, and I'm active on Twitter. So much of platform is building connections brick by brick. **ADVICE FOR WRITERS:** Write for you first. Write what you like. And keep at it. **NEXT UP:** A picture book from Viking Children's—*The Society for Underrepresented Animals*, illustrated by Charles Santoso—coming in 2017.

② Linda Liukas **WWW.HELLORUBY.COM**

Hello Ruby: Adventures in Coding (October 2015, Feiwel & Friends)

....

QUICK TAKE: *Hello Ruby* is the world's most whimsical way to learn about technology, computing, and coding. **WRITES FROM**: Helsinki, Finland. **PRE-BOOK**: I was teaching myself programming in 2009 and started doodling the Ruby character in my notes, inspired by the programming language Ruby. Whenever I ran into a question—such as how object oriented programming works—I'd try to imagine how little Ruby would explain it. The imaginative viewpoint of a small girl soon started to pop up everywhere in the technology world and I knew I had a book in my hands. **TIME FRAME**: The book was a side project I had worked on a few years, but things started to move when I put the book proposal on Kickstarter in January 2014. I had asked for $10,000 to cover self-publishing, but ended up gathering $380,000 dollars worth of pre-orders. *Hello Ruby* is still one of the most backed children's books on Kickstarter. **ENTER THE AGENT**: I found agent Jess Regel [of Foundry Literary + Media] through an old colleague whose wife worked in publishing. Jess's Norwegian roots immediately synced with my Finnish background, and we ended up working together. **WHAT I LEARNED**: For someone who comes from the web industry, where things are designed for change, a book feels very final. The book is a representation of who I am and what I know today. Five years from now it would look totally different. I would actually love to see artists redraw some of their early books. **WHAT I DID RIGHT**: Crowdfunding allowed me to directly reach out to people all over the world who want to teach their kids code. I'm not sure traditional publishers would have immediately seen the magic of Ruby's world—although now it's obvious that there is a huge market for material like this. Not all projects are ideal for a crowdfunding campaign, naturally. Running a successful campaign is partly luck, but mostly it's just hard work and dedication. Offering something that taps into a bigger theme enables your backers to dream with you. **PLATFORM**: I co-founded Rails Girls, the grassroots movement to encourage young women to get excited about coding, without the faintest idea about the role it would end up playing. Three years, one hundred cities, and innumerable discussions later, I had a pretty good understanding of what type of people could get excited about *Hello Ruby*. I spoke to everyone about her adventures, gave talks, and published drawings. I started a blog where I documented how I was learning drawing. I forced myself to practice daily by making a public Christmas calendar. I started an e-mail list for people who wanted to be notified about the progress with the book. And I think Rails Girls ended up paying a huge role in the success of the Kickstarter campaign.

MIDDLE-GRADE

③ Jenn Bishop WWW.JENNBISHOP.COM
The Distance to Home (June 2016, Alfred A. Knopf)

QUICK TAKE: The story of how eleven-year-old Quinnen finds her way back into baseball after losing her biggest sideline fan, her older sister, Haley. **WRITES FROM:** Watertown, Massachusetts. **PRE-BOOK:** Following college, I spent several years writing YA while working as a teen librarian in public libraries. I kept getting those "close, but not quite there yet" rejections from agents, which was both encouraging and frustrating. Basically, I knew that there was something that I didn't know about writing, but I couldn't figure out what exactly it was. That's when I decided to go back to school for writing and get an MFA to fill in that gap. **TIME FRAME:** I decided to try my hand at middle-grade during my second semester at Vermont College of Fine Arts's Writing for Children and Young Adults MFA program. I wrote the entire draft of what would become *The Distance To Home* during that semester. **ENTER THE AGENT:** I found my agent, Katie Grimm at Don Congdon Associates, the traditional way—querying. I think I sent out about sixty-ish queries for this project and connected with Katie about six months in. **WHAT I DID RIGHT:** Truthfully, I think not giving up is huge. If you keep at it and keep learning, you will get there. In many cases, "failure" or lack of success comes from not putting yourself out there enough. **I WISH I WOULD HAVE DONE DIFFERENT:** I would have revised more. Sometimes, even still, I'm so excited about a project and getting it out there that I don't take enough time to make sure that the book I think I wrote is actually all on the page (and not still in my head). **ADVICE FOR WRITERS:** [As a previous writing instructor once told me]: "Always keep writing the next thing." **NEXT UP:** I'm currently in revisions on the second book in my contract, a middle-grade novel tentatively titled *14 Hollow Road*, slated for summer 2017 with Knopf.

④ Lindsay Eagar WWW.TWITTER.COM/LINDSAYMCCALL
Hour of the Bees (March 2016, Candlewick Press)

QUICK TAKE: Twelve-year-old Carolina spends the summer moving her grandfather off his sheep ranch in the New Mexican desert and into a home for dementia patients, but she comes to believe his crazy stories about a healing tree and bees that stole a lake might be coming true. **WRITES FROM:** Salt Lake City, Utah. **PRE-BOOK:** My debut is my fourth novel. The first two were terrible YAs, and the third was a MG that I rewrote seven times before finally [stepping away from]. **TIME FRAME**: When I wrote the first paragraph, I had no idea what kind of book I was writing; by the next paragraph, the whole story flashed before my eyes, beginning to end, like lightning. I finished the first draft in ten days. **ENTER THE AGENT**: I sent out thirty query letters for *Bees*, and received four offers of representation. I chose to work with Sarah Davies of Greenhouse Literary because of her strong editorial background, her confidence and perspective on my career as an author, and her absolutely stellar background and reputation in children's publishing. **BIGGEST SURPRISE**: That I would come to appreciate and even crave the radio-silence quiet stretches of time between agent and editor contact, because those are the times when the writing gets done. Busy times when I have lots of "author" things to get done (blog posts, events, etc.) are wonderful, but I became an author so I could write stories. **WHAT I DID RIGHT**: My attitude was to interpret any "no" from the publishing industry as "not yet." I also viewed any feedback—whether a thoughtful critique or a full-on rejection with no explanation—as a gift. **I WISH I WOULD HAVE DONE DIFFERENT**: I spent a lot of energy feeling anxious for the next milestone in my publishing journey. As soon as I found an agent, I was hungry for a book deal—as soon as we sold the book, I was dying to get to release day. Now that I'm on the other side of the debut experience, I have a new perspective on my long-term career, and I wish I had celebrated more and been less hasty for time to rush past. **ADVICE FOR WRITERS**: Be willing to work harder than will show. No reader will know if you had to rewrite the opening chapter ten times, or cut an entire character. All that matters is the [final product]. **NEXT UP**: My next middle-grade comes out from Candlewick Press in fall of 2017, and a third middle-grade comes out from Candlewick Press in 2018.

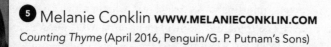

⑤ Melanie Conklin **WWW.MELANIECONKLIN.COM**
Counting Thyme (April 2016, Penguin/G. P. Putnam's Sons)

QUICK TAKE: When eleven-year-old Thyme's family moves across the country to New York City for her little brother's cancer treatment, she must find her place in her new life despite her yearning to return home to San Diego. **WRITES FROM**: South Orange, New Jersey. **PRE-BOOK**: I began exploring middle-grade stories about a year prior to writing one. After reading several books about kids facing difficult situations, I wondered what it would be like to be the sibling of a child facing a devastating illness. That was the nexus for *Counting Thyme*. **TIME FRAME**: I wrote the first draft in about six weeks, but many more drafts followed. The publication date is about three years after I began writing that first draft. **ENTER THE AGENT**: I connected with Pete Knapp [of New Leaf Literary & Media] the old-fashioned way: a cold query. I'd seen some of his insightful comments at a WriteOnCon feedback forum and I felt he would be a good fit for me. Luckily, he felt the same way! **BIGGEST SURPRISE:** That I still had a tremendous amount of creative freedom after we sold the book. I guess I was expecting to have more argument over choices, when that was not the case. My editor's notes and questions were intended to spark solutions, with the nature of the solutions very much up to me as the author. **WHAT I DID RIGHT:** The most valuable thing I did to improve my craft was finding critique partners and beta reading regularly for other writers. In addition to reading published books voraciously, providing beta feedback on manuscripts helped me study the craft of writing and gain perspective to judge my own work. **PLATFORM:** I started blogging on a simple website many years ago, and have since evolved that into a reader-focused author website. I also particularly enjoy Twitter, where there are so many good writing folks talking about fun and fascinating topics every day. **ADVICE FOR WRITERS:** Writing is rewriting. **NEXT UP:** Another middle-grade novel with Putnam.

6 Steve Bohls **WWW.JEDANDTHEJUNKYARDWAR.COM**
Jed and the Junkyard War (December 2016, Disney-Hyperion)

QUICK TAKE: *Jed and the Junkyard War* is [the] Pirates of the Caribbean [series] meets Thomas Edison middle-grade junkpunk adventure about an audacious boy who follows the trail of his kidnapped parents to a junkyard world riddled with warring pirates, floating cities, and violent junk storms. **WRITES FROM:** Daybreak, Utah. **PRE-BOOK:** Before this book, I wrote a little of everything. I believed (and still do) that every book we read contains—at least to some degree—elements of so many other genres. For that reason, the six novels I wrote in the twelve months preceding *Jed* were in the genres of thriller/suspense, romance, comedy, horror, literary/drama, and fantasy. I wanted the scenes and characters in future books to feel real, whether it was a suspenseful moment in a fantasy novel, or a romantic moment in a drama. **TIME FRAME:** From the moment I started, I was hooked. I finished the first draft in just under eight weeks. It was my eleventh novel, but it was the first one where I had the thought: "I don't care if no one likes it, or even if it never gets published. I love this book." Ever since then, it's been my sincerest endeavor to feel this way about each new book I write. **ENTER THE AGENT:** My agent is Marisa Corvisiero of Corvisiero Literary Agency. I endured hundreds of rejections over so many years. I sent a batch of twenty queries out on Memorial Day weekend for this book and received seven requests for the full within three days. Within a week, I had two offers of representation, and I joined Marisa's team. **WHAT I LEARNED:** Inspiration is overrated and ideas are cheap. Being a writer doesn't mean you're exceptionally smart, creative, or talented. Instead, it means that you put in your time. That you put in your million practice words. I found there to be so much less "luck" in the publishing process than I'd originally thought. I also learned (if quite late in the game) to be my own type of writer. Not to sound cheesy, but it was a huge epiphany to discover that my very best writing came when I was trying to be me, not someone else. **I WISH I WOULD HAVE DONE DIFFERENT**: If I could travel back in time and tell myself anything, it would be: "Finish that first novel, and then throw it away! Rinse and repeat. All the while, study writing. Study craft. Study stories."

7 Adam Furgang WWW.ADAMFURGANG.BLOGSPOT.COM
Braxton Woods Mystique (April 2016, Ravenswood Publishing)

QUICK TAKE: The new kid in town, Leo, tries to get a fresh start in a remote neighborhood, but he ends up leading his new friends into a world of mystery in the woods behind their homes, complete with monsters, supernatural events, and a buried carnival. **WRITES FROM**: Albany, New York. **PRE-BOOK**: I've written some work-for-hire nonfiction books purely on an assignment basis, so I don't even consider those my own projects. Before *Braxton Woods Mystique*, I had written [one kidlit novel that collected] rejection letters. **TIME FRAME**: It took me about two years to finish *Braxton Woods Mystique*. **ENTER THE AGENT:** My first round of submissions was mostly to publishers. When that was not working out, I doubled down on the agent search. I found Mark Gottlieb from Trident Media Group after scouring for reps that were seeking middle-grade. I read a few interviews with him and he seemed willing to work with new writers, so I added him to my list and gave it a shot. **WHAT I DID RIGHT**: I spent a very long time crafting an outline, a character bible, and a timeline for the story. I also worked very hard on my query letter. Also, no matter how complex a novel is, the writer should be able to describe a story quickly in a sentence or two. I learned that somewhere and it has served me well. **PLATFORM**: I've been extremely active online for many years now. I have been quietly running a gaming and pop culture blog, www.wizardsneverweararmor.com, for several years now. I started it up in 2013 when I rediscovered Dungeons and Dragons with my sons. I can also be found on Amazon, Facebook, Google+, Instagram, Twitter, Blogspot, Pinterest, Flickr, and Tumblr. **ADVICE FOR WRITERS**: Write what excites you as a reader. I like to write the kind of story I like to read, not what I think the market needs or wants. For me, writing is just a grown-up form of making up stories like a kid does while playing with toys. If you do not find yourself getting excited by what you have written, then it's a good warning sign that it should be rethought or rewritten. **NEXT UP**: My next project is also a middle-grade adventure story—with a few monsters in it.

YOUNG ADULT

8 Ava Jae **WWW.AVAJAE.BLOGSPOT.COM**

Beyond the Red (March 2016, Sky Pony Press)

QUICK TAKE: An uprising on a distant planet threatens the reign of a teen alien queen who turns to her rebel half-human bodyguard for help against her power-hungry twin brother. **WRITES FROM**: Michigan. **PRE-BOOK**: I started writing my very first manuscript in October 2005, wrote eight other young adult manuscripts, then started writing *Beyond the Red* in the summer of 2013, and began querying it that fall. **TIME FRAME**: *Beyond the Red* was my tenth manuscript, so at that point I'd pretty well figured out what writing process worked best for me. I wrote the first draft in three weeks. I revised it over the summer and began querying. **ENTER THE AGENT**: My agent, Louise Fury of The Bent Agency, actually found me through Miss Snark's First Victim's Secret Agent Blog Contest. I entered my work in the contest, and she chose me as a runner up, asking to see more of my work! The small partial request led to a request for the full manuscript, which led to a very happy phone call two months later. **BIGGEST SURPRISE:** How different the publishing timeline varies from publisher to publisher. I'm part of a debut group, The Sweet Sixteens, which has two hundred authors from all over the world whose books debut in 2016. Initially, I thought everyone's experience would be roughly the same, but that is so not the case. It really varies publisher to publisher, editor to editor, and even book to book. **WHAT I DID RIGHT**: Getting involved in the writer community online has been a key step toward my eventual publication. Twitter especially became a hub for me where I connected with other writers, met my future critique partners, became familiar with agents and industry professionals who share tips for aspiring writers online, and kept up to date with what was going on in the publishing industry. **PLATFORM**: I began both my Twitter and blog in 2011, both of which I post to regularly. I also post a vlog from my YouTube channel once a week, with more writing tips and advice. I cross-post all of my blog posts and vlogs to Tumblr and Facebook, which has helped me expand my audience, so my Twitter, blog, and YouTube channel have become popular over time. **ADVICE FOR WRITERS**: Get critique partners. Swapping manuscripts with critique partners is easily the best (and scariest) writing decision I ever made.

9 Anna-Marie McLemore **WWW.AUTHOR.ANNAMARIEMCLEMORE. COM** *The Weight of Feathers* (September 2015, Thomas Dunne Books/St. Martin's Press)

QUICK TAKE: The story of the romance between a Latina girl and a Romani boy, whose families each run rival traveling shows. **WRITES FROM**: Northern California. **TIME FRAME:** A few years ago, I was in the woods wearing a set of wings, and the idea for the book snuck up on me. I'd wanted to write about performing mermaids for a while, and when the image of winged tree performers came to me, that contrast fueled the story. I wrote fast, and then relied on notes from my critique partners and my agent to help me revise in the months that followed. I'd just finished writing a couple of short stories for literary journals, so I started working on novel ideas, and but this was the one that kept calling me back. **ENTER THE AGENT**: I had met Taylor Martindale Kean of Full Circle Literary at a conference, but didn't have a manuscript ready to pitch then. A few months later through an online contest, Taylor read a sample chapter of a book I was working on, and I was thrilled when she offered to represent me. Taylor really encouraged me to write what I was passionate about, and I realized more and more that my heart was in magical realism and my Mexican-American heritage. *The Weight of Feathers* was the result of following that passion. **BIGGEST SURPRISE:** The sheer number of people whose hard work, talent, and heart go into taking a story from file to shelves. **WHAT I DID RIGHT**: Seeking out and being open to advice and feedback. It's so important to be open to learning from others. **I WISH I WOULD HAVE DONE DIFFERENT**: I feel incredibly lucky to have debuted during a time where conversations about diversity were growing more visible. But a few years ago, I was afraid to write from my heritage, and that meant there were stories I was afraid to write. If I could do it again, I would have followed my heart sooner, in spite of that fear about where my stories might fit. **ADVICE FOR WRITERS:** Take in other art whenever you can—books, visual art, music, plays, movies that inspire you. It helps your brain rest, and gives you creative energy. **NEXT UP**: My second novel, *When the Moon Was Ours* (October 2016) also has magical realism and multicultural elements.

10 Julie Hammerle **WWW.JULIEHAMMERLE.COM** *The Sound of Us* (June 2016, Entangled Teen)

QUICK TAKE: A geeky, TV-obsessed high school student goes to opera camp for the summer. **WRITES FROM**: Chicago. **PRE-BOOK**: Prior to writing this novel, I was recapping TV shows on the Internet for money (kind of a dream job) and taking care of my infant son. I wasn't writing much, if any, fiction. **TIME FRAME**: I technically started writing this book back in 2002, while taking a class for my MFA (which I never finished). I put the idea on the back burner until 2009, when I bought one of those novel-in-a-month workbooks. I was committed to the process. I managed to crank out that first draft in a month, and I spent the next several years revising. Only one scene remains from that original version. **ENTER THE AGENT:** My agent is Beth Phelan of The Bent Agency. I went through several rounds of querying this novel over the course of about two years. Beth caught my attention because of the Guide to Literary Agents Blog. She was a new agent, and I was just about to start querying this manuscript (for the third time, after more revisions). I saw that she was looking for YA fiction and humor/pop culture nonfiction. Even though my book wasn't nonfiction, I reasoned that it did include humor and pop culture, so she might like it. **WHAT I DID RIGHT:** I was always open to learning about what I didn't know—whether that was the craft of writing itself or querying and publishing. I took workshop classes at StoryStudio Chicago. I read probably every craft book ever. I devoured a million blog posts about the querying process. I also kept a really positive, confident mindset. I decided early on that I simply was not going to fail. I was going to be a writer. I didn't set a timetable or anything. I just kept chugging along, plugging my ears and singing "la-la-la" whenever anyone landed a book deal before me. **I WISH I WOULD HAVE DONE DIFFERENT:** I queried too early the first time (back in January of 2011). I would've waited until both the manuscript and my query letter were in better shape. I received a whopping zero requests from that batch, but I learned some valuable lessons about handling rejection. **ADVICE FOR WRITERS:** Just write—wherever, whenever you can. If the product is garbage, you can always fix it, as they say in the film industry, in post.

11 Kathleen Glasgow WWW.KATHLEENGLASGOWBOOKS.COM
Girl in Pieces (August 2016, Delacorte Press)

QUICK TAKE: At seventeen, Charlotte Davis has already lost more than most people do in a lifetime, and she has the self-inflicted scars to prove it. Now she must find a way to put herself back together. **WRITES FROM:** Arizona. **PRE-BOOK:** I had published stories and poems in *Bellingham Review, Cimarron Review, Clackamas Literary Review*, and other journals prior to publishing *Girl in Pieces*. **TIME FRAME:** It took me eight years of writing and fourteen drafts before *Girl in Pieces* sold. I worked full time and relied on artist grants to take time off work in the summer to blaze out pages, then spent the rest of the year pecking out revisions late at night or early in the morning—whenever my son was sleeping. **ENTER THE AGENT:** My agent is Julie Stevenson of Waxman Leavell Literary Agency. I submitted to about twenty agents. Many agents never responded, but Julie was the first one to write back and her e-mail blew me away. She really *got* the book. I had found my champion. **BIGGEST SURPRISE:** My biggest surprise was learning that I actually *liked* the editing process. It was kind of a huge relief to have someone tell me to cut something or reimagine something. Fresh perspective is really invigorating after working on a book alone for a long time. You need new eyes, new thoughts. **WHAT I DID RIGHT**: I never gave up—plain and simple. **ADVICE FOR WRITERS**: (1) Never give up. Just don't. (2) Turn off the television and your i-Whatevers, and get to work. (3) Don't be afraid to revise and to listen to other people's suggestions about how to improve your writing. (4) Keep at it. There is someone out there who *needs* the story you are writing. **NEXT UP**: I am working on the follow-up to *Girl in Pieces*.

12 Penelope Wright WWW.PENELOPEWRIGHT.COM
No Use for a Name (April 2016, Reputation Books)

QUICK TAKE: A fifteen-year-old girl discovers her horrible parents never officially named her, and she embarks on a journey of self discovery in order to choose a name for herself that fits. **WRITES FROM**: Bothell, Washington. **PRE-BOOK**: I attended a writing conference in 2009 and agent Kate McKean [of Howard Morhaim Literary] gave a talk. She said that you should write against trope (for example, that not all cheerleaders were bitches). McKean's advice stayed with me, rattling around in my head, and several months later, I wrote a short 1,500-word piece for a writing contest, centered around an idea. I liked the characters so much and felt that they had so much more to do, that I fleshed it out into *No Use for a Name*. **TIME FRAME**: I wrote the first draft of the novel in six months. **ENTER THE AGENT**: My agent is Elizabeth Kracht [of Kimberly Cameron & Associates]. My friend (Chelly Wood) pitched to her at a writers conference and ultimately Liz offered her representation. A few months later, Chelly mentioned to Liz that she thought she would really like my work, and would she like me to query her. Kracht said sure, and Chelly was right; she *did* like my work. She offered me representation later that year. **WHAT I LEARNED**: The publishing process really does take forever. Everyone tells you it does, and you think you are prepared for how long it will be, but it still takes you by surprise. **WHAT I DID RIGHT**: Forcing myself to overcome my shy nature and hermit-like tendencies, and going to a conference, and—once there actually talking to people—was what made the difference for me. I wouldn't be where I am without my network of writer friends. We are all in this together. **ADVICE FOR WRITERS**: You must write. If you don't write, you won't have anything to edit later. You must get words down on the page. Even if you feel like what you are writing is terrible, at least it is on paper and you can fix it later. **NEXT UP**: A novel about a thirteen-year-old boy who becomes an assistant to the Tooth Fairy. I expect to go on submission with that manuscript soon.

13 Olivia Rivers **WWW.OLIVIARIVERSBOOKS.COM**

Tone Deaf (May 2016, Sky Pony Press)

QUICK TAKE: The story of a deaf girl who gets tangled up in the life of a young punk musician after winning back-stage passes to his concert. **WRITES FROM:** Sacramento, California. **PRE-BOOK:** As I got to know the online writing world better, I started to see lots of YA contemporary stories finding huge success on serial websites. So I decided to take a crack at writing my own. I started *Tone Deaf* in 2011 using www.watt pad.com as the hosting platform. Within months, I had thousands of people following the novel, and to this date, more than a million people have read the original serial online. **TIME FRAME:** The novel had an unusual timeline, since it began as a serial. I wrote the first twenty chapters in serial format in 2011-2012 and then paused for a year on the project. I returned to it in 2013 and made extensive changes to prepare the book for a more traditional publication method. After those rewrites, I signed with my agent in late 2013 and received my offer from Skyhorse Publishing in 2014. **ENTER THE AGENT:** I met Laurie McLean, co-founder of Fuse Literary, at the San Francisco Writers Conference in 2013. When we first met, I was interviewing to become her assistant at Fuse. After working with her for nearly a year, she kindly offered to give me a critique of my writing, so I sent *Tone Deaf* to her. She ended up enjoying it so much she offered me representation. **WHAT I DID RIGHT:** For me, "success" has come from getting repeatedly thrown flat on the ground—by harsh critiques, rejections, reviews, you name it—and then getting up, dusting myself off, and continuing to pursue publication. It's been three steps forward, two steps back. And in this industry, I think that's pretty normal. Success comes from a process of persistence. **I WISH I WOULD HAVE DONE DIFFERENT:** I would have spent less time discussing writing and more time *actually writing*. For a while, I was extremely intimidated by the novel writing process, so I tried to improve my craft just by listening to other people discuss writing (on blogs, social media, etc.). Once I began forcing myself to write about a thousand words a day, my writing improved immensely in a very short period of time. **PLATFORM:** I built an online platform on Wattpad before gaining an agent and a traditional deal. I continue to grow my online platform and expand it to other sites, including Tumblr, Facebook, and Twitter. While interacting with readers online is certainly important, I've found that the most reliable way to grow a readership is to consistently and frequently distribute quality content to readers. In this digital age, readers expect to be constantly entertained, so I'm trying to meet those expectations by putting out excerpts, short stories, and other free content to keep readers engaged in between my major releases. **ADVICE FOR WRITERS:** Instead of looking at other writers as competitors, look at them as allies and try to form a group of writer friends. **NEXT UP:**

I'm a hybrid author [self-published and traditionally published], so I have two indie novels releasing in 2016 along with *Tone Deaf*. My indie works are titled *This is What Goodbye Looks Like* and *In the Hope of Memories*, and both fall into the YA contemporary genre.

14 Margot Harrison WWW.MARGOTHARRISON.COM
The Killer in Me (July 2016, Disney-Hyperion)

QUICK TAKE: A girl believes she's the only person alive who knows the identity of an elusive serial killer—but when she tracks him to his home turf, prepared to stop him with deadly force, she gets to know him in a way that makes her question everything. **WRITES FROM**: Burlington, Vermont. **PRE-BOOK**: I've been a professional journalist and editor for nearly ten years, so I publish nonfiction every week—mostly book and film reviews. Before that, I published a couple of academic articles. I've been writing fiction since I was eight, but before this novel, I had only published one short story (for adults) in a literary journal. My debut is about the fifth complete novel I've written. **TIME FRAME**: I wrote the first draft in six months, then revised for a few more months. **ENTER THE AGENT**: I looked up agent listings and started querying in batches of five or ten. I took it slowly, revising my query with each batch and tinkering with my opening pages, testing the waters. I got a request for the full manuscript from Jessica Sinsheimer of Sarah Jane Freymann Literary Agency, and she ended up offering representation, giving me brilliant revision notes, and selling the book. **WHAT I DID RIGHT**: I didn't give up. **I WISH I WOULD HAVE DONE DIFFERENT**: I would have learned about the market earlier. I spent years writing what I liked with no concern about what might sell. That was great fun, and I'm still not someone who can ever write *just* for a market. I need a vision. But now I have a general sense of where my vision for a given book overlaps with the needs of a given market, and that's invaluable. **PLATFORM**: I've established an author site and become more active on Twitter and Instagram, and I've made connections with book bloggers. Perhaps the single most valuable step I took was joining a debut group, The Sweet Sixteens, which gives authors the opportunity to network and boost one another's signals. **ADVICE FOR WRITERS**: Read. Read widely, outside your chosen category and genre. Read things you're not sure you'll like. As a reviewer, I've read hundreds of books I would never have picked up on my own. I've learned something about writing from every single one of them, even if it was what not to do.

15 Marisa Reichardt WWW.MARISAREICHARDT.COM

Underwater (January 2016, Farrar Straus Giroux)

QUICK TAKE: In the aftermath of a deadly high school shooting, Seventeen-year-old Morgan Grant is an agoraphobe trapped in the apartment she shares with her mother and brother. When surfer boy Evan moves in next door, she has to face the life she's been missing. **WRITES FROM:** Los Angeles. **PRE-BOOK:** *Underwater* was the third YA novel I wrote but the first that led me to my agent. Before then, I'd been freelancing, writing content for websites, and not giving up on novel writing. **TIME FRAME:** I wrote the first draft of *Underwater* in 2013 in ten months. **ENTER THE AGENT:** My agent is Kate Testerman of KT Literary. I had queried her with a previous novel and she requested to read a partial but ultimately passed. I couldn't wait to query her again with *Underwater*, hoping this one would be the one. Luckily for me, it was. **BIGGEST SURPRISE:** How much I enjoyed the editing process. It was inspiring and I attribute most of that to my phenomenal editor, Joy Peskin. Each round of editing was exciting and made me a better writer. I am so thankful for that time. **WHAT I DID RIGHT:** I researched literary agents. The easiest thing you can do is find out what agents are looking for. It's all out there for you. I was a big fan of many of Kate's clients and I followed her on Twitter, so I was confident that she was a good fit for *Underwater* when I queried her. **I WISH I WOULD HAVE DONE DIFFERENT:** I would've tried to enjoy the process more. It's such an exciting time when you're querying, and agents are requesting to read your manuscript, but I spent a lot of that time feeling anxious and panicked. I wish I'd focused more on appreciating how amazing it all was. **PLATFORM:** I'm on Twitter and have joined two debut author groups: The Sweet Sixteens and Sixteen to Read. These are made up of MG and YA authors publishing their debut novels in 2016. These groups have been a great support system. **ADVICE FOR WRITERS:** I'm a big believer in writing what scares you. There were many elements of *Underwater* that scared me but I think those fears pushed me to write a better book. **NEXT UP:** I'm working on a second standalone YA contemporary novel and looking forward to upcoming foreign publications of *Underwater*.

16 Kara Storti WWW.KARASTORTI.COM

Tripping Back Blue (April 2016, Carolrhoda)

QUICK TAKE: A seventeen-year-old kid struggles with an addiction to heroin. It's "Breaking Bad" meets *The Catcher in the Rye* with a twist of magic. **WRITES FROM:** Cambridge, Massachusetts. **PRE-BOOK:** My previous young adult novel didn't get published, so I let myself wallow in self-pity for a moment and then forced myself to suck it up. Soon after, I happened to start watching "Breaking Bad." Next thing I knew, the characters in that show became my twisted little muses and I didn't have a social life for a month straight. **TIME FRAME:** I already had an agent for that previous novel. I wrote the first draft of *Tripping Back Blue* in a month through NaNoWriMo (National Novel Writing Month). It took me about five months to polish the manuscript. **ENTER THE AGENT**: A talented writing group buddy referred me to his agent, Rubin Pfeffer (Rubin Pfeffer Content, LLC). When Rubin heard a client vouching for me, he said that he had no choice but to check me out. It has been a gift working with such a knowledgeable, sincere, and warmhearted man. **WHAT I LEARNED**: The process always takes longer than you think it will. I also learned that persistence pays off just as much as talent. When I heard known authors say, "I was rejected a ton of times before I had any success," I never fully believed it. Lo and behold, I was rejected around forty times by different publishing companies, and it took me ten years of writing almost every day to get published. **WHAT I DID RIGHT**: Undying determination and persistence. Constant practice of the craft. I made sure to sit down and write on my busted couch, even if I had no motivation. Even if it was just one sentence, it was something, because I was honing the writing muscles I needed for the long haul. **I WISH I WOULD HAVE DONE DIFFERENT**: I wouldn't be so hard on myself. I'd say, "Kara, calm the heck down." I would have more faith in my passion and diligence and the priority I make to write. **ADVICE FOR WRITERS**: Anne Lamott's *Bird by Bird* taught me that I can't look at the entire story and its every twist and turn, layer, and subtlety all at once. That view will cripple a writer on the spot. My tactic is to chip away at a story bit by bit, turn that chunk of marble into something people want to look at. I focus only on a chapter, and brainstorm on one or two elements to include. But they have to be elements I feel excited about. My mentor would always say, "Write where the heat is." I find that heat and start running toward it. **NEXT UP**: I'm writing a book about a teenage girl with epilepsy, who develops a kind of magic from her seizures.

17 Meghan Rogers WWW.MEGHANROGERSBOOKS.COM
Crossing the Line (April 2016, Philomel/Penguin)

QUICK TAKE: After being kidnapped as a child and raised to be a North Korean spy, eighteen-year-old Jocelyn Steely must work with her enemies to escape her kidnappers and get revenge. **WRITES FROM**: Philadelphia. **PRE-BOOK**: I've been writing since I was in high school—always young adult, though more fantasy and sci-fi than thriller/spy. I was wrapping up my MFA program (and another young adult fantasy project) when I saw *The Avengers*. I became fascinated with the character of Black Widow, who worked for an enemy agency [in her backstory]. I couldn't stop thinking about what the enemy-to-ally transition must have been like, which is how I arrived at *Crossing the Line*. I hadn't written a spy or thriller book before, but it was a story I couldn't stop thinking about. I had to write it. **TIME FRAME**: From conception to query it took a year and four months. From conception to publication it was almost four years. The actual writing was about a year on my own, and then about another six months worth of work with my editor. **ENTER THE AGENT**: I found Michelle Wolfson [of Wolf Literary] with a cold query letter. I'd queried her for a previous project. She passed on that book, but gave me fantastic feedback. When I went to query *Crossing the Line*, Michelle was my top choice. I was so excited when she loved the book as much as I hoped she would. **WHAT I DID RIGHT**: My focus was always on learning to be a better writer. For me, this meant going to Rosemont College for my MFA. It totally revolutionized my process and my approach, and I don't think I would have gotten published without it (or at the very least, it would have taken a lot longer). **ADVICE FOR WRITERS**: Remember that what works for one writer might not necessarily be good for you. Try a lot of different approaches, but focus on creating a process that works for you. **NEXT UP:** The second book of The Raven Files.

DONNA KUZMA is a Philadelphia-based writer and freelance editor. Find her on Twitter @donnagambale.

NEW AGENT SPOTLIGHTS

Learn about new reps seeking clients.

by Chuck Sambuchino and Hannah Haney

One of the most popular columns on my Guide to Literary Agents Blog is my "New Agent Alerts," a series where I spotlight new/newer literary reps who are open to queries and looking for clients right now.

Newer agents are golden opportunities for aspiring authors because they are actively building their client lists. They're hungry to sign new clients and start the ball rolling with submissions to editors and get books sold. Where an established agent with forty clients may have little to no time to consider new writers' work (let alone help them shape it), a newer agent may be willing to sign a promising writer whose work is not a guaranteed huge payday.

THE CONS & PROS OF NEWER AGENTS

At writing conferences, a frequent question I get is "Is it OK to sign with a new agent?" The question comes about because people value experience and wonder about the skill of someone who's new to the scene. The concern is an interesting one, so let me try to list the downsides and upsides to choosing a rep who's in her first few years of agenting.

Possible cons

- They are less experienced in contract negotiations.
- They know fewer editors at this point than a rep who's been in business a while, meaning there is a smaller chance they can help you get published. This is a big, justified point—and writers' foremost concern.
- They are in a weaker position to demand a high advance for you.
- New agents come and some go. This means if your agent is in business for a year or two and doesn't find the success for which they hoped, they could bail on the biz altogether. That leaves you without a home. If you sign with an agent who's been in business for fourteen years, however, chances are they won't quit tomorrow.

Probable pros

- They are actively building their client lists—and that means they are anxious to sign new writers and lock in those first several sales.
- They are willing to give your work a longer look. They may be willing to work with you on a project to get it ready for submission, whereas a more established agent has lots of clients and no time—meaning they have no spare moments to help you with shaping your novel or proposal.
- With fewer clients under their wing, you will get more attention than you would with an established rep.
- If they've found their calling and don't seem like they're giving up anytime soon (and keep in mind, most do continue on as agents), you can have a decades-long relationship that pays off with lots of books.
- They have little going against them. An established agent once told me that a new agent is in a unique position because they have no duds under their belt. Their slates are clean.

HOW CAN YOU DECIDE FOR YOURSELF?

1. FIND OUT IF THE AGENT IS PART OF A LARGER AGENCY. Agents share contacts and resources. If your agent is the new girl at an agency with five people, those other four agents will help her (and you) with submissions. In other words, she's new, but not alone.

2. LEARN WHERE THE AGENT CAME FROM. Has she been an apprentice at the agency for two years? Was she an editor for seven years and just switched to agenting? If they already have a few years in publishing under their belt, they're not as green as you may think. Agents don't become agents overnight.

3. ASK WHERE SHE WILL SUBMIT THE WORK. This is a big one. If you fear the agent lacks proper contacts to move your work, ask straight out: "What editors do you see us submitting this book to, and have you sold to them before?" The question tests their plan for where to send the manuscript and get it in print.

4. ASK THE AGENT WHY SHE IS YOUR BEST OPTION. This is another straight-up question that gets right to the point. If she's new and has few (or no) sales at that point, she can't respond with "I sell tons of books and I make it rain cash money!! Dolla dolla bills, y'all!!!" She can't rely on her track record to entice you. So what's her sales pitch? Weigh her enthusiasm, her plan for the book, her promises of hard work and anything else she tells you. In the publishing business, you want communication and enthusiasm from agents (and editors). Both are invaluable. What's the point of signing with a huge agent when they don't return your e-mails and consider your book last on their list of priorities for the day?

5. IF YOU'RE NOT SOLD, YOU CAN ALWAYS SAY NO. It's as simple as that. Always query new/newer agents because, at the end of the day, receiving an offer of representation doesn't mean you're obligated to accept.

NEW AGENT SPOTLIGHTS

Peppered throughout this book's large number of agency listings are sporadic "New Agent Alert" sidebars. Look them over to see if these newer reps would be a good fit for your work. Always read personal information and submission guidelines carefully. Don't get rejected on a technicality because you submitted work incorrectly. Wherever possible, we have included a website address for their agency, as well as the Twitter handle for those reps that tweet.

Also please note that as of when this book went to press in fall 2016, all these agents were still active and looking for writers. That said, I cannot guarantee every one is still in their respective position when you read this, nor that they have kept their query inboxes open. I urge you to visit agency websites and double check before you query. (This is always a good idea in any case.) Good luck!

GLOSSARY OF INDUSTRY TERMS

Understand terminology and lingo.

//

AAR. Association of Authors' Representatives.

ABA. American Booksellers Association.

ABC. Association of Booksellers for Children.

ADVANCE. A sum of money a publisher pays a writer or illustrator prior to the publication of a book. It is usually paid in installments, such as one half on signing the contract, one half on delivery of a complete and satisfactory manuscript. The advance is paid against the royalty money that will be earned by the book.

ALA. American Library Association.

ALL RIGHTS. The rights contracted to a publisher permitting the use of material anywhere and in any form, including movie and book club sales, without additional payment to the creator.

ANTHOLOGY. A collection of selected writings by various authors or gatherings of works by one author.

ANTHROPOMORPHIZATION. The act of attributing human form and personality to things not human (such as animals).

ASAP. As soon as possible.

ASSIGNMENT. An editor or art director asks a writer, illustrator, or photographer to produce a specific piece for an agreed-upon fee.

B&W. Black and white.

BACKLIST. A publisher's list of books not published during the current season but still in print.

BEA. BookExpo America.

BIENNIALLY. Occurring once every two years.

BIMONTHLY. Occurring once every two months.

BIWEEKLY. Occurring once every two weeks.

BOOK PACKAGER. A company that draws all elements of a book together, from the initial concept to writing and marketing strategies, then sells the book package to a book publisher and/or movie producer. Also known as book producer or book developer.

BOOK PROPOSAL. Package submitted to a publisher for consideration, usually consisting of a synopsis and outline as well as sample chapters.

BUSINESS-SIZE ENVELOPE. Also known as a #10 envelope. The standard size used in sending business correspondence.

CAMERA-READY. Refers to art that is completely prepared for copy camera platemaking.

CAPTION. A description of the subject matter of an illustration or photograph; photo captions include persons' names where appropriate. Also called cutline.

CBC. Children's Book Council.

CLEAN-COPY. A manuscript free of errors that needs no editing; it is ready for typesetting.

CLIPS. Samples, usually from newspapers or magazines, of a writer's published work.

CONCEPT BOOKS. Books that deal with ideas, concepts and large-scale problems, promoting an understanding of what's happening in a child's world. Most prevalent are alphabet and counting books, but also includes books dealing with specific concerns facing young people (such as divorce, birth of a sibling, friendship, or moving).

CONTRACT. A written agreement stating the rights to be purchased by an editor, art director, or producer and the amount of payment the writer, illustrator, or photographer will receive for that sale.

CONTRIBUTOR'S COPIES. The magazine issues sent to an author, illustrator, or photographer in which her work appears.

CO-OP PUBLISHER. A publisher that shares production costs with an author but, unlike subsidy publishers, handles all marketing and distribution. An author receives a high percentage of royalties until her initial investment is recouped, then standard royalties. (*Children's Writer's & Illustrator's Market* does not include co-op publishers.)

COPY. The actual written material of a manuscript.

COPYEDITING. Editing a manuscript for grammar usage, spelling, punctuation, and other general style.

COPYRIGHT. A means to legally protect an author's/illustrator's/photographer's work. This can be shown by writing the creator's name and the year of the work's creation.

COVER LETTER. A brief letter, accompanying a complete manuscript, especially useful if responding to an editor's request for a manuscript. May also accompany a book proposal.

CUTLINE. See caption.

DIVISION. An unincorporated branch of a company.

DUMMY. A loose mock-up of a book showing placement of text and artwork.

ELECTRONIC SUBMISSION. A submission of material by e-mail or Web form.

FINAL DRAFT. The last version of a polished manuscript ready for submission to an editor.

FIRST NORTH AMERICAN SERIAL RIGHTS. The right to publish material in a periodical for the first time, in the US or Canada.

F&GS. Folded and gathered sheets. An early, not-yet-bound copy of a picture book.

FLAT FEE. A one-time payment.

GALLEYS. The first typeset version of a manuscript that has not yet been divided into pages.

GENRE. A formulaic type of fiction, such as horror, mystery, romance, fantasy, suspense, thriller, science fiction, or western.

GLOSSY. A photograph with a shiny surface, as opposed to one with a matte finish.

GOUACHE. Opaque watercolor with an appreciable film thickness and an actual paint layer.

HALFTONE. Reproduction of a continuous tone illustration with the image formed by dots produced by a camera lens screen.

HARD COPY. The printed copy of a computer's output.

HARDWARE. Refers to all the mechanically-integrated components of a computer that are not software—circuit boards, transistors and the machines that are the actual computer.

HI-LO. High interest, low reading level.

HOME PAGE. The first page of a website.

IBBY. International Board on Books for Young People.

IMPRINT. Name applied to a publisher's specific line of books.

IRA. International Reading Association.

IRC. International Reply Coupon. Sold at the post office to enclose with text or artwork sent to a recipient outside your own country to cover postage costs when replying or returning work.

KEYLINE. Identification of the positions of illustrations and copy for the printer.

LAYOUT. Arrangement of illustrations, photographs, text and headlines for printed material.

LGBTQ. Lesbian/gay/bisexual/trans/queer.

LINE DRAWING. Illustration done with pencil or ink using no wash or other shading.

MASS MARKET BOOKS. Paperback books directed toward an extremely large audience sold in supermarkets, drugstores, airports, newsstands, online retailers, and bookstores.

MECHANICALS. Paste-up or preparation of work for printing.

MIDDLE-GRADE OR MID-GRADE. See middle reader.

MIDDLE READER. The general classification of books written for readers approximately ages nine to twelve. Often called middle-grade or mid-grade.

MS (MSS). Manuscript(s).

MULTIPLE SUBMISSIONS. See simultaneous submissions.

NCTE. National Council of Teachers of English.

ONE-TIME RIGHTS. Permission to publish a story in periodical or book form one time only.

PACKAGE SALE. The sale of a manuscript and illustrations/photos as a "package" paid for with one check.

PAYMENT ON ACCEPTANCE. The writer, artist, or photographer is paid for her work at the time the editor or art director decides to buy it.

PAYMENT ON PUBLICATION. The writer, artist, or photographer is paid for her work when it is published.

PICTURE BOOK. A type of book aimed at preschoolers to eight-year-olds that tells a story using a combination of text and artwork, or artwork only.

PRINT. An impression pulled from an original plate, stone, block, screen, or negative; also a positive made from a photographic negative.

PROOFREADING. Reading text to correct typographical errors.

QUERY. A letter to an editor or agent designed to capture interest in an article or book you have written or propose to write. (See the article "Before Your First Sale.")

READING FEE. Money charged by some agents and publishers to read a submitted manuscript. (*Children's Writer's & Illustrator's Market* does not include agencies that charge reading fees.)

REPRINT RIGHTS. Permission to print an already published work whose first rights have been sold to another magazine or book publisher.

RESPONSE TIME. The average length of time it takes an editor or art director to accept or reject a query or submission, and inform the creator of the decision.

RIGHTS. The bundle of permissions offered to an editor or art director in exchange for printing a manuscript, artwork, or photographs.

ROUGH DRAFT. A manuscript that has not been checked for errors in grammar, punctuation, spelling, or content.

ROUGHS. Preliminary sketches or drawings.

ROYALTY. An agreed percentage paid by a publisher to a writer, illustrator, or photographer for each copy of her work sold.

SAE. Self-addressed envelope.

SASE. Self-addressed, stamped envelope.

SCBWI. The Society of Children's Book Writers and Illustrators.

SECOND SERIAL RIGHTS. Permission for the reprinting of a work in another periodical after its first publication in book or magazine form.

SEMIANNUAL. Occurring every six months or twice a year.

SEMIMONTHLY. Occurring twice a month.

SEMIWEEKLY. Occurring twice a week.

SERIAL RIGHTS. The rights given by an author to a publisher to print a piece in one or more periodicals.

SIMULTANEOUS SUBMISSIONS. Queries or proposals sent to several publishers at the same time. Also called multiple submissions. (See the article "Before Your First Sale.")

SLANT. The approach to a story or piece of artwork that will appeal to readers of a particular publication.

SLUSH PILE. Editors' term for their collections of unsolicited manuscripts.

SOFTWARE. Programs and related documentation for use with a computer.

SOLICITED MANUSCRIPT. Material that an editor has asked for or agreed to consider before being sent by a writer.

SPAR. Society of Photographers and Artists Representatives.

SPECULATION (SPEC). Creating a piece with no assurance from an editor or art director that it will be purchased or any reimbursements for material or labor paid.

SUBSIDIARY RIGHTS. All rights other than book publishing rights included in a book contract, such as paperback, book club, and movie rights.

SUBSIDY PUBLISHER. A book publisher that charges the author for the cost of typesetting, printing and promoting a book. Also called a vanity publisher. (Note: *Children's Writer's & Illustrator's Market* does not include subsidy publishers.)

SYNOPSIS. A summary of a story or novel. Usually a page to a page and a half, single-spaced, if part of a book submission.

TABLOID. Publication printed on an ordinary newspaper page turned sideways and folded in half.

TEARSHEET. Page from a magazine or newspaper containing your printed art, story, article, poem or photo.

THUMBNAIL. A rough layout in miniature.

TRADE BOOKS. Books sold in bookstores and through online retailers, aimed at a smaller audience than mass market books, and printed in smaller quantities by publishers.

TRANSPARENCIES. Positive color slides; not color prints.

UNSOLICITED MANUSCRIPT. Material sent without an editor's, art director's, or agent's request.

VANITY PUBLISHER. See subsidy publisher.

WORK-FOR-HIRE. An arrangement between a writer, illustrator, or photographer and a company under which the company retains complete control of the work's copyright.

YA. See young adult.

YOUNG ADULT. The general classification of books written for readers approximately ages twelve to sixteen. Often referred to as YA.

YOUNG READER. The general classification of books written for readers approximately ages five to eight.

BOOK PUBLISHERS

ABBEVILLE FAMILY

Abbeville Press, 116 W. 23rd St., New York NY 10011. (212)366-5585. **Fax:** (212)366-6966. **E-mail:** abbeville@abbeville.com. **Website:** www.abbeville.com. "Our list is full for the next several seasons." *Not accepting unsolicited book proposals at this time.* **Publishes 8 titles/year. 10% of books from first-time authors.**

FICTION Picture books: animal, anthology, concept, contemporary, fantasy, folktales, health, hi-lo, history, humor, multicultural, nature/environment, poetry, science fiction, special needs, sports, suspense. Average word length 300-1,000 words.

HOW TO CONTACT Please refer to website for submission policy.

ILLUSTRATION Works with approx 2-4 illustrators/year. Uses color artwork only.

PHOTOGRAPHY Buys stock and assigns work.

ABDO PUBLISHING CO.

8000 W. 78th St., Suite 310, Edina MN 55439. (800)800-1312. **Fax:** (952)831-1632. **E-mail:** nonfiction@abdopublishing.com. **Website:** www.abdopublishing.com. **Contact:** Paul Abdo, editor-in-chief. ABDO publishes nonfiction children's books (pre-kindergarten to 8th grade) for school and public libraries—mainly history, sports, biography, geography, science, and social studies. "Please specify each submission as either nonfic-

tion, fiction, or illustration." Publishes hardcover originals. **Publishes 300 titles/year.**

TERMS Guidelines online.

HARRY N. ABRAMS, INC.

115 W. 18th St., 6th Floor, New York NY 10011. (212)206-7715. **Fax:** (212)519-1210. **E-mail:** abrams@abramsbooks.com. **Website:** www.abramsbooks.com. **Contact:** Managing Editor. Publishes hardcover and a few paperback originals. **Publishes 250 titles/year.**

🔘 Does not accept unsolicited materials.

FICTION Publishes hardcover and "a few" paperback originals. Averages 150 total titles/year.

TIPS "We are one of the few publishers who publish almost exclusively illustrated books. We consider ourselves the leading publishers of art books and high-quality artwork in the US. Once the author has signed a contract to write a book for our firm, the author must finish the ms to agreed-upon high standards within the schedule agreed upon in the contract."

ABRAMS BOOKS FOR YOUNG READERS

115 W. 18th St., New York NY 10011. **Website:** www.abramsyoungreaders.com.

🔘 Abrams no longer accepts unsolicited mss or queries.

ILLUSTRATION Illustrations only: Do not submit original material; copies only. Contact: Chad Beckerman, art director.

ALADDIN

Simon & Schuster, 1230 Avenue of the Americas, 4th Floor, New York NY 10020. (212)698-7000. **Website:** www.simonandschuster.com. Aladdin also publishes Aladdin M!X, for those readers too old for kids' books, but not quite ready for adult or young adult novels. **Contact:** Acquisitions Editor. Aladdin publishes picture books, beginning readers, chapter books, middle-grade and tween fiction and nonfiction, and graphic novels and nonfiction in hardcover and paperback, with an emphasis on commercial, kid-friendly titles. Publishes hardcover/paperback originals and imprints of Simon & Schuster Children's Publishing Children's Division.

HOW TO CONTACT Simon & Schuster does not review, retain or return unsolicited materials or artwork. "We suggest prospective authors and illustrators submit their mss through a professional literary agent."

ALGONQUIN YOUNG READERS

P.O. Box 2225, Chapel Hill NC 27515. **Website:** algonquinyoungreaders.com. Algonquin Young Readers is a new imprint that features books for readers 7-17. "From short illustrated novels for the youngest independent readers to timely and topical crossover young adult fiction, what ties our books together are unforgettable characters, absorbing stories, and superior writing."

FICTION Algonquin Young Readers publishes ficiton and a limited number of narrative nonfiction titles for middle-grade and young adult readers. "We don't publish poetry, picture books, or genre fiction."

HOW TO CONTACT Query with 15-20 sample pages and SASE.

ILLUSTRATION "At this time, we do not accept unsolicited submissions for illustration."

TERMS Guidelines online.

AMBERJACK PUBLISHING

P.O. Box 4668 #89611, New York NY 10163. (888)959-3352. **Website:** www.amberjackpublishing.com. Amberjack Publishing offers authors the freedom to write without burdening them to promote the work themselves. Publisher retains all rights. "You will have no rights left to exploit, so you cannot resell, republish, or use your story again."

FICTION Amberjack Publishing is always on the lookout for the next great story. "We are interested in fiction, children's books, graphic novels, science fiction, fantasy, humor, and everything in between."

HOW TO CONTACT Submit via online query form with book proposal and first 10 pages of ms.

Ⓐ AMULET BOOKS

Imprint of Abrams, 115 W. 18th St., 6th Floor, New York NY 10001. **Website:** www.amuletbooks.com. **10% of books from first-time authors.**

Ⓞ *Does not accept unsolicited mss or queries.*

FICTION Middle readers: adventure, contemporary, fantasy, history, science fiction, sports. Young adults/teens: adventure, contemporary, fantasy, history, science fiction, sports, suspense.

ILLUSTRATION Works with 10-12 illustrators/year. Uses both color and b&w. Query with samples. Contact: Chad Beckerman, art director. Samples filed.

PHOTOGRAPHY Buys stock images and assigns work.

ARBORDALE PUBLISHING

612 Johnnie Dodds, Suite A2, Mt. Pleasant SC 29464. (843)971-6722. **Fax:** (843)216-3804. **E-mail:** katie@arbordalepublishing.com. **Website:** www.arbordalepublishing.com. **Contact:** Katie Hall. "The picture books we publish are usually, but not always, fictional stories with nonfiction woven into the story that relate to science or math. All books should subtly convey an educational theme through a warm story that is fun to read and that will grab a child's attention. Each book has a 4-page '*For Creative Minds*' section to reinforce the educational component. This section will have a craft and/or game as well as 'fun facts' to be shared by the parent, teacher, or other adult. Authors do not need to supply this information with their submission, but if their ms is accepted, they may be asked to provide additional information for this section. Mss should be less than 1,000 words and meet all of the following 4 criteria: fun to read—mostly fiction with nonfiction facts woven into the story; national or regional in scope; must tie into early elementary school curriculum; must be marketable through a niche market such as a zoo, aquarium, or museum gift shop." Publishes hardcover, trade paperback, and electronic originals. **Publishes 14 titles/year. 50% of**

books from first-time authors. 100% from unagented writers.

FICTION Picture books: animal, folktales, nature/environment, math-related. Word length—picture books: no more than 1,500.

HOW TO CONTACT 1,000 mss received/year. Accepts electronic submissions only. Snail mail submissions are discarded without being opened. Acknowledges receipt of ms submission within 1 month. Publishes book 18 months after acceptance. May hold onto mss of interest for 1 year until acceptance.

ILLUSTRATION Works with 20 illustrators/year. Prefers to work with illustrators from the US and Canada. Uses color artwork only. Submit Web link or 2-3 electronic images. Contact: Katie Hall.

TERMS Pays 6-8% royalty on wholesale price. Pays small advance. Book catalog and guidelines online. "All mss should be submitted via e-mail to Katie Hall. Mss should be less than 1,000 words."

TIPS "Please make sure that you have looked at our website to read our complete submission guidelines and to see if we are looking for a particular subject. Mss must meet all four of our stated criteria. We look for fairly realistic, bright, and colorful art (no cartoons). We want the children excited about the books. We envision the books being used at home and in the classroom."

ⒶATHENEUM BOOKS FOR YOUNG READERS

Simon & Schuster, 1230 Avenue of the Americas, New York NY 10020. **Website:** kids.simonandschuster.com. Publishes hardcover originals.

FICTION All in juvenile versions. "We have few specific needs except for books that are fresh, interesting, and well written. Fad topics are dangerous, as are works you haven't polished to the best of your ability. We also don't need safety pamphlets, ABC books, coloring books, and board books. In writing picture book texts, avoid the coy and 'cutesy,' such as stories about characters with alliterative names." Agented submissions only. No paperback romance-type fiction.

NONFICTION Publishes hardcover originals, picture books for young kids, nonfiction for ages 8-12 and novels for middle-grade and young adults. 100% require freelance illustration. Agented submissions only.

TERMS Guidelines for #10 SASE.

TIPS "Study our titles."

BAILIWICK PRESS

309 East Mulberry St., Fort Collins CO 80524. (970)672-4878. **Fax:** (970)672-4731. **E-mail:** info@bailiwickpress.com. **Website:** www.bailiwickpress.com. "We're a micro-press that produces books and other products that inspire and tell great stories. Our motto is 'books with something to say.' We are now considering submissions, agented and unagented, for children's and young adult fiction. We're looking for smart, funny, and layered writing that kids will clamor for. Authors who already have a following have a leg up. We are only looking for humorous children's fiction. Please do not submit work for adults. Illustrated fiction is desired but not required. (Illustrators are also invited to send samples.) Make us laugh out loud, ooh and aah, and cry, 'Eureka!'"

HOW TO CONTACT "Please read the Aldo Zelnick series to determine if we might be on the same page, then fill out our submission form. Please do not send submissions via snail mail or phone calls. You must complete the online submission form to be considered. If, after completing and submitting the form, you also need to send us an e-mail attachment (such as sample illustrations or excerpts of graphics), you may e-mail them to aldozelnick@gmail.com." Responds in 6 months.

ILLUSTRATION Illustrated fiction desired but not required. Send samples.

ⒶBALZER & BRAY

HarperCollins Children's Books, 10 E. 53rd St., New York NY 10022. **Website:** www.harpercollinschildrens.com. "We publish bold, creative, groundbreaking picture books and novels that appeal directly to kids in a fresh way." **Publishes 10 titles/year.**

FICTION Picture Books, Young Readers: adventure, animal, anthology, concept, contemporary, fantasy, history, humor, multicultural, nature/environment, poetry, science fiction, special needs, sports, suspense. Middle readers, young adults/teens: adventure, animal, anthology, contemporary, fantasy, history, humor, multicultural, nature/environment, poetry, science fiction, special needs, sports, suspense.

NONFICTION "We will publish very few nonfiction titles, maybe 1-2 per year."

143

HOW TO CONTACT Contact editor. Agented submissions only. Publishes book 18 months after acceptance.

ILLUSTRATION Works with 10 illustrators/year. Uses both color and b&w. Illustrations only: send tearsheets to be kept on file. Responds only if interested. Samples are not returned.

PHOTOGRAPHY Works on assignment only.

TERMS Offers advances. Pays illustrators by the project.

🅐 BANCROFT PRESS

P.O. Box 65360, Baltimore MD 21209-9945. (410)358-0658. **Fax:** (410)764-1967. **E-mail:** bruceb@bancroftpress.com. **Website:** www.bancroftpress.com. **Contact:** Bruce Bortz, editor/publisher (health, investments, politics, history, humor, literary novels, mystery/thrillers, chick lit, young adult). "Bancroft Press is a general trade publisher. We publish young adult fiction and adult fiction, as well as occasional nonfiction. Our only mandate is 'books that enlighten.'" Publishes hardcover and trade paperback originals. **Publishes 4-6 titles/year.**

FICTION "Our current list focuses are young adult fiction, women's fiction, and literary fiction."

NONFICTION "We advise writers to visit the website." All quality books on any subject of interest to the publisher.

HOW TO CONTACT Submit complete ms. Submit proposal package, outline, 5 sample chapters, competition/market survey. Responds in 6-12 months. Publishes book up to 3 years after acceptance of ms.

TERMS Pays 6-8% royalty. Pays various royalties on retail price. Pays $750 advance. Guidelines online.

TIPS "We advise writers to visit our website and to be familiar with our previous work. Patience is the number one attribute contributors must have. It takes us a very long time to get through submitted material, because we are such a small company. Also, we only publish 4-6 books per year, so it may take a long time for your optioned book to be published. We like to be able to market our books to be used in schools and in libraries. We prefer fiction that bucks trends and moves in a new direction. We are especially interested in mysteries and humor (especially humorous mysteries)."

🅐 BANTAM BOOKS

Imprint of Penguin Random House, Inc., 1745 Broadway, New York NY 10019. (212)782-9000. **Website:** www.randomhousebooks.com. *Not seeking mss at this time.*

BAREFOOT BOOKS

2067 Massachusettes Ave., 5th Floor, Cambridge MA 02140. (617)576-0660. **Fax:** (617)576-0049. **E-mail:** help@barefootbooks.com. **Website:** www.barefootbooks.com. "We are a small, independent publishing company that publishes high-quality picture books for children of all ages and specializes in the work of artists and writers from many cultures. We focus on themes that support independence of spirit, encourage openness to others, and foster a life-long love of learning. Prefers full ms." Publishes hardcover and trade paperback originals. **Publishes 30 titles/year. 35% of books from first-time authors. 60% from unagented writers.**

FICTION "Barefoot Books only publishes children's picture books and anthologies of folktales. We do not publish novels."

HOW TO CONTACT Barefoot Books is not currently accepting ms queries or submissions. 2,000 queries received/year. 3,000 mss received/year.

ILLUSTRATION Works with 20 illustrators/year. Uses color artwork only. Reviews ms/illustration packages from artists. Send query and art samples or dummy for picture books. Query with samples or send promo sheet and tearsheets. Responds only if interested. Samples returned with SASE. Pays authors royalty of 5% based on retail price. Offers advances. Sends galleys to authors. Originals returned to artist at job's completion.

TERMS Pays advance. Book catalog for 9x12 SASE stamped with $1.80 postage.

➕ BARRON'S EDUCATIONAL SERIES, INC.

250 Wireless Boulevard, Hauppauge NY 11788. **E-mail:** waynebarr@barronseduc.com. **Contact:** Wayne Barr, Acquisitions Manager. "Barron's Educational Series, Inc. rapidly became America's leading publisher of test preparation manuals and school directories." **Publishes 300+ titles/year.**

NONFICTION "We are currently interested in children and young adult fiction and nonfiction books, foreign language learning books, New Age books, cookbooks, business and financial advice books, parenting advice books, art instruction books, sports, fashion, crafts, and study guides. We do not publish poems, and we are not interested in books that have already been published. We would also like to hear from established authors of Test Prep books."

HOW TO CONTACT When submitting a proposal for a children's fiction book: Please include an outline summary; you may include sample pages (please DO NOT include the ms in its entirety); artwork is not necessary, but is helpful if author is also the illustrator (please only include a sample); author's credentials must be included. When submitting a work of adult or Juvenile Nonfiction: Include a Table of Contents, along with two sample chapters; a brief description of the work should be included in the cover letter, as well as an overview citing the market being targeted (e.g., children, ages 2–4; secondary school teachers, etc.); please include sample illustrations if the book is to be illustrated; author's credentials must also be included. Due to the large volume of unsolicited submissions received, a complete evaluation of a proposal may take 4-6 weeks. **Please do not call about the status of individual submissions.**

TERMS "A large, self-addressed, stamped envelope, with enough postage, must be included if you want your material returned. Only *queries* are accepted by e-mail."

BEHRMAN HOUSE INC.

11 Edison Place, Springfield NJ 07081. (973)379-7200. **Fax:** (973)379-7280. **E-mail:** customersupport@behrmanhouse.com. **Website:** www.behrmanhouse.com. Publishes books on all aspects of Judaism: history, cultural, textbooks, holidays. "Behrman House publishes quality books of Jewish content—history, Bible, philosophy, holidays, ethics—for children and adults." **12% of books from first-time authors.**

NONFICTION All levels: Judaism, Jewish educational textbooks. Average word length: young reader—1,200; middle reader—2,000; young adult—4,000.

HOW TO CONTACT Submit outline/synopsis and sample chapters. Responds in 1 month to queries; 2 months to mss. Publishes book 18 months after acceptance.

ILLUSTRATION Works with 6 children's illustrators/year. Reviews ms/illustration packages from artists. "Query first." Illustrations only: Query with sam-

ples; send unsolicited art samples by mail. Responds to queries in 1 month; mss in 2 months.

PHOTOGRAPHY Purchases photos from freelancers. Buys stock and assigns work. Uses photos of families involved in Jewish activities. Uses color and b&w prints. Photographers should query with samples. Send unsolicited photos by mail. Submit portfolio for review.

TERMS Pays authors royalty of 3-10% based on retail price or buys ms outright for $1,000-5,000. Offers advance. Pays illustrators by the project (range: $500-5,000). Book catalog free on request. Guidelines online.

BELLEBOOKS

P.O. Box 300921, Memphis TN 38130. (901)344-9024. **E-mail:** bellebooks@bellebooks.com. **Website:** www.bellebooks.com. BelleBooks began by publishing Southern fiction. It has become a "second home" for many established authors, who also continue to publish with major publishing houses. **Publishes 30-40 titles/year.**

FICTION "Yes, we'd love to find the next Harry Potter, but our primary focus for the moment is publishing for the teen market."

HOW TO CONTACT Query e-mail with brief synopsis and credentials/credits with full ms attached (RTF format preferred).

TERMS Guidelines online.

TIPS "Our list aims for the teen reader and the crossover market. If you're a 'Southern Louise Rennison,' that would catch our attention. Humor is always a plus. We'd love to see books featuring teen boys as protagonists. We're happy to see dark edgy books on serious subjects."

Ⓐ BERKLEY/NAL

Penguin Group (USA) Inc., 375 Hudson St., New York NY 10014. **Website:** penguin.com. **Contact:** Leslie Gelbman, president and publisher. The Berkley Publishing Group publishes a variety of general nonfiction and fiction including the traditional categories of romance, mystery and science fiction. Publishes paperback and mass market originals and reprints. **Publishes 700 titles/year.**

◯ "Due to the high volume of mss received, most Penguin Group Inc. imprints do not normally accept unsolicited mss. The preferred and standard method for having mss considered for publication by a major publisher is to submit them through an established literary agent."

FICTION No occult fiction.

NONFICTION No memoirs or personal stories.

HOW TO CONTACT Prefers agented submissions.

BETHANY HOUSE PUBLISHERS

Division of Baker Publishing Group, 6030 E. Fulton Rd., Ada MI 49301. (616)676-9185. **Fax:** (616)676-9573. **Website:** bakerpublishinggroup.com/bethanyhouse. Bethany House Publishers specializes in books that communicate Biblical truth and assist people in both spiritual and practical areas of life. Considers unsolicited work only through a professional literary agent or through ms submission services, Authonomy or Christian Ms Submissions. Guidelines online. *All unsolicited mss returned unopened.* Publishes hardcover and trade paperback originals, mass market paperback reprints. **Publishes 90-100 titles/year. 2% of books from first-time authors. 50% from unagented writers.**

HOW TO CONTACT Responds in 3 months to queries. Publishes a book 1 year after acceptance.

TERMS Pays royalty on net price. Pays advance. Book catalog for 9 x 12 envelope and 5 first-class stamps.

TIPS "Bethany House Publishers' publishing program relates Biblical truth to all areas of life—whether in the framework of a well-told story, of a challenging book for spiritual growth, or of a Bible reference work. We are seeking high-quality fiction and nonfiction that will inspire and challenge our audience."

BLACK HERON PRESS

P.O. Box 13396, Mill Creek WA 98082. **Website:** www.blackheronpress.com. "Black Heron Press publishes primarily literary fiction." Publishes hardcover and trade paperback originals, trade paperback reprints. **Publishes 4 titles/year. 50% of books from first-time authors. 90% from unagented writers.**

FICTION "All of our fiction is character driven. We don't want to see fiction written for the mass market. If it sells to the mass market, fine, but we don't see ourselves as a commercial press."

HOW TO CONTACT Submit proposal package, including cover letter and first 40-50 pages pages of your completed novel. Submit proposal package, include cover letter and first 30-50 pages of your completed novel. 1,500 queries received/year. Responds in 6 months. Publishes ms 2 years after acceptance.

TERMS Pays 8% royalty on retail price. Catalog available online.

TIPS "Our Readers love good fiction—they are scattered among all social classes, ethnic groups, and zip code areas. If you can't read our books, at least check out our titles on our website."

Ⓐ BLOOMSBURY CHILDREN'S BOOKS

Imprint of Bloomsbury USA, 1385 Broadway, 5th Floor, New York NY 10008. **Website:** www.bloomsbury.com/us/childrens. No phone calls or e-mails. *Agented submissions only.* **Publishes 60 titles/year. 25% of books from first-time authors.**

HOW TO CONTACT *Agented submissions only.* Responds in 6 months.

TERMS Pays royalty. Pays advance. Book catalog online. Guidelines online.

⊕ BLOOMSBURY SPARK

Website: www.bloomsbury.com/us/bloomsbury-spark. "Bloomsbury Spark is a one-of-a-kind, global, digital imprint from Bloomsbury Publishing dedicated to publishing a wide array of exciting fiction eBooks to teen, young adult, and new adult readers. Our outstanding list features multiple genres: romance, contemporary, dystopian, paranormal, science fiction, mystery, thriller, and more."

FICTION "We're always in the market for fast-paced, unputdownable young adult novels on the older end of the spectrum. Whether it's a pulse-pounding adventure set in a post-apocalyptic future or a heart-wrenching romance, we want it! Bring on the fantasy! Anything that puts a fresh spin on magic, wizards, and far-off lands will always grab our attention." Full wishlist available on website.

HOW TO CONTACT "If you have a ms between 25,000-100,000 words in one (or more) of our wishlist categories, please send us: a query letter, the first 3 chapters of your ms pasted into the body of the message, a brief biography, and links to your online presence. Due to the volume of e-mails we receive, we unfortunately cannot respond to each individual submission, but we will let you know within two months if we would like to read more of your fantastic ms."

BOOKFISH BOOKS

E-mail: bookfishbooks@gmail.com. **Website:** bookfishbooks.com. **Contact:** Tammy McKee, acquisitions editor. BookFish Books is looking for novel-length young adult, new adult, and middle-grade works in all subgenres. Both published and unpublished, agented or unagented authors are welcome to submit. "Sorry, but we do not publish novellas, picture books, early reader/chapter books or adult novels." Responds to every query.

HOW TO CONTACT Query via e-mail with a brief synopsis and first 3 chapters of ms.

TERMS Guidelines online.

TIPS "We only accept complete mss. Please do not query us with partial mss or proposals."

BOYDS MILLS PRESS

Highlights for Children, Inc., 815 Church St., Honesdale PA 18431. (570)253-1164. **Website:** www.boydsmillspress.com. Boyds Mills Press publishes picture books, nonfiction, activity books, and paperback reprints. Their titles have been named notable books by the International Reading Association, the American Library Association, and the National Council of Teachers of English. They've earned numerous awards, including the National Jewish Book Award, the Christopher Medal, the NCTE Orbis Pictus Honor, and the Golden Kite Honor. Boyds Mills Press welcomes unsolicited submissions from published and unpublished writers and artists. Submit a ms with a cover letter of relevant information, including experience with writing and publishing. Label the package "Ms Submission" and include a SASE. For art samples, label the package "Art Sample Submission." All submissions will be evaluated for all imprints.

FICTION Interested in picture books and middle-grade fiction. Do not send a query first. Send the entire ms of picture book or the first 3 chapters and a plot summary for middle-grade fiction (will request the balance of ms if interested).

NONFICTION Include a detailed bibliography with submission. The publisher highly recommend including an expert's review of your ms and a detailed explanation of the books in the marketplace that are similar to the one you propose. References to the need for this book (by the National Academy of Sciences or by similar subject-specific organizations) will strengthen your proposal. If you intend for the book to be illustrated with photos or other graphic elements (charts, graphs, etc.), it is your responsibility to find or create those elements and to include with the submission a permissions budget, if applicable. Finally, keep in mind that good children's nonfiction has a narrative quality—a story line—that encyclopedias do not; please consider whether both the subject and the language will appeal to children.

HOW TO CONTACT Responds to mss within 3 months.

ILLUSTRATION Illustrators submitting a picture book should include the ms, a dummy, and a sample reproduction of the final artwork that reflects the style and technique you intend to use. Do not send original artwork.

TERMS Catalog online. Guidelines online.

CALKINS CREEK

Boyds Mills Press, 815 Church St., Honesdale PA 18431. **Website:** www.calkinscreekbooks.com. "We aim to publish books that are a well-written blend of creative writing and extensive research, which emphasize important events, people, and places in U.S. history."

HOW TO CONTACT Submit outline/synopsis and 3 sample chapters.

ILLUSTRATION Accepts material from international illustrators. Works with 25 (for all Boyds Mills Press imprints) illustrators/year. Uses both color and b&w. Reviews ms/illustration packages. For ms/illustration packages: Submit ms with 2 pieces of final art. Submit ms/illustration packages to address above, label package "Mansuscript Submission." Reviews work for future assignments. If interested in illustrating future titles, query with samples. Submit samples to address above. Label package "Art Sample Submission."

PHOTOGRAPHY Buys stock images and assigns work. Submit photos to: address above, label package "Art Sample Submission." Uses color or b&w 8×10 prints. For first contact, send promo piece (color or b&w).

TERMS Pays authors royalty or work purchased outright. Guidelines online.

TIPS "Read through our recently published titles and review our catalog. When selecting titles to publish, our emphasis will be on important events, people, and places in US history. Writers are encouraged to submit a detailed bibliography, including secondary and primary sources, and expert reviews with their submissions."

Ⓐ CANDLEWICK PRESS

99 Dover St., Somerville MA 02144. (617)661-3330. **Fax:** (617)661-0565. **E-mail:** bigbear@candlewick. com. **Website:** www.candlewick.com. "Candlewick Press publishes high-quality, illustrated children's books for ages infant through young adult. We are a truly child-centered publisher." Publishes hardcover and trade paperback originals, and reprints. **Publishes 200 titles/year. 5% of books from first-time authors.**

○ *Candlewick Press is not accepting queries or unsolicited mss at this time.*

FICTION Picture books: animal, concept, contemporary, fantasy, history, humor, multicultural, nature/environment, poetry. Middle readers, young adults: contemporary, fantasy, history, humor, multicultural, poetry, science fiction, sports, suspense/mystery.

NONFICTION Picture books: concept, biography, geography, nature/environment. Young readers: biography, geography, nature/environment.

HOW TO CONTACT "We currently do not accept unsolicited editorial queries or submissions. If you are an author or illustrator and would like us to consider your work, please read our submissions policy (online) to learn more."

ILLUSTRATION "Candlewick prefers to see a range of styles from artists along with samples showing strong characters (human or animals) in various settings with various emotions."

TERMS Pays authors royalty of 2½-10% based on retail price. Offers advance.

TIPS *"We no longer accept unsolicited mss. See our website for further information about us."*

CAPSTONE PRESS

Capstone Young Readers, 1710 Roe Crest Dr., North Mankato MN 56003. **E-mail:** nf.il.sub@capstonepub. com; author.sub@capstonepub.com; il.sub@capstonepub.com. **Website:** www.capstonepub.com. The Capstone Press imprint publishes nonfiction with accessible text on topics kids love to capture interest and build confidence and skill in beginning, struggling, and reluctant readers, grades pre-K-9.

FICTION Send fiction submissions via e-mail (author.sub@capstonepub.com). Include the following, in the body of the e-mail: sample chapters, résumé, and a list of previous publishing credits.

NONFICTION Send nonfiction submissions via postal mail. Include the following: résumé, cover letter, and up to 3 writing samples.

HOW TO CONTACT Responds only if submissions fit needs. Mss and writing samples will not be returned. "If you receive no reply within 6 months, you should assume the editors are not interested."

ILLUSTRATION Send fiction illustration submissions via e-mail (il.sub@capstonepub.com). Include the following, in the body of the e-mail: sample artwork, résumé, and a list of previous publishing credits. For nonfiction illustrations, send via e-mail (nf. il.sub@capstonepub.com) sample artwork (2-4 pieces) and a list of previous publishing credits.

TERMS Catalog available upon request. Guidelines online.

CAPSTONE PROFESSIONAL

Maupin House, Capstone, 1710 Roe Crest Dr., North Mankato MN 56003. (312) 324-5200. **Fax:** (312) 324-5201. **E-mail:** info@maupinhouse.com. **Website:** www.capstonepd.com. **Contact:** Karen Soll, Managing Editor, acquisitions. Capstone Professional publishes professional learning resources for K-12 educators under the imprint of Maupin House. **Publishes 6-8 titles/year. 60% of books from first-time authors. 100% from unagented writers.**

NONFICTION Professional development offerings by Capstone Professional range from webinars and workshops to conference speakers and author visits. Submissions for products that speak to the needs of educators today are always accepted. "We continue to look for professional development resources that support grades K–8 classroom teachers in areas, such as these: literacy, language arts, content-area literacy, research-based practices, assessment, inquiry, technology, differentiation, standards-based instruction, school safety, classroom management, and school community."

HOW TO CONTACT Receives 25 submissions/year. Responds in less than 1 month. Publishes 6 months after acceptance.

CAROLRHODA BOOKS, INC.

1251 Washington Ave. N., Minneapolis MN 55401. **Website:** www.lernerbooks.com. "We will continue to seek targeted solicitations at specific reading levels and in specific subject areas. The company will list these targeted solicitations on our website and in national newsletters, such as the SCBWI Bulletin." Interested in "boundary-pushing" teen fiction. *Lerner Publishing Group no longer accepts submissions to any of their imprints except for Kar-Ben Publishing.*

Ⓐ CARTWHEEL BOOKS

Imprint of Scholastic Trade Division, 557 Broadway, New York NY 10012. (212)343-6100. **Website:** www.scholastic.com. Cartwheel Books publishes innovative books for children, up to age 8. "We are looking for 'novelties' that are books first, play objects second. Even without its gimmick, a Cartwheel Book should stand alone as a valid piece of children's literature." Publishes novelty books, easy readers, board books, hardcover and trade paperback originals.

FICTION Again, the subject should have mass market appeal for very young children. Humor can be helpful, but not necessary. Mistakes writers make are a reading level that is too difficult, a topic of no interest or too narrow, or mss that are too long.

NONFICTION Cartwheel Books publishes for the very young, therefore nonfiction should be written in a manner that is accessible to preschoolers through 2nd grade. "Often writers choose topics that are too narrow or 'special' and do not appeal to the mass market. Also, the text and vocabulary are frequently too difficult for our young audience."

HOW TO CONTACT *Accepts mss from agents only. Accepts mss from agents only.*

TERMS Guidelines available for free.

CEDAR FORT, INC.

2373 W. 700 S, Springville UT 84663. (801)489-4084. **Fax:** (801)489-1097. **Website:** www.cedarfort.com. "Each year we publish well over 100 books, and many of those are by first-time authors. At the same time, we love to see books from established authors. As one of the largest book publishers in Utah, we have the capability and enthusiasm to make your book a success, whether you are a new author or a returning one. We want to publish uplifting and edifying books that help people think about what is important in life, books people enjoy reading to relax and feel better about themselves, and books to help improve lives. Although we do put out several children's books each year, we are extremely selective. Our children's books must have strong religious or moral values, and must contain outstanding writing and an excellent storyline." Publishes hardcover, trade paperback originals and reprints, mass market paperback and electronic reprints. **Publishes 150 titles/year. 60% of books from first-time authors. 95% from unagented writers.**

HOW TO CONTACT Submit completed ms. Query with SASE; submit proposal package, including outline, 2 sample chapters; or submit completed ms. Receives 200 queries/year; 600 mss/year. Responds in 1 month on queries; 2 months on proposals; 4 months on mss. Publishes book 10-14 months after acceptance.

TERMS Pays 10-12% royalty on wholesale price. Pays $2,000-50,000 advance. Catalog and guidelines online.

TIPS "Our audience is rural, conservative, mainstream. The first page of your ms is very important because we start reading every submission, but good writing and plot keep us reading."

Ⓒ CHARLESBRIDGE PUBLISHING

85 Main St., Watertown MA 02472. (617)926-0329. **Fax:** (617)926-5720. **E-mail:** tradeeditorial@charlesbridge.com. **Website:** www.charlesbridge.com. "Charlesbridge publishes high-quality books for children, with a goal of creating lifelong readers and lifelong learners. Our books encourage reading and discovery in the classroom, library, and home. We believe that books for children should offer accurate information, promote a positive worldview, and embrace a child's innate sense of wonder and fun. To this end, we continually strive to seek new voices, new visions, and new directions in children's literature. As of September 2015, we are now accepting young adult novels for consideration." Publishes hardcover and trade paperback nonfiction and fiction, children's books for the trade and library markets. **Publishes 30 titles/year. 10-20% of books from first-time authors. 80% from unagented writers.**

FICTION Strong stories with enduring themes. Charlesbridge publishes both picture books and transitional bridge books (books ranging from early readers to middle-grade chapter books). Our fiction titles include lively, plot-driven stories with strong, engaging characters. No alphabet books, board books, coloring books, activity books, or books with audiotapes or CD-ROMs.

NONFICTION Strong interest in nature, environment, social studies, and other topics for trade and library markets.

HOW TO CONTACT Please submit only 1 ms at a time. For picture books and shorter bridge books, please send a complete ms. For fiction books longer than 30 pages, please send a detailed plot synopsis, a chapter outline, and 3 chapters of text. If sending a young adult novel, mark the front of the envelope w/ "Young adult novel enclosed." Please note, for young adult, e-mail submissions are preferred to the following address; yasubs@charlesbridge.com. Only responds if interested. Full guidelines on website. Please submit only 1-2 chapters at a time. For nonfiction books longer than 30 pages, send a detailed proposal, a chapter outline, and 1-3 chapters of text. Responds in 3 months. Publishes ms 2-4 years after acceptance.

TERMS Pays royalty. Pays advance. Guidelines online.

TIPS "To become acquainted with our publishing program, we encourage you to review our books and visit our website where you will find our catalog."

CHICAGO REVIEW PRESS

814 N. Franklin St., Chicago IL 60610. (312)337-0747. **Fax:** (312)337-5110. **E-mail:** frontdesk@chicagoreviewpress.com. **Website:** www.chicagoreviewpress.com. **Contact:** Cynthia Sherry, publisher; Yuval Taylor, senior editor; Jerome Pohlen, senior editor; Lisa Reardon, senior editor. "Chicago Review Press publishes high-quality, nonfiction, educational activity books that extend the learning process through hands-on projects and accurate and interesting text. We look for activity books that are as much fun as they are constructive and informative."

FICTION Guidelines now available on website.

NONFICTION Young readers, middle readers and young adults: activity books, arts/crafts, multicultural, history, nature/environment, science. "We're interested in hands-on, educational books; anything else probably will be rejected." Average length: young readers and young adults—144-160 pages.

HOW TO CONTACT Enclose cover letter and a brief synopsis of book in 1-2 paragraphs, table of contents and first 3 sample chapters; prefers not to receive e-mail queries. For children's activity books include a few sample activities with a list of the others. Full guidelines available on site. Responds in 2 months. Publishes a book 1-2 years after acceptance.

ILLUSTRATION Works with 6 illustrators/year. Uses primarily b&w artwork. Reviews ms/illustration packages from artists. Submit 1-2 chapters of ms with corresponding pieces of final art. Illustrations

only: Query with samples, résumé. Responds only if interested. Samples returned with SASE.

PHOTOGRAPHY Buys photos from freelancers ("but not often"). Buys stock and assigns work. Wants "instructive photos. We consult our files when we know what we're looking for on a book-by-book basis." Uses b&w prints.

TERMS Pays authors royalty of 7.5-12.5% based on retail price. Offers advances of $3,000-6,000. Pays illustrators and photographers by the project (range varies considerably). Book catalog available for $3. Ms guidelines available for $3.

TIPS "We're looking for original activity books for small children and the adults caring for them—new themes and enticing projects to occupy kids' imaginations and promote their sense of personal creativity. We like activity books that are as much fun as they are constructive. Please review our guidelines so you'll know what we're looking for."

CHILDREN'S BRAINS ARE YUMMY (CBAY) BOOKS

P.O. Box 670296, Dallas TX 75367. **E-mail:** submissions@cbaybooks.com. **Website:** www.cbaybooks.com. **Contact:** Madeline Smoot, publisher. "CBAY Books currently focuses on quality fantasy and science fiction books for the middle-grade and teen markets. We are not currently accepting unsolicited submissions." **Publishes 3-6 titles/year. 30% of books from first-time authors. 80% from unagented writers.**

HOW TO CONTACT Responds in 2 months. Publishes ms 24 months after acceptance.

ILLUSTRATION Accepts international material. Works with 0-1 illustrators/year. Uses color artwork only. Reviews artwork. Send mss with dummy. Send resume and tearsheets. Send samples to Madeline Smoot. Responds to queries only if interested.

PHOTOGRAPHY Buys stock images.

TERMS Pays authors royalty 10%-15% based on wholesale price. Offers advances against royalties. Average amount $500. Pays advance. "We are distributed by IPG. Our books can be found in their catalog at www.ipgbooks.com." Brochure and guidelines online.

CHOOSECO, LLC

P.O. Box 46, Waitsfield VT 05673. 1-800-564-3468; (802)496-2595. **Fax:** (802) 496-7965. **Website:** www.cyoa.com/pages/ms-submissions. **Contact:** Submissions. "Chooseco LLC was formed in 2003 by series founder R.A. Montgomery to republish some of the best-selling titles in the original Choose Your Own Adventure® series. We have also published 19 CYOA books for younger readers under our Dragonlarks imprint. These books are shorter, with a larger page format and vibrant color artwork (aimed at readers aged 5-8). Chooseco has introduced CYOA: The Golden Path, an original three volume hardcover series written by Anson Montgomery. The Golden Path series is our experiment with a 'longer form' version of interactive fiction for slightly older readers (Age 12+)."

HOW TO CONTACT "While Chooseco works with a team of very talented writers, we are able to review mss or writing samples from potential new writers. We receive many submissions each year, so please be patient awaiting a response."

ILLUSTRATION "We are always interested in hearing from artists. Please e-mail a link to a portfolio to art@chooseco.com."

TERMS "Chooseco does not accept online submissions of mss. If you are interested in submitting a ms, please print and fill out the submissions contract available online, and mail it to our address with a cover letter describing your ms. You will be notified you if they are interested in pursuing your submission. Any submissions not adhering to these guidelines will not be reviewed."

CHRONICLE BOOKS

680 Second St., San Francisco CA 94107. **E-mail:** submissions@chroniclebooks.com. **Website:** www.chroniclebooks.com. "We publish an exciting range of books, stationery, kits, calendars, and novelty formats. Our list includes children's books and interactive formats, young adult books, cookbooks, fine art, design, and photography, pop culture, craft, fashion, beauty and home decor, relationships, mind/body/spirit, and innovative formats (interactive journals, kits, decks, and stationery)." **Publishes 90 titles/year.**
FICTION Only interested in fiction for children and young adults. No adult fiction.
NONFICTION "We're always looking for the new and unusual. We do accept unsolicited mss and we review all proposals. However, given the volume of proposals we receive, we are not able to personally respond to unsolicited proposals unless we are interested in pursuing the project."

HOW TO CONTACT Submit complete ms (picture books); submit outline/synopsis and 3 sample chapters (for older readers). Will not respond to submissions unless interested. Will not consider submissions by fax, e-mail, or disk. Do not include SASE; do not send original materials. No submissions will be returned. Submit via mail or e-mail (prefers e-mail for adult submissions; only by mail for children's submissions). Submit proposal (guidelines online) and allow 3 months for editors to review and for children's submissions, allow 6 months. If submitting by mail, do not include SASE since our staff will not return materials. Responds to queries in 1 month. Publishes a book 1-3 years after acceptance.

ILLUSTRATION Works with 40-50 illustrators/year. Wants "unusual art, graphically strong, something that will stand out on the shelves. Fine art, not mass market." Reviews ms/illustration packages from artists. "Indicate if project *must* be considered jointly, or if editor may consider text and art separately." Illustrations only: Submit samples of artist's work (not necessarily from book, but in the envisioned style). Slides, tearsheets and color photocopies OK. (No original art.) Dummies helpful. Résumé helpful. Samples suited to our needs are filed for future reference. Samples not suited to our needs will be recycled. Queries and project proposals responded to in same time frame as author query/proposals."

PHOTOGRAPHY Purchases photos from freelancers. Works on assignment only.

TERMS Generally pays authors in royalties based on retail price, "though we do occasionally work on a flat fee basis." Advance varies. Illustrators paid royalty based on retail price or flat fee. Book catalog for 9x12 SAE and 8 first-class stamps. Ms guidelines for #10 SASE.

CHRONICLE BOOKS FOR CHILDREN

680 Second St., San Francisco CA 94107. (415)537-4200. **Fax:** (415)537-4460. **E-mail:** submissions@chroniclebooks.com. **Website:** www.chroniclekids.com. "Chronicle Books for Children publishes an eclectic mixture of traditional and innovative children's books. Our aim is to publish books that inspire young readers to learn and grow creatively while helping them discover the joy of reading. We're looking for quirky, bold artwork and subject matter." Publishes hardcover and trade paperback originals. **Publishes**

100-110 titles/year. **6% of books from first-time authors. 25% from unagented writers.**

FICTION Does not accept proposals by fax, e-mail, or disk. When submitting artwork, either as a part of a project or as samples for review, do not send original art.

HOW TO CONTACT Query with synopsis. 30,000 queries received/year. Responds in 2-4 weeks to queries; 6 months to mss. Publishes a book 18-24 months after acceptance.

TERMS Pays variable advance. Book catalog for 9x12 envelope and 3 first-class stamps. Guidelines online.

TIPS "We are interested in projects that have a unique bent to them—be it in subject matter, writing style, or illustrative technique. As a small list, we are looking for books that will lend our list a distinctive flavor. Primarily we are interested in fiction and nonfiction picture books for children ages up to 8 years, and nonfiction books for children ages up to 12 years. We publish board, pop-up, and other novelty formats as well as picture books. We are also interested in early chapter books, middle-grade fiction, and young adult projects."

CINCO PUNTOS PRESS

701 Texas Ave., El Paso TX 79901. (915)838-1625. **Fax:** (915)838-1635. **E-mail:** info@cincopuntos.com. **Website:** www.cincopuntos.com. **Contact:** Lee Byrd, acquisitions editor. "We don't always know what we're looking for until we actually see it, but the one thing that matters to us is that the writing is good, that it is work that comes from the heart and soul of the author and that it fits well with the concerns of our press."

FICTION "We do not look at unsolicited mss or at work that comes via e-mail."

TERMS Call first for submission details.

CLARION BOOKS

Houghton Mifflin Co., 215 Park Ave. S., New York NY 10003. **Website:** www.hmhco.com. "Clarion Books publishes picture books, nonfiction, and fiction for infants through grade 12. Avoid telling your stories in verse unless you are a professional poet. We are no longer responding to your unsolicited submission unless we are interested in publishing it. Please do not include a SASE. Submissions will be recycled, and you will not hear from us regarding the status of your submission unless we are interested. We regret that we cannot respond personally to each submission, but we do consider each and every submission we receive." Publishes hardcover originals for children. **Publishes 50 titles/year.**

FICTION "Clarion is highly selective in the areas of historical fiction, fantasy, and science fiction. A novel must be superlatively written in order to find a place on the list. Mss that arrive without a SASE of adequate size will *not* be responded to or returned. Accepts fiction translations."

NONFICTION No unsolicited mss.

HOW TO CONTACT Submit complete ms. No queries, please. Send to only *one* Clarion editor. Query with SASE. Submit proposal package, sample chapters, SASE. Responds in 2 months to queries. Publishes a book 2 years after acceptance.

ILLUSTRATION Pays illustrators royalty; flat fee for jacket illustration.

TERMS Pays 5-10% royalty on retail price. Pays minimum of $4,000 advance. Guidelines online.

TIPS "Looks for freshness, enthusiasm—in short, life."

CRAIGMORE CREATIONS

PMB 114, 4110 SE Hawthorne Blvd., Portland OR 97124. (503)477-9562. **E-mail:** info@craigmorecreations.com. **Website:** www.craigmorecreations.com.

NONFICTION "We publish books that make time travel seem possible: nonfiction that explores prehistory and Earth sciences for children."

HOW TO CONTACT Submit proposal package. See website for detailed submission guidelines. Submit proposal package. See website for detailed submission guidelines.

CREATIVE COMPANY

E-mail: info@thecreativecompany.us. **Website:** www.thecreativecompany.us. **Contact:** Kate Riggs, Managing Editor. "We are currently not accepting fiction submissions." **Publishes 140 titles/year.**

NONFICTION Picture books, young readers, young adults: animal, arts/crafts, biography, careers, geography, health, history, hobbies, multicultural, music/dance, nature/environment, religion, science, social issues, special needs, sports. Average word length: young readers—500; young adults—6,000.

HOW TO CONTACT Submit outline/synopsis and 2 sample chapters, along with division of titles within the series. Responds in 3-6 months. Publishes a book 2 years after acceptance.

PHOTOGRAPHY Buys stock. Contact: Photo Editor. Model/property releases not required; captions required. Uses b&w prints. Submit cover letter, promo piece. Ms and photographer guidelines available for SAE.

TERMS Guidelines available for SAE.

TIPS "We are accepting nonfiction, series submissions only. Fiction submissions will not be reviewed or returned. Nonfiction submissions should be presented in series (4, 6, or 8) rather than single."

CRESTON BOOKS

P.O. Box 9369, Berkeley CA 94709. **E-mail:** submissions@crestonbooks.co. **Website:** crestonbooks.co. Creston Books is author-illustrator driven, with talented, award-winning creators given more editorial freedom and control than in a typical New York house. **50% of books from first-time authors. 50% from unagented writers.**

HOW TO CONTACT Please paste text of picture books or first chapters of novels in the body of e-mail. Words of Advice for submitting authors listed on the site.

TERMS Pays advance. Catalog online. Guidelines available.

CURIOSITY QUILLS

Whampa, LLC, P.O. Box 2160, Reston VA 20195. (800)998-2509. **Fax:** (800)998-2509. **E-mail:** editor@curiosityquills.com. **Website:** curiosityquills.com. **Contact:** Alisa Gus. Curiosity Quills is a publisher of hard-hitting dark science fiction, speculative fiction, and paranormal works aimed at adults, young adults, and new adults. Firm publishes science fiction, speculative fiction, steampunk, paranormal and urban fantasy, and corresponding romance titles under its new Rebel Romance imprint. **Publishes 75 titles/year. 60% of books from first-time authors. 65% from unagented writers.**

FICTION Looking for "thought-provoking, mind-twisting rollercoasters—challenge our mind, turn our world upside down, and make us question. Those are the makings of a true literary marauder."

NONFICTION Writer's guides, on a strictly limited basis.

HOW TO CONTACT Submit ms using online submission form or e-mail to acquisitions@curiosityquills.com. 1,000 submissions/year. Responds in 1-6 weeks. Publishes ms 9 months after acceptance.

TERMS Pays variable royalty. Does not pay advance. Catalog available. Guidelines online.

✚ DAWN PUBLICATIONS

12402 Bitney Springs Rd., Nevada City CA 95959. (530)274-7775. **Fax:** (530)274-7778. **Website:** www.dawnpub.com. **Contact:** Glenn Hovemann, editor. "Dawn Publications is dedicated to inspiring in children a sense of appreciation for all life on earth. Dawn looks for nature awareness and appreciation titles that promote a relationship with the natural world and specific habitats, usually through inspiring treatment and nonfiction." Publishes hardcover and trade paperback originals. **Publishes 6 titles/year. 15% of books from first-time authors. 90% from unagented writers.**

HOW TO CONTACT Dawn accepts mss submissions by e-mail; follow instructions posted on website. Submissions by mail still OK.

ILLUSTRATION Works with 5 illustrators/year. Will review ms/illustration packages from artists. Query; send ms with dummy. Illustrations only: Query with samples, résumé.

TERMS Pays advance. Book catalog and guidelines online. Publishes book 1-2 years after acceptance.

TIPS "Publishes mostly creative nonfiction with lightness and inspiration." Looking for picture books expressing nature awareness with inspirational quality leading to enhanced self-awareness. Does not publish anthropomorphic works; no animal dialogue.

Ⓐ DELACORTE PRESS

An imprint of Random House Children's Books, a division of Penguin Random House LLC, New York, 1745 Broadway, New York NY 10019. (212)782-9000. **Website:** randomhousekids.com; randomhouseteens.com. Publishes middle-grade and young adult fiction in hard cover, trade paperback, mass market, and digest formats.

All query letters and ms submissions must be submitted through an agent or at the request of an editor.

DIAL BOOKS FOR YOUNG READERS

Imprint of Penguin Group (USA), 345 Hudson St., New York NY 10014. (212)366-2000. **Website:** www.penguin.com/children. "Dial Books for Young Readers publishes quality picture books for ages 18 months-6 years; lively, believable novels for middle readers and young adults; and occasional nonfiction for middle readers and young adults." Publishes hardcover originals. **Publishes 50 titles/year. 20% of books from first-time authors.**

FICTION Especially looking for lively and well-written novels for middle-grade and young adult children involving a convincing plot and believable characters. The subject matter or theme should not already be overworked in previously published books. The approach must not be demeaning to any minority group, nor should the roles of female characters (or others) be stereotyped, though we don't think books should be didactic, or in any way message-y. No topics inappropriate for the juvenile, young adult, and middle-grade audiences. No plays.

HOW TO CONTACT Accepts unsolicited queries and up to 10 pages for longer works and unsolicited mss for picture books. Will only respond if interested. Only responds if interested. "We accept entire picture book mss and a maximum of 10 pages for longer works (novels, easy-to-reads). When submitting a portion of a longer work, please provide an accompanying cover letter that briefly describes your ms's plot, genre (i.e. easy-to-read, middle-grade, or young adult novel), the intended age group, and your publishing credits, if any." 5,000 queries received/year. Responds in 4-6 months to queries.

ILLUSTRATION Send nonreturnable samples, no originals, to Lily Malcolm. Show children and animals.

TERMS Pays royalty. Pays varies advance. Book catalog and guidelines online.

TIPS "Our readers are anywhere from preschool age to teenage. Picture books must have strong plots, lots of action, unusual premises, or universal themes treated with freshness and originality. Humor works well in these books. A very well-thought-out and intelligently presented book has the best chance of being taken on. Genre isn't as much of a factor as presentation."

DUTTON CHILDREN'S BOOKS

Penguin Random House, 375 Hudson St., New York NY 10014. **Website:** www.penguin.com. **Contact:** Julie Strauss-Gabel, vice president and publisher. Dutton Children's Books publishes high-quality fiction and nonfiction for readers ranging from preschoolers to young adults on a variety of subjects. Currently emphasizing middle-grade and young adult novels

that offer a fresh perspective. De-emphasizing photographic nonfiction and picture books that teach a lesson. Publishes hardcover originals as well as novelty formats. **Publishes 100 titles/year. 15% of books from first-time authors.**

○ "Cultivating the creative talents of authors and illustrators and publishing books with purpose and heart continue to be the mission and joy at Dutton."

FICTION Dutton Children's Books has a diverse, general interest list that includes picture books; easy-to-read books; and fiction for all ages, from first chapter books to young adult readers.

HOW TO CONTACT Query. Responds only in interested.

TERMS Pays royalty on retail price. Offers advance. Pays royalty on retail price. Pays advance.

EDUPRESS, INC.

P.O. Box 8610, Madison WI 53708. (608)242-1201. **E-mail:** edupress@highsmith.com. **Website:** www.edupress.com. **Contact:** Liz Bowie. Edupress, Inc., publishes supplemental curriculum resources for Pre-K-6th grade. Currently emphasizing Common Core reading and math games and materials.

○ "Our mission is to create products that make kids want to go to school."

HOW TO CONTACT Submit complete ms via mail or e-mail with "Ms Submission" as the subject line. Responds in 2-4 months. Publishes ms 1-2 years after acceptance.

ILLUSTRATION Query with samples. Contact: Cathy Baker, product development manager. Responds only if interested. Samples returned with SASE.

PHOTOGRAPHY Buys stock.

TERMS Work purchased outright from authors. Catalog online.

TIPS "We are looking for unique, research-based, quality supplemental materials for Pre-K through 6th grade. We publish mainly reading and math materials in many different formats, including games. Our materials are intended for classroom and home schooling use. We do not publish picture books."

WILLIAM B. EERDMANS PUBLISHING CO.

2140 Oak Industrial Dr. NE, Grand Rapids MI 49505. (616)459-4591. **Fax:** (616)459-6540. **E-mail:** info@eerdmans.com. **Website:** www.eerdmans.com. "The majority of our adult publications are religious and most of these are academic or semi-academic in character (as opposed to inspirational or celebrity books), though we also publish general trade books on the Christian life. Our nonreligious titles, most of them in regional history or on social issues, aim, similarly, at an educated audience." Publishes hardcover and paperback originals and reprints.

NONFICTION "We prefer that writers take the time to notice if we have published anything at all in the same category as their ms before sending it to us."

HOW TO CONTACT Query with SASE. Query with TOC, 2-3 sample chapters, and SASE for return of ms. Responds in 4 weeks.

TERMS Book catalog and ms guidelines free.

ELM BOOKS

1175 Hwy. 130, Laramie WY 82070. (610)529-0460. **E-mail:** leila.elmbooks@gmail.com. **Website:** www.elm-books.com. **Contact:** Leila Monaghan, publisher. "We are eager to publish stories by new writers that have real stories to tell. We are looking for short stories (5,000-10,000 words) with real characters and true-to-life stories. Whether your story is fictionalized autobiography, or other stories of real-life mayhem and debauchery, we are interested in reading them!"

FICTION "We are looking for short stories (1,000-5,000 words) about kids of color that will grab readers' attentions—mysteries, adventures, humor, suspense, set in the present, near past, or near future that reflect the realities and hopes of life in diverse communities." Also looking for middle-grade novels (20,000-50,000 words).

HOW TO CONTACT Send complete ms for short stories; synopsis and 3 sample chapters for novels.

TERMS Pays royalties.

ENTANGLED TEEN

Website: www.entangledteen.com. "Entangled Teen and Entangled digiTeen, our young adult imprints, publish the swoonworthy young adult romances readers crave. Whether they're dark and angsty or fun and sassy, contemporary, fantastical, or futuristic. We are seeking fresh voices with interesting twists on popular genres."

FICTION "We are seeking novels in the subgenres of romantic fiction for contemporary, upper young adult with crossover appeal."

HOW TO CONTACT E-mail using site. "All submissions must have strong romantic elements. Young adult novels should be 50,000–100,000 words in length. Revised backlist titles will be considered on a case by case basis." Agented and unagented considered.

TERMS Pays royalty.

⊕ EVIL JESTER PRESS

46 Gull Dipp Rd., Attn: Charles Day, Ridge NY 11961. **Website:** eviljesterpress.com/for-authors/novel-submissions. **Contact:** Charles Day. "A respected small press committed to publishing the best in dark fiction and comics. Horror, thrillers, dark fantasy and science fiction—that's our game."

FICTION "We are looking for dark and thoughtful novels between 40,000-100,000 words for our selected tomes will fall somewhere in the horror, thriller, dark fantasy, or science fiction genres. Mash ups are fine, but we're tired of zombies." Starting to publish middle grade and young adult.

TERMS "Send the entire ms (no partials) to EJP's Acquisitions editor, atcharles@eviljesterpress.com. Include the following in the subject line: novel or comic submission, title, author's last name, word count. Include a short bio in the body of the e-mail, but do not send a synopsis. We want to discover the story as a reader would, and knowing where things are going will remove the element of surprise. Sell us with your prose, your craft, not your marketing copy." Send complete ms as one RTF file, double-spaced, Times New Roman (size 12). Page headers (in the upper right hand of every page except the title page) should include: author name/title/page number.

FACTS ON FILE, INC.

Infobase Learning, 132 W. 31st St., 17th Floor, New York NY 10001. (800)322-8755. **Fax:** (800)678-3633. **E-mail:** llikoff@factsonfile.com; custserv@factsonfile.com. **Website:** www.factsonfile.com. Facts On File produces high-quality reference materials in print and digital format on a broad range of subjects for the school and public library market and the general nonfiction trade. Publishes hardcover originals and reprints and e-books as well as reference databases. **Publishes 150-200 titles/year. 10% of books from first-time authors. 25% from unagented writers. NONFICTION** "We publish serious, informational books and e-books for a targeted audience. All our books must have strong library interest, but we also distribute books effectively to the trade. Our library books fit the junior and senior high school curriculum." No computer books, technical books, cookbooks, biographies (except young adult), pop psychology, humor, fiction, or poetry. **HOW TO CONTACT** Query or submit outline and sample chapter with SASE. No submissions returned without SASE. Responds in 2 months to queries. **ILLUSTRATION** Commissions line art only. **TERMS** Pays 10% royalty on retail price. Pays $5,000 advance. Book catalog available free. Guidelines online. **TIPS** "Our audience is school and public libraries for our more reference-oriented books and libraries, schools and bookstores for our less reference-oriented informational titles."

FAMILIUS

1254 Commerce Way, Sanger CA 93657. (559)876-2170. **Fax:** (559)876-2180. **E-mail:** bookideas@familius.com. **Website:** familius.com. **Contact:** Michele Robbins, acquisitions editor. Familius is all about strengthening families. Collective, the authors and staff have experienced a wide slice of the family-life spectrum. Some come from broken homes. Some are married and in the throes of managing a bursting household. Some are preparing to start families of their own. Together, they publish books and articles that help families be happy. Publishes hardcover, trade paperback, and electronic originals and reprints. **Publishes 40 titles/year. 30% of books from first-time authors. 70% from unagented writers.** **FICTION** All fiction must align with Familius values statement listed on the website footer. **NONFICTION** All mss must align with Familius mission statement to help families succeed. **HOW TO CONTACT** Submit a proposal package, including a synopsis, 3 sample chapters, and your author platform. Submit a proposal package, including an outline, one sample chapter, competition evaluation, and your author platform. 200 queries; 100 mss received/year. Responds in 1 month to queries and proposals; 2 months to mss. Publishes book 12 months after acceptance. **TERMS** Authors are paid 10-30% royalty on wholesale price. Catalog online. Guidelines online.

FARRAR, STRAUS & GIROUX FOR YOUNG

READERS

Macmillan Children's Publishing Group, 175 Fifth Ave., New York NY 10010. (212)741-6900. **Fax:** (212)633-2427. **Website:** www.fsgkidsbooks.com. **FICTION** All levels: all categories. "Seeking original and well-written material for all ages." **NONFICTION** All levels: all categories. "We publish only literary nonfiction." **HOW TO CONTACT** Submit cover letter, first 50 pages by mail only. **ILLUSTRATION** Works with 30-60 illustrators/year. Reviews ms/illustration packages from artists. Submit ms with 1 example of final art, remainder roughs. Do not send originals. Illustrations only: Query with tearsheets. Responds if interested in 3 months. Samples returned with SASE; samples sometimes filed. **TERMS** Book catalog available by request. Ms guidelines online. **TIPS** "Study our catalog before submitting. We will see illustrators' portfolios by appointment. Don't ask for criticism and/or advice—due to the volume of submissions we receive, it's just not possible. Never send originals. Always enclose SASE."

FATHER'S PRESS

590 NW 1921 St. Rd., Kingsville MO 64063. (816)566-0654. **Website:** www.fatherspress.com. **Contact:** Mike Smitley, owner (fiction, nonfiction). Publishes hardcover, trade paperback, and mass market paperback originals and reprints. **Publishes 6-10 titles/year.** **HOW TO CONTACT** Query with SASE. Unsolicited mss returned unopened. Call or e-mail first. Responds in 1-3 months. Publishes ms 6 months after acceptance. **TERMS** Pays 10-15% royalty on wholesale price. Guidelines online.

⊘ FEIWEL AND FRIENDS

Macmillan Children's Publishing Group, 175 Fifth Ave., New York NY 10010. (646)307-5151. **Website:** us.macmillan.com. Feiwel and Friends is a publisher of innovative children's fiction and nonfiction literature, including hardcover, paperback series, and individual titles. The list is eclectic and combines quality and commercial appeal for readers ages 0-16. The imprint is dedicated to "book by book" publishing, bringing the work of distinctive and oustanding authors, illustrators, and ideas to the marketplace. This market does not accept unsolicited mss due to the volume of submissions; they also do not accept unsolicited queries for interior art. The best way to submit a ms is through an agent.

TERMS Catalog online.

➕ FEY PUBLISHING

Website: www.feypublishing.com/submissions.html. "Young Fey is everything you've come to expect from Fey Publishing—quality science fiction, fantasy, horror, and speculative fiction, but written with a younger audience in mind. Young and old alike will love these tales of whimsy and triumph from some of the best up-and-coming authors of young adult and middle-grade fiction."

FICTION "We'd love to see more young adult books without romance as a focus, or if there is romance, we'd prefer it to be nontraditional and not the focus of the story. We want strong characters that teens can look up to. We'd love to find more stories with friendship, not just romance, as the focus. We also prefer young adult books with science fiction and fantasy elements, but it's not required. Young adult stories can feature darker stories and introduce some adult concepts within reason (issues that the age range may experience as they grow up). Middle-grade stories should be age appropriate."

HOW TO CONTACT Usually responds within 3 months.

TERMS "We are looking for full-length and completed mss only. No short story collections, just novels. We ask that they be at least 50,000 words in length; no novellas please. There is no maximum length; however, books that go more than 100,000 will have to be exceptional to be considered. We will accept series, but ask that the series be completed or be near completed before submission." Submit cover letter along with full ms. See website for formatting instructions and brands. Submit via link on website.

Ⓐ FIRST SECOND

Macmillan Children's Publishing Group, 175 5th Ave., New York NY 10010. **E-mail:** mail@firstsecondbooks. com. **Website:** www.firstsecondbooks.com. First Second is a publisher of graphic novels and an imprint of Macmillan Children's Publishing Group. First Second does not accept unsolicited submissions.

HOW TO CONTACT Responds in about 6 weeks.

TERMS Catalog online.

FLASHLIGHT PRESS

527 Empire Blvd., Brooklyn NY 11225. (718)288-8300. **Fax:** (718)972-6307. **Website:** www.flashlightpress. com. **Contact:** Shari Dash Greenspan, editor. Publishes hardcover and trade paperback original children's picture books for 4-8 year olds. **Publishes 2-3 titles/year. 50% of books from first-time authors. 50% from unagented writers.**

FICTION Average word length: 1,000 words. Picture books: contemporary, humor, multicultural.

HOW TO CONTACT "Query by e-mail only, after carefully reading our submission guidelines online. No e-mail attachments. Do not send anything by snail mail." 2000 queries received/year "Only accepts e-mail queries according to submission guidelines." Responds in 3 months to requested mss. Publishes ms up to 3 years after acceptance.

TERMS Pays 8-10% royalty on wholesale price. Pays advance. Book catalog available online. Guidelines online.

Ⓐ FLUX

Llewellyn Worldwide, Ltd., 2143 Wooddale Dr., Woodbury MN 55125. (651)312-8613. **Fax:** (651)291-1908. **Website:** www.fluxnow.com. "Flux seeks to publish authors who see young adult as a point of view, not a reading level. We look for books that try to capture a slice of teenage experience, whether in real or imagined worlds." **Publishes 21 titles/year. 50% of books from first-time authors.**

FICTION Young Adults: adventure, contemporary, fantasy, history, humor, problem novels, religion, science fiction, sports, suspense. Average word length: 50,000.

HOW TO CONTACT *Accepts agented submissions only.*

TERMS Pays royalties of 10-15% based on wholesale price. Book catalog and guidelines online.

TIPS "Read contemporary teen books. Be aware of what else is out there. If you don't read teen books, you probably shouldn't write them. Know your audience. Write incredibly well. Do not condescend."

FORWARD MOVEMENT

412 Sycamore St., Cincinnati OH 45202. (513)721-6659; (800)543-1813. **Fax:** (513)721-0729. **E-mail:** editorial@forwardmovement.org. **Website:** www.

forwardmovement.org. **Contact:** Richelle Thompson, managing editor. "Forward Movement was established to help reinvigorate the life of the church. Many titles focus on the life of prayer, where our relationship with God is centered, death, marriage, baptism, recovery, joy, the Episcopal Church and more. Currently emphasizing prayer/spirituality." **Publishes 30 titles/year.**

NONFICTION "We are an agency of the Episcopal Church. There is a special need for tracts of under 8 pages. (A page usually runs about 200 words.) On rare occasions, we publish a full-length book."

HOW TO CONTACT Query with SASE or by e-mail with complete ms attached. Responds in 1 month.

TERMS Book catalog free. Guidelines online.

TIPS "Audience is primarily Episcopalians and other Christians."

WALTER FOSTER, JR.

Quarto Publishing, 6 Orchard, Suite 100, Lake Forest CA 92630. (949)380-7510. **Fax:** (949)380-7575. **E-mail:** pauline.molinari@quartous.com. **Website:** www.quartoknows.com/Walter-Foster-Jr. **Contact:** Pauline Molinari, Editorial Director. Building on the success of Walter Foster Publishing, a leader in the art instruction field for more than 90 years, Walter Foster Jr. develops high-quality, affordable books that spark excitement and curiosity. As a creator of content for children and families, Walter Foster Jr. strives to bring out that childlike wonderment in all of us and inspire lifelong interests. Walter Foster Jr. publishes fun and imaginative books and kits for children of all ages. Encouraging learning and exploring, Walter Foster Jr. titles cover a wide range of subjects, including art, transportation, history, craft, gardening, and more.

TERMS "Walter Foster Publishing is always on the lookout for authors and artists with creative ideas that enhance and broaden our publishing list. Our topics span everything from traditional oil painting to newer art techniques like tangling and mixed media. See our submissions guidelines online if you are interested in submitting your ideas for consideration. - Asks authors to sign a submission agreement."

FREE SPIRIT PUBLISHING, INC.

6325 Sandburg Rd., Suite 100, Golden Valley MN 55427-3674. (612)338-2068. **Fax:** (612)337-5050. **E-mail:** acquisitions@freespirit.com. **Website:** www.freespirit.com. "We believe passionately in empowering kids to learn to think for themselves and make their own good choices." Free Spirit does not accept general fiction, poetry, or storybook submissions. Publishes trade paperback originals and reprints. **Publishes 25-30 titles/year.**

FICTION "Please review catalog and author guidelines (both available online) for details before submitting proposal. If you'd like material returned, enclose a SASE with sufficient postage."

NONFICTION "Many of our authors are educators, mental health professionals, and youth workers involved in helping kids and teens." No general fiction or picture storybooks, poetry, single biographies or autobiographies, books with mythical or animal characters, or books with religious or New Age content. We are not looking for academic or religious materials, or books that analyze problems with the nation's school systems.

HOW TO CONTACT Accepts queries only—not submissions—by e-mail. Query with cover letter stating qualifications, intent, and intended audience and market analysis (comprehensive list of similar titles and detailed explanation of how your book stands out from the field), along with your promotional plan, outline, 2 sample chapters (note: for early childhood submissions, the entire text is required for evaluation), résumé, SASE. Do not send original copies of work. Responds to proposals in 2-6 months.

ILLUSTRATION Works with 5 illustrators/year. Submit samples to creative director for consideration. If appropriate, samples will be kept on file and artist will be contacted if a suitable project comes up. Enclose SASE if you'd like materials returned.

PHOTOGRAPHY Uses stock photos. Does not accept photography submissions.

TERMS Pays advance. Book catalog and ms guidelines online.

TIPS "Our books are issue-oriented, jargon-free, and solution-focused. Our audience is children, teens, teachers, parents, and youth counselors. We are especially concerned with kids' social and emotional well-being and look for books with ready-to-use strategies for coping with today's issues at home or in school—written in everyday language. We are not looking for academic or religious materials, or books that analyze problems with the nation's school systems. Instead, we want books that offer practical, positive advice so kids can help themselves, and parents and teachers can help kids succeed."

○ FULCRUM PUBLISHING

4690 Table Mountain Dr., Suite 100, Golden CO 80403. **E-mail:** acquisitions@fulcrumbooks.com. **Website:** www.fulcrum-books.com. **Contact:** T. Baker, acquisitions editor.

NONFICTION Looking for nonfiction-based graphic novels and comics, US history and culture, Native American history or culture studies, conservation-oriented materials. "We do not accept memoir or fiction mss."

HOW TO CONTACT "Your submission must include: a proposal of your work, including a brief synopsis, 2-3 sample chapters, brief biography of yourself, description of your audience, your assessment of the market for the book, list of competing titles, and what you can do to help market your book. We are a green company and therefore only accept e-mailed submissions. Paper queries submitted via US Mail or any other means (including fax, FedEx/UPS, and even door-to-door delivery) will not be reviewed or returned. Please help us support the preservation of the environment by e-mailing your query to acquisitions@fulcrumbooks.com."

PHOTOGRAPHY Works on assignment only.

TERMS Pays authors royalty based on wholesale price. Offers advances. Catalog for SASE. Guidelines online.

TIPS "Research our line first. We look for books that appeal to the school market and trade. "

GIANT SQUID BOOKS

E-mail: editors@giantsquidbooks.com. **Website:** giantsquidbooks.com. "Our mission is to publish, support, and promote debut authors—and help them navigate the world of online publishing."

FICTION Giant Squid Books is currently closed to submissions. "See website or follow us on Twitter @giantsquidbooks to be notified when we reopen submissions." Accepts young adult novels in any genre.

HOW TO CONTACT Query with the first 3 chapters or 50 pages of book.

TERMS Guidelines online.

TIPS "We read every submission and try to respond within two weeks but due to a high volume of submissions sometimes get behind! If it's been more than 2 weeks since you queried us, please feel free to send a follow-up e-mail."

GIBBS SMITH

P.O. Box 667, Layton UT 84041. (801)544-9800. **Fax:** (801)544-8853. **E-mail:** debbie.uribe@gibbs-smith.com. **Website:** www.gibbs-smith.com. **Publishes 3 titles/year. 50% of books from first-time authors. 50% from unagented writers.**

NONFICTION Middle readers: activity, arts/crafts, cooking, how-to, nature/environment, science. Average word length: picture books—under 1,000 words; activity books—under 15,000 words.

HOW TO CONTACT Submit an outline and writing samples for activity books; query for other types of books. Responds in 2 months. Publishes ms 1-2 years after acceptance.

ILLUSTRATION Works with 2 illustrators/year. Reviews ms/illustration packages from artists. Query. Submit ms with 3-5 pieces of final art. Illustrations only: Query with samples; provide résumé, promo sheet, slides (duplicate slides, not originals). Responds only if interested. Samples returned with SASE; samples filed.

TERMS Pays illustrators by the project or royalty of 2% based on retail price. Sends galleys to authors; color proofs to illustrators. Original artwork returned at job's completion. Pays authors royalty of 2% based on retail price or work purchased outright ($500 minimum). Offers advances (average amount: $2,000). Book catalog available for 9×12 SAE and $2.30 postage. Ms guidelines available by e-mail.

TIPS "We target ages 5-11. We do not publish young adult novels or chapter books."

THE GLENCANNON PRESS

P.O. Box 1428, El Cerrito CA 94530. (510)528-4216. **E-mail:** merships@yahoo.com. **Website:** www.glencannon.com. **Contact:** Bill Harris (maritime, maritime children's). "We publish quality books about ships and the sea." Average print order: 1,000. Member PMA, BAIPA. Distributes titles through Baker & Taylor. Promotes titles through direct mail, magazine advertising and word of mouth. Accepts unsolicited mss. Often comments on rejected mss. Publishes hardcover and paperback originals and hardcover reprints. **Publishes 4-5 titles/year. 25% of books from first-time authors. 100% from unagented writers.**

HOW TO CONTACT Submit complete ms. Include brief bio, list of publishing credits. Send SASE for return of ms or send a disposable ms and SASE for reply only. Responds in 1 month to queries; 2 months to mss. Publishes ms 6-24 months after acceptance.

TERMS Pays 10-20% royalty.

TIPS "Write a good story in a compelling style."

Ⓐ DAVID R. GODINE, PUBLISHER

15 Court Square, Suite 320, Boston MA 02108. (617)451-9600. **Fax:** (617)350-0250. **E-mail:** info@godine.com. **Website:** www.godine.com. "We publish books that matter for people who care." This publisher is no longer considering unsolicited mss of any type. Only interested in agented material.

HOW TO CONTACT Only interested in agented material.

ILLUSTRATION Only interested in agented material. Works with 1-3 illustrators/year. "Please do not send original artwork unless solicited. Almost all of the children's books we accept for publication come to us with the author and illustrator already paired up. Therefore, we rarely use freelance illustrators."

Ⓐ☾ GOLDEN BOOKS FOR YOUNG READERS GROUP

1745 Broadway, New York NY 10019. **Website:** www.penguinrandomhouse.com. "Random House Books aims to create books that nurture the hearts and minds of children, providing and promoting quality books and a rich variety of media that entertain and educate readers from 6 months to 12 years." *Random House-Golden Books does not accept unsolicited mss, only agented material.* They reserve the right not to return unsolicited material. **2% of books from first-time authors.**

TERMS Pays authors in royalties; sometimes buys mss outright. Book catalog free on request.

GOOSEBOTTOM BOOKS

543 Trinidad Ln., Foster City CA 94404. **Fax:** (888)407-5286. **E-mail:** submissions@goosebottombooks.com. **Website:** goosebottombooks.com. **Contact:** Shirin Bridges. **50% of books from first-time authors. 100% from unagented writers.**

FICTION Gosling Press is a new partnership publishing imprint for children's, middle-grade, and young adult fiction. Please query with first ten pages. Any fiction for adults. Gosling Press focuses on picture book to young adult.

HOW TO CONTACT Query with first 10 pages. 1,000 submissions received/year. Responds in 1 month. Publishes ms 18 months after acceptance.

ILLUSTRATION Considers samples.

TERMS Goosebottom Books: Pays advance plus royalties; Gosling Press: Pays royalties only. Catalog online. Guidelines available.

GREENHAVEN PRESS

27500 Drake Rd., Farmington Hills MI 48331. (800)877-4523. **Website:** www.gale.com/greenhaven. Publishes 220 young adult academic reference titles/year. 50% of books by first-time authors. Greenhaven continues to print quality nonfiction anthologies for libraries and classrooms. "Our well-known Opposing Viewpoints series is highly respected by students and librarians in need of material on controversial social issues." Greenhaven accepts no unsolicited mss. Send query, résumé, and list of published works by e-mail. Work purchased outright from authors; write-for-hire, flat fee.

NONFICTION Young adults (high school): controversial issues, social issues, history, literature, science, environment, health.

Ⓐ GREENWILLOW BOOKS

HarperCollins Publishers, 10 E. 53rd St., New York NY 10022. (212)207-7000. **Website:** www.greenwillowblog.com. *Does not accept unsolicited mss.* "Unsolicited mail will not be opened and will not be returned." Publishes hardcover originals, paperbacks, e-books, and reprints. **Publishes 40-50 titles/year.**

HOW TO CONTACT *Agented submissions only.* Publishes ms 2 years after acceptance.

TERMS Pays 10% royalty on wholesale price for first-time authors. Offers variable advance.

Ⓐ GROSSET & DUNLAP PUBLISHERS

Penguin Random House, 345 Hudson St., New York NY 10014. **Website:** www.penguin.com. **Contact:** Francesco Sedita, president/publisher. Grosset & Dunlap publishes children's books that show children that reading is fun, with books that speak to their interests, and that are affordable so that children can build a home library of their own. Focus on licensed properties, series, and readers. "Grosset & Dunlap publishes high-interest, affordable books for children ages 0-10 years. We focus on original series, licensed properties, readers, and novelty books." Publishes hardcover (few) and mass market paperback originals. **Publishes 140 titles/year.**

HOW TO CONTACT *Agented submissions only.*

TERMS Pays royalty. Pays advance.

GRYPHON HOUSE, INC.

P.O. Box 10, 6848 Leon's Way, Lewisville NC 27023. (800)638-0928. **E-mail:** info@ghbooks.com. **Website:** www.gryphonhouse.com. "At Gryphon House, our goal is to publish books that help teachers and parents enrich the lives of children from birth through age 8. We strive to make our books useful for teachers at all levels of experience, as well as for parents, caregivers, and anyone interested in working with children." Query. Submit outline/synopsis and 2 sample chapters. Responds to queries/mss in 6 months. Publishes a book 18 months after acceptance. Will consider simultaneous submissions, e-mail submissions. Book catalog and ms guidelines available via website or with SASE. Publishes trade paperback originals. **Publishes 12-15 titles/year.**

NONFICTION Currently emphasizing social-emotional intelligence and classroom management; de-emphasizing literacy after-school activities.

HOW TO CONTACT "We prefer to receive a letter of inquiry and/or a proposal, rather than the entire ms. Please include: the proposed title, the purpose of the book, table of contents, introductory material, 20-40 sample pages of the actual book. In addition, please describe the book, including the intended audience, why teachers will want to buy it, how it is different from other similar books already published, and what qualifications you possess that make you the appropriate person to write the book. If you have a writing sample that demonstrates that you write clear, compelling prose, please include it with your letter." Responds in 3-6 months to queries.

ILLUSTRATION Works with 4-5 illustrators/year. Uses b&w realistic artwork only. Query with samples, promo sheet. Responds in 2 months. Samples returned with SASE; samples filed. Pays illustrators by the project.

PHOTOGRAPHY Pays photographers by the project or per photo. Sends edited ms copy to authors. Original artwork returned at job's completion.

TERMS Pays royalty on wholesale price. Guidelines available online.

TIPS "We are looking for books of creative, participatory learning experiences that have a common conceptual theme to tie them together. The books should be on subjects that parents or teachers want to do on a daily basis."

HACHAI PUBLISHING

527 Empire Blvd., Brooklyn NY 11225. (718)633-0100. **Fax:** (718)633-0103. **Website:** www.hachai.com. **Contact:** Devorah Leah Rosenfeld, editor. Hachai is dedicated to producing high quality Jewish children's literature, ages 2-10. Story should promote universal values such as sharing, kindness, etc. Publishes hardcover originals. **Publishes 5 titles/year. 75% of books from first-time authors.**

◯ "All books have spiritual/religious themes, specifically traditional Jewish content. We're seeking books about morals and values; the Jewish experience in current and Biblical times; and Jewish observance, Sabbath, and holidays."

FICTION Picture books and young readers: contemporary, historical fiction, religion. Middle readers: adventure, contemporary, problem novels, religion. Does not want to see fantasy, animal stories, romance, problem novels depicting drug use or violence.

HOW TO CONTACT Submit complete ms. Responds in 2 months to mss.

ILLUSTRATION Works with 4 illustrators/year. Uses primary color artwork, some b&w illustration. Reviews ms/illustration packages from authors. Submit ms with 1 piece of final art. Illustrations only: Query with samples; arrange personal portfolio review. Responds in 6 weeks. Samples returned with SASE; samples filed.

TERMS Work purchased outright from authors for $800-1,000. Guidelines online.

TIPS "We are looking for books that convey the traditional Jewish experience in modern times or long ago; traditional Jewish observance such as Sabbath and holidays and mitzvos such as mezuzah, blessings etc.; positive character traits (middos) such as honesty, charity, respect, sharing, etc. We are also interested in historical fiction for young readers (7-10) written with a traditional Jewish perspective and highlighting the relevance of Torah in making important choices. Please, no animal stories, romance, violence, preachy sermonizing. Write a story that incorporates a moral, not a preachy morality tale. Originality is the key. We feel Hachai publications will appeal to a wider readership as parents become more interested in positive values for their children."

Ⓐ HARLEQUIN TEEN

Harlequin, 195 Broadway, 24th Floor, New York NY 10007. **Website:** www.harlequin.com. **Contact:** Natashya Wilson, executive editor. Harlequin Teen is a single-title program dedicated to building authors and publishing unique, memorable young-adult fiction.

FICTION Harlequin Teen looks for fresh, authentic fiction featuring extraordinary characters and extraordinary stories set in contemporary, paranormal, fantasy, science-fiction, and historical worlds. Wants commercial, high-concept stories that capture the teen experience and will speak to readers with power and authenticity. All subgenres are welcome, so long as the book delivers a relevant reading experience that will resonate long after the book's covers are closed. Expects that most stories will include a compelling romantic element.

HOW TO CONTACT *Agented submissions only.*

HARMONY INK PRESS

5032 Capital Circle SW, Suite 2 PMB 279, Tallahassee FL 32305. (850)632-4648. **Fax:** (888)308-3739. **E-mail:** submissions@harmonyinkpress.com. **Website:** harmonyinkpress.com. Harmony Ink is accepting mss for teen and new adult fiction featuring at least 1 strong LGBTQ+ main character who shows significant personal growth through the course of the story.

FICTION "We are looking for stories in all subgenres, featuring primary characters across the whole LGBTQ+ spectrum between the ages of 14-21 that explore all the facets of young adult, teen, and new adult life. Sexual content should be appropriate for the characters and the story."

HOW TO CONTACT Submit complete ms.

TERMS Pays royalty. Pays $500-1,000 advance.

Ⓐ HARPERCOLLINS CHILDREN'S BOOKS/ HARPERCOLLINS PUBLISHERS

195 Broadway, New York NY 10007. (212)207-7000. **Website:** www.harpercollins.com. HarperCollins, one of the largest English language publishers in the world, is a broad-based publisher with strengths in academic, business and professional, children's, educational, general interest, and religious and spiritual books, as well as multimedia titles. Publishes hardcover and paperback originals and paperback reprints. **Publishes 500 titles/year.**

FICTION "We look for a strong story line and exceptional literary talent."

NONFICTION *No unsolicited mss or queries.*

HOW TO CONTACT Agented submissions only. *All unsolicited mss returned.* Responds in 1 month if interested. Does not accept any unsolicited texts.

TERMS Negotiates payment upon acceptance. Catalog online.

TIPS "We do not accept any unsolicited material."

Ⓐ HARPERTEEN

195 Broadway, New York NY 10007. (212)207-7000. **Website:** www.harpercollins.com. HarperTeen is a teen imprint that publishes hardcovers, paperback reprints and paperback originals. **Publishes 100 titles/year.**

○ *HarperCollins Children's Books is not accepting unsolicited and/or unagented mss or queries. Unfortunately the volume of these submissions is so large that they cannot receive the attention they deserve. Such submissions will not be reviewed or returned.*

HENDRICK-LONG PUBLISHING CO., INC.

10635 Tower Oaks, Suite D, Houston TX 77070. (832)912-READ. **Fax:** (832)912-7353. **E-mail:** hendrick-long@worldnet.att.net. **Website:** hendricklongpublishing.com. **Contact:** Vilma Long. "Hendrick-Long publishes historical fiction and nonfiction about Texas and the Southwest for children and young adults." Publishes hardcover and trade paperback originals and hardcover reprints. **Publishes 4 titles/year. 90% from unagented writers.**

NONFICTION Subject must be Texas related; other subjects cannot be considered. "We are particularly interested in material from educators that can be used in the classroom as workbooks, math, science, history with a Texas theme or twist."

HOW TO CONTACT Query with SASE. Submit outline, clips, 2 sample chapters. Responds in 3 months to queries. Publishes ms 18 months after acceptance.

TERMS No simultaneous submissions. Include SASE. Pays royalty on selling price. Pays advance. Book catalog available. Guidelines online.

HEYDAY BOOKS

c/o Acquisitions Editor, Box 9145, Berkeley CA 94709. **Fax:** (510)549-1889. **E-mail:** heyday@heydaybooks. com. **Website:** www.heydaybooks.com. **Contact:** Gayle Wattawa, acquisitions and editorial director. "Heyday Books publishes nonfiction books and literary anthologies with a strong California focus. We publish books about Native Americans, natural history, history, literature, and recreation, with a strong California focus." Publishes hardcover originals, trade paperback originals and reprints. **Publishes 12-15 titles/year. 50% of books from first-time authors. 90% from unagented writers.**

FICTION Publishes picture books, beginning readers, and young adult literature.

NONFICTION Books about California only.

HOW TO CONTACT Submit complete ms for picture books; proposal with sample chapters for longer works. Include a chapter by chapter summary. Mark attention: Children's Submission. Reviews ms/illustration packages; but may consider art and text separately. Tries to respond to query within 12 weeks. Query with outline and synopsis. "Query or proposal by traditional post. Include a cover letter introducing yourself and your qualifications, a brief description of your project, a table of contents and list of illustrations, notes on the market you are trying to reach and why your book will appeal to them, a sample chapter, and a SASE if you would like us to return these materials to you." Responds in 3 months. Publishes book 18 months after acceptance.

TERMS Pays 8% royalty on net price. Book catalog online. Guidelines online.

HOLIDAY HOUSE, INC.

425 Madison Ave., New York NY 10017. (212)688-0085. **Fax:** (212)421-6134. **E-mail:** info@holidayhouse. com. **Website:** holidayhouse.com. "Holiday House publishes children's and young adult books for the school and library markets. We have a commitment to publishing first-time authors and illustrators. We specialize in quality hardcovers from picture books to young adult, both fiction and nonfiction, primarily for the school and library market." Publishes hardcover originals and paperback reprints. **Publishes 50 titles/year. 5% of books from first-time authors. 50% from unagented writers.**

FICTION Children's books only.

HOW TO CONTACT Query with SASE. No phone calls, please. Please send the entire ms, whether submitting a picture book or novel. "All submissions should be directed to the Editorial Department, Holiday House. We do not accept certified or registered mail. There is no need to include a SASE. We do not consider submissions by e-mail or fax. Please note that you do not have to supply illustrations. However, if you have illustrations you would like to include with your submission, you may send detailed sketches or photocopies of the original art. Do not send original art." Responds in 4 months. Publishes 1-2 years after acceptance.

ILLUSTRATION Accepting art samples, not returned.

TERMS Pays royalty on list price, range varies. Guidelines for #10 SASE.

TIPS "We need mss with strong stories and writing."

HOUGHTON MIFFLIN HARCOURT BOOKS FOR CHILDREN

Imprint of Houghton Mifflin Trade & Reference Division, 222 Berkeley St., Boston MA 02116. (617)351-5000. **Fax:** (617)351-1111. **Website:** www.houghton-mifflinbooks.com. Houghton Mifflin Harcourt gives shape to ideas that educate, inform, and above all, delight. *Does not respond to or return mss unless interested.* Publishes hardcover originals and trade paperback originals and reprints. **Publishes 100 titles/year. 10% of books from first-time authors. 60% from unagented writers.**

NONFICTION Interested in innovative books and subjects about which the author is passionate.

HOW TO CONTACT Submit complete ms. Query with SASE. Submit sample chapters, synopsis. 5,000 queries received/year. 14,000 mss received/year. Responds in 4-6 months to queries. Publishes ms 2 years after acceptance.

TERMS Pays 5-10% royalty on retail price. Pays variable advance. Guidelines online.

ILLUSIO & BAQER

1827 W. Shannon Ave., Spokane WA 99205. **E-mail:** submissions@zharmae.com. **Website:** illusiobaqer. com. Illusio & Baqer publishes high quality middle-grade, young adult, and new adult fiction of all genres. "We are a young adult, new adult, and middle-grade imprint of The Zharmae Publishing Press."

HOW TO CONTACT Query with synopsis and 3-5 sample chapters.

IMMEDIUM

P.O. Box 31846, San Francisco CA 94131. (415)452-8546. **Fax:** (360)937-6272. **Website:** www.immedium.com. "Immedium focuses on publishing eye-catching children's picture books, Asian American topics, and contemporary arts, popular culture, and multicultural issues." Publishes hardcover and trade paperback originals. **Publishes 4 titles/year. 50% of books from first-time authors. 90% from unagented writers.**

HOW TO CONTACT Submit complete ms. Submit complete ms. 50 queries received/year. 25 mss received/year. Responds in 1-3 months. Publishes book 2 years after acceptance.

TERMS Pays 5% royalty on wholesale price. Pays on publication. Catalog online. Guidelines online.

TIPS "Our audience is children and parents. Please visit our site."

IMMORTAL INK PUBLISHING

E-mail: immortalinkpublishing@gmail.com. **Website:** www.immortalinkpublishing.com. Immortal Ink Publishing is open to most genres, but specifically wants literary fiction, women's fiction, crime/mystery/thriller, young adult, and dark and paranormal fiction that is original, character-based, and literary in flavor. Immortal Ink Publishing is currently closed to submissions.

HOW TO CONTACT Submit query with first 10 pages via e-mail.

TIPS "Due to time constraints, we will not be giving reasons for our rejections (as you really shouldn't be making changes just because of something we personally didn't like anyway), but we will get back to you with either a 'no thanks' or a request for your full ms."

IMPACT PUBLISHERS, INC.

5674 Shattuck Ave., Oakland CA 94609. **E-mail:** proposals@newharbinger.com. **Website:** www.newharbinger.com/imprint/impact-publishers. "Our purpose is to make the best human services expertise available to the widest possible audience. We publish only popular psychology and self-help materials written in everyday language by professionals with advanced degrees and significant experience in the human services." **Publishes 3-5 titles/year. 20% of books from first-time authors.**

NONFICTION Young readers, middle readers, young adults: self-help.

HOW TO CONTACT Query or submit complete ms, cover letter, résumé. Responds in 3 months.

ILLUSTRATION Works with 1 illustrator/year. Not accepting freelance illustrator queries.

TERMS Pays authors royalty of 10-12%. Offers advances. Book catalog for #10 SASE with 2 first-class stamps. Guidelines for SASE.

TIPS "Please do not submit fiction, poetry or narratives."

⊕ ISLANDPORT

P.O. Box 10, Yarmouth ME 04096. **Website:** www.islandportpress.com/submission-guidelines. **Contact:** Acquisitions editor, children's/young adult.

FICTION "We will consider picture books, story books, middle-grade chapter books, and young adult titles. We are not currently publishing poetry or early readers. As with our adult titles, all our children's books have New England sensibilities, and we do prefer to work with authors and illustrators who are connected to New England or the Northeast United States."

HOW TO CONTACT "We prefer paper copies of mss and written submissions (please do not submit children's books by e-mail). If you are submitting a children's book that you have illustrated, please include copies of your illustrations, but keep in mind that if we accept your ms, we still may decide to choose our own illustrator." Please include the following with your proposal: cover letter with the date and contact information, author bio, a copy of your ms, relevant marketing information, and publicity and social media contracts. Include SASE to have materials returned. Publisher cannot guarantee return of ms. Include e-mail address with materials as publisher will acknowledge receipt via e-mail. Note in query letter if your submission is a simultaneous submission. Please do not submit your only copy!"

ILLUSTRATION "We are committed to supporting artists who live and/or work in New England. We are always interested in seeing work from new illustrators. If you would like to send us samples of your portfolio, please send us copies (never send originals) to: Melissa Kim, senior editor, Children's Books, Islandport Press, P.O. Box 10, Yarmouth, Maine 04096. Please include a cover letter, artist bio, and full contact information including your e-mail address. You are also welcome to send a CD or send a link to an online portfolio."

JEWISH LIGHTS PUBLISHING

LongHill Partners, Inc., Sunset Farm Offices, Rt. 4, P.O. Box 237, Woodstock VT 05091. (802)457-4000. **Fax:** (802)457-4004. **E-mail:** editorial@jewishlights. com; sales@jewishlights.com. **Website:** www.jewishlights.com. **Contact:** Acquisitions Editor. "Jewish Lights publishes books for people of all faiths and all backgrounds who yearn for books that attract, engage, educate, and spiritually inspire. Our authors are at the forefront of spiritual thought and deal with the quest for the self and for meaning in life by drawing on the Jewish wisdom tradition. Our books cover topics including history, spirituality, life cycle, children, self-help, recovery, theology, and philosophy. We do not publish autobiography, biography, fiction, haggadot, poetry ,or cookbooks. At this point we plan to do only two books for children annually, and one will be for younger children (ages 4-10)." Publishes hardcover and trade paperback originals, trade paperback reprints. **Publishes 30 titles/year. 50% of books from first-time authors. 75% from unagented writers.**

FICTION Picture books, young readers, middle readers: spirituality. "We are not interested in anything other than spirituality."

NONFICTION Picture book, young readers, middle readers: activity books, spirituality. "We do *not* publish haggadot, biography, poetry, memoirs, or cookbooks."

HOW TO CONTACT Query with outline/synopsis and 2 sample chapters; submit complete ms for picture books. Query. Responds in 6 months to queries. Publishes ms 1 year after acceptance.

TERMS Pays authors royalty of 10% of revenue received; 15% royalty for subsequent printings. Book catalog and guidelines online.

TIPS "We publish books for all faiths and backgrounds that also reflect the Jewish wisdom tradition. Explain in your cover letter why you're submitting your project to us in particular. Make sure you know what we publish."

JOLLY FISH PRESS

P.O. Box 1773, Provo UT 84603. **E-mail:** submit@jollyfishpress.com. **Website:** jollyfishpress.com. **Publishes 17 titles/year. 70% of books from first-time authors. 70% from unagented writers.**

FICTION "We accept literary fiction, fantasy, science fiction, mystery, suspense, horror, thriller, children's literature, young adult, trade."

NONFICTION Nonfiction mss do not have to be completed, but the status of the ms should be noted.

HOW TO CONTACT Submit query with synopsis and first 3 chapters for fiction. Submit query and proposal for nonfiction. Publishes ms 2 years after acceptance.

TERMS Does not pay advance. Guidelines online.

JOURNEYFORTH

Imprint of BJU Press, 1700 Wade Hampton Blvd., Greenville SC 29614. (864)770-1317, 800-845-5731. **E-mail:** journeyforth@bjupress.com. **Website:** www.journeyforth.com. "Small independent publisher of trustworthy novels and biographies for readers in primary school through high school from a conservative Christian perspective as well as Christian living books and Bible studies for teens and adults." Publishes paperback originals. **Publishes 12 titles/year. 4% of books from first-time authors. 4% from unagented writers.**

FICTION "Our fiction is all based on a Christian worldview." Does not want short stories.

NONFICTION Christian living, Bible studies, church and ministry, church history. "We produce books for the adult Christian market that are from a conservative Christian worldview."

HOW TO CONTACT Submit 5 sample chapters, synopsis, market analysis of competing works. 400+ Responds in 1 month to queries; 3 months to mss. Publishes book 12-18 months after acceptance.

ILLUSTRATION Works with 2-4 illustrators/year. Query with samples. Send promo sheet; will review website portfolio if applicable. Responds only if interested. Samples returned with SASE; samples filed.

TERMS Pays authors royalty based on wholesale price. Pays illustrators by the project. Originals returned to artist at job's completion. Pays royalty. Book catalog available free or online. Guidelines online.

TIPS "Study the publisher's guidelines. No picture books. Fiction for the youth market only."

JUST US BOOKS, INC.

P.O. Box 5306, East Orange NJ 07019. (973)672-7701. **Fax:** (973)677-7570. **Website:** justusbooks. com. "Just Us Books is the nation's premier independent publisher of Black-interest books for young people. Our books focus primarily on the culture, history, and contemporary experiences of African Americans."

FICTION Just Us Books is currently accepting queries for chapter books and middle reader titles only. "We are not considering any other works at this time."

HOW TO CONTACT Query with synopsis and 3-5 sample pages.

TERMS Guidelines online.

TIPS "We are looking for realistic, contemporary characters; stories and interesting plots that introduce both conflict and resolution. We will consider various themes and story-lines, but before an author submits a query, we urge them to become familiar with our books."

KAEDEN BOOKS

P.O. Box 16190, Rocky River OH 44116. **Website:** www.kaeden.com. "Children's book publisher for education K-3 market: reading stories, fiction/nonfiction, chapter books, science, and social studies materials." Publishes paperback originals. **Publishes 12-20 titles/year. 30% of books from first-time authors. 95% from unagented writers.**

FICTION "We are looking for stories with humor, surprise endings, and interesting characters that will appeal to children in kindergarten through third grade." No sentence fragments. Please do not submit: queries, ms summaries, résumés, mss that stereotype or demean individuals or groups, or mss that present violence as acceptable behavior.

NONFICTION Mss should have interesting topics and information presented in language comprehensible to young students. Content should be supported with details and accurate facts.

HOW TO CONTACT Submit complete ms. "Can be as minimal as 25 words for the earliest reader or as much as 2,000 words for the fluent reader. Beginning chapter books are welcome. Our readers are in kindergarten to third grade, so vocabulary and sentence structure must be appropriate for young readers. Make sure that all language used in the story is of an appropriate level for the students to read independently. Sentences should be complete and grammatically correct." Responds only if interested. Publishes ms 6-9 months after acceptance.

ILLUSTRATION Work with 8-10 illustrators per year. Looking for samples that are appropriate for children's literature. Submit color samples no larger than 8.5x11. Samples kept on file. Responds only if interested. "No originals, disks or slides please." Samples not returned.

TERMS Works purchased outright from authors. Pays royalties to previous authors. Book catalog and guidelines online.

TIPS "Our audience ranges from kindergarten-third grade school children. We are an educational publisher. We are particularly interested in humorous stories with surprise endings and beginning chapter books."

Ⓐ KANE/MILLER BOOK PUBLISHERS

4901 Morena Blvd., Suite 213, San Diego CA 92117. (858)456-0540. **Fax:** (858)456-9641. **Website:** www. kanemiller.com. **Contact:** Editorial Department. "Kane/Miller Book Publishers is a division of EDC Publishing, specializing in award-winning children's books from around the world. Our books bring the children of the world closer to each other, sharing stories and ideas, while exploring cultural differences and similarities. Although we continue to look for books from other countries, we are now actively seeking works that convey cultures and communities within the US. We are committed to expanding our picture book list and are interested in great stories with engaging characters, especially those with particularly American subjects. When writing about the experiences of a particular community, we will express a preference for stories written from a firsthand experience." Submission guidelines on site.

FICTION Picture Books: concept, contemporary, health, humor, multicultural. Young Readers: contemporary, multicultural, suspense. Middle Readers: contemporary, humor, multicultural, suspense. "At this time, we are not considering holiday stories (in any age range) or self-published works."

HOW TO CONTACT If interested, responds in 90 days to queries.

TIPS "We like to think that a child reading a Kane/Miller book will see parallels between his own life and what might be the unfamiliar setting and characters of the story. And that by seeing how a character who is somehow or in some way dissimilar—an outsider—finds a way to fit comfortably into a culture or community or situation while maintaining a healthy sense of self and self-dignity, she might be empowered to do the same."

KAR-BEN PUBLISHING

Lerner Publishing Group, 241 First Ave. N, Minneapolis MN 55401. (612)215-6229. **E-mail:** editorial@karben.com. **Website:** www.karben.com. Kar-Ben publishes exclusively children's books on Jewish themes. Publishes hardcover, trade paperback and electronic originals. **Publishes 20 titles/year. 20% of books from first-time authors. 70% from unagented writers.**

FICTION "We seek picture book mss 800-1,000 words on Jewish-themed topics for children." Picture books: Adventure, concept, folktales, history, humor, multicultural, religion, special needs; must be on a Jewish theme. Average word length: picture books–1,000. Recently published titles: *The Count's Hanukkah Countdown, Sammy Spider's First Book of Jewish Holidays, The Cats of Ben Yehuda Street.*

NONFICTION "In addition to traditional Jewish-themed stories about Jewish holidays, history, folktales, and other subjects, we especially seek stories that reflect the rich diversity of the contemporary Jewish community." Picture books, young readers: activity books, arts/crafts, biography, careers, concept, cooking, history, how-to, multicultural, religion, social issues, special needs; must be of Jewish interest. No textbooks, games, or educational materials.

HOW TO CONTACT Submit full ms. Picture books only. Submit completed ms. 800 mss received/year. Responds in 6 weeks. Most mss published within 2 years.

TERMS Pays 5% royalty on net sale. Pays $500-2,500 advance. Book catalog online; free upon request. Guidelines online.

TIPS "Authors: Do a literature search to make sure similar title doesn't already exist. Illustrators: Look at our online catalog for a sense of what we like—bright colors and lively composition."

Ⓐ KATHERINE TEGEN BOOKS

HarperCollins, 10 E. 53rd St., New York NY 10022. **Website:** www.harpercollins.com. **Contact:** Katherine Tegen, vice-president and publisher. Katherine Tegen Books publishes high-quality, commercial literature for children of all ages, including teens. Talented authors and illustrators who offer powerful narratives that are thought-provoking, well-written, and entertaining are the core of the Katherine Tegen

Books imprint. *Katherine Tegen Books accepts agented work only.*

KREGEL PUBLICATIONS

2450 Oak Industrial Dr. NE, Grand Rapids MI 49505. (616)451-4775. **Fax:** (616)451-9330. **E-mail:** kregelbooks@kregel.com. **Website:** www.kregelpublications.com. **Contact:** Dennis R. Hillman, publisher. "Our mission as an evangelical Christian publisher is to provide—with integrity and excellence—trusted, Biblically based resources that challenge and encourage individuals in their Christian lives. Works in theology and Biblical studies should reflect the historic, orthodox Protestant tradition." Publishes hardcover and trade paperback originals and reprints. **Publishes 90 titles/year. 20% of books from first-time authors. 10% from unagented writers.**

FICTION Fiction should be geared toward the evangelical Christian market. Wants books with fast-paced, contemporary storylines presenting a strong Christian message in an engaging, entertaining style.

NONFICTION "We serve evangelical Christian readers and those in career Christian service."

HOW TO CONTACT Finds works through The Writer's Edge and Christian Ms Submissions ms screening services. Responds in 2-3 months. Publishes ms 12-16 months after acceptance.

TERMS Pays royalty on wholesale price. Pays negotiable advance. Guidelines online.

TIPS "Our audience consists of conservative, evangelical Christians, including pastors and ministry students."

LEE & LOW BOOKS

95 Madison Ave., #1205, New York NY 10016. (212)779-4400. **E-mail:** general@leeandlow.com. **Website:** www.leeandlow.com. "Our goals are to meet a growing need for books that address children of color, and to present literature that all children can identify with. We only consider multicultural children's books. Sponsors a yearly New Voices Award for first-time picture book authors of color. Contest rules online at website or for SASE." Publishes hardcover originals and trade paperback reprints. **Publishes 12-14 titles/year. 20% of books from first-time authors. 50% from unagented writers.**

FICTION Picture books, young readers: anthology, contemporary, history, multicultural, poetry. Picture book, middle reader: contemporary, history, multicultural, nature/environment, poetry, sports. Average word length: picture books—1,000-1,500 words. "We do not publish folklore or animal stories."

NONFICTION Picture books: concept. Picture books, middle readers: biography, history, multicultural, science and sports. Average word length: picture books—1,500-3,000.

HOW TO CONTACT Submit complete ms. Receives 100 queries/year; 1,200 mss/year. Responds in 6 months to mss if interested. Publishes book 2 years after acceptance.

ILLUSTRATION Works with 12-14 illustrators/year. Uses color artwork only. Reviews ms/illustration packages from artists. Contact: Louise May. Illustrations only: Query with samples, résumé, promo sheet and tearsheets. Responds only if interested. Original artwork returned at job's completion.

PHOTOGRAPHY Buys photos from freelancers. Works on assignment only. Model/property releases required. Submit cover letter, résumé, promo piece and book dummy.

TERMS Pays net royalty. Pays authors advances against royalty. Pays illustrators advance against royalty. Photographers paid advance against royalty. Book catalog available online. Guidelines available online or by written request with SASE.

TIPS "Check our website to see the kinds of books we publish. Do not send mss that don't fit our mission."

LEGACY PRESS

17909 Adria Maru, Carson CA 90746. (800)532-4278. **E-mail:** info@rainbowpublishers.com. **Website:** www.rainbowpublishers.com. "Our mission is to publish Bible-based, teacher resource materials that contribute to and inspire spiritual growth and development in kids ages 2-12." **Publishes Publishes 4 young readers/year; 4 middle readers/year; 4 young adult titles/year. titles/year. 50% of books from first-time authors.**

NONFICTION Young readers, middle readers, young adult/teens: activity books, arts/crafts, how-to, reference, religion.

HOW TO CONTACT Responds to queries in 6 weeks, mss in 3 months.

TERMS For authors: work purchased outright (range: $500 and up). Pays illustrators by the project (range: $300 and up). Sends galleys to authors.

TIPS "Our Rainbow imprint publishes reproducible books for teachers of children in Christian ministries, including crafts, activities, games, and puzzles. Our Legacy imprint publishes titles for children such as devotionals, fiction, and Christian living. Please see website and study the market before submitting material."

LERNER PUBLISHING GROUP

1251 Washington Ave. N., Minneapolis MN 55401. (800)452-7236; (612)332-3344. **Fax:** (612)337-7615. **Website:** www.karben.com; www.lernerbooks.com. Primarily publishes books for children ages 7-18. List includes titles in geography, natural and physical science, current events, ancient and modern history, high interest, sports, world cultures, and numerous biography series.

◯ Starting in 2007, Lerner Publishing Group no longer accepts submission in any of their imprints except for Kar-Ben Publishing.

HOW TO CONTACT "We will continue to seek targeted solicitations at specific reading levels and in specific subject areas. The company will list these targeted solicitations on our website and in national newsletters, such as the SCBWI *Bulletin*."

ARTHUR A. LEVINE BOOKS

Scholastic, Inc., 557 Broadway, New York NY 10012. (212)343-4436. **Fax:** (212)343-6143. **Website:** www. arthuralevinebooks.com. Publishes hardcover, paperback, and e-book editions.

FICTION "Arthur A. Levine is looking for distinctive literature, for children and young adults, for whatever's extraordinary." Averages 18-20 total titles/year.

HOW TO CONTACT Query. Please follow submission guidelines. Responds in 1 month to queries; 5 months to mss. Publishes a book 18 months after acceptance.

TERMS Picture Books: Query letter and full text of picture book. Novels: Send Query letter, first 2 chapters, and synopsis. Other: Query letter, 10-page sample, and synopsis/proposal.

Ⓐ LITTLE, BROWN BOOKS FOR YOUNG READERS

Hachette Book Group USA, 1290 Avenue of the Americas, New York NY 10104. (212)364-1100. **Fax:** (212)364-0925. **Website:** littlebrown.com. "Little, Brown and Co. Children's Publishing publishes all formats including board books, picture books, middle-grade fiction, and nonfiction young adult titles.

We are looking for strong writing and presentation, but no predetermined topics." *Only interested in solicited agented material.* **Publishes 100-150 titles/year.**

FICTION Average length: picture books—1,000; young readers—6,000; middle-grade—15,000-50,000; young adults—50,000 and up.

NONFICTION "Writers should avoid looking for the 'issue' they think publishers want to see, choosing instead topics they know best and are most enthusiastic about/inspired by."

HOW TO CONTACT *Agented submissions only.* Responds in 1-2 months. Publishes ms 2 years after acceptance.

ILLUSTRATION Works with 40 illustrators/year. Illustrations only: Query art director with b&w and color samples; provide résumé, promo sheet or tearsheets to be kept on file. Does not respond to art samples. Do not send originals; copies only. Accepts illustration samples by postal mail or e-mail.

PHOTOGRAPHY Works on assignment only. Model/property releases required; captions required. Publishes photo essays and photo concept books. Uses 35mm transparencies. Photographers should provide résumé, promo sheets or tearsheets to be kept on file.

TERMS Pays authors royalties based on retail price. Pays illustrators and photographers by the project or royalty based on retail price. Sends galleys to authors; dummies to illustrators. Pays negotiable advance.

TIPS "In order to break into the field, authors and illustrators should research their competition and try to come up with something outstandingly different."

LITTLE PICKLE PRESS

3701 Sacramento St., #494, San Francisco CA 94118. (415)340-3344. **Fax:** (415)366-1520. **E-mail:** info@littlepicklepress.com. **Website:** www.littlepicklepress.com. Little Pickle Press is a 21st-century publisher dedicated to helping parents and educators cultivate conscious, responsible little people by stimulating explorations of the meaningful topics of their generation through a variety of media, technologies, and techniques. Submit through submission link on site. Includes young adult imprint Relish Media

TERMS Uses www.author.me for submissions for Little Pickle and young adult imprint Relish Media. Guidelines available on website.

TIPS "We have lots of mss to consider, so it will take up to 8 weeks before we get back to you."

Ⓐ LITTLE SIMON

Imprint of Simon & Schuster, 1230 Avenue of the Americas, New York NY 10020. (212)698-1295. **Fax:** (212)698-2794. **Website:** www.simonandschuster.com/kids. "Our goal is to provide fresh material in an innovative format for preschool to age 8. Our books are often, if not exclusively, format driven." Publishes novelty and branded books only.

FICTION Novelty books include many things that do not fit in the traditional hardcover or paperback format, such as pop-up, board book, scratch and sniff, glow in the dark, lift the flap, etc. Children's/juvenile. No picture books. Large part of the list is holiday-themed.

NONFICTION "We publish very few nonfiction titles." No picture books.

HOW TO CONTACT *Currently not accepting unsolicited mss.*

TERMS Offers advance and royalties.

Ⓐ LIZZIE SKURNICK BOOKS

(718)797-0676. **Website:** lizzieskurnickbooks.com. Lizzie Skurnick Books, an imprint of Ig Publishing, is devoted to reissuing the very best in young adult literature, from the classics of the 1930s and 1940s to the social novels of the 1970s and 1980s. Ig does not accept unsolicited mss, either by e-mail or regular mail. If you have a ms that you would like Ig to take a look at, send a query through online contact form. If interested, they will contact. All unsolicited mss will be discarded.

MAGINATION PRESS

750 First St. NE, Washington DC 20002. (202)336-5618. **Fax:** (202)336-5624. **E-mail:** magination@apa.org. **Website:** www.apa.org. Magination Press is an imprint of the American Psychological Association. "We publish books dealing with the psycho/therapeutic resolution of children's problems and psychological issues with a strong self-help component." Submit complete ms. Full guidelines available on site. Materials returned only with SASE. **Publishes 12 titles/year. 75% of books from first-time authors.**

FICTION All levels: psychological and social issues, self-help, health, parenting concerns, and special needs. Seeks picture books, middle school readers.

NONFICTION All levels: psychological and social issues, self-help, health, multicultural, special needs.

HOW TO CONTACT Responds to queries in 1-2 months; mss in 2-6 months. Publishes a book 18-24 months after acceptance.

ILLUSTRATION Works with 10-15 illustrators/year. Reviews ms/illustration packages. Will review artwork for future assignments. Responds only if interested, or immediately if SASE or response card is included. "We keep samples on file."

MARTIN SISTERS PUBLISHING COMPANY

P.O. Box 1154, Barbourville KY 40906-1499. **E-mail:** submissions@martinsisterspublishing.com. **Website:** www.martinsisterspublishing.com. **Contact:** Publisher/Editor (fiction/nonfiction). Firm/imprint publishes trade and mass market paperback originals; electronic originals. **Publishes 12 titles/year. 75% of books from first-time authors. 100% from unagented writers.**

HOW TO CONTACT "Please place query letter, marketing plan, and the first 5-10 pages of your ms (if you are submitting fiction) directly into your e-mail." Guidelines available on site. Responds in 1 month on queries, 2 months on proposals, 3-6 months on mss. Publishes ms 9 months after acceptance.

TERMS Pays 7.5% royalty/max on print net. Pays 35% royalty/max on eBook net. No advance offered. Catalog and guidelines online.

⊙ MASTER BOOKS

P.O. Box 726, Green Forest AR 72638. (870)438-5288. **Fax:** (870)438-5120. **E-mail:** submissions@newleafpress.net. **Website:** www.masterbooks.com. **Contact:** Craig Froman, acquisitions editor. Publishes 3 middle readers/year; 2 young adult nonfiction titles/year; 10 homeschool curriculum titles; 20 adult trade books/year. **10% of books from first-time authors.**

NONFICTION Picture books: activity books, animal, nature/environment, creation. Young readers, middle readers, young adults: activity books, animal, biography, Christian, nature/environment, science, creation.

HOW TO CONTACT Submission guidelines on website. Responds in 90 days. Publishes book 1 year after acceptance.

TERMS Pays authors royalty of 3-15% based on wholesale price. Book catalog available upon request. Guidelines online.

TIPS "All of our children's books are creation-based, including topics from the Book of Genesis. We look

also for homeschool educational material that would be supplementary to a homeschool curriculum, especially elementary material."

MARGARET K. MCELDERRY BOOKS

Imprint of Simon & Schuster Children's Publishing Division, 1230 Sixth Ave., New York NY 10020. (212)698-7200. **Website:** imprints.simonandschuster.biz/margaret-k-mcelderry-books. "Margaret K. McElderry Books publishes hardcover and paperback trade books for children from pre-school age through young adult. This list includes picture books, middle-grade and teen fiction, poetry, and fantasy. The style and subject matter of the books we publish is almost unlimited. We do not publish textbooks, coloring and activity books, greeting cards, magazines, pamphlets, or religious publications." **Publishes 30 titles/year. 15% of books from first-time authors. 50% from unagented writers.**

FICTION *No unsolicited mss.*

NONFICTION *No unsolicited mss.*

HOW TO CONTACT *Agented submissions only.*

TERMS Pays authors royalty based on retail price. Pays illustrator royalty by the project. Pays photographers by the project. Original artwork returned at job's completion. Offers $5,000-8,000 advance for new authors. Guidelines for #10 SASE.

TIPS "Read! The children's book field is competitive. See what's been done and what's out there before submitting. We look for high quality: an originality of ideas, clarity and felicity of expression, an organized plot, and strong character-driven stories. We're looking for strong, original fiction, especially mysteries and middle-grade humor. We are always interested in picture books for the youngest age reader. Study our titles."

ANDREW MCMEEL

Andrew McMeel Publishing, Attn: Book Submissions, 1130 Walnut St., Kansas City MO 64106. **Website:** www.andrewsmcmeel.com/our-company/submissions. Andrews McMeel Publishing (AMP) is a leading publisher of cookbooks, gift books, humor books, middle-grade fiction titles, and cartoon collections, publishing as many as 250 new titles annually. AMP is also the premier calendar publisher in the country, annually publishing calendars based on many top-selling properties. **Publishes 250 titles/year.**

HOW TO CONTACT "Please allow at least 90 days to receive a response. We get many submissions a day, and we may not get to yours immediately."

TERMS Send cover letter with bio along with outline and first two chapters. "We are happy to consider submissions from both literary agents and directly from authors." Full submission guidelines listed on site.

MEDALLION PRESS

4222 Meridian Pkwy., Aurora IL 60504. (630)513-8316. **E-mail:** emily@medallionpress.com. **Website:** medallionpress.com. **Contact:** Emily Steele, editorial director. "We are an independent, innovative publisher looking for compelling, memorable stories told in distinctive voices." Publishes trade paperback, hardcover, e-book originals, book apps, and TREEbook.

FICTION Word count: 40,000-90,000 for young adult; 60,000-120,000 for all others. No short stories, anthologies, erotica.

NONFICTION *Agented only.*

HOW TO CONTACT Submit first 3 consecutive chapters and a synopsis through our online submission form. Please check if submissions are currently open before submitting. Please query. Responds in 2-3 months to mss. Publishes ms 1-2 years after acceptance.

TERMS Offers advance. Guidelines online. Currently closed to submissions.

TIPS "We are not affected by trends. We are simply looking for well-crafted, original, compelling works of fiction and nonfiction. Please visit our website for the most current guidelines prior to submitting anything to us. Please check if submissions are currently open before submitting."

⊕ MIGHTY MEDIA PRESS

1201 Currie Ave., Minneapolis MN 55403. (612)399-1969. **E-mail:** lauren@mightymedia.com. **Website:** mightymediapress.com. **Contact:** Lauren Kukla, publishing director. Mighty Media Press delivers captivating books and media that ignite a child's curiosity, imagination, social awareness, and sense of adventure.

FICTION "We only publish books that fit all parts of our mission. Why? Because we know the stories kids experience help shape their minds, and we want to produce books that guide kids on the path to becoming great adults." Publishes picture books and middle-grade. Only publishes about 6 titles per year. "We

seek out stories that leap off the page. We challenge our readers to think differently, be adventurous, build forts, find shapes in the clouds, explore new perspectives, be compassionate, and grow up to be mighty adults."

TERMS Enter e-mail on the website to receive a link with submission guidelines. Doesn't accept hard copy submissions. Only accepts submissions during our reading period (October 1–April 30). Please no phone calls regarding submissions

MILKWEED EDITIONS

1011 Washington Ave. S., Suite 300, Minneapolis MN 55415. (612)332-3192. **Fax:** (612)215-2550. **Website:** www.milkweed.org. Publishes 3-4 middle readers/year. 25% of books by first-time authors. **Contact:** Patrick Thomas, managing editor. "Milkweed Editions publishes with the intention of making a humane impact on society, in the belief that literature is a transformative art uniquely able to convey the essential experiences of the human heart and spirit. To that end, Milkweed Editions publishes distinctive voices of literary merit in handsomely designed, visually dynamic books, exploring the ethical, cultural, and esthetic issues that free societies need continually to address." Publishes hardcover, trade paperback, and electronic originals; trade paperback and electronic reprints. **Publishes 15-20 titles/year. 25% of books from first-time authors. 75% from unagented writers.**

FICTION Novels for adults and for readers 8-13. High literary quality. Middle readers: adventure, contemporary, fantasy, multicultural, nature/environment, suspense/mystery. Average length: middle readers—90-200 pages. No romance, mysteries, science fiction.

HOW TO CONTACT "Please submit a query letter with three opening chapters (of a novel) or three representative stories (of a collection)." Responds in 6 months. Publishes book in 18 months.

TERMS Pays authors variable royalty based on retail price. Offers advance against royalties. Pays varied advance from $500-10,000. Book catalog online. Only accepts submissions during open submission periods. See website for guidelines.

TIPS "We are looking for excellent writing with the intent of making a humane impact on society. Please read submission guidelines before submitting and acquaint yourself with our books in terms of style and quality before submitting. Many factors influence our selection process, so don't get discouraged. Nonfiction is focused on literary writing about the natural world, including living well in urban environments."

MILKWEED FOR YOUNG READERS

Milkweed Editions, Open Book Building, 1011 Washington Ave. S., Suite 300, Minneapolis MN 55415. (612)332-3192. **Fax:** (612)215-2550. **Website:** www.milkweed.org. **Contact:** Patrick Thomas, managing editor. "We are looking first of all for high quality literary writing. We publish books with the intention of making a humane impact on society." Publishes hardcover and trade paperback originals. **Publishes 3-4 titles/year. 25% of books from first-time authors. 50% from unagented writers.**

HOW TO CONTACT "Milkweed Editions now accepts mss online through our Submission Manager. If you're a first-time submitter, you'll need to fill in a simple form and then follow the instructions for selecting and uploading your ms. Please make sure that your ms follows the submission guidelines." Responds in 6 months to queries. Publishes ms 1 year after acceptance.

TERMS Pays 7% royalty on retail price. Pays variable advance. Book catalog for $1.50. Guidelines online.

○ THE MILLBROOK PRESS

Lerner Publishing Group, 1251 Washington Ave N, Minneapolis MN 55401. **E-mail:** info@lernerbooks.com. **Website:** www.lernerbooks.com. **Contact:** Carol Hinz, editorial director. "Millbrook Press publishes informative picture books, illustrated nonfiction titles, and inspiring photo-driven titles for grades K–5. Our authors approach curricular topics with a fresh point of view. Our fact-filled books engage readers with fun yet accessible writing, high-quality photographs, and a wide variety of illustration styles. We cover subjects ranging from the parts of speech and other language arts skills; to history, science, and math; to art, sports, crafts, and other interests. Millbrook Press is the home of the best-selling Words Are CATegorical® series and Bob Raczka's Art Adventures. We do not accept unsolicited mss from authors. Occasionally, we may put out a call for submissions, which will be announced on our website."

MITCHELL LANE PUBLISHERS, INC.

P.O. Box 196, Hockessin DE 19707. (302)234-9426. **Fax:** (866)834-4164. **E-mail:** barbaramitchell@mitch-elllane.com; customerservice@mitchelllane.com. **Website:** www.mitchelllane.com. **Contact:** Barbara Mitchell, publisher. Publishes hardcover and library bound originals. **Publishes 80 titles/year. 90% from unagented writers.**

NONFICTION Young readers, middle readers, young adults: biography, nonfiction, and curriculum-related subjects. Average word length: 4,000-50,000 words. Recently published: *My Guide to US Citizenship*, *Rivers of the World*, and *Vote America*.

HOW TO CONTACT Query with SASE. *All unsolicited mss discarded.* 100 queries received/year. Responds only if interested to queries. Publishes ms 1 year after acceptance.

ILLUSTRATION Works with 2-3 illustrators/year. Reviews ms/illustration packages from artists. Query. Illustration only: Query with samples; send résumé, portfolio, slides, tearsheets. Responds only if interested. Samples not returned; samples filed.

PHOTOGRAPHY Buys stock images. Needs photos of famous and prominent minority figures. Captions required. Uses color prints or digital images. Submit cover letter, résumé, published samples, stock photo list.

TERMS Work purchased outright from authors (range: $350-2,000). Pays illustrators by the project (range: $40-400). Book catalog available free.

TIPS "We hire writers on a 'work-for-hire' basis to complete book projects we assign. Send résumé and writing samples that do not need to be returned."

○ MOODY PUBLISHERS

Moody Bible Institute, 820 N. LaSalle Blvd., Chicago IL 60610. (800)678-8812. **Fax:** (312)329-4157. **E-mail:** authors@moody.edu. **Website:** www.moodypublishers.org. **Contact:** Acquisitions Coordinator. "The mission of Moody Publishers is to educate and edify the Christian and to evangelize the non-Christian by ethically publishing conservative, evangelical Christian literature and other media for all ages around the world, and to help provide resources for Moody Bible Institute in its training of future Christian leaders." Publishes hardcover, trade, and mass market paperback originals. **Publishes 60 titles/year. 80% from unagented writers.**

NONFICTION "We are no longer reviewing queries or unsolicited mss unless they come to us through an agent, are from an author who has published with us, an associate from a Moody Bible Institute ministry, or a personal contact at a writers conference. Unsolicited proposals will be returned only if proper postage is included. We are not able to acknowledge the receipt of your unsolicited proposal."

HOW TO CONTACT *Agented submissions only.* Does not accept unsolicited nonfiction submissions. 1,500 queries received/year. Responds in 2-3 months to queries. Publishes book 1 year after acceptance.

TERMS Royalty varies. Book catalog for 9×12 envelope and 4 first-class stamps. Guidelines online.

TIPS "In our fiction list, we're looking for Christian storytellers rather than teachers trying to present a message. Your motivation should be to delight the reader. Using your skills to create beautiful works is glorifying to God."

⊕ MOONDANCE PRESS

Quarto Publishing, 25 Whitman Rd., Morganville NJ 07751. **Website:** www.quartoknows.com/moondance-press. MoonDance Press is dedicated to entertaining, educating, and inspiring children with beautifully produced, content-rich books. "Our picture books capture young imaginations with enthralling stories brought to life by award-winning illustrators. Science, nature, and activity titles inspire the inquisitive mind with fun and fascinating information. The exquisitely produced Modern Retelling series, with unique and brilliant art, captures the essence of literature's timeless classics, bringing their characters and stories to the youngest minds. The literary world's best poets and award-winning illustrators introduce poetry to young children in the Poetry for Kids series. MoonDance publishes books for dreamers, thinkers, doodlers, puzzlers, the moon watchers, the question askers, and of course, the book lovers." **Publishes 20. titles/year.**

TERMS Complete information listed on website. Asks writers to sign submission agreement.

TIPS "If you are looking for something to enthrall a young child, our picture books do just that with stories that capture young imaginations and award-winning illustrators who bring them to life. To inspire the inquisitive mind, our science, nature, and activity-filled books, filled with fun and fascinating information, will do the trick."

MSI PRESS

1760-F Airline Hwy, #203, Hollister CA 95023. **Fax:** (831)886-2486. **E-mail:** editor@msipress.com. **Website:** www.msipress.com. **Contact:** Betty Leaver, managing editor (self-help, spirituality, religion, memoir, mind/body/spirit, some humor, popular psychology, foreign tales, parenting). "We are a small, 'boutique' press that specializes in award-winning quality publications, refined through strong personal interactions and productive working relationships between our editors and our authors. A small advance may be offered to previously published authors with a strong book and strong platform. We will accept first-time authors with credibility in their fields and a strong platform, but we do not offer advances to first-time authors. We may refer authors with a good book but little credibility or lacking a strong platform to San Juan Books, our co-publishing venture." Publishes trade paperback originals and corresponding e-books. **Publishes 20-25 titles/year.**

NONFICTION "We continue to expand our spirituality, psychology, and self-help lines and are interested in adding to our collection of books in Spanish. We do not do or publish translations." Does not want erotica.

HOW TO CONTACT Submit proposal package, including: outline, 1 sample chapter, professional resume, platform. Prefers electronic submissions. Note that we are open to foreign writers (non-native speakers of English), but please have an English editor proofread the submission prior to sending. Responds in 2 weeks to queries sent by e-mail and to proposals submitted via the template on our website. Publishes ms 8-12 months after acceptance.

TERMS Pays 10% royalty on retail price. Pays small advance to previously published authors with good sales history. Does not pay advance to first-time authors or to authors whose previously published books do not have a good track record. Catalog online. Guidelines online.

TIPS "Learn the mechanics of writing. Too many submissions are full of grammar and punctuation errors and poorly worded and trite expressions. Read to write; observe and analyze how the great authors of all time use language to good avail. Capture our attention with active verbs, not bland description. Before writing your book, determine its audience, write to that audience, and go about developing your credibility with that audience—and then tell us what you have done and are doing in your proposal."

Ⓐ NATIONAL GEOGRAPHIC CHILDREN'S BOOKS

1145 17th St. NW, Washington DC 20090-8199. (800)647-5463. **Website:** www.ngchildrensbooks.

org. National Geographic Children's Books provides quality nonfiction for children and young adults by award-winning authors. *This market does not currently accept unsolicited mss.*

NATUREGRAPH PUBLISHERS, INC.

P.O. Box 1047, 3543 Indian Creek Rd., Happy Camp CA 96039. (530)493-5353. **Fax:** (530)493-5240. **E-mail:** nature@sisqtel.net. **Website:** www.naturegraph.com. **Contact:** Barbara Brown, owner. Publishes trade paperback originals. **Publishes 2 titles/year. 80% of books from first-time authors.**

HOW TO CONTACT 300 queries; 12 mss received/year. Responds in 1 month to queries; 2 months to mss. Publishes ms 2 years after acceptance.

TERMS Pays royalties. Does not pay advance. Book catalog for #10 SASE.

TIPS "Please-always send a stamped reply envelope. Publishers get hundreds of mss yearly."

TOMMY NELSON

Imprint of Thomas Nelson, Inc., P.O. Box 141000, Nashville TN 37214-1000. (615)889-9000. **Fax:** (615)902-2219. **Website:** www.tommynelson.com. "Tommy Nelson publishes children's Christian nonfiction and fiction for boys and girls up to age 14. We honor God and serve people through books, videos, software, and Bibles for children that improve the lives of our customers." Publishes hardcover and trade paperback originals. **Publishes 50-75 titles/year.**

FICTION No stereotypical characters.

HOW TO CONTACT *Does not accept unsolicited mss.*

TERMS Guidelines online.

TIPS "Know the Christian Booksellers Association market. Check out the Christian bookstores to see what sells and what is needed."

NIGHTSCAPE PRESS

P.O. Box 1948, Smyrna TN 37167. **E-mail:** info@nightscapepress.com. **Website:** www.nightscapepress.com. Nightscape Press is seeking quality book-length words of at least 50,000 words (40,000 for young adult).

FICTION "We are not interested in erotica or graphic novels."

HOW TO CONTACT Query.

TERMS Pays monthly royalties. Offers advance. Guidelines online. Currently closed to submissions.

Will announce on site when they re-open to submissions.

NOMAD PRESS

2456 Christain St., White River Junction VT 05001. (802)649-1995. **E-mail:** rachel@nomadpress.net; info@nomadpress.net. **Website:** www.nomadpress.net. **Contact:** Alex Kahan, publisher. "We produce nonfiction children's activity books that bring a particular science or cultural topic into sharp focus. Nomad Press does not accept unsolicited mss. If authors are interested in contributing to our children's series, please send a writing résumé that includes relevant experience/expertise and publishing credits."

○ Nomad Press does not accept picture books, fiction, or cookbooks.

NONFICTION Middle readers: activity books, history, science. Average word length for middle readers—30,000.

HOW TO CONTACT Responds to queries in 3-4 weeks. Publishes book 1 year after acceptance.

TERMS Pays authors royalty based on retail price or work purchased outright. Offers advance against royalties. Catalog online.

TIPS "We publish a very specific kind of nonfiction children's activity book. Please keep this in mind when querying or submitting."

NORTHSOUTH BOOKS

600 Third Ave., 2nd Floor, New York NY 10016. (917)210-5868. **E-mail:** hlennon@northsouth.com. **Website:** www.northsouth.com.

FICTION Looking for fresh, original fiction with universal themes that could appeal to children ages 3-8. "We typically do not acquire rhyming texts, since our books must also be translated into German."

HOW TO CONTACT Submit picture book mss (1,000 words or less) via e-mail.

TERMS Guidelines online.

○ ONSTAGE PUBLISHING

190 Lime Quarry Rd., Suite 106-J, Madison AL 35758-8962. (256)461-0661. **E-mail:** onstage123@knology.net. **Website:** www.onstagepublishing.com. **Contact:** Dianne Hamilton, senior editor. "At this time, we only produce fiction books for ages 8-18. We have added an eBook only side of the house for mysteries for grades 6-12. See our website for more information. We will not do anthologies of any kind. Query first for

nonfiction projects as nonfiction projects must spark our interest. Now accepting e-mail queries and submissions. For submissions: Put the first 3 chapters in the body of the e-mail. Do not use attachments! We will no longer return any mss. Only a SASE envelope is needed. Send complete ms if under 20,000 words, otherwise send synopsis and first 3 chapters." **80% of books from first-time authors.**

◑ Suggested word count lengths: chapter books—3,000–9,000 words; middle-grade novels—10,000–40,000 words; young adult novels—40,000–60,000 words.

FICTION Middle readers: adventure, contemporary, fantasy, history, nature/environment, science fiction, suspense/mystery. Young adults: adventure, contemporary, fantasy, history, humor, science fiction, suspense/mystery. Average word length: chapter books—4,000-6,000 words; middle readers—5,000 words and up; young adults—25,000 and up. Recently published *Mission: Shanghai* by Jamie Dodson (an adventure for boys ages 12+); *Birmingham, 1933: Alice* (a chapter book for grades 3-5). "We do not produce picture books."

ILLUSTRATION Reviews ms/illustration packages from artists. Submit with 3 pieces of final art. **Contact:** Dianne Hamilton, senior editor. Illustrations only. Samples not returned.

TERMS Pays authors/illustrators/photographers advance plus royalties.

TIPS "Study our titles and get a sense of the kind of books we publish, so that you know whether your project is likely to be right for us."

OOLIGAN PRESS

369 Neuberger Hall, 724 SW Harrison St., Portland OR 97201. (503)725-9410. **Website:** ooligan.pdx.edu. **Contact:** Acquisitions co-managers. Publishes trade paperbacks, electronic originals, and reprints. **Publishes 3-4 titles/year.**

FICTION "We seek to publish regionally significant works of literary, historical, and social value. We define the Pacific Northwest as Northern California, Oregon, Idaho, Washington, British Columbia, and Alaska." We recognize the importance of diversity, particularly within the publishing industry, and are committed to building a literary community that includes traditionally underrepresented voices; therefore, we are interested in works originating from, or

focusing on, marginalized communities of the Pacific Northwest. Does not want romance, horror, westerns, incomplete mss.

NONFICTION Cookbooks, self-help books, how-to manuals.

HOW TO CONTACT Query with SASE. *"At this time we cannot accept science fiction or fantasy submissions."* Submit a query through Submittable. If accepted, then submit proposal package, outline, 4 sample chapters, projected page count, audience, marketing ideas, and a list of similar titles. 250-500 queries; 50-75 mss received/year. Responds in 2 weeks for queries; 3 months for proposals. Publishes ms 12-18 months after acceptance.

TERMS Pays negotiable royalty on retail price. Catalog online. Guidelines online.

TIPS "Search the blog for tips."

Ⓐ ORCHARD BOOKS (US)

557 Broadway, New York NY 10012. **Website:** www.scholastic.com. *Orchard is not accepting unsolicited mss.* **Publishes 20 titles/year. 10% of books from first-time authors.**

FICTION Picture books, early readers, and novelty: animal, contemporary, history, humor, multicultural, poetry.

TERMS Most commonly offers an advance against list royalties.

RICHARD C. OWEN PUBLISHERS, INC.

P.O. Box 585, Katonah NY 10536. (914)232-3903; (800)262-0787. **E-mail:** richardowen@rcowen.com. **Website:** www.rcowen.com. **Contact:** Richard Owen, publisher. "We publish child-focused books, with inherent instructional value, about characters and situations with which children ages 5-7 can identify—books that can be read for meaning, entertainment, enjoyment and information. We include multicultural stories that present minorities in a positive and natural way. Our stories show the diversity in America." Not interested in lesson plans, or books of activities for literature studies or other content areas. Submit complete ms and cover letter.

◑ "Due to high volume and long production time, we are currently limiting to nonfiction submissions only."

NONFICTION "Our books are for kindergarten, first- and second-grade children to read on their own. The stories are very brief—up to 2,000 words—yet well structured and crafted with memorable characters, language, and plots. Picture books, young readers: animals, careers, history, how-to, music/dance, geography, multicultural, nature/environment, science, sports. Multicultural needs include: Good stories respectful of all heritages, races, cultural—African-American, Hispanic, American Indian, Asian, European, Middle Eastern." Wants lively stories. No "encyclopedic" type of information stories. Average word length: under 500 words.

HOW TO CONTACT Responds to mss in 1 year. Publishes book 2-3 years after acceptance.

ILLUSTRATION Works with 20 illustrators/year. Uses color artwork only. Illustration only: Send color copies/reproductions or photos of art or provide tearsheets; do not send slides or originals. Include SASE and cover letter. Responds only if interested; samples filed.

TERMS Pays authors royalty of 5% based on net price or outright purchase (range: $25-500). Offers no advances. Pays illustrators by the project (range: $100-2,000) or per photo (range: $50-150). Book catalog available with SASE. Ms guidelines with SASE or online.

PAGESPRING PUBLISHING

P.O. Box 2113, Columbus OH 43221. **E-mail:** sales@pagespringpublishing.com. **Website:** www.pagespringpublishing.com. **Contact:** Lucky Marble Books editor or Cup of Tea Books editor. "PageSpring Publishing publishes young adult and middle-grade titles under the Lucky Marble Books imprint and women's fiction under the Cup of Tea imprint. See PageSpring website for submission details." Publishes trade paperback and electronic originals. **Publishes 7-10 titles/year. 75% of books from first-time authors. 100% from unagented writers.**

FICTION The Lucky Marble Books imprint of PageSpring Publishing specializes in fiction for middle-grade and young adult readers. Cup of Tea Books publishes women's fiction. Lucky Marble books specializes in middle-grade and young adult fiction.

HOW TO CONTACT submissions@pagespringpublishing.com Looking for young adult submissions. "Our favorite genres include historical fiction, fantasy, science fiction, mystery, supernatural fiction, romantic comedy, and humor." Send submissions to submissions@pagespringpublishing.com. Please send a query, synopsis, and the first 30 pages of your ms

in the body of the e-mail. No attachments, please. In the subject line, write "Young Adult Submission." The publisher endeavors to respond to all queries within 6 weeks. Publishes ms 9-12 months after acceptance.

TERMS Pays royalty on wholesale price. Catalog online. Guidelines online.

TIPS "Cup of Tea Books would love to see more cozy mysteries and humor. Lucky Marble Books is looking for humor and engaging contemporary stories for middle-grade and young adult readers."

PANTS ON FIRE PRESS

2062 Harbor Cove Way, Winter Garden FL 34787. (863)546-0760. **E-mail:** submission@pantsonfirepress.com. **Website:** www.pantsonfirepress.com. **Contact:** Becca Goldman, senior editor; Emily Gerety, editor. Pants On Fire Press is an award-winning book publisher of picture, middle-grade, young adult, and adult books. They are a digital-first book publisher, striving to follow a high degree of excellence while maintaining quality standards. Publishes hardcover originals and reprints, trade paperback originals and reprints, and electronic originals and reprints. **Publishes 10-15 titles/year. 60% of books from first-time authors. 80% from unagented writers.**

FICTION Publishes big story ideas with high concepts, new worlds, and meaty characters for children, teens, and discerning adults. Always on the lookout for action, adventure, animals, comedic, dramatic, dystopian, fantasy, historical, paranormal, romance, science fiction, supernatural, and suspense stories.

HOW TO CONTACT Submit a proposal package including a synopsis, 3 sample chapters, and a query letter via e-mail. Receives 2,500 queries and mss per year. Responds in 3 months. Publishes ms approximately 7 months after acceptance.

TERMS Pays 10-50% royalties on wholesale price. Catalog online. Guidelines online.

PARADISE CAY PUBLICATIONS

P.O. Box 29, Arcata CA 95518-0029. (800)736-4509. **Fax:** (707)822-9163. **E-mail:** info@paracay.com. **Website:** www.paracay.com. "Paradise Cay Publications, Inc. is a small independent publisher specializing in nautical books, videos, and art prints. Our primary interest is in mss that deal with the instructional and technical aspects of ocean sailing. We also publish and will consider fiction if it has a strong nautical theme." Publishes hardcover and trade paperback originals and reprints. **Publishes 5 titles/year. 10% of books from first-time authors. 100% from un-agented writers.**

FICTION All fiction must have a nautical theme.

NONFICTION Must have strong nautical theme.

HOW TO CONTACT Query with SASE. Submit proposal package, clips, 2-3 sample chapters. Include a cover letter containing a story synopsis and a short bio, including any plans to promote their work. The cover letter should describe the book's subject matter, approach, distinguishing characteristics, intended audience, author's qualifications, and why the author thinks this book is appropriate for Paradise Cay. Call first. 360-480 queries received/year. 240-360 mss received/year. Responds in 1 month to queries/proposals; 2 months to mss. Publishes book 4 months after acceptance.

TERMS Pays 10-15% royalty on wholesale price. Makes outright purchase of $1,000-10,000. Does not normally pay advances to first-time or little-known authors. Book catalog and ms guidelines free on request or online.

TIPS "Audience is recreational sailors. Call Matt Morehouse (publisher)."

PAUL DRY BOOKS

1700 Sansom St., Suite 700, Philadelphia PA 19103. (215)231-9939. **Fax:** (215)231-9942. **E-mail:** editor@pauldrybooks.com. **Website:** pauldrybooks.com. "We publish fiction, both novels and short stories, and nonfiction, biography, memoirs, history, and essays, covering subjects from Homer to Chekhov, bird watching to jazz music, New York City to shogunate Japan." Hardcover and trade paperback originals, trade paperback reprints.

○   "Take a few minutes to familiarize yourself with the books we publish. Then if you think your book would be a good fit in our line, we invite you to submit the following: A one- or two-page summary of the work. Be sure to tell us how many pages or words the full book will be; a sample of 20-30 pages; your bio. A brief description of how you think the book (and you, the author) could be marketed."

HOW TO CONTACT Submit sample chapters, clips, bio. Submit proposal package.

TERMS Book catalog available online. Guidelines available online.

TIPS "Our aim is to publish lively books 'to awaken, delight, and educate'—to spark conversation. We publish fiction and nonfiction, and essays covering subjects from Homer to Chekhov, bird watching to jazz music, New York City to shogunate Japan."

PAULINE BOOKS & MEDIA

50 St. Paul's Ave., Boston MA 02130. (617)522-8911. **Fax:** (617)541-9805. **E-mail:** design@paulinemedia.com; editorial@paulinemedia.com. **Website:** www.pauline.org. "Submissions are evaluated on adherence to Gospel values, harmony with the Catholic faith tradition, relevance of topic, and quality of writing." For board books and picture books, the entire ms should be submitted. For easy-to-read, young readers, and middle reader books and teen books, please send a cover letter accompanied by a synopsis and two sample chapters. "Electronic submissions are encouraged. We make every effort to respond to unsolicited submissions within 2 months." Publishes trade paperback originals and reprints. **Publishes 40 titles/ year; about 40% for children's books.**

FICTION Children's and teen fiction only. "We are now accepting submissions for easy-to-read and middle reader chapter, and teen well documented historical fiction. We would also consider well-written fantasy, fairy tales, myths, science fiction, mysteries, or romance if approached from a Catholic perspective and consistent with church teaching. Please see our guidelines."

NONFICTION Picture books, young readers, middle readers, teen: religion and fiction. Average word length: picture books—500-1,000; young readers—8,000-10,000; middle readers—15,000-25,000; teen—30,000-50,000. Recently published children's titles: *Bible Stores for Little Ones* by Genny Monchapm; *I Forgive You: Love We Can Hear, Ask For and Give* by Nicole Lataif; *Shepherds To the Rescue* (first place Catholic Book Award Winner) by Maria Grace Dateno; *FSP; Jorge from Argentina; Prayers for Young Catholics.* Teen Titles: *Teens Share the Mission* by Teens; *Martyred: The Story of Saint Lorenzo Ruiz; Ten Commandments for Kissing Gloria Jean* by Britt Leigh; *A.K.A. Genius* (second place Catholic Book Award Winner) by Marilee Haynes; *Tackling Tough Topics with Faith and Fiction* by Diana Jenkins. No memoir/autobiography, poetry, or strictly nonreligious works currently considered.

HOW TO CONTACT "Submit proposal package, including synopsis, 2 sample chapters, and cover letter; complete ms." Responds in 2 months to queries, proposals, and mss. Publishes a book approximately 11-18 months after acceptance.

ILLUSTRATION Works with 10-15 illustrators/year. Uses color and b&w- artwork. Samples and résumés will be kept on file unless return is requested and SASE provided.

TERMS Varies by project, but generally are royalties with advance. Flat fees sometimes considered for smaller works. Book catalog available online. Guidelines available online and by e-mail.

TIPS "Mss may or may not be explicitly catechetical, but we seek those that reflect a positive worldview, good moral values, awareness and appreciation of diversity, and respect for all people. All material must be relevant to the lives of readers and must conform to Catholic teaching and practice."

PAULIST PRESS

997 Macarthur Blvd., Mahwah NJ 07430. (201)825-7300. **Fax:** (201)825-8345. **E-mail:** submissions@paulistpress.com. **Website:** www.paulistpress.com. **Contact:** Trace Murphy, editorial director. Paulist Press publishes ecumenical theology, Roman Catholic studies, and books on scripture, liturgy, spirituality, church history, and philosophy, as well as works on faith and culture. "Our publishing is oriented toward adult-level nonfiction. We do not publish memoirs, poetry, or works of fiction, and we have scaled back on children's books. Offer of a subsidy is no guarantee of acceptance—we are not a vanity press." **10% of books from first-time authors. 95% from unagented writers.**

HOW TO CONTACT Accepts submissions via e-mail. Hard copy submissions returned only if accompanied by self-addressed envelope with adequate postage. Receives 250 submissions/year. Responds in 3 months to queries and proposals; 3-4 months on mss. Publishes a book 12-18 months after receipt of final, edited ms.

TERMS Royalties and advances are negotiable. Pays negotiable advance. Book catalog available online. Guidelines available on website and by e-mail.

Ⓐ PEACE HILL PRESS

Affiliate of W.W. Norton, 18021 The Glebe Ln., Charles City VA 23030. (804)829-5043. **Fax:** (804)829-5704.

Website: www.peacehillpress.com. Publishes hardcover and trade paperback originals. **Publishes 4-8 titles/year.**

HOW TO CONTACT Does not take unagented submissions. Publishes a book 18 months after acceptance.

TERMS Pays 6-10% royalty on retail price. Pays $500-1,000 advance.

PEACHTREE PUBLISHERS, LTD.

1700 Chattahoochee Ave., Atlanta GA 30318. (404)876-8761. **Fax:** (404)875-2578. **E-mail:** hello@peachtree-online.com. **Website:** www.peachtree-online.com. **Publishes 30-35 titles/year.**

FICTION Picture books, young readers: adventure, animal, concept, history, nature/environment. Middle readers: adventure, animal, history, nature/environment, sports. Young adults: fiction, mystery, adventure. Does not want to see science fiction, romance.

NONFICTION Picture books: animal, history, nature/environment. Young readers, middle readers, young adults: animal, biography, nature/environment. Does not want to see religion.

HOW TO CONTACT Submit complete ms or 3 sample chapters by postal mail only. Submit complete ms or 3 sample chapters by postal mail only. Responds in 6-7 months. Publishes book 1-2 years after acceptance.

ILLUSTRATION Works with 8-10 illustrators/year. Illustrations only: Query production manager or art director with samples, résumé, slides, color copies to keep on file. Responds only if interested. Samples returned with SASE; samples filed.

Ⓒ PELICAN PUBLISHING COMPANY

1000 Burmaster St., Gretna LA 70053. (504)368-1175. **Fax:** (504)368-1195. **E-mail:** editorial@pelicanpub.com. **Website:** www.pelicanpub.com. "We believe ideas have consequences. One of the consequences is that they lead to a best-selling book. We publish books to improve and uplift the reader. Currently emphasizing business and history titles." Publishes 20 young readers/year; 1 middle reader/year. "Our children's books (illustrated and otherwise) include history, biography, holiday, and regional. Pelican's mission is to publish books of quality and permanence that enrich the lives of those who read them." Publishes hardcover, trade paperback, and mass market paperback originals and reprints.

FICTION "We publish no adult fiction." Young readers: history, holiday, science, multicultural and regional. Middle readers: Louisiana History. Multicultural needs include stories about African-Americans, Irish-Americans, Jews, Asian-Americans, and Hispanics. Does not want animal stories, general Christmas stories, "day at school" or "accept yourself" stories. Maximum word length: young readers—1,100; middle readers—40,000. No young adult, romance, science fiction, fantasy, gothic, mystery, erotica, confession, horror, sex, or violence. Also no psychological novels.

NONFICTION "We look for authors who can promote successfully. We require that a query be made first. This greatly expedites the review process and can save the writer additional postage expenses." Young readers: biography, history, holiday, multicultural. Middle readers: Louisiana history, holiday, regional. No multiple queries or submissions.

HOW TO CONTACT Submit outline, clips, 2 sample chapters, SASE. Full guidelines on website. Responds in 1 month to queries; 3 months to mss. Requires exclusive submission. Publishes a book 9-18 months after acceptance.

ILLUSTRATION Works with 20 illustrators/year. Reviews ms/illustration packages from artists. Query first. Illustrations only: Query with samples (no originals). Responds only if interested. Samples returned with SASE; samples kept on file.

TERMS Pays authors in royalties; buys ms outright "rarely." Illustrators paid by "various arrangements." Advance considered. Book catalog and ms guidelines online.

TIPS "We do extremely well with cookbooks, popular histories, and business. We will continue to build in these areas. The writer must have a clear sense of the market and knowledge of the competition. A query letter should describe the project briefly, give the author's writing and professional credentials, and promotional ideas."

PENGUIN RANDOM HOUSE, LLC

Division of Bertelsmann Book Group, 1745 Broadway, New York NY 10019. (212)782-9000. **Website:** www.penguinrandomhouse.com. Penguin Random House LLC is the world's largest English-language general trade book publisher. *Agented submissions only. No unsolicited mss.*

PERSEA BOOKS

277 Broadway, Suite 708, New York NY 10007. (212)260-9256. **Fax:** (212)267-3165. **E-mail:** info@perseabooks.com. **Website:** www.perseabooks.com. The aim of Persea is to publish works that endure by meeting high standards of literary merit and relevance. "We have often taken on important books other publishers have overlooked, or have made significant discoveries and rediscoveries, whether of a single work or writer's entire oeuvre. Our books cover a wide range of themes, styles, and genres. We have published poetry, fiction, essays, memoir, biography, titles of Jewish and Middle Eastern interest, women's studies, American Indian folklore, and revived classics, as well as a notable selection of works in translation."

HOW TO CONTACT Queries should include a cover letter, author background and publication history, a detailed synopsis of the proposed work, and a sample chapter. Please indicate if the work is simultaneously submitted. Responds in 8 weeks to proposals; 10 weeks to mss.

TERMS Guidelines online.

PHAIDON PRESS

65 Bleecker St., 8th Floor, New York NY 10012. (212)652-5400. **Fax:** (212)652-5410. **Contact:** Meagan Bennet, art director and Cecily Kaiser, children's publishing director. "Phaidon is the premier global publisher of the creative arts with 1,500 titles in print. We work with the world's most influential artists, chefs, writers, and thinkers to produce innovative books on art, photography, design, architecture, fashion, food, and travel, and illustrated books for children."

TERMS "If you are interested in submitting a children's book proposal to us, please bear in mind that we currently publish for children ages 0-8 in the categories of: board book, novelty book, and picture book. Subject matter must be relevant to the target age group and quality must be commensurate with the Phaidon brand." Priority is given to submissions that have been solicited or agented, and we will not reply to those that are not. Appropriate submissions should be e-mailed to submissions@phaidon.com. Please do not send hard copies. Phaidon cannot assume responsibility for any submissions sent by postal mail.

PHILOMEL BOOKS

Imprint of Penguin Group (USA), Inc., 375 Hudson St., New York NY 10014. (212)414-3610. **Website:**

www.penguin.com. **Contact:** Michael Green, president/publisher. "We look for beautifully written, engaging mss for children and young adults." Publishes hardcover originals. **Publishes 8-10 titles/year. 5% of books from first-time authors.**

NONFICTION Picture books.

HOW TO CONTACT *No unsolicited mss. Agented submissions only.*

ILLUSTRATION Works with 8-10 illustrators/year. Reviews ms/illustration packages from artists. Query with art sample first. Illustrations only: Query with samples. Send résumé and tearsheets. Responds to art samples in 1 month. Original artwork returned at job's completion. Samples returned with SASE or kept on file.

TERMS Pays authors in royalties. Average advance payment "varies." Illustrators paid by advance and in royalties. Pays negotiable advance.

○ PIANO PRESS

P.O. Box 85, Del Mar CA 92014. (619)884-1401. **Fax:** (858)755-1104. **E-mail:** pianopress@pianopress.com. **Website:** www.pianopress.com. **Contact:** Elizabeth C. Axford, editor. "We publish music-related books, either fiction or nonfiction, music-related coloring books, songbooks, sheet music, CDs, and music-related poetry."

FICTION Picture books, young readers, middle readers, young adults: folktales, multicultural, poetry, music. Average word length: picture books—1,500-2,000.

NONFICTION Picture books, young readers, middle readers, young adults: multicultural, music/dance. Average word length: picture books—1,500-2,000.

HOW TO CONTACT Electronic queries ONLY may be sent to: pianopress@pianopress.com. Please include a brief bio and/or web link(s) with your inquiry. Please DO NOT send MP3s, ms .docs, or picture .jpgs unless requested to do so by the acquisitions editor. Responds if interested. Publishes book 1 year after acceptance.

ILLUSTRATION Works with 1 or 2 illustrators/year. Reviews ms/illustration packages from artists. Query. Illustrations only: Query with samples. Responds in 3 months. Samples returned with SASE; samples filed.

PHOTOGRAPHY Buys stock and assigns work. Looking for music-related, multicultural. Model/property releases required. Uses glossy or flat, color or b&w prints. Submit cover letter, résumé, client list, published samples, stock photo list.

TERMS Pays authors, illustrators, and photographers royalties based on the retail price. Book catalog available online.

TIPS "We are looking for music-related material only for the juvenile market. Please do not send non-music-related materials. Query by e-mail first before submitting anything."

PIÑATA BOOKS

Imprint of Arte Publico Press, University of Houston, 4902 Gulf Fwy., Bldg. 19, Room 100, Houston TX 77204-2004. (713)743-2845. **Fax:** (713)743-3080. **E-mail:** submapp@uh.edu. **Website:** www.artepublicopress.com. "Piñata Books is dedicated to the publication of children's and young adult literature focusing on US Hispanic culture by US Hispanic authors. Arte Publico's mission is the publication, promotion and dissemination of Latino literature for a variety of national and regional audiences, from early childhood to adult, through the complete gamut of delivery systems, including personal performance as well as print and electronic media." Publishes hardcover and trade paperback originals. **Publishes 10-15 titles/year. 80% of books from first-time authors.**

NONFICTION Piñata Books specializes in publication of children's and young adult literature that authentically portrays themes, characters and customs unique to US Hispanic culture.

HOW TO CONTACT Submissions made through online submission form. Submissions made through online submission form. Responds in 2-3 months to queries; 4-6 months to mss. Publishes book 2 years after acceptance.

ILLUSTRATION Works with 6 illustrators/year. Uses color artwork only. Reviews ms/illustration packages from artists. Query or send portfolio (slides, color copies). Illustrations only: Query with samples or send résumé, promo sheet, portfolio, slides, client list, and tearsheets. Responds only if interested. Samples not returned; samples filed.

TERMS Pays 10% royalty on wholesale price. Pays $1,000-3,000 advance. Book catalog and guidelines online.

TIPS "Include cover letter with submission explaining why your ms is unique and important, why we should publish it, who will buy it, etc."

PINEAPPLE PRESS, INC.

P.O. Box 3889, Sarasota FL 34230. (941)706-2507. **Fax:** (800)746-3275. **E-mail:** info@pineapplepress. com. **Website:** www.pineapplepress.com. **Contact:** June Cussen, executive editor. "We are seeking quality nonfiction on diverse topics for the library and book trade markets. Our mission is to publish good books about Florida." Publishes hardcover and trade paperback originals. **Publishes 21 titles/year.**

FICTION Picture books, young readers, middle readers, young adults: animal, folktales, history, nature/environment.

NONFICTION Picture books: animal, history, nature/environmental, science. Young readers, middle readers, young adults: animal, biography, geography, history, nature/environment, science.

HOW TO CONTACT Query or submit outline/synopsis and 3 sample chapters. 1,000 queries; 500 mss received/year. Responds in 2 months. Publishes a book 1 year after acceptance.

ILLUSTRATION Works with 2 illustrators/year. Reviews ms/illustration packages from artists. Query with nonreturnable samples. Contact: June Cussen, executive editor. Illustrations only: Query with brochure, nonreturnable samples, photocopies, résumé. Responds only if interested. Samples returned with SASE, but prefers nonreturnable; samples filed.

TERMS Pays authors royalty of 10-15%. Book catalog for 9×12 SAE with $1.32 postage. Guidelines online.

TIPS "Quality first novels will be published, though we usually only do one or two novels per year and they must be set in Florida. We regard the author/editor relationship as a trusting relationship with communication open both ways. Learn all you can about the publishing process and about how to promote your book once it is published. A query on a novel without a brief sample seems useless."

THE POISONED PENCIL

Poisoned Pen Press, 6962 E. First Ave., Suite 103, Scottsdale AZ 85251. (480)945-3375. **Fax:** (480)949-1707. **E-mail:** info@thepoisonedpencil.com. **Website:** www.thepoisonedpencil.com. **Contact:** Ellen Larson, editor. Publishes trade paperback and electronic originals. **Publishes 4-6 titles/year.**

Accepts young adult mysteries only.

FICTION "We publish only young adult mystery novels, 45,000 to 90,000 words in length. For our pur-

poses, a young adult book is a book with a protagonist between the ages of 13 and 18. We are looking for both traditional and cross-genre young adult mysteries. We encourage off-beat approaches and narrative choices that reflect the complexity and ambiguity of today's world. Submissions from teens are very welcome. Avoid serial killers, excessive gore, and vampires (and other heavy supernatural themes). We only consider authors who live in the US or Canada, due to practicalities of marketing promotion. Avoid coincidence in plotting. Avoid having your sleuth leap to conclusions rather than discover and deduce. Pay attention to the resonance between character and plot; between plot and theme; between theme and character. We are looking for clean style, fluid storytelling, and solid structure. Unrealistic dialogue is a real turn-off."

HOW TO CONTACT Submit proposal package including synopsis, complete ms, and cover letter. 150 submissions received/year. Responds in 6 weeks to mss. Publishes ms 15 months after acceptance.

TERMS Pays 9-15% for trade paperback; 25-35% for e-books. Pays advance of $1,000. Guidelines online.

TIPS "Our audience is made up of young adults and adults who love young adult mysteries."

POLIS BOOKS

E-mail: info@polisbooks.com. **Website:** www.polisbooks.com. "Polis Books is an independent publishing company actively seeking new and established authors for our growing list. We are actively acquiring titles in mystery, thriller, suspense, procedural, traditional crime, science fiction, fantasy, horror, supernatural, urban fantasy, romance, erotica, commercial women's fiction, commercial literary fiction, young adult and middle-grade books." **Publishes 40 titles/year. 33% of books from first-time authors. 10% from unagented writers.**

HOW TO CONTACT Query with 3 sample chapters and bio via e-mail. Only responds to submissions if interested For e-book originals, ms published 6-9 months after acceptance. For front list print titles, 9-15 months.

TERMS Offers advance against royalties. Guidelines online.

✚ POMEGRANATE KIDS

19018 NE Portal Way, Portland OR 97230. (503)328-6500; 1-800-227-1428. **Website:** www.pomegranate.

com/arsub.html. "With a focus on fine art and illustration, Pomegranate collaborates with individual artists as well as museums, galleries, and libraries across the world. We publish artful and educational items for adults and children. Popular product lines include art books, bookplates, calendars, children's books, coloring books, coloring cards, home décor, puzzles, stationery, and a myriad of other high-quality paper gift products. We continually introduce new formats and designs, with the mission to inspire through art. We delight in collaborating with many artists and writers in the creation of new products, so we're happy to review your work for possible publication."

ILLUSTRATION "If you are an artist looking to submit a query or proposal, visit our Art Submissions page. E-mail us with "[Your name]: Artist Submission" in the subject line. Please provide a link to your website, or digital portfolio, and if there is a specific body of work you would like us to consider, please provide a direct link. If you do not have a website, you may include 5-8 images of your work. Image resolution should be 72 dpi and the images under 1 MB each. Please attach a PDF of your résumé. You may mail a CD or flash drive with images, or you may mail color printouts/photocopies. Never send originals! We are careful and attentive, but we can't assume responsibility for lost or mangled materials. Please include your résumé."

⊕ POW!

37 Main St., Brooklyn NY 11201. (212)604-9074. **Website:** www.powkidsbooks.com. POW! publishes books for children that are visually striking, imaginative, funny, and have an offbeat or edgy sensibility. If you have a book project that meets these criteria, and you would like POW! to consider your book for publication, you can send us a submission. Publishes mainly picture books.

HOW TO CONTACT "Put together a proposal. It should include: a brief description of your book and why it's right for us an analysis of the market for your book and a list of recent comparable titles, the full text (if it's reasonably short; a sample chapter with illustrations otherwise). The best way to send it to us is by e-mail: info@powkidsbooks.com. No attachments please. Submissions containing attachments will be rejected. Please send a link instead."

Ⓐ PRICE STERN SLOAN, INC.

Penguin Group, 375 Hudson St., New York NY 10014. (212)366-2000. **Website:** www.penguin.com. **Contact:** Francesco Sedita, president/publisher. "Price Stern Sloan publishes quirky mass market novelty series for childrens as well as licensed movie tie-in books." Price Stern Sloan only responds to submissions it's interested in publishing.

FICTION Publishes picture books and novelty/board books.

HOW TO CONTACT *Agented submissions only.*

TERMS Book catalog online.

TIPS "Price Stern Sloan publishes unique, fun titles."

PRUFROCK PRESS, INC.

P.O. Box 8813, Waco TX 76714. (800)988-2208. **Fax:** (800)240-0333. **E-mail:** info@prufrock.com. **Website:** www.prufrock.com. **Contact:** Joel McIntosh, publisher and marketing director. "Prufrock Press offers award-winning products focused on gifted education, gifted children, advanced learning, and special needs learners, including trade nonfiction (not narrative nonfiction, however) for adults and children/teens. For more than 20 years, Prufrock has supported gifted children and their education and development. The company publishes more than 300 products that enhance the lives of gifted children and the teachers and parents who support them." Accepts simultaneous submissions, but must be notified about it. **20% of books from first-time authors. 100% from unagented writers.**

FICTION No picture books.

NONFICTION "We are always looking for truly original, creative materials for teachers."

HOW TO CONTACT "Prufrock Press does not consider unsolicited mss." Query with SASE. Submit outline, 1-3 sample chapters. 50 queries; 40 mss received/year. Publishes ms 1-2 year after acceptance.

TERMS Book catalog available. Guidelines online.

Ⓐ PUFFIN BOOKS

Imprint of Penguin Group (USA), Inc., 375 Hudson St., New York NY 10014. (212)366-2000. **Website:** www.penguin.com. **Contact:** Eileen Bishop Kreit, publisher. "Puffin Books publishes high-end trade paperbacks and paperback reprints for preschool children, beginning and middle readers, and young adults." Publishes trade paperback originals and reprints. **Publishes 175-200 titles/year.**

NONFICTION "Women in history books interest us."

HOW TO CONTACT *No unsolicited mss. Agented submissions only.* Publishes book 1 year after acceptance.

ILLUSTRATION Reviews artwork. Send color copies.

PHOTOGRAPHY Reviews photos. Send color copies.

TIPS "Our audience ranges from little children 'first books' to young adult (ages 14-16). An original idea has the best luck."

🅐 G.P. PUTNAM'S SONS HARDCOVER

Imprint of Penguin Group (USA), Inc., 375 Hudson, New York NY 10014. (212)366-2000. **Fax:** (212)366-2664. **Website:** www.penguin.com. **Contact:** Christine Ball, vice president/deputy publisher; Mark Tavani, vice president/executive editor. Publishes hardcover originals.

HOW TO CONTACT *Agented submissions only. No unsolicited mss.*

TERMS Pays variable royalties on retail price. Pays varies advance. Request book catalog through mail order department.

⊕ QUIRK BOOKS

215 Church St., Philadelphia PA 19106. **E-mail:** blair@quirkbooks.com, jason@quirkbooks.com. "Quirk Books is headquartered on a quiet cobblestone street in the historic Old City district of Philadelphia. Quirk publishes just 25 books per year and every title is a labor of love. Some of our more popular recent titles include the bestselling young adult series Miss Peregrine's Peculiar Children, the Edgar Award-winning mystery *The Last Policeman*, the legendary *Pride and Prejudice and Zombies*, and classroom favorite *William Shakespeare's Star Wars*." **Publishes 25 titles/year.**

FICTION "We publish across a broad range of categories—always with the goal of delivering innovative books to discerning readers. Put more simply, we publish books that are smart, original, cool, and fun."

HOW TO CONTACT "The easiest way to submit your idea is to e-mail a query letter to one of our editors. The query letter should be a short description of your project. Try to limit your letter to a single page. If you have sample chapters, go ahead and include them. You can also mail materials directly to our office. If you would like a reply, please include a SASE. If you

want your materials returned, please include adequate postage. If your project involves fiction (adult, young adult, or middle-grade), humor, pop culture, history, sports, literature, sex, monsters, or "guy stuff," send it to Jason Rekulak (jason@quirkbooks.com). If your project involves fiction (adult or young adult) about falling in love, avoiding falling in love, books-within-books, unconventional narrative (epistolary, text-message-o-lary, diary novels, etc.), wordplay, smart teenagers, travel, or medievalists, send a query letter and the first chapter pasted into the body of the e-mail (no attachments) to Blair Thornburgh (blair@quirkbooks.com)."

🅐 RANDOM HOUSE CHILDREN'S BOOKS

1745 Broadway, New York NY 10019. (212)782-9000. **Website:** www.randomhouse.com. "Producing books for preschool children through young adult readers, in all formats from board to activity books to picture books and novels, Random House Children's Books brings together world-famous franchise characters, multimillion-copy series and top-flight, award-winning authors, and illustrators." Submit mss through a literary agent.

FICTION "Random House publishes a select list of first chapter books and novels, with an emphasis on fantasy and historical fiction." Chapter books, middle-grade readers, young adult.

HOW TO CONTACT *Does not accept unsolicited mss.*

ILLUSTRATION The Random House publishing divisions hire their freelancers directly. To contact the appropriate person, send a cover letter and résumé to the department head at the publisher as follows: "Department Head" (e.g., art director, production director), "Publisher/Imprint" (e.g., Knopf, Doubleday, etc.), 1745 Broadway New York, NY 10019. Works with 100-150 freelancers/year. Works on assignment only. Send query letter with résumé, tearsheets, and printed samples; no originals. Samples are filed. Negotiates rights purchased. Assigns 5 freelance design jobs/year. Pays by the project.

TIPS "We look for original, unique stories. Do something that hasn't been done before."

RAZORBILL

Penguin Young Readers Group, 345 Hudson St., New York NY 10014. (212)414-3720. **E-mail:** jharriton@penguinrandomhouse.com; bschrank@penguinrandomhouse.com. **Website:** www.razorbillbooks.com. **Contact:** Jessica Almon, senior editor; Elizabeth Tingue, editor; Casey McIntyre, associate publisher; Deborah Kaplan, vice president and executive art director, Marissa Grossman; assistant editor, Tiffany Liao; associate editor. "This division of Penguin Young Readers is looking for the best and the most original of commercial contemporary fiction titles for middle-grade and young adult readers. A select quantity of nonfiction titles will also be considered." **Publishes 30 titles/year.**

FICTION Middle Readers: adventure, contemporary, graphic novels, fantasy, humor, problem novels. Young adults/teens: adventure, contemporary, fantasy, graphic novels, humor, multicultural, suspense, paranormal, science fiction, dystopian, literary, romance. Average word length: middle readers—40,000; young adult—60,000.

NONFICTION Middle readers and young adults/teens: concept.

HOW TO CONTACT Submit cover letter with up to 30 sample pages. Responds in 1-3 months. Publishes book 1-2 after acceptance.

TERMS Offers advance against royalties.

TIPS "New writers will have the best chance of acceptance and publication with original, contemporary material that boasts a distinctive voice and well-articulated world. Check out website to get a better idea of what we're looking for."

REDLEAF LANE

10 Yorkton Ct., St. Paul MN 55117. (800)423-8309. **E-mail:** info@redleafpress.org. **Website:** www.redleafpress.org. **Contact:** David Heath, director. Redleaf Lane publishes engaging, high-quality picture books for children. "Our books are unique because they take place in group-care settings and reflect developmentally appropriate practices and research-based standards."

TERMS Guidelines online.

RIPPLE GROVE PRESS

P.O. Box 86740, Portland OR 97286. **Website:** www.ripplegrovepress.com. "We started Ripple Grove Press because we have a passion for well-written and beautifully illustrated children's picture books. Each story selected has been read dozens of times, then slept on, then walked away from, then talked about again and again. If the story has the same intrigue and the same interest that it had when we first read it, we move forward." Publishes hardcover originals. **Publishes 3-6 titles/year.**

FICTION "We are looking for something unique, that hasn't been done before; an interesting story that captures a moment with a timeless feel. We are looking for picture driven stories for children ages 2-6. Please do not send early readers, middle-grade, or young adult mss. No religious or holiday themed stories. Please do not submit your story with page breaks or illustration notes. Do not submit a story with doodles or personal photographs. Do not send your 'idea' for a story, send your story in ms form."

HOW TO CONTACT Submit completed mss. Accepts submissions by mail and e-mail. Please submit a cover letter including a summary of your story, the age range of the story, a brief biography of yourself, and contact information. "Given the volume of submissions we receive we are no longer able to individually respond to each. Please allow 5 months for us to review your submission. If we are interested in your story, you can expect to hear from us within that time. If you do not hear from us after that time, we are not interested in publishing your story. It's not you, it's us! We receive thousands of submissions and only publish a few books each year. Don't give up!" Average length of time between acceptance of a book-length ms and publication is 12-18 months.

TERMS Authors receive between 10-12% royalty on net receipts. Catalog online. Guidelines online.

TIPS "Please read children's picture books. We create books that children and adults want to read over and over again. Our books showcase art as well as stories and tie them together to create a unique and creative product."

Ⓐ ROARING BROOK PRESS

Macmillan Children's Publishing Group, 175 Fifth Ave., New York NY 10010. (646)307-5151. **Website:** us.macmillan.com. Roaring Brook Press is an imprint of MacMillan, a group of companies that includes Henry Holt and Farrar, Straus & Giroux. *Roaring Brook is not accepting unsolicited mss.*

FICTION Picture books, young readers, middle readers, young adults: adventure, animal, contemporary, fantasy, history, humor, multicultural, nature/environment, poetry, religion, science fiction, sports, suspense/mystery.

NONFICTION Picture books, young readers, middle readers, young adults: adventure, animal, contemporary, fantasy, history, humor, multicultural, nature/environment, poetry, religion, science fiction, sports, suspense/mystery.

HOW TO CONTACT *Not accepting unsolicited mss or queries.*

ILLUSTRATION Works with 25 illustrators/year. Illustrations only: Query with samples. Do not send original art; copies only through the mail. Samples returned with SASE.

TERMS Pays authors royalty based on retail price.

TIPS "You should find a reputable agent and have him/her submit your work."

ROSEN PUBLISHING

29 E. 21st St., New York NY 10010. (800)237-9932. **Fax:** (888)436-4643. **Website:** www.rosenpublishing.com. Artists and writers should contact customer service team through online form for information about contributing to Rosen Publishing. Rosen Publishing is an independent educational publishing house, established to serve the needs of students in grades Pre-K-12 with high interest, curriculum-correlated materials. Rosen publishes more than 700 new books each year and has a backlist of more than 7,000.

SADDLEBACK EDUCATIONAL PUBLISHING

3120-A Pullman St., Costa Mesa CA 92626. (888)735-2225. **E-mail:** contact@sdlback.com. **Website:** www.sdlback.com. Saddleback is always looking for fresh, new talent. "Please note that we primarily publish books for kids ages 12-18."

FICTION "We look for diversity for our characters and content."

HOW TO CONTACT Mail typed submission along with a query letter describing the work simply and where it fits in with other titles.

SALINA BOOKSHELF

1120 W. University Ave., Suite 102, Flagstaff AZ 86001. (877)527-0070. **Fax:** (928)526-0386. **Website:** www.salinabookshelf.com. Publishes trade paperback originals and reprints. **Publishes 4-5 titles/year. 50% of books from first-time authors. 100% from unagented writers.**

FICTION Submissions should be in English or Navajo. "All our books relate to the Navajo language and culture."

NONFICTION "We publish children's bilingual readers." Nonfiction should be appropriate to science and social studies curriculum grades 3-8.

HOW TO CONTACT Query with SASE. Query with SASE. Responds in 3 months to queries. Publishes ms 1 year after acceptance.

TERMS Pays varying royalty. Pays advance.

SASQUATCH BOOKS

1904 Third Ave., Suite 710, Seattle WA 98101. (206)467-4300. **Fax:** (206)467-4301. **E-mail:** custserv@sasquatchbooks.com. **Website:** www.sasquatchbooks.com. "Sasquatch Books publishes books for and from the Pacific Northwest, Alaska, and California is the nation's premier regional press. Sasquatch Books' publishing program is a veritable celebration of regionally written words. Undeterred by political or geographical borders, Sasquatch defines its region as the magnificent area that stretches from the Brooks Range to the Gulf of California and from the Rocky Mountains to the Pacific Ocean. Our top-selling Best Places® travel guides serve the most popular destinations and locations of the West. We also publish widely in the areas of food and wine, gardening, nature, photography, children's books, and regional history, all facets of the literature of place. With more than 200 books brimming with insider information on the West, we offer an energetic eye on the lifestyle, landscape, and worldview of our region. Considers queries and proposals from authors and agents for new projects that fit into our West Coast regional publishing program. We can evaluate query letters, proposals, and complete mss." Publishes regional hardcover and trade paperback originals. **Publishes 30 titles/year. 20% of books from first-time authors. 75% from unagented writers.**

FICTION Young readers: adventure, animal, concept, contemporary, humor, nature/environment.

NONFICTION "We are seeking quality nonfiction works about the Pacific Northwest and West Coast regions (including Alaska to California). The literature of place includes how-to and where-to as well as history and narrative nonfiction." Picture books: activity books, animal, concept, nature/environment. "We publish a variety of nonfiction books, as well as children's books under our Little Bigfoot imprint."

HOW TO CONTACT Query first, then submit outline and sample chapters with SASE. Send submissions to The Editors. E-mailed submissions and queries are not recommended. Please include return postage if you want your materials back. Responds to queries in 3 months. Publishes book 6-9 months after acceptance.

ILLUSTRATION Accepts material from international illustrators. Works with 5 illustrators/year. Uses both color and b&w. Reviews ms/illustration packages. For ms/illustration packages: Query. Submit ms/illustration packages to The Editors. Reviews work for future assignments. If interested in illustrating future titles, query with samples. Samples returned with SASE. Samples filed.

TERMS Pays royalty on cover price. Pays wide range advance. Guidelines online.

TIPS "We sell books through a range of channels in addition to the book trade. Our primary audience consists of active, literate residents of the West Coast."

Ⓐ SCHOLASTIC LIBRARY PUBLISHING

90 Old Sherman Turnpike, Danbury CT 06816. (203)797-3500. **Fax:** (203)797-3197. **E-mail:** slpservice@scholastic.com. **Website:** www.scholastic.com/librarypublishing. **Contact:** Phil Friedman, vice president/publisher; Kate Nunn, editor-in-chief; Marie O'Neil, art director. "Scholastic Library is a leading publisher of reference, educational, and children's books. We provide parents, teachers, and librarians with the tools they need to enlighten children to the pleasure of learning and prepare them for the road ahead. Publishes informational (nonfiction) for K-12; picture books for young readers, grades 1-3." Publishes hardcover and trade paperback originals.

🗨 *Accepts agented submissions only.*

FICTION Publishes 1 picture book series, Rookie Readers, for grades 1-2. Does not accept unsolicited mss.

NONFICTION Photo-illustrated books for all levels: animal, arts/crafts, biography, careers, concept, geography, health, history, hobbies, how-to, multicultural, nature/environment, science, social issues, special needs, sports. Average word length: young readers—2,000; middle readers—8,000; young adult—15,000.

HOW TO CONTACT *Does not accept fiction proposals.* Query; submit outline/synopsis, resume, and/or list of publications, and writing sample. SASE required for response.

ILLUSTRATION Works with 15-20 illustrators/year. Uses color artwork and line drawings. Illustrations only: Query with samples or arrange personal portfolio review. Responds only if interested. Samples returned with SASE. Samples filed. Do not send originals. No phone or e-mail inquiries; contact only by mail.

TERMS Pays authors royalty based on net or work purchased outright. Pays illustrators at competitive rates.

Ⓐ SCHOLASTIC PRESS

Imprint of Scholastic, Inc., 557 Broadway, New York NY 10012. (212)343-6100. **Fax:** (212)343-4713. **Website:** www.scholastic.com. Scholastic Press publishes fresh, literary picture book fiction and nonfiction; fresh, literary nonseries or nongenre-oriented middle-grade and young adult fiction. Currently emphasizing subtly handled treatments of key relationships in children's lives; unusual approaches to commonly dry subjects, such as biography, math, history, or science. De-emphasizing fairy tales (or retellings), board books, genre, or series fiction (mystery, fantasy, etc.). Publishes hardcover originals. **Publishes 60 titles/year.**

FICTION Looking for strong picture books, young chapter books, appealing middle-grade novels (ages 8-11), and interesting and well-written young adult novels. Wants fresh, exciting picture books and novels—inspiring, new talent.

HOW TO CONTACT. Agented submissions and previously published authors only. 2,500 queries received/year. Responds in 3 months to queries; 6-8 months to mss. Publishes book 2 years after acceptance.

ILLUSTRATION Works with 30 illustrators/year. Uses both b&w and color artwork. Illustrations only: Query with samples; send tearsheets. Responds only if interested. Samples returned with SASE. Original artwork returned at job's completion.

TERMS Pays royalty on retail price. Pays variable advance.

TIPS "Read *currently* published children's books. Revise, rewrite, rework and find your own voice, style, and subject. We are looking for authors with a strong and unique voice who can tell a great story and have the ability to evoke genuine emotion. Children's publishers are becoming more selective, looking for irresistible talent and fairly broad appeal, yet still very willing to take risks, just to keep the game interesting."

SCHWARTZ & WADE BOOKS

1745 Broadway, 10-4, New York NY 10019. **Website:** www.penguinrandomhouse.com. Schwartz & Wade publishes 15-20 books a year—mostly picture books, as well as middle grade and young adult fiction, nontraditional nonfiction, and graphic novels.

HOW TO CONTACT "Schwartz & Wade accepts submissions directly from authors. Schwartz & Wade also accepts unsolicited picture book mss and proposals for longer books. However, we advise that you first take a look at a selection of our books to make sure that your submission is a good fit for our small imprint."

SEEDLING CONTINENTAL PRESS

520 E. Bainbridge St., Elizabethtown PA 17022. (800)233-0759; **Fax:** (888)834-1303. **Website:** www. continentalpress.com. "Continental publishes educational materials for grades K-12, specializing in reading, mathematics, and test preparation materials. We are not currently accepting submissions for Seedling leveled readers or instructional materials."

FICTION Young readers: adventure, animal, folktales, humor, multicultural, nature/environment. Does not accept texts longer than 12 pages or over 300 words. Average word length: young readers—100.

NONFICTION Young readers: animal, arts/crafts, biography, careers, concept, multicultural, nature/environment, science. Does not accept texts longer than 12 pages or over 300 words. Average word length: young readers—100.

HOW TO CONTACT Submit complete ms. Responds to mss in 6 months. Publishes book 1-2 years after acceptance.

ILLUSTRATION Works with 8-10 illustrators/year. Uses color artwork only. Reviews ms/illustration packages from artists. Submit ms with dummy. Illustrations only: Color copies or line art. Responds only if interested. Samples returned with SASE only; samples filed if interested.

PHOTOGRAPHY Buys photos from freelancers. Works on assignment only. Model/property releases required. Uses color prints and 35mm transparencies. Submit cover letter and color promo piece.

TERMS Work purchased outright from authors.

TIPS "See our website. Follow writers' guidelines carefully and test your story with children and educators."

SILVER DOLPHIN BOOKS

(858)457-2500. **E-mail:** infosilverdolphin@readerlink.com. **Website:** www.silverdolphinbooks.com. Silver Dolphin Books publishes activity, novelty, and educational nonfiction books for preschoolers to 12-year-olds. Highly interactive formats such as the Field Guides and Uncover series both educate and entertain older children. "We will consider submissions only from authors with previously published works."

HOW TO CONTACT Submit cover letter with full proposal and SASE.

SIMON & SCHUSTER BOOKS FOR YOUNG READERS

Imprint of Simon & Schuster Children's Publishing, 1230 Avenue of the Americas, New York NY 10020. (212)698-7000. **Fax:** (212)698-2796. **Website:** www. simonsayskids.com. "Simon and Schuster Books For Young Readers is the Flagship imprint of the S&S Children's Division. We are committed to publishing a wide range of contemporary, commercial, award-winning fiction and nonfiction that spans every age of children's publishing. BFYR is constantly looking to the future, supporting our foundation authors and franchises, but always with an eye for breaking new ground with every publication. We publish high-quality fiction and nonfiction for a variety of age groups and a variety of markets. Above all, we strive to publish books that we are passionate about." *No unsolicited mss.* All unsolicited mss returned unopened. Publishes hardcover originals. **Publishes 75 titles/year.**

NONFICTION Picture books: concept. All levels: narrative, current events, biography, history. "We're looking for picture books or middle-grade nonfiction that have a retail potential. No photo essays."

HOW TO CONTACT *Agented submissions only.* Publishes ms 2-4 years after acceptance.

ILLUSTRATION Works with 70 illustrators/year. Do not submit original artwork. Does not accept unsolicited or unagented illustration submissions.

TERMS Pays variable royalty on retail price. Guidelines online.

TIPS "We're looking for picture books centered on a strong, fully-developed protagonist who grows or changes during the course of the story; young adult novels that are challenging and psychologically complex; also imaginative and humorous middle-grade fiction. And we want nonfiction that is as engaging as fiction. Our imprint's slogan is 'Reading You'll Remember.' We aim to publish books that are fresh, accessible, and family-oriented; we want them to have an impact on the reader."

SKINNER HOUSE BOOKS

The Unitarian Universalist Association, 24 Farnsworth St., Boston MA 02210. (617)742-2100, ext. 603. **Fax:** (617)948-6466. **E-mail:** bookproposals@uua.org. **Website:** www.uua.org/publications/skinnerhouse. **Contact:** Betsy Martin. "We publish titles in Unitarian Universalist faith, liberal religion, history, biography, worship, and issues of social justice. Most of our children's titles are intended for religious education or worship use. They reflect Unitarian Universalist values. We also publish inspirational titles of poetic prose and meditations. Writers should know that Unitarian Universalism is a liberal religious denomination committed to progressive ideals. Currently emphasizing social justice concerns." Publishes trade paperback originals and reprints. **Publishes 10-20 titles/year. 30% of books from first-time authors. 100% from unagented writers.**

FICTION Only publishes fiction for children's titles for religious instruction.

NONFICTION All levels: activity books, multicultural, music/dance, nature/environment, religion.

HOW TO CONTACT Query. Query or submit proposal with cover letter, table of contents, 2 sample chapters. Responds to queries in 1 month. Publishes book 1 year after acceptance.

ILLUSTRATION Works with 2 illustrators/year. Uses both color and b&w. Reviews ms/illustration packages from artists. Query. Contact: Suzanne Morgan, design director. Responds only if interested. Samples returned with SASE.

PHOTOGRAPHY Buys stock images and assigns work. Contact: Suzanne Morgan, design director. Uses inspirational types of photos. Model/property releases required; captions required. Uses color, b&w. Submit cover letter, résumé.

TERMS Book catalog for 6×9 SAE with 3 first-class stamps. Guidelines online.

TIPS "From outside our denomination, we are interested in mss that will be of help or interest to liberal churches, Sunday School classes, parents, ministers, and volunteers. Inspirational/spiritual and children's titles must reflect liberal Unitarian Universalist values."

SKY PONY PRESS

307 W. 36th St., 11th Floor, New York NY 10018. (212)643-6816. **Fax:** (212)643-6819. **Website:** skyponypress.com. Sky Pony Press is the children's book imprint of Skyhorse Publishing. "Following in the footsteps of our parent company, our goal is to provide books for readers with a wide variety of interests."

FICTION "We will consider picture books, early readers, midgrade novels, novelties, and informational books for all ages."

NONFICTION "Our parent company publishes many excellent books in the fields of ecology, independent living, farm living, wilderness living, recycling, and other green topics, and this will be a theme in our children's books. We are also searching for books that have strong educational themes and that help inform children of the world in which they live."

HOW TO CONTACT Submit ms or proposal. Submit proposal via e-mail.

TERMS Guidelines online.

SLEEPING BEAR PRESS

2395 South Huron Parkway #200, Ann Arbor MI 48104. (800)487-2323. **Fax:** (734)794-0004. **E-mail:** submissions@sleepingbearpress.com. **Website:** www.sleepingbearpress.com. **Contact:** Ms Submissions.

FICTION Picture books: adventure, animal, concept, folktales, history, multicultural, nature/environment, religion, sports. Young readers: adventure, animal, concept, folktales, history, humor, multicultural, nature/environment, religion, sports. Average word length: picture books—1,800.

HOW TO CONTACT Accepts unsolicited queries three times per year. See website for details. Query with sample of work (up to 15 pages) and SASE. Please address packages to "Ms Submissions."

TERMS Book catalog available via e-mail.

SOURCEBOOKS FIRE

1935 Brookdale Rd., Suite 139, Naperville IL 60563. (630)961-3900. **Fax:** (630)961-2168. **E-mail:** submissions@sourcebooks.com. **Website:** www.sourcebooks.com. "We're actively acquiring knockout books for our young adult imprint. We are particularly looking for strong writers who are excited about promoting and building their community of readers, and whose books have something fresh to offer the ever-growing young adult audience. We are not accepting any unsolicited or unagented mss at this time. Unfortunately, our staff can no longer handle the large volume of mss that we receive on a daily basis. We will continue to consider agented mss." See website for details.

HOW TO CONTACT Query with the full ms attached in Word doc.

SPENCER HILL PRESS

P.O. Box 243, Marlborough CT 06447. (860)207-2206. **E-mail:** submissions@spencerhillpress.com. **Website:** www.spencerhillpress.com. **Contact:** Jennifer Carson. Spencer Hill Press is an independent publishing house specializing in science fiction, urban fantasy, and paranormal romance for young adult readers. "Our books have that 'I couldn't put it down!' quality."

FICTION "We are interested in young adult, new adult, and middle-grade science fiction, paranormal, or urban fantasy, particularly those with a strong and interesting voice."

HOW TO CONTACT Check website for open submission periods.

TERMS Guidelines online.

SPINNER BOOKS

University Games, 2030 Harrison St., San Francisco CA 94110. (415)503-1600. **Fax:** (415)503-0085. **E-mail:** info@ugames.com. **Website:** www.ugames.com. "Spinners Books publishes books of puzzles, games, and trivia."

NONFICTION Picture books: games and puzzles.

HOW TO CONTACT Query. Responds to queries in 3 months; mss in 2 months only if interested. Publishes book 6 months after acceptance.

ILLUSTRATION Only interested in agented material. Uses both color and b&w. Illustrations only: Query with samples. Responds in 3 months only if interested. Samples not returned.

SPLASHING COW BOOKS

P.O. Box 867, Manchester VT 05254. **Website:** www.splashingcowbooks.com. **Contact:** Gordon McClellan, publisher. Splashing Cow Books publishes books under three imprints: Splashing Cow (children), Blue Boot (women) and Yellow Dot (any other topic that interests us!). Four Splashing Cow authors in the last

year (our first year) won national awards for their work. Splashing Cow also recently launched DartFrog, which selects self-published books of distinction for distribution. Publishes mass market paperback and electronic originals. **Publishes 10 titles/year. 100% of books from first-time authors. 100% from unagented writers.**

FICTION Interested in a wide range of subject matter for children and women.

NONFICTION Open to any topic that would be of interest to children, women or general interest.

HOW TO CONTACT "Please check our website for submission guidelines. We try to respond in 1 week to all inquiries, but it can take longer."

TERMS Pays royalties on retail price. Does not offer an advance. Catalog available online. Guidelines available online.

STANDARD PUBLISHING

Standex International Corp., 4050 Lee Vance View, Colorado Springs CO 80918. (800)323-7543. **Fax:** (800)323-0726. **Website:** www.standardpub.com. Publishes resources that meet church and family needs in the area of children's ministry.

TERMS Guidelines online.

STAR BRIGHT BOOKS

13 Landsdowne St., Cambridge MA 02139. (617)354-1300. **Fax:** (617)354-1399. **E-mail:** info@starbrightbooks.com. **Website:** www.starbrightbooks.com. Star Bright Books does accept unsolicited mss and art submissions. "We welcome submissions for picture books and longer works, both fiction and nonfiction." Also beginner readers and chapter books. Query first. **Publishes 18 titles/year.**

NONFICTION Very keen on biographies and any thing of interest to children.

HOW TO CONTACT Responds in several months. Publishes ms 1-2 years after acceptance.

TERMS Pays advance. Catalog available.

STERLING PUBLISHING CO., INC.

1166 Avenue of the Americas, 17th Floor, New York NY 10036. (212)532-7160. **Fax:** (212)981-0508. **Website:** www.sterlingpublishing.com. "Sterling publishes highly illustrated, accessible, hands-on, practical books for adults and children. Our mission is to publish high-quality books that educate, entertain, and enrich the lives of our readers." Publishes hardcover and paperback originals and reprints. **15% of books from first-time authors.**

FICTION Publishes fiction for children.

NONFICTION Proposals on subjects such as crafting, decorating, outdoor living, and photography should be sent directly to Lark Books at their Asheville, North Carolina offices. Complete guidelines can be found on the Lark site: www.larkbooks.com/submissions. Publishes nonfiction only.

HOW TO CONTACT Submit to attention of "Children's Book Editor." Submit outline, publishing history, 1 sample chapter (typed and double-spaced), SASE. "Explain your idea. Send sample illustrations where applicable. For children's books, please submit full mss. We do not accept electronic (e-mail) submissions. Be sure to include information about yourself with particular regard to your skills and qualifications in the subject area of your submission. It is helpful for us to know your publishing history—whether or not you've written other books and, if so, the name of the publisher and whether those books are currently in print."

ILLUSTRATION Works with 50 illustrators/year. Reviews ms/illustration packages from artists. Illustrations only: Send promo sheet. Contact: Karen Nelson, creative director. Responds in 6 weeks. Samples returned with SASE; samples filed.

PHOTOGRAPHY Buys stock and assigns work. Contact: Karen Nelson.

TERMS Pays royalty or work purchased outright. Offers advances (average amount: $2,000). Catalog online. Guidelines online.

TIPS "We are primarily a nonfiction activities-based publisher. We have a picture book list, but we do not publish chapter books or novels. Our list is not trend-driven. We focus on titles that will backlist well. "

STONE ARCH BOOKS

1710 Roe Crest Rd., North Mankato MN 56003. **Website:** www.stonearchbooks.com.

FICTION Imprint of Capstone Publishers. Young readers, middle readers, young adults: adventure, contemporary, fantasy, humor, light humor, mystery, science fiction, sports, suspense. Average word length: young readers—1,000-3,000; middle readers and early young adults—5,000-10,000.

HOW TO CONTACT Submit outline/synopsis and 3 sample chapters. Electronic submissions preferred. Full guidelines available on website.

ILLUSTRATION Works with 35 illustrators/year. Uses both color and b&w.

TERMS Work purchased outright from authors. Catalog online.

TIPS "A high-interest topic or activity is one that a young person would spend their free time on without adult direction or suggestion."

STRAWBERRIES PRESS

750 Pinehurst Dr., Rio Vista CA 94571. (707)398-6430. **E-mail:** books@strawberriespress.com. **Website:** www.strawberriespress.com. **Contact:** Susan Zhang, Executive Editor. Strawberries Press publishes full-color, interactive and digitally enhanced, children's picture flipbooks on CDs that are designed to be viewed and read on computer screens and that explore exciting subjects that stimulate young minds. Publishes interactive flipbooks on CDs. **Publishes 6 titles/year. 50% of books from first-time authors. 100% from unagented writers.**

NONFICTION Interested in topics that explore exciting subjects that stimulate young minds in both the fiction and nonfiction genres. For examples of subject matter and format requirements, see online catalog of flipbook titles. "We only publish wholesome learning resources and educationally constructive subject matter that retains, promotes, and enhances the innocence of children. Political, immoral, antisocial, propagandist, and other age-inappropriate themes are strictly prohibited at Strawberries Press. We do not use our publications as social engineering and brainwashing tools."

HOW TO CONTACT Submit completed ms. Receives 12-20 queries/year; 12 mss/year. Responds in 1 month. Publishes mss in 3-4 months upon acceptance.

TERMS Pays for outright purchase between $250-500. Catalog available online. Guidelines available by e-mail.

TIPS "Although there are no restrictions on the number of sentences on a single page, all flipbooks are limited to 40 pages. For text, illustrating, and formatting examples, view our sample online flipbook."

SUNSTONE PRESS

Box 2321, Santa Fe NM 87504. (800)243-5644. **Website:** www.sunstonepress.com. **Contact:** Submissions Editor. Sunstone's original focus was on nonfiction subjects that preserved and highlighted the richness of the American Southwest, but it has expanded its view over the years to include mainstream themes and categories—both nonfiction and fiction—that have a more general appeal.

HOW TO CONTACT Query with 1 sample chapter. Query with 1 sample chapter.

TERMS Guidelines online.

THUNDERSTONE BOOKS

6575 Horse Dr., Las Vegas NV 89131. **E-mail:** info@thunderstonebooks.com. **Website:** www.thunderstonebooks.com. **Contact:** Rachel Noorda, editorial director. "At ThunderStone Books, we aim to publish children's books that have an educational aspect. We are not looking for curriculum for learning certain subjects, but rather stories that encourage learning for children, whether that be learning about a new language/culture or learning more about science and math in a fun, fictional format. We want to help children to gain a love for other languages and subjects so that they are curious about the world around them. We are currently accepting fiction and nonfiction submissions. Picture books without accompanying illustration will not be accepted." Publishes hardcover, trade paperback, mass market paperback, and electronic originals. **Publishes 2-5 titles/year. 100% of books from first-time authors. 100% from unagented writers.**

FICTION Interested in multicultural stories with an emphasis on authentic culture and language (these may include mythology).

NONFICTION Looking for engaging educational materials, not a set curriculum, but books that teach as well as have some fun. Open to a variety of educational subjects, but specialty and main interest lies in language exposure/learning, science, math, and history.

HOW TO CONTACT "If you think your book is right for us, send a query letter with a word attachment of the first 50 pages to info@thunderstonebooks.com. If it is a picture book or chapter book for young readers that is shorter than 50 pages send the entire ms." Receives 30 queries and mss/year. Responds in 3 months. Publishes ms 6 months after acceptance.

TERMS Pays 5-15% royalties on retail price. Pays $300-1,000 advance. Catalog available for SASE. Guidelines available.

TILBURY HOUSE PUBLISHERS

WordSplice Studio, Inc., 12 Starr St., Thomaston ME 04861. (800)582-1899. **Fax:** (207)582-8772. **E-mail:** tilbury@tilburyhouse.com. **Website:** www.tilburyhouse.com. **Contact:** Audrey Maynard, children's book editor; Jonathan Eaton, publisher. **Publishes 10 titles/year.**

FICTION Picture books: multicultural, nature/environment. Special needs include books that teach children about tolerance and honoring diversity.

NONFICTION Regional adult biography/history/maritime/nature, and children's picture books that deal with issues, such as bullying, multiculturalism, etc., science/nature.

HOW TO CONTACT Send art/photography samples and/or complete ms to Audrey Maynard, children's book editor. Submit complete ms for picture books or outline/synopsis for longer works. Now uses online submission form. Responds to mss in 3 months. Publishes ms 1 year after acceptance.

ILLUSTRATION Works with 2-3 illustrators/year. Illustrations only: Query with samples. Responds in 1 month. Samples returned with SASE. Original artwork returned at job's completion.

PHOTOGRAPHY Buys photos from freelancers. Works on assignment only.

TERMS Pays royalty based on wholesale price. Guidelines and catalog online.

TIPS "We are always interested in stories that will encourage children to understand the natural world and the environment, as well as stories with social justice themes. We really like stories that engage children to become problem solvers as well as those that promote respect, tolerance and compassion." We do not publish books with personified animal characters, historical fiction, or fantasy."

TOR BOOKS

Tom Doherty Associates, 175 Fifth Ave., New York NY 10010. **Website:** www.tor-forge.com. Tor Books is the "world's largest publisher of science fiction and fantasy, with strong category publishing in historical fiction, mystery, western/Americana, thriller, young adult." **Publishes 10-20 titles/year.**

HOW TO CONTACT Submit first 3 chapters, 3-10 page synopsis, dated cover letter, SASE.

TERMS Pays author royalty. Pays illustrators by the project. Book catalog available. Guidelines online.

TRIANGLE SQUARE

Seven Stories Press, 140 Watts St., New York NY 10013. (212)226-8760. **Fax:** (212)226-1411. **E-mail:**

info@sevenstories.com. **Website:** www.sevenstories. com/trianglesquare. Triangle Square is a children's and young adult imprint of Seven Story Press.

HOW TO CONTACT Send a cover letter with 2 sample chapters and SASE. Send c/o Acquisitions.

TU BOOKS

Lee & Low Books, 95 Madison Ave., Suite #1205, New York NY 10016. **Website:** www.leeandlow.com/imprints/3. **Contact:** Stacy Whitman, publisher. The Tu imprint spans many genres: science fiction, fantasy, mystery, contemporary, and more. "We don't believe in labels or limits, just great stories. Join us at the crossroads where fantasy and real life collide. You'll be glad you did." **25% of books from first-time authors.**

FICTION "At Tu Books, an imprint of Lee & Low Books, our focus is on well-told, exciting, adventurous fantasy, science fiction, and mystery novels starring people of color. We also selectively publish realism that explores the contemporary and historical experiences of people of color. We look for fantasy set in worlds inspired by non-Western folklore or culture, contemporary mysteries and fantasy set all over the world starring people of color, and science fiction that centers the possibilities for people of color in the future. We welcome intersectional narratives that feature LGBTQIA and disabled POC as heroes in their own stories. We are looking specifically for stories for both middle-grade (ages 8-12) and young adult (ages 12-18) readers. Occasionally a ms might fall between those two categories; if your ms does, let us know. We are not looking for picture books, chapter books, or short stories at this time. Please do not send submissions in these categories. (See the Lee & Low Books guidelines for books for younger readers.)"

HOW TO CONTACT Submit via Submittable page. Only submissions sent through Submittable or regular post will be considered. "We cannot accept submissions through e-mail or fax. Mss should be accompanied by a cover letter that includes a brief biography of the author, including publishing history. The letter should also state if the ms is a simultaneous or an exclusive submission. Include a synopsis and the first 3 chapters of the novel. Include full contact information on the cover letter and the first page of the ms." Responds only if interested.

ILLUSTRATION "Tu Books, an imprint of Lee & Low Books, is not interested in illustrations for picture books, but will consider artwork for book covers and spot illustrations, for novels aimed at older readers (ages 8-18). Artists are welcome to submit a sample with the address of their website portfolio following the guidelines below. Our books feature children and teens of color and include a variety of fantasy, science fiction, and mystery. We are particularly interested in hearing from illustrators whose cultural, ethnic, or racial backgrounds and experiences support their knowledge of diverse cultures. We are open to seeing work from professional illustrators and artists at all levels of experience. Illustrators who have worked in other fields and are interested in creating cover and spot art for novels are also welcome."

TERMS Pays advance. Guidelines online. Electronic submissions can be submitted here (only): www.tubooks.submittable.com/submit.

TUMBLEHOME LEARNING

P.O. Box 71386, Boston MA 02117. **E-mail:** info@tumblehomelearning.com. **Website:** www.tumblehomelearning.com. **Contact:** Pendred Noyce, editor. Tumblehome Learning helps kids imagine themselves as young scientists or engineeers and encourages them to experience science through adventure and discovery. "We do this with exciting mystery and adventure tales as well as experiments carefully designed to engage students from ages 8 and up." Publishes hardcover, trade paperback, and electronic originals. **Publishes 8-10 titles/year. 50% of books from first-time authors. 100% from unagented writers.**

FICTION "All our fiction has science at its heart. This can include using science to solve a mystery (see *The Walking Fish* by Rachelle Burk or *Something Stinks!* by Gail Hedrick), realistic science fiction, books in our Galactic Academy of Science series, science-based adventure tales, and the occasional picture book with a science theme, such as appreciation of the stars and constellations in *Elizabeth's Constellation Quilt* by Olivia Fu. A graphic novel about science would also be welcome."

NONFICTION Rarely publishes nonfiction. Book would need to be sold to trade, not just the school market.

HOW TO CONTACT Submit completed ms electronically. Receives 20 queries and 20 mss/year. Responds in 1 month to queries and proposals, and 2 months to mss. Publishes ms 8 months after acceptance.

TERMS Pays authors 8-12% royalties on retail price. Pays $500 advance. Catalog available online. Guidelines available on request for SASE.

TIPS "Please don't submit to us if your book is not about science. We don't accept generic books about animals or books with glaring scientific errors in the first chapter. That said, the book should be fun to read and the science content can be subtle. We work closely with authors, including first-time authors, to edit and improve their books. As a small publisher, the greatest benefit we can offer is this friendly and respectful partnership with authors."

✛ TUTTLE PUBLISHING

364 Innovation Dr., Editorial Acquisitions, North Clarendon VT 05759. (800)526-2778. **Fax:** (800)329-8885. **Website:** www.tuttlepublishing.com. **Contact:** Editorial acquisitions. "Since 1948, Tuttle has been a leader in the field of Asian cultures, language, and martial arts. Genres include children's books. Today, we currently have a backlist of 6,000 titles and publish 150 new titles per year." **Publishes 150 titles/year.**

FICTION Publishes children's craft, origami, and activity kits, folktales, celebrations, customs, and traditions, and young adult.

HOW TO CONTACT If you wish to submit a project for consideration for publication, please send a complete book proposal consisting of: a cover letter, annotated table of contents, and 1-2 sample chapters. Include a description of your target audience and comparison titles.

ⒶTYNDALE HOUSE PUBLISHERS, INC.

351 Executive Dr., Carol Stream IL 60188. (800)323-9400. **Fax:** (800)684-0247. **Website:** www.tyndale.com. "Tyndale House publishes practical, user-friendly Christian books for the home and family." Publishes hardcover and trade paperback originals and mass paperback reprints. **Publishes 15 titles/year.**

FICTION "Christian truths must be woven into the story organically. No short story collections. Youth books: character building stories with Christian perspective. Especially interested in ages 10-14. We primarily publish Christian historical romances, with occasional contemporary, suspense, or standalones."

HOW TO CONTACT *Agented submissions only. No unsolicited mss.*

ILLUSTRATION Uses full-color for book covers, b&w or color spot illustrations for some nonfiction.

Illustrations only: Query with photocopies (color or b&w) of samples, résumé.

PHOTOGRAPHY Buys photos from freelancers. Works on assignment only.

TERMS Pays negotiable royalty. Pays negotiable advance. Guidelines online.

TIPS "All accepted mss will appeal to evangelical Christian children and parents."

Ⓐ VIKING CHILDREN'S BOOKS

375 Hudson St., New York NY 10014. **Website:** www.penguin.com. "Viking Children's Books is known for humorous, quirky picture books, in addition to more traditional fiction. We publish the highest quality fiction, nonfiction, and picture books for pre-schoolers through young adults." *Does not accept unsolicited submissions.* Publishes hardcover originals. **Publishes 70 titles/year.**

FICTION All levels: adventure, animal, contemporary, fantasy, history, humor, multicultural, nature/environment, poetry, problem novels, romance, science fiction, sports, suspense/mystery.

NONFICTION All levels: biography, concept, history, multicultural, music/dance, nature/environment, science, and sports.

HOW TO CONTACT *Agented submissions only.* Responds in 6 months. Publishes book 1-2 years after acceptance.

ILLUSTRATION Works with 30 illustrators/year. Responds to artist's queries/submissions only if interested. Samples returned with SASE only or samples filed. Originals returned at job's completion.

TERMS Pays 2-10% royalty on retail price or flat fee. Pays negotiable advance.

TIPS "No 'cartoony' or mass-market submissions for picture books."

WESTERN PSYCHOLOGICAL SERVICES

625 Alaska Ave., Torrance CA 90503. (424)201-8800 or (800)648-8857. **Fax:** (424)201-6950. **Website:** www.wpspublish.com. "Western Psychological Services publishes psychological and educational assessments that practitioners trust. Our products allow helping professionals to accurately screen, diagnose, and treat people in need. WPS publishes practical books and games used by therapists, counselors, social workers, and others in the helping professions who work with children and adults." Publishes psychological and educational assessments and some trade paperback

originals. **Publishes 2 titles/year. 90% of books from first-time authors. 95% from unagented writers.**

NONFICTION "We publish children's books dealing with feelings, anger, social skills, autism, family problems."

HOW TO CONTACT Submit complete ms. 60 queries received/year. 30 mss received/year. Responds in 2 months to queries. Publishes ms 1 year after acceptance.

TERMS Pays 5-10% royalty on wholesale price. Book catalog available free. Guidelines online.

WHITE MANE KIDS

73 W. Burd St., P.O. Box 708, Shippensburg PA 17257. (717)532-2237. **Fax:** (717)532-6110. **E-mail:** marketing@whitemane.com. **Website:** www.whitemane.com. **Contact:** Harold Collier, acquisitions editor.

FICTION Middle readers, young adults: history (primarily American Civil War). Average word length: middle readers—30,000. Does not publish picture books.

NONFICTION Middle readers, young adults: history. Average word length: middle readers—30,000. Does not publish picture books.

HOW TO CONTACT Query. Submit outline/synopsis and 2-3 sample chapters. Book proposal form on website. Responds to queries in 1 month, mss in 6-9 months. Publishes book 18 months after acceptance.

ILLUSTRATION Works with 4 illustrators/year. Illustrations used for cover art only. Responds only if interested. Samples returned with SASE.

PHOTOGRAPHY Buys stock and assigns work. Submit cover letter and portfolio.

TERMS Pays authors royalty of 7-10%. Pays illustrators and photographers by the project. Book catalog and writer's guidelines available for SASE.

TIPS "Make your work historically accurate. We are interested in historically accurate fiction for middle and young adult readers. We do *not* publish picture books. Our primary focus is the American Civil War and some America Revolution topics."

ALBERT WHITMAN & COMPANY

250 S. Northwest Hwy., Suite 320, Park Ridge IL 60068. (800)255-7675. **Fax:** (847)581-0039. **E-mail:** submissions@albertwhitman.com. **Website:** www.albertwhitman.com. Albert Whitman & Company publishes books for the trade, library, and school library market. Interested in reviewing the following types of projects: Picture book mss for ages 2-8; novels and chapter books for ages 8-12; young adult novels; nonfiction for ages 3-12 and young adult; art samples showing pictures of children. Best known for the classic series The Boxcar Children® Mysteries. "We are no longer reading unsolicited queries and mss sent through the US mail. We now require these submissions to be sent by e-mail. You must visit our website for our guidelines, which include instructions for formatting your e-mail. E-mails that do not follow this format may not be read. We read every submission within 4 months of receipt, but we can no longer respond to every one. If you do not receive a response from us after four months, we have declined to publish your submission." Publishes in original hardcover, paperback, boardbooks. **Publishes 60 titles/year. 10% of books from first-time authors. 50% from unagented writers.**

FICTION Picture books (up to 1,000 words); middle-grade (up to 35,000 words); young adult (up to 70,000 words).

NONFICTION Picture books up to 1,000 words.

HOW TO CONTACT For picture books, submit cover letter and brief description. For middle-grade and young adult, send query, synopsis, and first 3 chapters. Submit cover letter, brief description.

TERMS Guidelines online.

WILLIAMSON BOOKS

6100 Tower Circle, Suite 210, Franklin TN 37067. **Website:** www.idealsbooks.com. Publishes "very successful nonfiction series (Kids Can! Series) on subjects such as history, science, arts/crafts, geography, diversity, multiculturalism. Little Hands series for ages 2-6, Kaleidoscope Kids series (age 7 and up) and Quick Starts for Kids! series (ages 8 and up) Our goal is to help every child fulfill his/her potential and experience personal growth."

NONFICTION Hands-on active learning books, animals, African-American, arts/crafts, Asian, biography, diversity, careers, geography, health, history, hobbies, how-to, math, multicultural, music/dance, nature/environment, Native American, science, writing and journaling. Does not want to see textbooks, picture books, fiction. "Looking for all things African American, Asian American, Hispanic, Latino, and Native American including crafts and traditions, as well as their history, biographies, and personal retrospectives of growing up in US for grades K-8. We are looking for books in which learning and doing are inseparable."

HOW TO CONTACT Query with annotated table of contents (or synopsis) and 1 sample chapter. Responds in 4 months. Publishes book 1 year after acceptance.

ILLUSTRATION Works with at least 2 illustrators and 2 designers/year. "We're interested in expanding our illustrator and design freelancers." Uses primarily 2-color and 4-color artwork. Responds only if interested. Samples returned with SASE; samples filed.

PHOTOGRAPHY Buys photos from freelancers; uses archival art and photos.

TERMS Pays authors advance against future royalties based on wholesale price or purchases outright. Pays illustrators by the project. Pays photographers per photo. Guidelines online.

WINDWARD PUBLISHING

Finney Company, 5995 149th St. W., Suite 105, Apple Valley MN 55124. **E-mail:** info@finneyco.com. **Website:** www.finneyco.com. **Contact:** Alan E. Krysan, president. Windward publishes illustrated natural history, recreation books, and children's books. "Covers topics of natural history and science, outdoor recreation, and children's literature. Its principal markets are book, retail, and specialty stores. While primarily a nonfiction publisher, we will occasionally accept fiction books with educational value." Publishes trade paperback originals. **Publishes 6-10 titles/year. 50% of books from first-time authors. 100% from unagented writers.**

NONFICTION Young readers, middle readers, young adults: activity books, animal, careers, nature/environment, science. Young adults: textbooks.

HOW TO CONTACT Query with SASE. Does not accept e-mail or fax submissions. 120 queries received/year. 50 mss received/year. Responds in 8-10 weeks to queries. Publishes book 1 year after acceptance.

ILLUSTRATION Reviews ms/illustration packages from artists. Send ms with dummy. Query with samples. Responds in 2 months. Samples returned with SASE; samples filed.

TERMS Pays 10% royalty on wholesale price. Pays advance.

Ⓐ PAULA WISEMAN BOOKS

1230 Sixth Ave., New York NY 10020. (212)698-7000. **Fax:** (212)698-2796. **E-mail:** paula.wiseman@simo-

nandschuster.com; sylvie.frank@simonandschuster.com; sarahjane.abbott@simonandschuster.com. **Website:** kids.simonandschuster.com. Paula Wiseman Books is an imprint of Simon & Schuster Children's Publishing that launched in 2003. It has since gone on to publish over 70 award-winning and bestselling books, including picture books, novelty books, and novels. The imprint focuses on stories and art that are childlike, timeless, innovative, and centered in emotion. "We strive to publish books that entertain while expanding the experience of the children who read them, as well as stories that will endure, including those based in other cultures. We are committed to publishing new talent in both picture books and novels. We are actively seeking submissions from new and published authors and artists through agents and from SCBWI conferences." **Publishes 30 titles/year. 15% of books from first-time authors.**

FICTION Considers all categories. Average word length: picture books—500; others standard length.

NONFICTION Picture books: animal, biography, concept, history, nature/environment. Young readers: animal, biography, history, multicultural, nature/environment, sports. Average word length: picture books—500; others standard length.

HOW TO CONTACT Does not accept unsolicited or unagented mss.

ILLUSTRATION Works with 15 illustrators/year. Does not accept unsolicited or unagented illustrations or submissions.

WOODBINE HOUSE

6510 Bells Mill Rd., Bethesda MD 20817. (301)897-3570. **Fax:** (301)897-5838. **E-mail:** info@woodbinehouse.com. **Website:** www.woodbinehouse.com. **Contact:** Acquisitions editor. Woodbine House publishes books for or about individuals with disabilities to help those individuals and their families live fulfilling and satisfying lives in their homes, schools, and communities. Publishes trade paperback originals. **Publishes 10 titles/year. 15% of books from first-time authors. 90% from unagented writers.**

FICTION Receptive to stories regarding developmental and intellectual disabilities, e.g., autism and cerebral palsy.

NONFICTION Publishes books for and about children with disabilities. No personal accounts or general parenting guides.

HOW TO CONTACT Submit complete ms with SASE. Submit outline, and at least 3 sample chapters. Responds in 3 months to queries. Publishes ms 18 months after acceptance.

TERMS Pays 10-12% royalty. Guidelines online.

TIPS "Do not send us a proposal on the basis of this description. Examine our catalog or website and a couple of our books to make sure you are on the right track. Put some thought into how your book could be marketed (aside from in bookstores). Keep cover letters concise and to the point; if it's a subject that interests us, we'll ask to see more."

ⓐ WORDSONG

815 Church St., Honesdale PA 18431. **Fax:** (570)253-0179. **Website:** www.wordsongpoetry.com. "We publish fresh voices in contemporary poetry."

HOW TO CONTACT Responds to mss in 3 months.

ILLUSTRATION Works with 7 illustrators/year. Reviews ms/illustration packages from artists. Submit complete ms with 1 or 2 pieces of art. Illustrations only: Query with samples best suited to the art (postcard, 8½×11, etc.). Label package "Art Sample Submission." Responds only if interested. Samples returned with SASE.

PHOTOGRAPHY Assigns work.

TERMS Pays authors royalty or work purchased outright.

TIPS "Collections of original poetry, not anthologies, are our biggest need at this time. Keep in mind that the strongest collections demonstrate a facility with multiple poetic forms and offer fresh images and insights. Check to see what's already on the market and on our website before submitting."

WORKMAN BOOKS

225 Varick St., New York NY 10014. **Website:** www.workman.com.

TERMS "When submitting work to us, please send as much of the proposed book or calendar as possible. If the project contains or consists primarily of artwork, please send photocopies or another type of reproduction. We will contact you if we need to see the originals. We prefer electronic submissions, which may be sent to submissions@workman.com in the form of a Word document or a PDF. You may also send hard-copy submissions to the attention of the editorial department. For children's book submissions, please note that we do not publish picture books or middle-grade

and young adult fiction. Send your submissions to the attention of the Children's Department."

WORLD BOOK, INC.

180 N. LaSalle St., Suite 900, Chicago IL 60601. (312)729-5800. **Fax:** (312)729-5600. **E-mail:** service@worldbook.com. **Website:** www.worldbook.com. World Book, Inc. (publisher of The World Book Encyclopedia) publishes reference sources and nonfiction series for children and young adults in the areas of science, mathematics, English-language skills, basic academic and social skills, social studies, history, and health and fitness. "We publish print and non-print material appropriate for children ages 3-14. WB does not publish fiction, poetry, or wordless picture books."

NONFICTION Young readers: animal, arts/crafts, careers, concept, geography, health, reference. Middle readers: animal, arts/crafts, careers, geography, health, history, hobbies, how-to, nature/environment, reference, science. Young adult: arts/crafts, careers, geography, health, history, hobbies, how-to, nature/environment, reference, science.

HOW TO CONTACT Query. Responds to queries in 2 months. Publishes book 18 months after acceptance.

ILLUSTRATION Works with 10-30 illustrators/year. Illustrations only: Query with samples. Responds only if interested. Samples returned with SASE; samples filed "if extra copies and if interested."

PHOTOGRAPHY Buys stock and assigns work. Needs broad spectrum; editorial concept, specific natural, physical, and social science spectrum. Model/property releases required; captions required. Submit cover letter, résumé, promo piece (color and b&w).

TERMS Payment negotiated on project-by-project basis.

WORLD WEAVER PRESS

E-mail: submissions@worldweaverpress.com. **Website:** www.worldweaverpress.com. **Contact:** WWP Editors. World Weaver Press publishes digital and print editions of speculative fiction at various lengths for adult, young adult, and new adult audiences. We believe in great storytelling. **Publishes 10-12 titles/year. 85% from unagented writers.**

FICTION "We believe that publishing speculative fiction isn't just printing words on the page — it's the act of weaving brand new worlds. Seeking speculative fiction in many varieties: protagonists who have strength, not fainting spells; intriguing worlds with well-developed settings; characters that are to die for (we'd rather find ourselves in love than just in lust)." Full list of interests on website. Does not want giant bugs, ghosts, post-apocalyptic and/or dystopia, angels, zombies, magical realism, surrealism, middle-grade (MG) or younger.

NONFICTION "We're interested in nonfiction that relates to pop culture and genre studies (i.e. essays on genre fiction/TV/film), folklore and fairy tale explorations, and books on writing and/or for genre writers. Unless you walked the Hobbit path to Mordor, we don't want your travelogue or memoir."

HOW TO CONTACT Query letter with first 5,000 words in body of e-mail. Queries accepted only during February and September annually, unless agented. Responds to query letters within 3 weeks. Responses to mss requests take longer. Publishes ms 6-24 months after acceptance.

TERMS Average royalty rate of 39% net on all editions. No advance. Catalog online. Guidelines online.

TIPS "Use your letter to pitch us the story, not talk about its themes or inception."

WORTHYKIDS/IDEALS

Worthy Publishing Group, 6100 Tower Circle, Suite 210, Franklin TN 37067. (615)932-7600. **E-mail:** idealsinfo@worthy-ideals.com. **Website:** www.idealsbooks.com. "WorthyKids/Ideals publishes 30-35 new children's titles a year, primarily for ages 2-8. Our backlist includes 400 titles, and we publish picture books, activity books, board books, and novelty and sound books covering a wide array of topics, such as Bible stories, holidays, early learning, history, family relationships, and values. Our bestselling titles include *The Story of Christmas*, *The Story of Easter*, *Seaman's Journal*, *How Do I Love You?*, *God Made You Special* and *A View at the Zoo*. Through our dedication to publishing high-quality and engaging books, we never forget our obligation to our littlest readers to help create those special moments with books."

FICTION WorthyKids/Ideals publishes fiction and nonfiction picture books for children ages 2-8. Subjects include holiday, inspirational, and patriotic themes; relationships and values; and general fiction. Picture book mss should be no longer than 800 words. Board book mss should be no longer than 250 words.

HOW TO CONTACT Submission guidelines available on website.

YALI BOOKS

Website: www.yalibooks.com. **E-mail:** yalibooks@gmail.com **Contact:** Kala and Ambika Sambasivan. Yali Books is an independent publisher of books with a focus on South Asian cultures. "We are open to hearing from writers and illustrators who would like to introduce the world to South Asia—the people, places and cultures of India, Pakistan, Bhutan, Nepal, Afghanistan, Bangladesh, and Sri Lanka. We are looking for stories that educate and entertain, with an emphasis on entertainment. We would like humor to be hallmark of Yali Books. We enjoy making people, particularly children, laugh!"

HOW TO CONTACT "Send a query letter and 3 sample chapters to yalibooks@gmail.com. For picture books, please send us the entire ms. Your entry must be original, unpublished, and not accepted by any other publisher or producer at the time of submission."

ILLUSTRATION "Send us your bio, a link to your portfolio, and 2 sample images. Submissions sent through social media will not be considered."

ZEST BOOKS

2443 Fillmore St., Suite 340, San Francisco CA 94115. (415)777-8654. **Fax:** (415)777-8653. **Website:** zestbooks.net. **Contact:** Dan Harmon, publishing director. Zest Books is a leader in young adult nonfiction, publishing books on entertainment, history, science, health, fashion, and lifestyle advice since 2006. Zest Books is distributed by Houghton Mifflin Harcourt.

HOW TO CONTACT Submit proposal.

ILLUSTRATION "If you are interested in becoming part of our team of illustrators, please send examples of printed work to adam@zestbooks.net."

TERMS Guidelines online.

TIPS "If you're interested in becoming a member of our author pool, send a cover letter stating why you are interested in young adult nonfiction, plus your specific areas of interest and specialties, your resume, 3-5 writing samples."

ZUMAYA PUBLICATIONS, LLC

3209 S. Interstate 35, Austin TX 78741. (512)537-3145. **Fax:** (512)276-6745. **E-mail:** business@zumayapublishing.com. **Website:** www.zumayapublications.com. **Contact:** Rie Sheridan Rose, acquisitions editor. Zumaya Publications is a digitally-based micro-press publishing mainly on-demand trade paperback and e-book formats. "We currently offer approximately

190 fiction titles in the mystery, science fiction, fantasy, historical, romance, LGBTQ, horror, and occult genres in adult, young adult, and middle reader categories. In 2016, we plan to officially launch our graphic and illustrated novel imprint, Zumaya Fabled Ink. We publish approximately 10-15 new titles annually, at least five of which are from new authors. We do not publish erotica or graphic erotic romance at this time. We accept only electronic queries; all others will be discarded unread. A working knowledge of computers and relevant software is a necessity, as our production process is completely digital." Publishes trade paperback and electronic originals and reprints. **Publishes 10-15 titles/year. 5% of books from first-time authors. 98% from unagented writers.**

FICTION "We are open to all genres, particularly GLBT and young adult/middle-grade, historical and western, New Age/inspirational (no overtly Christian materials, please), non-category romance, thrillers. We encourage people to review what we've already published so as to avoid sending us more of the same, at least, insofar as the plot is concerned. While we're always looking for good mysteries, especially cozies, mysteries with historical settings, and police procedurals, we want original concepts rather than slightly altered versions of what we've already published. We do not publish erotica or graphically erotic romance at this time." Does not want erotica, graphically erotic romance, experimental, literary (unless it fits into one of the house's established imprints).

NONFICTION "The easiest way to figure out what we're looking for is to look at what we've already done. Our main nonfiction interests are in collections of true ghost stories, ones that have been investigated or thoroughly documented, memoirs that address specific regions and eras from a 'normal person' viewpoint and books on the craft of writing. That doesn't mean we won't consider something else."

HOW TO CONTACT "A copy of our rules of submission is posted on our website and can be downloaded. They are rules rather than guidelines and should be read carefully before submitting. It will save everyone time and frustration." Electronic query only. 1,000 queries received/year. 50 mss requested/year. Responds in 3 months to queries and proposals; 6 months to mss. Publishes book 2 years after acceptance.

TERMS Pay 20% of net on paperbacks, net defined as cover price minus printing and other associated costs; 50% of net on all e-books. Does not pay advance. Guidelines online.

TIPS "We're catering to readers who may have loved last year's best seller but not enough to want to read 10 more just like it. Have something different. If it does not fit standard pigeonholes, that's a plus. On the other hand, it has to have an audience. And if you're not prepared to work with us on promotion and marketing, particularly via social media, it would be better to look elsewhere."

CANADIAN & INTERNATIONAL BOOK PUBLISHERS

///

◐ ALLEN & UNWIN

406 Albert St., East Melbourne VIC 3002, Australia. (61)(3)9665-5000. **E-mail:** fridaypitch@allenandunwin.com. **Website:** www.allenandunwin.com. Allen & Unwin publish more than 80 new books for children and young adults each year, many of these from established authors and illustrators. "However, we know how difficult it can be for new writers to get their work in front of publishers, which is why we've decided to extend our innovative and pioneering Friday Pitch service to emerging writers for children and young adults."

TERMS Guidelines online.

◐ ANDERSEN PRESS

20 Vauxhall Bridge Rd., London SW1V 2SA, United Kingdom. **E-mail:** andersoneditorial@randomhouse.co.uk. **Website:** www.andersenpress.co.uk. Andersen Press is a specialist children's publisher. "We publish picture books, for which the required text would be approximately 500 words (maximum 1,000), juvenile fiction for which the text would be approximately 3,000-5,000 words, and older fiction up to 75,000 words. We do not publish adult fiction, nonfiction, poetry, or short story anthologies."

HOW TO CONTACT Send all submissions by post: Query and full ms for picture books; synopsis and 3 chapters for longer fiction.

TERMS Guidelines online.

◑ ANNICK PRESS, LTD.

15 Patricia Ave., Toronto ON M2M 1H9, Canada. (416)221-4802. **Fax:** (416)221-8400. **Website:** www.annickpress.com. **Contact:** The Editors. "Annick Press maintains a commitment to high-quality books that entertain and challenge. Our publications share fantasy and stimulate imagination, while encouraging children to trust their judgment and abilities." *Does not accept unsolicited mss.* Publishes picture books, juvenile, and young adult fiction and nonfiction; specializes in trade books. **Publishes 25 titles/year. 20% of books from first-time authors. 80-85% from unagented writers.**

FICTION Publisher of children's books. Not accepting picture books at this time.

HOW TO CONTACT 5,000 queries received/year. 3,000 mss received/year. Publishes a book 2 years after acceptance.

TERMS Pays authors royalty of 5-12% based on retail price. Offers advances (average amount: $3,000). Pays illustrators royalty of 5% minimum. Book catalog and guidelines online.

◐◑ BLACK AND WHITE PUBLISHING

29 Ocean Dr., Edinburgh EH6 6JL, Scotland. **E-mail:** mail@blackandwhitepublishing.com. **Website:** blackandwhitepublishing.com. **Contact:** Alison McBride, publishing director. Black and White Publishing was founded in 1999. Since then, the business has grown

into one of Scotland's leading independent publishers with more than 300 books in print across a variety of genres. We are committed to publishing the best books from the most talented writers in the UK and beyond. "We produce an extensive range of titles, including general nonfiction, biography, sport, and humor, as well as selected fiction, young adult, and children's books."

HOW TO CONTACT If you would like us to consider your ms, please submit the following as a single Word document or PDF: a blurb, a one-page chapter-by-chapter breakdown of the entire book, the first 3 chapters or first 30 pages of your ms, a cover letter telling us about yourself and your writing experience, the readership for your book (it might help to highlight a similar title that has had success), and why your work stands out from the crowd. To send, add "New Submission" and the title of your book at the start of the e-mail subject field. Then e-mail your material to: submissions@blackandwhitepublishing.com. Responds in 3 months, if interested.

TIPS "Itchy Coo is our award-winning Scots language imprint for children. Producing timeless children's books written in Scots for all ages, which have included original works such as the Katy series of books and Animal ABC, as well as translations of bestselling favourite children's authors including Julia Donaldson (*The Gruffalo*) and David Walliams."

THE BRUCEDALE PRESS

P.O. Box 2259, Port Elgin ON N0H 2C0, Canada. (519)832-6025. **E-mail:** info@brucedalepress.ca. **Website:** brucedalepress.ca. The Brucedale Press publishes books and other materials of regional interest and merit, as well as literary, historical, and/or pictorial works. Publishes hardcover and trade paperback originals. **Publishes 3 titles/year. 75% of books from first-time authors. 100% from unagented writers.**

Accepts works by Canadian authors only. Book submissions reviewed November–January. Submissions to The Leaf Journal *accepted in September and March only. Mss must be in English and thoroughly proofread before being sent. Use Canadian spellings and style.*

HOW TO CONTACT 50 queries received/year. 30 mss received/year. Publishes book 1 year after acceptance.

TERMS Pays royalty. Book catalog online. "Unless responding to an invitation to submit, query first by

Canada Post with outline and sample chapter to book-length mss. Send full mss for work intended for children." Guidelines online.

TIPS "Our focus is very regional. In reading submissions, I look for quality writing with a strong connection to the Queen's Bush area of Ontario. All authors should visit our website, get a catalog, and read our books before submitting."

BUSTER BOOKS

16 Lion Yard, Tremadoc Rd., London WA SW4 7NQ, United Kingdom. (020)7720-8643. **Fax:** (022)7720-8953. **E-mail:** enquiries@mombooks.com. **Website:** www.busterbooks.co.uk. "We are dedicated to providing irresistible and fun books for children of all ages. We typically publish black and white nonfiction for children aged 8-12, and novelty titles (including doodle books)."

HOW TO CONTACT Prefers synopsis and sample text over complete ms.

TIPS "We do not accept picture book or poetry submissions. Please do not send original artwork, as we cannot guarantee its safety." Visit website before submitting.

CHILD'S PLAY (INTERNATIONAL) LTD.

Child's Play, Ashworth Rd. Bridgemead, Swindon, Wiltshire SN5 7YD, United Kingdom. **E-mail:** neil@childs-play.com; office@childs-play.com. **Website:** www.childs-play.com. **Contact:** Sue Baker, Neil Burden, ms acquisitions. Specializes in nonfiction, fiction, educational material, multicultural material. Produces 30 picture books/year; 10 young readers/year. "A child's early years are more important than any other. This is when children learn most about the world around them and the language they need to survive and grow. Child's Play aims to create exactly the right material for this all-important time." **Publishes 40 titles/year.**

"Due to a backlog of submissions, Child's Play is currently no longer able to accept any more mss."

FICTION Picture books: adventure, animal, concept, contemporary, folktales, multicultural, nature/environment. Young readers: adventure, animal, anthology, concept, contemporary, folktales, humor, multicultural, nature/environment, poetry. Average word length: picture books—1,500; young readers—2,000.

NONFICTION Picture books: activity books, animal, concept, multicultural, music/dance, nature/

environment, science. Young readers: activity books, animal, concept, multicultural, music/dance, nature/environment, science. Average word length: picture books—2,000; young readers—3,000.

HOW TO CONTACT Publishes book 2 years after acceptance.

ILLUSTRATION Accepts material from international illustrators. Works with 10 illustrators/year. Uses color artwork only. Reviews ms/illustration packages. For ms/illustration packages: Query or submit ms/illustration packages to Sue Baker, editor. Reviews work for future assignments. If interested in illustrating future titles, query with samples, CD, website address. Submit samples to Annie Kubler, art director. Responds in 10 weeks. Samples not returned. Samples filed.

TIPS "Look at our website to see the kind of work we do before sending. Do not send cartoons. We do not publish novels. We do publish lots of books with pictures of babies/toddlers."

CHRISTIAN FOCUS PUBLICATIONS

Geanies House, Fearn, Tain, Ross-shire Scotland IV20 1TW, United Kingdom. (44)1862-871-011. **Fax:** (44)1862-871-699. **E-mail:** submissions@christianfocus.com. **Website:** www.christianfocus.com. **Contact:** Director of Publishing. Specializes in Christian material, nonfiction, fiction, educational material. **Publishes 22-32 titles/year. 2% of books from first-time authors.**

FICTION Picture books, young readers, adventure, history, religion. Middle-grade: adventure, problem novels, religion. Young adult/teens: adventure, history, problem novels, religion. Average word length: young readers—5,000; middle-grade—max 10,000; young adult/teen—max 20,000.

NONFICTION All levels: activity books, biography, history, religion, science. Average word length: picture books—5,000; young readers—5,000; middle readers—5,000-10,000; young adult/teens—10,000-20,000.

HOW TO CONTACT Query or submit outline/synopsis and 3 sample chapters. Include Author Information Form from site with submission. Will consider electronic submissions and previously published work. Responds to queries in 2 weeks; mss in 3-6 months. Publishes book 1 year after acceptance.

ILLUSTRATION Works on 15-20 potential projects. "Some artists are chosen to do more than one. Some projects just require a cover illustration, some

require full color spreads, others black and white line art." **Contact:** Catherine Mackenzie, children's editor. Responds in 2 weeks only if interested. Samples are not returned.

PHOTOGRAPHY "We purchase only royalty-free photos from particular photographic associations. However portfolios can be presented to our designer." **Contact:** Daniel van Straaten. Photographers should send cover letter, résumé, published samples, client list, portfolio.

TIPS "Be aware of the international market in regards to writing style/topics as well as illustration styles. Our company sells rights to European as well as Asian countries. Fiction sales are not as good as they were. Christian fiction for youngsters is not a product that is performing well in comparison to nonfiction such as Christian biography/Bible stories/church history, etc."

✪ COTEAU BOOKS

Thunder Creek Publishing Co-operative Ltd., 2517 Victoria Ave., Regina SK S4P 0T2, Canada. (306)777-0170. **Fax:** (306)522-5152. **E-mail:** coteau@coteaubooks.com. **Website:** www.coteaubooks.com. **Contact:** Geoffrey Ursell, publisher. "Our mission is to publish the finest in Canadian fiction, nonfiction, poetry, drama, and children's literature, with an emphasis on Saskatchewan and prairie writers. De-emphasizing science fiction, picture books." Publishes chapter books for young readers aged 9-12 and novels for older kids ages 13-15, as well as ages 15 and up. Publishes trade paperback originals and reprints. **Publishes 12 titles/year. 25% of books from first-time authors. 90% from unagented writers.**

FICTION No science fiction or children's picture books.

NONFICTION *Canadian authors only.*

HOW TO CONTACT Query. Submit hard copy query, bio, 3-4 sample chapters, SASE. 200 queries received/year. 40 mss received/year. Responds in 3 months. Publishes book 1 year after acceptance.

TERMS Pays 10% royalty on retail price. Book catalog available free. Guidelines online.

TIPS "Look at past publications to get an idea of our editorial program. We do not publish romance, horror, or picture books, but we are interested in juvenile and teen fiction from Canadian authors. Submissions, even queries, must be made in hard copy only. We do not accept simultaneous/multiple submissions. Check our website for new submission timing guidelines."

CURIOUS FOX

Brunel Rd., Houndmills, Basingstoke Hants RG21 6XS, United Kingdom. **E-mail:** submissions@curi-ous-fox.com. **Website:** www.curious-fox.com. "Do you love telling good stories? If so, we'd like to hear from you. Curious Fox is on the lookout for UK-based authors, whether new talent or established authors with exciting ideas. We take submissions for books aimed at ages 3-young adult. If you have story ideas that are bold, fun, and imaginative, then please do get in touch!"

HOW TO CONTACT "Send your submission via e-mail to submissions@curious-fox.com. Include the following in the body of the e-mail, not as attachments: sample chapters, résumé, list of previous publishing credits, if applicable. We will respond only if your writing samples fit our needs."

ILLUSTRATION Please submit any illustrations/artwork by e-mail.

TERMS Guidelines online.

ECW PRESS

665 Gerrard St. E, Toronto Ontario M4M 1Y2, Canada. (416)694-3348. **E-mail:** info@ecwpress.com. **Contact:** Athmika Punja, corporate sales manager. "*Publishers Weekly* recognized ECW Press as one of the most diversified independent publishers in North America. ECW Press has published close to 1,000 books that are distributed throughout the English-speaking world and translated into dozens of languages. In the next year, we'll release 50+ new titles and will continue to support and promote a vibrant backlist that includes poetry and fiction, pop culture and political analysis, sports books, biography, and travel guides. We proudly publish an eclectic list of nonfiction, poetry, and fiction—but we don't publish in every category under the sun. We are committed to publishing diverse voices and experiences." **Note:** ECW accepts fiction and poetry submissions by Canadians only; there are no citizenship restrictions on writers submitting nonfiction.

TERMS Please send your proposal to submissions@ecwpress.com and include: a cover letter explaining what your book is about and why you think it's a good fit with ECW, a brief bio and publication history, a sample of the ms. Concerning samples, for poetry, approximately 10–15 pages is fine; for fiction and nonfiction, 15–25 pages is best. For nonfiction, please also send an outline of the entire work and suggested

marketing ideas. We heartily prefer electronic submissions; sending by e-mail will save you time, resources, and money. We prefer .doc or .docx format, but accept text in the body of your e-mail or PDFs."

EK BOOKS

230 Narone Creek Rd., Wollombi NSW 2325, Australia. For New Zealand specific titles: EK Books, Exisle Publishing Ltd., PO Box 60490, Titirangi, Waitakere 0642, New Zealand. "Our motto is 'great story, great characters, great message' and our books are aimed primarily at children aged 4-8. EK is a publisher of children's picture books only. We welcome submissions from literary agents, as well as new and established authors. Submissions should be sent to your nearest EK office. If in doubt, send to the Australian address."

HOW TO CONTACT E-query. We respond in 3 months if interested.

TERMS Submission guidelines available on website

FAT FOX BOOKS

The Den, P.O. Box 579, Tonbridge TN9 9NG, United Kingdom. (44)(0)1580-857249. **E-mail:** hello@fat-foxbooks.com. **Website:** fatfoxbooks.com. "Can you write engaging, funny, original, and brilliant stories? We are looking for fresh new talent as well as exciting new ideas from established writers and illustrators. We publish books for children from 3-14, and if we think the story is brilliant and fits our list, then as one of the few publishers who accepts unsolicited material, we will take it seriously. We will consider books of all genres."

HOW TO CONTACT For picture books, send complete ms; for longer works, send first 3 chapters and estimate of final word count.

ILLUSTRATION "We are looking for beautiful, original, distinctive illustration that stands out."

TERMS Guidelines online. Currently closed to submissions.

DAVID FICKLING BOOKS

31 Beamont St., Oxford OX1 2NP, United Kingdom. (018)65-339000. **Fax:** (018)65-339009. **Website:** www.davidficklingbooks.co.uk. **Contact:** Simon Mason, managing editor. David Fickling Books is a story house." For nearly 12 years, DFB has been run as an imprint—first as part of Scholastic, then of Random House. Now we've set up as an independent business." **Publishes 12-20 titles/year.**

FICTION Considers all categories.

HOW TO CONTACT Submit cover letter and 3 sample chapters as PDF attachment saved in format "Author Name_Full Title." Responds to mss in 3 months if interested.

ILLUSTRATION Reviews ms/illustration packages from artists. Illustrations only: query with samples.

PHOTOGRAPHY Submit cover letter, résumé, promo pieces.

TERMS Guidelines online. Closed to submissions. Check website for when they open to submissions and for details on the Inkpot competition.

TIPS "We adore stories for all ages, in both text and pictures. Quality is our watch word."

FITZHENRY & WHITESIDE, LTD.

195 Allstate Pkwy., Markham ON L3R 4T8, Canada. (905)477-9700. **Fax:** (905)477-9179. **E-mail:** fitzkids@fitzhenry.ca; godwit@fitzhenry.ca. **Website:** www.fitzhenry.ca/. **Contact:** Sharon Fitzhenry (adult books); Cheryl Chen (children's books). Emphasis on Canadian authors and illustrators, subject, or perspective. **Publishes 15 titles/year. 10% of books from first-time authors.**

HOW TO CONTACT For picture book submissions, please include the entire text. For novels, please submit a proposal/synopsis and the first 3 chapters only. Full guidelines on site. For works of nonfiction, please include a proposal with 2-3 sample chapters. Publishes book 1-2 years after acceptance.

ILLUSTRATION Works with approximately 10 illustrators/year. Reviews ms/illustration packages from artists. Submit outline and sample illustration (copy). Illustrations only: Query with samples and promo sheet. Samples not returned unless requested.

PHOTOGRAPHY Buys photos from freelancers. Buys stock and assigns work. Captions required. Uses black and white 8×10 prints; 35mm and 4×5 transparencies, 300+ dpi digital images. Submit stock photo list and promo piece.

TERMS Pays authors 8-10% royalty with escalations. Offers "respectable" advances for picture books, split 50/50 between author and illustrator. Pays illustrators by project and royalty. Pays photographers per photo.

TIPS "We respond to quality."

FLYING EYE BOOKS

62 Great Eastern St., London EC2A 3QR, United Kingdom. (44)(0)207-033-4430. **E-mail:** picturbksubs@nobrow.net. **Website:** flyingeyebooks.com. Flying Eye Books is the children's imprint of award-winning visual publishing house Nobrow. FEB seeks to retain the same attention to detail and excellence in illustrated content as its parent publisher, but with a focus on the craft of children's storytelling and nonfiction.

TERMS Guidelines online.

FORMAC LORIMER BOOKS

317 Adelaide St. W, Suite 1002, Toronto ON M5V 1P9, Canada. **Website:** www.formaclorimerbooks.ca/childrens-author-guidelines.html. **Contact:** Children's book editor.

"Our first priority is good writing, with believable characters, situations, and dialogue. All settings must be Canadian, with storylines that take place in the child or teen world with minimal adult involvement." James Lorimer & Company is currently seeking mss for the following series: sports stories series—hi-lo, sports-themed fiction for ages 10 to 13; side-streets series—edgy, issues-based novels for ages 13 and up; recordbooks series—nonfiction sports bios/issues for reluctant readers ages 12 and up.

HOW TO CONTACT See online guidelines. Respinds in 2-16 months

TERMS "We are only considering mss from Canadian writers. Mss should be typed and double-spaced on one side only of 8.5x11 white paper." All mss should be accompanied by a typed cover letter of no more than 1 page. Also include a short (1-2 page) synopsis that outlines both plot and sub-plot(s), setting, and characters. Include word count and the name of the series the ms is intended for. Also include a brief bio of yourself and a list of previously published works. Query letters, cover letters, and the first page of mss should include the author's name, address, and phone number. Please enclose a SASE for the return of your material.

TIPS "We strongly recommend that you review the relevant sections on our website, www.lorimer.ca, to familiarize yourself with the types of books we publish before sending in your submission. Lorimer welcomes submissions by first-time and emerging authors. As publishers of novels and short stories based on the original Degrassi TV series, we share the commitment evident in that pioneering series to serious engagement with themes and issues in a way that reaches a contemporary youth audience. At this time, we do not publish picture books, seasonal stories, cookbooks, board books, activity books, historical fiction, or fantasy. We are not interested in stories written to convey a lesson or moral."

🔵 FRANCES LINCOLN CHILDREN'S BOOKS

Frances Lincoln, 74-77 White Lion St., Islington, London N1 9PF, United Kingdom. (44)(20)7284-4009. **Website:** www.quartoknows.com. "Our company was founded by Frances Lincoln in 1977. We published our first books 2 years later, and we have been creating illustrated books of the highest quality ever since, with special emphasis on gardening, walking and the outdoors, art, architecture, design, and landscape. In 1983, we started to publish illustrated books for children. Since then we have won many awards and prizes with both fiction and nonfiction children's books." **Publishes 100 titles/year. 6% of books from first-time authors.**

FICTION Average word length: picture books—1,000; young readers—9,788; middle readers—20,653; young adults—35,407.

NONFICTION Average word length: picture books—1,000; middle readers—29,768.

HOW TO CONTACT Query by e-mail. Responds in 6 weeks to mss. Publishes book 18 months after acceptance.

ILLUSTRATION Works with approx 56 illustrators/year. Uses both color and b&w. Reviews ms/illustration packages from artist. Sample illustrations. Illustrations only: Query with samples. Responds only if interested. Samples are returned with SASE. Samples are kept on file only if interested.

PHOTOGRAPHY Buys stock images and assign work. Uses children, multicultural photos. Submit cover letter, published samples, or portfolio.

🅐🔵 FRANKLIN WATTS

Hachette Children's Books, Carmelite House, 50 Victoria Embankment, London EC4Y 0DZ, United Kingdom. (44)(20)7873-6000. **Fax:** (44)(20)7873-6024. **E-mail:** ad@hachettechildrens.co.uk. **Website:** www. franklinwatts.co.uk. Franklin Watts is well known for its high quality and attractive information books, which support the National Curriculum and stimulate children's enquiring minds. *Generally does not accept unsolicited mss.*

🔵➕ GECKO PRESS

P.O. Box 9335, Marion Square, Wellington 6141, New Zealand. **Website:** www.geckopress.co.nz. **Contact:** Editor. "Gecko Press, founded in 2005, is an independent publisher of curiously good books. We translate and publish children's books by some of the world's best writers and illustrators. We choose books that are excellent in story, illustration and design, with a strong 'heart factor.'"

FICTION "We always like to read picture book texts with energy and originality and a strong story/narrative (not "ideas" stories). Please note we do not publish educational books or didactic books. At the moment we are looking for junior fiction—novels for ages 7-12. We are looking for character-driven work, with a strong plot and voice. We also consider nonfiction and digital-only ideas."

HOW TO CONTACT For novel submissions, submit the first 2-3 chapters only. Does not accept e-mailed submissions. Will ask for electronic version if requesting full ms. Include a proposal. For novel submissions, include a synopsis. Include a SASE if you want your submission returned "We accept submissions if you are: a previously published author, or if your work is recommended to us by a person known to us whose opinion we trust." Responds within 16 weeks if interested.

➕💬 GROUNDWOOD BOOKS

128 Sterling Rd., Lower Level, Attn: Submissions, Toronto Ontario M6R 2B7, Canada. (416)363-4343. **Fax:** (416)363-1017. **E-mail:** submissions@groundwoodbooks.com. **Website:** www.groundwoodbooks.com. "We are always looking for new authors of novel-length fiction for children of all ages. Our mandate is to publish quality, character-driven literary fiction. We do not generally publish stories with an obvious moral or message, or genre fiction such as thrillers or fantasy."

FICTION Recently published: *Lost Girl Found*, by Leah Bassoff and Laura Deluca; *A Simple Case of Angels*, by Carolnie Adderson; *This One Summer*, by Mariko Tamaki and Jillian Tamaki.

NONFICTION Recently published: *The Amazing Travels of IBN Batutta*, by Fatima Sharafeddine, illustrated by Intelaq Mohammed Ali.

HOW TO CONTACT Submit a cover letter, synopsis, and sample chapters via e-mail. "Due to the large number of submissions we receive, Groundwood regrets that we cannot accept unsolicited manuscripts for picture books." Responds to mss in 6-8 months.

TERMS Offers advances. Visit website for guidelines: www.houseofanansi.com/Groundwoodsubmissions.aspx.

○⊕ HOT KEY BOOKS

Bonnier Publishing Fiction, 80-81 Wimpole St., London W1G 9RE, United Kingdom. **Website:** hotkeybooks.com/about-us. "We are Hot Key Books, a brand new division of Bonnier Publishing, publishing books for ages 9-19. We publish standout, quality fiction that people like to talk about. We publish books that people want to talk about, like *Maggot Moon* by Sally Gardner, *We Were Liars* by E. Lockhart, and *The Savages* by Matt Whyman."

FICTION Publishes young adult and middle-grade fiction.

HOW TO CONTACT "Due to volume of submissions, we are only able to get back to writers we are interested in pursuing. But we do read everything that comes in."

TERMS Send full ms via e-mail to: at enquiries@hotkeybooks.com along with a synopsis. Only accepts electronic submissions (any format but prefers Word or PDF).

○ KIDS CAN PRESS

25 Dockside Dr., Toronto ON M5A 0B5, Canada. (416)479-7000. **Fax:** (416)960-5437. **Website:** www.kidscanpress.com. **Contact:** Corus Quay, acquisitions.

○ *Kids Can Press is currently accepting unsolicited mss from Canadian adult authors only.*

FICTION Picture books, young readers: concepts. "We do not accept young adult fiction or fantasy novels for any age." Adventure, animal, contemporary, folktales, history, humor, multicultural, nature/environment, special needs, sports, suspense/mystery. Average word length: picture books—1,000-2,000; young readers—750-1,500; middle-grade—10,000-15,000; young adult—15,000+.

NONFICTION Picture books: activity books, animal, arts/crafts, biography, careers, concept, health, history, hobbies, how-to, multicultural, nature/environment, science, social issues, special needs, sports. Young readers: activity books, animal, arts/crafts, biography, careers, concept, history, hobbies, how-to, multicultural. Middle readers: cooking, music/dance. Average word length: picture

books—500-1,250; young readers—750-2,000; middle-grade—5,000-15,000.

HOW TO CONTACT Submit outline/synopsis and 2-3 sample chapters. For picture books, submit complete ms. Responds in 6 months only if interesed. Publishes book 18-24 months after acceptance.

ILLUSTRATION Works with 40 illustrators/year. Reviews ms/illustration packages from artists. Send color copies of illustration portfolio, cover letter outlining other experience. Contact: Art Director. Illustrations only: Send tearsheets, color photocopies. Responds only if interested.

○⊕ LANTANA PUBLISHING

London, United Kingdom. **E-mail:** info@lantanapublishing.com. **Website:** www.lantanapublishing.com. "Lantana Publishing is an independent publishing company committed to addressing the widespread lack of cultural diversity in children's publishing in the UK. As a publishing house with a strong social mission to increase the availability and visibility of diverse children's writing, we provide opportunities for authors and illustrators of minority backgrounds to create children's books that are resonant of their own experiences, places and cultures."

○ "We are currently focusing on picture books for ages 4-8."

FICTION "We love writing that is new, unusual, or quirky, and that interweaves mythic, historical, or spiritual elements into fun, contemporary stories full of color and excitement. We particularly like stories with modern-day settings and strong role models, positive relationships between communities and their environment, and evocative storylines that can provide a glimpse into the belief systems, traditions, or worldviews of other cultures." No nonfiction.

HOW TO CONTACT "If you are a picture book author, please send us the complete text of your ms. Illustrations are not necessary. If we like your story, we will commission an illustrator to work with you. A picture book ms should not normally exceed 1,000 words. If your story does exceed this word limit, please include a justification for its length in your covering letter." Responds in 6 weeks.

TERMS Pays royalty. Pays advance. Guidelines online.

○ LES ÉDITIONS DU VERMILLON

305 Saint Patrick St., Ottawa ON K1N 5K4, Canada. (613)241-4032. **Fax:** (613)241-3109. **E-mail:** lesedition-

sduvermillon@rogers.com. **Website:** www.leseditionsduvermillon.ca. Publishes trade paperback originals. **Publishes 15-20 titles/year.**
HOW TO CONTACT Responds in 6 months to mss. Publishes ms 18 months after acceptance.
TERMS Pays 10% royalty. Book catalog available free.

LITTLE TIGER PRESS

1 The Coda Centre, 189 Munster Rd., London SW6 6AW, United Kingdom. (44)(20)7385-6333. **Website:** www.littletigerpress.com. Little Tiger Press is a dynamic and busy independent publisher. Also includes imprints: Caterpillar Books and Stripes Publishing.
FICTION Picture books: animal, concept, contemporary, humor. Average word length: picture books—750 words or fewer.
HOW TO CONTACT "We are no longer accepting unsolicited mss. We will, however, continue to accept illustration submissions and samples."
ILLUSTRATION Digital submissions preferred please send in digital samples as PDF or JPG attachments to artsubmissions@littletiger.co.uk. Files should be flattened and no bigger than 1 mb per attachment. Include name and contact details on any attachments. Printed submissions: Please send in printed color samples as A4 printouts. Do not send in original artwork, as we cannot be held responsible for unsolicited original artwork being lost or damaged in the post. We aim to acknowledge unsolicited material and to return material if so requested within 3 months. Please include SAE if return of material is requested.

MANOR HOUSE PUBLISHING, INC.

452 Cottingham Crescent, Ancaster ON L9G 3V6, Canada. **E-mail:** mbdavie@manor-house.biz. **Website:** manor-house.ca. **Contact:** Mike Davie, president (novels and nonfiction). Publishes hardcover, trade paperback, and mass-market paperback originals reprints. **Publishes 5-6 titles/year. 90% of books from first-time authors. 90% from unagented writers.**
FICTION Stories should have Canadian settings and characters should be Canadian, but content should have universal appeal to wide audience.
NONFICTION "We are a Canadian publisher, so mss should be Canadian in content and aimed as much as possible at a wide, general audience. At this point in time, we are publishing books only by Canadian citizens residing in Canada."

HOW TO CONTACT Query via e-mail. Submit proposal package, clips, bio, 3 sample chapters. Submit complete ms. Queries and mss to be sent by e-mail only. "We will respond in 30 days if interested. Do not follow up unless asked to do so." Publishes book 1 year after acceptance.
TERMS Pays 10% royalty on retail price. Book catalog online. Guidelines available via e-mail.
TIPS "Our audience includes everyone—the general public/mass audience. Self-edit your work first; make sure it is well written with strong Canadian content."

MOGZILLA

8 Maud Jane's Close, Ivinghoe, Bucks LU7 9ED, United Kingdom. (44)(0)845-838-5526. **E-mail:** info@mogzilla.co.uk. **Website:** mogzilla.co.uk. "Mogzilla is an independent company on a mission. We want to get children into history through storytelling and fire their imagination with brilliant books and graphic novels."
FICTION "Mogzilla started off specializing in fiction for pre-teens and younger teenagers, although we are also getting into color books for younger readers and graphic novels, too. As a rough guide, a novel for this age range would be 45,000-75,000 words."
HOW TO CONTACT Query by mail or e-mail. Guidelines online.
TIPS "If we do not respond to your e-mail, please assume that we are not interested. We receive a great deal of proposals every week, and we regret that we cannot get into correspondence about why we did not want to progress your proposal."

NOSY CROW PUBLISHING

The Crow's Nest, 10a Lant St., London SE1 1QR, United Kingdom. (44)(0)207-089-7575. **Fax:** (44)(0)207-089-7576. **E-mail:** hello@nosycrow.com. **Website:** nosycrow.com. "We publish books for children 0-14. We're looking for 'parent-friendly' books, and we don't publish books with explicit sex, drug use, or serious violence, so no edgy young adult or edgy cross-over. And whatever new adult is, we don't do it. We also publish apps for children from 2-7, and may publish apps for older children if the idea feels right."
FICTION "As a rule, we don't like books with 'issues' that are in any way overly didactic."
HOW TO CONTACT Prefers submissions by e-mail, but post works if absolutely necessary. Prefers submis-

sions by e-mail, but post works if absolutely necessary. Guidelines online.

TIPS "Please don't be too disappointed if we reject your work! We're a small company and can only publish a few new books and apps each year, so do try other publishers and agents: publishing is necessarily a hugely subjective business. We wish you luck!"

⦿⊕ OFTOMES PUBLISHING

Website: www.oftomes.com. Oftomes Publishing is run by Benjamin Alderson, alternatively known as Benjaminoftomes, a UK booktuber.

FICTION Publishes young adult and teen fiction: series, paranormal, supernatural, fantasy, science fiction, romance, thriller, and horror.

TERMS "If you feel like your submission fits our family, then please follow our instructions. Send the first 5 chapters and summary of your novel to oftomes@oftomes.com. Oftomes does not offer an advance to authors looking to be published. But the royalty rates are fair and split 50% for both ecopy and physical sales. All novels will be edited before publication. We may ask for changes to be made which we ask that authors are open minded about."

☺ ON THE MARK PRESS

15 Dairy Ave., Napanee ON K7R 1M4, Canada. (800)463-6367. **Fax:** (800)290-3631. **Website:** www.onthemarkpress.com. Publishes books for the Canadian curriculum. **15% of books from first-time authors.**

PHOTOGRAPHY Buys stock images.

☺ ORCA BOOK PUBLISHERS

P.O. Box 5626, Stn. B, Victoria BC V8R 6S4, Canada. (250)380-1229. **Fax:** (877)408-1551. **E-mail:** orca@orcabook.com. **Website:** www.orcabook.com. **Contact:** Amy Collins, editor (picture books); Sarah Harvey, editor (young readers); Andrew Wooldridge, editor (juvenile and teen fiction); Bob Tyrrell, publisher (young adult, teen); Ruth Linka, associate editor (rapid reads). Publishes only Canadian authors. Publishes hardcover and trade paperback originals, and mass market paperback originals and reprints. **Publishes 30-50 titles/year. 20% of books from first-time authors. 75% from unagented writers.**

FICTION Picture books: animals, contemporary, history, nature/environment. Middle readers: contemporary, history, fantasy, nature/environment, problem novels, graphic novels. Young adults: ad-

venture, contemporary, hi-lo (Orca Soundings), history, multicultural, nature/environment, problem novels, suspense/mystery, graphic novels. Average word length: picture books—500-1,500; middle readers—20,000-35,000; young adult—25,000-45,000; Orca Soundings—13,000-15,000; Orca Currents—13,000-15,000. No romance, science fiction.

NONFICTION Publishes only Canadian authors.

HOW TO CONTACT Query with SASE. Submit proposal package, outline, clips, 2-5 sample chapters, SASE. Query with a SASE. 2,500 queries received/year; 1,000 mss received/year. Responds in 1 month to queries; 2 months to proposals and mss. Publishes book 12-18 months after acceptance.

ILLUSTRATION Works with 8-10 illustrators/year. Reviews ms/illustration packages from artists. Submit ms with 3-4 pieces of final art. "Reproductions only, no original art please." Illustrations only: Query with samples; provide résumé, online portfolio. Responds in 2 months. Samples returned with SASE; samples filed. Send 4-8 copies, digital proofs, tear sheets, press sheets.

TERMS Pays 10% royalty. Book catalog for 8.5x11 SASE. Guidelines online.

TIPS "Our audience is students in grades K-12. Know our books and know the market."

☺ PAJAMA PRESS

181 Carlaw Ave., Suite 207, Toronto ON M4M 2S1, Canada. **E-mail:** info@pajamapress.ca. **Website:** pajamapress.ca. "We publish picture books—both for the very young and for school-aged readers—as well as novels for middle-grade readers and for young adults aged 12+. Our nonfiction titles typically contain a strong narrative element."

HOW TO CONTACT Query with an excerpt. Guidelines on site.

Ⓐ☻ RANDOM HOUSE CHILDREN'S PUBLISHERS UK

20 Vauxhall Bridge Rd., London SW1V 2SA, United Kingdom. **Website:** www.randomhousechildrens.co.uk. *Only interested in agented material.* **Publishes 250 titles/year.**

FICTION Picture books: adventure, animal, anthology, contemporary, fantasy, folktales, humor, multicultural, nature/environment, poetry, suspense/mystery. Young readers: adventure, animal, anthology, contemporary, fantasy, folktales, humor, multicultural, nature/environment, poetry, sports, suspense/mystery. Middle readers: adventure, animal, anthology, contemporary, fantasy, folktales, humor, multicultural, nature/environment, problem novels, romance, sports, suspense/mystery. Young adults: adventure, contemporary, fantasy, humor, multicultural, nature/environment, problem novels, romance, science fiction, suspense/mystery. Average word length: picture books—800; young readers—1,500-6,000; middle readers—10,000-15,000; young adults—20,000-45,000.

ILLUSTRATION Works with 50 illustrators/year. Reviews ms/illustration packages from artists. Query with samples. Contact: Margaret Hope. Samples are returned with SASE (international reply coupons).

PHOTOGRAPHY Buys photos from freelancers. Contact: Margaret Hope. Photo captions required. Uses color or b&w prints. Submit cover letter, published samples.

TERMS Pays authors royalty. Offers advances.

TIPS "Although Random House is a big publisher, each imprint only publishes a small number of books each year. Our lists for the next few years are already full. Any book we take on from a previously unpublished author has to be truly exceptional. Mss should be sent to us via literary agents."

○ **REBELIGHT PUBLISHING, INC.**

23-845 Dakota St., Suite 314, Winnipeg Manitoba R2M 5M3, Canada. **Website:** www.rebelight.com. **Contact:** Editor. Rebelight Publishing is interested in "crack the spine, blow your mind" mss for middle-grade, young adult, and new adult novels. *Only considers submissions from Canadian writers.* Publishes paperback and electronic originals. **Publishes 6-10 titles/year. 25-50% of books from first-time authors. 100% from unagented writers.**

FICTION All genres are considered, provided they are for a middle-grade, young adult, or new adult audience. "Become familiar with our books. Study our website. Stick within the guidelines. Our tagline is 'crack the spine, blow your mind.' We are looking for well-written, powerful, fresh, fast-paced fiction. Keep us turning the pages. Give us something we just have to spread the word about."

HOW TO CONTACT Submit proposal package, including a synopsis and 3 sample chapters. Read guidelines carefully. Receive about 500 submissions/year. Responds in 3 months to queries and mss. Submis-

sions accepted via e-mail only. Publishes ms 12-18 months after acceptance.

TERMS Pays 12-22% royalties on retail price. Does not offer an advance. Catalog online or PDF available via e-mail request. Guidelines online.

TIPS "Review your ms for passive voice prior to submitting (and that means get rid of it)."

○ **RED DEER PRESS**

195 Allstate Pkwy., Markham ON L3R 4TB, Canada. (905)477-9700. **Fax:** (905)477-9179. **E-mail:** rdp@reddeerpress.com. **Website:** www.reddeerpress.com. **Contact:** Richard Dionne, publisher.

○ Red Deer Press is an award-winning publisher of children's and young adult literary titles.

FICTION Publishes young adult, adult science fiction, fantasy, and paperback originals "focusing on books by, about, or of interest to Canadians." Average print order: 5,000. First novel print order: 2,500. Distributes titles in Canada and the US, the UK, Australia, and New Zealand. Young adult (juvenile and early reader): contemporary. No romance or horror.

HOW TO CONTACT Accepts unsolicited mss. Query with SASE. No submissions on disk. Submit query with outline and sample chapter. Responds to queries in 6 months. Publishes ms 18 months after acceptance.

ILLUSTRATION Works with 4-6 illustrators/year. Illustrations only: Query with samples. Responds only if interested. Samples not returned; samples filed for six months. Canadian illustrators only.

PHOTOGRAPHY Buys stock and assigns work. Model/property releases required. Submit cover letter, résumé and color promo piece.

TERMS Pays illustrators and photographers by the project or royalty (depends on the project). Originals returned to artist at job's completion. Pays 8-10% royalty. Book catalog for 9 x 12 SASE.

TIPS "We're very interested in young adult and children's fiction from Canadian writers with a proven track record (either published books or widely published in established magazines or journals) and for mss with regional themes and/or a distinctive voice. We publish Canadian authors exclusively."

○ **RONSDALE PRESS**

3350 W. 21st Ave., Vancouver BC V6S 1G7, Canada. (604)738-4688. **Fax:** (604)731-4548. **Website:** ronsdalepress.com. **Contact:** Ronald B. Hatch (fiction, poetry, nonfiction, social commentary); Veronica Hatch (young adult novels and short stories). "Ronsdale Press is a Canadian literary publishing house that publishes 12 books each year, 4 of which are young adult titles. Of particular interest are books involving children exploring and discovering new aspects of Canadian history." Publishes trade paperback originals. **Publishes 12 titles/year. 40% of books from first-time authors. 95% from unagented writers.**

FICTION Young adults: Canadian novels. Average word length: middle readers and young adults—50,000.

NONFICTION Middle readers, young adults: animal, biography, history, multicultural, social issues. "We publish a number of books for children and young adults in the age 10-15 age range. We are especially interested in young adult historical novels. We regret that we can no longer publish picture books."

HOW TO CONTACT Submit complete ms. Submit complete ms. 40 queries received/year; 800 mss received/year. Responds to queries in 2 weeks; mss in 2 months. Publishes book 1 year after acceptance.

ILLUSTRATION Works with 2 illustrators/year. Reviews ms/illustration packages from artists. Requires only cover art. Responds in 2 weeks. Samples returned with SASE. Originals returned to artist at job's completion.

TERMS Pays 10% royalty on retail price. Book catalog for #10 SASE. Guidelines online.

TIPS "Ronsdale Press is a literary publishing house, based in Vancouver, and dedicated to publishing books from across Canada, books that give Canadians new insights into themselves and their country. We aim to publish the best Canadian writers."

SCHOLASTIC CHILDREN'S UK

Euston House, 24 Eversholt St., London VI NW1 1DB, United Kingdom. **E-mail:** contactus@scholastic.co.uk. **Website:** www.scholastic.co.uk.

Scholastic UK does not accept unsolicited submissions. Unsolicited illustrations are accepted, but please do not send any original artwork as it will not be returned.

TIPS "Getting work published can be a frustrating process, and it's often best to be prepared for disappointment, but don't give up."

SEAGRASS PRESS

Quarto Publishing, The Old Brewery, 6 Blundell St., London N7 9BH, United Kingdom. **Website:** www.quartoknows.com/SeagrassPress. **Contact:** The Quarto Group, Inc. Like the flora that inspired its name,

Seagrass Press aims to nurture young readers as they grow by offering a range of informative and entertaining titles. Children will learn about the fascinating world around them in nonfiction titles written by award-winning children's authors.

NONFICTION "Seagrass Press is always on the lookout for authors and artists with creative ideas that enhance and broaden our publishing list. Our children's books focus on all the wonders of the Earth."

SECOND STORY PRESS

20 Maud St., Suite 401, Toronto ON M5V 2M5, Canada. (416)537-7850. **Fax:** (416)537-0588. **E-mail:** info@secondstorypress.ca. **Website:** secondstorypress.ca.

FICTION Considers non-sexist, non-racist, and non-violent stories, as well as historical fiction, chapter books, picture books.

NONFICTION Picture books: biography.

HOW TO CONTACT Accepts appropriate material from residents of Canada only. "Send a synopsis and up to 3 sample chapters. If you are submitting a picture book you can send the entire ms. Illustrations are not necessary." No electronic submissions or queries. Guidelines on website.

SIMPLY READ BOOKS

501-5525 W. Blvd., Vancouver BC V6M 3W6, Canada. **E-mail:** go@simplyreadbooks.com. **Website:** www.simplyreadbooks.com. Simply Read Books is currently seeking mss in picture books, early readers, early chapter books, middle-grade fiction, and graphic novels.

HOW TO CONTACT Query or submit complete ms.

SWEET CHERRY PUBLISHING

Unit E, Vulcan Business Complex, Vulcan Rd., Leicester Leicestershire LE5 3EB, United Kingdom. **E-mail:** info@sweetcherrypublishing.com. **Website:** www.sweetcherrypublishing.com. Sweet Cherry Publishing publishes fiction for children ages 0-16. "We specialize in sets and series. Our aim is to give our readers the opportunity to revisit their favorite characters again and again, and to create stories that will stand the test of time. If you have written an original series with strong themes and characters, we would like to hear from you."

FICTION No erotica.

HOW TO CONTACT Submit a cover letter and a synopsis with 3 sample chapters via post or e-mail.

"Please note that we strongly prefer e-mail submissions."

ILLUSTRATION Submissions may include illustrations, but Sweet Cherry employs in-house illustrators and would therefore by unlikely to utilize them in the event of publication.

TERMS Offers a one-time fee for work that is accepted. Guidelines online.

TIPS "If your work is accepted, Sweet Cherry may consider commissioning you for future series."

TAFELBERG PUBLISHERS

Imprint of NB Publishers, P.O. Box 879, Cape Town 8000, South Africa. (27)(21)406-3033. **Fax:** (27) (21)406-3812. **E-mail:** kristin@nb.co.za. **Website:** www.tafelberg.com. **Contact:** Kristin Paremoer. General publisher best known for Afrikaans fiction, authoritative political works, children's/youth literature, and a variety of illustrated and non-illustrated nonfiction. **Publishes 10 titles/year.**

FICTION Picture books, young readers: animal, anthology, contemporary, fantasy, folktales, hi-lo, humor, multicultural, nature/environment, scient fiction, special needs. Middle readers, young adults: animal (middle reader only), contemporary, fantasy, hi-lo, humor, multicultural, nature/environment, problem novels, science fiction, special needs, sports, suspense/mystery. Average word length: picture books—1,500-7,500; young readers—25,000; middle readers—15,000; young adults—40,000.

HOW TO CONTACT Submit complete ms. Submit outline, information on intended market, bio, and 1-2 sample chapters. Responds to queries in 2 weeks; mss in 6 months. Publishes book 1 year after acceptance.

ILLUSTRATION Works with 2-3 illustrators/year. Reviews ms/illustration packages from artists. Send ms with dummy or e-mail and JPGs. Contact: Louise Steyn, publisher. Illustrations only: Query with brochure, photocopies, résumé, URL, JPGs. Responds only if interested. Samples not returned.

TERMS Pays authors royalty of 15-18% based on wholesale price.

TIPS "Writers: Story needs to have a South African or African style. Illustrators: I'd like to look, but the chances of getting commissioned are slim. The market is small and difficult. Do not expect huge advances. Editorial staff attended or plans to attend the following conferences: IBBY, Frankfurt, SCBWI Bologna."

TEXT PUBLISHING

Swann House, 22 Wiliam St., Melbourne VIC 3000, Australia. "Text Publishing is an independent, Melbourne-based publisher of literary fiction and nonfiction. Text won the Australian Book Industry Awards (ABIA) Small Publisher of the Year in 2012, 2013, and 2014. Text is broadly interested in publishing fiction and nonfiction, including upper primary and young adult. Please note that we are not accepting poetry or stage play scripts at present."

HOW TO CONTACT Accepts hard copy submissions only, in double-spaced and single-sided format. Send query letter, first three chapters and synopsis. "Make sure your ms has your full contact details, including e-mail address, so we can reach you easily if we need to. Do not send original material as it will not be held for collection or be returned. Due to the large number of mss we receive and consider we are unable to provide individual editorial advice."

THAMES & HUDSON

181A High Holborn, London WC1V 7QX, United Kingdom. **Website:** www.thamesandhudson.com. Thames & Hudson publishes approximately 180 new titles each year and has a current backlist of more than 2,000 titles. The company specializes in the arts (fine, applied, decorative, performing), archaeology and history, architecture, design, photography, travel, and popular culture—but also publishes in a variety of other areas, especially those of visual interest. Publishes some children titles. **Publishes 180 titles/year.**

NONFICTION From beautifully produced activity titles such as *My Big World* to fun, fact-filled surveys on art history or the environment, our children's books are guaranteed to inform, entertain and engage young minds everywhere.

HOW TO CONTACT "If we are interested, we will contact you for further information."

TERMS "If you are interested in submitting a book proposal to us, please keep in mind that we specialize in illustrated books in the categories you can see on this website. We do not publish works of fiction. If you have a proposal, please send a short outline only, without attachments, plus your CV via e-mail to: editorial@thameshudson.co.uk"

THISTLEDOWN PRESS LTD.

410 2nd Ave., Saskatoon SK S7K 2C3, Canada. (306)244-1722. **Fax:** (306)244-1762. **E-mail:** edito-

rial@thistledownpress.com. **Website:** www.thistle-downpress.com. **Contact:** Allan Forrie, publisher. "Thistledown originates books by Canadian authors only, although we have co-published titles by authors outside Canada. We do not publish children's picture books."

FICTION Young adults: adventure, anthology, contemporary, fantasy, humor, poetry, romance, science fiction, suspense/mystery, short stories. Average word length: young adults—40,000.

HOW TO CONTACT Submit outline/synopsis and sample chapters. *Does not accept mss.* Do not query by e-mail. "Please note: we are not accepting middle years (ages 8-12) nor children's mss at this time." See submission guidelines on website. Responds to queries in 6 months. Publishes book 1 year after acceptance.

ILLUSTRATION Prefers agented illustrators but "not mandatory." Works with few illustrators. Illustrations only: Query with samples, promo sheet, slides, tearsheets. Responds only if interested. Samples returned with SASE; samples filed.

TERMS Pays authors royalty of 10-12% based on net dollar sales. Pays illustrators and photographers by the project (range: $250-750). Book catalog on website.

TIPS "Send cover letter, including publishing history and SASE."

⊘ TRADEWIND BOOKS

202-1807 Maritime Mews, Granville Island, Vancouver BC V6H 3W7, Canada. (604)662-4405. **Website:** tradewindbooks.com. "Tradewind Books publishes juvenile picture books and young adult novels. Requires that submissions include evidence that author has read at least 3 titles published by Tradewind Books." Publishes hardcover and trade paperback originals. **Publishes 5 titles/year. 15% of books from first-time authors. 50% from unagented writers.**

FICTION Average word length: 900 words.

HOW TO CONTACT Send complete ms for picture books. *Young adult novels by Canadian authors only. Chapter books by US authors considered.* For chapter books/middle-grade fiction, submit the first 3 chapters, a chapter outline, and plot summary. Responds to mss in 2 months. Publishes book 3 years after acceptance.

ILLUSTRATION Works with 3-4 illustrators/year. Reviews ms/illustration packages from artists. Send illustrated ms as dummy. Illustrations only: Query

with samples. Responds only if interested. Samples returned with SASE; samples filed.

TERMS Pays 7% royalty on retail price. Pays variable advance. Book catalog and ms guidelines online.

Ⓐ◍ USBORNE PUBLISHING

83-85 Saffron Hill, London En EC1N 8RT, United Kingdom. (44)207430-2800. **Fax:** (44)207430-1562. **E-mail:** mail@usborne.co.uk. **Website:** www.usborne.com. "Usborne Publishing is a multiple-award-winning, worldwide children's publishing company publishing almost every type of children's book for every age from baby to young adult."

FICTION Young readers, middle readers: adventure, contemporary, fantasy, history, humor, multicultural, nature/environment, science fiction, suspense/mystery, strong concept-based or character-led series. Average word length: young readers—5,000-10,000; middle readers—25,000-50,000; young adult—50,000-100,000.

HOW TO CONTACT *Agented submissions only.*

ILLUSTRATION Works with 100 illustrators per year. Illustrations only: Query with samples. Samples not returned; samples filed.

PHOTOGRAPHY Contact: Usborne Art Department. Submit samples.

TERMS Pays authors royalty.

TIPS "Do not send any original work and, sorry, but we cannot guarantee a reply."

⊘ WHITECAP BOOKS, LTD.

314 W. Cordova St., Suite 210, Vancouver BC V6B 1 E8, Canada. (604)681-6181. **Fax:** (905)477-9179. **E-mail:** steph@whitecap.ca. **Website:** www.whitecap.ca. "Whitecap Books is a general trade publisher with a focus on food and wine titles. Although we are interested in reviewing unsolicited ms submissions, please note that we accept only submissions that meet the needs of our current publishing program. Please see some of most recent releases to get an idea of the kinds of titles we are interested in." Publishes hardcover and trade paperback originals. **Publishes 30 titles/year. 20% of books from first-time authors. 90% from unagented writers.**

FICTION No children's picture books or adult fiction.

NONFICTION Young children's and middle reader's nonfiction focusing mainly on nature, wildlife, and animals. "Writers should take the time to research our list and read the submission guidelines on our website. This is especially important for children's writers and cookbook authors. We will consider only submissions that fall into these categories: cookbooks, wine and spirits, regional travel, home and garden, Canadian history, North American natural history, juvenile series-based fiction. At this time, we are not accepting the following categories: self-help or inspirational books, political, social commentary or issue books, general how-to books, biographies or memoirs, business and finance, art and architecture, religion and spirituality."

HOW TO CONTACT Submit cover letter, synopsis, SASE via ground mail. See guidelines online. 500 queries received/year; 1,000 mss received/year. Responds in 2-3 months to proposals. Publishes book 1 year after acceptance.

ILLUSTRATION Works with 1-2 illustrators/year. Uses color artwork only. Reviews ms/illustration packages from artists. Query. Contact: Rights and Acquisitions. Illustrations only: Send postcard sample with tearsheets. Contact: Michelle Furbacher, art director. Responds only if interested.

PHOTOGRAPHY Accepts only digital photography. Submit stock photo list. Buys stock and assigns work. Model/property releases required.

TERMS Pays royalty and negotiated advance. Catalog and guidelines online.

TIPS "We want well-written, well-researched material that presents a fresh approach to a particular topic."

MAGAZINES

AQUILA

Studio 2 Willowfield Studios, 67a Willowfield Rd., Eastbourne BN22 8AP, England. (44)(132)343-1313. **E-mail:** editor@aquila.co.uk. **Website:** www.aquila. co.uk. *"Aquila* is an educational magazine for readers ages 8-13 including factual articles (no pop/celebrity material), arts/crafts, and puzzles." Entire publication aimed at juvenile market. Estab. 1993. Circ. 40,000.

FICTION Young readers: animal, contemporary, fantasy, folktales, health, history, humorous, multicultural, nature/environment, problem solving, religious, science fiction, sports, suspense/mystery. Middle readers: animal, contemporary, fantasy, folktales, health, history, humorous, multicultural, nature/environment, problem solving, religious, romance, science fiction, sports, suspense/mystery. Length: 1,000-1,150 words. Pays £90.

NONFICTION Young readers: animal, arts/crafts, concept, cooking, games/puzzles, health, history, how-to, interview/profile, math, nature/environment, science, sports. Middle readers: animal, arts/crafts, concept, cooking, games/puzzles, health, history, interview/profile, math, nature/environment, science, sports. Query. length: 600-800 words. Pays £90.

HOW TO CONTACT Accepts queries by mail, e-mail.

TERMS Pays on publication. Sample copy: £5. Guidelines online.

TIPS "We only accept a high level of educational material for children ages 8-13 with a good standard of literacy and ability."

ASCENT ASPIRATIONS

1560 Arbutus Dr., Nanoose Bay British Columbia C9P 9C8, Canada. **E-mail:** ascentaspirations@shaw. ca. **Website:** www.ascentaspirations.ca. **Contact:** David Fraser, editor. E-zine specializing in short fiction (all genres) and poetry, spoken work videos, essays, visual art. *"Ascent Aspirations* magazine publishes monthly online and once in print. The print issues are operated as contests. Please refer to current guidelines before submitting. *Ascent Aspirations* is a quality electronic publication dedicated to the promotion and encouragement of aspiring writers of any genre. The focus, however, is toward interesting experimental writing in dark mainstream, literary, science fiction, fantasy, and horror. Poetry can be on any theme. Essays need to be unique, current, and have social, philosophical commentary." Estab. 1997.

Magazine: 40 electronic pages, illustrations, photos. Receives 100-200 unsolicited mss/month. Accepts 40 mss/issue, 240 mss/year. Publishes ms 3 months after acceptance. Publishes 10-50 new writers/year. Has published work by Taylor Graham, Janet Buck, Jim Manton, Steve Cartwright, Don Stockard, Penn

Kemp, Sam Vargo, Vernon Waring, Margaret Karmazin, Bill Hughes, and recently spoken-word artists Sheri-D Wilson, Missy Peters, Ian Ferrier, Cathy Petch, and Bob Holdman.

FICTION Query by e-mail with Word attachment. Include estimated word count, brief bio, and list of publications. "If you have to submit by mail because it is your only avenue, provide a SASE with either international coupons or Canadian stamps only." Length: up to 1,000 words. Publishes short shorts. "No payment at this time."

NONFICTION Query by e-mail with Word attachment. Include estimated word count, brief bio, and list of publications. "If you have to submit by mail because it is your only avenue, provide a SASE with either international coupons or Canadian stamps only." Length: up to 1,000 words. "No payment at this time."

POETRY Submit 1-5 poems at a time. Prefers e-mail submissions (pasted into body of message or as attachment in Word); no disk submissions. "If you must submit by postal mail because it is your only avenue, provide a SASE with IRCs or Canadian stamps." Reads submissions on a regular basis year round. "We accept all forms of poetry on any theme. Poetry needs to be unique and touch the reader emotionally with relevant human, social, and philosophical imagery." Considers poetry by children and teens. Does not want poetry "that focuses on mainstream, overtly religious verse. No payment at this time.

HOW TO CONTACT Responds in 1 week to queries, 3 months to mss. Sometimes comments on rejected mss.

TERMS Rights remain with author. Guidelines by e-mail or on website. Accepts multiple submissions and reprints.

TIPS "Short fiction should first of all tell a good story, take the reader to new and interesting imaginary or real places. Short fiction should use language lyrically and effectively, be experimental in either form or content, and take the reader into realms where they can analyze and think about the human condition. Write with passion for your material, be concise and economical, and let the reader work to unravel your story. In terms of editing, always proofread to the point where what you submit is the best it possibly can be. Never be discouraged if your work is not accepted; it may just not be the right fit for a current publication."

ASK

E-mail: ask@askmagkids.com. **Website:** www.cricketmag.com. "*Ask* is a magazine of arts and sciences for curious kids ages 7-10 who like to find out how the world works." Estab. 2002.

NONFICTION Needs humor, photo feature, profile. "*ASK* commissions most articles but welcomes queries from authors on all nonfiction subjects. Particularly looking for odd, unusual, and interesting stories likely to interest science-oriented kids. Writers interested in working for *ASK* should send a résumé and writing sample (including at least 1 page unedited) for consideration." Length: 200-1,600.

HOW TO CONTACT Send submissions to: Art Submissions Coordinator, Cricket Media, 70 E. Lake St., Suite 800, Chicago IL 60601. Accepts queries by e-mail, online submission form.

ILLUSTRATION Illustrations are by assignment only. PLEASE DO NOT send original artwork. Send postcards, promotional brochures, or color photocopies. Be sure that each sample is marked with your name, address, phone number, and website or blog. Art submissions will not be returned.

PHOTOS

TERMS Rights vary. Byline given. Guidelines available online.

BABYBUG

Cricket Media, Inc., 13625A Dulles Technology Dr., Herndon VA 20171. (703)885-3400. **Website:** www.cricketmedia.com. "*Babybug*, a look-and-listen magazine, presents simple poems, stories, nonfiction, and activities that reflect the natural playfulness and curiosity of babies and toddlers." Estab. 1994. Circ. 45,000.

FICTION Wants very short, clear fiction. Submit complete ms via online submissions manager. Length: up to 6 sentences. Pays up to 25¢/word.

NONFICTION "First Concepts," a playful take on a simple idea, expressed through very short nonfiction. See recent issues for examples. Submit through online submissions manager: cricketmag.submittable.com/submit. Length: up to 6 sentences. Pays up to 25¢/word.

POETRY "We are especially interested in rhythmic and rhyming poetry. Poems may explore a baby's day, or they may be more whimsical." Submit via online submissions manager. Pays up to $3/line; $25 minimum.

HOW TO CONTACT Send submissions to: Art Submissions Coordinator, Cricket Media, 70 E. Lake St., Suite 800, Chicago IL 60601. Responds in 3-6 months to mss.

ILLUSTRATION "Please **do not** send original artwork. Send postcards, promotional brochures, or color photocopies. Be sure that each sample is marked with your name, address, phone number, and website or blog. Art submissions will not be returned."

TERMS Rights vary. Byline given. Pays on publication. 50% freelance written. Guidelines available online: www.cricketmedia.com/babybug-submission-guidelines.

TIPS "We are particularly interested in mss that explore simple concepts, encourage very young children's imaginative play, and provide opportunities for adult readers and babies to interact. We welcome work that reflects diverse family cultures and traditions."

BOYS' LIFE

Boy Scouts of America, P.O. Box 152079, 1325 W. Walnut Hill Ln., Irving TX 75015. **Website:** www.boyslife. org. **Contact:** Paula Murphey, senior editor; Clay Swartz, associate editor. *Boys' Life* is a monthly four-color general interest magazine for boys 7-18, most of whom are Cub Scouts, Boy Scouts, or Venturers. Estab. 1911. Circ. 1.1 million.

NONFICTION Subjects of interest include scouting activities and general interests. Length: 500-1,500 words.

HOW TO CONTACT Query senior editor with SASE. No phone or e-mail queries. Responds to queries/mss in 2 months. Publishes ms approximately 1 year after acceptance. Accepts queries by mail.

ILLUSTRATION Buys 10-12 illustrations/issue; 100-125 illustrations/year. Works on assignment only. Reviews ms/illustration packages from artists. "Query first." Illustrations only: Send tearsheets. Responds to art samples only if interested. Samples returned with SASE. Original artwork returned at job's completion. Works on assignment only.

PHOTOS Photo guidelines free with SASE. Pays $500 base editorial day rate against placement fees, plus expenses. **Pays on acceptance.** Buys one-time rights.

TERMS Buys one-time rights. Byline given. Pays on acceptance. 75% freelance written. Prefers to work with published/established writers; works with small number of new/unpublished writers each year. Sample copy: $3.95 plus 9x12 SASE. Guidelines online. Pay ranges from $400-1,500.

TIPS "We strongly recommend reading at least 12 issues of the magazine before submitting queries. We are a good market for any writer willing to do the necessary homework. Write for a boy you know who is 12. Our readers demand punchy writing in relatively short, straightforward sentences. The editors demand well-reported articles that demonstrate high standards of journalism. We follow the *Associated Press* manual of style and usage. Learn and read our publications before submitting anything."

BREAD FOR GOD'S CHILDREN

P.O. Box 1017, Arcadia FL 34265. (863)494-6214. **E-mail:** bread@breadministries.org. **Website:** www.breadministries.org. **Contact:** Judith M. Gibbs, editor. An interdenominational Christian teaching publication published 4-6 times/year written to aid children and youth in leading a Christian life. Estab. 1972. Circ. 10,000 (US and Canada).

FICTION "We are looking for writers who have a solid knowledge of Biblical principles and are concerned for the youth of today living by those principles. Stories must be well written, with the story itself getting the message across—no preaching, moralizing, or tag endings." Young readers, middle readers, young adult/teen: adventure, religious, problem-solving, sports. Looks for "teaching stories that portray Christian lifestyles without preaching." Send complete ms. Length: 600-800 words for young children; 900-1,500 words for older children. Pays $40-50.

NONFICTION All levels: how-to articles. "We do not want anything detrimental to solid family values. Most topics will fit if they are slanted to our basic needs." Send complete ms. Length: 500-800 words.

HOW TO CONTACT Responds in 6 months to mss. Publishes ms an average of 6 months after acceptance. Accepts queries by mail.

ILLUSTRATION "The only illustrations we purchase are those occasional good ones accompanying an accepted story."

TERMS Pays on publication. Pays $30-50 for stories; $30 for articles. Sample copies free for 9x12 SAE and 5 first-class stamps (for 2 copies). Buys first rights. Byline given. No kill fee. 10% freelance written. Sample copy for 9x12 SAE and 5 first-class stamps. Guidelines for #10 SASE.

TIPS "We want stories or articles that illustrate overcoming obstacles by faith and living solid, Christian lives. Know our publication and what we have used in the past. Know the readership and publisher's guidelines. Stories should teach the value of morality and honesty without preaching. Edit carefully for content and grammar."

BRILLIANT STAR

1233 Central St., Evanston IL 60201. (847)853-2354. **E-mail:** brilliant@usbnc.org, sengle@usbnc.org. **Website:** www.brilliantstarmagazine.org. **Contact:** Susan Engle, associate editor. "*Brilliant Star* presents Bahá'í history and principles through fiction, nonfiction, activities, interviews, puzzles, cartoons, games, music, and art. Universal values of good character, such as kindness, courage, creativity, and helpfulness are incorporated into the magazine." Estab. 1969.

FICTION We print fiction with kids 10-12 as the protagonists who resolve their problems themselves. Submit complete ms. Length: 700-1,400 words. Pays 2 contributor's copies.

NONFICTION Middle readers: arts/crafts, games/puzzles, geography, how-to, humorous, multicultural, nature/environment, religion, social issues. Query. Length: 300-700 words. Pays 2 contributor's copies.

POETRY "We only publish poetry written by children at the moment."

HOW TO CONTACT Accepts queries by e-mail.

ILLUSTRATION Reviews ms/illustration packages from artists. Illustrations only; query with samples. Contact: Aaron Kreader, graphic designer, at brilliant@usbnc.org. Responds only if interested. Samples kept on file. Credit line given.

PHOTOS Buys photos with accompanying ms only. Model/property release required; captions required. Responds only if interested.

TERMS Buys first rights and reprint rights for mss, artwork, and photos. Byline given. Guidelines available for SASE or via e-mail.

TIPS "*Brilliant Star*'s content is developed with a focus on children in their 'tween' years, ages 8-12. This is a period of intense emotional, physical, and psychological development. Familiarize yourself with the interests and challenges of children in this age range. Protagonists in our fiction are usually in the upper part of our age range: 10-12 years old. They solve their problems without adult intervention. We appreciate seeing a sense of humor but not related to bodily functions or put-downs. Keep your language and concepts age-appropriate. Use short words, sentences, and paragraphs. Activities and games may be submitted in rough or final form. Send us a description of your activity along with short, simple instructions. We avoid long, complicated activities that require adult supervision. If you think they will be helpful, please try to provide step-by-step rough sketches of the instructions. You may also submit photographs to illustrate the activity."

CADET QUEST MAGAZINE

1333 Alger St. SE, Grand Rapids MI 49507. (616)241-5616. **Fax:** (616)241-5558. **E-mail:** submissions@calvinistcadets.org. **Website:** www.calvinistcadets.org. **Contact:** Steve Bootsma, editor. Magazine published 7 times/year. *Cadet Quest Magazine* shows boys 9-14 how God is at work in their lives and in the world around them. Estab. 1958. Circ. 6,000.

FICTION "Fast-moving, entertaining stories that appeal to a boy's sense of adventure or to his sense of humor are welcomed. Stories must present Christian life realistically and help boys relate Christian values to their own lives. Stories must have action without long dialogues. Favorite topics for boys include sports and athletes, humor, adventure, mystery, friends, etc. They must also fit the theme of that issue of *Cadet Quest*. Stories with preachiness and/or clichés are not of interest to us." We seek the following subjects for middle readers, boys/early teens: adventure, arts/craft, games/puzzles, hobbies, humorous, multicultural, religious, science, sports. No fantasy, science fiction, fashion, horror, or erotica. Send complete ms by postal mail or e-mail (in body of e-mail; no attachments). Length: 1,000-1,300 words. Pays 5¢/word and 1 contributor copy.

NONFICTION Needs how-to, humor, inspirational, interview, personal experience, informational. Send complete ms via postal mail or e-mail (in body of e-mail; no attachments). Length: up to 1,500 words. Pays 5¢/word and 1 contributor's copy.

HOW TO CONTACT Responds in 2 months to mss. Publishes ms 4-11 months after acceptance.

ILLUSTRATION Works on assignment only. Reviews ms/illustration packages from artists.

PHOTOS Pays $5 each for photos purchased with ms.

TERMS Buys all rights, first rights, and second rights. Rights purchased vary with author and material. Byline given. Pays on acceptance. No kill fee. Sample copy for 9x12 SASE and $1.45 postage. Guidelines online.

TIPS "The best time to submit stories/articles is early in the year (January-April). Also remember readers are boys ages 9-14. Stories must reflect or add to the theme of the issue and be from a Christian perspective."

⊙ CHEMMATTERS

American Chemical Society, Education Division, 1155 16th St. NW, Washington DC 20036. (202)872-6164. **Fax:** (202)872-8068. **E-mail:** chemmatters@acs.org. **Website:** www.acs.org/chemmatters. **Contact:** Patrice Pages, editor; Cornithia Harris, art director. Covers topics of interest to teenagers and that can be explained with chemistry. *ChemMatters*, published 4 times/year, is a magazine that helps high school students find connections between chemistry and the world around them. Estab. 1983. Circ. 30,000.

NONFICTION Query with published clips. Pays $700-$1,000 for article.

HOW TO CONTACT Responds in 4 weeks to queries and mss. Publishes ms 6 months after acceptance. Accepts queries by mail, e-mail.

ILLUSTRATION Buys 3 illustrations/issue; 12 illustrations/year. Uses color artwork only. Works on assignment only. Reviews ms/illustration packages from artists. Illustrations only: Query with promo sheet, résumé. Samples returned with SASE; samples not filed. Credit line given.

PHOTOS Looking for photos of high school students engaged in science-related activities. Model/property release required; captions required. Uses color prints, but prefers high-resolution PDFs. Query with samples. Responds in 2 weeks.

TERMS Minimally buys first North American serial rights but prefers to buy all rights, reprint rights, electronic rights for ms. Buys all rights for artwork; nonexclusive first rights for photos. Byline given. Pays on acceptance. 100% freelance written. Sample copies and writer's guidelines free (available as e-mail attachment upon request).

TIPS "Be aware of the content covered in a standard high school chemistry textbook. Choose themes and topics that are timely, interesting, fun, *and* that relate to the content and concepts of the first-year chemistry course. Articles should describe real people involved with real science. Best articles feature young people making a difference or solving a problem."

CICADA

E-mail: cicada@cicadamag.com. **Website:** www.cricketmag.com/cicada. "*Cicada* is a young adult lit/comics magazine fascinated with the lyric and strange and committed to work that speaks to teens' truths. We publish poetry, realistic and genre fiction, essay, and comics by adults and teens. (We are also inordinately fond of Viking jokes.) Our readers are smart and curious; submissions are invited but not required to engage young adult themes." Bimonthly literary magazine for ages 14 and up. Publishes 6 issues/year. Estab. 1998. Circ. 6,000.

FICTION Areas of interest are realism, science fiction, fantasy, historical fiction. Wants everything from flash fiction to novellas. Length: up to 9,000 words. Pays up to 25¢/word.

NONFICTION Seeks narrative nonfiction (especially teen-written), essays on literature, culture, and the arts. Submit complete ms via online submissions manager (www.cricketmag.submittable.com). Length: up to 5,000 words. Pays up to 25¢/word.

POETRY Reviews serious, humorous, free verse, rhyming. Length: no limit. Pays up to $3/line ($25 minimum).

HOW TO CONTACT Responds in 3-6 months to mss. Accepts queries by online submission form.

ILLUSTRATION Send portfolio with samples to cicada@cricketmedia.com with "Online Portfolio Sample" as the subject line. For comic submissions, e-mail a short pitch/sketch(es) and a link to online portfolio with "Comic Submission" as the subject line. Please do not send final art. Please allow up to 3-6 months response time.

TERMS Rights vary. Pays after publication. Sample copy available online. Guidelines available online.

TIPS "Favorite writers, young adult and otherwise: Bennett Madison, Sarah McCarry, Leopoldine Core, J. Hope Stein, José Olivarez, Sofia Samatar, Erica Lorraine Scheidt, David Levithan, Sherman Alexie, Hilary Smith, Nnedi Okorafor, Teju Cole, Anne Boyer, Malory Ortberg. @cicadamagazine; cicadamagazine.tumblr.com."

CLICK

E-mail: click@cricketmedia.com. **Website:** www.cricketmag.com. "*Click* is a science and exploration magazine for children ages 3-7. Designed and written with the idea that it's never too early to encourage a child's natural curiosity about the world, *Click*'s 40 full-color pages are filled with amazing photographs, beautiful illustrations, and stories and articles that are both entertaining and thought-provoking."

🚫 *Does not accept unsolicited mss.*

NONFICTION Query by e-mail with résumé and published clips. Length: 200-500 words.

HOW TO CONTACT Send submissions to: Art Submissions Coordinator, Cricket Media, 70 E. Lake St., Suite 800, Chicago IL 60601. Buys print, digital, promotional rights. Accepts queries by e-mail.

ILLUSTRATION Illustrations are by assignment only. Please do not send original artwork. Send postcards, promotional brochures, or color photocopies. Be sure that each sample is marked with your name, address, phone number, and website or blog. Art submissions will not be returned.

TERMS Rights vary. Sample copy available online. Guidelines available online.

TIPS "The best way for writers to understand what *Click* is looking for is to read the magazine. Writers are encouraged to examine several past copies before submitting a query."

COBBLESTONE

E-mail: cobblestone@cricketmedia.com. **Website:** www.cricketmedia.com. "*Cobblestone* is interested in articles of historical accuracy and lively, original approaches to the subject at hand." American history magazine for ages 8-14. Circ. 15,000.

🚫 "*Cobblestone* stands apart from other children's magazines by offering a solid look at 1 subject and stressing strong editorial content, color photographs throughout, and original illustrations." *Cobblestone* themes and deadline are available on website or with SASE.

FICTION Needs adventure stories. Query by e-mail with published clips. Length: up to 800 words. Pays 20-25¢/word.

NONFICTION Needs historical, humor, interview, personal experience, photo feature. Query by e-mail with published clips. Length: 700-800 words for feature articles; 300-600 words for supplemental nonfiction. Pays 20-25¢/word.

POETRY Serious and light verse considered. Must have clear, objective imagery. Length: up to 100 lines/poem. Pays on an individual basis.

HOW TO CONTACT Send submissions to: Art Submissions Coordinator, Cricket Media, 70 E. Lake St., Suite 800, Chicago IL 60601. Accepts queries by e-mail.

ILLUSTRATION Illustrations are by assignment only. Please do not send original artwork. Send postcards, promotional brochures, or color photocopies. Be sure that each sample is marked with your name, address, phone number, and website or blog. Art submissions will not be returned.

TERMS Buys all rights. Byline given. Pays on publication. Offers 50% kill fee. 50% freelance written. Sample copy available online. Guidelines available online.

TIPS "Review theme lists and past issues to see what we're looking for."

COLLEGEXPRESS MAGAZINE

Carnegie Communications, LLC, 2 LAN Dr., Suite 100, Westford MA 01886. **E-mail:** info@carnegiecomm.com. **Website:** www.collegexpress.com. *CollegeXpress Magazine*, formerly *Careers and Colleges*, provides juniors and seniors in high school with editorial, tips, trends, and websites to assist them in the transition to college, career, young adulthood, and independence.

🚫 Distributed to 10,000 high schools and reaches 1.5 million students.

TIPS "Articles with great quotes, good reporting, good writing. Rich with examples and anecdotes. Must tie in with the objective to help teenaged readers plan for their futures. Seeks articles about current trends, policy changes, and information—regarding college admissions, financial aid, and career opportunities."

CRICKET

Website: www.cricketmag.com. *Cricket* is a monthly literary magazine for ages 9-14. Publishes 9 issues/year. Estab. 1973. Circ. 73,000.

FICTION Realistic, contemporary, historic, humor, mysteries, fantasy, science fiction, folk/fairy tales, legend, myth. No didactic, sex, religious, or horror stories. Submit via online submissions manager (www.cricketmag.submittable.com). Length: 1,200-1,800 words. Pays up to 25¢/word.

NONFICTION *Cricket* publishes thought-provoking nonfiction articles on a wide range of subjects: history, biography, true adventure, science and technology, sports, inventors and explorers, architecture and engineering, archaeology, dance, music, theater, and art. Articles should be carefully researched and include a solid bibliography that shows that research has gone beyond reviewing websites. Submit via online submissions manager (www.cricketmag.submittable. com). Length: 1,200-1,800 words. Pays up to 25¢/word.

POETRY *Cricket* publishes both serious and humorous poetry. Poems should be well-crafted, with precise and vivid language and images. Poems can explore a variety of themes, from nature, to family and friendships, to whatever you can imagine that will delight our readers and invite their wonder and emotional response. Length: up to 35 lines/poem. Most poems run 8-15 lines. Pays up to $3/line.

HOW TO CONTACT Send submissions to: Art Submissions Coordinator, Cricket Media, 70 E. Lake St., Suite 800, Chicago IL 60601. Responds in 3-6 months to mss. Accepts queries by online submission form.

ILLUSTRATION "Please do not send original artwork. Send postcards, promotional brochures, or color photocopies. Be sure that each sample is marked with your name, address, phone number, and website or blog. Art submissions will not be returned."

TERMS Byline given. Pays on publication. Sample copy available online. Guidelines available online.

TIPS Writers: "Read copies of back issues and current issues. Adhere to specified word limits." Would currently like to see more fantasy and science fiction. Illustrators: "Send only your best work and be able to reproduce that quality in assignments. Put name and address on *all* samples. Know a publication before you submit."

DIG INTO HISTORY

E-mail: dig@cricketmedia.com. **Website:** www.cricketmedia.com. *Dig into History* is an archaeology magazine for kids ages 10-14. Publishes entertaining and educational stories about discoveries, artifacts, and archaeologists. Estab. 1999.

FICTION Authentic historical and biographical fiction, adventure, and retold legends relating to the theme. Query by e-mail with brief cover letter, one-page outline, bibliography. Length: 750-1,000 words.

NONFICTION Query by e-mail with brief cover letter, one-page outline, bibliography. Length: 750-900 words for feature articles; 250-500 words for supplemental nonfiction; up to 700 words for activities.

HOW TO CONTACT Send submissions to: Art Submissions Coordinator, Cricket Media, 70 E. Lake St., Suite 800, Chicago IL 60601. Buys print, digital, promotional rights. Accepts queries by e-mail.

ILLUSTRATION Illustrations are by assignment only. Please do not send original artwork. Send postcards, promotional brochures, or color photocopies. Be sure that each sample is marked with your name, address, phone number, and website or blog. Art submissions will not be returned.

TERMS Pays on publication. Sample copy available online. Guidelines available online.

TIPS "We are looking for writers who can communicate archaeological concepts in a conversational, interesting, informative, and *accurate* style for kids. Writers should have some idea of where photography can be located to support their articles."

DRAMATICS MAGAZINE

Educational Theatre Association, 2343 Auburn Ave., Cincinnati OH 45219. (513)421-3900. **E-mail:** dcorathers@schooltheatre.org. **Website:** schooltheatre.org. **Contact:** Don Corathers, editor. *Dramatics* is for students (mainly high school age) and teachers of theater. The magazine wants student readers to grow as theater artists and become a more discerning and appreciative audience. Material is directed to both theater students and their teachers, with strong student slant. Tries to portray the theater community in all its diversity. Estab. 1929. Circ. 45,000.

FICTION Young adults: drama (one-act and full-length plays). "We prefer unpublished scripts that have been produced at least once." Does not want to see plays that show no understanding of the conventions of the theater. No plays for children, no Christmas or didactic "message" plays. Submit complete ms. Buys 5-9 plays/year. Emerging playwrights have better chances with résumé of credits. Length: 10 minutes to full length. Pays $100-500 for plays.

NONFICTION Needs how-to; profile; practical articles on acting, directing, design, production, and other facets of theater; career-oriented profiles of working theater professionals. Submit complete ms. Length: 750-3,000 words. Pays $50-500 for articles.

HOW TO CONTACT Publishes ms 3 months after acceptance. Accepts queries by mail, e-mail.

ILLUSTRATION Buys 3-8 illustrations/year. Works on assignment only. Arrange portfolio review; send résumé, promo sheets, and tearsheets. Responds only if interested. Samples returned with SASE; sample not filed. Credit line given. Pays up to $300 for illustrations.

PHOTOS Buys photos with accompanying ms only. Looking for "good-quality production or candid photography to accompany article. We very occasionally publish photo essays." Model/property release and captions required. Prefers hi-res JPG files. Will consider prints or transparencies. Query with résumé of credits. Responds only if interested.

TERMS Byline given. Pays on acceptance. Sample copy available for 9x12 SAE with four-ounce first-class postage. Guidelines available for SASE.

TIPS "Obtain our writers' guidelines and look at recent back issues. The best way to break in is to know our audience—drama students, teachers, and others interested in theater—and write for them. Writers who have some practical experience in theater, especially in technical areas, have an advantage, but we'll work with anybody who has a good idea. Some freelancers have become regular contributors."

FACES

E-mail: faces@cricketmedia.com. **Website:** www.cricketmedia.com. "Published 9 times/year, *Faces* covers world culture for ages 9-14. It stands apart from other children's magazines by offering a solid look at 1 subject and stressing strong editorial content, color photographs throughout, and original illustrations. *Faces* offers an equal balance of feature articles and activities, as well as folktales and legends." Estab. 1984. Circ. 15,000.

FICTION Fiction accepted: retold legends, folktales, stories, and original plays from around the world, etc., relating to the theme. Needs ethnic material and stories. Query with cover letter, one-page outline, bibliography. Pays 20-25¢/word.

NONFICTION Needs historical, interview, personal experience, photo feature, feature articles (in-depth nonfiction highlighting an aspect of the featured culture, interviews, and personal accounts); length of 700-800 words; supplemental nonfiction (subjects directly and indirectly related to the theme)should be 300-600 words. Query by e-mail with cover letter, one-page outline, bibliography. Pays 20-25¢/word.

HOW TO CONTACT Send submissions to: Art Submissions Coordinator, Cricket Media, 70 E. Lake St., Suite 800, Chicago IL 60601.

ILLUSTRATION Illustrations are by assignment only. Please do not send original artwork. Send postcards, promotional brochures, or color photocopies. Be sure that each sample is marked with your name, address, phone number, and website or blog. Art submissions will not be returned.

TERMS Buys print, digital, promotional rights. Buys all rights. Byline given. Pays on publication. Offers 50% kill fee. 90-100% freelance written. Sample copy available online. Guidelines available online.

TIPS "Writers are encouraged to study past issues of the magazine to become familiar with our style and content. Writers with anthropological and/or travel experience are particularly encouraged; *Faces* is about world cultures. All feature articles, recipes, and activities are freelance contributions."

FCA MAGAZINE

Fellowship of Christian Athletes, 8701 Leeds Rd., Kansas City MO 64129. (816)921-0909, (800)289-0909. **Fax:** (816)921-8755. **E-mail:** mag@fca.org. **Website:** www.fca.org/mag. **Contact:** Clay Meyer, editor; Matheau Casner, creative director. Published 6 times/year. *FCA Magazine*'s mission is to serve as a ministry tool of the Fellowship of Christian Athletes by informing, inspiring, and involving coaches, athletes and all whom they influence, that they may make an impact for Jesus Christ. Estab. 1959. Circ. 75,000.

NONFICTION Needs inspirational, personal experience, photo feature. Articles should be accompanied by at least 3 quality photos. Query and submit via e-mail. Length: 1,000-2,000 words. Pays $150-400 for assigned and unsolicited articles.

HOW TO CONTACT Responds to queries/mss in 3 months. Publishes ms an average of 4 months after acceptance.

PHOTOS Purchases photos separately. Looking for photos of sports action. Uses color prints and high resolution electronic files of 300 dpi or higher. State availability. Reviews contact sheets. Payment based on size of photo.

TERMS Buys first rights and second serial (reprint) rights. Byline given. Pays on publication. No kill fee. 50% freelance written. Prefers to work with published/established writers, but works with a growing number of new/unpublished writers each year. Sample copy for $2 and 9x12 SASE with 3 first-class stamps. Guidelines available at www.fca.org/mag/media-kit.

TIPS "Profiles and interviews of particular interest to coed athlete, primarily high school and college age. Our graphics and editorial content appeal to youth. The area most open to freelancers is profiles on or interviews with well-known athletes or coaches (male, female, minorities) who have been or are involved in some capacity with FCA."

THE FRIEND MAGAZINE

The Church of Jesus Christ of Latter-day Saints, 50 E. North Temple St., Salt Lake City UT 84150. **E-mail:** friend@ldschurch.org. **Website:** www.lds.org/friend. **Contact:** Paul B. Pieper, editor; Mark W. Robison, art director. Monthly magazine for ages 3-12. Estab. 1971.

FICTION Wants illustrated stories and "For Little Friends" stories. See guidelines online.

NONFICTION Needs historical, humor, inspirational.

POETRY Pays $30 for poems.

ILLUSTRATION Illustrations only: Query with samples; arrange personal interview to show portfolio; provide résumé and tearsheets for files.

TERMS Available online.

FUN FOR KIDZ

P.O. Box 227, Bluffton OH 45817. 419-358-4610. **Website:** funforkidz.com. **Contact:** Marilyn Edwards, articles editor. "*Fun For Kidz* is an activity magazine that maintains the same wholesome values as the other publications. Each issue is also created around a theme. There is nothing in the magazine to make it outdated. *Fun For Kidz* offers creative activities for children with extra time on their hands." Estab. 2002.

NONFICTION Picture-oriented material, young readers, middle readers: animal, arts/crafts, cooking, games/puzzles, history, hobbies, how-to, humorous, problem-solving, sports, carpentry projects. Submit complete ms with SASE, contact info, and notation of which upcoming theme your content should be considered for. Length: 300-750 words. Pays minimum 5¢/word for articles; variable rate for games and projects, etc.

HOW TO CONTACT Accepts queries by mail.

ILLUSTRATION Works on assignment mostly. "We are anxious to find artists capable of illustrating stories and features. Our inside art is pen and ink." Query with samples. Samples kept on file. Pays $35 for full page and $25 for partial page.

PHOTOS "We use a number of b&w photos inside the magazine; most support the articles used." Photos should be in color. Pays $5 per photo.

TERMS Buys first North American serial rights. Byline given. Pays on acceptance. Sample copy: $6 in US, $9 in Canada, and $12.25 internationally. Guidelines online.

TIPS "Our point of view is that every child deserves the right to be a child for a number of years before he or she becomes a young adult. As a result, *Fun for Kidz* looks for activities that deal with timeless topics, such as pets, nature, hobbies, science, games, sports, careers, simple cooking, and anything else likely to interest a child."

GIRLS' LIFE

3 S. Frederick St., Suite 806, Baltimore MD 21202. (410)426-9600. **Fax:** (866)793-1531. **Website:** www.girlslife.com. **Contact:** Karen Bokram, founding editor and publisher; Kelsey Haywood, senior editor; Chun Kim, art director. Bimonthly magazine covering girls ages 9-15. Estab. 1994. Circ. 2.16 million.

FICTION "We accept short fiction. They should be standalone stories and are generally 2,500-3,500 words." Needs short stories.

NONFICTION Needs book excerpts, essays, general interest, how-to, humor, inspirational, interview, new product, travel. Query by mail with published clips. Submit complete ms on spec only. "Features and articles should speak to young women ages 10-15 looking for new ideas about relationships, family, friends, school, etc. with fresh savvy advice. Front-of-the-book columns and quizzes are a good place to start." Length: 700-2,000 words. Pays $350/regular column; $500/feature.

HOW TO CONTACT Editorial lead time 4 months. Responds in 1 month to queries. Publishes an average of 3 months after acceptance. Accepts queries by mail, e-mail.

PHOTOS State availability with submission if applicable. Reviews contact sheets, negatives, transparencies. Negotiates payment individually. Captions, identification of subjects, model releases required. State availability. Captions, identification of subjects, model releases required. Reviews contact sheets, negatives, transparencies. Negotiates payment individually.

TERMS Buys all rights. Byline given. Pays on publication. Sample copy for $5 or online. Guidelines available online.

TIPS "Send thought-out queries with published writing samples and detailed résumé. Have fresh ideas and a voice that speaks to our audience—not down to them. And check out a copy of the magazine or visit girlslife.com before submitting."

☯ GREEN TEACHER

Green Teacher, 95 Robert St., Toronto Ontario M2S 2K5, Canada. (416)960-1244. **Fax:** (416)925-3474. **E-mail:** tim@greenteacher.com, info@greenteacher.com. **Website:** www.greenteacher.com. **Contact:** Tim Grant, co-editor; Amy Stubbs, editorial assistant. "We're a nonprofit organization dedicated to helping educators, both inside and outside of schools, promote environmental awareness among young people aged 6-19." Estab. 1991. Circ. 15,000.

NONFICTION Multicultural, nature, environment. Query. Submit one-page summary or outline. Length: 1,500-3,500 words.

HOW TO CONTACT Responds to queries in 1 week. Publishes ms 8 months after acceptance. Accepts queries by mail, e-mail.

ILLUSTRATION Buys 3 illustrations/issue from freelancers; 10 illustrations/year from freelancers. Black and white artwork only. Works on assignment only. Reviews ms/illustration packages from artists. Query with samples; tearsheets. Responds only if interested. Samples not returned. Samples filed. Credit line given.

PHOTOS Purchases photos both separately and with accompanying mss. "Activity photos, environmental photos." Query with samples. Responds only if interested.

TERMS Pays on acceptance.

GUIDE

Pacific Press Publishing Association, P.O. Box 5353, Nampa ID 83653. (208)465-2579. **E-mail:** guide@pacificpress.com. **Website:** www.guidemagazine.org. **Contact:** Randy Fishell, editor; Brandon Reese, designer. *Guide* is a Christian story magazine for young people ages 10-14. The 32-page, four-color publication is published weekly by the Pacific Press. Their mission is to show readers, through stories that illustrate Bible truth, how to walk with God now and forever. Estab. 1953.

NONFICTION Needs humor, personal experience, religious. Send complete ms. "Each issue includes 3-4 true stories. *Guide* does not publish fiction, poetry, or articles (devotionals, how-to, profiles, etc.). However, we sometimes accept quizzes and other unique nonstory formats. Each piece should include a clear spiritual element." Looking for pieces on adventure, personal growth, Christian humor, inspiration, biography, story series, and nature. Length: 1,000-1,200 words. Pays 7-10¢/word.

HOW TO CONTACT Responds in 6 weeks to mss. Accepts queries by mail, e-mail.

TERMS Buys first serial rights. Byline given. Pays on acceptance. Sample copy free with 6x9 SAE and 2 first-class stamps. Guidelines available on website.

TIPS "Children's magazines want mystery, action, discovery, suspense, and humor—no matter what the topic. For us, truth is stronger than fiction."

HIGHLIGHTS FOR CHILDREN

803 Church St., Honesdale PA 18431. (570)253-1080. **Fax:** (570)251-7847. **Website:** www.highlights.com. **Contact:** Christine French Cully, editor-in-chief. Monthly magazine for children up to ages 6-12. "This book of wholesome fun is dedicated to helping children grow in basic skills and knowledge, in creativeness, in ability to think and reason, in sensitivity to others, in high ideals, and worthy ways of living—for children are the world's most important people. We publish stories for beginning and advanced readers. Up to 500 words for beginning readers, up to 800 words for advanced readers." Estab. 1946. Circ. approximately 1.5 million.

FICTION Meaningful stories appealing to both girls and boys, up to age 12. Vivid, full of action. Engaging plot, strong characterization, lively language. Prefers stories in which a child protagonist solves a dilemma through his or her own resources. Seeks stories that the child ages 8-12 will eagerly read, and the younger child will like to hear when read aloud (500-800 words). Stories require interesting plots and a number of illustration possiblities. Also need rebuses (picture stories of 100 words), stories with urban settings, stories for beginning readers (100-500 words), sports and humorous stories, adventures, holiday stories, and mysteries. We also would like to see more material of one-page length (300 words), both fiction and factual. Needs adventure, fantasy, historical, humorous, animal, contemporary, folktales, multicultural, problem-solving, sports. No stories glorifying war, crime or violence. Send complete ms. Pays $150 minimum plus 2 contributor's copies.

NONFICTION "Generally we prefer to see a manuscript rather than a query. However, we will review queries regarding nonfiction." Length: 800 words maximum. Pays $25 for craft ideas and puzzles; $25 for fingerplays; $150 and up for articles.

POETRY Lines/poem: 16 maximum ("most poems are shorter"). Considers simultaneous submissions (please indicate); no previously published poetry. No e-mail submissions. Submit typed manuscript with very brief cover letter. Occasionally comments on submissions "if manuscript has merit or author seems to have potential for our market." Guidelines available for SASE. Responds "generally within 2 months." Always sends prepublication galleys. Pays 2 contributor's copies; "money varies." Acquires all rights.

HOW TO CONTACT Responds in 2 months to queries. Accepts queries by mail.

PHOTOS Reviews electronic files, color 35mm slides, photos.

TERMS Buys all rights. Pays on acceptance. 80% freelance written. Sample copy free. Guidelines on website in "Company" area.

TIPS "Know the magazine's style before submitting. Send for guidelines and sample issue if necessary." Writers: "At *Highlights* we're paying closer attention to acquiring more nonfiction for young readers than we have in the past." Illustrators: "Fresh, imaginative work encouraged. Flexibility in working relationships a plus. Illustrators presenting their work need not confine themselves to just children's illustrations as long as work can translate to our needs. We also use animal illustrations, real and imaginary. We need crafts, puzzles, and any activity that will stimulate children mentally and creatively. Know our publication's standards and content by reading sample issues, not just the guidelines. Avoid tired themes, or put a fresh twist on an old theme so that its style is fun and lively. Write what inspires you, not what you think the market needs. We are pleased that many authors of children's literature report that their first published work was in the pages of *Highlights*. It is not our policy to consider fiction on the strength of the reputation of the author. We judge each submission on its own merits. Query with simple letter to establish whether the nonfiction subject is likely to be of interest. Expert reviews and complete bibliography required for nonfiction. A beginning writer should first become familiar with the type of material that *Highlights* publishes. Include special qualifications, if any, of author. Write for the child, not the editor. Write in a voice that children understand and relate to. Speak to today's kids, avoiding didactic, overt messages. Even though our general principles haven't changed over the years, we are contemporary in our approach to issues. Avoid worn themes."

●◔● HUNGER MOUNTAIN

Vermont College of Fine Arts, 36 College St., Montpelier VT 05602. (802)828-8517. **E-mail:** hungermtn@vcfa.edu. **Website:** www.hungermtn.org. "We accept picture book, middle-grade, young adult, and young adult crossover work (text only—for now). We're looking for polished pieces that entertain, that show the range of adolescent experience, and that are compelling, creative, and will appeal to the devoted followers of the kidlit craft, as well as the child inside us all." **Contact:** Samantha Kolber, managing editor. Monthly online publication and annual perfect-bound journal covering high-quality fiction, poetry, creative nonfiction, craft essays, writing for children, and artwork. Accepts high-quality work from unknown, emerging, or successful writers. Publishing fiction, creative nonfiction, poetry, young adult, and children's writing. Four writing contests annually. Estab. 2002. Circ. 1,000.

○ *Hunger Mountain* is a print an online journal of the arts. The print journal is about 200 pages, 7x9, professionally printed, perfect-bound, with full-bleed color artwork on cover. Press run is 1,000. Over 10,000 visits online monthly. Uses online submissions manager (Submittable). Member: CLMP.

FICTION "We look for work that is beautifully crafted and tells a good story, with characters that are alive and kicking, storylines that stay with us long after we've finished reading, and sentences that slay us with their precision." Needs experimental, humorous, novel excerpts, short stories, slice-of-life vignettes. No genre fiction (science fiction, fantasy, horror, detective, erotic, etc). Submit ms using online submissions manager: hungermtn.submittable.com/submit. Length: up to 10,000 words. $50 for general fiction

NONFICTION "We welcome an array of traditional and experimental work, including, but not limited to, personal, lyrical, and meditative essays, memoirs, collages, rants, and humor. The only requirements are recognition of truth, a unique voice with a firm command of language, and an engaging story with multiple pressure points." Submit complete ms using online submissions manager at Submittable: hungermtn.submittable.com/submit. Length: up to 10,000 words. $50 for general fiction or creative nonfiction, for both children's lit and general adult lit; $50 for general fiction or creative nonfiction, for both children's lit and general adult lit; $50 for general fiction or creative nonfiction, for both children's lit and general adult lit.

POETRY Submit 1-5 poems at a time. "We are looking for truly original poems that run the aesthetic gamut: lively engagement with language in the act of pursuit. Some poems remind us in a fresh way of our own best thoughts; some poems bring us to a place beyond language for which there aren't quite words; some poems take us on a complicated language ride that is, itself, its own aim. Complex poem-architectures thrill us and still-points in the turning world do, too. Send us the best of what you have." Submit using online submissions manager. No light verse, humor/quirky/catchy verse, greeting card verse. $25 for poetry up to two poems (plus $5 per poem for additional poems); $25 for poetry up to two poems (plus $5 per poem for additional poems).

HOW TO CONTACT Responds in 4 months to mss. Publishes ms an average of 1 year after acceptance. Accepts queries by online submission form.

PHOTOS Send photos. Reviews contact sheets, transparencies, prints, GIF/JPG files. Slides preferred. Negotiates payment individually.

TERMS Buys first worldwide serial rights. Byline given. Pays on publication. No kill fee. Single issue: $12; subscription: $18 for 2 issues/2 years; back issue: $8. Checks payable to Vermont College of Fine Arts, or purchase online hungermtn.org/subscribe Guidelines online at hungermtn.org/submit.

TIPS "Mss must be typed, prose double-spaced. Poets submit poems as one document. No multiple genre submissions. Fresh viewpoints and human interest are very important, as is originality and diversity. We are committed to publishing an outstanding journal of the arts. Do not send entire novels, mss, or short story collections. Do not send previously published work."

IMAGINATION CAFÉ

Imagination Café, P.O. Box 1536, Valparaiso IN 46384. (219)510-4467. **E-mail:** editor@imagination-cafe.com. **Website:** www.imagination-cafe.com. "*Imagination Café* is dedicated to empowering kids and tweens by encouraging curiosity in the world around them, as well as exploration of their talents and aspirations. *Imagination Café*'s mission is to offer children tools to discover their passions by providing

them with reliable information, resources and safe opportunities for self-expression." Estab. 2006.

NONFICTION Manuscripts are preferred over queries. Varies. Under 1,000 words.

HOW TO CONTACT Accepts queries by e-mail.

JUNIOR BASEBALL

JSAN Publishing LLC, 14 Woodway Ln., Wilton CT 06897. **E-mail:** publisher@juniorbaseball.com. **Website:** www.juniorbaseball.com. **Contact:** Jim Beecher, editor and publisher. Bimonthly magazine focused on youth baseball players ages 7-17 (including high school) and their parents/coaches. Edited to various reading levels, depending upon age/skill level of feature. Estab. 1996. Circ. 20,000.

NONFICTION Query. Length: 500-1,000 words. Pays $50-100.

HOW TO CONTACT Editorial lead time 3 months. Responds in 2 weeks to queries; in 1 month to mss. Publishes ms an average of 4 months after acceptance. Accepts queries by e-mail.

PHOTOS Photos can be e-mailed in 300 dpi JPGs. State availability. Captions, identification of subjects required. Offers $10-100/photo; negotiates payment individually.

TERMS Buys all rights. Byline given. Pays on publication. No kill fee. 25% freelance written. Sample copy: $5 or free online.

TIPS "Must be well-versed in baseball! Have a child who is very involved in the sport, or have extensive hands-on experience in coaching baseball at the youth, high school, or higher level. We can always use accurate, authoritative skills information, and good photos to accompany is a big advantage! This magazine is read by experts. No fiction, poems, games, puzzles, etc."

KEYS FOR KIDS DEVOTIONAL

E-mail: editorial@keysforkids.org. **Website:** www.keysforkids.org. **Contact:** Courtney Lasater. "*Keys for Kids Devotional*, published by Keys for Kids Ministries, features stories and key verses of the day for children ages 6-12. Our devotions teach kids about God's love." Estab. 1982. Circ. 60,000 print (not including digital circulation).

"Please put your name and contact information on each page of your submission. We strongly prefer receiving submissions via e-mail with Word attachments. Story length is typically between 340-375 words. Please see writers' guidelines on website for more information."

FICTION "Propose a title and suggest an appropriate Scripture passage, generally 3-10 verses, to reinforce the theme of your story. Tell a contemporary story (not a Bible story) with a spiritual application. Avoid fairy-tale endings. Include some action and message illustration—not conversation only. Some humor is good." Needs religious. Submit complete ms. Length: up to 350 words. Pays $25.

HOW TO CONTACT Editorial lead time 6-8 months. Responds in 2-4 months. Publishes ms 6-9 months after acceptance. Accepts queries by e-mail.

TERMS Buys all rights. Byline given. Pays on acceptance. 90% Sample copy online. Guidelines online.

TIPS "Please follow writers' guidelines at www.keysforkids.org/forkids/keysforkids/readlisten.aspx."

LADYBUG

Website: www.cricketmag.com. *Ladybug* magazine is an imaginative magazine with art and literature for young children ages 3-6. Publishes 9 issues/year. Estab. 1990. Circ. 125,000.

FICTION Imaginative contemporary stories, original retellings of fairy and folk tales, multicultural stories. Submit via online submissions manager: www.cricket.submittable.com. Length: up to 800 words. Pays up to 25¢/word.

NONFICTION Seeks "simple explorations of interesting places in a young child's world (such as the library and the post office), different cultures, nature, and science. These articles can be straight nonfiction, or they may include story elements, such as a fictional child narrator." Submit via online submissions manager: www.cricketmag.submittable.com. Length: up to 400 words. Pays up to 25¢/word.

POETRY Wants poetry that is "rhythmic, rhyming; serious, humorous." Submit via online submissions manager: www.cricket.submittable.com. Length: up to 20 lines/poem. Pays up to $3/line ($25 minimum).

HOW TO CONTACT Send submissions to: Art Submissions Coordinator, Cricket Media, 70 E. Lake St., Suite 800, Chicago IL 60601. Please allow 3-6 months response time. Responds in 6 months to mss. Accepts queries by online submission form.

ILLUSTRATION Prefers "bright colors; all media, but uses watercolor and acrylics most often; same size as magazine is preferred but not required." To be considered for future assignments: "Please do not send original artwork. Send postcards, promotional brochures, or color photocopies. Be sure that each sample is marked with your name, address, phone number, and website or blog. Art submissions will not be returned."

TERMS Acquires print and digital rights, plus promotional rights. Byline given. Pays on publication. Guidelines available online.

THE LOUISVILLE REVIEW

Spalding University, 851 S. Fourth St., Louisville KY 40203. (502)873-4398. **Fax:** (502)992-2409. **E-mail:** louisvillereview@spalding.edu. **Website:** www.louisvillereview.org. **Contact:** Ellyn Lichvar, managing editor. *The Louisville Review*, published twice/year, prints poetry, fiction, nonfiction, and drama. Has a section devoted to poetry by writers under age 18 (grades K-12) called The Children's Corner. Estab. 1976.

○ *The Louisville Review* is 150 pages, digest-sized, flat-spined. Receives about 700 submissions/year, accepts about 10%.

POETRY Accepts submissions via online manager; please see website for more information. "Poetry by children must include permission of parent to publish if accepted. Address those submissions to The Children's Corner." Reads submissions year round. Has published poetry by Wendy Bishop, Gary Fincke, Michael Burkard, and Sandra Kohler. Pays in contributor's copies.

TERMS Sample: $5. Single copy: $8. Subscription: $14/year, $27/2 years, $40/3 years (foreign subscribers add $6/year for shipping and handling). Guidelines online.

MAGIC DRAGON

Association for Encouragement of Children's Creativity, P.O. Box 687, Webster NY 14580. **E-mail:** magicdragonmagazine@gmail.com; info@magicdragonmagazine.com. **Website:** www.magicdragonmagazine.com. Quarterly magazine publishes children's writing and art (no photography). "All work is created by children age 12 and younger (elementary school grades). We consider stories, poems, and artwork. Queries, writing, and art accepted by USPS mail and by e-mail." Estab. 2005. Circ. 3,500.

FICTION Needs adventure, fantasy, historical, humorous. Submit complete ms. Pays 1 contributor's copy.

NONFICTION Needs essays, humor, inspirational, personal experience. Send complete ms. Length: up to 250 words. Pays 1 contributor's copy.

POETRY Length: up to 30 lines/poem. Pays 1 contributor's copy.

HOW TO CONTACT Editorial lead time 3-6 months. Time between acceptance and publication varies. Accepts queries by mail, e-mail.

TERMS Byline given. Pays contributor's copy on publication. No kill fee. Sample: $4. Guidelines available online.

TIPS "Artists: Include a SASE with adequate postage with all original artwork. If it's a copy, make sure the colors and copy are the same and the lines are clear. Include an explanation of how you created the art (crayon, watercolor, paper sculpture, etc.)."

MUSE

E-mail: muse@cricketmedia.com. **Website:** www.cricketmag.com. "The goal of *Muse* is to give as many children as possible access to the most important ideas and concepts underlying the principal areas of human knowledge. Articles should meet the highest possible standards of clarity and transparency, aided, wherever possible, by a tone of skepticism, humor, and irreverence." Estab. 1996. Circ. 40,000.

FICTION Needs science fiction. Query with published clips. Length: 1,000-1,600 words

NONFICTION Needs interviews, photo feature, profile, as well as entertaining stories from the fields of science, technology, engineering, art, and math. Query by e-mail with published clips. Length: 1,200-1,800 words for features; 500-800 words for profiles and interviews; 100-300 words for photo essays.

HOW TO CONTACT Send submissions to: Art Submissions Coordinator, Cricket Media, 70 E. Lake St., Suite 800, Chicago IL 60601. Accepts queries by e-mail.

ILLUSTRATION Illustrations are by assignment only. Please do not send original artwork. Send postcards, promotional brochures, or color photocopies. Be sure that each sample is marked with your name, address, phone number, and website or blog. Art submissions will not be returned.

NATIONAL GEOGRAPHIC KIDS

National Geographic Society, 1145 17th St. NW, Washington DC 20036. **E-mail:** ashaw@ngs.org. **Website:** www.kids.nationalgeographic.com. **Con-**tact: Catherine Hughes, science editor; Andrea Silen, associate editor; Kay Boatner, associate editor; Jay Sumner, photo director. Magazine published 10 times/year. "It's our mission to find fresh ways to entertain children while educating and exciting them about their world." Estab. 1975. Circ. 1.3 million.

○ "We do not want poetry, sports, fiction, or story ideas that are too young—our audience is between ages 6-14."

NONFICTION Needs general interest, humor, interview, technical. Query with published clips and résumé. Length: 100-1,000 words. Pays $1/word for assigned articles.

HOW TO CONTACT Editorial lead time 6+ months. Publishes ms an average of 6 months after acceptance. Accepts queries by mail.

PHOTOS State availability. Captions, identification of subjects, model releases required. Reviews contact sheets, negatives, transparencies, prints. Negotiates payment individually.

TERMS Buys all rights. Makes work-for-hire assignments. Byline given. Pays on acceptance. Offers 10% kill fee. 70% freelance written. Sample copy for #10 SASE. Guidelines online.

TIPS "Submit relevant clips. Writers must have demonstrated experience writing for kids. Read the magazine before submitting."

○ ☺ ⊕ NATURE FRIEND MAGAZINE

4253 Woodcock Lane, Dayton VA 22821. (540)867-0764. **E-mail:** info@naturefriendmagazine.com, editor@naturefriendmagazine.com, photos@naturefriendmagazine.com. **Website:** www.naturefriendmagazine.com. **Contact:** Kevin Shank, editor. Monthly children's magazine covering creation-based nature. "*Nature Friend* includes stories, puzzles, science experiments, nature experiments—all submissions need to honor God as creator." Estab. 1982. Circ. 13,000.

○ Picture-oriented material and conversational material needed.

NONFICTION Needs how-to. Send complete ms. Length: 250-900 words. Pays 5¢/word.

HOW TO CONTACT Editorial lead time 4 months. Responds in 6 months to mss.

PHOTOS Send photos. Captions, identification of subjects required. Reviews prints. Offers $20-75/photo.

TERMS Buys first rights and one-time rights. Byline given. Pays on publication. No kill fee. 80% freelance written. Sample copy: $5, postage paid. Guidelines available on website.

TIPS "We want to bring joy and knowledge to children by opening the world of God's creation to them. We endeavor to create a sense of awe about nature's Creator and a respect for His creation. We'd like to see more submissions on hands-on things to do with a nature theme (not collecting rocks or leaves—real stuff). Also looking for good stories that are accompanied by good photography."

NEW MOON GIRLS

New Moon Girl Media, P.O. Box 161287, Duluth MN 55816. (218)728-5507. **Fax:** (218)728-0314. **Website:** www.newmoon.com. Bimonthly magazine covering girls ages 8-14, edited by girls ages 8-14. "*New Moon Girls* is for every girl who wants her voice heard and her dreams taken seriously. *New Moon* celebrates girls, explores the passage from girl to woman, and builds healthy resistance to gender inequities. The *New Moon* girl is true to herself, and *New Moon Girls* helps her as she pursues her unique path in life, moving confidently into the world." Estab. 1992. Circ. 30,000.

○ In general, all material should be pro-girl and feature girls and women as the primary focus.

FICTION Prefers girl-written material. All girl-centered. Needs adventure, fantasy, historical, humorous, slice-of-life vignettes. Send complete ms by e-mail. Length: 900-1,600 words. Pays 6-12¢/word.

NONFICTION Needs essays, general interest, humor, inspirational, interview, opinion, personal experience, photo feature, religious. Send complete ms by e-mail. Publishes nonfiction by adults in Herstory and Women's Work departments only. Length: 600 words. Pays 6-12¢/word.

POETRY No poetry by adults.

HOW TO CONTACT Editorial lead time 6 months. Responds in 2 months to mss. Publishes ms an average of 6 months after acceptance. Accepts queries by mail, e-mail, fax.

ILLUSTRATION Buys 6-12 illustrations/year from freelancers. *New Moon* seeks 4-color cover illustrations. Reviews ms/illustrations packages from artists. Query. Submit ms with rough sketches. Illustration only: Query; send portfolio and tearsheets. Samples not returned; samples filed. Responds in 6 months only if interested. Credit line given.

PHOTOS State availability. Captions, identification of subjects required. Negotiates payment individually.

TERMS Buys all rights. Byline given. Pays on publication. 25% freelance written. Sample copy: $7.50 or online. Guidelines available at website.

TIPS "We'd like to see more girl-written feature articles that relate to a theme. These can be about anything the girl has done personally, or she can write about something she's studied. Please read *New Moon Girls* before submitting to get a sense of our style. Writers and artists who comprehend our goals have the best chance of publication. We love creative articles—both nonfiction and fiction—that are not condescending to our readers. Keep articles to suggested word lengths; avoid stereotypes. Refer to our guidelines and upcoming themes online."

ONCOURSE

The General Council of the Assemblies of God, 1445 Boonville Ave., Springfield MO 65802-1894. (417)862-2781. **Fax:** (417)862-1693. **E-mail:** oncourse@ag.org. **Website:** www.oncourse.ag.org. **Contact:** Amber Weigand-Buckley, editor; Josh Carter, art director. *ONCOURSE* is a magazine to empower students to grow in a real-life relationship with Christ. Estab. 1991.

○ *ONCOURSE* no longer uses illustrations, only photos. Works on assignment basis only. Résumés and writing samples will be considered for inclusion in Writer's File to receive story assignments.

FICTION Length: 800 words.

NONFICTION "Submit an audition manuscript of less than 1,200 words. *ONCOURSE* evaluates manuscripts to determine if you, as a writer, fit our magazine. We will not print them—we do not purchase unsolicited articles. Article assignments go to writers listed in our Writer's File and focus on scheduled topics. If we approve you for our Writers File, we will also issue you a password for Writers Only, where we post these themes." Pays $40 for columns, $80 for two-page features, $15 for sidebars/reviews, and $30 for Web-only features.

PHOTOS Buys photos from freelancers. "Teen life, church life, college life; unposed; often used for illustrative purposes." Model/property releases required. Uses color glossy prints and 35mm or 2½×2¼ transparencies. Query with samples; send business card, promotional literature, tearsheets or catalog. Responds only if interested.

TERMS Buys first or reprint rights for mss. Byline given. Pays on acceptance. Sample copy free for 9x11 SASE. Guidelines on website.

POCKETS

The Upper Room, P.O. Box 340004, Nashville TN 37203. (615)340-7333. **E-mail:** pockets@upperroom. org. **Website:** pockets.upperroom.org. **Contact:** Lynn W. Gilliam, editor. Magazine published 11 times/year. "*Pockets* is a Christian devotional magazine for children ages 6-12. All submissions should address the broad theme of the magazine. Each issue is built around a theme with material which can be used by children in a variety of ways. Scripture stories, fiction, poetry, prayers, art, graphics, puzzles and activities are included. Submissions do not need to be overtly religious. They should help children experience a Christian lifestyle that is not always a neatly wrapped moral package but is open to the continuing revelation of God's will. Seasonal material, both secular and liturgical, is desired." Estab. 1981.

◯ Does not accept e-mail or fax submissions.

FICTION "Stories should contain lots of action, use believable dialogue, be simply written, and be relevant to the problems faced by this age group in everyday life." Submit complete ms by mail. No e-mail submissions. Length: 600-1,000 words.

NONFICTION Picture-oriented, young readers, middle readers: cooking, games/puzzles. Submit complete ms by mail. No e-mail submissions. Length: 400-1,000 words. Pays 14¢/word.

POETRY Both seasonal and theme poems needed. Considers poetry by children. Length: up to 20 lines. Pays $25 minimum.

HOW TO CONTACT Responds in 8 weeks to mss. Publishes ms an average of 1 year after acceptance.

PHOTOS Send 4-6 close-up photos of children actively involved in peacemakers at work activities. Send photos, contact sheets, prints, or digital images. Must be 300 dpi. Pays $25/photo.

TERMS Buys first North American serial rights. Byline given. Pays on acceptance. No kill fee. 60% freelance written. Each issue reflects a specific theme. Guidelines online.

TIPS "Theme stories, role models, and retold scripture stories are most open to freelancers. Poetry is also open. It is very helpful if writers read our writers' guidelines and themes on our website."

RAINBOW RUMPUS

P.O. Box 6881, Minneapolis MN 55406. **Website:** www.rainbowrumpus.org. **Contact:** Liane Bonin Starr, editor in chief and fiction editor. "*Rainbow Rumpus* is the world's only online literary magazine for children and youth with lesbian, gay, bisexual, and transgender (LGBT) parents. We are creating a new genre of children's and young adult fiction. Please carefully read and observe the guidelines on our website." Estab. 2005. Circ. 300 visits/day.

FICTION "Stories should be written from the point of view of children or teens with lesbian, gay, bisexual, or transgender parents or other family members, or who are connected to the LGBT community. Stories featuring families of color, bisexual parents, transgender parents, family members with disabilities, and mixed-race families are particularly welcome." Query editor through website's Contact page. Be sure to select the Submissions category. Length: 800-2,500 words for stories for 4- to 12-year-olds; up to 5,000 words for stories for 13- to 18-year-olds. Pays $300/story.

ILLUSTRATION Buys 1 illustration/issue. Uses both b&w and color artwork. Reviews ms/illustration packages from artists: Query. Illustrations only: Query with samples. Contact: Beth Wallace, fiction editor. Samples not returned; samples filed depending on the level of interest. Credit line given.

TERMS Buys first North American online rights for mss; may request print anthology and audio rights; may buy recording rights. Byline given. Pays on publication. Guidelines available online.

TIPS "Emerging writers encouraged to submit. You do not need to be a member of the LGBT community to participate."

SCIENCE WEEKLY

P.O. Box 70638, Chevy Chase MD 20813. (301)680-8804. **E-mail:** info@scienceweekly.com. **Website:** www.scienceweekly.com. **Contact:** Dr. Claude Mayberry, publisher. *Science Weekly* uses freelance writers to develop and write an entire issue on a single science topic. Send résumé only, not submissions. Authors preferred within the greater D.C./Virginia/Maryland area. *Science Weekly* works on assignment only. Estab. 1984. Circ. 200,000.

◯   Submit résumé only.

NONFICTION Young readers, middle readers (grades K-6): science/math education, education, problem-solving.

TERMS Pays on publication. Sample copy free online.

Ⓐ SEVENTEEN MAGAZINE

300 W. 57th St., 17th Floor, New York NY 10019. (917)934-6500. **Fax:** (917)934-6574. **E-mail:** mail@seventeen.com. **Website:** www.seventeen.com. **Contact:** Consult masthead to contact appropriate editor. Monthly magazine covering topics geared toward young adult American women. "We reach 14.5 million girls each month. Over the past 6 decades, *Seventeen* has helped shape teenage life in America. We represent an important rite of passage, helping to define, socialize, and empower young women. We create notions of beauty and style, proclaim what's hot in popular culture, and identify social issues." Estab. 1944. Circ. 2,000,000.

◯   *Seventeen* no longer accepts fiction submissions.

NONFICTION Query by mail. Consult masthead to pitch appropriate editor. Length: 200-2,000 words.

HOW TO CONTACT Accepts queries by mail.

ILLUSTRATION *Only interested in agented material.* Buys 10 illustrations/issue; 120 illustrations/year. Works on assignment only. Reviews ms/illustration packages. Illustrations only: Query with samples. Responds only if interested. Samples not returned; samples filed. Credit line given.

PHOTOS Looking for photos to match current stories. Model/property releases required; captions required. Uses color, 8×10 prints; 35mm, 2¼×2¼, 4×5, or 8×10 transparencies. Query with samples or résumé of credits, or submit portfolio for review. Responds only if interested.

TERMS Buys first North American serial rights, first rights, or all rights. Buys excusive rights for 3 months. Byline sometimes given. Pays on publication. Guidelines for SASE.

TIPS "Send for guidelines before submitting."

SHINE BRIGHTLY

GEMS Girls' Clubs, 1333 Alger St., SE, Grand Rapids MI 49507. (616)241-5616. **Fax:** (616)241-5558. **E-mail:** shinebrightly@gemsgc.org. **Website:** www.gemsgc.org. **Contact:** Kelli Gilmore, managing editor. Monthly magazine (with combined May/June/July/August summer issue). "Our purpose is to lead girls into a living relationship with Jesus Christ and to help them see how God is at work in their lives and the world around them. Puzzles, crafts, stories, and articles for girls ages 9-14." Estab. 1970. Circ. 14,000.

FICTION Does not want "unrealistic stories and those with trite, easy endings. We are interested in manuscripts that show how real girls can change the world." Needs ethnic, historical, humorous, mystery, religious, slice-of-life vignettes. Believable only. Nothing too preachy. Submit complete ms in body of e-mail. No attachments. Length: 700-900 words. Pays up to $35, plus 2 copies.

NONFICTION Needs humor, inspirational, interview, personal experience, photo feature, religious, travel, adventure, mystery. Submit complete ms in body of e-mail. No attachments. Length: 100-800 words. Pays up to $35, plus 2 copies.

POETRY Limited need for poetry. Pays $5-15.

HOW TO CONTACT Responds in 2 months to mss. Publishes ms an average of 4 months after acceptance.

ILLUSTRATION Samples returned with SASE. Credit line given.

PHOTOS Purchased with or without ms. Appreciate multicultural subjects. Reviews 5x7 or 8x10 clear color glossy prints. Pays $25-50 on publication.

TERMS Buys first North American serial rights, buys second serial (reprint) rights, buys simultaneous rights. Byline given. Pays on publication. No kill fee. 60% freelance written. Works with new and published/established writers. Sample copy with 9x12 SASE with 3 first class stamps and $1. Guidelines available online.

TIPS Writers: "Please check our website before submitting. We have a specific style and theme that deals with how girls can impact the world. The stories should be current, deal with pre-adolescent problems and joys, and help girls see God at work in their lives through humor as well as problem-solving." Prefers not to see anything on the adult level, secular material, or violence. Writers frequently oversimplify the articles and often write with a Pollyanna attitude. An author should be able to see his/her writing style as exciting and appealing to girls ages 9-14. The style can be fun, but also teach a truth. Subjects should be current and important to *SHINE brightly* readers. Use our theme update as a guide. We would like to receive material with a multicultural slant."

SKIPPING STONES: A MULTICULTURAL LITERARY MAGAZINE

P.O. Box 3939, Eugene OR 97403-0939. (541)342-4956. **E-mail:** editor@skippingstones.org. **Website:** www.skippingstones.org. **Contact:** Arun Toké, editor. "*Skipping Stones* is an award-winning multicultural, nonprofit magazine designed to promote cooperation, creativity, and celebration of cultural and ecological richness. We encourage submissions by children of color, minorities, and under-represented populations. We want material meant for children and young adults/teenagers with multicultural or ecological awareness themes. Think, live and write as if you were a child, tween, or teen. We want material that gives insight to cultural celebrations, lifestyle, customs and traditions, or glimpses of daily life in other countries and cultures. Photos, songs, artwork are most welcome if they illustrate/highlight the points. Translations are invited if your submission is in a language other than English." Themes may include cultural celebrations, living abroad, challenging disability, hospitality customs of various cultures, cross-cultural understanding, African, Asian and Latin American cultures, humor, international understanding, turning points and magical moments in life, caring for the earth, spirituality, and multicultural awareness. *Skipping Stones* is magazine-sized, saddle-stapled, printed on recycled paper. Published quarterly during the school year (4 issues). Estab. 1988. Circ. 1,600 print, plus Web.

FICTION Middle readers, young adult/teens: contemporary, meaningful, humorous. All levels: folktales, multicultural, nature/environment. Multicultural needs include: bilingual or multilingual pieces, use of words from other languages, settings in other countries, cultures or multi-ethnic communities. Needs adventure, ethnic, historical, humorous, multicultural, international, social issues. No suspense or romance stories. Send complete ms. Length: 1,000 words maximum. Pays 6 contributor's copies.

NONFICTION Needs essays, general interest, humor, inspirational, interview, opinion, personal experience, photo feature, travel. All levels: animal, biography, cooking, games/puzzles, history, humorous, interview/profile, multicultural, nature/environment, creative problem-solving, religion, cultural celebrations, sports, travel, and social and international awareness. Does not want to see preaching, violence, or abusive language. Send complete ms. Length: 1,000 words maximum. Pays 6 contributor's copies.

POETRY Submit up to 5 poems at a time. Considers simultaneous submissions; no previously published poems. Accepts e-mail submissions. Cover letter is preferred. "Include your cultural background, experiences, and the inspiration behind your creation." Time between acceptance and publication is 6-9 months. "A piece is chosen for publication when most of the editorial staff feel good about it." Seldom comments on rejected poems. Publishes multi-theme issues. Responds in up to 4 months. Length: 30 lines maximum. Pays 2 contributor's copies, offers 40% discount for more copies and subscription, if desired.

HOW TO CONTACT Editorial lead time 3-4 months. Responds only if interested. Send nonreturnable samples. Publishes ms an average of 4-8 months after acceptance. Accepts queries by mail, e-mail.

ILLUSTRATION Prefers illustrations by teenagers and young adults. Will consider all illustration packages. Manuscript/illustration packages: Query; submit complete ms with final art; submit tearsheets. Responds in 4 months. Credit line given.

PHOTOS Black & white photos preferred, but color photos with good contrast are welcome. Needs: youth material for ages 7-17, international, nature, celebrations. Send photos. Captions required. Reviews 4x6 prints, low-res JPG files. Offers no additional payment for photos.

TERMS Buys first North American serial rights, non-exclusive reprint, and electronic rights. Byline given. sends comp. contributor copies upon publication No kill fee. 80% freelance written. Sample: $7. Subscription: $25. Guidelines available online or for SASE.

TIPS "Be original and innovative. Use multicultural, nature, or cross-cultural themes. Multilingual submissions are welcome."

SPARKLE

GEMS Girls' Clubs, 1333 Alger St. SE, Grand Rapids MI 49507. (616)241-5616. **Fax:** (616)241-5558. **E-mail:** kelli@gemsgc.org. **Website:** www.gemsgc.org. **Contact:** Kelli Gilmore, managing editor; Lisa Hunter, art director/photo editor. Monthly magazine for girls ages 6-9 from October to March. Mission is to prepare young girls to live out their faith and become world-changers. Strives to help girls make a difference in the world. Looks at the application of scripture to everyday life. Also strives to delight the reader and cause the reader to evalute her own life in light of the truth presented. Finally, attempts to teach practical life skills. Estab. 2002. Circ. 9,000.

FICTION Young readers: adventure, animal, contemporary, ethnic/multicultural, fantasy, folktale, health, history, humorous, music and musicians, mystery, nature/environment, problem-solving, religious, recipes, service projects, slice-of-life, sports, suspense/mystery, vignettes, interacting with family and friends. Send complete ms. Length: 100-400 words. Pays $35 maximum.

NONFICTION Young readers: animal, arts/crafts, biography, careers, cooking, concept, games/puzzles, geography, health, history, hobbies, how-to, humor, inspirational, interview/profile, math, multicultural, music/drama/art, nature/environment, personal experience, photo feature, problem-solving, quizzes, recipes, religious, science, social issues, sports, travel. Looking for inspirational biographies, stories from Zambia, and ideas on how to live a green lifestyle. Send complete ms. Length: 100-400 words. Pays $35 maximum.

POETRY Prefers rhyming. "We do not wish to see anything that is too difficult for a first grader to read. We wish it to remain light. The style can be fun but should also teach a truth." No violence or secular material.

HOW TO CONTACT Editorial lead time 3 months. Responds 3 months to mss. Accepts queries by e-mail.

ILLUSTRATION Buys 1-2 illustrations/issue; 8-10 illustrations/year. Uses color artwork only. Works on assignment only. Reviews ms/illustration packages from artists. Send ms with dummy. Illustrations only: send promo sheet. Contact: Sara DeRidder. Responds in 3 weeks only if interested. Samples returned with SASE; samples filed. Credit line given.

PHOTOS Send photos. Identification of subjects required. Reviews at least 5x7 clear color glossy prints, GIF/JPG files on CD. Offers $25-50/photo.

TERMS Buys first North American serial rights, first rights, one-time rights, second serial (reprint) rights. Byline given. Pays on publication. 40% freelance written. Sample copy for 9x13 SAE, 3 first-class stamps, and $1 for coverage/publication cost. Guidelines available for #10 SASE or online.

TIPS "Keep it simple. We are writing to first to third graders. It must be simple yet interesting. Mss should build girls up in Christian character but not be preachy. They are just learning about God and how He

wants them to live. Mss should be delightful as well as educational and inspirational. Writers should keep stories simple but not write with a 'Pollyanna' attitude. Authors should see their writing style as exciting and appealing to girls ages 6-9. Subjects should be current and important to *Sparkle* readers. Use our theme as a guide. We would like to receive material with a multicultural slant."

SPIDER

Website: www.cricketmag.com. Monthly reading and activity magazine for children ages 6-9. "*Spider* introduces children to the highest-quality stories, poems, illustrations, articles, and activities. It was created to foster in beginning readers a love of reading and discovery that will last a lifetime. We're looking for writers who respect children's intelligence." Estab. 1994. Circ. 70,000.

FICTION Wants "complex and believable" stories. Needs fantasy, humorous. No romance, horror, religious. Submit complete ms via online submissions manager (www.cricketmag.submittable.com). Length: 300-1,000 words. Pays up to 25¢/word.

NONFICTION Submit complete ms via online submissions manager (cricketmag.submittable.com). Length: 300-800 words. Pays up to 25¢/word.

POETRY Submit up to 5 poems via online submissions manager (cricketmag.submittable.com). "Poems should be succinct, imaginative, and accessible; we tend to avoid long narrative poems." Length: up to 20 lines/poem. Pays up to $3/line.

HOW TO CONTACT Send submissions to: Art Submissions Coordinator, Cricket Media, 70 E. Lake St., Suite 800, Chicago IL 60601. Responds in 6 months to mss. Accepts queries by online submission form.

ILLUSTRATION "Please do not send original artwork. Send postcards, promotional brochures, or color photocopies. Be sure that each sample is marked with your name, address, phone number and website or blog. Art submissions will not be returned."

TERMS Rights purchased vary. Byline given. Pays on publication. 85% freelance written. Sample copy available online. Guidelines available online.

TIPS "We'd like to see more of the following: engaging nonfiction, fillers and 'takeout page' activities, folktales, fairy tales, science fiction, and humorous stories. Most importantly, do not write down to children."

STONE SOUP

Children's Art Foundation, P.O. Box 83, Santa Cruz CA 95063-0083. (831)426-5557. **E-mail:** editor@stonesoup.com. **Website:** stonesoup.com. **Contact:** Ms. Gerry Mandel, editor. Bimonthly magazine of writing and art by children age 13 under, including fiction, poetry, book reviews, and art. *Stone Soup* is 48 pages, 7x10, professionally printed in color on heavy stock, saddle-stapled, with coated cover with full-color illustration. Receives 5,000 poetry submissions/year, accepts about 12. Press run is 15,000. Subscription: $37/year (US). "We have a preference for writing and art based on real-life experiences; no formula stories or poems. We only publish writing by children ages 8-13. We do not publish writing by adults." Estab. 1973.

○ "Stories and poems from past issues are available online."

FICTION Needs adventure, ethnic, experimental, fantasy, historical, humorous, mystery, science fiction, slice-of-life vignettes, suspense. "We do not like assignments or formula stories of any kind." Send complete ms; no SASE. Length: 150-2,500 words. Pays $40 for stories, a certificate and 2 contributor's copies, plus discounts.

NONFICTION Needs historical, humor, memoir, personal experience, reviews. Submit complete ms; no SASE. Pays $40, a certificate and 2 contributor's copies, plus discounts.

POETRY Wants free verse poetry. Does not want rhyming poetry, haiku, or cinquain. Pays $40/poem, a certificate, and 2 contributor's copies, plus discounts.

HOW TO CONTACT Publishes ms an average of 4 months after acceptance.

TERMS Buys all rights. Pays on publication. 100% freelance written. View a PDF sample copy at www.stonesoup.com. Guidelines available at www.stonesoup.com/stone-soup-contributor-guideline/

TIPS "All writing we publish is by young people ages 13 and under. We do not publish any writing by adults. We can't emphasize enough how important it is to read a couple of issues of the magazine. You can read stories and poems from past issues online. We have a strong preference for writing on subjects that mean a lot to the author. If you feel strongly about something that happened to you or something you observed, use that feeling as the basis for your story or poem. Stories should have good descriptions, realistic dialogue, and a point to make. In a poem, each word must be chosen carefully. Your poem should present a view of your subject, and a way of using words that are special and all your own."

TC MAGAZINE (TEENAGE CHRISTIAN)

HU Box 10750, Searcy AR 72149. (501)279-4530. **E-mail:** season@harding.edu. **Website:** www.tcmagazine.org. "*TC Magazine* is published by the Mitchell Center for Leadership & Ministry. We are dedicated to the idea that it is not only possible but entirely excellent to live in this world with a vibrant and thriving faith. That, and an awesome magazine." Estab. 1961.

NONFICTION Query or submit complete ms.

HOW TO CONTACT Accepts queries by e-mail.

ILLUSTRATION Works on assignment only. Send ms with dummy. Illustrations only. Responds only if interested.

PHOTOS Buys photos separately. Model/property release required. Uses hi-res color digital photos. E-mail. Responds only if interested.

TERMS Pays on publication. Guidelines available online.

YOUNG RIDER

Irvine CA 92618. (949) 855-8822. **Fax:** (949) 855-3045. **E-mail:** yreditor@i5publishing.com. **Website:** www.youngrider.com. "*Young Rider* magazine teaches young people, in an easy-to-read and entertaining way, how to look after their horses properly, and how to improve their riding skills safely."

FICTION Young adults: adventure, animal, horses. "We would prefer funny stories, with a bit of conflict, which will appeal to the 13-year-old age group. They should be written in the third person, and about kids.". Query. Length: 800-1,000 words. Pays $150.

NONFICTION Young adults: animal, careers, famous equestrians, health (horse), horse celebrities, riding. Query with published clips. Length: 800-1,000 words. Pays $200/story.

PHOTOS Buys photos with accompanying ms only. Uses high-res digital images only—in focus, good light. Model/property release required; captions required.

TERMS Byline given. Guidelines available online.

TIPS "Fiction must be in third person. Read magazine before sending in a query. No 'true story from when I was a youngster.' No moralistic stories. Fiction must be up-to-date and humorous, teen-oriented. No practical or how-to articles—all done in-house."

AGENTS & ART REPS

///

Literary agents listed in this section do not charge for reading or considering your ms or book proposal. It's the goal of an agent to find salable manuscripts: Her income depends on finding the best publisher for your manuscript.

Since an agent's time is better spent meeting with editors, she will have little or no time to critique your writing. Agents who don't charge fees must be selective and often prefer to work with established authors, celebrities, or those with professional credentials in a particular field.

SUBHEADS

Each agency listing is broken down into subheads to make locating specific information easier. In the first section, you'll find contact information for each agency. Additional information in this section includes the size of each agency, its willingness to work with new or unpublished writers, and its general areas of interest.

MEMBER AGENTS: Agencies comprised of more than one agent list member agents and their individual specialties. This information will help you determine the appropriate person to whom you should send your query letter.

REPRESENTS: This section allows agencies to specify what nonfiction and fiction subjects they represent. Make sure you query only those agents who represent the type of material you write.

Look for the key icon to quickly learn an agent's areas of specialization. In this portion of the listing, agents mention the specific subject areas they're currently seeking as well as those subject areas they do not consider.

HOW TO CONTACT: Most agents open to submissions prefer an initial query letter that briefly describes your work. You should send additional material only if the agent requests it. In this section, agents also mention if they accept queries by fax or e-mail, if they consider simultaneous submissions, and how they prefer to obtain new clients.

TERMS: Provided here are details of an agent's commission, whether a contract is offered and for how long, and what additional office expenses you might have to pay if the agent agrees to represent you. Standard commissions range from 10–15 percent for domestic sales and 15–25 percent for foreign or dramatic sales (with the difference going to the co-agent who places the work).

RECENT SALES: Some agencies have chosen to list recent book sales in their listing. To get to know an agency better, investigate these published titles and learn about writing styles that the agency has bonded with.

WRITERS CONFERENCES: A great way to meet an agent is at a writers conference. Here agents list the conferences they usually attend. For more information about a specific conference, check the Conferences & Workshops section starting on page 314.

TIPS: In this section, agents offer advice and additional instructions for writers.

ADAMS LITERARY

7845 Colony Rd., C4 #215, Charlotte NC 28226. (704)542-1440. **Fax:** (704)542-1450. **E-mail:** info@adamsliterary.com. **Website:** www.adamsliterary.com. **Contact:** Tracey Adams, Josh Adams. Adams Literary is a full-service literary agency exclusively representing children's and young adult authors and artists. Estab. 2004. Member of AAR. Other memberships include SCBWI and WNBA.

MEMBER AGENTS Tracey Adams, Josh Adams, Samantha Bagood (assistant).

REPRESENTS Considers these fiction areas: middle-grade, picture books, young adult.

- Represents "the finest children's book and young adult authors and artists."

HOW TO CONTACT **Submit through online form on website only.** This agency accepts submissions only through its website submission form. (You can query by e-mail if the website form is not operating correctly.) No snail mail submissions. Before submitting work for consideration, review complete guidelines online, as the agency sometimes closes to new submissions. Accepts simultaneous submissions. "While we have an established client list, we do seek new talent—and we accept submissions from both published and aspiring authors and artists."

TERMS Agent receives 15% commission on domestic sales; 20% on foreign sales. Offers written contract.

RECENT SALES *The Cruelty* by Scott Bergstrom (Feiwel & Friends), *The Little Fire Truck* by Margery Cuyler (Christy Ottaviano), *Unearthed* by Amie Kaufman and Meagan Spooner (Disney-Hyperion), *A Handful of Stars* by Cynthia Lord (Scholastic), *Under Their Skin* by Margaret Peterson Haddix (Simon & Schuster).

TIPS "Guidelines are posted (and frequently updated) on our website."

BETSY AMSTER LITERARY ENTERPRISES

6312 SW Capitol Hwy., #503, Portland OR 97239. **E-mail:** b.amster.assistant@gmail.com (for adult titles), b.amster.kidsbooks@gmail.com (for children's and young adult). **Website:** www.amsterlit.com. **Contact:** Betsy Amster (adult books), Mary Cummings (children's and young adult). Estab. 1992. Member of AAR. Represents 65+ clients.

- Prior to opening her agency, Ms. Amster was an editor at Pantheon and Vintage for 10 years

and served as editorial director for the Globe Pequot Press for 2 years.

REPRESENTS Nonfiction, novels, juvenile books. **Considers these nonfiction areas:** business, cooking, creative nonfiction, decorating, gardening, history, horticulture, interior design, investigative, memoirs, money, multicultural, parenting, popular culture, psychology, self-help, women's issues. **Considers these fiction areas:** crime, detective, juvenile, literary, middle-grade, multicultural, mystery, picture books, police, women's, young adult.

- "Actively seeking strong narrative nonfiction, particularly by journalists; outstanding literary fiction (the next Jennifer Haigh or Jess Walter); witty, intelligent commercial women's fiction (the next Elinor Lipman); mysteries that open new worlds to us; and high-profile self-help and psychology, preferably research-based." Does not want to receive poetry, children's books, romances, western, science fiction, action/adventure, screenplays, fantasy, techno-thrillers, spy capers, apocalyptic scenarios, or political or religious arguments.

HOW TO CONTACT For adult titles: b.amster.assistant@gmail.com. "For fiction or memoirs, please [paste] the first 3 pages in the body of your e-mail. For nonfiction, please [paste] your proposal [into the e-mail]." For children's and young adult: b.amster.kidsbooks@gmail.com. See submission requirements online. "For picture books, please [paste] the entire text in the body of your e-mail. For novels, please [paste] the first 3 pages [into the e-mail]." Accepts simultaneous submissions. Responds in 1 month to queries; in 2 months to mss. Obtains most new clients through recommendations from others, solicitations, conferences.

TERMS Agent receives 15% commission on domestic sales; 20% commission on foreign sales. Offers written contract, binding for 1 year. Three-month notice must be given to terminate contract. Charges for photocopying, postage, messengers, galleys/books used in submissions to foreign and film agents and to magazines for first serial rights. (Please note that it is rare to incur much in the way of expenses now that most submissions are made by e-mail.)

RECENT SALES *Kachka: The Recipes, Stories, and Vodka That Started a Russian Food Revolution* by Bonnie Morales (Flatiron), *It Takes One to Tango* by Winifred Reilly (Touchstone), *Plus One* by Christopher Noxon (Prospect Park Books), *Animals Spell Love: I*

NEW AGENT SPOTLIGHT

MICHAEL HOOGLAND
DYSTEL & GODERICH LITERARY MANAGEMENT

www.dystel.com
@mike_hoogland

ABOUT MICHAEL: Michael Hoogland joined Dystel & Goderich Literary Management after completing an internship at Sterling Lord Literistic. Before pursuing a career in publishing, Mike studied at Colgate University and graduated with a degree in political science and the intention to work in government. He interned with the US Department of Homeland Security, but soon realized his interests and passions were better suited to a career in the publishing industry. After Colgate, Mike went on to gain a valuable education at the Columbia Publishing Course and discovered his passion for the agenting side of the business.

HE IS SEEKING: Science fiction, fantasy, thrillers, upmarket women's fiction, and some children's books (picture books, middle-grade, and young adult). He also seeks a wide variety of narrative nonfiction, including science, history, and politics. He is particularly interested in seeing thought-provoking, realistic speculative fiction.

HOW TO CONTACT: Send a query to mhoogland@dystel.com. "Synopses, outlines, or sample chapters (say, one chapter or the first twenty-five pages of your manuscript) should either be included below the cover letter or attached as a separate document. We won't open attachments if they come with a blank e-mail, by the way. We will respond to most query letters within eight weeks. If you don't hear from us within that time frame, chances are we did not receive yours. Feel free to resend it."

Love You in Sixteen Languages by David Cundy (David R. Godine), *Monster Trucks* by Joy Keller (Holt Children's).

ANDERSON LITERARY MANAGEMENT, LLC

244 Fifth Ave., Floor 11, New York NY 10001. (212)645-6045. **Fax:** (212)741-1936. **E-mail:** info@andersonliterary.com. **Website:** www.andersonliterary.com. **Contact:** Kathleen Anderson. Estab. 2006. Member of AAR. Represents 100+ clients.

MEMBER AGENTS Kathleen Anderson, kathleen@andersonliterary.com; **Adam Friedstein**, adam@andersonliterary.com; **Tess Taylor**, tess@andersonliterary.com.
REPRESENTS Nonfiction, novels. **Considers these nonfiction areas:** anthropology, architecture, biography, creative nonfiction, cultural interests, current affairs, environment, ethnic, history, music, politics, psychology, religious, science, spirituality, travel,

women's studies, literary journalism, narrative non-fiction, social science, nature. **Considers these fiction areas:** ethnic, historical, humor, literary, middle-grade, multicultural, suspense, thriller, women's, young adult, contemporary, international.

☞ "We do not represent plays or screenplays. We do not represent science fiction, cookbooks, gardening, craft books, or children's picture books. While we love literature in translation, we cannot accept samples of work written in languages other than English."

HOW TO CONTACT Query with SASE. Submit synopsis, first 3 sample chapters, proposal (for nonfiction). Snail mail queries only. Accepts simultaneous submissions. Responds in 6 weeks to queries.

AZANTIAN LITERARY AGENCY

E-mail: queries@azantianlitagency.com. **Website:** www.azantianlitagency.com. **Contact:** Jennifer Azantian. Estab. 2014. Member of AAR. Signatory of WGA.

○ Prior to her current position, Ms. Azantian was with Sandra Dijkstra Literary Agency.

REPRESENTS Novels. **Considers these fiction areas:** fantasy, horror, middle-grade, science fiction, young adult.

☞ Actively seeking fantasy, science fiction, and psychological horror for adult, young adult, and middle-grade readers. Does not want to receive nonfiction or picture books.

HOW TO CONTACT Send your query letter, a synopsis of 1-2 pages, and the first 10-15 pages of your ms all pasted in an e-mail (no attachments) to queries@azantianlitagency.com. Please note in the e-mail subject line if your work was requested at a conference, is an exclusive submission, or was referred by a current client. Accepts simultaneous submissions. Responds within 6 weeks. Check the website before submitting to make sure the agency is currently open to queries.

THE BENT AGENCY

E-mail: info@thebentagency.com. **Website:** www.thebentagency.com. Estab. 2009. Member of AAR.

○ Prior to forming her own agency, Ms. Bent was an agent and vice president at Trident Media Group.

MEMBER AGENTS Jenny Bent, queries@thebentagency.com (adult fiction including women's fiction, romance, and crime/suspense; she particularly likes novels with magical or fantasy elements that fall outside of genre fiction; young adult and middle-grade fiction; nonfiction interests are memoir and humor); **Susan Hawk**, kidsqueries@thebentagency.com (young adult, middle-grade, picture books; within the realm of kids stories, she likes contemporary, mystery, fantasy, science fiction, and historical stories); **Molly Ker Hawn**, queries@thebentagency.com (young adult and middle-grade books, including contemporary, historical, fantasy, science fiction, thrillers, and mystery); **Gemma Cooper**, cooperqueries@thebentagency.com (all ages of children's and young adult books, including picture books; she likes historical, contemporary, thrillers, mystery, humor, and science fiction); **Louise Fury**, furyqueries@thebentagency.com (picture books, literary middle-grade, all young adult subgenres, speculative fiction, suspense/thriller, commercial fiction, all sub-genres of romance, erotic novels; her nonfiction interest are cookbooks and pop culture); **Brooks Sherman**, shermanqueries@thebentagency.com (speculative and literary adult fiction, select narrative nonfiction, all ages of children's and young adult books; he enjoys historical, contemporary, thrillers, humor, fantasy, and horror); **Beth Phelan**, phelanqueries@thebentagency.com (young adult, thrillers, suspense and mystery, romance, women's fiction, literary fiction, general fiction, cookbooks, lifestyle and pets); **Victoria Lowes**, lowesqueries@thebentagency.com (romance, women's fiction, thrillers, mystery, and young adult); **Heather Flaherty**, flahertyqueries@thebentagency.com (all genres of young adult and middle-grade fiction; she represents select adult fiction upmarket fiction—women's fiction, and female-centric thrillers; she also takes select nonfiction—pop culture, humorous, and social media based projects, as well as teen memoir).

REPRESENTS Nonfiction, novels, juvenile books. **Considers these nonfiction areas:** animals, cooking, creative nonfiction, foods, juvenile nonfiction, popular culture, women's issues, young adult. **Considers these fiction areas:** commercial, crime, erotica, fantasy, feminist, historical, horror, juvenile, literary, mainstream, middle-grade, multicultural, mystery, picture books, romance, suspense, thriller, women's, young adult.

HOW TO CONTACT E-query. "Tell us briefly who you are, what your book is, and why you're the one to write it. Then include the first 10 pages of your material in the body of your e-mail. We respond to all queries; please resend your query if you haven't had a response within 4 weeks." Accepts simultaneous submissions.

RECENT SALES *Caraval* by Stephanie Garber (Flatiron), *The Smell of Other People's Houses* by Bonnie-Sue Hitchcock (Wendy Lamb Books/Random House), *My Perfect Me* by J.M.M. Nuanez (Kathy Dawson Books/Penguin BFYR), *The Square Root of Summer* by Harriet Reuter Hapgood (Roaring Brook/Macmillan), *Dirty Money* by Lisa Renee Jones (Simon & Schuster), *True North* by Liora Blake (Pocket Star).

DAVID BLACK LITERARY AGENCY

335 Adams St., Suite 2707, Brooklyn NY 11201. (718)852-5500. **Fax:** (718)852-5539. **Website:** www.davidblackagency.com. **Contact:** David Black, owner. Member of AAR. Represents 150 clients.

MEMBER AGENTS David Black, Jenny Herrera, Gary Morris, Joy E. Tutela (narrative nonfiction, memoir, history, politics, self-help, investment, business, science, women's issues, LGBT issues, parenting, health, humor, craft, cooking, lifestyle and entertainment, commercial fiction, literary fiction, middle-grade, young adult); **Susan Raihofer** (commercial fiction and nonfiction, memoir, pop culture, music, inspirational, thrillers, literary fiction); **Sarah Smith** (memoir, biography, food, music, narrative history, social studies, literary fiction); **Heather Jackson,** (commercial nonfiction, commercial fiction, popular culture; also seeks fresh narrative voices that inform, entertain, and shift the cultural conversation).

REPRESENTS Nonfiction, novels. **Considers these nonfiction areas:** biography, business, cooking, crafts, gay/lesbian, health, history, humor, inspirational, memoirs, music, parenting, popular culture, politics, science, self-help, sociology, sports, women's issues. **Considers these fiction areas:** commercial, literary, middle-grade, thriller, young adult.

HOW TO CONTACT "To query an individual agent, please follow the specific query guidelines outlined in the agent's profile on our website. Not all agents are currently accepting unsolicited queries. To query the agency, please send a query letter of 1-2 pages describing your book, and include information about any previously published works, your audience, and your platform." Do not e-mail your query unless an agent specifically asks for it. Accepts simultaneous submissions. Responds in 2 months to queries.

RECENT SALES Some of the agency's best-selling authors include Erik Larson, Stuart Scott, Jeff Hobbs, Mitch Albom, Gregg Olsen, Jim Abbott, and John Bacon.

BOND LITERARY AGENCY

4340 E. Kentucky Ave., Suite 471, Denver CO 80246. (303)781-9305. **E-mail:** queries@bondliteraryagency.com. **Website:** www.bondliteraryagency.com. **Contact:** Sandra Bond.

○ Prior to her current position, Ms. Bond worked with agent Jody Rein.

MEMBER AGENTS Sandra Bond; Becky LeJeune, associate agent.

REPRESENTS Nonfiction, novels, juvenile books. **Considers these nonfiction areas:** biography, business, history, juvenile nonfiction, popular culture, science, young adult. **Considers these fiction areas:** commercial, crime, detective, family saga, historical, horror, juvenile, literary, mainstream, middle-grade, mystery, police, suspense, thriller, women's, young adult.

⌐ The agency represents adult and young adult fiction—both literary and commercial, including mysteries and women's fiction. The agency also seeks many categories of nonfiction, including narrative, health, science, memoir, biography, and business. It does not represent romance, adult fantasy, science fiction, poetry, children's picture books, or screenplays. Becky LeJeune is particularly looking for thriller and horror.

HOW TO CONTACT Please submit query by e-mail (absolutely no attachments unless requested). They will let you know if they are interested in seeing more material. *No unsolicited mss or phone calls.* Accepts simultaneous submissions.

RECENT SALES *The Ninja's Daughter* by Susan Spann, *Amelia Earhart: Beyond the Grave* by W.C. Jameson, *The Gathering Jar* by Margo Catts.

BOOKENDS LITERARY AGENCY

Website: bookendsliterary.com. **Contact:** Jessica Faust, Kim Lionetti, Jessica Alvarez, Moe Ferrara, Beth Campbell. "Representing fiction and nonfiction primarily for the adult, young adult, and middle-grade markets, BookEnds agents continue to live their dreams while helping authors achieve theirs." Estab. 1999. Member of AAR, RWA, MWA, SCBWI. Represents 50+ clients.

MEMBER AGENTS Jessica Faust, jfsubmissions@ bookendsliterary.com (women's fiction, mysteries, thrillers, suspense); **Kim Lionetti**, klsubmissions@ bookendsliterary.com (contemporary romance, women's fiction, cozies, new adult, and contemporary young adult); **Jessica Alvarez,** jasubmissions@book-endsliterary.com (romance, women's fiction, erotica, romantic suspense); **Beth Campbell,** bcsubmissions@ bookendsliterary.com (urban fantasy, science fiction, young adult, suspense, romantic suspense, and mystery); **Moe Ferrara,** mfsubmissions@bookendsliter-ary.com (adult science fiction and fantasy).

REPRESENTS Nonfiction, novels. **Considers these nonfiction areas:** business, creative nonfiction, ethnic, how-to, money, women's issues. **Considers these fiction areas:** crime, detective, erotica, fantasy, gay, lesbian, mainstream, middle-grade, multicultural, mystery, police, romance, science fiction, thriller, urban fantasy, women's, young adult.

☛ "BookEnds is currently accepting queries from published and unpublished writers in the areas of romance (and all its subgenres), erotica, mystery, suspense, thrillers, science fiction, fantasy, urban fantasy, young adult, middle-grade, and women's fiction." BookEnds does not want to receive children's books, screenplays, poetry, or technical/military thrillers.

HOW TO CONTACT Visit http://bookendsliterary. com/index.php/submissions for the most up-to-date submission instructions, as they change. BookEnds is no longer accepting unsolicited proposal packages or snail mail queries. Send query in the body of e-mail to only 1 agent. No attachments. Accepts simultaneous submissions. "Our response time goals are 6 weeks for queries and 12 weeks on requested partials and fulls."

✚ ◎ BOOKMARK LITERARY

189 Berdan Ave., #101, Wayne NJ 07470 **E-mail:** teresa@bookmarkliterary.com. **Website:** http://book markliterary.com. **Contact:** Teresa Kietlinski, foundere.

☛ This agency specializes in books for young children, including picture books, early reader books, and chapter books. Seeks submissions from authors, illustrators, and author-illustrators.

HOW TO CONTACT "Bookmark Literary has an open door policy when it comes to Illustrator submissions. Illustrators are welcome to submit by snail mail

with postcards and promo. If submitting a dummy via e-mail, PDF proposals must have a file size under 1MB. Please do not send multiple attachments of art samples. We will automatically delete any e-mails with large files or multiple attachments. We are not accepting self-publishing or previously published projects. Submit to submissions@bookmarkliterary. com." Writers of picture books, beginning readers, and early chapter books can submit to the same e-mail above. Again, no self-publishing or previously published projects. There is also an online submission form.

BOOKSTOP LITERARY AGENCY

67 Meadow View Rd., Orinda CA 94563. (925)254-2664. **E-mail:** info@bookstopliterary.com. **Website:** www.bookstopliterary.com. Represents authors and illustrators of books for children and young adults. Estab. 1984.

REPRESENTS Nonfiction, novels, short story collections, juvenile books, poetry books. **Considers these nonfiction areas:** juvenile nonfiction, young adult. **Considers these fiction areas:** hi-lo, middle-grade, picture books, plays, poetry, young adult.

☛ "Special interest in Hispanic, Asian-American, African-American, and multicultural writers. Also seeking quirky picture books, clever mystery novels, eye-opening nonfiction, heartfelt middle-grade, and unusual teen romance."

HOW TO CONTACT For picture books, send a cover letter and the entire ms. For novels, send a query and the first 10 pages. For nonfiction, send a proposal and sample chapters. E-query info@bookstopliterary. com. Send sample illustrations only if you are an illustrator. Illustrators, send a postcard or link to online portfolio. Do not send original artwork. Accepts simultaneous submissions.

TERMS Agent receives 15% commission on domestic sales. Offers written contract, binding for 1 year.

BRADFORD LITERARY AGENCY

5694 Mission Center Rd., #347, San Diego CA 92108. (619)521-1201. **E-mail:** queries@bradfordlit.com. **Website:** www.bradfordlit.com. **Contact:** Laura Bradford, Natalie Lakosil, Sarah LaPolla, Monica Odom. "The Bradford Literary Agency is a boutique agency that offers a full range of representation services to authors who are both published and pre-published. Our mission at the Bradford Literary Agency is to form true partnerships with our clients and build long-term relationships that extend from writing the first draft through the length of the author's career." Estab. 2001. Member of AAR, RWA, SCBWI, ALA. Represents 130 clients.

MEMBER AGENTS Laura Bradford (romance [historical, romantic suspense, paranormal, category, contemporary, erotic], mystery, women's fiction, thrillers, suspense, and young adult); **Natalie Lakosil** (children's literature [from picture book through teen and new adult], romance [contemporary and historical], cozy mystery/crime, upmarket women's/general fiction and select children's nonfiction); **Sarah LaPolla** (YA, middle-grade, literary fiction, science fiction, magical realism, dark/psychological mystery, literary horror, and upmarket contemporary fiction); **Monica Odom** (nonfiction by authors with demonstrable platforms in the areas of pop culture, illustrated/graphic design, food and cooking, humor, history, and social issues; she also seeks narrative nonfiction, memoir, literary fiction, upmarket commercial fiction, compelling speculative fiction, magical realism, historical fiction, alternative histories, dark and edgy fiction, literary psychological thrillers, and illustrated/picture books).

REPRESENTS Nonfiction, novels, juvenile books. **Considers these nonfiction areas:** biography, business, cooking, creative nonfiction, cultural interests, foods, history, humor, juvenile nonfiction, memoirs, parenting, popular culture, politics, self-help, women's issues, women's studies, young adult. **Considers these fiction areas:** erotica, juvenile, middle-grade, multicultural, mystery, new adult, paranormal, picture books, romance, science fiction, thriller, women's, young adult.

8→   Laura Bradford does not want to receive poetry, screenplays, short stories, westerns, horror, New Age, religion, crafts, cookbooks, or gift books. Natalie Lakosil does not want to receive inspirational novels, memoir, romantic suspense, adult thrillers, poetry, or screenplays. Sarah LaPolla does not want to receive nonfiction, picture books, inspirational/spiritual novels, romance, or erotica. Monica Odom does not want to receive genre romance, erotica, military, poetry, or inspirational/spiritual works.

HOW TO CONTACT Accepts e-queries only. For submissions to Laura Bradford or Natalie Lakosil, send to queries@bradfordlit.com. For submissions to Sarah LaPolla, send to sarah@bradfordlit.com. For submissions to Monica Odom, send to monica@bradfordlit.com. The entire submission must appear in the body of the e-mail and not as an attachment. The subject line should begin as follows: "QUERY: [the title of the ms]." For fiction: e-mail a query letter along with the first chapter of ms and a synopsis. Include the genre and word count in your query letter. Nonfiction writers should e-mail a full nonfiction proposal, including a query letter and a sample chapter. Accepts simultaneous submissions. Responds in 4 weeks to queries. Obtains most new clients through queries.

TERMS Agent receives 15% commission on domestic sales; 25% commission on foreign sales. Offers written contract.

RECENT SALES Sold 115 titles in the last year, including *All the Secrets We Keep* by Megan Hart (Montlake), *Magnate* by Joanna Shupe (Kensington), *Always and Forever* by Soraya Lane (Amazon), *Billionaire After Dark* by Katie Lane (Grand Central), *Coming Back* by Lauren Dane (Grand Central).

WRITERS CONFERENCES RWA National Conference, Romantic Times Booklovers Convention.

BRANDT & HOCHMAN LITERARY AGENTS, INC.

1501 Broadway, Suite 2310, New York NY 10036. (212)840-5760. **Fax:** (212)840-5776. **Website:** brandthochman.com. **Contact:** Gail Hochman. Member of AAR. Represents 200 clients.

MEMBER AGENTS Gail Hochman (works of literary fiction, idea-driven nonfiction, literary memoir, and children's books); **Marianne Merola** (fiction, nonfiction, and children's books with strong and unique narrative voices); **Bill Contardi** (voice-driven young adult and middle-grade fiction, commercial thrillers, psychological suspense, quirky mysteries, high fantasy, commercial fiction, and memoir); **Emily Forland** (voice-driven literary fiction and nonfiction, memoir, narrative nonfiction, history, biography, food writing, cultural criticism, graphic novels, and young adult fiction); **Emma Patterson** (fiction— from dark, literary novels to upmarket women's and historical fiction; she also seeks narrative nonfiction that includes memoir, investigative journalism, and popular history); **Jody Kahn** (literary and upmarket fiction, narrative nonfiction [particularly books related to sports, food, history, science, and pop culture], literary memoir, and journalism); **Henry Thayer** (nonfiction on a wide variety of subjects and fiction that inclines toward the literary). The e-mail addresses and specific preferences of each of these agents is listed on the agency website.

REPRESENTS Nonfiction, novels. **Considers these nonfiction areas:** biography, cooking, current affairs, foods, health, history, memoirs, music, popular culture, science, sports, narrative nonfiction, journalism. **Considers these fiction areas:** fantasy, historical, literary, middle-grade, mystery, suspense, thriller, women's, young adult.

☞ No screenplays or textbooks.

HOW TO CONTACT "We accept queries by e-mail and postal mail; however, we cannot guarantee a response to e-mailed queries. For queries via postal mail, be sure to include a SASE for our reply. Query letters should be no more than 2 pages and should include a convincing overview of the book project and information about the author and his or her writing credits. Address queries to the specific Brandt & Hochman agent whom you would like to consider your work. Agent e-mail addresses and query preferences may be found at the end of each agent profile on the 'Agents' page of our website." Accepts simultaneous submissions. Obtains most new clients through recommendations from others.

TERMS Agent receives 15% commission on domestic sales; 20% commission on foreign sales.

RECENT SALES This agency sells 40-60 new titles each year. A full list of their clients is on the agency website.

TIPS "Write a letter that will give the agent a sense of you as a professional writer—your long-term interests, as well as a short description of the work at hand."

CURTIS BROWN, LTD.

10 Astor Place, New York NY 10003-6935. (212)473-5400. **Website:** www.curtisbrown.com. Represents authors and illustrators of fiction, nonfiction, picture books, middle-grade, young adult. Member of AAR. Signatory of WGA.

MEMBER AGENTS Noah Ballard (literary debuts, upmarket thrillers, and narrative nonfiction; he is always on the hunt for honest and provocative new writers); **Ginger Clark** (science fiction, fantasy, paranormal romance, literary horror, young adult, middle-grade); **Kerry D'Agostino** (a wide range of literary and commercial fiction, as well as narrative

nonfiction and memoir); **Katherine Fausset** (literary fiction, upmarket commercial fiction, journalism, memoir, popular science, and narrative nonfiction); **Holly Frederick; Peter Ginsberg**, president; **Elizabeth Harding**, vice president (authors and illustrators of juvenile, middle-grade, and young adult fiction); **Steve Kasdin** (mysteries/thrillers, romantic suspense [emphasis on the suspense], historical fiction, young adult fiction [particularly with crossover appeal]; he also seeks narrative nonfiction, including biography, history, and current affairs); **Ginger Knowlton**, executive vice president (authors and illustrators of children's books in all genres); **Timothy Knowlton,** chief executive officer; **Jonathan Lyons** (biographies, history, science, pop culture, sports, general narrative nonfiction, mysteries, thrillers, science fiction, fantasy, and young adult fiction); **Laura Blake Peterson**, vice president (memoir and biography, natural history, literary fiction, mystery, suspense, women's fiction, health and fitness, children's and young adult, faith issues, popular culture); **Maureen Walters**, senior vice president (women's fiction, and nonfiction projects on subjects as eclectic as parenting, popular psychology, inspirational topics, and medical books); **Mitchell Waters** (literary and commercial fiction and nonfiction—including mystery, history, biography, memoir, young adult, cookbooks, self-help, and pop culture).

REPRESENTS Nonfiction, novels. **Considers these nonfiction areas:** biography, computers, cooking, current affairs, ethnic, health, history, humor, memoirs, popular culture, psychology, science, self-help, spirituality, sports. **Considers these fiction areas:** fantasy, horror, humor, juvenile, literary, mainstream, middle-grade, mystery, paranormal, picture books, religious, romance, spiritual, sports, suspense, thriller, women's, young adult.

HOW TO CONTACT Please refer to the "Agents" page on the website for each agent's submission guidelines. Accepts simultaneous submissions. Responds in 3 weeks to queries; 5 weeks to mss. Obtains most new clients through recommendations from others, solicitations, conferences.

TERMS Agent receives 15% commission on domestic sales; 20% on foreign sales. Offers written contract. Seventy-five-day notice must be given to terminate contract. Charges for some postage (overseas, etc.).

RECENT SALES This agency prefers not to share information on specific sales.

NEW AGENT SPOTLIGHT

SUZY EVANS
SANDRA DIJKSTRA LITERARY AGENCY

www.dijkstraagency.com
@thehistorychef

ABOUT SUZY: Suzy Evans is an attorney, author, and agent who holds a PhD in history from University of California, Berkeley. Her most recent books include *Machiavelli for Moms* (Simon & Schuster) and *Forgotten Crimes*. She is also a ghostwriter for a best-selling author with more than 15 million copies in print. Her first children's book will be published by HarperCollins in 2018.

SHE IS SEEKING: General fiction, suspense/thriller, juvenile fiction, biography, business/investing, history, health, travel, lifestyle, cookbooks, middle-grade, young adult, sports, and science. "In the adult market, I'm particularly on the hunt for great serious nonfiction, especially by established historians who are looking to make the transition from an academic to trade readership, as well as journalists who have something truly unique and significant to say. I'm also on the lookout for smart parenting books with useful, original, unexpected hooks that fill a gap in the market (bonus points for humor). On the children's front, I have a great love of middle-grade and am particularly on the hunt for engaging, original nonfiction that pops off the page and makes kids excited about learning. I also have a huge soft spot for contemporary young adult fiction that tackles difficult issues in bold, daring ways and with inventive formats that can be brought into the classroom to stimulate meaningful discussion and debate.

HOW TO CONTACT: Contact suzy@dijkstraagency.com. For fiction, please send a synopsis and the first chapter of your polished manuscript pasted below your query. For nonfiction, send your query and first chapter with a concise author bio. Response time varies from a few minutes to a few weeks.

MARIE BROWN ASSOCIATES, INC.
412 W. 154th St., New York NY 10032-6302. (212)939-9725 for Marie Brown; or (678)515-7907 for Janell Walden Agyeman. **Fax:** (212)939-9728. **E-mail:** info@janellwaldenagyeman.com. **Website:** www.janellwaldenagyeman.com. **Contact:** Marie Brown, Janell Walden Agyeman. Estab. 1984. Memberships include Authors Guild, Independent Book Publishers Association, SCBWI.

MEMBER AGENTS Marie Brown, Janell Walden Agyeman.

REPRESENTS Nonfiction, novels, juvenile books. **Considers these nonfiction areas:** creative nonfiction, cultural interests, education, ethnic, history, inspirational, juvenile nonfiction, memoirs, multicultural, popular culture, spirituality, sports, women's studies, young adult. **Considers these fiction areas:** contemporary issues, ethnic, hi-lo, historical, juvenile, literary, mainstream, middle-grade, multicultural, new adult, paranormal, picture books, supernatural, urban fantasy, women's, young adult. "We welcome debut fiction for adults (literary and popular) and for young readers."

☛ Marie Brown does not want to receive genre fiction, poetry, true crime, high fantasy.

HOW TO CONTACT Marie Dutton Brown: Query first via snail mail. For fiction, you may include your first 20-25 pages. With nonfiction, include an annotated table of contents. **Janell Walden Agyeman:** E-submissions only. Queries should include a brief pitch of no more than 150 words. Fiction submissions may also include an attached Word document containing the first 20-25 pages. For nonfiction, attach the completed proposal. Responds within 12 weeks. Obtains most new clients through recommendations from others, conferences

TERMS Agent receives 15% commission on domestic sales; 20% commission on foreign sales. Offers written contract.

RECENT SALES *The Man in 3B* by Carl Weber, *Pushout* by Monique Morris, *Born Bright* by C. Nicole Mason, *Degree Zombie Zone* by Patrick Henry Bass, *Harlem Renaissance Party* by Faith Ringgold, *Stella by Starlight* by Sharon M. Draper, *Grant Park* by Leonard H. Pitts, Jr.

TIPS "Have your project professionally edited and/or critiqued before submitting. Show us your very best work."

BROWNE & MILLER LITERARY ASSOCIATES, LLC

410 S. Michigan Ave., Suite 460, Chicago IL 60605. (312)922-3063. **Fax:** (312)922-1905. **E-mail:** mail@browneandmiller.com. **Website:** www.browneandmiller.com. Estab. 1971. Member of AAR, RWA, MWA. Signatory of WGA.

○ Prior to opening the agency, Ms. Egan-Miller worked as an editor.

MEMBER AGENTS Danielle Egan-Miller; Abby Saul (runs the gamut from literary newbies and classics, to cozy mysteries, to sappy women's fiction, to dark and twisted thrillers); Joanna MacKenzie (women's fiction, thrillers, new adult, and young adult).

REPRESENTS Nonfiction, novels. **Considers these fiction areas:** commercial, crime, historical, inspirational, literary, romance, women's, young adult, Amish fiction, time-travel.

☛ Browne & Miller is most interested in literary fiction, commercial fiction, women's fiction, women's historical fiction, literary-leaning crime fiction, romance, and Amish fiction. We are also interested in time travel stories, Christian/inspirational fiction by established authors, literary and commercial young adult fiction, and a broad array of nonfiction by nationally-recognized author/experts. "We do not represent children's picture books, horror, science fiction, short stories, poetry, original screenplays, articles, or software."

HOW TO CONTACT E-query. No attachments. Do not send unsolicited mss. Accepts simultaneous submissions.

TIPS "We are very hands-on and do much editorial work with our clients. We are passionate about the books we represent and work hard to help clients reach their publishing goals."

ANDREA BROWN LITERARY AGENCY, INC.

Website: www.andreabrownlit.com. Member of AAR.

○ Prior to opening her agency, Ms. Brown served as an editorial assistant at Random House and Dell Publishing and an editor with Knopf.

MEMBER AGENTS Andrea Brown, andrea@andreabrownlit.com (president); Laura Rennert, lauraqueries@gmail.com (executive agent); Caryn Wiseman, caryn@andreabrownlit.com (senior agent); Jennifer Laughran, jennL@andreabrownlit.com (senior agent); Jennifer Rofé, jennifer@andreabrownlit.com (senior agent); Kelly Sonnack, kelly@andreabrownlit.com (agent); Jamie Weiss Chilton, jamie@andreabrownlit.com (agent); Jennifer Mattson, jmatt@andreabrownlit.com (agent); Kathleen Rushall, kathleen@andreabrownlit.com (agent); Lara Perkins, lara@andreabrownlit.com (associate agent, digital manager); Jennifer March Soloway, soloway@andreabrownlit.com (assistant agent).

REPRESENTS Nonfiction, novels, juvenile books. **Considers these nonfiction areas:** juvenile nonfiction, young adult, narrative. **Considers these fiction areas:** picture books, young adult, middle-grade, all juvenile genres.

☛   Specializes in all kinds of children's books—illustrators and authors.

HOW TO CONTACT For picture books, submit a query letter and complete ms in the body of the e-mail. For fiction, submit a query letter and the first 10 pages in the body of the e-mail. For nonfiction, submit proposal, first 10 pages in the body of the e-mail. Illustrators: submit a query letter and 2-3 illustration samples (in JPEG format), link to online portfolio, and text of picture book, if applicable. "We only accept queries via e-mail. No attachments, with the exception of JPEG illustrations from illustrators. Visit the agents' bios on our website and choose only 1 agent to whom you will submit your e-query. Send a short e-mail query letter to that agent with 'QUERY' in the subject line. If we are interested in your work, we will certainly follow up by e-mail or by phone. However, if you haven't heard from us within 8 weeks, please assume that we are passing on your project." Obtains most new clients through referrals from editors, clients, and agents. Check website for guidelines and information. Accepts simultaneous submissions.

TERMS Agent receives 15% commission on domestic sales; 25% commission on foreign sales. Offers written contract.

WRITERS CONFERENCES SCBWI, Asilomar; Maui Writers' Conference, Southwest Writers' Conference, San Diego State University Writers' Conference, Big Sur Children's Writing Workshop, William Saroyan Writers' Conference, Columbus Writers' Conference, Willamette Writers' Conference, La Jolla Writers' Conference, San Francisco Writers' Conference, Hilton Head Writers' Conference, Pacific Northwest Conference, Pikes Peak Conference.

KIMBERLEY CAMERON & ASSOCIATES

1550 Tiburon Blvd., #704, Tiburon CA 94920. (415)789-9191. **Website:** www.kimberleycameron. com. **Contact:** Kimberley Cameron. Member of AAR. Signatory of WGA.

○   Kimberley Cameron & Associates (formerly The Reece Halsey Agency) has had an illustrious client list of established writers, including Aldous Huxley, Upton Sinclair, William Faulkner, and Henry Miller.

MEMBER AGENTS Kimberley Cameron; Elizabeth Kracht, liz@kimberleycameron.com (literary, commercial, women's, thrillers, mysteries, historical, young adult with crossover appeal, health, science, environment, prescriptive, investigative, true crime, memoir, sexuality, spirituality, animal/pet stories); **Pooja Menon**, pooja@kimberleycameron.com (currently closed to unsolicited submissions); **Amy Cloughley**, amyc@kimberleycameron.com (literary and upmarket fiction, women's, historical, narrative nonfiction, travel or adventure memoir); **Mary C. Moore** (currently closed to submissions); **Lisa Abellera**, lisa@kimberlycameron.com (currently closed to unsolicited submissions).

REPRESENTS **Considers these nonfiction areas:** animals, environment, health, memoirs, science, spirituality, travel, true crime, narrative nonfiction. **Considers these fiction areas:** commercial, fantasy, historical, literary, mystery, romance, science fiction, thriller, women's, young adult, LGBT.

☛   "We are looking for a unique and heartfelt voice that conveys a universal truth."

HOW TO CONTACT Prefers e-mail queries. Visit the page for each agent on the agency website to see his or her individual online submission form. Accepts simultaneous submissions. Obtains new clients through recommendations from others, solicitations.

MARIA CARVAINIS AGENCY, INC.

Rockefeller Center, 1270 Avenue of the Americas, Suite 2320, New York NY 10020. (212)245-6365. **Fax:** (212)245-7196. **E-mail:** mca@mariacarvainisagency.com. **Website:** mariacarvainisagency.com. Estab. 1977. Member of AAR, Authors Guild, Women's Media Group, ABA, MWA, RWA. Signatory of WGA.

○   Prior to opening her agency, Ms. Carvainis spent more than 10 years in the publishing industry as a senior editor with Macmillan Publishing, Basic Books, Avon Books, and Crown Publishers. Ms. Carvainis has served as a member of the AAR Board of Directors and AAR Treasurer, as well as serving as chair of the AAR Contracts Committee.

MEMBER AGENTS Maria Carvainis, president/agent; **Elizabeth Copps**, associate agent.

REPRESENTS Nonfiction, novels. **Considers these nonfiction areas:** biography, business, history, memoirs, popular culture, psychology, science. **Considers these fiction areas:** action, adventure, commercial, contemporary issues, crime, historical, horror, humor, juvenile, literary, mainstream, middle-grade, multicultural, mystery, romance, suspense, thriller, women's, young adult.

☛　The agency does not represent screenplays, children's picture books, science fiction, or poetry.

HOW TO CONTACT Send us a query letter, a synopsis of the work, the first 5-10 pages of the ms, and an explanation of any writing credentials. E-mail queries to mca@mariacarvainisagency.com. All attachments must be either Word documents or PDF files. "We typically respond to queries within 1 month, if not earlier." Accepts simultaneous submissions. Obtains most new clients through recommendations from others, conferences, query letters.

TERMS Agent receives 15% commission on domestic sales; 20% commission on foreign sales. Offers written contract. Charges clients for foreign postage and bulk copying.

RECENT SALES *Only Beloved* by Mary Balogh (Signet), *Friction* by Sandra Brown (Grand Central), *Enraptured* by Candace Camp (Pocket Books), *The Infinite* by Nicholas Mainieri (Harper Perennial), *If You Only Knew* by Kristan Higgins (HQN Books), *Anatomy of Evil* by Will Thomas (Minotaur Books).

CHALBERG & SUSSMAN

115 W. 29th St., Third Floor, New York NY 10001. (917)261-7550. **Website:** www.chalbergsussman.com. Member of AAR. Signatory of WGA.

◖　Prior to her current position, Ms. Chalberg held a variety of editorial positions and was an agent with The Susan Golomb Literary Agency. Ms. Sussman was an agent with Zachary Shuster Harmsworth. Ms. James was with The Aaron Priest Literary Agency.

MEMBER AGENTS Terra Chalberg; Rachel Sussman (narrative journalism, memoir, psychology, history, humor, pop culture, literary fiction); **Nicole James** (plot-driven fiction, psychological suspense, uplifting female-driven memoir, upmarket self-help, and lifestyle books); **Lana Popovic** (young adult, middle-grade, contemporary realism, speculative fiction, fantasy, horror, sophisticated erotica, romance, select nonfiction, international stories).

REPRESENTS Nonfiction, novels. **Considers these nonfiction areas:** history, humor, memoirs, psychology, self-help, narrative journalism, pop culture. **Considers these fiction areas:** erotica, fantasy, horror, literary, middle-grade, romance, science fiction, suspense, young adult, contemporary realism, speculative fiction.

HOW TO CONTACT To query by e-mail, please contact 1 of the following: terra@chalbergsussman.com, rachel@chalbergsussman.com, nicole@chalbergsussman.com, lana@chalbergsussman.com. To query by regular mail, please address your letter to 1 agent and include a SASE. Accepts simultaneous submissions.

RECENT SALES The agents' sales and clients are listed on their website.

◎　THE CHUDNEY AGENCY

72 N. State Rd., Suite 501, Briarcliff Manor NY 10510. (201)758-8739. **E-mail:** steven@thechudneyagency.com. **Website:** www.thechudneyagency.com. **Contact:** Steven Chudney. Estab. 2001.

◖　Prior to becoming an agent, Mr. Chudney held various sales positions with major publishers.

REPRESENTS Novels. **Considers these fiction areas:** historical, juvenile, literary, middle-grade, picture books, young adult.

☛　"At this time, the agency is only looking for author/illustrators (1 individual), who can both write and illustrate wonderful picture books. Storylines should be engaging, fun, with a hint of a life lessons and cannot be longer than 800 words. With chapter books, middle-grade, and teen novels, I'm primarily looking for quality, contemporary literary fiction. I seek novels that are exceedingly well-written, with wonderful settings and developed, unforgettable characters. I'm looking for historical fiction that will excite me, young readers, editors, and reviewers, and will introduce us to unique characters in settings and situations, countries, and eras we haven't encountered too often yet in children's and teen literature." Does not want to receive any fantasy, science fiction, board books, fables, fairytales, poetry, "stories for all ages," or stage plays.

HOW TO CONTACT No snail mail submissions. E-queries only. Submit a proposal package and 4-6 sample chapters. For picture books, submit full text and 3-5 illustrations. Accepts simultaneous submissions. Responds if interested. Responds in 3 weeks to queries.

WM CLARK ASSOCIATES

186 Fifth Ave., 2nd Floor, New York NY 10010. (212)675-2784. **E-mail:** general@wmclark.com. **Website:** www.wmclark.com. Estab. 1997. Member of AAR.

○ Prior to opening WCA, Mr. Clark was an agent at the William Morris Agency.

REPRESENTS Nonfiction, novels. **Considers these nonfiction areas:** architecture, art, autobiography, biography, cultural interests, current affairs, dance, design, ethnic, film, history, inspirational, memoirs, music, popular culture, politics, religious, science, sociology, technology, theater, translation, travel. **Considers these fiction areas:** contemporary issues, ethnic, historical, literary, mainstream, young adult.

⌐ William Clark represents a wide range of titles across all formats to the publishing, motion picture, TV, and multimedia fields. "Offering individual focus and a global reach, we move quickly and strategically on behalf of domestic and international clients ranging from authors of award-winning, best-selling narrative nonfiction, to authors in translation, chefs, musicians, and artists. The agency undertakes to discover, develop, and market today's most interesting content and the talent that creates it, and forge sophisticated and innovative plans for self-promotion, reliable revenue streams, and an enduring creative career. It is advised that before querying you become familiar with the kinds of books we handle by browsing our book list, which is available on our website." Does not represent screenplays or respond to screenplay pitches.

HOW TO CONTACT Accepts queries via online form only. "We will endeavor to respond as soon as possible as to whether or not we'd like to see a proposal or sample chapters from your ms." Responds in 2 months to queries.

TERMS Agent receives 15% commission on domestic sales; 20% commission on foreign sales. Offers written contract.

DON CONGDON ASSOCIATES INC.

110 William St., Suite 2202, New York NY 10038. (212)645-1229. **Fax:** (212)727-2688. **E-mail:** dca@doncongdon.com. **Website:** http://doncongdon.com. **Contact:** Michael Congdon, Susan Ramer, Cristina Concepcion, Maura Kye Casella, Katie Kotchman, Katie Grimm. Member of AAR.

MEMBER AGENTS Christina Concepcion (crime fiction, narrative nonfiction, political science, journalism, history, books about cities or classical music, biography, science for a popular audience, philosophy, food and wine, iconoclastic books on health and human relationships, essays, and arts criticism); **Michael Congdon** (commercial and literary fiction, suspense, mystery, thriller, history, military history, biography, memoir, current affairs, and narrative nonfiction [adventure, medicine, science, and nature]); **Katie Grimm** (literary fiction, historical, women's fiction, short story collections, graphic novels, mysteries, young adult, middle-grade, memoirs, science, academic); **Katie Kotchman** (business [all areas], narrative nonfiction [particularly popular science and cultural issues], self-help, success, motivation, psychology, pop culture, women's fiction, realistic young adult, literary fiction, and psychological thrillers); **Maura Kye-Casella** (narrative nonfiction, cookbooks, self-help, pop culture, sports, humor, and parenting; for fiction, she seeks literary works, women's fiction, horror, multicultural voices, young adult, and middle-grade); **Susan Ramer** (literary fiction, upmarket commercial fiction [contemporary and historical], narrative nonfiction, social history, cultural history, smart pop culture [music, film, food, art], women's issues, psychology and mental health, and memoir).

REPRESENTS Nonfiction, novels, short story collections, graphic novels. **Considers these nonfiction areas:** art, biography, business, cooking, creative nonfiction, cultural interests, current affairs, film, foods, history, humor, medicine, memoirs, military, multicultural, music, parenting, philosophy, popular culture, politics, psychology, science, self-help, sociology, sports, women's issues, journalism, relationships, essays/criticism, nature, adventure, academic, mental health. **Considers these fiction areas:** crime, historical, literary, middle-grade, mystery, suspense, thriller, young adult.

NEW AGENT SPOTLIGHT

ANJALI SINGH
AYESHA PANDE LITERARY

www.pandeliterary.com

ABOUT ANJALI: Before joining Ayesha Pande Literary, Anjali Singh started her career in publishing in 1996 as a literary scout. Most recently editorial director at Other Press, she has also worked as an editor at Simon & Schuster, Houghton Mifflin Harcourt, and Vintage Books. She is a member of the International Committee of the Brooklyn Book Festival.

SHE IS SEEKING: She is looking for new voices, character-driven fiction or nonfiction works that reflect an engagement with the world around us, literary thrillers, memoirs, young adult literature, and graphic novels.

HOW TO SUBMIT: Use the agency's online submissions form here: www.pande literary.com/queries.

Susan Ramer is not looking for romance, science fiction, fantasy, espionage, mysteries, politics, health/diet/fitness, self-help, or sports. Katie Kotchman is not looking for screenplays or poetry.
HOW TO CONTACT "For queries via e-mail, you must include the word 'Query' and the agent's full name in your subject line. Please also include your query and a sample chapter in the body of the e-mail, as we do not open attachments for security reasons. Please query only 1 agent within the agency at a time. If you are sending your query via regular mail, please enclose a SASE for our reply. If you would like us to return your materials, please make sure your postage will cover their return." Does not accept unsolicited mss. Accepts simultaneous submissions.
RECENT SALES This agency represents many bestselling clients such as David Sedaris and Kathryn Stockett.

CONNOR LITERARY AGENCY

Website: www.connorliteraryagency.webs.com. **Contact:** Marlene Connor Lynch, Deborah Connor Coker.

Prior to opening her agency, Ms. Connor served at the Literary Guild of America, Simon & Schuster, and Random House. She is author of *Welcome to the Family: Memories of the Past for a Bright Future* (Broadway Books) and *What is Cool: Understanding Black Manhood in America* (Crown).
MEMBER AGENTS Marlene Connor Lynch; Deborah Coker (young adult, mainstream fiction and nonfiction, suspense, historical fiction, humor, illustrated books, children's books).
REPRESENTS Nonfiction, novels. **Considers these fiction areas:** historical, literary, mainstream, picture books, suspense, young adult.
HOW TO CONTACT Inquire via form on website. "Please include information about your writing experience and your general bio with your inquiry. Whenever submitting sample material, remember to add headers or footers to your material that identify you and the name of your material." Accepts simultaneous submissions.

⊙ JILL CORCORAN LITERARY AGENCY

P.O. Box 4116, Palos Verdes Peninsula CA 90274. E-mail: query@jillcorcoranliteraryagency.com. Website: http://jillcorcoranliteraryagency.com. Contact: Jill Corcoran. Ms. Corcoran previously worked with the Herman Agency for 4 years. Estab. 2013. Member of AAR. Signatory of WGA.

REPRESENTS Considers these fiction areas: juvenile, middle-grade, picture books, romance, young adult.

HOW TO CONTACT Send a query and the first 10 pages of your ms embedded into your e-mail, plus a link to your portfolio (illustrators) to query@jill-corcoranliteraryagency.com. Accepts simultaneous submissions.

RECENT SALES *Guy-Write: What Every Guy Writer Needs to Know* by Ralph Fletcher, *Kiss, Kiss Good Night* by Kenn Nesbitt, *The Plot Whisperer: Secrets of Story Structure Any Writer Can Master* by Martha Alderson, *Blind Spot* by Laura Ellen, *How I Lost You* by Janet Gurtler.

CORVISIERO LITERARY AGENCY

275 Madison Ave., at 40th, 14th Floor, New York NY 10016. E-mail: query@corvisieroagency.com. Website: www.corvisieroagency.com. Contact: Marisa A. Corvisiero, senior agent and literary attorney. Member of AAR. Signatory of WGA.

MEMBER AGENTS Marisa A. Corvisiero, senior agent and literary attorney (contemporary romance, thrillers, adventure, paranormal, urban fantasy, science fiction, middle-grade, young adult, picture books, Christmas themes, time travel, space science fiction, nonfiction, self-help, science business); **Saritza Hernandez**, senior agent (all kinds of romance, LGBT, young adult, erotica); **Sarah Negovetich** (young adult); **Doreen McDonald** (no submissions); **Cate Hart** (young adult, fantasy, magical realism, middle-grade, mystery, fantasy, adventure, historical romance, LGBT, erotic, history, biography); **Samantha Bremekamp** (children's, middle-grade, young adult, and new adult—closed to unsolicited queries); **Veronica Park** (dark or edgy young adult and new adult, commercial fiction, romance and romantic suspense, adult nonfiction [funny, current, controversial]); **Vanessa Robins** (new adult, young adult, thrillers, romance, science fiction, sports-centric plots, memoirs, humor, medical narratives); **Kelly Peterson** (middle-grade, fantasy, paranormal, young adult, science fiction, steampunk, historical, dystopian, sword and sorcery, new adult, romance, historical romance, fantasy, romance).

REPRESENTS Nonfiction, novels. **Considers these nonfiction areas:** biography, business, history, medicine, memoirs, science, self-help, spirituality. **Considers these fiction areas:** adventure, erotica, fantasy, gay, historical, lesbian, middle-grade, mystery, paranormal, picture books, romance, science fiction, suspense, thriller, urban fantasy, young adult, magical realism, steampunk, dystopian, sword and sorcery.

HOW TO CONTACT Accepts submissions via e-mail only. Include 5 pages of a complete and polished ms pasted into the body of an e-mail, and a synopsis of 1-2 pages. For nonfiction, include a proposal instead of the synopsis. Put "Query for [Agent]" in the e-mail subject line. Accepts simultaneous submissions.

D4EO LITERARY AGENCY

7 Indian Valley Rd., Weston CT 06883. (203)544-7180. **Fax:** (203)544-7160. **Website:** www.d4eoliteraryagency.com. **Contact:** Bob Diforio. Estab. 1990.

⚲   Prior to opening his agency, Mr. Diforio was a publisher.

MEMBER AGENTS Bob Diforio (prefers to see recommendations from clients and writers with previously published works); **Joyce Holland**; **Pam Howell** (genre fiction, middle-grade, young adult, new adult).

REPRESENTS Nonfiction, novels. **Considers these nonfiction areas:** biography, business, health, history, humor, money, psychology, science, sports. **Considers these fiction areas:** adventure, detective, erotica, juvenile, literary, mainstream, middle-grade, mystery, new adult, romance, sports, thriller, young adult.

HOW TO CONTACT Each of these agents has a different submission e-mail and different tastes regarding how they review material. See all on their individual agent pages on the agency website.

LAURA DAIL LITERARY AGENCY, INC.

350 Seventh Ave., Suite 2003, New York NY 10001. (212)239-7477. **E-mail:** ldail@ldlainc.com. **E-mail:** queries@ldlainc.com. **Website:** www.ldlainc.com. Member of AAR.

MEMBER AGENTS Laura Dail, Tamar Rydzinski, Elana Roth Parker.

REPRESENTS Nonfiction, novels, juvenile books. **Considers these nonfiction areas:** biography, cooking, creative nonfiction, current affairs, government, history, investigative, juvenile nonfiction, memoirs, multicultural, popular culture, politics, psychology, sociology, true crime, war, women's studies, young adult. **Considers these fiction areas:** commercial, crime, detective, fantasy, feminist, historical, juvenile, mainstream, middle-grade, multicultural, mystery, picture book, thriller, women's, young adult.

☞ Specializes in women's fiction, literary fiction, young adult fiction, as well as both practical and idea-driven nonfiction. Tamar is not interested in prescriptive or practical nonfiction, humor, coffee table books, or children's books (anything younger than middle-grade). She is interested in everything that is well-written and has great characters, including graphic novels. "Due to the volume of queries and mss received, we apologize for not answering every e-mail and letter. None of us handles children's picture books or chapter books. No New Age. We do not handle screenplays or poetry." Elana, who joined the agency in 2016, specializes in children's books.

HOW TO CONTACT "If you would like, you may include a synopsis and no more than 10 pages. If you are mailing your query, please be sure to include a SASE; without it, you may not hear back from us. To save money, time, and trees, we prefer queries by e-mail to queries@ldlainc.com. We get a lot of spam and are wary of computer viruses, so please use the word 'Query' in the subject line and include your detailed materials in the body of your message, not as an attachment." Accepts simultaneous submissions.

DARHANSOFF & VERRILL LITERARY AGENTS

133 W. 72nd St., Room 304, New York NY 10023. (917)305-1300. **E-mail:** submissions@dvagency.com. **Website:** www.dvagency.com. "We are most interested in literary fiction, narrative nonfiction, memoir, sophisticated suspense, and both fiction and nonfiction for younger readers. We do not represent theatrical plays or film scripts." Member of AAR.
MEMBER AGENTS Liz Darhansoff, Chuck Verrill, Michele Mortimer, Eric Amling.
REPRESENTS Nonfiction, novels. **Considers these nonfiction areas:** creative nonfiction, juvenile nonfiction, memoirs, young adult. **Considers these fiction areas:** literary, middle-grade, suspense, young adult.

HOW TO CONTACT Send queries via e-mail (submissions@dvagency.com). Accepts simultaneous submissions.
RECENT SALES A full list of clients is available on their website.

LIZA DAWSON ASSOCIATES

350 Seventh Ave., Suite 2003, New York NY 10001. (212)465-9071. **Website:** www.lizadawsonassociates. com. **Contact:** Caitie Flum. Member of AAR, MWA, Women's Media Group. Represents 50+ clients.

◯ Prior to becoming an agent, Ms. Dawson was an editor for 20 years, spending 11 years at William Morrow as vice president and 2 years at Putnam as executive editor. Ms. Blasdell was a senior editor at HarperCollins and Avon.

MEMBER AGENTS Liza Dawson, queryliza@ lizadawsonassociates.com (plot-driven literary and popular fiction, historicals, thrillers, suspense, history, psychology [both popular and clinical], politics, narrative nonfiction, and memoirs); **Caitlin Blasdell**, querycaitlin@lizadawsonassociates.com (science fiction, fantasy [both adult and young adult], parenting, business, thrillers, women's fiction); **Hannah Bowman**, queryhannah@lizadawsonassociates.com (commercial fiction—especially science fiction and fantasy, young adult; she also seeks nonfiction in the areas of mathematics, science, spirituality); **Jennifer Johnson-Blalock**, queryjennifer@lizadawsonassociates.com (nonfiction interests include current events, social sciences, women's issues, law, business, history, the arts and pop culture, lifestyle, sports, and food; fiction interests include commercial and upmarket fiction—especially thrillers/mysteries, women's fiction, contemporary romance, young adult, and middle-grade); **Caitie Flum**, querycaitie@lizadawsonassociates.com (commercial fiction—especially historical, women's, mysteries, young adult, middle-grade, and crossover fantasy; her nonfiction interests are theater, memoir, current affairs, pop culture).
REPRESENTS **Considers these nonfiction areas:** agriculture, Americana, animals, anthropology, archeology, architecture, art, autobiography, biography, business, computers, cooking, creative nonfiction, cultural interests, current affairs, environment, ethnic, film, gardening, gay/lesbian, history, humor, investigative, juvenile nonfiction, memoirs, multicultural, parenting, popular culture, politics, psychology, religious, science, sex, sociology, spirituality,

NEW AGENT SPOTLIGHT

DANIELLE BARTHEL
NEW LEAF LITERARY & MEDIA

www.newleafliterary.com
@debarthel

ABOUT DANIELLE: Following her completion of the Denver Publishing Institute after graduation, Danielle began interning at Writers House. While there, she realized she wanted to put her English degree and love of the written word to work at a literary agency. She worked as a full-time assistant for three years, and continues to help keep the New Leaf offices running smoothly in her role of team and client services coordinator, and associate agent.

SHE IS SEEKING: Upper middle-grade, young adult, adult fiction, and adult nonfiction. She'd love to find an amazing middle-grade epistolary, engrossing young adult realistic contemporary stories like *This is What Happy Looks Like* and *Anna and the French Kiss*, well-crafted fantasies, and retellings that truly twist a story from its original version. Adult family dramas akin to *This is Where I Leave You* and upmarket women's fiction are also high on her wish list. A strong romantic subplot, especially with expertly crafted tension, is never a bad thing, and she's particularly fond of historical romance (especially set in England). For nonfiction, she's excited about unique and poignant lifestyle and cookbooks.

HOW TO SUBMIT: Contact query@newleafliterary.com. "The word 'Query' must be in the subject line, plus the agent's name—for example 'Query for Danielle: [Title].' You may include up to five double-spaced sample pages within the body of the e-mail. No attachments, unless specifically requested. We respond if we are interested in seeing more work."

theater, travel, true crime, women's issues, women's studies, young adult. **Considers these fiction areas:** action, adventure, commercial, contemporary issues, crime, detective, ethnic, family saga, fantasy, feminist, gay, historical, horror, humor, juvenile, lesbian, mainstream, middle-grade, multicultural, mystery, new adult, police, romance, science fiction, supernatural, suspense, thriller, urban fantasy, women's, young adult.

This agency specializes in readable literary fiction, thrillers, mainstream historicals, women's fiction, young adult, middle-grade, academics, historians, journalists, and psychology. **HOW TO CONTACT** Query by e-mail only. No phone calls. Each of these agents has specific submission requirements, which you can find on their website. Accepts simultaneous submissions. Responds in 6 weeks to queries; 8 weeks to mss.

TERMS Agent receives 15% commission on domestic sales; 20% commission on foreign sales. Offers written contract.

THE JENNIFER DE CHIARA LITERARY AGENCY

31 E. 32nd St., Suite 300, New York NY 10016. (212)481-8484. **Fax:** (212)481-9582. **Website:** www.jdlit.com. **Contact:** Jennifer De Chiara. Estab. 2001.

MEMBER AGENTS Jennifer DeChiara, jenndec@aol.com (literary, commercial, women's fiction [no bodice-rippers, please], chick-lit, mysteries, suspense, thrillers, funny/quirky picture books, middle-grade, and young adult; for nonfiction: celebrity memoirs and biographies, LGBT, memoir, books about the arts and performing arts, behind-the-scenes-type books, and books about popular culture); **Stephen Fraser,** fraserstephena@gmail.com (one-of-a-kind picture books; strong chapter book series; whimsical, dramatic, or humorous middle-grade; dramatic or high-concept young adult; powerful and unusual nonfiction; nonfiction with a broad audience on topics as far reaching as art history, theater, film, literature, and travel); **Marie Lamba,** marie.jdlit@gmail.com (young adult and middle-grade fiction, along with general and women's fiction and some memoir; interested in established illustrators and picture book authors); **Roseanne Wells,** queryroseanne@gmail.com (literary fiction, young adult, middle-grade, narrative nonfiction, select memoir, science [popular or trade, not academic], history, religion [not inspirational], travel, humor, food/cooking, and similar subjects); **Victoria Selvaggio,** vselvaggio@windstream.net (lyrical picture books, middle-grade, young adult, mysteries, suspense, thrillers, paranormal, fantasy, narrative nonfiction); **Alex Weiss.**

REPRESENTS Nonfiction, novels, juvenile books. **Considers these nonfiction areas:** art, autobiography, biography, child guidance, cooking, creative nonfiction, cultural interests, current affairs, dance, film, foods, gay/lesbian, health, history, humor, investigative, juvenile nonfiction, literature, memoirs, multicultural, parenting, philosophy, popular culture, politics, psychology, religious, science, self-help, sex, spirituality, theater, travel, true crime, war, women's issues, women's studies, young adult. **Considers these fiction areas:** commercial, contemporary

issues, crime, ethnic, family saga, fantasy, feminist, gay, historical, horror, humor, inspirational, juvenile, lesbian, literary, mainstream, middle-grade, multicultural, mystery, new adult, New Age, paranormal, picture books, suspense, thriller, urban fantasy, women's, young adult.

HOW TO CONTACT Each agent has an individual e-mail submission address and submission instructions. Check the website for the current updates, as policies do change. Accepts simultaneous submissions. Obtains most new clients through recommendations from others, conferences, query letters.

TERMS Agent receives 15% commission on domestic sales; 20% commission on foreign sales. Offers written contract.

DEFIORE & CO. LITERARY MANAGEMENT, INC.

47 E. 19th St., Third Floor, New York NY 10003. (212)925-7744. **Fax:** (212)925-9803. **E-mail:** info@defliterary.com; submissions@defliterary.com. **Website:** www.defliterary.com. Member of AAR. Signatory of WGA.

Prior to becoming an agent, Mr. DeFiore was publisher of Villard Books (1997-1998), editor-in-chief of Hyperion (1992-1997), editorial director of Delacorte Press (1988-1992), and an editor at St. Martin's Press (1984-88).

MEMBER AGENTS Brian DeFiore (popular nonfiction, business, pop culture, parenting, commercial fiction); **Laurie Abkemeier** (memoir, parenting, business, how-to, self-help, popular science); **Matthew Elblonk** (young adult, popular culture, narrative nonfiction); **Caryn Karmatz-Rudy** (popular fiction, self-help, narrative nonfiction); **Adam Schear** (commercial fiction, humor, young adult, smart thrillers, historical fiction, and quirky debut literary novels; for nonfiction: popular science, politics, popular culture, and current events); **Meredith Kaffel Simonoff** (smart upmarket women's fiction, literary fiction [especially debut], literary thrillers, narrative nonfiction, nonfiction about science and tech, sophisticated pop culture, humor books); **Rebecca Strauss** (literary and commercial fiction, women's fiction, urban fantasy, romance, mystery, young adult, memoir, pop culture, and select nonfiction); **Lisa Gallagher** (fiction and nonfiction); **Nicole Tourtelot** (narrative and prescriptive nonfiction, food, lifestyle, wellness, pop culture, history, humor, memoir, select young adult and adult fiction); **Ashley Collum** (women's fiction, books for kids and teens, psychological thrillers, memoir, politics, photography, cooking, narrative nonfiction, LGBT issues, feminism, and the occult); **Colin Farstad** (literary fiction, upmarket fiction, young adult, narrative nonfiction, graphic novels, science fiction, fantasy); **Miriam Altshuler** (adult literary and commercial fiction, narrative nonfiction, middle-grade, young adult, memoir, narrative nonfiction, self-help, family sagas, historical novels); **Reiko Davis** (adult literary and upmarket fiction, narrative nonfiction, young adult, middle-grade, memoir).

REPRESENTS Novels, nonfiction. **Considers these nonfiction areas:** autobiography, biography, business, child guidance, cooking, economics, foods, how-to, inspirational, money, multicultural, parenting, photography, popular culture, politics, psychology, religious, science, self-help, sports, technology, travel, women's issues, young adult. **Considers these fiction areas:** commercial, ethnic, literary, mainstream, middle-grade, mystery, paranormal, picture books, romance, short-story collections, suspense, thriller, urban fantasy, women's, young adult.

HOW TO CONTACT Query with a SASE or e-mail to submissions@defliterary.com. "Please include the word 'Query' in the subject line. All attachments will be deleted; please insert all text in the body of the e-mail. For more information about our agents, their individual interests, and their query guidelines, please visit our 'About Us' page on our website." Accepts simultaneous submissions. Obtains most new clients through recommendations from others.

TERMS Agent receives 15% commission on domestic sales; 20% commission on foreign sales. Offers written contract; 10-day notice must be given to terminate contract. Charges clients for photocopying and overnight delivery (deducted only after a sale is made).

JOELLE DELBOURGO ASSOCIATES, INC.

101 Park St., Montclair NJ 07042 USA. (973)773-0836. **Fax:** (973)783-6802. **E-mail:** joelle@delbourgo.com. **E-mail:** submissions@delbourgo.com. **Website:** www.delbourgo.com. "We are a boutique agency representing a wide range of nonfiction and fiction."

Prior to becoming an agent, Ms. Delbourgo was an editor and senior publishing executive at HarperCollins and Random House. She began her editorial career at Bantam Books

where she discovered the Choose Your Own Adventure series. Ms. Flynn was executive editor at Amacom for more than 15 years.

MEMBER AGENTS Joelle Delbourgo, Jacqueline Flynn.

REPRESENTS Novels, nonfiction. **Considers these nonfiction areas:** Americana, animals, anthropology, archeology, autobiography, biography, business, child guidance, cooking, creative nonfiction, current affairs, dance, decorating, diet/nutrition, design, economics, education, environment, film, gardening, gay/lesbian, government, health, history, how-to, humor, inspirational, interior design, investigative, juvenile nonfiction, literature, medicine, memoirs, military, money, multicultural, music, parenting, philosophy, popular culture, politics, psychology, science, self-help, sex, sociology, spirituality, sports, translation, travel, true crime, war, women's issues, women's studies. **Considers these fiction areas:** adventure, commercial, contemporary issues, crime, detective, fantasy, feminist, juvenile, literary, mainstream, middle-grade, military, mystery, new adult, New Age, romance, science fiction, thriller, urban fantasy, women's, young adult.

"We are former publishers and editors with deep knowledge and an insider perspective. We have a reputation for individualized attention to clients, strategic management of authors' careers, and creating strong partnerships with publishers for our clients."

HOW TO CONTACT Submit via e-mail to a specific agent. Query 1 agent only. No attachments. Put the word "Query" in the subject line. "While we do our best to respond to each query, if you have not received a response in 60 days, you may consider that a pass. Please do not send us copies of self-published books unless requested. Let us know if you are sending your query to us exclusively or if this is a multiple submission. For nonfiction, let us know if a proposal and sample chapters are available. If not, you should probably wait to send your query when you have a completed proposal. For fiction and memoir, embed the *first* 10 pages of the ms into the e-mail after your query letter. Please no attachments. If we like your first pages, we may ask to see your synopsis and more ms. Please do not cold call us or make a follow-up call unless we call you." Accepts simultaneous submissions.

TERMS Agent receives 15% commission on domestic sales; 20% commission on foreign sales. Offers written contract. Charges clients for postage and photocopying.

RECENT SALES *Searching for Sappho* by Philip Freeman (Norton), *UnSelfie: The Habits of Empathy* by Dr. Michele Borba (Touchstone/Simon & Schuster), *Underground Airlines* by Ben H. Winters (Mulholland/Little Brown).

TIPS "Do your homework. Do not cold call. Read and follow submission guidelines before contacting us. Do not call to find out if we received your material. No e-mail queries. Treat agents with respect, as you would any other professional, such as a doctor, lawyer, or financial advisor."

SANDRA DIJKSTRA LITERARY AGENCY

1155 Camino del Mar, PMB 515, Del Mar CA 92014. E-mail: elise@dijkstraagency.com. **E-mail:** queries@dijkstraagency.com. **Website:** www.dijkstraagency.com. The Dijkstra Agency was established more than 30 years ago and is known for guiding the careers of many best-selling fiction and nonfiction authors, including Amy Tan, Lisa See, Maxine Hong Kingston, Chitra Divakaruni, Eric Foner, Marcus Rediker, and many more. "We handle nearly all genres, except for poetry." Member of AAR, Authors Guild, Organization of American Historians, RWA. Represents 100+ clients.

MEMBER AGENTS Sandra Dijkstra; Elise Capron (adult books only); Jill Marr (adult books only); Thao Le (adult books and young adult); Roz Foster (adult books and young adult); Jessica Watterson (subgenres of adult and new adult romance, as well as women's fiction).

REPRESENTS Nonfiction, novels, short story collections, juvenile books, scholarly books. **Considers these nonfiction areas:** Americana, anthropology, art, biography, business, creative nonfiction, cultural interests, current affairs, design, economics, environment, ethnic, gardening, government, health, history, juvenile nonfiction, literature, memoirs, multicultural, popular culture, politics, psychology, science, self-help, true crime, young adult, narrative. **Considers these fiction areas:** commercial, horror, literary, middle-grade, new adult, romance, science fiction, suspense, thriller, women's, young adult.

HOW TO CONTACT "Please see submission guidelines on our website, as they can change. Please note that we accept only e-mail submissions. Due to the large number of unsolicited submissions we receive, we are able to respond only to those submissions in which we are interested." Accepts simultaneous submissions. Responds to queries of interest within 6 weeks.

TERMS Works in conjunction with foreign and film agents. Agent receives 15% commission on domestic sales; 20% commission on foreign sales. Offers written contract.

TIPS "Remember that publishing is a business. Do your research and present your project in as professional a way as possible. Only submit your work when you are confident that it is polished and ready. Make yourself a part of the active writing community by getting stories and articles published, networking with other writers, and getting a good sense of where your work fits in the market."

◎ DONADIO & OLSON, INC.

40 W. 27th St., 5th Floor, New York NY 10001. (212)691-8077. **Fax:** (212)633-2837. **E-mail:** neil@donadio.com. **E-mail:** mail@donadio.com. **Website:** http://donadio.com. **Contact:** Neil Olson. Member of AAR.

MEMBER AGENTS Neil Olson (no queries); Edward Hibbert (no queries); Carrie Howland, carrie@donadio.com (adult literary fiction, narrative nonfiction, young adult, middle-grade, picture books).

REPRESENTS Nonfiction, novels. **Considers these nonfiction areas:** creative nonfiction. **Considers these fiction areas:** literary, middle-grade, picture books, young adult.

☞ This agency represents mostly fiction and is very selective.

HOW TO CONTACT "Please send a query letter and the first 3 chapters (or first 25 pages) of the ms to mail@donadio.com. Please allow a minimum of 1 month for a reply. Accepts simultaneous submissions.

DONAGHY LITERARY GROUP

6-14845 Yonge St., Suite # 123, Aurora, Ontario L4G 6H8, Canada, (647)527-4353. **E-mail:** stacey@donaghyliterary.com. **E-mail:** query@donaghyliterary.com. **Website:** www.donaghyliterary.com. **Contact:** Stacey Donaghy. "Donaghy Literary Group provides full-service literary representation to our clients at every stage of their writing career. Specializing in commercial fiction, we seek young adult, new adult, and adult novels."

◖ Prior to opening her agency, Ms. Donaghy served as an agent at the Corvisiero Literary

Agency. Ms. Noble interned for Jessica Sinsheimer of Sarah Jane Freymann Literary Agency. Ms. Miller previously worked in children's publishing with Scholastic Canada and also interned with Bree Ogden during her time at the D4EO Agency.

MEMBER AGENTS Stacey Donaghy (romantic suspense, LGBT, thriller, mystery, contemporary romance, erotic romance, young adult, and quirky middle-grade); **Valerie Noble** (historical, science fiction and fantasy [think Kristin Cashore and Suzanne Collins] for young adults and adults); **Sue Miller** (young adult, urban fantasy, contemporary romance).

REPRESENTS Considers these fiction areas: commercial, erotica, ethnic, fantasy, gay, juvenile, lesbian, mainstream, multicultural, mystery, new adult, police, psychic, romance, science fiction, sports, suspense, thriller, urban fantasy, young adult.

HOW TO CONTACT Query via e-mail with no attachments. Visit agency website for submission guidelines to view agent bios. Do not e-mail agents directly. Accepts simultaneous submissions. Responds in 8 weeks to queries. Time may vary during holidays and closures.

TERMS Agent receives 15% commission on domestic sales; 20% commission on foreign sales.

WRITERS CONFERENCES Toronto Writing Workshop, Romantic Times Booklovers Convention, Windsor International Writers Conference, OWC Ontario Writers Conference.

TIPS "Submit to only 1 DLG agent. We work collaboratively and often share projects that may be better suited to another agent at the agency."

DUNHAM LITERARY, INC.

110 William St., Suite 2202, New York NY 10038. (212)929-0994. **E-mail:** query@dunhamlit.com. **Website:** www.dunhamlit.com. **Contact:** Jennie Dunham. Estab. 2000. Member of AAR, SCBWI.

Prior to opening her agency, Ms. Dunham worked as a literary agent for Russell & Volkening. The Rhoda Weyr Agency is now a division of Dunham Literary, Inc.

MEMBER AGENTS Jennie Dunham, Bridget Smith.

REPRESENTS Nonfiction, novels, juvenile books. **Considers these nonfiction areas:** anthropology, archeology, biography, creative nonfiction, cultural interests, environment, health, history, language, literature, medicine, memoirs, multicultural, parenting, popular culture, politics, psychology, science, technology, women's issues, women's studies, young adult. **Considers these fiction areas:** fantasy, historical, humor, juvenile, literary, mainstream, middle-grade, multicultural, mystery, picture books, science fiction, women's, young adult.

HOW TO CONTACT E-queries preferred, with all materials pasted in the body of the e-mail. Attachments will not be opened. Paper queries are also accepted. Please include a SASE for response and return of materials. If submitting to Bridget, please include the first 5 pages with the query. Accepts simultaneous submissions. Responds in 4 weeks to queries; 2 months to mss. Obtains most new clients through recommendations from others, solicitations.

TERMS Agent receives 15% commission on domestic sales; 20% commission on foreign sales.

RECENT SALES *The White House* by Robert Sabuda (Simon & Schuster), *The Gollywhopper Games* and sequels by Jody Feldman (HarperCollins), *First & Then* by Emma Mills (Macmillan).

DUNOW, CARLSON, & LERNER AGENCY

27 W. 20th St., Suite 1107, New York NY 10011. (212)645-7606. **E-mail:** mail@dclagency.com. **E-mail:** mail@dclagency.com. **Website:** www.dclagency.com. Member of AAR.

MEMBER AGENTS Jennifer Carlson (narrative nonfiction by journalists covering current events, ideas, and cultural history; she also seeks literary and upmarket commercial novelists); **Henry Dunow** (quality fiction—literary, historical, strongly written commercial—and with voice-driven nonfiction across a range of areas [narrative history, biography, memoir, current affairs, cultural trends and criticism, science, sports]); **Erin Hosier** (popular culture, music, sociology, and memoir); **Betsy Lerner** (nonfiction writers in the areas of psychology, history, cultural studies, biography, current events, business; fiction interests include literary, dark, funny, voice-driven works); **Yishai Seidman** (broad range of fiction: literary, postmodern, and thrillers; nonfiction interests include sports, music, and pop culture); **Amy Hughes** (history, cultural studies, memoir, current events, wellness, health, food, pop culture, biography, literary fiction); **Eleanor Jackson** (literary, commercial, memoir, art, food, science, history); **Julia Kenny** (fiction—adult, middle-grade, and young adult—and is especially interested in dark thrillers and suspense); **Edward Necarsulmer IV** (strong new voices in teen and middle-grade, as well as picture books); **Stacia Decker**; **Arielle Datz** (young adult, middle-grade, literary, commercial; nonfiction interests include essays, unconventional memoir, pop culture, and sociology).

REPRESENTS Nonfiction, novels. **Considers these nonfiction areas:** art, biography, creative nonfiction, cultural interests, current affairs, foods, health, history, memoirs, music, popular culture, psychology, science, sociology, sports. **Considers these fiction areas:** commercial, literary, mainstream, middle-grade, mystery, picture books, thriller, young adult.

HOW TO CONTACT Query via snail mail with SASE, or by e-mail. Paste 10 sample pages below your query letter. No attachments. Will respond only if interested. Accepts simultaneous submissions.

RECENT SALES A full list of agency clients is on the website.

DYSTEL & GODERICH LITERARY MANAGEMENT

1 Union Square W., Suite 904, New York NY 10003. (212)627-9100. **Fax:** (212)627-9313. **Website:** www.dystel.com. Estab. 1994. Member of AAR, SCBWI. Represents 600+ clients.

MEMBER AGENTS Jane Dystel; Miriam Goderich, miriam@dystel.com (literary and commercial fiction, some genre fiction, narrative nonfiction, pop culture, psychology, history, science, art, business books, and biography/memoir); **Stacey Kendall Glick**, sglick@dystel.com (adult narrative nonfiction [including memoir, parenting, cooking, and food], psychology, science, health and wellness, lifestyle, current events, pop culture, young adult, middle-grade, children's nonfiction, and select adult contemporary fiction); **Michael Bourret**, mbourret@dystel.com (middle-grade and young adult fiction, commercial adult fiction; varied nonfiction interests, such as food and cocktail books, memoir, popular history, politics, religion [though not spirituality], popular science, and current events); **Jim McCarthy**, jmccarthy@dystel.com (literary women's fiction, underrepresented voices, mysteries, romance, paranormal fiction, narrative nonfiction, memoir, and paranormal nonfiction); **Jessica Papin**, jpapin@dystel.com (plot-driven literary and smart commercial fiction, narrative nonfiction across a range of subjects [history, medicine, science, economics, and women's issues]); **Lauren E. Abramo**, labramo@dystel.com (humorous middle-grade, contemporary young adult, upmarket commercial fiction, and well-paced literary fiction; she's also interested in adult narrative nonfiction—especially pop culture, psychology, pop science, reportage, media, and contemporary culture); **John Rudolph**, jrudolph@dystel.com (picture book author/illustrators, middle-grade, young adult, select commercial fiction, and narrative nonfiction [music, sports, history, popular science], performing arts, health, business, memoir, military history, and humor); **Sharon Pelletier**, spelletier@dystel.com (smart commercial fiction, upmarket women's fiction, domestic suspense, literary thrillers, strong contemporary romance novels; she seeks compelling nonfiction projects, especially feminism and religion); **Michael Hoogland**, mhoogland@dystel.com (thriller, science fiction, fantasy, young adult, upmarket women's fiction, narrative nonfiction); **Erin Young**, eyoung@dystel.com (young adult, middle-grade, literary and intellectual commercial thrillers, memoirs, biographies, sport and science narratives); **Amy Bishop**, abishop@dystel.com (commercial and literary women's fiction, fiction from diverse authors, historical fiction, young adult, personal narratives, and biographies); **Kemi Faderin**, kfaderin@dystel.com (plot-driven young adult, historical fiction and nonfiction, contemporary women's fiction, literary fiction); **Eric Myers**, emyers@dystel.com (young adult and middle-grade; he also seeks adult nonfiction in the categories of history, biography, psychology, health and wellness, pop culture, thriller, and memoir).

REPRESENTS **Considers these nonfiction areas:** animals, art, autobiography, biography, business, cooking, cultural interests, current affairs, ethnic, foods, gay/lesbian, health, history, humor, inspirational, investigative, medicine, memoirs, metaphysics, military, New Age, parenting, popular culture, politics, psychology, religious, science, sports, women's issues, women's studies. **Considers these fiction areas:** commercial, ethnic, gay, lesbian, literary, mainstream, middle-grade, mystery, paranormal, romance, suspense, thriller, women's, young adult.

☛ "We are actively seeking fiction for all ages, in all genres." No plays, screenplays, or poetry.

HOW TO CONTACT Query via e-mail and put "Query" in the subject line. "Synopses, outlines, or sample chapters (for example, 1 chapter or the first

25 pages of your ms) should either be included below the cover letter or attached as a separate document. We won't open attachments if they come with a blank e-mail." Accepts simultaneous submissions. Responds in 8 weeks to queries; within 8 weeks to mss. Obtains most new clients through recommendations from others, solicitations, conferences.

TIPS "DGLM prides itself on being a full-service agency. We're involved in every stage of the publishing process, from offering substantial editing on mss and proposals, to coming up with book ideas for authors looking for their next project, to negotiating contracts and collecting monies for our clients. We follow a book from its inception through its sale to a publisher, its publication, and beyond. Our commitment to our writers does not, by any means, end when we have collected our commission. This is one of the many things that makes us unique in a very competitive business."

EDEN STREET LITERARY

P.O. Box 30, Billings NY 12510. **E-mail:** info@edenstreetlit.com. **E-mail:** submissions@edenstreetlit.com. **Website:** www.edenstreetlit.com. **Contact:** Liza Voges. Eden Street represents more than 40 authors and author-illustrators of books for young readers from pre-school through young adult. Their books have won numerous awards over the past 30 years. Member of AAR. Signatory of WGA.

REPRESENTS Novels, juvenile books. **Considers these fiction areas:** juvenile, middle-grade, picture books, young adult.

HOW TO CONTACT Check the website before submitting, as the agency will close itself off to submissions sometimes. When open, contact submissions@edenstreetlit.com. Accepts simultaneous submissions. Responds only to submissions of interest.

RECENT SALES *Dream Dog* by Lou Berger, *Biscuit Loves the Library* by Alyssa Capucilli, *The Scraps Book* by Lois Ehlert, *Two Bunny Buddies* by Kathryn O. Galbraith, *Between Two Worlds* by Katherine Kirkpatrick.

EINSTEIN LITERARY MANAGEMENT

27 W. 20th St., No. 1003, New York NY 10011. **E-mail:** submissions@einsteinliterary.com. **Website:** http://einsteinliterary.com. **Contact:** Susanna Einstein. Estab. 2015. Member of AAR. Signatory of WGA.

Prior to her current position, Ms. Einstein was with LJK Literary Management and the Einstein Thompson Agency.

MEMBER AGENTS Susanna Einstein.

REPRESENTS Nonfiction, fiction. **Considers these nonfiction areas:** cooking, creative nonfiction, memoirs, blog-to-book projects. **Considers these fiction areas:** commercial, crime, historical, literary, romance, women's.

"We represent a broad range of literary and commercial fiction, including upmarket women's fiction, crime fiction, historical fiction, romance, and books for middle-grade and young adults. We also handle nonfiction, including cookbooks, memoir and narrative, and blog-to-book projects." Does not want picture books, poetry, textbooks, or screenplays.

HOW TO CONTACT Please submit a query letter and the first 10 double-spaced pages of your ms in the body of the e-mail (no attachments). Does not respond to snail mail queries, phone queries, or queries that are not specifically addressed to this agency. Accepts simultaneous submissions. Responds in 6 weeks if interested.

ETHAN ELLENBERG LITERARY AGENCY

155 Suffolk St., No. 2R, New York NY 10002. (212)431-4554. **E-mail:** agent@ethanellenberg.com. **Website:** http://ethanellenberg.com. **Contact:** Ethan Ellenberg. This agency specializes in commercial fiction and nonfiction. Estab. 1984. Member of AAR, Science Fiction and Fantasy Writers of America, SCBWI, RWA, MWA.

MEMBER AGENTS Ethan Ellenberg, president; Evan Gregory, senior agent; Bibi Lewis, associate agent (young adult and women's fiction).

REPRESENTS Nonfiction, fiction. **Considers these nonfiction areas:** biography, cooking, current affairs, health, history, memoirs, New Age, popular culture, psychology, science, spirituality, true crime, adventure. **Considers these fiction areas:** commercial, ethnic, fantasy, literary, middle-grade, mystery, picture books, romance, science fiction, thriller, women's, young adult, general.

"We specialize in commercial fiction and children's books. In commercial fiction, we want to see science fiction, fantasy, romance, mystery, thriller, and women's fiction. In children's books, we want to see everything: picture books, early reader, middle-grade, and young adult. We do some nonfiction: history, biography, military, popular science, and cutting edge books about any subject." Does not want to receive poetry, short stories, or screenplays.

HOW TO CONTACT Query by e-mail. Paste all of the material in the order listed. Fiction: query letter, synopsis, first 50 pages. Nonfiction: query letter, book proposal. Picture books: query letter, complete ms, 4-5 sample illustrations (if available), link to online portfolio (if available). Will not respond unless interested. Accepts simultaneous submissions. Responds in 2 weeks.

➕ EMERALD CITY LITERARY AGENCY

2522 N. Proctor St., Suite 359, Tacoma WA 98406. **Website:** http://emeraldcityliterary.com.
MEMBER AGENTS Mandy Hubbard, querymandy@emeraldcityliterary.com (young adult, middle-grade, adult romance; she has specific tastes for each genre, and those are available on the website); **Linda Epstein**, querylinda@emeraldcityliterary.com (picture books, middle-grade, young adult, and children's nonfiction; she does not represent adult literature); **Lindsay Mealing** (agency assistant).
REPRESENTS Nonfiction, fiction. **Considers these nonfiction areas:** juvenile. **Considers these fiction areas:** middle-grade, picture books, romance, young adult.
HOW TO CONTACT Each agent has different submission guidelines. Those guidelines are explained on the agency website.

MARY EVANS INC.

242 E. Fifth St., New York NY 10003. (212)979-0880. **Fax:** (212)979-5344. **E-mail:** info@maryevansinc.com. **Website:** http://maryevansinc.com. Member of AAR.
MEMBER AGENTS Mary Evans (progressive politics, alternative medicine, science and technology, social commentary, American history and culture); **Julia Kardon** (literary and upmarket fiction, narrative nonfiction, journalism, history); **Mary Gaule** (picture books, middle-grade, young adult).
REPRESENTS Nonfiction, novels. **Considers these nonfiction areas:** creative nonfiction, cultural interests, history, medicine, politics, science, technology, social commentary, journalism. **Considers these fiction areas:** literary, middle-grade, picture books, young adult, upmarket.

No screenplays or stage plays.
HOW TO CONTACT Query by mail or e-mail. If querying by mail, include a SASE. If querying by e-mail, put "Query" in the subject line. For fiction, include the first few pages or opening chapter of your novel as a single Word attachment. For nonfiction, include your book proposal as a single Word attachment. Accepts simultaneous submissions. Responds within 8 weeks.

DIANA FINCH LITERARY AGENCY

116 W. 23rd St., Suite 500, New York NY 10011. (917)544-4470. **E-mail:** diana.finch@verizon.net. **Website:** http://dianafinchliteraryagency.blogspot.com. **Contact:** Diana Finch. Estab. 2003. Member of AAR. Represents 40 clients.

Seeking to represent books that change lives. Prior to opening her agency in 2003, Ms. Finch worked at Ellen Levine Literary Agency for 18 years.

REPRESENTS Nonfiction, novels. **Considers these nonfiction areas:** autobiography, biography, business, child guidance, computers, cultural interests, current affairs, dance, economics, environment, ethnic, film, government, health, history, how-to, humor, investigative, juvenile nonfiction, law, medicine, memoirs, military, money, music, parenting, photography, popular culture, politics, psychology, satire, science, self-help, sports, technology, theater, translation, true crime, war, women's issues, women's studies. **Considers these fiction areas:** action, adventure, contemporary issues, crime, detective, ethnic, historical, literary, mainstream, police, sports, thriller, young adult.

"Does not want romance, mysteries, or children's picture books."

HOW TO CONTACT This agency prefers submissions via its online form: https://dianafinchliteraryagency.submittable.com/submit. Accepts simultaneous submissions.

TERMS Agent receives 15% commission on domestic sales; 20% commission on foreign sales. Offers written contract. "I charge for overseas postage, galleys, and books purchased, and try to recoup these costs from earnings received for a client, rather than charging outright."

TIPS "Do as much research as you can on agents before you query. Have someone critique your query letter before you send it. It should be only 1 page and describe your book clearly—and why you are writing it—but also demonstrate creativity and a sense of your writing style."

FINEPRINT LITERARY MANAGEMENT

115 W. 29th, Third Floor, New York NY 10001. (212)279-1282. **Website:** www.fineprintlit.com. Member of AAR.

MEMBER AGENTS Peter Rubie, CEO, peter@fineprintlit.com (nonfiction interests include narrative nonfiction, popular science, spirituality, history, biography, pop culture, business, technology, parenting, health, self help, music, and food; fiction interests include literary thrillers, crime fiction, science fiction and fantasy, military fiction, literary fiction, middle-grade, and boy-oriented young adult); **Stephany Evans**, stephany@fineprintlit.com (nonfiction interests include health and wellness, spirituality, lifestyle [including home renovating, decorating, food and drink, and sustainability], running and fitness, memoir, and narrative nonfiction; fiction interests include women's fiction [from literary to romance, including mystery, historical, and romantic suspense]); **Janet Reid**, janet@fineprintlit.com (crime fiction and narrative nonfiction); **Laura Wood**, laura@fineprintlit.com (serious nonfiction—especially in the areas of science and nature, business, history, religion, and other areas by academics and professionals; she seeks select genre fiction [no poetry, literary fiction, or memoir] in the categories of science fiction, fantasy, and mystery); **June Clark**, june@fineprintlit.com (nonfiction projects in the areas of entertainment, self-help, parenting, reference, how-to books, food and wine, style/beauty, and prescriptive business titles); **Penny Moore**, penny@fineprintlit.com (all genres of middle-grade and young adult fiction; she seeks adult fiction in the genres of upmarket, speculative, science fiction, fantasy, psychological thrillers, and select romance; nonfiction projects in the realm of pop culture, humor, travel, food, and pets); **Jacqueline Murphy**, jacqueline@fineprintlit.com.

REPRESENTS Considers these nonfiction areas: biography, business, foods, health, history, how-to, humor, memoirs, music, parenting, popular culture, science, self-help, spirituality, technology, travel, fitness, lifestyle. **Considers these fiction areas:** commercial, crime, fantasy, historical, middle-grade, mystery, romance, science fiction, suspense, thriller, women's, young adult.

HOW TO CONTACT E-query. For fiction, send a query, synopsis, bio, and 30 pages pasted into the e-mail. No attachments. For nonfiction, send a query only, with the proposal requested later if the agent is interested. Accepts simultaneous submissions. Obtains most new clients through recommendations from others, solicitations.

TERMS Agent receives 15% commission on domestic sales; 20% commission on foreign sales.

FLANNERY LITERARY

1140 Wickfield Court, Naperville IL 60563. **E-mail:** jennifer@flanneryliterary.com. **Contact:** Jennifer Flannery. "Flannery Literary is a Chicago-area literary agency representing writers of books for children and young adults." Estab. 1992. Represents 40 clients.

REPRESENTS Nonfiction, novels, juvenile books. **Considers these nonfiction areas:** young adult. **Considers these fiction areas:** juvenile, middle-grade, new adult, picture books, young adult.

> This agency specializes in children's and young adult fiction and nonfiction. It also accepts picture books. 100% juvenile books.

HOW TO CONTACT Query by e-mail. "Simultaneous submissions are fine, but please inform us. No attachments. If you're sending a query about a novel, please include, in the e-mail, the first 5-10 pages. If it's a picture book, please include the entire text." Accepts simultaneous submissions. Responds in 2 weeks to queries; 1 month to mss.

TERMS Agent receives 15% commission on domestic sales; 20% commission on foreign sales.

TIPS "Write an engrossing, succinct query describing your work. We are always looking for a fresh new voice."

FOLIO LITERARY MANAGEMENT, LLC

The Film Center Building, 630 Ninth Ave., Suite 1101, New York NY 10036. (212)400-1494. **Fax:** (212)967-0977. **Website:** www.foliolit.com. Member of AAR. Represents 100+ clients.

> Prior to creating Folio Literary Management, Mr. Hoffman worked for several years at another agency; Mr. Kleinman was an agent at Graybill & English.

MEMBER AGENTS Claudia Cross (romance novels, commercial women's fiction, cooking and food writing, serious nonfiction on religious and spiritual topics); **Scott Hoffman** (literary and commercial fiction, journalistic or academic nonfiction, narrative nonfiction, pop culture books, business, history,

STACEY GRAHAM
RED SOFA LITERARY

www.redsofaliterary.com
@staceyigraham

ABOUT STACEY: Stacey is an associate agent for Red Sofa Literary after years of being on the other side of the literary blanket. She is the author of four books, as well as being a freelance editor, ghostwriter, and screenwriter. She works closely with Boundary Stone Films.

SHE IS SEEKING: Humor books, humorous memoir along the lines of Jenny Lawson or John Cleese, dark middle-grade, New Age with a strong platform, quirky nonfiction (young adult, middle-grade, and adult), history, and horror. She is *not* looking for young adult fiction or adult fantasy.

HOW TO SUBMIT: Contact stacey@redsofaliterary.com. If it's a good fit, she will request the first three chapters or a finished book proposal.

AGENTS & ART REPS

politics, spiritual or religious fiction and nonfiction, science fiction, fantasy, literary fiction, heartbreaking memoirs, humorous nonfiction); **Jeff Kleinman** (bookclub fiction [not genre commercial, like mysteries or romances], literary fiction, thrillers and suspense, narrative nonfiction, memoir); **Dado Derviskadic** (nonfiction interests include cultural history, biography, memoir, pop science, motivational self-help, health, pop culture, cookbooks; also seeks fiction that's gritty, introspective, or serious); **Frank Weimann** (biography, business, finance, history, religious, health, lifestyle, cookbooks, sports, African-American, science, memoir, military, prescriptive nonfiction, humor, celebrity; also seeks adult and children's fiction); **Michael Harriot** (commercial nonfiction [both narrative and prescriptive], fantasy, science fiction); **Erin Harris** (book club, historical fiction, literary, narrative nonfiction, psychological suspense, young adult); **Molly Jaffa** (middle-grade, young adult, select nonfiction); **Katherine Latshaw** (blog-to-book projects, food/cooking, middle-grade, narrative and prescriptive nonfiction); **Annie Hwang** (literary and upmarket fiction with commercial appeal; select nonfiction in the areas of popular science, health, lifestyle, narrative nonfiction, pop culture, and humor); **Erin Niumata** (commercial women's fiction, romance, historical fiction, mysteries, psychological thrillers, suspense, humor, self-help, women's issues, pop culture and humor, pets, memoirs, and anything by successful bloggers); **Ruth Pomerance** (narrative nonfiction and commercial fiction); **Marcy Posner** (commercial women's fiction, historical fiction, mystery, biography, history, health, lifestyle, thrillers, narrative nonfiction; for kidlit, she seeks contemporary young adult and middle-grade, mystery series for boys, and select historical fiction and fantasy); **Jeff Silberman** (narrative nonfiction, biography, history, politics, current affairs, health, lifestyle, humor, food, memoir, pop culture, sports, science, technology; his fiction interests include commercial, literary, and book club fiction); **Steve Troha**; **Emily van Beek** (young adult, middle-grade, picture books), **Melissa White** (general nonfiction, literary and commercial fiction, middle-grade, young adult); **John Cusick** (middle-grade, picture books, young adult).

REPRESENTS Nonfiction, novels. **Considers these nonfiction areas:** animals, art, biography, business, cooking, creative nonfiction, economics, environment, foods, health, history, how-to, humor, inspirational, memoirs, military, parenting, popular culture, politics, psychology, religious, satire, science, self-help, technology, war, women's issues, women's studies. **Considers these fiction areas:** commercial, fantasy, horror, literary, middle-grade, mystery, picture books, religious, romance, thriller, women's, young adult.

☛ No poetry, stage plays, or screenplays.

HOW TO CONTACT Query via e-mail only (no attachments). Read agent bios online for specific submission guidelines and e-mail addresses, and to check if someone is closed to queries. "All agents respond to queries as soon as possible, whether interested or not. If you haven't heard back from the individual agent within the time period that they specify on their bio page, it's possible that something has gone wrong, and you can e-mail a follow-up."

TIPS "Please do not submit simultaneously to more than 1 agent at Folio. If you're not sure which of us is exactly right for your book, don't worry. We work closely as a team, and if 1 of our agents gets a query that might be more appropriate for someone else, we'll always pass it along. It's important that you check each agent's bio page for clear directions as to how to submit, as well as when to expect feedback."

FOUNDRY LITERARY + MEDIA

33 W. 17th St., PH, New York NY 10011. (212)929-5064. **Fax:** (212)929-5471. **Website:** www.foundrymedia.com.

MEMBER AGENTS Peter McGuigan, pmsubmissions@foundrymedia.com (smart, offbeat voices in all genres of fiction and nonfiction); **Yfat Reiss Gendell**, yrgsubmissions@foundrymedia.com (practical nonfiction in the areas of health and wellness, diet, lifestyle, how-to, and parenting; seeks a range of narrative nonfiction that includes humor, memoir, history, science, pop culture, psychology, and adventure/travel stories; seeks unique commercial fiction, including young adult fiction, speculative fiction, thrillers, and historical fiction); **Chris Park**, cpsubmissions@foundrymedia.com (memoirs, narrative nonfiction, sports books, Christian nonfiction,

Christian character-driven fiction); **Hannah Brown Gordon**, hbgsubmissions@foundrymedia.com (stories and narratives that blend genres, including thriller, suspense, historical, literary, speculative, memoir, pop-science, psychology, humor, and pop culture); **Brandi Bowles**, bbsubmissions@foundrymedia.com (nonfiction ranges from cookbooks to prescriptive books, science, pop culture, and real-life inspirational stories; seeks high-concept novels that feature strong female bonds and psychological or scientific themes); **Kirsten Neuhaus**, knsubmissions@foundrymedia.com (platform-driven narrative nonfiction in the areas of memoir, business, lifestyle [fashion/relationships], current events, history, and stories with strong female voices; seeks smart fiction that appeals to a wide market); **Jessica Regel**, jrsubmissions@foundrymedia.com (young adult and middle-grade books, as well as a select list of adult general fiction, women's fiction, and adult nonfiction); **Anthony Mattero**, amsubmissions@foundrymedia.com (smart, platform-driven nonfiction in the areas of pop culture, humor, music, sports, and popular business); **Peter Steinberg**, pssubmissions@foundrymedia.com (narrative nonfiction, commercial and literary fiction, memoir, health, history, lifestyle, humor, sports, and young adult); **Roger Freet**, rfsubmissions@foundrymedia.com (narrative and idea-driven nonfiction clients in the areas of religion, spirituality, memoir, and cultural issues; represents leading scholars, pastors, historians, activists, and musicians); **Adriann Ranta** arsubmissions@foundrymedia.com (accepts all genres and age groups; loves gritty, realistic, true-to-life narratives, women's fiction and nonfiction, accessible pop nonfiction [science, history, and craft], and fresh genre-bending works for children).

REPRESENTS **Considers these nonfiction areas:** creative nonfiction, current affairs, diet/nutrition, health, history, how-to, humor, medicine, memoirs, music, parenting, popular culture, psychology, science, sports, travel. **Considers these fiction areas:** commercial, historical, humor, literary, middle-grade, suspense, thriller, women's, young adult.

HOW TO CONTACT Target 1 Foundry agent only. Send queries to the specific submission e-mail of the agent. For fiction, send a query, synopsis, author bio, and the first 3 chapters—all pasted in the e-mail. For nonfiction, send a query, sample chapters, table of contents, and author bio (all pasted). "If you do not receive a response within 8 weeks, your submission is not right for our lists at this time." Accepts simultaneous submissions.

RECENT SALES *The Last September* by Nina de Gramont, *The Hired Girl* by Laura Amy Schlitz, *The Power of Broke* by Daymond John with Daniel Paisner, *The Suja Juice Solution* by Annie Lawless and Jeff Church, *NFL Confidential* by Johnny Anonymous.

TIPS "Consult our website for each agent's individual submission instructions."

FOX LITERARY

110 W. 40th St., Suite 2305, New York NY 10018. E-mail: submissions@foxliterary.com. **Website:** www.publishersmarketplace.com/members/fox/. Fox Literary is a boutique agency that represents commercial fiction, along with select works of literary fiction and nonfiction with broad commercial appeal.

MEMBER AGENTS Diana Fox.

REPRESENTS Nonfiction, fiction, graphic novels. **Considers these nonfiction areas:** biography, creative nonfiction, history, popular culture, mind/body. **Considers these fiction areas:** fantasy, historical, romance, science fiction, thriller, young adult, general.

HOW TO CONTACT E-mail a query and first 5 pages in body of e-mail. No attachments. Accepts simultaneous submissions.

RECENT SALES *Black Ships* by Jo Graham (Orbit), Evernight series by Claudia Gray (HarperCollins), October Daye series by Seanan McGuire (DAW), *Salt and Silver* by Anna Katherine (Tor), *Alcestis* by Katharine Beutner (Soho Press).

⊕ FRASER-BUB LITERARY, LLC

410 Park Ave. S, Tenth Floor, New York NY 10016. (917)524-6982. **E-mail:** mackenzie@fraserbubliterary.com. **Website:** www.fraserbubliterary.com. **Contact:** MacKenzie Fraser-Bub. Estab. 2015.

○ Prior to forming her own agency, Ms. Fraser-Bub worked as an editor before becoming an agent at Trident Media Group..

REPRESENTS Nonfiction, novels. **Considers these nonfiction areas:** cookbooks (especially healthy eating and baking), design, diet, fashion, food, popular psychology, relationships, self-help, true crime. **Considers these fiction areas:** crime, historical fiction, mystery (female-driven), new adult, romance, thriller, women's fiction, young adult (with crossover appeal).

⊶ Does not want to receive children's picture books, middle-grade, screenplays, poetry, graphic novels, or comics. Rarely represents or requests science fiction, fantasy, westerns, philosophy, or sports.

HOW TO CONTACT "I only accept e-queries. Please do not query via phone. Include the world 'Query' in your subject line. For fiction submissions, your query may include the first chapter in the body of the e-mail. I will not open attachments. For nonfiction submissions, your query may include the first 10 pages in the body of the e-mail."

SARAH JANE FREYMANN LITERARY AGENCY

(212)362-9277. **E-mail:** sarah@sarahjanefreymann.com. **E-mail:** submissions@sarahjanefreymann.com. **Website:** www.sarahjanefreymann.com.

MEMBER AGENTS Sarah Jane Freymann (nonfiction interests include spiritual, psychology, self-help, women/men's issues, books by health experts [conventional and alternative], cookbooks, narrative nonfiction, natural science, nature, memoirs, cutting-edge journalism, travel, multicultural issues, parenting, lifestyle; fiction interests include literary, mainstream, young adult); **Jessica Sinsheimer**, jessica@sarahjanefreymann.com (young adult, thrillers, picture books); **Steven Schwartz**, steve@sarahjanefreymann.com (popular fiction [crime, thrillers, and historical novels], world and national affairs, business books, self-help, psychology, humor, sports and travel).

REPRESENTS Nonfiction, novels. **Considers these nonfiction areas:** business, cooking, creative nonfiction, current affairs, health, humor, memoirs, multicultural, parenting, psychology, science, self-help, spirituality, sports, travel, women's issues, men's issues, nature, journalism, lifestyle. **Considers these fiction areas:** crime, historical, literary, mainstream, thriller, young adult, popular fiction.

HOW TO CONTACT Query via e-mail. No attachments. Below the query, please paste the first 10 pages of your work. Accepts simultaneous submissions.

TERMS Charges clients for long distance, overseas postage, photocopying. 100% of business is derived from commissions on ms sales.

RECENT SALES *Your Life is a Book: How to Craft and Publish Your Memoir* by Brenda Peterson and Sarah Jane Freymann (Sasquatch Books), *The Soul of an Octopus: A Surprising Exploration into the Wonder of*

NEW AGENT SPOTLIGHT

AMANDA JAIN
INKLINGS LITERARY AGENCY

www.inklingsliterary.com
@wensday95

ABOUT AMANDA: After earning a bachelor of arts in English, Amanda Jain worked in the trade department at W.W. Norton for seven years before leaving to pursue graduate studies. She graduated in 2011 with a master of arts in the history of decorative arts. Amanda joined Inklings in 2014. She is now building her client list and seeking submissions.

SHE IS SEEKING: Historical fiction (in all genres), women's fiction, book club/upmarket fiction, romance (particularly historical, suspenseful, or with a comedic bent), and mysteries (particularly historical, cozy, or historical cozies). She also seeks narrative nonfiction in the areas of social history, archaeology, art history, and material culture. She is interested in select young adult and middle-grade projects with unique hooks and a strong voice. In all cases, what Amanda is most looking for is a story that completely immerses the reader in the world of the book. Amanda is *not* the agent to query with picture books, memoirs, self-help, poetry, erotica, science fiction, fantasy, horror, or inspirational fiction.

HOW TO CONTACT: Type "Query for Amanda: [Title]" in the subject line to query@inklingsliterary.com. No attachments. In the body of the e-mail, send a query letter that includes the title, genre, and word count of your project. Also include a brief pitch about the story, a brief bo (including any publishing credits), the first 10 pages of your manuscript, and a brief synopsis (one or two pages). "Our response time varies, but the general response time is within three months for queries, and four months for manuscripts. If you have not received an answer for your query after three months," the agency is not interested in the project."

Consciousness by Sy Montgomery (Atria Books), *The Bird Has My Wings: The Autobiography of an Innocent Man on Death Row* by Jarvis Jay Masters (HarperOne).

REBECCA FRIEDMAN LITERARY AGENCY

E-mail: Abby@rfliterary.com. **Website:** www.rfliterary.com. Estab. 2013. Member of AAR. Signatory of WGA.

○ Prior to opening her agency in 2013, Ms. Friedman was with Sterling Lord Literistic from 2006 to 2011, then with Hill Nadell Agency.

MEMBER AGENTS Rebecca Friedman, brandie@rfliterary.com (commercial and literary fiction with a focus on literary novels of suspense, women's fiction, contemporary romance, young adult, as well as journalistic nonfiction and memoir); **Kimberly Brower**, kimberly@rfliterary.com (commercial and literary fiction, with an emphasis in contemporary romance, women's fiction, mysteries/thrillers, young adult); **Rachel Marks**, rachel@rfliterary.com (young adult, fantasy, science fiction, new adult, and romance); **Susan Finesman**, susan@rfliterary.com (fiction, cookbooks, lifestyle); **Jess Dallow**, jess@rfliterary.com (young adult and adult literary and commercial fiction—with a focus in romance, thrillers, and women's fiction).

REPRESENTS Nonfiction, fiction. **Considers these nonfiction areas:** memoirs, journalistic nonfiction. **Considers these fiction areas:** commercial, fantasy, literary, mystery, new adult, romance, science fiction, suspense, women's, young adult.

HOW TO CONTACT Please submit your query letter and first chapter (no more than 15 pages, double-spaced). If querying Kimberly, paste a full synopsis into the e-mail submission. No attachments. Accepts simultaneous submissions. Tries to respond in 8 weeks.

RECENT SALES A complete list of agency authors is available online.

FULL CIRCLE LITERARY, LLC

Website: www.fullcircleliterary.com. **Contact:** Stefanie Von Borstel. Estab. 2005. Member of AAR, SCBWI, Authors Guild. Represents 100+ clients.

○ Please read the "Our Agents" page on our website and determine the Full Circle Literary agent who is the best fit for your work.

MEMBER AGENTS Stefanie Von Borstel; **Adriana Dominguez**; **Taylor Martindale** (multicultural voices); **Lilly Ghahremani**.

REPRESENTS Considers these nonfiction areas: creative nonfiction, how-to, interior design, multicultural, women's issues, young adult. **Considers these fiction areas:** literary, middle-grade, multicultural, picture books, women's, young adult.

☛ Actively seeking nonfiction by authors with a unique voice and strong platform, projects that offer new and diverse viewpoints, and literature with a global or multicultural perspective. We are particularly interested in books with a Latino or Middle Eastern angle.

HOW TO CONTACT Online submissions only via the submissions form at www.fullcircleliterary.com Please complete the form and submit a cover letter, author information, and sample writing. Concerning the sample writing, fiction submissions should include the first 10 ms pages. For nonfiction, include a proposal with 1 sample chapter. Accepts simultaneous submissions. "Due to the high volume of submissions, please keep in mind we are no longer able to personally respond to every submission. If you have not heard from us in 8 weeks, your project is not right for our agency at the current time."

TERMS Agent receives 15% commission on domestic sales; 25% commission on foreign sales. Offers written contract which outlines responsibilities of the author and the agent.

RECENT SALES "Please visit our website to learn about our latest deals and book news. Follow our agency on Twitter @fullcirclelit."

FUSE LITERARY

Website: www.fuseliterary.com. Member of AAR. Signatory of WGA.

MEMBER AGENTS Laurie McLean (only accepting referral inquiries and submissions requested at conferences or online events, with the exception of unsolicited adult and children's science fiction); **Gordon Warnock**, querygordon@fuseliterary.com (fiction interests include high-concept commercial fiction, literary fiction [adult and young adult], graphic novels [adult, young adult, middle-grade]; nonfiction interests include memoir [adult, young adult, new adult, graphic novels], cookbooks, food, illustrated art and photography [especially graphic nonfiction], political and current events, pop science, pop culture [especially punk culture and geek culture], self-help, how-to, humor, pets, business, career); **Connor Goldsmith**, queryconnor@fuseliterary.com (fiction interests include science fiction, fantasy, horror, thrillers, and upmarket commercial fiction with a unique and memorable hook; seeks books by and about people from marginalized perspectives, such as LGBT people and/or racial minorities; seeks nonfiction from recognized experts with established platforms in the areas of history [partic-

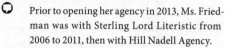

ularly of the ancient world], theater, cinema, music, television, mass media, popular culture, feminism and gender studies, LGBT issues, race relations, and the sex industry); **Sara Sciuto**, querysara@fuseliterary.com (middle-grade, young adult, standout picture books); **Michelle Richter**, querymichelle@fuseliterary.com (book club reads, literary fiction, mystery, suspense, thrillers; for nonfiction, she seeks fashion, pop culture, science, medicine, sociology, and economics); **Emily S. Keyes**, queryemily@fuseliterary.com (young adult, middle-grade, fantasy, science fiction, women's fiction, new adult fiction, pop culture, and humor); **Tricia Skinner**, querytricia@fuseliterary.com (romance in the subgenres of science fiction, futuristic, fantasy, military/special ops, medieval historical, diversity); **Jennifer Chen Tran**, queryjennifer@fuseliterary.com (literary fiction, commercial fiction, women's fiction, upmarket fiction, contemporary romance, mature young adult, new adult, suspense, thriller, select graphic novels [adult, young adult, middle-grade], memoir; seeks narrative nonfiction in the areas of adventure, biography, business, current affairs, medical, history, how-to, pop culture, psychology, social entrepreneurism, social justice, travel, and lifestyle books [home, design, fashion, food]).

HOW TO CONTACT E-query an individual agent. Check the website to see if any individual agent has closed themselves to submissions, as well as each agent's individual query preferences. Accepts simultaneous submissions.

WRITERS CONFERENCES Agents from this agency attend many conferences. A full list of their appearances is available on the agency website.

⊙ NANCY GALLT LITERARY AGENCY

273 Charlton Ave., South Orange NJ 07079. (973)761-6358. **Website:** www.nancygallt.com. **Contact:** Nancy Gallt, Marietta Zacker. "At the Nancy Gallt Literary Agency, we represent people, not projects, and we focus solely on writers and illustrators of children's books." Estab. 2000. Represents 60 clients.

Prior to opening her agency, Ms. Gallt was subsidiary rights director of the children's book division at Morrow, Harper, and Viking.

MEMBER AGENTS Nancy Gallt, Marietta Zacker.

REPRESENTS Considers these fiction areas: juvenile, middle-grade, picture books, young adult.

Actively seeking picture books, middle-grade, and young adult novels. No adult fiction.

HOW TO CONTACT Submit through online submission form on agency website. No e-queries, please. Accepts simultaneous submissions.

TERMS Agent receives 15% commission on domestic sales; 20% commission on foreign sales. Offers written contract; 30-day notice must be given to terminate contract.

RECENT SALES *Toya* by Randi Revill, Rick Riordan's books (Hyperion), *Something Extraordinary* by Ben Clanton (Simon & Schuster), *The Baby Tree* by Sophie Blackall (Nancy Paulsen Books/Penguin), *Fenway and Hattie* by Victoria J. Coe (Putnam/Penguin).

TIPS "Writing and illustrations stand on their own, so submissions should tell the most compelling stories possible—whether visually, in words, or both."

GELFMAN SCHNEIDER / ICM PARTNERS

850 Seventh Ave., Suite 903, New York NY 10019. **E-mail:** mail@gelfmanschneider.com. **Website:** www.gelfmanschneider.com. **Contact:** Jane Gelfman, Deborah Schneider. Member of AAR. Represents 300+ clients.

MEMBER AGENTS Deborah Schneider (all categories of literary and commercial fiction and nonfiction); **Jane Gelfman**; **Victoria Marini**, victoria.gsliterary@gmail.com (literary fiction, commercial fiction, pop culture nonfiction, young adult and middle-grade fiction; she has a particular interest in engaging literary fiction and mysteries/suspense, commercial women's fiction [suspense, mystery, thriller, magical realism, fantasy], and young adult [contemporary and speculative]); **Heather Mitchell** (particularly interested in narrative nonfiction, historical fiction, and young debut authors with strong voices); **Penelope Burns**, penelope.gsliterary@gmail.com (literary and commercial fiction and nonfiction, as well as a variety of young adult and middle-grade).

REPRESENTS Nonfiction, fiction, juvenile books. **Considers these nonfiction areas:** creative nonfiction, popular culture. **Considers these fiction areas:** commercial, fantasy, historical, literary, mainstream, middle-grade, mystery, science fiction, suspense, women's, young adult.

Does not currently accept screenplays or scripts, poetry, or picture book queries.

HOW TO CONTACT Query. Check the submissions page of the website to see which agents are open to queries and further instructions. To query Victoria or Penelope, please send a query letter and 1-3 sample chapters (pasted, no attachments) to their individual e-mails. Please include "Query" in the subject line. If you are contacting Victoria, please check victoriamarini.com/submissions for updates and response times, as they may vary. Accepts simultaneous submissions. **TERMS** Agent receives 15% commission on domestic sales; 20% commission on foreign sales. Offers written contract. Charges clients for photocopying and messengers/couriers.

GLOBAL LION INTELLECTUAL PROPERTY MANAGEMENT, INC.

P.O. Box 669238, Pompano Beach FL 33066. **E-mail:** queriesgloballionmgt@gmail.com. **Website:** www.globallionmanagement.com. **Contact:** Peter Miller. Estab. 2013. Member of AAR. Signatory of WGA.

○ Prior to his current position, Mr. Miller was formerly the founder of PMA Literary & Film Management Inc. of New York.

☛ "I look for cutting-edge authors of both fiction and nonfiction with global marketing and motion picture (or TV) production potential."

HOW TO CONTACT E-query. Global Lion Intellectual Property Management, Inc. accepts exclusive submissions only. "If your work is under consideration by another agency, please do not submit it to us." Below the query, paste a one-page synopsis, a sample of your book (20 pages is typical), a short author bio, and any impressive social media links.

BARRY GOLDBLATT LITERARY LLC

320 Seventh Ave. #266, Brooklyn NY 11215. **E-mail:** query@bgliterary.com. **Website:** www.bgliterary.com. **Contact:** Barry Goldblatt. Estab. 2000. Member of AAR. Signatory of WGA.

MEMBER AGENTS Barry Goldblatt; Jennifer Udden, query.judden@gmail.com (speculative fiction of all stripes [especially innovative science fiction or fantasy], romance [contemporary, erotic, LGBT, paranormal, historical], contemporary or speculative young adult, mysteries, thrillers, and urban fantasies).

REPRESENTS Fiction. **Considers these fiction areas:** fantasy, middle-grade, mystery, romance, science fiction, thriller, young adult.

☛ "Please see our website for specific submission guidelines and information on our particular tastes."

HOW TO CONTACT "E-mail queries can be sent to query@bgliterary.com and should include the word 'Query' in the subject line. To query Jen specifically, e-mail queries can be sent to query.judden@gmail.com. Please know that we will read and respond to every e-query that we receive, provided it is properly addressed and follows the submission guidelines below. We will not respond to e-queries that are addressed to no one or to multiple recipients. While we do not require exclusivity, exclusive submissions will receive priority review. If your submission is exclusive to Barry Goldblatt Literary, please indicate so by including the word 'Exclusive' in the subject line of your e-mail. Your e-query should include the following within the body of the e-mail: your query letter, a synopsis of the book, and the first 5 pages of your ms. We will not open or respond to any e-mails that have attachments. Our response time is 4 weeks on queries, 8 weeks on full mss. If you haven't heard from us within that time, feel free to check in via e-mail." Accepts simultaneous submissions. Obtains clients through referrals, queries, conferences.

TERMS Agent receives 15% commission on domestic sales; 20% on foreign and dramatic sales. Offers written contract.

RECENT SALES *Other Broken Things* by C. Desir, *Masks and Shadows* by Stephanie Burgis, *Wishing Day* by Lauren Myracle, *Mother-Daughter Book Camp* by Heather Vogel Frederick.

TIPS "We're a hands-on agency, focused on building an author's career, not just making an initial sale. We don't care about trends or what's hot; we just want to sign great writers."

IRENE GOODMAN LITERARY AGENCY

27 W. 24th St., Suite 700B, New York NY 10010. **Website:** www.irenegoodman.com. Member of AAR.

MEMBER AGENTS Irene Goodman, irene.queries@irenegoodman.com; Miriam Kriss, miriam.queries@irenegoodman.com; Barbara Poelle, barbara.queries@irenegoodman.com; Rachel Ekstrom, rachel.queries@irenegoodman.com; Beth Vesel, beth.queries@irenegoodman.com; Kim Perel, kim.queries@irenegoodman.com; Anne Baltazar; Brita Lundberg.

REPRESENTS Nonfiction, novels, juvenile books. **Considers these nonfiction areas:** parenting, social issues, francophilia, anglophilia, Judaica, lifestyles, cooking, memoir. **Considers these fiction areas:**

NEW AGENT SPOTLIGHT

TANUSRI PRASANNA
HANNIGAN SALKY GELTZER

www.hsgagency.com
@tanusriprasanna

ABOUT TANUSRI: A lawyer by training, Tanusri Prasanna has a PhD in legal philosophy and human rights from Oxford University, and a master's degree from Harvard Law School. Along the way, she worked in the legal department of the World Bank in Washington and as a fellow at Columbia Law School. An avid fan of children's literature, Tanusri joined a book club devoted to kidlit in 2012, which sowed the seeds of her decision to become a literary agent specializing in children's books. To this end, before joining HSG, she gained valuable experience interning at Knopf Young Readers and Foundry Literary + Media. Tanusri was born and raised in India, though she has lived in the United Kingdom and New York for the past fourteen years.

SHE IS SEEKING: All sorts of kidlit, ranging from picture books and middle-grade to young adult (including young adult/adult crossovers). And while her primary interest is kidlit, she is also open to selective domestic suspense (Tana French and Sophie Hannah are two of her favorite authors in the genre) and voice-driven narrative nonfiction on social justice issues.

HOW TO SUBMIT: Send a query letter and the first five pages of your manuscript (within the e-mail—no attachments) to tprasanna@hsgagency.com. If it is a picture book, please include the entire manuscript. "If you were referred to us, please mention it in the first line of your query. We generally respond to queries within six weeks, although we do get behind occasionally."

crime, detective, historical, mystery, romance, thriller, women's, young adult.

8— Seeking commercial fiction, literary fiction, and commercial nonfiction. No children's picture books, screenplays, poetry, or inspirational fiction.

HOW TO CONTACT Query. Also submit a synopsis and the first 10 pages pasted into the body of the e-mail. E-mail queries only. No attachments. Query 1 agent only. Accepts simultaneous submissions. Responds in 2 months to queries. Consult website for each agent's specific submission guidelines.

TIPS "We are receiving an unprecedented amount of e-queries. If you find that the mailbox is full, please try again in 2 weeks. E-queries to our personal inboxes will be deleted."

DOUG GRAD LITERARY AGENCY, INC.

68 Jay St., Suite N3, Brooklyn NY 11201. (718)788-6067. **E-mail:** query@dgliterary.com. **Website:** www.

dgliterary.com. **Contact:** Doug Grad. Estab. 2008. Member of AAR. Signatory of WGA.

○ Prior to being an agent, Mr. Grad spent 22 years as an editor at imprint at 4 major publishing houses—Simon & Schuster, Random House, Penguin, and HarperCollins.

MEMBER AGENTS Doug Grad (narrative nonfiction, military, sports, celebrity memoir, thrillers, mysteries, historical fiction, music, style, business, home improvement, cookbooks, science, and theater).

REPRESENTS Nonfiction, novels. **Considers these nonfiction areas:** Americana, autobiography, business, cooking, creative nonfiction, current affairs, diet/nutrition, design, film, government, history, humor, military, music, popular culture, politics, science, sports, technology, theater, travel, true crime, war. **Considers these fiction areas:** action, adventure, commercial, crime, detective, historical, horror, literary, mainstream, military, mystery, police, science fiction, suspense, thriller, war, young adult.

☛ Does not want fantasy, young adult, or children's picture books.

HOW TO CONTACT Query by e-mail. No sample material unless requested; no printed submissions by mail. Accepts simultaneous submissions.

RECENT SALES *The Earthend Saga* by Gillian Anderson and Jeff Rovin (Simon451), *Bounty* by Michael Byrnes (Bantam), *Sports Idioms and Words* by Josh Chetwynd (Ten Speed Press).

ASHLEY GRAYSON LITERARY AGENCY

1342 W. 18th St., San Pedro CA 90732. **E-mail:** graysonagent@earthlink.net. **Website:** www.publishersmarketplace.com/members/CGrayson. Estab. 1976. Member of AAR.

MEMBER AGENTS Ashley Grayson (fantasy, mystery, thrillers, young adult); Carolyn Grayson, carolyngraysonagent@earthlink.net (women's fiction, romance, urban fantasy, paranormal romance, mysteries, thrillers, children's books, nonfiction); Lois Winston, lois.graysonagent@earthlink.net (women's fiction, romance, chick lit, mystery).

REPRESENTS Nonfiction, novels. **Considers these nonfiction areas:** business, parenting, popular culture, science, spirituality, true crime. **Considers these fiction areas:** fantasy, juvenile, middle-grade, mystery, romance, thriller, women's, young adult.

☛ "We represent literary and commercial fiction, as well as nonfiction for adults (self-help, parenting, pop culture, mind/body/spirit, true crime, business, science). We also represent fiction for younger readers (chapter books through young adult). We are seeking more mysteries and thrillers."

HOW TO CONTACT "The agency is temporarily closed to queries from fiction writers who are not previously published at book length (self-published or print-on-demand titles do not count). However, we will take contacts through client referrals, conference meetings, and from unpublished authors who have received an offer from a reputable publisher (who need an agent before beginning contract negotiations). Nonfiction authors who are recognized within their field or area may still query with proposals. We cannot review self-published, subsidy-published, and POD-published works to evaluate moving them to mainstream publishers. If you meet the criteria above, send a query letter with a list of your publication credits. Do not include attachments to your e-mail unless requested. Do not query more than 1 agent in our agency, whether by e-mail or post." Accepts simultaneous submissions.

TERMS Agent receives 15% commission on domestic sales; 20% commission on foreign sales.

SANFORD J. GREENBURGER ASSOCIATES, INC.

55 Fifth Ave., New York NY 10003. (212)206-5600. **Fax:** (212)463-8718. **Website:** www.greenburger.com. Member of AAR. Represents 500 clients.

MEMBER AGENTS Matt Bialer, lribar@sjga.com (fantasy, science fiction, thrillers, mysteries, select group of literary writers; also seeks smart narrative nonfiction—including books about current events, popular culture, biography, history, music, race, and sports); Brenda Bowen, querybb@sjga.com (literary fiction, writers and illustrators of picture books, chapter books, middle-grade, young adult); Faith Hamlin, fhamlin@sjga.com (submissions by referral only); Heide Lange, queryhl@sjga.com (submissions by referral only); Daniel Mandel, querydm@sjga.com (literary and commercial fiction, memoirs; seeks nonfiction about business, art, history, politics, sports, and popular culture); Courtney Miller-Callihan, cmiller@sjga.com (young adult, middle-grade, women's fiction, romance, historical novels; seeks nonfiction projects on unusual topics, humor, pop culture, and lifestyle); Nicholas Ellison, nellison@sjga.com; Chelsea Lindman, clindman@sjga.com (playful literary fiction, upmarket crime fiction, and forward-thinking or boundary-pushing nonfiction); **Rachael Dillon Fried**, rfried@sjga.com (both fiction and nonfiction authors—with a keen interest in unique literary voices, women's fiction, narrative nonfiction, memoir, and comedy); **Lindsay Ribar**, co-agents with Matt Bialer (young adult and middle-grade fiction); **Bethany Buck**, querybbuck@sjga.com (middle-grade, chapter books, teen fiction, and a select list of picture book authors and illustrators); **Stephanie Delman**, sdelman@sjga.com (literary/upmarket contemporary fiction, psychological thrillers and suspense, atmospheric near-historical fiction); **Ed Maxwell**, emaxwell@sjga.com (expert and narrative nonfiction authors, novelists and graphic novelists, as well as children's book authors and illustrators).

REPRESENTS Nonfiction, novels, juvenile books. **Considers these nonfiction areas:** art, biography, business, creative nonfiction, current affairs, ethnic, history, humor, memoirs, music, popular culture, politics, sports. **Considers these fiction areas:** commercial, crime, family saga, fantasy, feminist, historical, literary, middle-grade, multicultural, mystery, picture books, romance, science fiction, thriller, women's, young adult.

HOW TO CONTACT E-query. "Please look at each agent's profile page for current information about what each agent is looking for and for the correct e-mail address to use for queries to that agent. Please be sure to use the correct query e-mail address for each agent." Agents will respond within 8 weeks if interested.

TERMS Agent receives 15% commission on domestic sales; 20% commission on foreign sales.

RECENT SALES *Inferno* by Dan Brown, *Sweet Pea and Friends: A Sheepover* by John Churchman and Jennifer Churchman, *Code of Conduct* by Brad Thor.

◉ **THE GREENHOUSE LITERARY AGENCY**

E-mail: submissions@greenhouseliterary.com. **Website:** www.greenhouseliterary.com. Member of AAR, SCBWI. Represents 20 clients.

○ Ms. Davies has had an editorial and management career in children's publishing spanning 25 years.

MEMBER AGENTS Sarah Davies (fiction by North American authors—from middle-grade through young adult); **Polly Nolan** (fiction by authors in the United Kingdom, Ireland, and the Commonwealth [including Australia, New Zealand, and India], plus European authors writing in English—from picture books (fewer than 1,000 words) to young adult).

🖙 "We exclusively represent authors writing fiction for children and teens. The agency has offices in both the US and the United Kingdom. Does not want to receive picture books texts (i.e., written by writers who aren't also illustrators), short stories, educational works, religious/inspirational work, preschool material, novelty material, screenplays, or writing aimed at adults.

HOW TO CONTACT Query 1 agent only. Put the target agent's name in the subject line. Paste the first 5 pages of your story (or your complete picture book) after the query. Accepts simultaneous submissions.

TERMS Agent receives 15% commission on domestic sales; 25% commission on foreign sales. Offers written contract.

RECENT SALES *Hour of the Bees* by Lindsay Eager (Candlewick), *Triangles: The Points of Love* by Natalie C. Parker (HarperCollins), *Maudeville* by Michelle Schusterman (Random House), *The Radiant Man* by Tami Lewis Brown (FSG, Macmillan).

TIPS "Before submitting material, authors should read the Greenhouse's 'Top 10 Tips for Authors of Children's Fiction' on our website and carefully follow our online submission guidelines."

KATHRYN GREEN LITERARY AGENCY, LLC

250 W. 57th St., Suite 2302, New York NY 10107. (212)245-4225. **Fax:** (212)245-4042. **E-mail:** query@kgreenagency.com. **Website:** www.kathryngreenliteraryagency.com. **Contact:** Kathy Green. Represents approximately 20 clients.

○ Prior to becoming an agent, Ms. Green was a book and magazine editor.

REPRESENTS Considers these nonfiction areas: history, humor, memoirs, parenting, popular culture, psychology. **Considers these fiction areas:** crime, detective, family saga, historical, humor, juvenile, literary, mainstream, middle-grade, mystery, police, romance, satire, suspense, thriller, women's, young adult.

🖙 Considers all types of fiction but particularly likes historical fiction, cozy mysteries, young adult, and middle-grade. "For nonfiction, I am interested in memoir, parenting, humor with a pop culture bent, and history. Quirky nonfiction is also a particular favorite." Does not want to receive science fiction, fantasy, children's picture books, screenplays, or poetry.

HOW TO CONTACT Send a query to query@kgree-nagency.com. Send no attachments unless requested. Do not send queries via postal mail. Responds in 4 weeks. "Queries do not have to be exclusive; however, if further material is requested, please be in touch before accepting other representation."

TERMS Agent receives 15% commission on domestic sales; 20% commission on foreign sales.

JILL GRINBERG LITERARY MANAGEMENT

392 Vanderbilt Ave., Brooklyn NY 11238. (212)620-5883. **E-mail:** info@jillgrinbergliterary.com. **Website:** www.jillgrinbergliterary.com. Estab. 1999.

○ Prior to her current position, Ms. Grinberg was at Anderson Grinberg Literary Management.

MEMBER AGENTS Jill Grinberg; Cheryl Pientka, cheryl@jillgrinbergliterary.com; **Katelyn Detweiler**, katelyn@jillgrinbergliterary.com.

REPRESENTS Nonfiction, novels. **Considers these nonfiction areas:** biography, cooking, ethnic, history, science, travel. **Considers these fiction areas:** fantasy, juvenile, literary, mainstream, middle-grade, romance, science fiction, young adult.

HOW TO CONTACT Please send your query letter to info@jillgrinbergliterary.com and attach the first 50 pages (fiction) or full proposal (nonfiction) as a Word doc file. All submissions will be read, but electronic submissions are preferred. Accepts simultaneous submissions.

RECENT SALES *Cinder* by Marissa Meyer, *The Hero's Guide to Saving Your Kingdom* by Christopher Healy, *Kiss and Make Up* by Katie Anderson and T.J. Stiles, *Eon* and *Eona* by Alison Goodman, *American Nations* by Colin Woodard, HALO trilogy by Alexandra Adornetto, *Liar* by Justine Larbalestier, *Turtle in Paradise* by Jennifer Holm, *Wisdom's Kiss* and *Dairy Queen* by Catherine Gilbert Murdock.

TIPS "We prefer submissions by e-mail."

✪ HELEN HELLER AGENCY, INC.

4-216 Heath St. W, Toronto, Ontario M5P 1N7 Canada. (416)489-0396. **E-mail:** info@helenhelleragency.com. **Website:** www.helenhelleragency.com. **Contact:** Helen Heller. Represents 30+ clients.

○ Prior to her current position, Ms. Heller worked for Cassell & Co. (England), was an editor for Harlequin Books, a senior editor for Avon Books, and editor in chief for Fitzhenry & Whiteside.

MEMBER AGENTS Helen Heller, helen@helenhelleragency.com (thrillers and front-list general fiction); **Sarah Heller**, sarah@helenhelleragency.com (front list commercial young adult and adult fiction, with a particular interest in high-concept historical fiction); **Barbara Berson**, barbara@helenhelleragency.com (literary fiction, nonfiction, young adult).

REPRESENTS Nonfiction, novels. **Considers these fiction areas:** commercial, crime, historical, literary, mainstream, thriller, young adult.

HOW TO CONTACT E-mail info@helenheller agency.com. Submit a brief synopsis, publishing history, author bio, and writing sample—pasted in the body of the e-mail. No attachments. Accepts simultaneous submissions. Responds within 3 months if interested. Accepts simultaneous submissions. Obtains most new clients through recommendations from others, solicitations.

RECENT SALES *Broken Promise* by Linwood Barclay, *When the Moon is Low* by Nadia Hashimi, *Fear the Darkness* by Becky Masterman.

TIPS "Whether you are an author searching for an agent, or whether an agent has approached you, it is in your best interest to first find out who the agent represents, what publishing houses has that agent sold to recently, and what foreign sales have been made. You should be able to go to the bookstore or search online and find the books the agent refers to. Many authors acknowledge their agents in the front or back or their books."

RONNIE ANN HERMAN

350 Central Park West, New York NY 10025. **E-mail:** ronnie@hermanagencyinc.com. **E-mail:** ronnie@hermanagencyinc.com. **Website:** www.hermanagencyinc.com. **Contact:** Ronnie Ann Herman. "We are a small boutique literary agency that represent authors and artists for the children's book market. We are only accepting submissions for middle-grade and young adult books at this time." Estab. 1999. Member of SCBWI. Represents 19 clients.

MEMBER AGENTS Ronnie Ann Herman, Katia Herman.

REPRESENTS Juvenile books. **Considers these nonfiction areas:** juvenile nonfiction. **Considers these fiction areas:** juvenile.

⊶ Middle-grade and young adult (all genres).

HOW TO CONTACT Submit via e-mail Accepts simultaneous submissions.

HOLLOWAY LITERARY

Raleigh NC. **E-mail:** submissions@hollowayliterary-agency.com. **Website:** http://hollowayliteraryagency.com. **Contact:** Nikki Terpilowski. Estab. 2011. Member of AAR, ITW, RWA. Signatory of WGA.
MEMBER AGENTS Nikki Terpilowski (romance, women's fiction, Southern fiction, historical fiction, cozy mysteries); **Rachel Burkot** (young adult contemporary, women's fiction, upmarket/book club fiction, contemporary romance, Southern fiction, urban fiction, literary fiction).
REPRESENTS Fiction. **Considers these fiction areas:** erotica, ethnic, fantasy, glitz, historical, literary, mainstream, middle-grade, multicultural, regional, romance, thriller, women's, young adult.

⊶ "Note to self-published authors: While we are happy to receive submissions from authors who have previously self-published novels, we do not represent self-published works. Send us your unpublished mss only." Nikki is open to submissions and is selectively reviewing queries for cozy mysteries with culinary, historical or book/publishing industry themes written in the vein of Jaclyn Brady, Laura Childs, Julie Hyzy, and Lucy Arlington. Nikki also seeks women's fiction with strong magical realism similar to Meena van Praag's *The Dress Shop of Dreams*. She would love to find a wine-themed mystery series similar to Nadia Gordon's Sunny McCoskey series or Ellen Crosby's Wine County mysteries that combine culinary themes with lots of great Southern history.

HOW TO CONTACT Send your query and the first 15 pages of your ms pasted into the body of your e-mail to submissions@hollowayliteraryagency.com. In the subject header, write: "[agent name]/[title]/[genre]." You can expect a response in 4-6 weeks. Responds if interested. Accepts simultaneous submissions.
RECENT SALES A list of agency clients is available on the website.

HSG AGENCY

37 W. 28th St, Eighth Floor, New York NY 10001. **E-mail:** channigan@hsgagency.com, jsalky@hsgagency.com, jgetzler@hsgagency.com, dburby@hsgagency.com, tprasanna@hsgagency.com, leigh@hsgagency.com. **Website:** http://hsgagency.com. Estab. 2011. Member of AAR. Signatory of WGA.

○ Prior to opening HSG Agency, Ms. Hannigan, Ms. Salky, and Mr. Getzler were agents at Russell & Volkening.

MEMBER AGENTS Carrie Hannigan (fiction and nonfiction children's books in the picture book and middle-grade age range, as well as adult women's fiction and select photography projects that would appeal to a large audience); **Jesseca Salky** (literary and mainstream fiction); **Josh Getzler** (foreign and historical fiction, women's fiction, straight-ahead historical fiction, thrillers, mysteries); **Danielle Burby** (young adult, women's fiction, mysteries, fantasy); **Tanusri Prasanna** (picture books, middle-grade, young adult, voice-driven narrative nonfiction on social justice issues); **Leigh Eisenman** (literary and commercial fiction, foodie/cookbooks, health and fitness, lifestyle, select narrative nonfiction).
REPRESENTS Nonfiction, novels, juvenile books. **Considers these nonfiction areas:** business, creative nonfiction, current affairs, diet/nutrition, education, environment, foods, memoirs, multicultural, photography, politics, psychology, science, self-help, women's issues, women's studies. **Considers these fiction areas:** adventure, commercial, contemporary issues, crime, detective, ethnic, family saga, historical, juvenile, literary, mainstream, middle-grade, multicultural, mystery, picture books, thriller, translation, women's, young adult.
HOW TO CONTACT Electronic submissions only. Send query letter and the first 5 pages of ms within an e-mail to the appropriate agent. Avoid submitting to multiple agents within the agency. Picture books submissions should include the entire ms. Accepts simultaneous submissions. Responds in 4-6 weeks.
RECENT SALES *The Beginner's Goodbye* by Anne Tyler (Knopf), *Blue Sea Burning* by Geoff Rodkey (Putnam), *The Partner Track* by Helen Wan (St. Martin's Press), *The Thrill of the Haunt* by E.J. Copperman (Berkley), *Aces Wild* by Erica Perl (Knopf Books for Young Readers), *Steve & Wessley: The Sea Monster* by Jennifer Morris (Scholastic), *Infinite Worlds* by Michael Soluri (Simon & Schuster).

ICM PARTNERS

730 Fifth Ave., New York NY 10019. (212)556-5600. **Website:** www.icmtalent.com. **Contact:** Literary Department. Member of AAR. Signatory of WGA.
REPRESENTS Nonfiction, novels.
HOW TO CONTACT The best way to query this agency is through a referral or by meeting an agent at an industry event, such as a writers conference.

INKLINGS LITERARY AGENCY

3419 Virginia Beach Blvd., #183, Virginia Beach VA 23452. (757)340-1070. **Fax:** (904)758-5440. **E-mail:** michelle@inklingsliterary.com. **E-mail:** query@inklingsliterary.com. **Website:** www.inklingsliterary.com. Inklings Literary Agency is a full-service, hands-on literary agency seeking submissions from established authors, as well as talented new authors. "We represent a broad range of commercial and literary fiction, as well as memoirs and true crime. We are not seeking other nonfiction, short stories, poetry, screenplays, or children's picture books." Estab. 2013. Member of RWA, SinC, HRW.

○   "We offer our clients interactive representation for their work, as well as developmental guidance for their author platforms, working with them as they grow."

MEMBER AGENTS Michelle Johnson, michelle@inklingsliterary.com (adult and young adult fiction interests include contemporary, suspense, thriller, mystery, horror, fantasy [including paranormal and supernatural elements within those genres], romance of every level; also seeks nonfiction in the areas of memoir and true crime); **Dr. Jamie Bodnar Drowley**, jamie@inklingsliterary.com (new adult fiction in the areas of romance [all subgenres], fantasy [urban fantasy, light science fiction, steampunk], mystery, thrillers, young adult [all subgenres], and middle-grade); **Margaret Bail**, margaret@inklingsliterary.com (romance, science fiction, mystery, thrillers, action adventure, historical fiction, western, some fantasy, memoir, cookbooks, true crime); **Naomi Davis**, naomi@inklingsliterary.com (romance of any variety [including paranormal, fresh urban fantasy, general fantasy, new adult and light science fiction], young adult in any of those same genres, memoirs about living with disabilities, facing criticism, and mental illness); **Whitley Abell**, whitley@inklingsliterary.com (young adult, middle-grade, and select upmarket women's fiction); **Alex

Barba**, alex@inklingsliterary.com (young adult); **Amanda Jain** (historical fiction [in all genres], women's, book club fiction, upmarket fiction, romance [particularly historical, suspenseful, or with a comedic bent], mysteries [particularly historical or cozy, or historical cozies]; also seeks narrative nonfiction in the areas of social history, archaeology, art history, and material culture).
REPRESENTS Nonfiction, novels, juvenile books. **Considers these nonfiction areas:** cooking, creative nonfiction, diet/nutrition, gay/lesbian, memoirs, true crime, women's issues. **Considers these fiction areas:** action, adventure, commercial, contemporary issues, crime, detective, erotica, ethnic, fantasy, feminist, gay, historical, horror, juvenile, lesbian, mainstream, metaphysical, middle-grade, military, multicultural, multimedia, mystery, new adult, New Age, occult, paranormal, police, psychic, regional, romance, science fiction, spiritual, sports, supernatural, suspense, thriller, urban fantasy, war, women's, young adult.
HOW TO CONTACT E-queries only. To query, type "Query (Agent Name)" plus the title of your novel in the subject line, then please send your query letter, short synopsis, and first 10 pages pasted into the body of the e-mail to query@inklingsliterary.com. Check the agency website to make sure that your targeted agent is currently open to submissions. Accepts simultaneous submissions. For queries, no response in 3 months is considered a rejection.

INKWELL MANAGEMENT, LLC

521 Fifth Ave., 26th Floor, New York NY 10175. (212)922-3500. **Fax:** (212)922-0535. **E-mail:** submissions@inkwellmanagement.com. **Website:** www.inkwellmanagement.com. Represents 500 clients.
MEMBER AGENTS Stephen Barbara (select adult fiction and nonfiction); **William Callahan** (nonfiction of all stripes—especially American history and memoir, pop culture and illustrated books, as well as voice-driven fiction that stands out from the crowd); **Michael V. Carlisle**; **Catherine Drayton** (books for children, young adults, and women readers); **David Forrer** (literary, commercial, historical, crime fiction, suspense/thriller, humorous nonfiction, and popular history); **Alexis Hurley** (literary and commercial fiction, memoir, narrative nonfiction); **Nathaniel Jacks** (memoir, narrative nonfiction, social sciences, health, current affairs, business, religion, popular history; fic-

tion interests include literary, commercial, women's, young adult, historical, short stories); **Jacqueline Murphy** (fiction, children's books, graphic novels and illustrated works, compelling narrative nonfiction); **Richard Pine; Eliza Rothstein** (literary and commercial fiction, narrative nonfiction, memoir, popular science, and food writing); **Emma Schlee** (literary fiction, the occasional thriller, travel and adventure books, popular culture, and philosophy books); **Hannah Schwartz; David Hale Smith; Lauren Smythe** (smart narrative nonfiction [narrative journalism, modern history, biography, cultural criticism, personal essay, humor], personality-driven practical nonfiction [cookbooks, fashion, and style], and contemporary literary fiction); **Kimberly Witherspoon; Monika Woods** (literary and commercial fiction, young adult, memoir; also seeks compelling nonfiction in popular culture, science, and current affairs); **Lena Yarbrough** (literary fiction, upmarket commercial fiction, memoir, narrative nonfiction, history, investigative journalism, and cultural criticism); **Jenny Witherell; Charlie Olson; Liz Parker** (commercial and upmarket women's fiction; also seeks narrative, practical, and platform-driven nonfiction); **George Lucas; Alyssa diPierro**.

REPRESENTS Novels, nonfiction. **Considers these nonfiction areas:** biography, business, cooking, creative nonfiction, current affairs, foods, health, history, humor, memoirs, popular culture, religious, science. **Considers these fiction areas:** commercial, crime, historical, literary, middle-grade, picture books, romance, short story collections, suspense, thriller, women's, young adult.

HOW TO CONTACT "In the body of your e-mail, please include a query letter and a short writing sample (1-2 chapters). We currently accept submissions in all genres except screenplays. Due to the volume of queries we receive, our response time may take up to 2 months. Feel free to put 'Query for [Agent Name]: [Your Book Title]' in the e-mail subject line." Accepts simultaneous submissions. Obtains most new clients through recommendations from others.

TERMS Agent receives 15% commission on domestic sales; 20% commission on foreign sales. Offers written contract.

TIPS "We will not read a ms before receiving a letter of inquiry."

JABBERWOCKY LITERARY AGENCY

49 W. 45th St., New York NY 10036. (917)388-3010. **Website:** www.awfulagent.com. **Contact:** Joshua Bilmes. Memberships include SFWA. Represents 40 clients.

MEMBER AGENTS Joshua Bilmes, Eddie Schneider, Lisa Rodgers, Sam Morgan.

REPRESENTS Nonfiction, novels. **Considers these nonfiction areas:** autobiography, biography, business, cooking, current affairs, economics, film, foods, gay/lesbian, government, health, history, humor, language, law, literature, medicine, money, popular culture, politics, satire, science, sociology, sports, theater, war, women's issues, women's studies, young adult. **Considers these fiction areas:** action, adventure, contemporary issues, crime, detective, ethnic, family saga, fantasy, gay, glitz, historical, horror, humor, lesbian, literary, mainstream, middle-grade, police, psychic, regional, satire, science fiction, sports, supernatural, thriller, young adult.

This agency represents quite a lot of genre fiction and is actively seeking to increase the amount of nonfiction projects. It does not handle children's or picture books. Book-length material only—no poetry, articles, or short fiction.

HOW TO CONTACT "We are currently open to unsolicited queries. No e-mail, phone, or fax queries, please. Query with a SASE. Please check our website, as there may be times during the year when we are not accepting queries. Only send a query letter; no ms material unless requested." Accepts simultaneous submissions. Responds in 3 weeks to queries. Obtains most new clients through solicitations, recommendation by current clients.

TERMS Agent receives 15% commission on domestic sales; 20% commission on foreign sales. Offers written contract, binding for 1 year. Charges clients for book purchases, photocopying, international book/ms mailing.

J DE S ASSOCIATES, INC.

9 Shagbark Rd., Wilson Point, South Norwalk CT 06854. (203)838-7571. **E-mail:** Jdespoel@aol.com. **Website:** www.jdesassociates.com. **Contact:** Jacques de Spoelberch.

Prior to opening his agency, Mr. de Spoelberch was an editor with Houghton Mifflin.

REPRESENTS Novels, nonfiction. **Considers these nonfiction areas:** biography, business, cultural interests, current affairs, economics, ethnic, government, health, history, law, medicine, metaphysics, military, New Age, politics, self-help, sociology, sports, translation. **Considers these fiction areas:** crime, detective, frontier, historical, juvenile, literary, mainstream, mystery, New Age, police, suspense, westerns, young adult.

HOW TO CONTACT "Brief queries by regular mail and e-mail are welcomed for fiction and nonfiction, but kindly do not include sample proposals or other material unless specifically requested to do so." Accepts simultaneous submissions. Responds in 2 months to queries.

TERMS Agent receives 15% commission on domestic sales; 20% commission on foreign sales. Charges clients for foreign postage and photocopying.

RECENT SALES Joshilyn Jackson's new novel *A Grown-Up Kind of Pretty* (Grand Central), Margaret George's final Tudor historical *Elizabeth I* (Penguin), the fifth in Leighton Gage's series of Brazilian thrillers *A Vine in the Blood* (Soho), Genevieve Graham's romance *Under the Same Sky* (Berkley Sensation).

HARVEY KLINGER, INC.

300 W. 55th St., Suite 11V, New York NY 10019. (212)581-7068. **E-mail:** queries@harveyklinger.com. **Website:** www.harveyklinger.com. **Contact:** Harvey Klinger. Always interested in considering new clients, both published and unpublished. Member of AAR. Represents 100 clients.

MEMBER AGENTS Harvey Kliinger; David Dunton (popular culture, music-related books, literary fiction, young adult, fiction, memoirs); **Sara Crowe** (children's and young adult authors, adult fiction and nonfiction, foreign rights sales); **Andrea Somberg** (literary fiction, commercial fiction, romance, science fiction, fantasy, mysteries/thrillers, young adult, middle-grade, quality narrative nonfiction, popular culture, how-to, self-help, humor, interior design, cookbooks, health/fitness); **Wendy Levinson** (literary and commercial fiction, occasional children's young adult or middle-grade, wide variety of nonfiction).

REPRESENTS Nonfiction, novels, juvenile books. **Considers these nonfiction areas:** autobiography, biography, business, child guidance, cooking, crafts, creative nonfiction, cultural interests, current affairs, diet/nutrition, foods, health, history, how-to, inves-

tigative, literature, medicine, memoirs, psychology, science, self-help, spirituality, sports, technology, true crime, women's issues, women's studies, young adult. **Considers these fiction areas:** action, adventure, commercial, crime, detective, erotica, family saga, fantasy, gay, glitz, historical, horror, juvenile, lesbian, literary, mainstream, middle-grade, mystery, police, suspense, thriller, women's, young adult.

☞ This agency specializes in big, mainstream, contemporary fiction and nonfiction.

HOW TO CONTACT Use submission form on the website, or query with SASE via snail mail. No phone or fax queries. Don't send unsolicited mss or e-mail attachments. Make submission letter to the point and as brief as possible. Accepts simultaneous submissions. Responds in 4 weeks to queries, if interested. Obtains most new clients through recommendations from others.

TERMS Agent receives 15% commission on domestic sales; 25% commission on foreign sales.

RECENT SALES *Land of the Afternoon Sun* by Barbara Wood, *I Am Not a Serial Killer* by Dan Wells, *Me, Myself and Us* by Brian Little, *The Secret of Magic* by Deborah Johnson, *Children of the Mist* by Paula Quinn.

THE KNIGHT AGENCY

570 East Ave., Madison GA 30650. **E-mail:** submissions@knightagency.net. **Website:** http://knightagency.net/. **Contact:** Elaine Spencer. The Knight Agency is a full-service literary agency with a focus on genre-based adult fiction, young adult, middle-grade and select nonfiction projects. Estab. 1996. Member of AAR, SCWBI, WFA, SFWA, RWA. Represents 200+ clients.

MEMBER AGENTS Deidre Knight (romance, women's fiction, erotica, commercial fiction, inspirational, memoir and nonfiction narrative, personal finance, true crime, business, popular culture, self-help, religion, and health); **Pamela Harty** (romance, women's fiction, young adult, business, motivational, diet and health, memoir, parenting, pop culture, and true crime); **Elaine Spencer** (romance [single title and category], women's fiction, commercial "book-club" fiction, cozy mysteries, young adult, and middle-grade); **Lucienne Diver** (fantasy, science fiction, romance, suspense, and young adult); **Nephele Tempest** (literary fiction, commercial fiction, women's fiction, fantasy, science fiction, romantic suspense, paranormal romance, contemporary romance, historical fic-

NEW AGENT SPOTLIGHT

MOLLY O'NEILL
WAXMAN LEAVELL LITERARY AGENCY

www.waxmanleavell.com
@molly_oneill

ABOUT MOLLY: Prior to becoming an agent, Molly O'Neill spent thirteen years working in various roles inside the publishing industry. She served as an editor at HarperCollins Children's Books, where she acquired Veronica Roth's juggernaut Divergent series, among many other fantastic projects. She also served as head of editorial at Storybird, a publishing/tech startup. She loves the creative process and project development, is invigorated by business strategy and entrepreneurial thinking, and is fascinated by the intersections of art, commerce, creativity, and innovation. Molly is especially passionate about the people behind books, and takes pride in discovering and evangelizing talented authors and illustrators, expanding the global reach of their work, and finding new ways to build connections and community among creators, readers, stories, and their champions. Molly is an alum of Marquette University, an erstwhile Texan, and a current dweller of Brooklyn.

SHE IS SEEKING: Young adult and middle-grade fiction. She is also seeking a select number of children's illustrators (illustrators who write are especially welcome), and authors of juvenile nonfiction (any age), early readers, chapter books, and children's graphic novels. She is *not* currently seeking picture book texts unless the author is also a professional illustrator, a writer of nonfiction, or a referral from an industry contact that she knows personally.

HOW TO CONTACT: E-mail your query to mollysubmit@waxmanleavell.com and include a description of your project, biographical information (including details about any relevant credentials, subject area expertise, stats, or existing platform), and a pitch summary. If applicable, speak of prior published works, agent representation, and/or publisher submission history. Please also be sure to include your phone number, e-mail address, and any relevant Internet/social media links.

tion, young adult, and middle-grade); **Melissa Jeglinski** (romance [contemporary, category, historical, inspirational], young adult, middle-grade, women's fiction, mystery); **Kristy Hunter** (romance, women's fiction, commercial fiction, young adult, and middle-grade), **Travis Pennington** (young adult, middle-grade, mysteries, thrillers, commercial fiction, and romance [nothing paranormal/fantasy in any genre for now]).

REPRESENTS Nonfiction, novels. **Considers these nonfiction areas:** current affairs, diet/nutrition, design, economics, gay/lesbian, health, juvenile nonfiction, memoirs, politics, self-help, sociology, travel, true crime, women's issues, young adult. **Considers these fiction areas:** commercial, fantasy, middle-grade, new adult, romance, science fiction, thriller, women's, young adult.

☞ Actively seeking romance in all subgenres (both category and single-title), science fiction, fantasy, historical fiction, mysteries in both traditional and cozy arena, middle-grade, young adult, nonfiction, and memoir. Does not want to receive screenplays, short stories, poetry, essays, or children's picture books.

HOW TO CONTACT E-queries only. "Your submission should include a one-page query letter and the first 5 pages of your ms. All text must be contained in the body of your e-mail. Attachments will not be opened nor included in the consideration of your work. Queries must be addressed to a specific agent. Please do not query multiple agents at our agency." Accepts simultaneous submissions.

EDITE KROLL LITERARY AGENCY, INC.

20 Cross St., Saco ME 04072. (207)283-8797. **Fax:** (207)283-8799. **E-mail:** ekroll@maine.rr.com. **Contact:** Edite Kroll. Represents 45 clients.

○ Prior to opening her agency, Ms. Kroll served as a book editor and translator.

☞ "We represent writers and writer-artists of both adult and children's books. We have a special focus on international feminist writers, women writers of nonfiction, and artists who write their own books (including children's and humor books)." Actively seeking artists who write their own books and international feminists who write in English. Does not represent genre fiction (mysteries, thrillers, diet, cookery, etc.), photography books, coffee table books, romance, or commercial fiction.

HOW TO CONTACT Query with SASE or by e-mail. Submit outline/proposal, synopsis, 1-2 sample chapters, author bio, and the entire ms (or dummy)

if sending a picture book. No phone queries. Accepts simultaneous submissions.

TERMS Agent receives 15% commission on domestic sales; 20% commission on foreign sales.

RECENT SALES Sold 12 domestic titles and 30 foreign titles in the last year. Clients include Shel Silverstein and Charlotte Zolotow estates.

TIPS "Please do your research so you won't send me books/proposals I specifically excluded."

LAUNCHBOOKS LITERARY AGENCY

E-mail: david@launchbooks.com. **Website:** www.launchbooks.com. **Contact:** David Fugate. Represents 45 clients.

○ Mr. Fugate has been an agent for 20 years and has successfully represented more than 1,000 book titles. He left another agency to start LaunchBooks in 2005.

REPRESENTS Nonfiction, novels. **Considers these nonfiction areas:** autobiography, biography, business, creative nonfiction, current affairs, diet/nutrition, environment, health, history, how-to, humor, investigative, medicine, memoirs, money, parenting, popular culture, politics, psychology, recreation, science, self-help, sex, sociology, sports, technology, travel. **Considers these fiction areas:** action, adventure, crime, fantasy, horror, mainstream, military, satire, science fiction, suspense, thriller, urban fantasy, war, westerns, young adult.

☞ "We're looking for genre-breaking fiction. Do you have the next *The Martian*? Or maybe the next *Red Rising*, *Ready Player One*, *Ancillary Sword*, or *The Bone Clocks*? We're on the lookout for fun, engaging, contemporary novels that appeal to a broad audience. In nonfiction, we're interested in a broad range of topics. Check www.launchbooks.com/submissions for a complete list."

HOW TO CONTACT Query via e-mail. Accepts simultaneous submissions. Responds in 1 week to queries. Responds in 4 weeks to mss. Obtains most new clients through recommendations from others, solicitations.

TERMS Agent receives 15% commission on domestic sales; 25% commission on foreign sales. Offers written contract; 30-day notice to terminate contract. Charges occur very seldom. This agency's agreement limits any charges to $50 unless the author gives a written consent.

RECENT SALES *The Martian* by Andy Weir (Random House), *The Remaining: Allegiance* by DJ Molles (Orbit), *The Fold* by Peter Clines (Crown), *Faster, Higher, Stronger* by Mark McClusky (Hudson Street Press), *Fluent in Three Months* by Benny Lewis (HarperOne).

THE LESHNE AGENCY

16 W. 23rd St., Fourth Floor, New York NY 10010. **E-mail:** info@leshneagency.com. **E-mail:** submissions@leshneagency.com. **Website:** www.leshneagency.com. **Contact:** Lisa Leshne, agent and owner. "We are a full-service literary agency committed to the success of our authors. We represent a select and growing number of established and new writers interested in developing long-term relationships. We work closely with authors to develop their ideas for impact and audience reach, across print, digital, and other formats—providing hands-on guidance and networking for success. We also offer our services to authors who may wish to explore the self-publishing route via a variety of platforms." Member of AAR. Signatory of WGA.

○ Prior to founding the agency, Ms. Leshne was a literary agent at LJK Literary.

MEMBER AGENTS Lisa Leshne, agent and owner; Sandy Hodgman, director of foreign rights. **REPRESENTS Considers these nonfiction areas:** business, creative nonfiction, health, memoirs, parenting, politics, sports. **Considers these fiction areas:** commercial, middle-grade, young adult.

☛ Wants authors across all genres. "We are interested in narrative, memoir, and prescriptive nonfiction—with a particular interest in sports, wellness, business, politics, and parenting topics. We will also look at truly terrific commercial fiction, young adult, and middle-grade books."

HOW TO CONTACT "Submit all materials in the body of an e-mail. No attachments. Be sure to include the word 'QUERY' and the title of your ms in the subject line. Include brief synopsis, table of contents or chapter outline, 10 sample pages, bio, any previous publications, word count, how much of the ms is complete, and the best way to reach you." Accepts simultaneous submissions.

LEVINE GREENBERG ROSTAN LITERARY

AGENCY, INC.

307 Seventh Ave., Suite 2407, New York NY 10001. (212)337-0934. **Fax:** (212)337-0948. **E-mail:** submit@lgrliterary.com. **Website:** www.lgrliterary.com. Member of AAR. Represents 250 clients.

○ Prior to opening his agency, Mr. Levine served as vice president of the Bank Street College of Education.

MEMBER AGENTS Jim Levine (nonfiction—including business, science, narrative nonfiction, social and political issues, psychology, health, spirituality, parenting); Stephanie Rostan (adult and young adult fiction; nonfiction interests include parenting, health and wellness, sports, memoir); Melissa Rowland; Daniel Greenberg (popular culture, narrative nonfiction, memoir, humor; also seeks literary fiction); Victoria Skurnick; Danielle Svetcov (nonfiction); Lindsay Edgecombe (narrative nonfiction, memoir, lifestyle and health, illustrated books; also seeks literary fiction); Monika Verma (nonfiction interests include humor, pop culture, memoir, narrative nonfiction, style, and fashion; also represents some young adult fiction [paranormal, historical, contemporary]); Kerry Sparks (young adult, middle-grade, select adult fiction, and occasional nonfiction); Tim Wojcik (food narratives, humor, pop culture, popular history, science, literary fiction); Arielle Eckstut (no queries).

REPRESENTS Nonfiction, novels. **Considers these nonfiction areas:** business, creative nonfiction, health, history, humor, memoirs, parenting, popular culture, science, spirituality, sports. **Considers these fiction areas:** literary, mainstream, middle-grade, young adult.

HOW TO CONTACT E-query to submit@lgrliterary.com, or use the agency's online submission form. "If you would like to direct your query to 1 of our agents specifically, please feel free to name them in the online form or in the e-mail you send." Cannot respond to submissions by mail. Do not attach more than 50 pages. "Due to the volume of submissions we receive, we are unable to respond to each individually. If we would like more information about your project, we'll contact you within 3 weeks (though we do get backed up on occasion)." Accepts simultaneous submissions. Obtains most new clients through recommendations from others.

TERMS Agent receives 15% commission on domestic sales; 20% commission on foreign sales. Offers written contract.

TIPS "We focus on editorial development, business representation, publicity, and marketing strategy."

PAUL S. LEVINE LITERARY AGENCY

(310)450-6711. **Fax:** (310)450-0181. **E-mail:** paul@paulslevinelit.com. **Website:** www.paulslevinelit.com. **Contact:** Paul S. Levine. Other memberships include the State Bar of California. Represents 100 clients.

MEMBER AGENTS Paul S. Levine (children's and young adult fiction; also seeks adult fiction and nonfiction excluding science fiction, fantasy, and horror); Loren R. Grossman (archeology, art/photography, architecture, parenting, coffee table books, gardening, education, health, science, law, religion, memoir, sociology).

HOW TO CONTACT E-mail queries preferred. Send a one-page, single-spaced query letter. In your query letter, note your target market with a summary of specifics on how your work differs from other authors' previously published work. Accepts simultaneous submissions.

TERMS Agent receives 15% commission on domestic sales. Offers written contract. Charges for postage and actual, out-of-pocket costs only.

WRITERS CONFERENCES Willamette Writers Conference, San Francisco Writers Conference, Santa Barbara Writers Conference, Las Vegas Writing Workshop, and many others.

LIPPINCOTT MASSIE MCQUILKIN

27 W. 20th St., Suite 305, New York NY 10011. **E-mail:** info@lmqlit.com. **Website:** www.lmqlit.com.

MEMBER AGENTS Laney Katz Becker, laney@lmqlit.com (book club fiction, upmarket women's fiction, suspense, thrillers, and memoir); Ethan Bassoff, ethan@lmqlit.com (literary fiction, crime fiction; also seeks narrative nonfiction in the areas of history, sports writing, journalism, science writing, pop culture, humor, and food writing); Jason Anthony, jason@lmqlit.com (commercial fiction of all types including young adult; also seeks nonfiction in the areas of memoir, pop culture, true crime, general psychology, and sociology); Will Lippincott, will@lmqlit.com (narrative nonfiction and prescriptive nonfiction in the areas of politics, history, biography, foreign affairs, and health); Rob McQuilkin, rob@lmqlit.com (literary fiction; also seeks narrative nonfiction and nonfiction in the areas of memoir, history, biography, art history, cultural criticism, popular sociology, and psychology); Rayhane Sanders, rayhane@lmqlit.com (literary fiction, historical fiction, upmarket commercial fiction [including select young adult], narrative nonfiction [including essays], and select memoir); Stephanie Abou (literary and upmarket commercial fiction [including select young adult and middle-grade], crime fiction, memoir, and narrative nonfiction).

REPRESENTS Nonfiction, novels. **Considers these nonfiction areas:** art, biography, cultural interests, foods, health, history, humor, memoirs, popular culture, politics, psychology, science, sociology, sports, true crime. **Considers these fiction areas:** commercial, crime, literary, mainstream, middle-grade, suspense, thriller, women's.

> "Lippincott Massie McQuilkin is a full-service literary agency that focuses on bringing fiction and nonfiction of quality to the largest possible audience."

HOW TO CONTACT E-queries preferred. Include the word "Query" in the subject line of your e-mail. Review the agency's online page of agent bios (www.lmqlit.com/contact.html), as some agents want sample pages with their submissions and some do not. If you have not heard back from the agency in 4 weeks, assume they are not interested in seeing more. Accepts simultaneous submissions. Obtains most new clients through recommendations from others, solicitations, conferences.

TERMS Agent receives 15% commission on domestic sales; 20% commission on foreign sales. Offers written contract; 30-day notice must be given to terminate contract. Only charges for reasonable business expenses upon successful sale.

RECENT SALES Clients include Peter Ho Davies, Kim Addonizio, Natasha Trethewey, David Sirota, Katie Crouch, Uwen Akpan, Lydia Millet, Tom Perrotta, Jonathan Lopez, Chris Hayes, and Caroline Weber.

LKG AGENCY

465 West End Ave., 2A, New York NY 10024. **E-mail:** query@lkgagency.com. **Website:** http://lkgagency.com. The LKG Agency was founded in 2005 and is based on the Upper West Side of Manhattan. "We are a boutique literary agency that specializes in middle-

grade and young adult fiction, as well as nonfiction, both practical and narrative, with a particular interest in women-focused how-to. We invest a great deal of care and personal attention in each of our authors with the aim of developing long-term relationships that last well beyond the sale of a single book." Estab. 2005. Member of AAR. Signatory of WGA.

MEMBER AGENTS Lauren Galit (nonfiction, middle-grade, young adult); **Caitlen Rubino-Bradway** (middle-grade and young adult, some nonfiction). **REPRESENTS** Nonfiction, juvenile books. **Considers these nonfiction areas:** animals, child guidance, creative nonfiction, diet/nutrition, design, health, how-to, humor, juvenile nonfiction, memoirs, parenting, popular culture, psychology, women's issues, young adult. **Considers these fiction areas:** middle-grade, young adult.

8→ Seeking books on parenting, beauty, celebrity, dating and relationships, entertainment, fashion, health, diet and fitness, home and design, lifestyle, memoir, narrative, pets, psychology, middle-grade, and young adult fiction.

HOW TO CONTACT For nonfiction submissions, send a query letter to nonfiction@lkgagency.com, along with a table of contents and 2 sample chapters. The table of contents should be fairly detailed, with 1-2 paragraphs for an overview of the content of each chapter. Please also make sure to mention any publicity you have at your disposal. For middle-grade and young adult submissions, send a query, synopsis, and 3 chapters, and address all submissions to mgya@lkgagency.com. On a side note, while both Lauren and Caitlen consider young adult and middle-grade, Lauren tends to look more for middle-grade, while Caitlen deals more with young adult fiction. Responds if interested. Accepts simultaneous submissions.

STERLING LORD LITERISTIC, INC.

65 Bleecker St., New York NY 10012. **Fax:** (212)780-6095. **E-mail:** info@sll.com. **Website:** www.sll.com. Estab. 1987. Member of AAR. Signatory of WGA.
MEMBER AGENTS Philippa Brophy (represents journalists, nonfiction writers, and novelists; she is most interested in current events, memoir, science, politics, biography, and women's issues); **Laurie Liss** (represents authors of commercial and literary fiction and nonfiction whose perspectives are well developed and unique); **Sterling Lord**; **Peter Matson** (abiding interest in storytelling, whether in the service of history,

fiction, or the sciences); **Douglas Stewart** (fiction for all ages, from the innovatively literary to the unabashedly commercial); **Neeti Madan** (memoir, journalism, popular culture, lifestyle, women's issues, multicultural books, and virtually any intelligent writing on intriguing topics); **Robert Guinsler** (literary and commercial fiction [including young adult], journalism, narrative nonfiction with an emphasis on pop culture, science and current events, memoirs and biographies); **Jim Rutman**; **Celeste Fine** (expert, celebrity, and corporate clients with strong national and international platforms, particularly in the health, science, self-help, food, business, and lifestyle fields); **Erica Rand Silverman** (represents picture books through young adult novels, both fiction and nonfiction; adult interests include parenting and humor nonfiction); **Martha Millard** (fiction and nonfiction, including well-written science fiction and young adult); **Mary Krienke** (literary fiction, memoir, and narrative nonfiction [psychology, popular science, and cultural commentary]); **Jenny Stephens** (nonfiction interests include cookbooks, practical lifestyle projects, transportive travel and nature writing, and creative nonfiction; fiction interests include contemporary literary narratives strongly rooted in place); **Alison MacKeen** (idea-driven research books in the categories of social scientific, scientific, historical, relationships, parenting, learning and education, sexuality, technology, health, the environment, politics, economics, psychology, geography, and culture; also seeks literary fiction, literary nonfiction, memoirs, essays, and travel writing); **John Maas** (serious nonfiction—specifically business, personal development, science, self-help, health, fitness, and lifestyle); **Sarah Passick** (commercial nonfiction in the categories of celebrity, food, blogger, lifestyle, health, diet, fitness, and fashion).

REPRESENTS Nonfiction, fiction. **Considers these nonfiction areas:** biography, business, cooking, creative nonfiction, current affairs, economics, education, foods, gay/lesbian, history, humor, memoirs, multicultural, parenting, popular culture, politics, psychology, science, technology, travel, women's issues, fitness. **Considers these fiction areas:** commercial, juvenile, literary, middle-grade, picture books, science fiction, young adult.

HOW TO CONTACT Query via snail mail. "Please submit a query letter, a synopsis of the work, a brief proposal or the first 3 chapters of the ms, a brief bio, and a SASE for reply. Original artwork is not accepted. Enclose sufficient postage if you wish to have your materials returned to you. We do not respond to unsolicited e-mail inquiries." Accepts simultaneous submissions.

TERMS Agent receives 15% commission on domestic sales; 20% commission on foreign sales. Offers written contract.

GINA MACCOBY LITERARY AGENCY

P.O. Box 60, Chappaqua NY 10514. (914)238-5630. **E-mail:** query@maccobylit.com. **Website:** www.publishersmarketplace.com/members/GinaMaccoby/. **Contact:** Gina Maccoby. Member of AAR, Authors Guild. Represents 25 clients.

MEMBER AGENTS Gina Maccoby.

REPRESENTS Nonfiction, novels. **Considers these nonfiction areas:** autobiography, biography, cultural interests, current affairs, ethnic, history, juvenile nonfiction, popular culture, women's issues, women's studies. **Considers these fiction areas:** juvenile, literary, mainstream, mystery, thriller, young adult.

HOW TO CONTACT Query by e-mail only. Accepts simultaneous submissions. Owing to volume of submissions, may not respond to queries unless interested. Obtains most new clients through recommendations from clients and publishers.

TERMS Agent receives 15% commission on domestic sales; 20-25% commission on foreign sales, which includes subagents commissions. May recover certain costs, such as legal fees or the cost of shipping books by air to Europe or Japan.

MANSION STREET LITERARY MANAGEMENT

Website: http://mansionstreet.com. **Contact:** Jean Sagendorph, Michelle Witte. Member of AAR. Signatory of WGA.

MEMBER AGENTS Jean Sagendorph, querymansionstreet@gmail.com (pop culture, gift books, cookbooks, general nonfiction, lifestyle, design, brand extensions); Michelle Witte, querymichelle@mansionstreet.com (young adult, middle-grade, early readers, picture books [especially from author-illustrators], juvenile nonfiction).

REPRESENTS Nonfiction, novels. **Considers these nonfiction areas:** cooking, design, popular culture. **Considers these fiction areas:** juvenile, middle-grade, young adult.

☛ Jean is not interested in memoirs or medical/reference. Typically sports, travel, and self-help books are also not a good fit. Michelle is not interested in fiction or nonfiction for adults.

HOW TO CONTACT Send a query letter and no more than the first 10 pages of your ms in the body of an e-mail. Query 1 specific agent at this agency. No attachments. You must list the genre in the subject line. If the genre is not in the subject line, your query will be deleted. Accepts simultaneous submissions. Responds in up to 6 weeks.

RECENT SALES *Shake and Fetch* by Carli Davidson, *Bleed, Blister, Puke, and Purge* by J. Marin Younker, *Spectrum* by Ginger Johnson, *I Left You a Present* and *Movie Night Trivia* by Robb Pearlman, *Open Sesame!* by Ashley Evanson, *Fox Hunt* by Nilah Magruder, *ABC Now You See Me* by Kim Siebold.

MARSAL LYON LITERARY AGENCY, LLC

PMB 121, 665 San Rodolfo Dr. 124, Solana Beach CA 92075. **Website:** www.marsallyonliteraryagency.com. **Contact:** Kevan Lyon, Jill Marsal. Member of AAR. Signatory of WGA.

MEMBER AGENTS Kevan Lyon, kevan@marsallyonliteraryagency.com (commercial women's fiction, young adult fiction, and all genres of romance); Jill Marsal, jill@marsallyonliteraryagency.com (all types of women's fiction, all types of romance, mysteries, cozies, suspense, and thrillers; also seeks nonfiction in the areas of current events, business, health, self-help, relationships, psychology, parenting, history, science, and narrative nonfiction); Patricia Nelson, patricia@marsallyonliteraryagency.com (literary fiction, commercial fiction, all types of women's fiction, contemporary and historical romance, young adult, middle-grade, and LGBTQ fiction for both young adult and adult); Deborah Ritchkin, deborah@marsallyonliteraryagency.com (lifestyle books [specifically in the areas of food, design and entertaining], pop culture, women's issues, biography, and current events; her niche interest is projects about France, including fiction); Shannon Hassan, shannon@marsallyonliteraryagency.com (literary and commercial fiction, young adult and middle-grade fiction, and select nonfiction).

REPRESENTS Nonfiction, novels, juvenile books. **Considers these nonfiction areas:** animals, biography, business, cooking, creative nonfiction, current affairs, diet/nutrition, history, investigative, memoirs, parenting, popular culture, politics, psychology, science, self-help, sports, women's issues, women's studies. **Considers these fiction areas:** commercial, juvenile, literary, mainstream, middle-grade, multicultural, mystery, paranormal, romance, suspense, thriller, women's, young adult.

HOW TO CONTACT Query by e-mail. Query only 1 agent at this agency at a time. "Please visit our website to determine who is best suited for your work. Write 'Query' in the subject line of your e-mail. Please allow up to several weeks to hear back on your query." Accepts simultaneous submissions.

TIPS "Our agency's mission is to help writers achieve their publishing dreams. We want to work with authors not just for a book but for a career. We are dedicated to building long-term relationships with our authors and publishing partners. Our goal is to help find homes for books that engage, entertain, and make a difference."

THE EVAN MARSHALL AGENCY

Indie Rights Agency, 1 Pacio Court, Roseland NJ 07068-1121. (973)287-6216. **Fax:** (973)488-7910. **E-mail:** evan@evanmarshallagency.com. **Website:** www.evanmarshallagency.com. **Contact:** Evan Marshall. Founded in 1987, the Evan Marshall Agency is a leading literary management firm specializing in adult and young adult fiction. "We handle a wide-ranging roster of writers in numerous genres, from romance to mystery and thriller to literary fiction. We take pride in providing careful career guidance and strategizing to our clients." Member of AAR, Novelists, Inc. Represents 50+ clients.

○ Prior to becoming an agent, Mr. Marshall held senior editorial positions at Houghton Mifflin, Ariel Books, New American Library, and Everest House, where he acquired national and international bestsellers.

MEMBER AGENTS Evan Marshall.

REPRESENTS Fiction. **Considers these fiction areas:** action, adventure, crime, detective, erotica, ethnic, family saga, fantasy, feminist, frontier, gay, glitz, historical, horror, humor, inspirational, lesbian, literary, mainstream, military, multicultural, multimedia, mystery, new adult, New Age, occult, paranormal, police, psychic, regional, religious, satire, science fiction, spiritual, sports, supernatural, suspense, thriller, translation, urban fantasy, war, westerns, women's,

young adult, romance (contemporary, gothic, historical, regency).

☛ We represent all genres of adult and young adult full-length fiction. Does not want to receive articles, children's books, essays, memoirs, nonfiction, novellas, poetry, screenplays, short stories, or stage plays.

HOW TO CONTACT Actively seeking new clients. E-mail a query letter, synopsis, and the first 3 chapters of your novel within the body of an e-mail. Accepts simultaneous submissions.

TERMS Agent receives 15% commission on domestic sales; 20% commission on foreign sales. Offers written contract.

RECENT SALES *The Language of Sisters* by Cathy Lamb (Kensington), *A Husband for Mari* by Emma Miller (Love Inspired), *A Taste of Fire* by Hannah Howell (Kensington), *Murder Has Nine Lives* by Laura Levine (Kensington), *Fortune's Secret Husband* by Karen Rose Smith (Harlequin).

MARTIN LITERARY MANAGEMENT

914 164th St. SE, Suite B12, #307, Mill Creek WA 98012. **E-mail:** sharlene@martinliterarymanagement.com. **Website:** www.MartinLit.com. **Contact:** Sharlene Martin. "Please see our website at www.MartinLit.com for company overview, testimonials, bios of literary managers." Estab. 2002.

○ Prior to becoming an agent, Ms. Martin worked in film/TV production and acquisitions.

MEMBER AGENTS Sharlene Martin (nonfiction); Clelia Gore (children's, middle-grade, young adult).

REPRESENTS Nonfiction, juvenile books. **Considers these nonfiction areas:** autobiography, biography, business, child guidance, current affairs, economics, health, history, how-to, humor, inspirational, investigative, medicine, memoirs, parenting, popular culture, psychology, satire, self-help, true crime, war, women's issues, women's studies. **Considers these fiction areas:** juvenile, middle-grade, young adult.

☛ This agency has strong ties to film/TV. Actively seeking nonfiction that is highly commercial and that can be adapted to film. "We are being inundated with queries and submissions that are wrongfully being submitted to us, which only results in more frustration for the writers."

HOW TO CONTACT Query via e-mail with no attachments; place text in the body of the e-mail. Accepts simultaneous submissions. Responds in 2 weeks to queries. Obtains most new clients through recommendations from others.

TERMS Agent receives 15% commission on domestic sales. Offers written contract, binding for 1 year; 1-month notice must be given to terminate contract.

RECENT SALES *Breakthrough* by Jack Andraka, *In the Matter of Nikola Tesla: A Romance of the Mind* by Anthony Flacco, *Honor Bound: My Journey to Hell and Back With Amanda Knox* by Raffaele Sollecito.

TIPS "Have a strong platform for nonfiction. Please don't call. (I can't tell how well you write by the sound of your voice.) I welcome e-mail. I'm very responsive when I'm interested in a query and work hard to get my clients' materials in the best possible shape before submissions. Do your homework prior to submission and only submit your best efforts. Please review our website carefully to make sure we're a good match for your work. If you read my book, *Publish Your Nonfiction Book: Strategies For Learning the Industry, Selling Your Book and Building a Successful Career* (Writer's Digest Books), you'll know exactly how to charm me."

THE MCCARTHY AGENCY, LLC

456 Ninth St., No. 28, Hoboken NJ 07030. **E-mail:** McCarthylit@aol.com. **Contact:** Shawna McCarthy. Member of AAR.

MEMBER AGENTS Shawna McCarthy.

REPRESENTS Novels. **Considers these fiction areas:** fantasy, middle-grade, mystery, new adult, science fiction, women's, young adult.

☛ This agency represents mostly novels. No picture books.

HOW TO CONTACT E-queries only. Accepts simultaneous submissions.

SEAN MCCARTHY LITERARY AGENCY

E-mail: submissions@mccarthylit.com. **Website:** www.mccarthylit.com. **Contact:** Sean McCarthy. Estab. 2013.

◐ Prior to his current position, Mr. McCarthy began his publishing career as an editorial intern at Overlook Press and then moved over to the Sheldon Fogelman Agency.

REPRESENTS **Considers these nonfiction areas:** juvenile nonfiction, young adult. **Considers these fiction areas:** juvenile, middle-grade, picture books, young adult.

☛ Sean is drawn to flawed, multifaceted characters with devastatingly concise writing in young adult, and boy-friendly mysteries or adventures in middle-grade. In picture books, he looks more for unforgettable characters, off-beat humor, and especially clever endings. He is not currently interested in high fantasy, message-driven stories, or query letters that pose too many questions.

HOW TO CONTACT E-query. "Please include a brief description of your book, your biography, and any literary or relevant professional credits in your query letter. If you are a novelist, submit the first 3 chapters of your ms (or roughly 25 pages) and a one-page synopsis in the body of the e-mail or as a Word or PDF attachment. If you are a picture book author, submit the complete text of your ms. We are not currently accepting picture book mss of more than 1,000 words. If you are an illustrator, attach up to 3 JPEGs or PDFs of your work, along with a link to your website." Accepts simultaneous submissions.

☉ ANNE MCDERMID & ASSOCIATES LITERARY, LTD

320 Front St. W, Suite 1105, Toronto, Ontario M5V 3B6 Canada. (647)788-4016. **Fax:** (416)324-8870. **E-mail:** info@mcdermidagency.com. **Website:** www.mcdermidagency.com. **Contact:** Anne McDermid. Estab. 1996.

MEMBER AGENTS Anne McDermid, Martha Webb, Monica Pacheco, and Chris Bucci.

REPRESENTS Nonfiction, novels.

☛ The agency represents literary novelists and commercial novelists of high quality, and also writers of nonfiction in the areas of memoir, biography, history, literary travel, narrative science, and investigative journalism. "We also represent a certain number of children's and young adult writers and writers in the genres of science fiction and fantasy."

HOW TO CONTACT Query via e-mail or mail with a brief bio, description, and first 5 pages of project only. Accepts simultaneous submissions. *No unsolicited mss.* Obtains most new clients through recommendations from others.

MCINTOSH & OTIS, INC.

353 Lexington Ave., New York NY 10016. (212)687-7400. **Fax:** (212)687-6894. **E-mail:** info@mcintoshan-

NEW AGENT SPOTLIGHT

RACHEL BURKOT
HOLLOWAY LITERARY

www.hollowayliteraryagency.com
@Rachel_Burkot

ABOUT RACHEL: Rachel Burkot of Holloway Literary has been in the publishing industry since 2009. After completing an internship with two literary agencies, she worked as an editor for Harlequin. Rachel's career highlights include helping her authors achieve prestigious romance book nominations and two selective awards, including the National Readers' Choice Award, and several top reviews in *Romantic Times* magazine for her writers' books.

SHE IS SEEKING: Voice-driven fiction, particularly in young adult books. She enjoys quirky, three-dimensional, flawed characters—especially secondary characters. She seeks beautiful writing, books that explore good people in morally complicated situations, and complex, detailed plots. Rachel is interested in representing women's fiction, upmarket/book club fiction (e.g., Emily Giffin and Diane Chamberlain), young adult (no fantasy or paranormal unless it's very light), contemporary romance (i.e., Kristan Higgins), category romance with unique plots (e.g., Natalie Charles), Southern fiction, "dark" women's thrillers (e.g., Gillian Flynn or Mary Kubica), urban fiction, and literary fiction

HOW TO SUBMIT: Send your query to submissions@hollowayliteraryagency. com. E-mail a brief query and the first five pages of your manuscript pasted in the body of your e-mail. In the e-mail subject header, write "Query: [Title/ Genre]." If Rachel is interested, she'll respond via e-mail with a request for more material.

dotis.com. **Website:** www.mcintoshandotis.com. **Contact:** Eugene H. Winick, Esq. McIntosh & Otis has a long history of representing authors of adult and children's books. The children's department is a separate division. Estab. 1927. Member of AAR, SCBWI. Signatory of WGA.
MEMBER AGENTS Elizabeth Winick Rubinstein, ewrquery@mcintoshandotis.com (literary fiction, women's fiction, historical fiction, mystery/suspense, narrative nonfiction, spiritual, self-help, history, and current affairs); **Shira Hoffman**, shquery@mcintoshandotis.com (young adult, middle-grade, mainstream commercial fiction, mystery, literary fiction, women's fiction, romance, urban fantasy, fantasy, science fiction, horror, and dystopian); **Christa Heschke**, chquery@mcintoshandotis.com (picture

books, middle-grade, young adult, and new adult); **Adam Muhlig**, amquery@mcintoshandotis.com (music books [from jazz to classical to punk], popular culture, natural history, travel and adventure, and sports); **Eugene Winick**; **Shannon Powers**, spquery@mcintoshandotis.com (literary fiction, mystery, horror, popular history, and romance; also seeks young adult, middle-grade, mysteries and thrillers with high emotional stakes, projects with romantic elements, horror, light science fiction or fantasy, and contemporary fiction with a unique premise); **Amelia Appel**, aaquery@mcintoshandotis.com (literary fiction, mystery, thriller, historical fiction, science fiction, fantasy, horror, and some young adult).

REPRESENTS Considers these nonfiction areas: creative nonfiction, current affairs, history, popular culture, self-help, spirituality, sports, travel. **Considers these fiction areas:** fantasy, historical, horror, literary, middle-grade, mystery, new adult, paranormal, picture books, romance, science fiction, suspense, urban fantasy, women's, young adult.

☛ Actively seeking "books with memorable characters, distinctive voices, and great plots."

HOW TO CONTACT E-mail submissions only. For fiction, please send a query letter, synopsis, author bio, and the first 3 consecutive chapters (no more than 30 pages) of your novel. For nonfiction, please send a query letter, proposal, outline, author bio, and 3 sample chapters (no more than 30 pages) of the ms. For children's and young adult, please send a query letter, synopsis, and the first 3 consecutive chapters (not to exceed 25 pages) of the ms. Accepts simultaneous submissions. Obtains clients through recommendations from others, editors, conferences, and queries.

HOWARD MORHAIM LITERARY AGENCY

30 Pierrepont St., Brooklyn NY 11201. (718)222-8400. **Fax:** (718)222-5056. **Website:** www.morhaimliterary.com. Member of AAR.

MEMBER AGENTS Howard Morhaim (no unsolicited submissions), **Kate McKean**, kmckean@morhaimliterary.com (fiction interests include contemporary romance, contemporary women's fiction, literary fiction, historical fiction set in the 20th century, high fantasy, magical realism, science fiction, middle-grade, young adult; nonfiction interests include books by authors with demonstrable platforms in the areas of sports, food writing, humor, design, creativity, and craft [sewing, knitting, etc.]; also seeks narrative

nonfiction by authors with or without an established platform, and some memoir); **DongWon Song**, dongwon@morhaimliterary.com (science fiction, fantasy; nonfiction interests include food writing, science, pop culture); **Kim-Mei Kirtland**, kimmei@morhaimliterary.com (hard science fiction, literary fiction, history, biography, business, economics).

REPRESENTS Considers these nonfiction areas: biography, business, cooking, crafts, creative nonfiction, design, economics, foods, health, humor, memoirs, parenting, self-help, sports. **Considers these fiction areas:** fantasy, historical, literary, middle-grade, new adult, romance, science fiction, women's, young adult, LGBTQ young adult, magical realism.

☛ Kate is open to many subgenres and categories of young adult and middle-grade fiction. Check the website for the most details. Actively seeking fiction, nonfiction, and young adult novels.

HOW TO CONTACT Query via e-mail with cover letter and 3 sample chapters. See each agent's website listing for further specifics. Accepts simultaneous submissions.

DEE MURA LITERARY

P.O. Box 131, Massapequa NY 11762. (516)795-1616. **E-mail:** info@deemuraliterary.com. **E-mail:** query@deemuraliterary.com. **Website:** www.deemuraliterary.com. "We focus on developing our clients' careers to publication and beyond by providing personalized editorial feedback, social media and platform marketing, and thorough rights management. Both new and experienced authors are welcome to submit." Signatory of WGA. Member of Women's National Book Association, GrubStreet.

🗨 Prior to opening her agency, Ms. Mura was a public relations executive with a roster of film and entertainment clients. She is the president and CEO of both Dee Mura Literary and Dee Mura Entertainment.

MEMBER AGENTS Dee Mura, Kimiko Nakamura, Kaylee Davis.

REPRESENTS Nonfiction, novels, short story collections, juvenile books. **Considers these nonfiction areas:** agriculture, Americana, animals, anthropology, archeology, architecture, art, autobiography, biography, business, child guidance, cooking, crafts, creative nonfiction, cultural interests, current affairs, dance, decorating, diet/nutrition, design, economics, education, environment, ethnic, film, foods, gardening, gay/lesbian, government, health, history, hobbies, horticulture, how-to, humor, inspirational, interior design, investigative, juvenile nonfiction, language, law, literature, medicine, memoirs, metaphysics, military, money, multicultural, music, New Age, parenting, photography, popular culture, politics, psychology, recreation, religious, science, self-help, sex, sociology, spirituality, sports, technology, travel, true crime, war, women's issues, women's studies, young adult, Judaism. **Considers these fiction areas:** action, adventure, comic books, commercial, contemporary issues, crime, detective, erotica, ethnic, family saga, fantasy, feminist, frontier, gay, glitz, historical, horror, humor, inspirational, juvenile, lesbian, literary, mainstream, metaphysical, middle-grade, military, multicultural, multimedia, mystery, new adult, New Age, occult, paranormal, police, psychic, regional, religious, romance, satire, science fiction, short story collections, spiritual, sports, supernatural, suspense, thriller, translation, urban fantasy, war, westerns, women's, young adult, espionage, magical realism, speculative.

☞ No screenplays, poetry, or children's picture books.

HOW TO CONTACT E-mail query@deemuraliterary.com. Please include the first 25 pages in the body of the e-mail, as well as a short author bio and synopsis of the work. Responds to queries in 5 weeks.

TERMS Agent receives 15% commission on domestic sales; 20% commission on foreign sales. Offers written contract.

RECENT SALES *An Infinite Number of Parallel Universes* by Randy Ribay, *The Number 7* by Jessica Lidh.

WRITERS CONFERENCES BookExpo America, New England Crime Bake, New England SCBWI Agent Day, The Writer's Institute Conference at UW-Madison, Writer's Digest Annual Conference.

⊘ ◉ ERIN MURPHY LITERARY AGENCY

824 Roosevelt Trail, #290, Windham ME 04062. **Website:** http://emliterary.com. **Contact:** Erin Murphy, president; Ammi-Joan Paquette, senior agent; Tricia Lawrence, agent.

REPRESENTS Considers these fiction areas: middle-grade, picture books, young adult.

☞ Specializes in children's books only.

HOW TO CONTACT This agency does not take unsolicited submissions. Query only after a referral or meeting an agent at a conference.

JEAN V. NAGGAR LITERARY AGENCY, INC.

JVNLA, Inc., 216 E. 75th St., Suite 1E, New York NY 10021. (212)794-1082. **Website:** www.jvnla.com. **Contact:** Jennifer Weltz. Estab. 1978. Member of AAR, Women's Media Group, SCBWI. Represents 450 clients.

MEMBER AGENTS Jennifer Weltz (well researched and original historicals, thrillers with a unique voice, wry dark humor, voice-driven young adult, middle-grade, magical realism; also seeks enthralling narrative nonfiction); **Alice Tasman** (literary, commercial, young adult, middle-grade; seeks nonfiction in the categories of narrative, biography, music, and pop culture); **Laura Biagi** (literary fiction, magical realism, psychological thrillers, young adult novels, middle-grade novels, and picture books).

REPRESENTS Nonfiction, novels, short story collections, novellas, juvenile books, scholarly books, poetry books.

☞ This agency specializes in mainstream fiction and nonfiction and literary fiction with commercial potential. The agency also seeks young adult, middle-grade, and picture books. Does not want to receive screenplays.

HOW TO CONTACT "Visit our website to send submissions [via an online form] and see what our individual agents are looking for. No snail mail submissions." Accepts simultaneous submissions. Responds if interested.

TERMS Agent receives 15% commission on domestic sales; 20% commission on foreign sales.

RECENT SALES *Mort(e)* by Robert Repino, *The Paying Guests* by Sarah Waters, *Violent Crimes* by Phillip Margolin, *An Unseemly Wife* by E.B. Moore, *The Man Who Walked Away* by Maud Casey, *Dietland* by Sarai Walker, *In the Land of Armadillos* by Helen Maryles Shankman, *Not If I See You First* by Eric Lindstrom.

TIPS "We recommend the courage to be true to your own vision, the fortitude to finish a novel and polish it again and again before sending it out, and the patience to accept rejection gracefully and wait for the stars to align themselves appropriately for success."

NELSON LITERARY AGENCY

1732 Wazee St., Suite 207, Denver CO 80202. (303)292-2805. **E-mail:** querykristin@nelsonagency.com. **Website:** http://nelsonagency.com. **Contact:** Kristin Nelson, President. Kristin Nelson established Nelson Literary Agency, LLC, in 2002 and over the last decade of her career, she has represented 35 *New York Times* best-selling titles and many *USA Today* bestsellers. Member of AAR, RWA, SCBWI, SFWA. Represents 33 clients.

REPRESENTS Fiction. **Considers these fiction areas:** commercial, fantasy, literary, mainstream, middle-grade, romance, science fiction, women's, young adult.

- ☞ NLA specializes in representing commercial fiction and high-caliber literary fiction. They represent many pop genre categories, including things like historical romance, steampunk, and all subgenres of young adult—good stories well told. Please remember that NLA does not look at submissions for nonfiction, memoir, screenplays, short story collections, poetry, children's picture books, early reader chapter books, or material for the Christian/inspirational market.

HOW TO CONTACT "Please visit our website to carefully read our submission guidelines." Kristin does not accept any queries by Facebook or Twitter. Query by e-mail only. Put the word "Query" in the e-mail subject line along with the title of your novel. No attachments, but it is OK to include the first 10 pages of your novel in the body of the e-mail. Accepts simultaneous submissions. Tries to respond to all queries within 10 business days. Full ms requests can take 2 months or more.

NEW LEAF LITERARY & MEDIA, INC.

110 W. 40th St., Suite 2201, New York NY 10018. (646)248-7989. **Fax:** (646)861-4654. **E-mail:** query@newleafliterary.com. **Website:** www.newleafliterary.com. Estab. 2012. Member of AAR.

MEMBER AGENTS Joanna Volpe (women's fiction, thriller, horror, speculative fiction, literary fiction, historical fiction, young adult, middle-grade, art-focused picture books); **Kathleen Ortiz**, director of subsidiary rights and literary agent (new voices in young adult, as well as animator/illustrator talent); **Suzie Townsend** (new adult, young adult, middle-grade, romance [all subgenres], fantasy [urban fantasy, science fiction, steampunk, epic fantasy], and crime fiction [mysteries, thrillers]); **Pouya Shahbazian**, director of film and television (no unsolicited queries); **Mackenzie Brady** (science books, memoirs, "lost history" nonfiction, epic sports narratives, true crime, and gift/lifestyle books; she represents select adult and young adult fiction projects, as well); **Peter Knapp** (middle-grade, young adult, general adult fiction, grounded science fiction, genre-agnostic for all); **Jaida Temperly** (magical realism, historical fiction, literary fiction, stories that are quirky and fantastical; nonfiction interests include niche, offbeat books, or anything that is a bit strange); **J.L. Stermer** (nonfiction and some fiction).

REPRESENTS Nonfiction, novels, novellas, juvenile books, poetry books. **Considers these nonfiction areas:** cooking, crafts, creative nonfiction, science, technology, women's issues, young adult. **Considers these fiction areas:** crime, fantasy, historical, horror, literary, mainstream, middle-grade, mystery, new adult, paranormal, picture books, romance, thriller, women's, young adult.

HOW TO CONTACT Send a query to query@newleafliterary.com. Please do not query via phone. The word "Query" must be in the subject line, plus the agent's name. You may include up to 5 double-spaced sample pages within the body of the e-mail. No attachments unless specifically requested. Include all necessary contact information. You will receive an auto-response confirming receipt of your query. Responds only if interested. All queries read within 2 weeks.

RECENT SALES *Red Queen* by Victoria Aveyard (HarperCollins), *Lobster is the Best Medicine* by Liz Climo (Running Press), *Six of Crows* by Leigh Bardugo (Henry Holt), *A Snicker of Magic* by Natalie Lloyd (Scholastic).

⊘◎ RUBIN PFEFFER CONTENT

648 Hammond St., Chestnut Hill MA 02467. **E-mail:** info@rpcontent.com. **Website:** www.rpcontent.com. **Contact:** Rubin Pfeffer. Rubin Pfeffer Content is a literary agency exclusively representing children's and young adult literature, as well as content that will serve educational publishers and digital developers. Estab. 2014. Member of AAR. Signatory of WGA.

- ○ Mr. Pfeffer has previously worked as the vice president and publisher of Simon & Schuster

Children's Books and as an independent agent at East West Literary Agency.

REPRESENTS Considers these fiction areas: juvenile, middle-grade, picture books, young adult.

HOW TO CONTACT *This agent accepts submissions by referral only. Specify the contact information of your reference when submitting.* Authors/illustrators should send a query and 1-3 chapters of their ms via e-mail (no postal submissions). The query, placed in the body of the e-mail, should include a pitch, as well as any relevant information regarding previous publications, referrals, websites, and biographies. The ms may be attached as a .doc or a PDF file. Specifically for illustrators, attach a PDF of the dummy or artwork to the e-mail. Accepts simultaneous submissions. Responds within 8 weeks.

RECENT SALES *Marti Feels Proud* by Micha Archer, *Burning* by Elana K. Arnold, *Junkyard* by Mike Austin, *Little Dog, Lost* by Marion Dane Bauer, *Not Your Typical Dragon* by Tim Bowers, *Ghost Hawk* by Susan Cooper.

◉ PIPPIN PROPERTIES, INC.

110 W. 40th St., Suite 1704, New York NY 10018. (212)338-9310. **Fax:** (212)338-9579. **E-mail:** info@pippinproperties.com. **Website:** www.pippinproperties.com. **Contact:** Holly McGhee.

◐ Prior to becoming an agent, Ms. McGhee was an editor for 7 years and in book marketing for 4 years.

MEMBER AGENTS Holly McGhee, Elena Giovinazzo, Heather Alexander. Although each of the agents take children's books, you can find in-depth preferences for each agency on their website.

REPRESENTS Juvenile books. **Considers these fiction areas:** middle-grade, picture books, young adult.

☛ "We are strictly a children's literary agency devoted to the management of authors and artists in all media. We are small and discerning in choosing our clientele."

HOW TO CONTACT Query via e-mail. Include a synopsis of the work(s), your background and/or publishing history, and anything else you think is relevant. Accepts simultaneous submissions. Obtains most new clients through recommendations from others.

TIPS "Please do not start calling after sending a submission."

AARON M. PRIEST LITERARY AGENCY

200 W. 41st St., 21st Floor, New York NY 10036. (212)818-0344. **Fax:** (212)573-9417. **E-mail:** info@aaronpriest.com. **Website:** www.aaronpriest.com. Estab. 1974. Member of AAR.

MEMBER AGENTS Aaron Priest, querypriest@aaronpriest.com (thrillers, commercial fiction, biographies); **Lisa Erbach Vance**, queryvance@aaronpriest.com (contemporary fiction, thrillers/suspense, international fiction, narrative nonfiction); **Lucy Childs Baker**, querychilds@aaronpriest.com (literary and commercial fiction, memoir, edgy women's fiction); **Melissa Edwards**, queryedwards@aaronpriest.com (middle-grade, young adult, women's fiction, thrillers); **Mitch Hoffman** (thrillers, suspense, crime fiction, and literary fiction, as well as narrative nonfiction, politics, popular science, history, memoir, current events, and pop culture).

REPRESENTS Considers these nonfiction areas: biography, current affairs, history, memoirs, popular culture, politics, science. **Considers these fiction areas:** commercial, contemporary issues, crime, literary, middle-grade, suspense, thriller, women's, young adult.

☛ Does not want to receive poetry, screenplays, horror, or science fiction.

HOW TO CONTACT "Please do not submit to more than 1 agent at this agency. We urge you to check our website and consider each agent's emphasis before submitting. Your query letter should be about 1 page long and describe your work, as well as your background. You may also paste the first chapter of your work in the body of the e-mail. Do not send attachments." Accepts simultaneous submissions. Responds in 4 weeks, only if interested.

TERMS Agent receives 15% commission on domestic sales.

RECENT SALES *The Hit* by David Baldacci, *Six Years* by Harlan Coben, *Suspect* by Robert Crais, *Permanent Record* by Leslie Stella.

PROSPECT AGENCY

551 Valley Rd., PMB 377, Upper Montclair NJ 07043. (718)788-3217. **Fax:** (718)360-9582. **Website:** www.prospectagency.com. "Prospect Agency focuses on adult and children's literature, and is currently looking for the next generation of writers and illustrators to shape the literary landscape." Estab. 2005. Member of AAR. Signatory of WGA.

MEMBER AGENTS Emily Sylvan Kim, esk@ prospectagency.com (romance, women's, commercial, young adult, new adult); **Rachel Orr**, rko@prospectagency.com (picture books, illustrators, middle-grade, young adult); **Becca Stumpf**, becca@prospectagency.com (young adult and middle-grade [all genres for both, especially novels featuring diverse protagonists and life circumstances]; also seeks adult science fiction and fantasy, upmarket women's fiction, spicy romance novels); **Carrie Pestritto**, carrie@ prospectagency.com (narrative nonfiction, general nonfiction, biography, and memoir; fiction interests include commercial fiction with a literary twist, women's fiction, romance, upmarket, historical fiction, high-concept young adult and upper middle-grade); **Linda Camacho,** linda@prospectagency.com (middle-grade, young adult, and adult fiction across all genres—especially women's fiction/romance, horror, fantasy, science fiction, graphic novels, contemporary, select literary fiction, and fiction featuring diverse/ marginalized groups); **Kirsten Carleton**, kcarleton@ prospectagency.com (upmarket speculative, thriller, and literary fiction for adult and young adult).

REPRESENTS Nonfiction, novels, novellas, juvenile books. **Considers these nonfiction areas:** biography, memoirs. **Considers these fiction areas:** commercial, contemporary issues, crime, ethnic, family saga, fantasy, feminist, gay, historical, horror, humor, juvenile, lesbian, literary, mainstream, middle-grade, multicultural, mystery, new adult, picture books, romance, science fiction, suspense, thriller, urban fantasy, women's, young adult.

☞   "We're looking for strong, unique voices and unforgettable stories and characters."

HOW TO CONTACT Note that each agent at this agency has a different submission e-mail address and different submission policies. Check the agency website for the latest formal guideline per each agent. Accepts simultaneous submissions. Obtains new clients through conferences, recommendations, queries, and some scouting.

THE PURCELL AGENCY

E-mail: tpaqueries@gmail.com. **Website:** www.thepurcellagency.com. **Contact:** Tina P. Schwartz. This is an agency for authors of children's and teen literature. Estab. 2012. Member of AAR. Signatory of WGA.
MEMBER AGENTS Tina P. Schwartz, Kim Blair McCollum, Mary Buza.

REPRESENTS Nonfiction, novels. **Considers these nonfiction areas:** juvenile nonfiction. **Considers these fiction areas:** juvenile, middle-grade, young adult.

☞   This agency also takes juvenile nonfiction for middle-grade and young adult markets. At this point, the agency is not considering fantasy, science fiction, or picture book submissions.

HOW TO CONTACT Check the website to see if agency is open at this time (as they can close submissions off).

RECENT SALES *I'm Not Her* by Cara Sue Achterberg, *Shyness: The Ultimate Teen Guide* by Bernardo J. Carducci and Lisa Kaiser, *Out of the Dragon's Mouth* by Joyce Burn Zeiss, *A Work of Art* by Melody Maysonet.

⊘⊙ RED FOX LITERARY

129 Morro Ave., Shell Beach CA 93449. (805)459-3327. **E-mail:** info@redfoxliterary.com. **Website:** http:// redfoxliterary.com. This agency specializes in books for children, looking for both authors and illustrators. Member of AAR. Signatory of WGA.

🗩   Before co-founding Red Fox Literary with Ms. Grencik in 2011, Ms. Samoun was an in-house children's book editor for 10 years. Ms. Smith was formerly with Red Fox Literary.

MEMBER AGENTS Abigail Samoun, Karen Grencik, Danielle Smith, Stephanie Fretwell-Hill.

REPRESENTS **Considers these fiction areas:** juvenile, middle-grade, picture books, young adult.

HOW TO CONTACT Only accepts submissions by invitation, conference meetings, and referrals. A full list of book sales and clients (and illustrator portfolios) is available on the agency website.

RED SOFA LITERARY

P.O. Box 40482, St. Paul MN 55104. (651)224-6670. **E-mail:** dawn@redsofaliterary.com, jennie@redsofaliterary.com, laura@redsofaliterary.com, bree@redsofaliterary.com, amanda@redsofaliterary.com, stacey@redsofaliterary.com, erik@redsofaliterary.com. **Website:** http://redsofaliterary.com.

REPRESENTS Nonfiction, novels, juvenile books. **Considers these nonfiction areas:** Americana, animals, anthropology, archeology, crafts, creative nonfiction, cultural interests, current affairs, dance, film, gay/lesbian, government, health, history, hobbies, humor, investigative, juvenile nonfiction, popular culture, politics, recreation, satire, sociology, true crime, women's issues, women's studies, extreme sports. **Considers these fiction areas:** erotica, fantasy, feminist, gay, humor, juvenile, lesbian, literary, middle-grade, romance, science fiction, suspense, thriller, young adult.

HOW TO CONTACT Query by e-mail or mail with SASE. No attachments. Submit full proposal plus 3 sample chapters (or first 50 pages) and any other pertinent writing samples upon request by the specific agent. Accepts simultaneous submissions.

TERMS Agent receives 15% commission on domestic sales; 20% commission on foreign sales. Offers written contract.

RECENT SALES *Branded* by Eric Smith (Bloomsbury Spark), *Seeking Mansfield* by Kate Watson (Jolly Fish Press), *Behind the Books: How Debut Authors Navigate From the Idea to the End* by Chris Jones (University of Chicago Press), *Ten Years an Orc: A Decade in the World of Warcraft* by Tony Palumbi (Chicago Review Press), *Bad Bitch* by Christina Saunders (SMP Swerve).

TIPS "Always remember the benefits of building an author platform and the accessibility of accomplishing this task in today's industry. Most importantly, research the agents queried. Avoid contacting every literary agent about a book idea."

REES LITERARY AGENCY

14 Beacon St., Suite 710, Boston MA 02108. (617)227-9014. **Website:** http://reesagency.com. Estab. 1983. Member of AAR. Represents more than 100 clients.

MEMBER AGENTS Ann Collette, agent10702@aol.com (fiction interests include literary, upscale commercial women's, crime [including mystery, thriller and psychological suspense], upscale western, historical, military and war, horror; nonfiction interests include narrative, military and war, books on race and class, works set in Southeast Asia, biography, pop culture, books on film and opera, humor, and memoir); **Lorin Rees**, lorin@reesagency.com (literary fiction, memoirs, business books, self-help, science, history, psychology, and narrative nonfiction); **Rebecca Podos**, rebecca@reesagency.com (young adult and middle-grade fiction, particularly books about complex female relationships, beautifully written contemporary, genre novels with a strong focus on character, romance with more at stake than "will they/won't they," and LGBTQ books across all genres).

REPRESENTS Novels, nonfiction. **Considers these nonfiction areas:** biography, business, film, history,

humor, memoirs, military, popular culture, psychology, science, war. **Considers these fiction areas:** commercial, crime, historical, horror, literary, middle-grade, mystery, suspense, thriller, westerns, women's, young adult.

HOW TO CONTACT Consult website for each agent's submission guidelines, as they differ. Accepts simultaneous submissions. Obtains most new clients through recommendations from others, conferences, submissions.

TERMS Agent receives 15% commission on domestic sales; 20% commission on foreign sales.

RECENT SALES *The Marauders* by Tom Cooper, *The Gentleman's Guide to Vice and Virtue* by Mackenzi Lee, *Regret Nothing* by Sarah Nicolas, *Suffer Love* by Ashley Herring Blake, *Superbosses* by Sydney Finkelstein, *Idyll Threats* by Stephanie Gayle.

REGAL HOFFMANN & ASSOCIATES, LLC

242 W. 38th St., Floor 2, New York NY 10018. (212)684-7900. **Fax:** (212)684-7906. **E-mail:** submissions@regal-literary.com. **Website:** www.regal-literary.com. Member of AAR. Represents 70 clients.

MEMBER AGENTS Claire Anderson-Wheeler (nonfiction interests include memoirs and biographies, narrative histories, popular science, popular psychology; adult fiction interests include primarily character-driven literary fiction; also seeks all genres of young adult and middle-grade fiction); **Markus Hoffmann** (international and literary fiction, crime, [pop] cultural studies, current affairs, economics, history, music, popular science, and travel literature); **Joseph Regal** (literary fiction, international thrillers, history, science, photography, music, culture, and whimsy).

REPRESENTS **Considers these nonfiction areas:** biography, creative nonfiction, current affairs, economics, history, memoirs, music, psychology, science, travel. **Considers these fiction areas:** literary, mainstream, middle-grade, thriller, young adult.

➥ "We represent works in a wide range of categories, with an emphasis on literary fiction, outstanding thriller and crime fiction, and serious narrative nonfiction." Actively seeking literary fiction and narrative nonfiction. Does not want romance, science fiction, poetry, or screenplays.

HOW TO CONTACT Query with SASE or via e-mail to submissions@rhaliterary.com. No phone calls. Submissions should consist of a one-page query letter detailing the book in question, as well as the qualifications of the author. For fiction, submissions may also include the first 10 pages of the novel or 1 short story from a collection. Responds if interested. Accepts simultaneous submissions. Responds in 8 weeks.

TERMS Agent receives 15% commission on domestic sales; 20% commission on foreign sales. "We charge no reading fees."

RECENT SALES *This Is How It Really Sounds* by Stuart Archer Cohen, *Autofocus* by Lauren Gibaldi, *We've Already Gone This Far* by Patrick Dacey, *A Fierce and Subtle Poison* by Samantha Mabry, *The Life of the World to Come* by Dan Cluchey, *Willful Disregard* by Lena Andersson, *The Sweetheart* by Angelina Mirabella.

TIPS "We are deeply committed to every aspect of our clients' careers, and are engaged in everything from the editorial work of developing a great book proposal or line editing a fiction ms to negotiating state-of-the-art book deals and working to promote and publicize the book when it's published."

✪ THE RIGHTS FACTORY

P.O. Box 499, Station C, Toronto Ontario M6J 3P6 Canada. (416)966-5367. **E-mail:** sam@therightsfactory.com. **Website:** www.therightsfactory.com. "The Rights Factory is an international literary agency." Estab. 2004. Represents 150 clients.

MEMBER AGENTS Sam Hiyate (fiction, nonfiction, and graphic novels); **Kelvin Kong** (clients by referral only); **Ali McDonald** (young adult and children's literature of all kinds); **Olga Filina** (commercial fiction, historical fiction, mystery, romance; seeks nonfiction in the field of business, wellness, lifestyle, and memoir; also seeks young adult and middle-grade novels with memorable characters); **Cassandra Rogers** (literary fiction, commercial women's fiction, historical fiction; also seeks nonfiction on politics, history, science, and finance; enjoys humorous, heartbreaking, and inspiring memoir); **Lydia Moed** (science fiction and fantasy, historical fiction, diverse voices; seeks narrative nonfiction on a wide variety of topics, including history, popular science, biography, and travel); **Natalie Kimber** (literary and commercial fiction; also seeks creative nonfiction in categories such as memoir, cooking, pop culture, spirituality, and sustainability); **Harry Endrulat** (children's literature, especially author/illustrators and Canadian voices); **Haskell Nussbaum** (literature of all kinds).

REPRESENTS Nonfiction, novels, short story collections, novellas, juvenile books. **Considers these nonfiction areas:** biography, business, cooking, environment, foods, gardening, health, history, inspirational, juvenile nonfiction, memoirs, money, music, popular culture, politics, science, travel, women's issues, young adult. **Considers these fiction areas:** commercial, crime, family saga, fantasy, gay, hi-lo, historical, horror, juvenile, lesbian, literary, mainstream, middle-grade, multicultural, mystery, new adult, paranormal, picture books, romance, science fiction, short story collections, suspense, thriller, urban fantasy, women's, young adult.

☞ Does not want to receive plays, screenplays, textbooks.

HOW TO CONTACT There is a submission form on this agency's website. Accepts simultaneous submissions.

RLR ASSOCIATES, LTD.

Literary Department, 7 W. 51st St., New York NY 10019. **E-mail:** sgould@rlrassociates.net. **Website:** www.rlrassociates.net. **Contact:** Scott Gould. Member of AAR. Represents 50 clients.

REPRESENTS Nonfiction, novels. **Considers these nonfiction areas:** biography, creative nonfiction, foods, history, humor, popular culture, sports. **Considers these fiction areas:** commercial, literary, mainstream, middle-grade, picture books, romance, women's, young adult, genre.

☞ "We provide a lot of editorial assistance to our clients and have connections." Does not want to receive screenplays.

HOW TO CONTACT Query by either e-mail or snail mail. For fiction, send a query and 1-3 chapters (pasted in the body of the e-mail). For nonfiction, send query or proposal. Accepts simultaneous submissions. "If you do not hear from us within 3 months, please assume that your work is out of active consideration." Obtains most new clients through recommendations from others.

TERMS Agent receives 15% commission on domestic sales; 20% commission on foreign sales. Offers written contract.

RECENT SALES Clients include Shelby Foote, The Grief Recovery Institute, Don Wade, David Plowden, Nina Planck, Karyn Bosnak, Gerald Carbone, Jason Lethcoe, and Andy Crouch.

RODEEN LITERARY MANAGEMENT

3501 N. Southport, No. 497, Chicago IL 60657. **E-mail:** submissions@rodeenliterary.com. **Website:** www.rodeenliterary.com. **Contact:** Paul Rodeen. Estab. 2009. Member of AAR. Signatory of WGA.

Mr. Rodeen established Rodeen Literary Management in 2009 after 7 years of experience with the literary agency Sterling Lord Literistic, Inc.

REPRESENTS Nonfiction, novels, juvenile books, illustrations, graphic novels. **Considers these fiction areas:** juvenile, middle-grade, picture books, young adult, graphic novels, comics.

Actively seeking "writers and illustrators of all genres of children's literature—including picture books, early readers, middle-grade fiction and nonfiction, graphic novels and comic books, as well as young adult fiction and nonfiction." This is primarily an agency devoted to children's books.

HOW TO CONTACT Unsolicited submissions are accepted by e-mail to submissions@rodeenliterary.com. Cover letters with a synopsis and contact information should be included in the body of your e-mail. An initial submission of 50 pages from a novel or a longer work of nonfiction will suffice and should be pasted into the body of your e-mail. Electronic portfolios from illustrators are accepted, but please keep the images at 72 dpi; a link to your website or blog is also helpful. Electronic picture book dummies and picture book texts are accepted. Graphic novels and comic books are welcome. Accepts simultaneous submissions. You will receive an auto-generated response to confirm your submission, but please understand that further contact will be made only if we feel we can represent your work. Accepts simultaneous submissions.

ANDY ROSS LITERARY AGENCY

767 Santa Ray Ave., Oakland CA 94610. (510)238-8965. **E-mail:** andyrossagency@hotmail.com. **Website:** www.andyrossagency.com. **Contact:** Andy Ross. Estab. 2008. Member of AAR.

REPRESENTS Considers these nonfiction areas: anthropology, autobiography, biography, child guidance, creative nonfiction, cultural interests, current affairs, education, environment, ethnic, government, history, language, law, literature, military, parenting, popular culture, politics, psychology, science, sociol-

ogy, technology, war. **Considers these fiction areas:** commercial, juvenile, literary, young adult.

"This agency specializes in general nonfiction, politics and current events, history, biography, journalism and contemporary culture, as well as literary, commercial, and young adult fiction." Actively seeking literary, commercial, and young adult fiction. Does not want to receive poetry.

HOW TO CONTACT Queries should be less than a half page. Please put the word "query" in the title header of the e-mail. In the first sentence, state the category of the project. Give a short description of the book and your qualifications for writing. Accepts simultaneous submissions. Responds in 1 week to queries.

TERMS Agent receives 15% commission on domestic sales; 20% commission on foreign sales or other deals made through a sub-agent. Offers standard written contract.

JANE ROTROSEN AGENCY, LLC

(212)593-4330. **Fax:** (212)935-6985. **Website:** www.janerotrosen.com. Estab. 1974. Member of AAR. Other memberships include Authors Guild. Represents more than 100 clients.

MEMBER AGENTS Jane Rotrosen Berkey (not taking on new clients); **Andrea Cirillo**, acirillo@janerotrosen.com (general fiction, suspense, and women's fiction); **Annelise Robey**, arobey@janerotrosen.com (women's fiction, suspense, mystery, literary fiction, and select nonfiction); **Meg Ruley**, mruley@janerotrosen.com (commercial fiction—including suspense, mysteries, romance, and general fiction); **Christina Hogrebe**, chogrebe@janerotrosen.com (young adult, new adult, book club fiction, romantic comedies, mystery, and suspense); **Amy Tannenbaum**, atannenbaum@janerotrosen.com (contemporary romance, psychological suspense, thrillers, new adult, as well as women's fiction that falls into that sweet spot between literary and commercial; also seeks memoir, narrative, and prescriptive nonfiction in the areas of health, business, pop culture, humor, and popular psychology); **Rebecca Scherer** rscherer@janerotrosen.com (women's fiction, mystery, suspense, thriller, romance, upmarket, and literary-leaning fiction); **Jessica Errera** (assistant).

REPRESENTS Nonfiction, novels. **Considers these nonfiction areas:** business, health, humor, memoirs,

CAITLIN MCDONALD
DONALD MAASS LITERARY AGENCY

www.maassagency.com
@literallycait

ABOUT CAITLIN: Caitlin McDonald joined the agency in 2015, and was previously at Sterling Lord Literistic. She represents adult and young adult speculative fiction, primarily science fiction, fantasy, horror, and related subgenres, as well as contemporary fiction about geeky characters. She also handles a small amount of nonfiction in geeky areas, with a focus on feminist theory, women's issues, and pop culture. Caitlin grew up overseas and has a bachelor of arts in creative writing from Columbia University.

SHE IS SEEKING: All science fiction and fantasy fiction (and subgenres) for adult, young adult, and middle-grade—especially secondary world fantasy and alternate history. She enjoys genre-bending or cross-genre fiction, and stories that examine tropes from a new angle. She especially likes diversity of all kinds, including (but not limited to) race, gender, sexuality, and ability, in both characters and world-building.

HOW TO CONTACT: Contact query.cmcdonald@maassagency.com with the query letter, synopsis, and first ten pages of your novel pasted into the body of the e-mail. Responds to queries within four weeks.

popular culture, psychology, narrative nonfiction. **Considers these fiction areas:** commercial, literary, mainstream, mystery, new adult, romance, suspense, thriller, women's, young adult.

8—▸ "Jane Rotrosen Agency is best known for representing writers of commercial fiction: thrillers, mystery, suspense, women's fiction, romance, historical novels, mainstream fiction, young adult, etc. We also work with authors of memoirs, narrative, and prescriptive nonfiction."

HOW TO CONTACT "Please e-mail the agent you think would best align with you and your work. Send a query letter that includes a concise description of your work, relevant biographical information, and any relevant publishing history. Also include a brief synopsis and the first 3 chapters of your novel or proposal for nonfiction. Paste all text in the body of your e-mail. We will not open e-mail attachments." Accepts simultaneous submissions. Obtains most new clients through recommendations from others.

TERMS Agent receives 15% commission on domestic sales; 20% commission on foreign sales. Offers written contract, binding for 3 years; two-month notice must be given to terminate contract. Charges clients for photocopying, express mail, overseas postage, book purchase.

SADLER CHILDREN'S LITERARY

(815)209-6252. **E-mail:** submissions.sadlerliterary@gmail.com. **Website:** www.sadlerchildrensliterary.

com. **Contact:** Jodell Sadler. "Sadler Children's Literary is an independent literary agency, serving aspiring authors and illustrators and branding careers through active media and marketing management in the field of children's literature." Member of AAR. Signatory of WGA.

REPRESENTS Nonfiction, novels, juvenile books. **Considers these nonfiction areas:** creative nonfiction, juvenile nonfiction, young adult. **Considers these fiction areas:** juvenile, middle-grade, picture books, young adult.

HOW TO CONTACT "We only take submissions from writers we've met through conferences, events, webinars, or other meeting opportunities. Your subject line should read 'CODE PROVIDED—(Genre), (Title), by (Author),' and specifically addressed to me. I prefer a short letter: hook (why my agency), pitch for you project, and bio (brief background and other categories you work in). All submissions should be in the body of the e-mail; no attachments. If you are submitting a picture book, send the entire text. If you are submitting young adult or middle-grade, submit the first 10 pages. If you are an illustrator or author-illustrator, I encourage you to contact me, and please send a link to your online portfolio. I only obtain clients through writing conferences, SCBWI, Writer's Digest, and KidLitCollege.com webinars and events." Accepts simultaneous submissions.

VICTORIA SANDERS & ASSOCIATES

440 Buck Rd., Stone Ridge NY 12484. (212)633-8811. **Fax:** (212)633-0525. **E-mail:** queriesvsa@gmail.com. **Website:** www.victoriasanders.com. **Contact:** Victoria Sanders. Estab. 1992. Member of AAR. Signatory of WGA. Represents 135 clients.

MEMBER AGENTS Victoria Sanders, Chris Kepner, Bernadette Baker-Baughman.

REPRESENTS Nonfiction, novels, juvenile books. **Considers these nonfiction areas:** autobiography, biography, cultural interests, current affairs, ethnic, film, gay/lesbian, government, history, humor, law, literature, music, popular culture, politics, psychology, satire, theater, translation, women's issues, women's studies. **Considers these fiction areas:** action, adventure, comic books, contemporary issues, crime, detective, ethnic, family saga, feminist, lesbian, literary, mainstream, middle-grade, mystery, new adult, picture books, thriller, young adult.

HOW TO CONTACT Query by e-mail only. "We will not respond to e-mails with attachments or attached files." Accepts simultaneous submissions.

TERMS Agent receives 15% commission on domestic sales; 20% commission on foreign/film sales. Offers written contract.

RECENT SALES Sold 20+ titles in the last year.

TIPS "Limit query to a letter (no calls) and give it your best shot. A good query is going to get a good response."

WENDY SCHMALZ AGENCY

402 Union St., #831, Hudson NY 12534. (518)672-7697. **E-mail:** wendy@schmalzagency.com. **Website:** www. schmalzagency.com. **Contact:** Wendy Schmalz. Estab. 2002. Member of AAR.

REPRESENTS Nonfiction, novels, juvenile books. **Considers these nonfiction areas:** biography, cultural interests, history, popular culture, young adult. Many nonfiction subjects are of interest to this agency. **Considers these fiction areas:** literary, mainstream, middle-grade, young adult.

○— Not looking for picture books, science fiction, or fantasy.

HOW TO CONTACT Accepts only e-mail queries. Paste synopsis into the e-mail. Do not attach the ms or sample chapters or synopsis. Please do not send genre fiction or children's picture books. If you do not hear from this agency within 2 weeks, consider that a no. Accepts simultaneous submissions. Obtains clients through recommendations from others.

TERMS Agent receives 15% commission on domestic sales; 20% on foreign sales; 25% for Asian sales.

SERENDIPITY LITERARY AGENCY, LLC

305 Gates Ave., Brooklyn NY 11216. **E-mail:** rbrooks@ serendipitylit.com; info@serendipitylit.com. **Website:** www.serendipitylit.com. **Contact:** Regina Brooks. Represents 50 clients.

○ Prior to becoming an agent, Ms. Brooks was an acquisitions editor for John Wiley & Sons, Inc. and McGraw-Hill Companies.

MEMBER AGENTS Regina Brooks; Dawn Michelle Hardy (nonfiction—including sports, pop culture, blog and trend, music, lifestyle, and social science); Folade Bell (literary and commercial women's fiction, young adult, literary mysteries and thrillers, historical fiction, African-American issues, gay/ lesbian, Christian fiction, humor, and books that deeply explore other cultures; also seeks nonfiction that reads like fiction, including blog-to-book or pop culture); **Nadeen Gayle** (romance, memoir, pop culture, inspirational/religious, women's fiction, parenting, young adult, mystery, political thrillers, and all forms of nonfiction); **Chelcee Johns** (narrative nonfiction, investigative journalism, memoir, inspirational self-help, religion/spirituality, international, popular culture, current affairs; also seeks literary and commercial fiction).

REPRESENTS **Considers these nonfiction areas:** creative nonfiction, current affairs, inspirational, memoirs, music, parenting, popular culture, religious, self-help, spirituality, sports. **Considers these fiction areas:** commercial, gay, historical, lesbian, literary, middle-grade, mystery, romance, thriller, women's, young adult, Christian.

HOW TO CONTACT Check the website, as there are online submission forms for fiction, nonfiction, and juvenile. "Website will also state if we're temporarily closed to submissions to any areas." Accepts simultaneous submissions. Obtains most new clients through conferences, referrals.

TERMS Agent receives 15% commission on domestic sales; 20% commission on foreign sales. Offers written contract; 2-month notice must be given to terminate contract. Charges clients for office fees, which are taken from any advance.

TIPS "See the books *Writing Great Books for Young Adults* and *You Should Really Write a Book: How to Write Sell and Market Your Memoir.* We are looking for high-concept ideas with big hooks. If you get writer's block, try www.possibiliteas.co."

THE SEYMOUR AGENCY

Website: www.theseymouragency.com. Member of AAR, RWA, Authors Guild, HWA. Signatory of WGA.

Ms. Resciniti was recently named "Agent of the Year" by the ACFW.

MEMBER AGENTS **Nicole Resciniti,** nicole@ theseymouragency.com (accepts all genres of romance, young adult, middle-grade, new adult, suspense, thriller, mystery, science fiction, fantasy); **Julie Gwinn,** julie@theseymouragency.com (Christian and inspirational fiction and nonfiction, women's fiction [contemporary and historical], new adult, Southern fiction, literary fiction, and young adult); **Lane Heymont,** lane@theseymouragency.com (science fiction, fantasy, romance, nonfiction).

REPRESENTS Nonfiction, novels. **Considers these nonfiction areas:** business, health, how-to, Christian books, cookbooks, any well-written nonfiction that includes a proposal in standard format and 1 sample chapter. **Considers these fiction areas:** action, fantasy, inspirational, middle-grade, mystery, new adult, religious, romance, science fiction, suspense, thriller, young adult.

HOW TO CONTACT E-mail the query plus first 5 pages of the ms pasted into the e-mail. Accepts simultaneous submissions. Responds in 1 month to queries.

TERMS Agent receives 12-15% commission on domestic sales.

THE SPIELER AGENCY

27 W. 20 St., Suite 305, New York NY 10011. **E-mail:** thespieleragency@gmail.com. **Website:** http://thespieleragency.com. **Contact:** Joe Spieler. Represents 160 clients.

Prior to opening his agency, Mr. Spieler was a magazine editor.

MEMBER AGENTS **Victoria Shoemaker,** victoria@thespieleragency.com (environment and natural history, popular culture, memoir, photography and film, literary fiction, poetry, food/cooking); **John Thornton,** john@thespieleragency.com (nonfiction); **Joe Spieler,** joe@thespieleragency.com (nonfiction and fiction and books for children and young adults); **Helen Sweetland,** helen@TheSpielerAgency.com (children's—from board books through young adult fiction; also seeks adult general interest nonfiction, including nature, green living, gardening, architecture, interior design, health, and popular science).

REPRESENTS Nonfiction, novels, juvenile books. **Considers these nonfiction areas:** architecture, biography, cooking, environment, film, foods, gardening, health, history, memoirs, photography, popular culture, science, sociology, spirituality. **Considers these fiction areas:** literary, middle-grade, New Age, picture books, thriller, young adult.

HOW TO CONTACT "Before submitting projects to the Spieler Agency, check the listings of our individual agents and see if any particular agent shows a general interest in your subject (e.g., history, memoir, young adult, etc.). Please send all queries either by e-mail or regular mail. If you query us by regular mail, we can only reply to you if you include a SASE." Accepts simultaneous submissions. Cannot guarantee a personal response to all queries. Obtains most new

NEW AGENT SPOTLIGHT

TRACY MARCHINI

BOOKENDS LITERARY AGENCY

www.bookendsliterary.com
@tracymarchini

ABOUT TRACY: After four years as an agency assistant at Curtis Brown, Tracy Marchini left to pursue her own editorial business and to earn her MFA in writing for children from Simmons College. Her editorial clients have gone on to secure representation, sell books to traditional publishers, win awards, and become bestsellers in the United Kingdom. She's looking forward to being able to work with her BookEnds clients throughout their careers and to see them grow as authors in the same way. Growing up, Tracy made it a personal goal to read every Nancy Drew Case Files title in her school's library and still has a soft spot for a good girl detective story. As an adult, she loves the sense of possibility in children's and young adult literature—and can still empathize with the soul-crushing feeling that is mandatory gym class.

SHE IS SEEKING: Picture books, middle-grade, and young adult manuscripts across most genres—including contemporary, mysteries, thrillers, magical realism, historical fiction, and nonfiction. For picture books, she's particularly interested in manuscripts that are laugh-out-loud funny or deliciously dark. For middle-grade and young adult, she's interested in underdogs, strong female characters, and/or unreliable narrators. She believes that it's important for readers of all backgrounds to see themselves reflected in the media they consume, and is looking to bring that diversity to her list. She is *not* a good fit for young adult horror, true crime, hard science fiction, or high fantasy. At this time, she is also not looking for board books, early chapter books, or nonfiction for the educational market.

HOW TO CONTACT: Contact tmsubmissions@bookendsliterary.com.

clients through recommendations, listing in *Guide to Literary Agents*.
TERMS Agent receives 15% commission on domestic sales. Charges clients for messenger bills, photocopying, postage.
WRITERS CONFERENCES London Book Fair.

TIPS "Check www.publishersmarketplace.com/members/spielerlit."

STIMOLA LITERARY STUDIO

308 Livingston Court, Edgewater NJ 07020. **E-mail:** info@stimolaliterarystudio.com. **Website:** www.

stimolaliterarystudio.com. **Contact:** Rosemary B. Stimola. "A full-service literary agency devoted to representing authors and author/illustrators of fiction and nonfiction, pre-school through young adult, who bring unique and substantive contributions to the industry." Estab. 1997. Member of AAR. Represents 45 clients.

○ Agency is owned and operated by a former educator and children's bookseller with a Ph.D in linguistics.

MEMBER AGENTS Rosemary B. Stimola.

REPRESENTS Juvenile books. **Considers these nonfiction areas:** cooking. **Considers these fiction areas:** young adult.

☛ Actively seeking remarkable middle-grade, young adult, and debut picture book author/ illustrators. No institutional books.

HOW TO CONTACT Query via e-mail. Author/illustrators of picture books may attach text and sample art. A PDF dummy is preferred. Accepts simultaneous submissions. Responds in 3 weeks to queries if interested. Responds in 2 months to requested mss. While unsolicited queries are welcome, most clients come through editor, agent, and client referrals.

TERMS Agent receives 15% commission on domestic sales; 20% (if subagents are employed) commission on foreign sales. Offers written contract, binding for all children's projects. 60 days notice must be given to terminate contract.

TIPS Agent is hands-on, no-nonsense. May request revisions. Does not line edit but may offer suggestions for improvement before submission.

STONESONG

270 W. 39th St., No. 201, New York NY 10018. (212)929-4600. **Fax:** (212)486-9123. **E-mail:** editors@ stonesong.com. **E-mail:** submissions@stonesong.com. **Website:** http://stonesong.com. Member of AAR. Signatory of WGA.

MEMBER AGENTS Alison Fargis, Ellen Scordato, Judy Linden, Emmanuelle Morgen, Leila Campoli (business, science, technology, and self improvement); Maria Ribas (cookbooks, self-help, health, diet, home, parenting, and humor, all from authors with demonstrable platforms; she's also interested in narrative nonfiction and select memoir).

REPRESENTS Nonfiction, novels, juvenile books. **Considers these nonfiction areas:** architecture, art, biography, business, cooking, crafts, creative nonfic-

tion, cultural interests, current affairs, dance, decorating, diet/nutrition, design, economics, foods, gay/ lesbian, health, history, hobbies, how-to, humor, interior design, investigative, literature, memoirs, money, music, New Age, parenting, photography, popular culture, politics, psychology, science, self-help, sociology, spirituality, sports, technology, women's issues, young adult.

☛ Does not represent plays, screenplays, picture books, or poetry.

HOW TO CONTACT Accepts electronic queries for fiction and nonfiction. Submit query addressed to 1 agent. Include first chapter or first 10 pages of ms. Accepts simultaneous submissions.

RECENT SALES *Revolutionary* by Alex Myers, *Rebel* by Amy Tintera, *Dangerous Curves Ahead* by Sugar Jamison, *Sunday Suppers* by Karen Mordechai, *Find Momo* by Andrew Knapp, *Smitten Kitchen* by Deb Perelman.

THE STRINGER LITERARY AGENCY LLC

P.O. Box 770365, Naples FL 34107. **E-mail:** mstringer@stringerlit.com. **Website:** www.stringerlit.com. **Contact:** Marlene Stringer. This agency focuses on commercial fiction for adults and teens. Estab. 2008; previously an agent with Barbara Bova Literary Agency. Member of AAR, RWA, MWA, ITW, SBCWI. Signatory of WGA. Represents 50 clients.

REPRESENTS Fiction. **Considers these fiction areas:** commercial, crime, detective, fantasy, historical, mainstream, multicultural, mystery, new adult, paranormal, police, romance, science fiction, suspense, thriller, urban fantasy, women's, young adult.

☛ This agency specializes in fiction. "We are an editorial agency and work with clients to make their mss the best they can be in preparation for submission. We focus on career planning and help our clients reach their publishing goals. Because we are so hands-on, we limit the size of our list; however, we are always looking for exceptional voices and stories that demand we read to the end. You never know where the next great story is coming from." This agency is seeking thrillers, crime fiction (not true crime), mystery, women's fiction, single-title and category romance, fantasy (all subgenres), earth-based science fiction (no space opera, aliens, etc.), and young adult. Does not want to receive picture books, middle-grade, plays, short stories, or poetry. This is not the agency for inspirational romance or erotica. The agency is not seeking nonfiction as of this time (2016).

HOW TO CONTACT Electronic submissions through website submission form only. Please make sure your ms is as good as it can be before you submit. Accepts simultaneous submissions. "We strive to respond quickly, but current clients' work always comes first."

RECENT SALES *The Conqueror's Wife* by Stephanie Thornton, *When I'm Gone* by Emily Bleeker, *Magic Bitter, Magic Sweet* by Charlie N. Holmberg, *Belle Chasse* by Suzanne Johnson, *Chapel of Ease* by Alex Bledsoe, *Wilds of the Bayou* by Susannah Sandlin, *Summit Lake* by Charlie Donlea.

TIPS "If your ms falls between categories, or you are not sure of the category, query and we'll let you know if we'd like to take a look. We strive to respond as quickly as possible. If you have not received a response in the time period indicated on website, please re-query."

THE STROTHMAN AGENCY, LLC

63 E. 9th St., 10X, New York NY 10003. **E-mail:** info@strothmanagency.com. **Website:** www.strothmanagency.com. **Contact:** Wendy Strothman, Lauren MacLeod. Member of AAR, Authors Guild. Represents 50 clients.

⭕ Prior to becoming an agent, Ms. Strothman was head of Beacon Press (1983-1995) and executive vice president of Houghton Mifflin's Trade & Reference Division (1996-2002).

MEMBER AGENTS Wendy Strothman (history, narrative nonfiction, narrative journalism, science and nature, and current affairs); **Lauren MacLeod** (young adult fiction and nonfiction, middle-grade novels, highly polished literary fiction, and narrative nonfiction [particularly food writing, science, pop culture and history]).

REPRESENTS Nonfiction, novels, juvenile books. **Considers these nonfiction areas:** business, current affairs, economics, environment, foods, history, language, popular culture, science. **Considers these fiction areas:** literary, middle-grade, young adult.

🔑 "The Strothman Agency seeks out scholars, journalists, and other acknowledged and emerging experts in their fields. We specialize in history, science, narrative journalism, nature and the environment, current affairs, narrative nonfiction, business and economics,

young adult fiction and nonfiction, and middle-grade fiction and nonfiction. Browse the 'Recent News' on our website to get an idea of the types of books that we represent. We are not signing up projects in romance, science fiction, picture books, or poetry." Does not want to receive adult fiction or self-help.

HOW TO CONTACT Accepts queries only via e-mail, through strothmanagency@gmail.com. See submission guidelines online. Accepts simultaneous submissions. "All e-mails received will be responded to with an auto-reply. If we have not replied to your query within 6 weeks, we do not feel that it is right for us." Accepts simultaneous submissions. Obtains most new clients through recommendations from others.

TERMS Agent receives 15% commission on domestic sales; 20% commission on foreign sales. Offers written contract; 30-day notice must be given to terminate contract.

TALCOTT NOTCH LITERARY

31 Cherry St., Suite 104, Milford CT 06460. (203)876-4959. **Fax:** (203)876-9517. **E-mail:** editorial@talcottnotch.net. **Website:** www.talcottnotch.net. **Contact:** Gina Panettieri, president. Represents 150 clients.

⭕ Prior to becoming an agent, Ms. Panettieri was a freelance writer and editor. Ms. Munier was director of acquisitions for Adams Media Corporation and had previously worked for Disney. Ms. Dugas and Ms. Sulaiman had both completed internships with Sourcebooks prior to joining Talcott Notch.

MEMBER AGENTS Gina Panettieri, gpanettieri@talcottnotch.net (history, business, self-help, science, gardening, cookbooks, crafts, parenting, memoir, true crime, travel, young adult, middle-grade, women's fiction, paranormal, urban fantasy, horror, science fiction, historical, mystery, thrillers and suspense); **Paula Munier**, pmunier@talcottnotch.net (mystery, thriller, science fiction, fantasy, romance, young adult, memoir, humor, pop culture, health and wellness, cooking, self-help, pop psych, New Age, inspirational, technology, science, and writing); **Rachael Dugas**, rdugas@talcottnotch.net (young adult, middle-grade, romance, and women's fiction); **Saba Sulaiman**, ssulaiman@talcottnotch.net (upmarket literary and commercial fiction, romance [all subgenres except paranormal], character-driven psychological thrillers, cozy mysteries, memoir, young adult [except paranormal and science fiction], middle-grade, and nonfiction humor).

REPRESENTS Nonfiction, novels, juvenile books. **Considers these nonfiction areas:** business, cooking, crafts, gardening, health, history, humor, inspirational, memoirs, parenting, popular culture, psychology, science, self-help, technology, travel, true crime. **Considers these fiction areas:** commercial, fantasy, historical, horror, literary, mainstream, middle-grade, mystery, New Age, paranormal, romance, science fiction, suspense, thriller, urban fantasy, women's, young adult.

HOW TO CONTACT Query via e-mail (preferred) with first 10 pages of the ms pasted within the body of the e-mail, not as an attachment. Accepts simultaneous submissions. Responds in 2 weeks to queries. Responds in 6-10 weeks to mss.

TERMS Agent receives 15% commission on domestic sales; 20% commission on foreign sales. Offers written contract, binding for 1 year.

RECENT SALES *Tier One* by Brian Andrews and Jeffrey Wilson (Thomas & Mercer), *Firestorm* by Nancy Holzner (Berkley Ace Science Fiction), *The New Jersey Mob* by Scott Deitche (Rowman and Littlefield).

TIPS "Know your market and how to reach them. A strong platform is essential in your book proposal. Can you effectively use social media? Are you a strong networker? Are you familiar with the book bloggers in your genre? Are you involved with the interest-specific groups that can help you? What can you do to break through the 'noise' and help present your book to your readers? Check our website for more tips and information on this topic."

THOMPSON LITERARY AGENCY

115 W. 29th St., Third Floor, New York NY 10001. (347)281-7685. **E-mail:** info@thompsonliterary.com; meg@thompsonliterary.com, submissions@thompsonliterary.com. **Website:** http://thompsonliterary.com. **Contact:** Meg Thompson. Estab. 2014. Member of AAR. Signatory of WGA.

○ Before her current position, Ms. Thompson was with LJK Literary and the Einstein Thompson Agency.

MEMBER AGENTS Meg Thompson; Cindy Uh (senior agent), (picture book, middle-grade, and young adult submissions [including nonfiction queries]; she loves compelling characters and distinct voices, and

more diversity of all types is welcome); **John Thorn** (affiliate agent); **Sandy Hodgman** (director of foreign rights).

REPRESENTS Nonfiction, novels, juvenile books. **Considers these nonfiction areas:** autobiography, biography, business, cooking, crafts, creative nonfiction, diet/nutrition, design, education, foods, health, history, how-to, humor, inspirational, interior design, juvenile nonfiction, memoirs, multicultural, popular culture, politics, science, self-help, sports, travel, women's issues, women's studies, young adult. **Considers these fiction areas:** commercial, historical, juvenile, literary, middle-grade, picture books, women's, young adult.

☛ The agency is always on the lookout for both commercial and literary fiction, as well as young adult and children's books. "Nonfiction, however, is our specialty, and our interests include biography, memoir, music, popular science, politics, blog-to-book projects, cookbooks, sports, health and wellness, fashion, art, and popular culture. Please note that we do not accept submissions for poetry collections or screenplays, and we only consider picture books by established illustrators."

HOW TO CONTACT "For fiction: Please send a query letter, including any salient biographical information or previous publications, and attach the first 25 pages of your ms. For nonfiction: Please send a query letter and a full proposal, including biographical information, previous publications, credentials that qualify you to write your book, marketing information, and sample material. You should address your query to whichever agent you think is best suited for your project." Accepts simultaneous submissions. Responds in 6 weeks if interested.

THREE SEAS LITERARY AGENCY

P.O. Box 8571, Madison WI 53708. (608)834-9317. **E-mail:** queries@threeseaslit.com. **Website:** http://threeseasagency.com. **Contact:** Michelle Grajkowski, Cori Deyoe. Estab. 2000. Member of AAR, RWA, SCBWI. Represents 55 clients.

○ Since its inception, Three Seas has sold more than 500 titles worldwide. Ms. Grajkowski's authors have appeared on all the major lists including *The New York Times*, *USA Today* and *Publishers Weekly*. Prior to joining the agency in 2006, Ms. Deyoe was a multi-published author. She represents a wide range of authors and has sold many projects at auction.

MEMBER AGENTS Michelle Grajkowski (romance, women's fiction, young adult and middle-grade fiction, select nonfiction); **Cori Deyoe** (romance [all types], women's fiction, young adult, middle-grade, picture books, thrillers, mysteries, and select nonfiction); **Linda Scalissi** (women's fiction, thrillers, young adult, mysteries and romance).

REPRESENTS Nonfiction, novels. **Considers these fiction areas:** middle-grade, mystery, picture books, romance, thriller, women's, young adult.

☛   "Currently, we are looking for fantastic authors with a voice of their own." Three Seas does not represent poetry or screenplays.

HOW TO CONTACT E-mail queries only; no attachments, unless requested by agents. For fiction, please e-mail the first chapter and synopsis along with a cover letter. Also, be sure to include the genre and the number of words in your ms, as well as pertinent writing experience in your query letter. For nonfiction, e-mail a complete proposal, including a query letter and your first chapter. For picture books, query with complete text. Accepts simultaneous submissions. Obtains most new clients through recommendations from others, conferences.

TERMS Agent receives 15% commission on domestic sales; 20% commission on foreign sales. Offers written contract.

⊙ TRANSATLANTIC LITERARY AGENCY

2 Bloor St. E, Suite 3500, Toronto Ontario M4W 1A8 Canada. (416)488-9214. **E-mail:** info@transatlanticagency.com. **Website:** http://transatlanticagency.com. "The Transatlantic Agency represents adult and children's authors of all genres, including illustrators. We do not handle stage plays, musicals, or screenplays." Please review the agency website and guidelines carefully before making any inquiries, as each agent has her own particular submission guidelines.

MEMBER AGENTS Trena White (upmarket/accessible nonfiction in the categories of current affairs, business, culture, politics, technology, and the environment); **Amy Tompkins** (literary fiction, historical fiction, women's fiction [including smart romance], narrative nonfiction, and quirky or original how-to books; also seeks early readers, middle-grade, young adult, and new adult); **Stephanie Sinclair** (literary fiction, upmarket women's and commercial fiction, literary thriller and suspense, young adult crossover, narrative nonfiction, memoir, investigative journalism, and true crime); **Samantha Haywood** (literary fiction and upmarket commercial fiction—specifically literary thrillers and upmarket mystery; also seeks historical fiction, smart contemporary fiction, upmarket women's fiction, and cross-over novels; enjoys narrative nonfiction, including investigative journalism, politics, women's issues, memoirs, environmental issues, historical narratives, sexuality, true crime; graphic novels [fiction and nonfiction, preferably full length], story collections, memoirs, biographies, travel narratives); **Jesse Finkelstein** (nonfiction in the categories of current affairs, business, culture, politics, technology, religion, and the environment); **Marie Campbell** (middle-grade); **Shaun Bradley** (referrals only; adult literary fiction and narrative nonfiction, primarily science and investigative journalism); **Sandra Bishop** (biography, memoir; also seeks positive or humorous how-to books on advice/relationships, mind/body, religion, healthy living, finances, life hacks, traveling, living a better life); **Fiona Kenshole** (children's and young adult; only accepting submissions from referrals or conferences she attends as faculty); **Lynn Bennett** (not accepting submissions or new clients); **David Bennett**.

REPRESENTS Nonfiction, novels, juvenile books.

☛   "In both children's and adult literature, we market directly into the US, the United Kingdom, and Canada." Represents adult and children's authors of all genres, including illustrators. Does not want to receive picture books, musicals, screenplays, or stage plays.

HOW TO CONTACT Always refer to the website, as guidelines will change, and only various agents are open to new clients at any given time. Obtains most new clients through recommendations from others.

TERMS Agent receives 15% commission on domestic sales; 20% commission on foreign sales. Offers written contract; 45-day notice must be given to terminate contract. This agency charges for photocopying and postage when it exceeds $100.

RECENT SALES Sold 250 titles in the past year.

TRIADA US LITERARY AGENCY, INC.

P.O. Box 561, Sewickley PA 15143 USA. (412)401-3376. **E-mail:** uwe@triadaus.com; brent@triadaus.com; laura@triadaus.com; mallory@triadaus.com. **Web-**

ALEXANDRA WEISS
JENNIFER DE CHIARA LITERARY AGENCY

www.jdlit.com
@akaweiss

ABOUT ALEXANDRA: Alexandra Weiss recently joined the agency as an associate agent and is currently building her client list. She's also a writer for www.bustle.com and PR manager for a Chicago circus. She previously worked as an acquisitions editor for an award-winning anthology and holds a BFA in creative writing and publishing from Columbia College Chicago.

SHE IS SEEKING: In young adult, she seeks realism, magical realism, science fiction (especially if it includes real science and or astronomy), paranormal, historical fiction, and fantasy. She's searching for beautiful writing, diverse voices, and subjects that go beyond the coming-of-age story. Pirates are cool, space travelers are awesome, and talented magicians are the way to her heart. For middle-grade and children's fiction, she is open to all genres. She loves adventurous, silly, out-of-the-box, and character-driven stories. Adult literary fiction and magical realism are welcome. She's *not* interested in nonfiction, heavy mysteries, horror, or thriller novels. If you have a short story collection, essay collection, or happen to use unique forms in your novel (letters, how-to, photos, poetry, or screenplays) and fit her other criteria, she's interested to hear from you.

HOW TO CONTACT: E-mail a query letter with the word "Query" in the subject line to alexweiss.jdlit@gmail.com. Send the first twenty pages in the body of the e-mail, along with a one-paragraph bio and one-paragraph pitch. Established picture book authors should e-mail a query and bio with the complete picture book manuscript pasted into the body of the e-mail.

site: www.triadaus.com. **Contact:** Dr. Uwe Stender. Estab. 2004. Member of AAR.
MEMBER AGENTS Uwe Stender, Brent Taylor, Laura Crockett, Mallory Brown.
REPRESENTS Nonfiction, novels, juvenile books. **Considers these nonfiction areas:** biography, business, cooking, crafts, current affairs, diet/nutrition, economics, education, environment, foods, gardening, health, history, how-to, memoirs, music, parenting, popular culture, politics, science, self-help, sports, true crime, young adult. **Considers these fiction areas:** action, adventure, contemporary issues, crime, detective, ethnic, fantasy, gay, historical, horror, juvenile, literary, mainstream, middle-grade, multicultural, mystery, new adult, occult, police, romance, suspense, thriller, urban fantasy, women's, young adult.

☞ "We are looking for great writing and story platforms. Our response time is fairly unique. We recognize that neither we nor the authors have time to waste, so we guarantee a 5-day response time. We usually respond within 24 hours." Actively looking for both fiction and nonfiction in all areas.

HOW TO CONTACT E-mail queries preferred. Accepts simultaneous submissions. Obtains most new clients through recommendations from others, conferences.

TERMS Agent receives 15% commission on domestic sales; 20% commission on foreign sales. Offers written contract; 30-day notice must be given to terminate contract.

RECENT SALES *Gettysburg Rebels* by Tom McMillan (Regency), *Who's That Girl* by Blair Thornburgh (Harper Collins Children's), *Perfect Ten* by L.Philips (Viking Children's), *You're Welcome Universe* by Whitney Gardner (Knopf Children's), *Timekeeper* by Tara Sim (Sky Pony).

TIPS "We comment on all requested mss that we reject."

TRIDENT MEDIA GROUP

41 Madison Ave., 36th Floor, New York NY 10010. (212)333-1511. **Website:** www.tridentmediagroup. com. Member of AAR.

MEMBER AGENTS Kimberly Whalen, ws.assistant@tridentmediagroup (commercial fiction and nonfiction—including women's fiction, romance, suspense, and paranormal; also seeks pop culture); **Alyssa Eisner Henkin** (picture books through young adult fiction—in the genres of mysteries, period pieces, contemporary school-settings, issues of social justice, family sagas, eerie magical realism, and retellings of classics); **Scott Miller**, smiller@tridentmediagroup.com (commercial fiction—including thrillers, crime fiction, women's, book club fiction, middle-grade, young adult; nonfiction interests include military, celebrity and pop culture, narrative, sports, prescriptive, and current events); **Melissa Flashman**, mflashman@tridentmediagroup. com (nonfiction interests include pop culture, memoir, wellness, popular science, business and economics, technology; fiction interests include adult and young adult, literary and commercial); **Don Fehr**, dfehr@tridentmediagroup.com (literary and commercial fiction, young adult fiction, narrative non-

fiction, memoirs, travel, science, and health); **John Silbersack**, silbersack.assistant@tridentmediagroup. com (literary fiction, crime fiction, science fiction, fantasy, children's, thrillers/suspense; nonfiction interests include narrative nonfiction, science, history, biography, current events, memoirs, finance, pop culture); **Erica Spellman-Silverman; Ellen Levine**, levine.assistant@tridentmediagroup.com (popular commercial fiction; also seeks compelling nonfiction—including memoir, popular culture, narrative nonfiction, history, politics, biography, science, and the odd quirky book); **Mark Gottlieb** (science fiction, fantasy, young adult, graphic novels, historical, middle-grade, mystery, romance, suspense, thrillers; nonfiction interests include business, finance, history, religious, health, cookbooks, sports, African-American, biography, memoir, travel, mind/body/spirit, narrative nonfiction, science, technology); **Alexander Slater**, aslater@tridentmediagroup.com (children's, middle-grade, young adult); **Amanda O'Connor**, aoconnor@tridentmediagroup.com; **Alexa Stark**, astark@tridentmediagroup.com (literary fiction, upmarket commercial fiction, young adult, memoir, narrative nonfiction, popular science, cultural criticism, and women's issues); **Katie Bush** (women's fiction).

REPRESENTS Considers these nonfiction areas: biography, business, cooking, creative nonfiction, current affairs, economics, health, history, memoirs, military, popular culture, politics, religious, science, sports, technology, travel, women's issues, young adult, middle-grade. **Considers these fiction areas:** commercial, crime, fantasy, historical, juvenile, literary, middle-grade, mystery, new adult, paranormal, picture books, romance, science fiction, suspense, thriller, women's, young adult.

☞ Actively seeking new or established authors in a variety of fiction and nonfiction genres.

HOW TO CONTACT Submit through the agency's online submission form on the website. Query only 1 agent at a time. If you e-query, include no attachments. Accepts simultaneous submissions.

RECENT SALES *Fish Wielder* by J.R.R.R. (Jim) Hardison, *How to Steal the Mona Lisa (And Six Other World-Famous Treasures)* by Taylor Bayouth.

TIPS "If you have any questions, please check our FAQ page online before e-mailing us."

THE UNTER AGENCY

23 W. 73rd St., Suite 100, New York NY 10023. (212)401-4068. **E-mail:** Jennifer@theunteragency. com. **Website:** www.theunteragency.com. **Contact:** Jennifer Unter. Estab. 2008. Member of AAR. Signatory of WGA.

○ Ms. Unter began her book publishing career in the editorial department at Henry Holt & Co. She later worked at the Karpfinger Agency while she attended law school. She then became an associate at the entertainment firm of Cowan, DeBaets, Abrahams & Sheppard, where she practiced primarily in the areas of publishing and copyright law.

REPRESENTS Nonfiction, novels, short story collections, juvenile books. **Considers these nonfiction areas:** animals, art, autobiography, biography, cooking, creative nonfiction, current affairs, diet/nutrition, environment, foods, health, history, how-to, humor, juvenile nonfiction, law, memoirs, popular culture, politics, spirituality, sports, travel, true crime, women's issues, young adult, nature subjects. **Considers these fiction areas:** action, adventure, cartoon, commercial, family saga, inspirational, juvenile, mainstream, middle-grade, mystery, paranormal, picture books, thriller, women's, young adult.

☛ This agency specializes in children's and nonfiction, but also takes quality adult fiction.

HOW TO CONTACT Send an e-query. There is also an online submission form. If you do not hear back from this agency within 3 months, consider that a no. Accepts simultaneous submissions.

RECENT SALES A full list of recent sales/titles is available on the agency website.

UPSTART CROW LITERARY

244 Fifth Ave., 11th Floor, New York NY 10001. **E-mail:** danielle.submission@gmail.com. **Website:** www.upstartcrowliterary.com. **Contact:** Danielle Chiotti, Alexandra Penfold. Estab. 2009. Member of AAR. Signatory of WGA.

MEMBER AGENTS Michael Stearns (not accepting submissions); **Danielle Chiotti** (all genres of young adult and middle-grade fiction, adult upmarket commercial fiction [not considering romance, mystery/suspense/thriller, science fiction, horror, or erotica]; also seeks nonfiction in the areas of narrative/memoir, lifestyle, relationships, humor, current events, food, wine, and cooking); **Ted Malawer** (not

accepting submissions); **Alexandra Penfold** (not accepting submissions).

REPRESENTS **Considers these nonfiction areas:** cooking, current affairs, foods, humor, memoirs. **Considers these fiction areas:** commercial, mainstream, middle-grade, picture books, young adult.

HOW TO CONTACT Submit a query and 20 pages of your ms pasted into an e-mail. Accepts simultaneous submissions.

VERITAS LITERARY AGENCY

601 Van Ness Ave., Opera Plaza, Suite E, San Francisco CA 94102. (415)647-6964. **Fax:** (415)647-6965. **E-mail:** submissions@verasliterary.com. **Website:** www.veritasliterary.com. **Contact:** Katherine Boyle. Member of AAR, Authors Guild, SCBWI.

MEMBER AGENTS Katherine Boyle, katherine@ veritasliterary.com (literary fiction, middle-grade, young adult, narrative nonfiction, memoir, historical fiction, crime, suspense, history, pop culture, popular science, business/career); **Michael Carr**, michael@ veritasliterary.com (historical fiction, women's fiction, science fiction, fantasy, nonfiction), **Chiara Rosati**, chiara@veritasliterary.com (literary fiction, middlegrade, young adult, new adult, women's studies, narrative nonfiction).

REPRESENTS Nonfiction, novels. **Considers these nonfiction areas:** business, history, memoirs, popular culture, women's issues. **Considers these fiction areas:** commercial, crime, fantasy, historical, literary, middle-grade, new adult, science fiction, suspense, women's, young adult.

HOW TO CONTACT This agency accepts short queries or proposals via e-mail only. "Fiction submissions: Please include a cover letter listing previously published work, a one-page query and the first 5 pages in the body of the e-mail (not as an attachment). Nonfiction submissions: If you are sending a proposal, please include an author biography, an overview, a chapter-by-chapter summary, and an analysis of competitive titles. We do our best to review all queries within 4-6 weeks; however, if you have not heard from us in 12 weeks, consider that a no." Accepts simultaneous submissions. If you have not heard from this agency in 12 weeks, consider that a no.

WAXMAN LEAVELL LITERARY AGENCY, INC.

443 Park Ave. S, Suite 1004, New York NY 10016. (212)675-5556. **Fax:** (212)675-1381. **Website:** www. waxmanleavell.com.

NEW AGENT SPOTLIGHT

KELLY PETERSON
CORVISIERO LITERARY AGENCY

www.corvisieroagency.com
@yafantasyfan

ABOUT KELLY: Kelly Peterson has spent her whole life with a book in her hands. Whether it's from reading, writing, or daydreaming, her mind has always been up in the clouds wishing her fantasy stories would come true. A graduate of West Chester University, she earned her BSEd in English.

SHE IS SEEKING: Kelly is seeking middle-grade in the areas of fantasy, paranormal, and science fiction. She seeks young adult in the areas of fantasy (all types), steampunk, science fiction, paranormal, historical (nineteenth century and earlier, with strong heroines), dystopian (hold the cyborgs, the scorch, and diseases, please), sword and sorcery, a very selective few for contemporary romance, and any combination of the above with strong female main characters. In new adult, she likes the areas of fantasy, paranormal, romance, and historical romance. Lastly, she seeks adult fantasy and adult romance. Her truest passion is for young adult fantasy.

HOW TO CONTACT: Contact query@corvisieroagency.com. In the e-mail subject line, write "Query for Kelly: [Title]." For fiction, provide a query letter pasted into the body of your e-mail along with a short synopsis and the first five pages of your manuscript either attached as two separate Word files or pasted into the query e-mail.

MEMBER AGENTS Scott Waxman (history, biography, health and science, adventure, business, inspirational sports); **Byrd Leavell** (narrative nonfiction, sports, humor, and select commercial fiction); Holly Root (middle-grade, young adult, women's fiction [commercial and upmarket], urban fantasy, romance, select nonfiction); **Larry Kirschbaum** (fiction and nonfiction; also represents select self-published breakout books); **Rachel Vogel** (subject-driven narratives, memoirs and biography, journalism, popular culture, and the occasional humor/gift book; also seeks selective fiction); **Taylor Haggerty** (young adult, historical, contemporary and historical romance, middle-grade, women's, new adult); **Cassie Hanjian** (new adult novels, plot-driven commercial and upmarket women's fiction, historical fiction, psychological suspense, cozy mysteries, and contemporary romance; nonfiction interests include mind/body/spirit, self-help, health and wellness, inspirational memoir, food/wine (narrative and prescriptive), and a limited number of accessible cookbooks); **Fleetwood Robbins** (fantasy and speculative fiction—all subgenres); **Molly O'Neill** (middle-grade and young adult fiction, picture book author/illustrators, and selective narrative nonfiction [including kidlit, pop science, pop culture, lifestyle, food, and travel projects by authors with established platforms]).

REPRESENTS Nonfiction, novels. **Considers these nonfiction areas:** biography, business, foods, health, history, humor, inspirational, memoirs, popular culture, science, sports, adventure. **Considers these fiction areas:** fantasy, historical, literary, mainstream, middle-grade, mystery, paranormal, romance, science fiction, suspense, thriller, urban fantasy, women's, young adult.

HOW TO CONTACT To submit a project, please send a query letter only via e-mail to 1 of the e-mail addresses included on the website. Do not send attachments, though for fiction you may include 5-10 pages of your ms in the body of your e-mail. "Due to the high volume of submissions, agents will reach out to you directly if interested. The typical time range for consideration is 6-8 weeks." Accepts simultaneous submissions.

CK WEBBER ASSOCIATES, LITERARY MANAGEMENT

E-mail: carlie@ckwebber.com. **Website:** http://ck-webber.com. **Contact:** Carlie Webber. CK Webber Associates is a literary agency open to commercial fiction and high-interest nonfiction. Our mission is to develop long-term careers for writers in a variety of genres. Our prime directive is outstanding fiduciary and editorial services for our clients. Member of AAR. Signatory of WGA.

○   Ms. Webber's professional publishing experience includes an internship at Writers House and work with the Publish or Perish Agency/New England Publishing Associates and the Jane Rotrosen Agency.

REPRESENTS Nonfiction, novels. **Considers these nonfiction areas:** memoirs. **Considers these fiction areas:** fantasy, literary, mainstream, middle-grade, mystery, new adult, romance, science fiction, suspense, thriller, women's, young adult.

☛   "We are currently not accepting: picture books, easy readers, poetry, scripts, and curriculum nonfiction."

HOW TO CONTACT To submit your work for consideration, please send a query letter, synopsis, and the first 30 pages (or 3 chapters) of your work, whichever is more, to carlie@ckwebber.com and put the word "Query" in the subject line of your e-mail. You may

include your materials either in the body of your e-mail or as a Word or PDF attachment. Blank e-mails that include an attachment will be deleted unread. We only accept queries via e-mail. Accepts simultaneous submissions.

◎   WELLS ARMS LITERARY

E-mail: info@wellsarms.com. **Website:** www.wellsarms.com. **Contact:** Victoria Wells Arms. Wells Arms Literary represents children's book authors and illustrators to the trade children's book market. Estab. 2013. Member of SCBWI. Represents 25 clients.

○   Ms. Arms's career began as an editor at Dial Books for Young Readers, then G. P. Putnam's Sons, and then as the founding editorial director and associate publisher of Bloomsbury USA's Children's Division.

REPRESENTS Nonfiction fiction, juvenile books, illustrators. **Considers these nonfiction areas:** juvenile nonfiction. **Considers these fiction areas:** juvenile, middle-grade, picture books, young adult.

☛   We focus on books for young readers of all ages: board books, picture books, readers, chapter books, middle-grade, and young adult fiction. We do not represent to the textbook, magazine, adult romance, or fine art markets.

HOW TO CONTACT E-query. Put "query" and your title in your e-mail subject line. No attachments. Accepts simultaneous submissions. "We try to respond in a month's time."

WERNICK & PRATT AGENCY

E-mail: info@wernickpratt.com. **Website:** www.wernickpratt.com. **Contact:** Marcia Wernick, Linda Pratt, Emily Mitchell. "Wernick & Pratt Agency provides each client with personal attention and the highest quality of advice and service that has been the hallmark of our reputations in the industry. We have the resources and accumulated knowledge to assist clients in all aspects of their creative lives, including editorial input, contract negotiations, and subsidiary rights management. Our goal is to represent and manage the careers of our clients so they may achieve industry-wide and international recognition, as well as the highest level of financial potential." Member of AAR, SCBWI. Signatory of WGA.

○   Prior to co-founding Wernick & Pratt Agency, Ms. Wernick worked at the Sheldon Fogelman Agency in subsidiary rights, advancing to director of subsidiary rights; Ms. Pratt also worked at the Sheldon Fogelman Agency.

MEMBER AGENTS Marcia Wernick, Linda Pratt, Emily Mitchell.

☞ "Wernick & Pratt Agency specializes in children's books of all genres, from picture books through young adult literature and everything in between. We represent both authors and illustrators. We do not represent authors of adult books." Actively seeking people who both write and illustrate in the picture book genre, humorous young chapter books with strong voice, and middle-grade and young adults novels in both the literary and commercial realms. No picture book mss of more than 750 words or mood pieces. Does not want work specifically targeted to the educational market, fiction about the American Revolution, Civil War, or World War II unless it is told from a very unique perspective.

HOW TO CONTACT Submit via e-mail only to submissions@wernickpratt.com. "Please indicate to which agent you are submitting." Detailed submission guidelines available on website. "Submissions will only be responded to further if we are interested in them. If you do not hear from us within 6 weeks of your submission, it should be considered declined."

WOLFSON LITERARY AGENCY

P.O. Box 266, New York NY 10276. **E-mail:** query@wolfsonliterary.com. **Website:** www.wolfsonliterary.com. **Contact:** Michelle Wolfson. Estab. 2007. Adheres to AAR canon of ethics.

○ Prior to forming her own agency in December 2007, Ms. Wolfson spent 2 years with Artists & Artisans, Inc., and 2 years with Ralph Vicinanza, Ltd.

REPRESENTS Nonfiction, fiction. **Considers these nonfiction areas:** creative nonfiction, health, humor, medicine, parenting, popular culture, relationships. **Considers these fiction areas:** mainstream, mystery, new adult, romance, suspense, thriller, women's, young adult.

☞ Actively seeking young adult, mainstream fiction, mysteries, thrillers, suspense, women's fiction, romance. Fiction interests include fun, practical advice books in any area, but particularly those that are of interest to women. Also seeks books on relationships, parenting,

health/medical, humor, pop culture, and narrative nonfiction.

HOW TO CONTACT E-queries only. Accepts simultaneous submissions. Responds only if interested. Positive response is generally given within 2-4 weeks. Obtains most new clients through queries or recommendations from others.

TERMS Agent receives 15% commission on domestic sales; receives 25% commission on foreign sales. Offers written contract; 30-day notice must be given to terminate contract.

TIPS "Be persistent."

WRITERS HOUSE

21 W. 26th St., New York NY 10010. (212)685-2400. **Fax:** (212)685-1781. **Website:** www.writershouse.com. Estab. 1973. Member of AAR.

MEMBER AGENTS Amy Berkower, Stephen Barr, Susan Cohen, Dan Conaway, Lisa DiMona, Susan Ginsburg, Susan Golomb, Merrilee Heifetz, Brianne Johnson, Daniel Lazar, Simon Lipskar, Steven Malk, Jodi Reamer, Esq., Robin Rue, Rebecca Sherman, Geri Thoma, Albert Zuckerman, Alec Shane, Stacy Testa, Victoria Doherty-Munro, Beth Miller, Andrea Morrison, Soumeya Roberts.

REPRESENTS Nonfiction, novels. **Considers these nonfiction areas:** biography, business, cooking, economics, history, how-to, juvenile nonfiction, memoirs, parenting, psychology, science, self-help. **Considers these fiction areas:** commercial, fantasy, juvenile, literary, mainstream, middle-grade, picture books, science fiction, women's, young adult.

☞ This agency specializes in all types of popular fiction and nonfiction, for both adult and juvenile books, as well as illustrators. Does not want to receive scholarly, professional, poetry, plays, or screenplays.

HOW TO CONTACT Individual agent e-mail addresses are available on the website. "Please e-mail us a query letter, which includes your credentials, an explanation of what makes your book unique and special, and a synopsis. Some agents within our agency have different requirements. Please consult their individual Publishers Marketplace profile for additional details. We respond to all queries, generally within 8 weeks." If you prefer to submit my mail, address it to an individual agent, and please include a SASE for our reply. (If submitting to Steven Malk: Writers House, 7660 Fay Ave., #338H, La Jolla, CA 92037.) Accepts simultaneous submissions. Obtains most new clients through recommendations from authors and editors.

TERMS Agent receives 15% commission on domestic sales; 20% commission on foreign sales. Offers written contract, binding for 1 year. Agency charges fees for copying mss/proposals and overseas airmail of books.

TIPS "Do not send mss. Write a compelling letter. If you do, we'll ask to see your work. Follow submission guidelines and please do not simultaneously submit your work to more than 1 Writers House agent."

ART REPS

CAROL BANCROFT & FRIENDS

P.O. Box 2030, Danbury CT 06813. (203)730-8270 or (800)720-7020. **Fax:** (203)730-8275. **E-mail:** cbfriends@sbcglobal.net. **Website:** www.carolbancroft.com. **Contact:** Joy Elton Tricarico, owner; Carol Bancroft, founder. "Internationally known for representing artists who specialize in illustrating art for all aspects of the children's market. We also represent many artists who are well known in other aspects of the field of illustration." Clients include, but not limited to, Scholastic, Houghton Mifflin Harcourt, HarperCollins, Marshall Cavendish, McGraw Hill, Hay House.

HANDLES Specializes in illustration for children's publishing-text and trade; any children's-related material.

TERMS Rep receives 25% commission. Advertising costs are split: 75% paid by talent; 25% paid by representative.

HOW TO CONTACT Mail e-mail 2-3 samples with your contact information/website Accepts simultaneous submissions.

TIPS "We look for artists who can draw animals and people with imagination and energy, depicting engaging characters with action in situational settings."

CORNELL & COMPANY, ILLUSTRATION AND DESIGN

44 Jog Hill Rd., Trumbull CT 06611. (203) 454-4210. **E-mail:** merial@cornellandco.com. **Website:** www.cornellandco.com. **Contact:** Merial Cornell. Cornell & Company, LLC represents a diverse group of talented, professional illustrators and author/illustrators specializing in children's picture books, jackets, educational materials, magazines, stationary, licensing, and toys. Please visit our website for an overview

of our group of illustrators. Additional portfolio samples are available on request. Cornell & Company also provides art buying services and support for large projects.

www.cornellandco.com

HANDLES Specializes in children's books illustration: trade, mass market, educational. Obtains new talent through recommendations, solicitation, conferences. Also represents author/illustrators

TERMS Agent receives 25% commission on illustration work. Advertising costs are split: 75% paid by talent; 25% paid by representative.

HOW TO CONTACT For first contact, send query letter, direct mail flier/brochure, tearsheets, photocopies and SASE or preferably e-mail. For promotional purposes, talent must provide 10-12 strong portfolio pieces relating to children's publishing. Accepts simultaneous submissions.

CREATIVE FREELANCERS, INC.

(888)398-9540. **E-mail:** crea@illustratorsonline.com. **Website:** www.illustratorsonline.com. **Contact:** Marilyn Howard.

HANDLES Specializes in children's books, advertising, architectural, conceptual. Markets include: advertising agencies; corporations/client direct; design firms; editorial/magazines; paper products/greeting cards; publishing/books; sales/promotion firms.

HOW TO CONTACT Accepts simultaneous submissions.

MARLENA AGENCY

278 Hamilton Ave., Princeton NJ 08540. (609)252-9405. **Fax:** (609)252-9408. **E-mail:** marlena@marlenaagency.com. **Website:** www.marlenaagency.com. Represents illustrators including Gerard Dubois, Linda Helton, Paul Zwolak, Serge Bloch, Hadley Hooper, Jean-François Martin, Perre Mornet, Pep Montserrat, Tomasz Walenta, Istvan Orosz, Lorenzo Petrantoni, Scott Mckowen, Olimpia Zagnoli, Francesco Bongiorni, Lincoln Agnew, Frederic Benaglia, Natalya Balnova, Umberto Mischi, Federico Jordan, Agata Endo Nowicka, Mariko Jesse and Carmen Segovia.

HANDLES Currently open to illustrators seeking representation. Open to both new and established illustrators.

RECENT SALES *Sees Behind Trees*, by Linda Helton (Harcourt); *Ms. Rubinstein's Beauty,* by Pep Montserrat (Sterling); *My Cat,* by Linda Helton (Scho-

AGENTS AND ART REPS

lastic); *The McElderry Book of Greek Myths*, by Pep Monserrat (McElderly Books); *You are What You Eat*, by Serge Bloch (Sterling); *The Arabian Nights*, by Carole Henaff (Barefoot); *36 Hours Book Series*, by Olimpia Zagnoli (Tashen).

TERMS Exclusive representation required. Offers written contract.

HOW TO CONTACT For first contact, send tearsheets, photocopies, or e-mail low resolution samples only. Submission guidelines available for #10 SASE. Accepts simultaneous submissions. Finds illustrators through queries/solicitations, magazines and graphic design.

TIPS "Be creative and persistent."

MB ARTISTS

775 Sixth Ave., #6, New York NY 10001. (212)689-7830. **E-mail:** mela@mbartists.com. **Website:** www.mbartists.com. **Contact:** Mela Bolinao. MB Artists represents illustrators whose work is primarily intended for the juvenile market in books, editorial publications, licensing merhandise, advertising, games, puzzles, and toys.

HANDLES Specializes in illustration for juvenile markets. Markets include: advertising agencies; editorial/magazines; publishing/books, board games, stationary, etc.

TERMS Rep receives 25% commission. No geographic restrictions. Advertising costs are split: 75% paid by talent; 25% paid by representative.

HOW TO CONTACT For first contact, send query letter, direct mail flier/brochure, website address, tearsheets, slides, photographs or color copies and SASE or send website link to mela@mbartists.com. Portfolio should include at least 12 images appropriate for the juvenile market. Accepts simultaneous submissions.

LIZ SANDERS AGENCY

2415 E. Hangman Creek Lane, Spokane WA 99224-8514. (509)993-6400. **E-mail:** liz@lizsanders.com; artsubmissions@lizsanders.com. **Website:** www.lizsanders.com. **Contact:** Liz Sanders, owner. Commercial illustration representative. Represents Kyle Poling, Amy Ning, Sue Rama, Sudi McCollum, Suzanne Beaky, Judy Reed Silver, Craig Orback and more.

HANDLES Markets include publishing, licensed properties, entertainment and advertising. Current-

ly open to illustrators seeking representation. Open to both new and established illustrators.

TERMS Receives 30% commission. Offers written contract.

HOW TO CONTACT For first contact, send tearsheets, direct mail flier/brochure, color copies, non-returnable or e-mail to artsubmissions@lizsanders.com. Accepts simultaneous submissions. Obtains new talent through recommendations from industry contacts, conferences and queries/solicitations, Literary Market Place.

GWEN WALTERS ARTIST REPRESENTATIVE

20 Windsor Ln., Palm Beach Garden FL 33418. (561)805-7739. **E-mail:** artincgw@gmail.com. **Website:** www.gwenwaltersartrep.com. **Contact:** Gwen Walters.

HANDLES Currently open to illustrators seeking representation. Looking for established illustrators only.

RECENT SALES Sells to "All major book publishers."

TERMS Receives 30% commission. Artist needs to supply all promo material. Offers written contract.

HOW TO CONTACT For first contact, send e-mail including samples. Accepts simultaneous submissions. Finds illustrators through recommendations from others.

TIPS "You need to pound the pavement for a couple of years to get some experience under your belt. Don't forget to sign all artwork. So many artists forget to stamp their samples."

DEBORAH WOLFE, LTD.

731 N. 24th St., Philadelphia PA 19130. (215)232-6666. **Fax:** (215)232-6585. **E-mail:** info@illustrationonline.com. **Website:** www.illustrationonline.com. Commercial illustration and animation representative. Member of Graphic Artist Guild. Represents 40 illustrators. Currently open to illustrators and animators seeking representation. **Contact:** Deborah Wolfe.

HANDLES Illustration.

TERMS Receives 25% commission. Exclusive representation required. Offers written contract.

HOW TO CONTACT Portfolio should be sent as a JPEG or you should direct us to your website." Finds illustrators through queries/solicitations. Accepts simultaneous submissions.

CLUBS & ORGANIZATIONS

AMERICAN ALLIANCE FOR THEATRE & EDUCATION

4908 Auburn Ave., Bethesda MD 20814. (301)200-1944. **Fax:** 301-280-1682. **E-mail:** info@aate.com. **Website:** www.aate.com. Purpose of organization: to promote standards of excellence in theatre and drama education. "We achieve this by assimilating quality practices in theatre and theatre education; connecting artists, educators, researchers, and scholars with one another, and by providing opportunities for our members to learn, exchange, and diversify their work, their audiences, and their perspectives." Membership cost: $115 annually for individual in US and Canada, $220 annually for organization, $60 annually for students, $70 annually for retired people, $310 annually for University Departmental memberships; add $30 outside Canada and US. Holds annual conference (July or August). Contests held for unpublished play reading project and annual awards in various categories. Awards plaque and stickers for published playbooks. Publishes list of unpublished plays deemed worthy of performance and stages readings at conference. Contact national office at number above or see website for contact information for Playwriting Network Chairpersons. **Contact:** Alexis Truitt, operations manager.

AMERICAN SOCIETY OF JOURNALISTS AND AUTHORS

1501 Broadway, Suite 403, New York NY 10036. (212)997-0947. **Website:** www.asja.org. Qualifications for membership: "Need to be a professional freelance nonfiction writer. Refer to website for further qualifications." Membership cost: application fee—$50; annual dues—$210. Group sponsors national conferences. Professional seminars online and in person around the country. Workshops/conferences open to non-members. Publishes a newsletter for members that provides confidential information for nonfiction writers. **Contact:** Alexandra Owens, executive director.

ARIZONA AUTHORS' ASSOCIATION

6939 East Chaparral Rd., Paradise Valley AZ 85253. (602)554-8101. **E-mail:** azauthors@gmail.com. **Website:** www.azauthors.com. Since 1978, Arizona Authors' Association has served to offer professional, educational, and social opportunities to writers and authors and serves as an informational and referral network for the literary community. Members must be authors, writers working toward publication, agents, publishers, publicists, printers, illustrators, etc. AZ Authors' publishes a bimonthly newsletter and the renown annual *Arizona Literary Magazine*. The Association sponsors the international Arizona Literary Contest, including poetry, essays, short stories, new drama writing, novels, and published books with cash prizes and awards bestowed at a fall ceremony. Winning entries are published or advertised in the *Arizona Literary Magazine*. First and second place winners in poetry, essay and short story categories are entered in the annual Pushcart Prize. Learn more online. **Contact:** Lisa Aquilina, President.

THE AUTHORS GUILD, INC.

31 E. 32nd St., 7th Floor, New York NY 10016. (212)563-5904. **Fax:** (212)564-5363. **E-mail:** staff@authorsguild.org. **Website:** www.authorsguild.org. Purpose of organization: to offer services and materials intended to help authors with the business and legal aspects of their work, including contract problems, copyright matters, freedom of expression, and taxation. Guild has 8,000 members. Qualifications for membership: Must be book author published by an established American publisher within 7 years or any author who has had 3 works (fiction or nonfiction) published by a magazine or magazines of general circulation in the past 18 months. Associate membership also available. Different levels of membership include: associate membership with all rights except voting available to an author who has a firm contract offer or is currently negotiating a royalty contract from an established American publisher. "The Guild offers free contract reviews to its members. The Guild conducts several symposia each year at which experts provide information, offer advice, and answer questions on subjects of interest and concern to authors. Typical subjects have been the rights of privacy and publicity, libel, wills and estates, taxation, copyright, editors and editing, the art of interviewing, standards of criticism, and book reviewing. Transcripts of these symposia are published and circulated to members. The *Authors Guild Bulletin*, a quarterly journal, contains articles on matters of interest to writers, reports of Guild activities, contract surveys, advice on problem clauses in contracts, transcripts of Guild and League symposia, and information on a variety of professional topics. Subscription included in the cost of the annual dues. **Contact:** Mary Rasenberger, executive director.

�় CANADIAN SOCIETY OF CHILDREN'S AUTHORS, ILLUSTRATORS AND PERFORMERS

104-40 Orchard View Blvd., Lower Level, Toronto ON M4R 1B9, Canada. (416)515-1559. **E-mail:** office@canscaip.org. **Website:** www.canscaip.org. Purpose of organization: development of Canadian children's culture and support for authors, illustrators, and performers working in this field. Qualifications for membership: Members—professionals who have been pub-

lished (not self-published) or have paid public performances/records/tapes to their credit; friends—share interest in field of children's culture. Sponsors workshops/conferences. Ms evaluation services; publishes newsletter: includes profiles of members; news roundup of members' activities countrywide; market news; news on awards, grants, etc.; columns related to professional concerns. **Contact:** Lena Coakley, administrative director.

LEWIS CARROLL SOCIETY OF NORTH AMERICA

11935 Beltsville Dr., Beltsville MD 20705. **E-mail:** secretary@lewiscarroll.org. **Website:** www.lewiscarroll.org. "We are an organization of Carroll admirers of all ages and interests and a center for Carroll studies." Qualifications for membership: "an interest in Lewis Carroll and a simple love for Alice (or the Snark for that matter)." Membership cost: $35 (regular membership), $50 (foreign membership), $100 (sustaining membership). The Society meets twice a year—in spring and in fall; locations vary. Publishes a semi-annual journal, *Knight Letter*, and maintains an active publishing program. **Contact:** Clare Imholtz, secretary.

GRAPHIC ARTISTS GUILD

32 Broadway, Suite 1114, New York NY 10004. (212)791-3400. **Fax:** 212-791-0333. **E-mail:** admin@gag.org. **Website:** www.graphicartistsguild.org. Purpose of organization: "to promote and protect the economic interests of member artists. It is committed to improving conditions for all creators of graphic arts and raising standards for the entire industry." Qualification for full membership: 50 percent of income derived from the creation of graphic artwork. Associate members include those in allied fields and students. Initiation fee $30. Membership costs: full memberships $200/year; student membership $75/year; associate membership $170/year. Publishes *Graphic Artists Guild Handbook*, *Pricing and Ethical Guidelines* (members receive a copy as part of their membership). **Contact:** Patricia McKiernan, executive director.

HORROR WRITERS ASSOCIATION

244 Fifth Ave., Suite 2767, New York NY 10001. **E-mail:** hwa@horror.org; membership@horror.org. **Website:** horror.org. Purpose of organization: to encourage public interest in horror and dark fantasy and to provide networking and career tools for members.

Qualifications for membership: Complete membership rules online at www.horror.org/memrule.htm. At least one low-level sale is required to join as an affiliate. Non-writing professionals who can show income from a horror-related field may join as an associate (booksellers, editors, agents, librarians, etc.). To qualify for full active membership, you must be a published, professional writer of horror. Membership cost: $69 annually. Holds annual Stoker Awards Weekend and HWA Business Meeting. Publishes monthly newsletter focusing on market news, industry news, HWA business for members. Sponsors awards. We give the Bram Stoker Awards annually for superior achievement in horror. Awards include a handmade Stoker trophy designed by sculptor Stephen Kirk. Awards open to non-members. **Contact:** James Chambers, membership chair.

INTERNATIONAL LITERACY ASSOCIATION

P.O. Box 8139, Newark DE 19714. (302)731-1600 ext. 293. **Fax:** (302)731-1057. **E-mail:** councils@reading. org. **Website:** www.literacyworldwide.org. The International Literary Association seeks to promote high levels of literacy for all by improving the quality of reading instruction through studying the reading process and teaching techniques; serving as a clearinghouse for the dissemination of reading research through conferences, journals, and other publications; and actively encouraging the lifetime reading habit. Its goals include professional development, advocacy, partnerships, research, and global literacy development. Sponsors annual convention. Publishes a newsletter called "Reading Today." Sponsors a number of awards and fellowships. More information online.

INTERNATIONAL WOMEN'S WRITING GUILD

274 Madison Ave., Suite 1202, New York NY 10016. (917)720-6959. **E-mail:** iwwgquestions@gmail.com. **Website:** www.iwwg.wildapricot.org. IWWG is a network for the personal and professional empowerment of women through writing. Open to any woman connected to the written word regardless of professional portfolio. IWWG sponsors several annual conferences per year in all areas of the US. The major conference, held in summer, is a week-long conference attracting hundreds of women writers from across the globe. **Contact:** Kristin Rath, director of operations.

LITERARY MANAGERS AND DRAMATURGS OF THE AMERICAS

P.O. Box 36, 20985 P.A.C.C., New York NY 10129. (800)680-2148. **E-mail:** info@lmda.org. **Website:** www.lmda.org. LMDA is a not-for-profit service organization for the professions of literary management and dramaturgy. Student membership: $30/ year. Open to students in dramaturgy, performing arts and literature programs, or related disciplines. Proof of student status required. Includes national conference, New Dramaturg activities, local symposia, job phone, and select membership meetings. Individual membership: $75/year. Open to full-time and part-time professionals working in the fields of literary management and dramaturgy. All privileges and services including voting rights and eligibility for office. Institutional membership: $200/ year. Open to theaters, universities, and other organizations. Includes all privileges and services except voting rights and eligibility for office. Publishes a newsletter featuring articles on literary management, dramaturgy, LMDA program updates and other articles of interest. Spotlight sponsor membership $500/year; Open to theatres, universities, and other organizations; includes all privileges for up to 6 individual members, plus additional promotional benefits.

THE NATIONAL LEAGUE OF AMERICAN PEN WOMEN

Pen Arts Building, 1300 17th St. NW, Washington D.C. 20036-1973. (202)785-1997. **Fax:** (202)452-8868. **E-mail:** contact@nlapw.org. **Website:** www.nlapw. org. Purpose of organization: to promote professional female work in art, letters, and music since 1897. Qualifications for membership: An applicant must show "proof of sale" in each chosen category—art, letters, and music. Levels of membership include: active, associate, international affiliate, members-at-large, honorary members (in one or more of the following classifications: art, letters, and music). Holds workshops/conferences. Publishes magazine 4 times/year titled *The Pen Woman*. Sponsors various contests in areas of art, letters, and music. Awards made at biennial convention. Biannual scholarships awarded to non-Pen Women for mature women. Awards include cash prizes—up to $1,000. Specialized contests open to non-members. **Contact:** Nina Brooks, corresponding secretary.

NATIONAL WRITERS ASSOCIATION

10940 S. Parker Rd., #508, Parker CO 80138. (303)841-0246. **Fax:** (303)841-2607. **E-mail:** natlwritersassn@hotmail.com. **Website:** www.nationalwriters.com. Association for freelance writers. Qualifications for membership: associate membership—must be serious about writing; professional membership—must be published and paid writer (cite credentials). Sponsors workshops/conferences: TV/screenwriting workshops, NWAF Annual Conferences, Literary Clearinghouse, editing and critiquing services, local chapters, National Writer's School. Open to non-members. Publishes industry news of interest to freelance writers, how-to articles, market information, member news, and networking opportunities. Sponsors poetry contest, short story contest, article contest, novel contest. Awards cash for top 3 winners, books and/or certificates for other winners, honorable mention certificates for places 5-10. Contests open to non-members.

NATIONAL WRITERS UNION

256 W. 38th St., Suite 703, New York NY 10018. (212)254-0279. **Fax:** (212)254-0673. **E-mail:** nwu@nwu.org. **Website:** nwu.org. Advocacy for freelance writers. Qualifications for membership: "Membership in the NWU is open to all qualified writers, and no one shall be barred or in any manner prejudiced within the Union on account of race, age, sex, sexual orientation, disability, national origin, religion, or ideology. You are eligible for membership if you have published a book, a play, 3 articles, 5 poems, 1 short story, or an equivalent amount of newsletter, publicity, technical, commercial, government, or institutional copy. You are also eligible for membership if you have written an equal amount of unpublished material, and you are actively writing and attempting to publish your work." Holds workshops throughout the country. Members-only section on website offers rich resources for freelance writers. Skilled contract advice and grievance help for members.

PEN AMERICAN CENTER

588 Broadway, Suite 303, New York NY 10012. (212)334-1660. **Fax:** (212)334-2181. **E-mail:** info@pen.org. **Website:** pen.org. "An association of writers working to advance literature, to defend free expression, and to foster international literary fellowship. PEN welcomes to its membership all writers and those belonging to the larger literary community. We ask that writers have at least 1 book published or be writers with proven records as professional writers; playwrights and screenwriters should have at least one work produced in a professional setting. Others should have achieved recognition in the literary field. Editors, literary agents, literary scouts, publicists, journalists, bloggers, and other literary professionals are all invited to join as professional members. If you feel you do not meet these guidelines, please consider joining as an Advocate Member. Candidates for membership may be nominated by a PEN member, or they may nominate themselves with the support of 2 references from the literary community or from a current PEN member. PEN members receive a subscription to the PEN journal, the PEN Annual Report, and have access to medical insurance at group rates. Members living in the New York metropolitan and tri-state area, or near the Branches, are invited to PEN events throughout the year. Membership in PEN American Center includes reciprocal privileges in PEN American Center branches and in foreign PEN Centers for those traveling abroad. Application forms are available online. PEN American Center is the largest of the 141 centers of PEN International, the world's oldest human rights organization and the oldest international literary organization. PEN International was founded in 1921 to dispel national, ethnic, and racial hatreds and to promote understanding among all countries. PEN American Center, founded a year later, works to advance literature, to defend free expression, and to foster international literary fellowship. The Center has a membership of 3,400 distinguished writers, editors, and translators. In addition to defending writers in prison or in danger of imprisonment for their work, PEN American Center sponsors public literary programs and forums on current issues, sends prominent authors to inner-city schools to encourage reading and writing, administers literary prizes, promotes international literature that might otherwise go unread in the United States, and offers grants and loans to writers facing financial or medical emergencies."

PUPPETEERS OF AMERICA, INC.

Sabathani Community Center, 310 East 38th St., Suite 127, Minneapolis MN 55409. (888)568-6235. **E-mail:** membership@puppeteers.org; execdir@puppeteers.org. **Website:** www.puppeteers.org. Purpose of organization: to promote the art and appreciation of puppetry as a means of communications and as a performing art. The Puppeteers of America boasts an international membership. There are 9 different levels of membership, from family to youth to library to senior and more. See the website for all details. Costs are $35-90 per year.

SCIENCE FICTION AND FANTASY WRITERS OF AMERICA, INC.

P.O. Box 3238, Enfield CT 06083. **Website:** www.sfwa. org. Purpose of organization: to encourage public interest in science fiction literature and provide organization format for writers/editors/artists within the genre. Qualifications for membership: at least 1 professional sale or other professional involvement within the field. Different levels of membership include: active—requires 3 professional short stories or 1 novel published; associate—requires 1 professional sale; or affiliate—which requires some other professional involvement such as artist, editor, librarian, bookseller, teacher, etc. Workshops/conferences: annual awards banquet, usually in April or May. Open to non-members. Publishes quarterly journal, the *SFWA Bulletin*. Sponsors Nebula Awards for best published science fiction or fantasy in the categories of novel, novella, novelette, and short story. Awards trophy. Also presents the Damon Knight Memorial Grand Master Award for Lifetime Achievement and, beginning in 2006, the Andre Norton Award for Outstanding Young Adult Science Fiction or Fantasy Book of the Year.

SOCIETY OF CHILDREN'S BOOK WRITERS AND ILLUSTRATORS

8271 Beverly Blvd., Los Angeles CA 90048. (323)782-1010. **Fax:** (323)782-1892. **E-mail:** scbwi@scbwi.org; membership@scbwi.org. **Website:** www.scbwi.org. Purpose of organization: to assist writers and illustrators working or interested in the field. Qualifications for membership: an interest in children's literature and illustration. Membership cost: $80/year plus one-time $95 initiation fee. Different levels of membership include: P.A.L. membership—published by publisher listed in SCBWI Market Surveys; full membership—published authors/illustrators (includes self-published); associate membership—unpublished writers/illustrators. Holds 100 events (workshops/conferences) worldwide each year. National Conference open to non-members. Publishes bimonthly magazine on writing and illustrating children's books. Sponsors

annual awards and grants for writers and illustrators who are members. **Contact:** Stephen Mooser, president; Lin Oliver, executive director.

SOCIETY OF ILLUSTRATORS

128 E. 63rd St., New York NY 10065. (212)838-2560. **Fax:** (212)838-2561. **E-mail:** info@societyillustrators. org. **Website:** www.societyillustrators.org. "Our mission is to promote the art and appreciation of illustration, its history, and evolving nature through exhibitions, lectures, and education. Membership costs: nnual dues for non-resident illustrator members (those living more than 125 air miles from SI's headquarters): $300. Dues for resident illustrator members: $500/year; resident associate members: $500. Artist members shall include those who make illustration their profession and earn at least 60 percent of their income from their illustration. Associate members are those who earn their living in the arts or who have made a substantial contribution to the art of illustration. This includes art directors, art buyers, creative supervisors, instructors, publishers, and like categories. The candidate must complete and sign the application form, which requires a brief biography, a listing of schools attended, other training, and a résumé of his or her professional career. Candidates for illustrators membership, in addition to the above requirements, must submit examples of their work." **Contact:** Anelle Miller, executive director.

SOCIETY OF MIDLAND AUTHORS

P.O. Box 10419, Chicago IL 60610. **Website:** www. midlandauthors.com. Purpose of organization: to create closer association among writers of the Middle West, stimulate creative literary effort, maintain collection of members' works, encourage interest in reading and literature by cooperating with other educational and cultural agencies. Qualifications for membership: membership by invitation only. Must be author or co-author of a book demonstrating literary style published by a recognized publisher, and be identified through residence with Illinois, Indiana, Iowa, Kansas, Michigan, Minnesota, Missouri, Nebraska, North Dakota, Ohio, South Dakota, or Wisconsin. Open to students (if authors). Membership cost: $40/year dues. Different levels of membership include: regular—published book authors; associate non-voting—not published as above but having some connection with literature, such as librarians, teachers, publishers, and editors. Program meetings held

5 times/year, featuring authors, publishers, editors or the like, individually or on panels. Usually second Tuesday of October, November, February, March, and April. Also holds annual awards dinner in May. Publishes a newsletter focusing on news of members and general items of interest to writers. Sponsors contests. "Annual awards in 6 categories given at annual dinner in May. Monetary awards for books published that premiered professionally in previous calendar year. Send SASE to contact person for details." Categories include adult fiction, adult nonfiction, juvenile fiction, juvenile nonfiction, poetry, biography. No picture books. Contest open to non-members. **Contact:** Robert Loerzel, president.

THE SOCIETY OF SOUTHWESTERN AUTHORS

Fax: (520)751-7877. **E-mail:** azwritten@gmail.com. **Website:** www.ssa-az.org. Purpose of organization: to promote fellowship among professional and associate members of the writing profession, to recognize members' achievements, to stimulate further achievement, and to assist persons seeking to become professional writers. Qualifications for membership: Professional membership: proof of publication of a book, articles, TV screenplay, etc. Associate membership: proof of desire to write, and/or become a professional. Self-published authors may receive status of Professional Membership at the discretion of the board of directors. Membership cost: see website. Sometimes this organization hosts writing events, such as its co-sponsorship of the Arizona Writing Workshops in Phoenix and Tucson in t6he past. **Contact:** Chris Stern.

○ TEXT & ACADEMIC AUTHORS ASSOCIATION (TAA)

P.O. Box 56359, St. Petersburg FL 33732. (727)563-0020. **E-mail:** richard.hull@taaonline.net; kim.pawlak@taaonline.net. **Website:** www.taaonline.net. TAA's overall mission is "to support textbook and academic authors in the creation of top-quality educational and scholarly works that stimulate the love of learning and foster the pursuit of knowledge." Qualifications for membership: All authors and prospective authors are welcome. Membership cost: $20-200. Workshops/conferences: June each year. Newsletter focuses on all areas of interest to textbook and academic authors. **Contact:** Richard T. Hall, executive director; Kim Pawlick, associate executive director.

THEATRE FOR YOUNG AUDIENCES

c/o The Theatre School, 2135 N. Kenmore Ave., Chicago IL 60657. (773)325-7981. **Fax:** (773)325-7920. **E-mail:** info@tyausa.org. **Website:** www.assitej-usa.org. Purpose of organization: to promote theater for children and young people by linking professional theaters and artists together; sponsoring national, international, and regional conferences; and providing publications and information. Also serves as US Center for International Association of the Theatre for Children and Young People. Different levels of memberships include: organizations, individuals, students, retirees, libraries. *TYA Today* includes original articles, reviews, and works of criticism and theory, all of interest to theater practitioners (included with membership). Publishes *Marquee*, a directory that focuses on information on members in US.

VOLUNTEER LAWYERS FOR THE ARTS

1 E. 53rd St., 6th Floor, New York NY 10022. (212)319-2787, ext. 1. **Fax:** (212)752-6575. **E-mail:** vlany@vlany.org. **Website:** vlany.org. Purpose of organization: Volunteer Lawyers for the Arts is dedicated to providing free arts-related legal assistance to low-income artists and not-for-profit arts organizations in all creative fields. More than 1,000 attorneys in the New York area donate their time through VLA to artists and arts organizations unable to afford legal counsel. Everyone is welcome to use VLA's Art Law Line, a legal hotline for any artist or arts organization needing quick answers to arts-related questions. VLA also provides clinics, seminars, and publications designed to educate artists on legal issues that affect their careers. Members receive discounts on publications and seminars as well as other benefits.

○ WRITERS' FEDERATION OF NEW BRUNSWICK

P.O. Box 306, Moncton NB E1C 8L4, Canada. (506)459-7228. **E-mail:** info@wfnb.ca. **Website:** wfnb.ca. Purpose of organization: "to promote New Brunswick writing and to help writers at all stages of their development." Qualifications for membership: interest in writing. Membership cost: $50 basic annual membership; $5 for high school students; $50 for an institutional membership. Holds workshops/conferences. Publishes a newsletter with articles concerning the craft of writing, member news, contests, markets, workshops, and conference listings. Sponsors annual literary competition, $20-35 entry fee for members, $25-40 for non-members. Categories: fiction, nonfiction, poetry, children's literature. **Contact:** Lee Thompson, executive director.

◑ WRITERS' FEDERATION OF NOVA SCOTIA

1113 Marginal Rd., Halifax NS B3H 4P7, Canada. (902)423-8116. **Fax:** (902)422-0881. **E-mail:** director@writers.ns.ca. **Website:** www.writers.ns.ca. Purpose of organization: "to foster creative writing and the profession of writing in Nova Scotia, to provide advice and assistance to writers at all stages of their careers, and encourage greater public recognition of Nova Scotian writers and their achievements." Regional organization open to anybody who writes. Currently has 800+ members. Offerings include resource library with more than 2,500 titles, promotional services, workshop series, annual festivals, mentorship program. Publishes *Eastword*, a bimonthly newsletter containing "a plethora of information on who's doing what, markets and contests, and current writing events and issues." Members and nationally known writers give readings that are open to the public. Additional information online.

◑ WRITERS GUILD OF ALBERTA

11759 Groat Rd., Edmonton AB T5M 3K6, Canada. (780)422-8174. **E-mail:** mail@writersguild.ab.ca. **Website:** writersguild.ab.ca. Purpose of organization: to support, encourage and promote writers and writing; to safeguard the freedom to write and to read; and to advocate for the well-being of writers in Alberta. Currently has more than 1,000 members. Offerings include retreats/conferences, monthly events, bimonthly magazine that includes articles on writing and a market section, weekly electronic bulletin with markets and event listings, and the Stephan G. Stephansson Award for Poetry (Alberta residents only). Holds workshops/conferences. Publishes a newsletter focusing on markets, competitions, contemporary issues related to the literary arts (writing, publishing, censorship, royalties, etc.). Sponsors annual literary awards in 5 categories (novel, nonfiction, children's literature, poetry, drama). Awards include $1,500. Open to non-members.

CONFERENCES & WORKSHOPS

Attending a writers conference that includes agents gives you the opportunity to learn more about what agents do and to show an agent your work. Ideally, a conference should include a panel or two with a number of agents to give writers a sense of the variety of personalities and tastes of different agents.

Not all agents are alike: Some are more personable, and sometimes you simply click better with one agent versus another. When only one agent attends a conference, there is a tendency for every writer at that conference to think, "Ah, this is the agent I've been looking for!" When the number of agents attending is larger, you have a wider group from which to choose, and you may have less competition for the agent's time.

Besides including panels of agents discussing what representation means and how to go about securing it, many of these gatherings also include time—either scheduled or impromptu—to meet briefly with an agent to discuss your work.

If they're impressed with what they see and hear about your work, they will invite you to submit a query, a proposal, a few sample chapters, or possibly your entire ms. Some conferences even arrange for agents to review mss in advance and schedule one-on-one sessions during which you can receive specific feedback or advice regarding your work. Such meetings often cost a small fee, but the input you receive is usually worth the price.

Ask writers who attend conferences and they'll tell you that, at the very least, you'll walk away with new knowledge about the industry. At the very best, you'll receive an invitation to send an agent your material!

Many writers try to make it to at least one conference a year, but cost and location can count as much as subject matter when determining which one to attend. There are conferences in almost every state and province that can provide answers to your questions about writing and the publishing industry. Conferences also connect you with a community of other writers. Such connections help you learn about the pros and cons of different agents, and they can also give you a renewed sense of purpose and direction in your own writing.

SUBHEADS

Each listing is divided into subheads to make locating specific information easier. In the first section, you'll find contact information for conference contacts. You'll also learn conference dates, specific focus, and the average number of attendees. Finally, names of agents who will be speaking or have spoken in the past are listed along with details about their availability during the conference. Calling or e-mailing a conference director to verify the names of agents in attendance is always a good idea.

COSTS: Looking at the price of events, plus room and board, may help writers on a tight budget narrow their choices.

ACCOMMODATIONS: Here conferences list overnight accommodations and travel information. Often conferences held in hotels will reserve rooms at a discount rate and may provide a shuttle bus to and from the local airport.

ADDITIONAL INFORMATION: This section includes information on conference-sponsored contests, individual meetings, the availability of brochures, and more.

ABROAD WRITERS CONFERENCES

17363 Sutter Creek Rd., (209)296-4052. **E-mail:** abroadwriters@yahoo.com; nancy@abroadwritersconference.com. **Website:** abroadwritersconference.com. "Abroad Writers Conferences are devoted to introducing our participants to world views here in the United States and abroad. Throughout the world we invite authors to give readings and to participate on panels. Our discussion groups touch upon a wide range of topics. Our objective is to broaden our cultural and scientific perspectives of the world through discourse and writing." Conferences are held throughout the year in various places worldwide. See website for scheduling details. Conference duration: 7-10 days. "Instead of being lost in a crowd at a large conference, Abroad Writers' Conference prides itself on holding small group meetings where participants have personal contact with everyone. Stimulating talks, interviews, readings, Q&As, writing workshops, film screenings, private consultations, and social gatherings all take place within 7-10 days. Abroad Writers' Conference promises you true networking opportunities and full detailed feedback on your writing submissions."
COSTS See website for pricing details.
ADDITIONAL INFORMATION Agents participate in conferences. Application is online at website.

ALASKA WRITERS CONFERENCE

Alaska Writers Guild, P.O. Box 670014, Chugiak AK 99567. **E-mail:** alaskawritersguild.awg@gmail.com. **Website:** alaskawritersguild.com. Annual event held in the fall—usually September. Duration: 2 days. There are many workshops and instructional tracks of courses. This event sometimes teams up with SCBWI and Alaska Pacific University to offer courses at the event. Literary agents are in attendance each year to hear pitches and meet writers.

ALGONKIAN FIVE DAY NOVEL CAMP

2020 Pennsylvania Ave. NW, Suite 443, Washington DC 20006. **E-mail:** info@algonkianconferences.com. **Website:** http://algonkianconferences.com/index.htm. Conference duration: 5 days. Average attendance: 12 students maximum per workshop. "During 45+ hours of actual workshop time, students will engage in those rigorous exercises necessary to produce a publishable ms. Genres we work with include general commercial fiction, literary fiction, serious and light women's fiction, mystery/cozy/thriller, science fiction, fantasy, young adult, memoir, and narrative nonfiction. The 3 areas of workshop emphasis will be premise, platform, and execution.

AMERICAN CHRISTIAN WRITERS CONFERENCES

P.O. Box 110390, Nashville TN 37222-0390. (800)219-7483, (800)21-WRITE. **E-mail:** ACWriters@aol.com. **Website:** www.ACWriters.com. **Contact:** Reg Forder, director. Estab. 1981. ACW hosts a dozen annual two-day writers conferences and mentoring retreats across America. These are taught by editors and professional freelance writers. These events provide excellent instruction, networking opportunities, and valuable one-on-one time with editors. Annual conferences promoting all forms of Christian writing (fiction, nonfiction, scriptwriting). Conferences are held between March and November during each year.
COSTS Costs vary based on conference. Prices also depend on whether it is a conference or a mentoring retreat.
ACCOMMODATIONS Special rates are available at the host hotel (usually a major chain like Holiday Inn).
ADDITIONAL INFORMATION E-mail or call for conference brochures.

ANTIOCH WRITERS' WORKSHOP

c/o Antioch University Midwest, 900 Dayton St., Yellow Springs OH 45387. (937)769-1803. **E-mail:** info@antiochwritersworkshop.com. **Website:** www.antiochwritersworkshop.com. **Contact:** Sharon Short, director. Estab. 1986. Average attendance: 80. Programs are offered year-round; see the website for details. The dates of the 2016 conference are July 9-16. Workshop concentration: fiction, poetry, personal essay, memoir. Workshop located at Antioch University Midwest in the Village of Yellow Springs. Literary agents attend. Writers of all levels (beginner to advanced) of fiction, memoir, personal essay, and poetry are warmly welcomed to discover their next steps on their writing paths—whether that's developing craft or preparing to submit for publication. An agent and an editor will be speaking and available for meetings with attendees.
ACCOMMODATIONS Accommodations are available at local hotels.
ADDITIONAL INFORMATION The easiest way to contact this event is through the online website contact form.

ATLANTA WRITERS CONFERENCE

Atlanta Writers Club, Westin Atlanta Airport Hotel, 4736 Best Rd., Atlanta GA 30337. **E-mail:** awconference@gmail.com. **E-mail:** gjweinstein@yahoo.com. **Website:** www.atlantawritersconference.com. **Contact:** George Weinstein. Estab. 2008. The Atlanta Writers Conference happens twice a year (May and October/November) with 10 agents and publishing editors attending each event. These agents and editors critique ms samples and query letters, and also respond to pitches. There also is a self-editing workshop with editor Angela James and instructional sessions with local authors as well as separate Q&A panels with the editors and agents. The first 2016 event is May 6-7.

COSTS Ms critiques are $160 each. Pitches on Saturday are $60 each. The query letter critique on Friday is $60 (you may register for only 1 spot). Other workshops and panels may also cost extra—check the website. The conference "All Activities" option (which includes 2 ms critiques, 2 pitches, and 1 of each remaining activity) is $560.

ACCOMMODATIONS Westin Airport Atlanta Hotel.

ADDITIONAL INFORMATION There is a free shuttle that runs between the airport and the hotel.

BALTIMORE WRITERS' CONFERENCE

English Department, Liberal Arts Bldg., Towson University, 8000 York Rd., Towson MD 21252. (410)704-3695. **E-mail:** prwr@towson.edu. **Website:** baltimorewritersconference.org. Estab. 1994. "Annual conference held in November at Towson University. Conference duration: 1 day. Average attendance: 150-200. Covers all areas of writing and getting published. Held at Towson University. Session topics include fiction, nonfiction, poetry, magazine, journals, agents, and publishers. Sign up the day of the conference for quick critiques to improve your stories, essays, and poems."

ACCOMMODATIONS Hotels are close by, if required.

ADDITIONAL INFORMATION Writers may register through the BWA website. Send inquiries via e-mail.

BAY TO OCEAN WRITERS CONFERENCE

P.O. Box 1773, Easton MD 21601. (410)482-6337. **E-mail:** info@baytoocean.com. **Website:** www.baytoocean.com. Estab. 1998. Annual conference held the second Saturday in March. Average attendance: 200. Approximately 30 speakers conduct workshops on publishing, agents, editing, marketing, craft, the Internet, poetry, fiction, nonfiction, and freelance writing. The location is Chesapeake College, Rt. 213 and Rt. 50, Wye Mills, on Maryland's historic eastern shore. Accessible to individuals with disabilities.

COSTS Adults $115, students $55. A paid ms review is also available—details on website. Includes continental breakfast and networking lunch.

ADDITIONAL INFORMATION Registration is on website. Pre-registration is required; no registration at door. Conference usually sells out 1 month in advance. Conference is for all levels of writers.

BIG SUR WRITING WORKSHOP

Henry Miller Library, Hwy. 1, Big Sur CA 93920. (831)667-2574. **E-mail:** writing@henrymiller.org. **Website:** http://bigsurwriting.wordpress.com. Annual workshops focusing on children's and young adult writing (picture books, middle-grade, and young adult). 2016 dates: March 4-6. Workshop held in Big Sur Lodge in Pfeiffer State Park. Cost of workshop includes meals, lodging, workshop, Saturday evening reception. This event is helmed by the literary agents of the Andrea Brown Literary Agency, which is the most successful agency nationwide in selling children's books. All attendees meet with at least 2 faculty members, and their work is critiqued.

BLUE RIDGE MOUNTAINS CHRISTIAN WRITERS CONFERENCE

(800)588-7222. **E-mail:** alton@altongansky.com. **Website:** www.brmcwc.com. Annual conference held in May. Conference duration: Sunday through lunch on Thursday. Average attendance: 350. The conference is a training and networking event for both seasoned and aspiring writers that allows attendees to interact with editors, agents, professional writers, and readers. Workshops and continuing classes in a variety of creative categories are offered.

COSTS $325 for the conference; meal package is $145 per person (12 meals beginning with dinner Sunday and ending with lunch on Thursday). $350 conference fee for those not staying on campus. Room rates vary from $60-70 per night.

ADDITIONAL INFORMATION For a PDF of the complete BRMCWC schedule (typically posted in April), visit the website.

BOOKS-IN-PROGRESS CONFERENCE

Carnegie Center for Literacy and Learning, 251 W. Second St., Lexington KY 40507. (859)254-4175. **E-mail:** lwhitaker@carnegiecenterlex.org. **Website: www.** carnegiecenterlex.org. **Contact:** Laura Whitaker. Estab. 2010. This is an annual writing conference at the Carnegie Center for Literacy and Learning in Lexington. It typically happens in June. "Each conference will offer writing and publishing workshops and includes a keynote presentation." Literary agents are flown in to meet with writers and hear pitches. Website is updated several months prior to each annual event.

ACCOMMODATIONS Several area hotels are nearby.

BREAD LOAF WRITERS' CONFERENCE

Middlebury College, Middlebury VT 05753. (802)443-5286. **Fax:** (802)443-2087. **E-mail:** blwc@middlebury. edu. **Website:** www.middlebury.edu/bread-loaf-con ferences/bl_writers. Estab. 1926. Annual conference held in late August. Conference duration: 10 days. Offers workshops for fiction, nonfiction, and poetry. Agents and editors will be in attendance.

ACCOMMODATIONS Bread Loaf Campus in Ripton, Vermont.

ADDITIONAL INFORMATION 2016 Conference Dates: August 10-20. Location: Bread Loaf campus of Middlebury College in Vermont. Average attendance: 230. There is a $15 application fee.

CAPE COD WRITERS CENTER ANNUAL CONFERENCE

P.O. Box 408, Osterville MA 02655. **E-mail:** writers@ capecodwriterscenter.org. **Website:** www.capecod writerscenter.org. **Contact:** Nancy Rubin Stuart, executive director. Duration: 3 days; held during first week in August. Offers workshops in fiction, commercial fiction, nonfiction, poetry, writing for children, memoir, pitching your book, screenwriting, digital communications, and getting published. There are ms evaluation and mentoring sessions with faculty.

COSTS Costs vary, depending on the number of courses selected.

ACCOMMODATIONS Held at Resort and Conference Center of Hyannis, Hyannis, Massachusetts. Pricing varies.

CELEBRATION OF SOUTHERN LITERATURE

Southern Lit Alliance, 3069 S. Broad St., Suite 2, Chattanooga TN 37408-3056. (423)267-1218. **Fax:** (866)483-6831. **E-mail:** srobinson@southernlital liance.org. **Website:** www.southernlitalliance. org. **Contact:** Susan Robinson. "The Celebration of Southern Literature stands out because of its unique collaboration with the Fellowship of Southern Writers, an organization founded by towering literary figures like Eudora Welty, Cleanth Brooks, Walker Percy, and Robert Penn Warren to recognize and encourage literature in the South. The 2015 celebration marked 26 years since the Fellowship selected Chattanooga for its headquarters and chose to collaborate with the Celebration of Southern Literature. The Fellowship awards 11 literary prizes and induct new members, making this event the place to discover up-and-coming voices in Southern literature. The Southern Lit Alliance's Celebration of Southern Literature attracts more than 1,000 readers and writers from all over the US. It strives to maintain an informal atmosphere where conversations will thrive, inspired by a common passion for the written word. The Southern Lit Alliance (formerly The Arts & Education Council) started as one of 12 pilot agencies founded by a Ford Foundation grant in 1952. The Alliance is the only organization of the 12 still in existence. The Southern Lit Alliance celebrates southern writers and readers through community education and innovative literary arts experiences."

CHICAGO WRITERS CONFERENCE

E-mail: mare@chicagowritersconference.org. **Website:** chicagowritersconference.org. **Contact:** Mare Swallow. Estab. 2011. This conference happens every year in the fall (typically September or October). Find them on Twitter at @ChiWritersConf. The conference brings together a variety of publishing professionals (agents, editors, authors) and brings together several Chicago literary, writing, and bookselling groups. The conference often sells out. Past speakers have included *New York Times* best-selling author Sara Paretsky, children's author Allan Woodrow, young adult author Erica O'Rourke, novelist Eric Charles May, and novelist Loretta Nyhan.

CHRISTOPHER NEWPORT UNIVERSITY WRITERS' CONFERENCE & WRITING CONTEST

(757)269-4368. **E-mail:** eleanor.taylor@cnu.edu. **Website:** writers.cnu.edu. Estab. 1981. 2016 conference held in May. This is a working conference. Presentations made by editors, agents, fiction writers, poets, and more. Breakout sessions in fiction, nonfiction, poetry, juvenile fiction, and publishing. Previous panels included "Publishing," "Proposal Writing," and "Internet Research."

ACCOMMODATIONS Provides list of area hotels.
ADDITIONAL INFORMATION 2016 conference dates were May 6-7.

CLARION WEST WRITERS WORKSHOP

P.O. Box 31264, Seattle WA 98103-1264. (206)322-9083. **E-mail:** info@clarionwest.org. **Website:** www.clarionwest.org. "Contact us through our webform." **Contact:** Nelle Graham, workshop director. Clarion West is an intensive six-week workshop for writers preparing for professional careers in science fiction and fantasy, held annually in Seattle. Usually goes from mid-June through end of July. Conference duration: 6 weeks. Average attendance: 18. Held near the University of Washington. Deadline for applications is March 1. Instructors are well-known writers and editors in the field.

COSTS $3,800 (for tuition, housing, most meals). Limited scholarships are available based on financial need.

ACCOMMODATIONS Workshop tuition, dormitory housing, and most meals: $3,800. Students stay onsite in workshop housing at one of the University of Washington's sorority houses. "Students write their own stories every week while preparing critiques of all the other students' work for classroom sessions. This gives participants a more focused, professional approach to their writing. The core of the workshop remains about speculative fiction and short stories (not novels)." Conference information available in fall. For brochure/guidelines send a SASE, visit website, e-mail, or call. Students must submit 20-30 pages of ms with four-page biography and $50 fee ($30 if received prior to February 10) for applications sent by mail or e-mail to qualify for admission.

ADDITIONAL INFORMATION This is a critique-based workshop. Students are encouraged to write a story every week; the critique of student material produced at the workshop forms the principal activity of the workshop. Students and instructors critique mss as a group. Visit the website for updates and complete details.

CLARKSVILLE WRITERS CONFERENCE

1123 Madison St., Clarksville TN 37040. (931)551-8870. **E-mail:** artsandheritage@cdelightband.net,

burawac@apsu.edu. **E-mail:** artsandheritage@cdelightband.net, burawac@apsu.edu. **Website:** www.artsandheritage.us/writers. **Contact:** Ellen Kanervo. Annual conference held in the summer at Austin Peay State University. The conference features a variety of presentations on fiction, nonfiction, and more. Past presenting authors include Tom Franklin, Frye Gaillard, William Gay, Susan Gregg Gilmore, Will Campbell, John Seigenthaler Sr., Alice Randall, George Singleton, Alanna Nash, and Robert Hicks. Our presentations and workshops are valuable to writers and interesting to readers.

COSTS Costs available online; prices vary depending on how long attendees stay and if they attend the banquet dinner.

ADDITIONAL INFORMATION Multiple literary agents are flown in to the event every year to meet with writers and take pitches.

COMMUNITY OF WRITERS AT SQUAW VALLEY

Community of Writers at Squaw Valley, P.O. Box 1416, Nevada City CA 95959-1416. (530)470-8440. **E-mail:** info@communityofwriters.org. **Website:** www.communityofwriters.org. **Contact:** Brett Hall Jones, executive director. Estab. 1969.

COSTS Tuition is $1,075, which includes 6 dinners. Limited financial aid is available.

ACCOMMODATIONS The Community of Writers rents houses and condominiums in the Valley for participants to live in during the week of the conference. Single room (1 participant): $700/week. Double room (twin beds, with room shared by conference participant of the same sex): $465/week. Multiple room (bunk beds, room shared with 2 or more participants of the same sex): $295/week. All rooms subject to availability; early requests are recommended. Can arrange airport shuttle pickups for a fee.

ADDITIONAL INFORMATION More information is online at www.communityofwriters.org/workshops/writers-workshops.

CONFERENCE FOR WRITERS & ILLUSTRATORS OF CHILDREN'S BOOKS

Book Passage, 51 Tamal Vista Blvd., Corte Madera CA 94925. (415)927-0960, ext. 234. **E-mail:** lberkler@bookpassage.com. **Website:** www.bookpassage.com. Conference for writers and illustrators geared toward beginner and intermediate levels. Sessions cover such topics as the nuts and bolts of writing and illustrating, publisher's spotlight, market trends, developing characters, finding voice in your writing, and the author/agent relationship. 2016 dates: Jan. 23-24.

CRESTED BUTTE WRITERS CONFERENCE

P.O. Box 1361, Crested Butte CO 81224. **E-mail:** coordinator@conf.crestedbuttewriters.org. **Website:** www.crestedbuttewriters.org/conf.php. **Contact:** Barbara Crawford or Theresa Rizzo, co-coordinators. Estab. 2006. Annual conference held in June. Previous faculty members have included numerous literary agents as well as some Writer's Digest Books staffers. There was no event in 2015, but there could be future summer conferences. Check the website.

COSTS Previous prices: $330 nonmembers; $300 members; $297 early bird; The Sandy Writing Contest finalist $280; and groups of 5 or more $280.

ACCOMMODATIONS The conference is held at The Elevation Hotel, located at the Crested Butte Mountain Resort at the base of the ski mountain. The quaint historic town lies nestled in a stunning mountain valley 3 short miles from the resort area of Mt. Crested Butte. A free bus runs frequently between the 2 towns. The closest airport is 30 miles away in Gunnison. The conference website lists 3 lodging options besides rooms at the event facility. All condos, motels, and hotel options offer special conference rates. No special travel arrangements are made through the conference; however, information for car rental from Gunnison airport or the Alpine Express shuttle is listed on the online conference FAQ page.

ADDITIONAL INFORMATION "Our conference workshops address a wide variety of writing craft and business. Our most popular workshop is our "First Pages Reading"—with a twist. Agents and editors read opening pages volunteered by attendees, with a few best-selling authors' openings mixed in. Writers may request additional conference information by e-mail."

DETROIT WORKING WRITERS ANNUAL WRITERS CONFERENCE

Detroit Working Writers, Box 82395, Rochester MI 48308. **E-mail:** conference@detworkingwriters.org. **Website:** dww-writers-conference.org. Estab. 1961. 2016 dates: May 21. Location: MSU Management Education Center, Troy, Michigan. Conference is 1 day, with breakfast, luncheon and keynote speaker, 4 breakout sessions, and 3 choices of workshop sessions. Much more info is available online. Detroit

Working Writers was founded on June 5, 1900, as the Detroit Press Club, Detroit's first press club. Today, more than a century later, it is a 501(c)(6) organization, and Michigan's oldest writers' organization. There are 5 writing competitions with cash prizes in different categories: young adult/new adult, creative nonfiction, poetry, children's, and adult fiction. Registration and competition entry begins each January, online.

COSTS Costs vary, depending on early bird registration and membership status within the organization.

FLORIDA CHRISTIAN WRITERS CONFERENCE

Word Weavers International, Inc., 530 Lake Kathryn Circle, Casselberry FL 32707. (386)295-3902. **E-mail:** FloridaCWC@aol.com. **Website:** floridacwc.net. **Contact:** Eva Marie Everson & Mark T. Hancock. Estab. 1988. Annual conference during the last Wednesday of February to the first Sunday in March at Lake Yale Conference Center, Leesburg, Florida. Workshops/classes geared toward all levels, from beginners to published authors. Open to students. FCWC offers 6 keynote addresses, 8 continuing classes, and a number of three-hour workshops, one-hour workshops, and after hours workshops. FCWC brings in the finest the industry as to offer in editors, agents, freelancers, and marketing/media experts. Additionally, FCWC provides a book proposal studio and a pitch studio. For those flying in to Orlando or Sanford, FCWC provides a shuttle from and to the conference center. Accommodations for both single- and double-room occupancy. Meals provided. The awards banquet is Saturday night. Advanced critique services offered. Scholarships offered. For more information or to register, go to the conference website.

COSTS Ranges: $275 (daily rate—in advance, includes lunch and dinner; specify days); $1,495 (full attendee and participating spouse/family member in same room).

ACCOMMODATIONS Private rooms and double-occupancy.

GREEN MOUNTAIN WRITERS CONFERENCE

47 Hazel St., Rutland VT 05701. (802)236-6133. **E-mail:** ydaley@sbcglobal.net. **E-mail:** yvonnedaley@me.com. **Website:** www.vermontwriters.com. **Contact:** Yvonne Daley, director. Estab. 1998. "Annual conference held in the summer. Covers fiction, creative nonfiction, poetry, young adult fiction, journal-

ism, nature writing, essay, memoir, personal narrative, and biography. Held at The Mountain Top Inn and Resort, a lakeside inn located in Chittenden, Vermont. Speakers have included Grace Paley, Ruth Stone, Howard Frank Mosher, Chris Bohjalian, Yvonne Daley, David Huddle, David Budbill, Jeffrey Lent, Verandah Porche, Tom Smith, and Chuck Clarino."

COSTS $575 before April 15; $625 before May 15; $650 before June 1. Partial scholarships are available.

ACCOMMODATIONS Dramatically reduced rates at The Mountain Top Inn and Resort for attendees. Close to other area hotels in Rutland County, Vermont.

ADDITIONAL INFORMATION Participants' mss can be read and commented on at a cost. Sponsors contests. Conference publishes a literary magazine featuring work of participants. Brochures available on website or e-mail. "We offer the opportunity to learn from some of the nation's best writers at a small, supportive conference in a lakeside setting that allows one-to-one feedback. Participants often continue to correspond and share work after conferences."

HAMPTON ROADS WRITERS CONFERENCE

P.O. Box 56228, Virginia Beach VA 23456. **E-mail:** hrwriters@cox.net. **Website:** www.hamptonroadswriters.org. Annual conference usually held in September. Workshops cover fiction, nonfiction, memoir, poetry, and the business of getting published. A bookshop, 3 free contests with cash prizes, free evening networking social, and many networking opportunities will be available. Multiple literary agents are in attendance each year to meet with writers and hear 10-minute pitches. Much more information available on the website.

COSTS Costs vary. There are discounts for members, for early bird registration, for students, and more.

HIGHLIGHTS FOUNDATION FOUNDERS WORKSHOPS

814 Court St., Honesdale PA 18431. (570)253-1122. **Fax:** (570)253-0179. **E-mail:** klbrown@highlightsfoundation.org. **Website:** highlightsfoundation.org. **Contact:** Kent Brown, director. Workshops geared toward those interested in writing and illustrating for children, intermediate and advanced levels. Classes offered include: "Writing Novels for Young Adults," "Biography," "Nonfiction Writing," "Writing Historical Fiction," "Wordplay: Writing Poetry for Children," "Heart of the Novel," "Nature Writing for Kids," "Visual Art of the Picture Book," "The Whole Novel Workshop," and more. See the website for an updated list. Workshops held near Honesdale, PA. Workshops limited to between 8-14 people. Cost of workshops range from $695 up. Cost of workshop includes tuition, meals, conference supplies, and private housing. Call for application and more information. Offers more than three dozen workshops per year. Conference duration: 3-7 days. Genre specific workshops and retreats on children's writing: fiction, nonfiction, poetry, promotions. "Our goal is to improve, over time, the quality of literature for children by educating future generations of children's authors." Coordinates pickup at local airport. Offers overnight accommodations. Participants stay in guest cabins on the wooded grounds surrounding Highlights Founders' home adjacent to the house/conference center.

COSTS Prices vary based on workshop. Check website for details.

ADDITIONAL INFORMATION Some workshops require pre-workshop assignment. Brochure available for SASE, by e-mail, on website, by phone, by fax. Editors attend conference. "Applications will be reviewed and accepted on a first-come, first-served basis. Applicants must demonstrate specific experience in writing area of workshop they are applying for—writing samples are required for many of the workshops."

HOUSTON WRITERS GUILD CONFERENCE

P.O. Box 42255, Houston TX 77242. (281)736-7168. **E-mail:** HoustonWritersGuild@Hotmail.com. **Website:** houstonwritersguild.org. 2016 dates: April 29 through May 1. This annual conference, organized by the Houston Writers Guild, happens in the spring, and has concurrent sessions and tracks on the craft and business of writing. Each year, multiple agents are in attendance taking pitches from writers. The 2016 special guest speaker was Jamie Ford.

COSTS Costs are different for members and non-members. Costs depend on how many days and events you sign up for.

ADDITIONAL INFORMATION There is a writing contest at the event. There is also a for-pay pre-conference workshop the day before the conference.

IDAHO WRITERS LEAGUE WRITERS' CONFERENCE

601 W. 75 S., Blackfoot ID 83221-6153. (208)684-4200. **Website:** www.idahowritersleague.org. Estab. 1940. Annual floating conference, usually held in September. This conference has at least 1 agent in attendance every year, along with other writers and presenters.

COSTS Pricing varies. Check website for more information. The location within Idaho changes each year.

IOWA SUMMER WRITING FESTIVAL

The University of Iowa, C215 Seashore Hall, University of Iowa, Iowa City IA 52242. (319)335-4160. **Fax:** (319)335-4743. **E-mail:** iswfestival@uiowa.edu. **Website:** www.iowasummerwritingfestival.org. Annual festival held in June and July. Workshops are 1 week or a weekend. Average attendance: Limited to 12 people/class, with more than 1,500 participants throughout the summer. "We offer courses across the genres: novel, short story, poetry, essay, memoir, humor, travel, playwriting, screenwriting, writing for children, and women's writing. Held at the University of Iowa campus." Speakers have included Marvin Bell, Lan Samantha Chang, John Dalton, Hope Edelman, Katie Ford, Patricia Foster, Bret Anthony Johnston, and Barbara Robinette Moss, among others. Accommodations available at area hotels. Information on overnight accommodations available by phone or on website.

ADDITIONAL INFORMATION Brochures are available in February. Inquire via e-mail or on website.

JACKSON HOLE WRITERS CONFERENCE

P.O. Box 1974, Jackson WY 83001. (307)413-3332. **E-mail:** connie@blackhen.com. **Website:** jacksonhole writersconference.com. Estab. 1991. Annual conference. 2016 dates: June 23-25. Conference duration: 3-4 days. Average attendance: 110. Covers fiction, creative nonfiction, and young adult. Offers ms critiques from authors, agents, and editors. Agents in attendance will take pitches from writers. Paid ms critique programs are available.

ADDITIONAL INFORMATION Held at the Center for the Arts in Jackson, Wyoming, and online.

JAMES RIVER WRITERS CONFERENCE

2319 E. Broad St., Richmond VA 23223. (804)433-3790. **Fax:** (804)291-1466. **E-mail:** info@jamesriverwriters.com; fallconference@jamesriverwriters.com. **Website:** www.jamesriverwriters.com. Estab. 2003. Annual conference held in October. The event has master classes, agent pitching, editor pitching, critiques, sessions, panels, and more. Previous attending agents have included Kimiko Nakamura, Kaylee Davis, Peter Knapp, and more.

COSTS Check website for updated pricing.

KACHEMAK BAY WRITERS' CONFERENCE

Kenai Peninsula College, Kachemak Bay Campus, 533 E. Pioneer Ave., Homer AK 99603. (907)235-7743. **E-mail:** iconf@uaa.alaska.edu. **Website:** writ ersconf.kpc.alaska.edu. Annual writers conference held in June. 2016 dates: June 10-14. The 2016 keynote speaker was Natasha Tretheway. Sponsored by Kachemak Bay Campus, Kenai Peninsula College /UAA. This nationally recognized writing conference features workshops, readings, and panel presentations in fiction, poetry, nonfiction, and the business of writing. There are "open mic" sessions for conference registrants, evening readings open to the public, agent/editor consultations, and more.

COSTS See the website. Some scholarships available.

ACCOMMODATIONS Homer is 225 miles south of Anchorage on the southern tip of the Kenai Peninsula and the shores of Kachemak Bay. There are multiple hotels in the area.

KENTUCKY WOMEN WRITERS CONFERENCE

University of Kentucky College of Arts & Sciences, 232 E. Maxwell St., Lexington KY 40506. (859)257-2874. **E-mail:** kentuckywomenwriters@gmail.com. **Website:** www.kentuckywomenwriters.org. **Contact:** Julie Wrinn, director. Estab. 1979. Conference held in second or third weekend of September. The location is the Carnegie Center for Literacy in Lexington, Kentucky. Conference duration: 2 days. Average attendance: 150-200. Conference covers poetry, fiction, creative nonfiction, and playwriting. Writing workshops, panels, and readings featuring contemporary women writers.

COSTS $200 for general admission and a workshop; $125 for admission with no workshop. Check website for most current pricing.

ADDITIONAL INFORMATION Sponsors prizes in poetry ($200), fiction ($200), nonfiction ($200), playwriting ($500), and spoken word ($500). Winners also invited to read during the conference. Pre-registration opens May 1.

KENTUCKY WRITERS CONFERENCE

Southern Kentucky Book Fest, Knicely Conference Center, 2355 Nashville Rd., Bowling Green KY 42101. (270)745-4502. **E-mail:** sara.volpi@wku.edu]. **Website:** www.sokybookfest.org/kywritersconf. **Contact:** Sara Volpi. This event is entirely free to the public. 2016 date: April 23. Duration: 1 day. Precedes the

Southern Kentucky Book Fest the next day. Authors who will be participating in the book fest on Saturday will give attendees at the writers' conference the benefit of their wisdom on Friday. Free workshops on a variety of writing topics will be presented during this day-long event. Sessions run for 75 minutes, and the day begins at 9 a.m. and ends at 3:30 p.m. The conference is open to anyone who would like to attend, including high school students, college students, teachers, and the general public.

KINDLING WORDS EAST

Website: www.kindlingwords.org. Annual retreat held early in the year near Burlington, VT. 2017 dates: January 28-31. A retreat with three strands: writer, illustrator, and editor. Intensive workshops for each strand, and an open schedule for conversations and networking. Registration limited to approximately 70. Hosted by the 4-star Inn at Essex (room and board extra). Participants must be published by a CCBC listed publisher, or if in publishing, occupy a professional position. Registration opens August 1 or as posted on the website, and fills quickly. Check website to see if spaces are available, to sign up to be notified when registration opens each year, or for more information. No contact e-mail is available for this organization, but there is a contact form on the website.

LA JOLLA WRITERS CONFERENCE

P.O. Box 178122, San Diego CA 92177. **E-mail:** akuritz@san.rr.com. **Website:** www.lajollawritersconference.com. **Contact:** Jared Kuritz, director. Estab. 2001. Annual conference held in November. 2016 dates: November 11-13. Conference duration: 3 days. Average attendance: 200. The LJWC covers all genres and both fiction and nonfiction as well as the business of writing. "We take particular pride in educating our attendees on the business aspect of the book industry and have agents, editors, publishers, publicists, and distributors teach classes. There is unprecedented access to faculty at the LJWC. Our conference offers lecture sessions that run for 50 minutes, and workshops that run for 110 minutes. Each block period is dedicated to either workshop or lecture-style classes, with 6-8 classes on various topics available each block. For most workshop classes, you are encouraged to bring written work for review. Literary agents from prestigious agencies have participated in the past, teaching workshops in which they are familiarized with attendee work. Late night and early bird sessions are also available. The conference creates a strong sense of community, and it has seen many of its attendees successfully published."

COSTS $395 for full 2016 conference registration (doesn't include lodging or breakfast). Conference limited to 200 attendees.

LAS VEGAS WRITERS CONFERENCE

Henderson Writers' Group, P.O. Box 92032, Henderson NV 89009. (702)564-2488; (866)869-7842. **E-mail:** lasvegaswritersconference@gmail.com. **Website:** www.lasvegaswritersconference.com. Annual event. 2016 dates: April 28-30. Conference duration: 3 days. Average attendance: 150 maximum. "Join writing professionals, agents, industry experts, and your colleagues for 3 days in Las Vegas as they share their knowledge on all aspects of the writer's craft. While there are formal pitch sessions, panels, workshops, and seminars, the faculty is also available throughout the conference for informal discussions and advice. Workshops, seminars, and expert panels cover topics in both fiction and nonfiction, screenwriting, marketing, indie publishing, and the craft of writing itself. There will be many Q&A panels for attendees to ask the experts questions." Site: Sam's Town Hotel and Gambling Hall in Las Vegas (Henderson, Nevada). The 2016 keynote was Larry Brooks.

COSTS Costs vary depending on the package. See the website. There are early bird rates as well as deep discounts for Clark County high school students.

ADDITIONAL INFORMATION Sponsors contest. Agents and editors participate in conference.

LAS VEGAS WRITING WORKSHOP

Writing Day Workshops. **E-mail:** writingdayworkshops@gmail.com. **Website:** www.lasvegaswritingworkshop.com. Estab. 2016. One-day conference. 2016 date: November 19. Presentions on publishing options today, literary agents and queries, marketing and promotion, first pages, and how to make a living as a writer. Several literary agents are in attendance to meet with writers and take pitches. See the website for the names of the attending agents.

COSTS $149 basic registration; add-on costs include query critiques and consultations/pitches.

ACCOMMODATIONS The event venue has hotel rooms available. The 2016 venue is the Embassy Suites.

ADDITIONAL INFORMATION Multiple writers have come out of a Writing Day Workshops event with a literary agent to show for it.

MIDWEST WRITERS WORKSHOP

Ball State University, Department of English, Muncie IN 47306. (765)282-1055. **E-mail:** midwestwriters@yahoo.com. **Website:** www.midwestwriters.org. **Contact:** Jama Kehoe Bigger, director. Annual workshop held in July in east central Indiana. Writer workshops geared toward writers of all levels, including craft and business sessions. Topics include most genres. Faculty/speakers have included Joyce Carol Oates, George Plimpton, Clive Cussler, Haven Kimmel, William Kent Krueger, William Zinsser, John Gilstrap, Lee Martin, Jane Friedman, Chuck Sambuchino, and numerous bestselling mystery, literary fiction, young adult, and children's authors. Workshop also includes agent pitch sessions, ms evaluation, and query letter critiques. Registration tentatively limited to 240.

COSTS $155-400. Most meals included.

ADDITIONAL INFORMATION Offers scholarships. See website for more information.

MISSOURI WRITERS' GUILD CONFERENCE

St. Louis MO **E-mail:** mwgconferenceinfo@gmail.com. **Website:** www.missouriwritersguild.org. **Contact:** Tricia Sanders, vice president/conference chairman. Writer and illustrator workshops geared to all levels. **Open to students.** Conference "gives writers the opportunity to hear outstanding speakers and to receive information on marketing, research, and writing techniques." Agents, editors, and published authors in attendance. 2016 dates were April 29-May 1. 2016 keynote speakers include Rachel R. Russell and Pamela Grout. The keynote speaker in 2014 was Writer's Digest Books editor Chuck Sambuchino.

ADDITIONAL INFORMATION The primary contact individual changes every year, because the conference chair changes every year. See the website for contact info.

MONTROSE CHRISTIAN WRITERS' CONFERENCE

218 Locust St., Montrose PA 18801. (570)278-1001. **Fax:** (570)278-3061. **E-mail:** mbc@montrosebible.org. **Website:** www.montrosebible.org. Estab. 1990. "Annual conference held in July. Offers workshops, editorial appointments, and professional critiques. We try to meet writing needs, for beginners and advanced, covering fiction, poetry, and writing for children. It is small enough to allow personal interaction between attendees and faculty. Speakers have included William Petersen, Mona Hodgson, Jim Fletcher, and Terri Gibbs." Held in Montrose.

COSTS Tuition is $180.

ACCOMMODATIONS Will meet planes in Binghamton, New York, and Scranton, Pennsylvania. On-site accommodations: room and board $340-475/conference, including food. RV court available.

ADDITIONAL INFORMATION Writers can send work ahead of time and have it critiqued for a small fee. The attendees are usually church-related. The writing has a Christian emphasis. Conference information available in April. For brochure, visit website, e-mail, or call. Accepts inquiries by phone or e-mail.

MOUNT HERMON CHRISTIAN WRITERS CONFERENCE

P.O. Box 413, Mount Hermon CA 95041. **E-mail:** info@mounthermon.org. **Website:** writers.mounthermon.org. Annual professional conference. 2016 dates: March 18-22. Average attendance: 450. Sponsored by and held at the 440-acre Mount Hermon Christian Conference Center near San Jose, California, in the heart of the coastal redwoods. "We are a broad-ranging conference for all areas of Christian writing, including fiction, nonfiction, fantasy, children's, teen, young adult, poetry, magazines, inspirational, and devotional writing. This is a working, how-to conference, with major morning tracks in all genres (including a track especially for teen writers), and as many as 20 optional workshops each afternoon. Faculty-to-student ratio is about 1 to 6. The bulk of our more than 70 faculty members are editors and publisher representatives from major Christian publishing houses nationwide." Past speakers have included T. Davis Bunn, Debbie Macomber, Jerry Jenkins, Bill Butterworth, Dick Foth, and others.

MUSE AND THE MARKETPLACE

Grub Street, 162 Boylston St., Fifth Floor, Boston MA 02116. (617)695-0075. **E-mail:** info@grubstreet.org. **Website:** http://museandthemarketplace.com. The conferences are held in the late spring, such as early May. (2016 dates were April 29 through May 1.) Conference duration: 3 days. Average attendance: 400. Dozens of agents are in attendance to meet writers and take pitches. The conference has workshops on all aspects of writing.

ACCOMMODATIONS Boston Park Plaza Hotel.

NAPA VALLEY WRITERS' CONFERENCE

Napa Valley College, 1088 College Ave., St. Helena CA 94574. (707)967-2900. **E-mail:** writecon@napa valley.edu. **Website:** www.napawritersconference.org. **Contact:** Andrea Bewick, managing director. Estab. 1981. Established 1981. Annual weeklong event. 2016 dates: July 24 through July 29. Location: Upper Valley Campus in the historic town of St. Helena, 25 miles north of Napa in the heart of the valley's wine growing community. Average attendance: 48 in poetry and 48 in fiction. "Serious writers of all backgrounds and experience are welcome to apply." Offers poets and fiction writers workshops, lectures, faculty readings at Napa Valley wineries, and one-on-one faculty counseling. "Poetry session provides the opportunity to work both on generating new poems and on revising previously written ones."

COSTS $975; $25 application fee.

NETWO WRITERS CONFERENCE

Northeast Texas Writers Organization, P.O. Box 411, Winfield TX 75493. (469)867-2624 or Paul at (903)573-6084. **E-mail:** jimcallan@winnsboro.com. **Website:** www.netwo.org. Estab. 1987. Annual conference held in April. (2016 dates were April 22-23.) Conference duration: 2 days. Presenters include agents, writers, editors, and publishers. Agents in attendance will take pitches from writers. The conference features a writing contest, pitch sessions, critiques from professionals, as well as dozens of workshops and presentations.

COSTS $90 for members before February 29, and $100 after. $112.50 for non-members before February 29, and $125 after.

ACCOMMODATIONS "On the website, we have posted information on lodging. The conference is held at the Titus County Civic Center in Mt. Pleasant, Texas."

ADDITIONAL INFORMATION Conference is cosponsored by the Texas Commission on the Arts. See website for current updates.

NORTH CAROLINA WRITERS' NETWORK FALL CONFERENCE

P.O. Box 21591, Winston-Salem NC 27120. (336)293-8844. **E-mail:** mail@ncwriters.org. **Website:** www.ncwriters.org. Estab. 1985. Annual conference held in November in different state venues. Average attendance: 250. This organization hosts 2 conferences: 1 in the spring and 1 in the fall. Each conference is a weekend full of workshops, panels, book signings, and readings (including open mic). There will be a keynote speaker, a variety of sessions on the craft and business of writing, and opportunities to meet with agents and editors.

COSTS Approximately $250 (includes 4 meals).

ACCOMMODATIONS Special rates are usually available at the conference hotel, but conferees must make their own reservations.

NORTHERN COLORADO WRITERS CONFERENCE

2107 Thunderstone Court, Fort Collins CO 80525. (970)556-0908. **E-mail:** kerrie@northerncolorado writers.com. **Website:** www.northerncoloradowriters. com. Estab. 2006. Annual conference held in March in Fort Collins. 2016 dates: April 22-23. Conference duration: 2-3 days. The conference features a variety of speakers, agents, and editors. There are workshops and presentations on fiction, nonfiction, screenwriting, children's books, marketing, magazine writing, staying inspired, and more. Previous agents who have attended and taken pitches from writers include Jessica Regel, Kristen Nelson, Rachelle Gardner, Andrea Brown, Ken Sherman, Jessica Faust, Gordon Warnock, and Taylor Martindale. Each conference features more than 30 workshops from which to choose from. Previous keynotes include Chuck Sambuchino, Andrew McCarthy, and Stephen J. Cannell.

COSTS $250-550+, depending on what package the attendee selects, whether you're a member or nonmember, and whether you're renewing your NCW membership.

NORWESCON

100 Andover Park W. PMB 150-165, Tukwila WA 98188. (425)243-4692. **E-mail:** info@norwescon.org. **Website:** www.norwescon.org. Estab. 1978. Annual conference held on Easter weekend. Average attendance: 2,800-3,000. General convention (with multiple tracks) focusing on science fiction and fantasy literature with wide coverage of other media. Tracks cover science, sociocultural, literary, publishing, editing, writing, art, and other media of a science fictionandfantasy orientation. Literary agents will be speaking and available for meetings with attendees.

ACCOMMODATIONS Conference is held at the Doubletree Hotel Seattle Airport.

ODYSSEY FANTASY WRITING WORKSHOP

P.O. Box 75, Mont Vernon NH 03057. (603)673-6234. **E-mail:** jcavelos@sff.net. **Website:** www.odyssey workshop.org. **Contact:** Jeanne Cavelos. Saint Anselm College, 100 Saint Anselm Dr., Manchester, New Hampshire, 03102. Estab. 1996. Annual workshop held in June (through July). Conference duration: 6 weeks. Average attendance: 15. This is a workshop for fantasy, science fiction, and horror writers that combines an intensive learning and writing experience with in-depth feedback on students' mss. Held on the campus of Saint Anselm College in Manchester, New Hampshire. Speakers have included George R.R. Martin, Elizabeth Hand, Jane Yolen, Harlan Ellison, Melissa Scott, and Dan Simmons.

COSTS In 2016: $2,025 tuition, $850 housing (double room), $1,700 housing (single room), $40 application fee, $600 food (approximate), $700 optional processing fee to receive college credit.

ADDITIONAL INFORMATION Students must apply and include a writing sample. Application deadline: April 8. Students' works are critiqued throughout the 6 weeks. Workshop information available in October. For brochure/guidelines, send SASE, e-mail, visit website, or call.

OHIO KENTUCKY INDIANA CHILDREN'S LITERATURE CONFERENCE

Northern Kentucky University, 405 Steely Library, Highland Heights KY 41099. (859)572-6620. **Fax:** (859)572-5390. **E-mail:** smithjen@nku.edu. **Website:** oki.nku.edu. **Contact:** Jennifer Smith. Annual conference for writers and illustrators geared toward all levels. Emphasizes multicultural literature for children and young adults. Conference held annually in November. Contact Jennifer Smith for more information.

COSTS $85. Includes registration/attendance at all workshop sessions, continental breakfast, lunch, author/illustrator signings. Manuscript critiques are available for an additional cost. E-mail or call for more information.

OKLAHOMA WRITERS' FEDERATION, INC. ANNUAL CONFERENCE

9800 South Hwy. 137, Miami OK 74354. **Website:** www.owfi.org. Annual conference held just outside Oklahoma City. Held first weekend in May each year. Writer workshops geared toward all levels. The goal of the conference is to create good stories with strong bones. We will be exploring cultural writing and cultural sensitivity in writing. Several literary agents are in attendance each year to meet with writers and hear pitches.

COSTS Costs vary depending on when registrants sign up. Cost includes awards banquet and famous author banquet. Three extra sessions are available for an extra fee. Visit the eventwebsite for a complete faculty list and conference information

OKLAHOMA WRITERS' FEDERATION, INC. ANNUAL CONFERENCE

9800 South Hwy. 137, Miami OK 74354. **Website:** www.owfi.org. Annual conference held just outside Oklahoma City. Held first weekend in May each year. Writer workshops geared toward all levels. The goal of the conference is to create good stories with strong bones. We will be exploring cultural writing and cultural sensitivity in writing. Several literary agents are in attendance each year to meet with writers and hear pitches.

COSTS Costs vary depending on when registrants sign up. Cost includes awards banquet and famous author banquet. Three extra sessions are available for an extra fee. Visit the event website for a complete faculty list and conference information

OREGON CHRISTIAN WRITERS SUMMER CONFERENCE

Red Lion Hotel on the River, 909 N. Hayden Island Dr., Portland OR 97217. **E-mail:** summerconf@ oregonchristianwriters.org. **Website:** www.oregon christianwriters.org. **Contact:** Lindy Jacobs, OCW Summer Conference director. Estab. 1989. Held annually in August at the Red Lion Hotel on the River, a full-service hotel. Conference duration: 4 days. 2016 dates: August 15-18. Average attendance: 225 (175 writers, 50 faculty). Top national editors, agents, and authors in the field of Christian publishing teach 12 intensive coaching classes and 30 workshops plus critique sessions. Published authors as well as emerging writers have opportunities to improve their craft, get feedback through ms reviews, meet one-on-one with editors and agents, and have half-hour mentoring appointments with published authors. Classes include fiction, nonfiction, memoir, young adult, poetry, magazine articles, devotional writing, children's books, and marketing. Daily general sessions include worship and an inspirational keynote address. Each year contacts made during the OCW summer conference lead to publishing contracts. The 2016 conference theme was "Vision and Voice," based on Psalm 19:14. 2016 Keynote speakers: James Scott Bell and Angela Hunt. Past agents in attendance include Chip MacGregor of MacGregor Literary, Nick Harrison of WordServe Agency, Sally Apokedak of Les Stobbe Agency, Bill Jensen of William K. Jensen Literary, Karen Ball of the Steve Laube Agency, and more. Past editors in attendance include personnel from Revell, Bethany/Chosen, HarperCollins, LIVE, Grace Publishing, Focus on the Family Clubhouse, The Upper Room, Bible Advocate, and *Splickety Magazine*.

COSTS $525 for OCW members; $560 for nonmembers. Registration fee includes all classes, workshops, and 2 lunches and 3 dinners. Lodging additional. Full-time registered registrants may also pre-submit 3 proposals for review by an editor (or agent) through the conference, plus sign up for a half-hour mentoring appointment with an author.

ACCOMMODATIONS Conference is held at the Red Lion on the River Hotel. Conferees wishing to stay at the hotel must make a reservation through the hotel. A block of rooms has been reserved at the hotel at a special rate for conferees and held until mid-July. The hotel reservation link will be posted on the website in late spring. Shuttle bus transportation will be provided by the hotel for conferees from Portland Airport (PDX) to the hotel, which is 20 minutes away.

ADDITIONAL INFORMATION Conference details will be posted online beginning in January. All attendees are welcome to attend the Cascade Awards ceremony, which takes place Wednesday evening during the conference. For more information about the Cascade Writing Contest, please check the website.

OZARK CREATIVE WRITERS, INC. CONFERENCE

P.O. Box 9076, Fayetteville AR 72703. **E-mail:** ozarkcreativewriters1@gmail.com. **Website:** www.ozarkcreativewriters.org. The annual event is held in October at the Inn of the Ozarks, in the resort town of Eureka Springs, Arkansas. The event has approximately 200 attend each year; many also enter the creative writing competitions. Open to professional and amateur writers, workshops are geared to all levels and all forms of the creative process and literary arts. Sessions sometimes include songwriting, with presentations by best-selling authors, editors, and agents.

The OCW Conference promotes writing by offering writing competitions in all genres.

PACIFIC COAST CHILDREN'S WRITERS WHOLE-NOVEL WORKSHOP: FOR ADULTS AND TEENS

P.O. Box 244, Aptos CA 95001. **Website:** www.childrenswritersworkshop.com. 2016 dates: Sept. 23-25. "Our seminar offers semi-advanced through published adult writers an editor and/or agent critique on their full novel or 15-30 page partial. (Mid-book and synopsis critique may be included with the partial.) A concurrent workshop is open to students age 13 and up, who give adults target-reader feedback. There is a focus on craft as a marketing tool. Team-taught master classes (open clinics for manuscript critiques) explore such topics as 'Story Architecture and Arcs.'" Continuous close contact with faculty, who have included Andrea Brown, agent, and Simon Boughton, VP/executive editor at 3 Macmillan imprints. **Past seminars:** Annually, late September or early October. Registration limited to 16 adults and 10 teens. For the most critique options, submit sample chapters and synopsis with e-application by mid May; open until filled. **Content:** Character-driven novels with protagonists ages 11 and older. Collegial format; 90 percent hands-on. Our pre-workshop anthology of peer manuscripts maximizes learning and networking. Several past attendees have landed contracts as a direct result of our seminar.

PENNWRITERS CONFERENCE

5706 Sonoma Ridge, Missouri City TX 77459. **E-mail:** conferenceco@pennwriters.org, info@pennwriters.org. **Website:** http://pennwriters.org/conference. Estab. 1987. The Mission of Pennwriters Inc. is to help writers of all levels, from the novice to the award-winning and multi-published, improve and succeed in their craft. The annual Pennwriters conference is held every year in May in Pennsylvania, switching between locations—Lancaster in even years and Pittsburgh in odd years. 2016 event dates: May 20-22 in Lancaster. Literary agents are in attendance meeting with writers.

ACCOMMODATIONS Costs vary. Pennwriters members in good standing get a slightly reduced rate.

ADDITIONAL INFORMATION Sponsors contest. Published authors judge fiction in various categories. Agent/editor appointments are available on a first-come, first serve basis.

PHILADELPHIA WRITERS' CONFERENCE

P.O. Box 7171, Elkins Park PA 19027-0171. (215)619-7422. **E-mail:** info@pwcwriters.org. **E-mail:** info@pwcwriters.org. **Website:** www.pwcwriters.org. Estab. 1949. Annual. Conference held in June. Average attendance: 160-200. Conference covers many forms of writing: novel, short story, genre fiction, nonfiction book, magazine writing, blogging, juvenile, poetry.

ACCOMMODATIONS Wyndham Hotel (formerly the Holiday Inn), Independence Mall, Fourth and Arch streets, Philadelphia, PA 19106-2170. Hotel offers discount for early registration.

ADDITIONAL INFORMATION Accepts inquiries by e-mail. Agents and editors attend the conference. Many questions are answered online.

PIKES PEAK WRITERS CONFERENCE

Pikes Peak Writers, P.O. Box 64273, Colorado Springs CO 80962. (719)244-6220. **Website:** www.pikespeak writers.com/ppwc. Estab. 1993. Annual conference held in April. 2016 dates: April 15-17. Conference duration: 3 days. Average attendance: 300. Workshops, presentations, and panels focus on writing and publishing. Attention is paid to both mainstream and genre fiction (romance, science fiction, fantasy, suspense/thrillers, action/adventure, mysteries, children's, young adult). Agents and editors are available for meetings with attendees on Saturday. 2016 speakers included Jeff Lindsay, Rachel Caine, and Kevin J. Anderson.

COSTS $395-465 (includes all 7 meals).

ACCOMMODATIONS Marriott Colorado Springs holds a block of rooms at a special rate for attendees until late March.

ADDITIONAL INFORMATION Readings with critiques are available on Friday afternoon. Registration forms are online; brochures are available in January. Send inquiries via e-mail.

PNWA SUMMER WRITERS CONFERENCE

317 NW Gilman Blvd., Suite 8, Issaquah WA 98027. (425)673-2665. **E-mail:** pnwa@pnwa.org. **Website:** www.pnwa.org. Estab. 1955. Annual conference held in July. Conference duration: 4 days. Average attendance: 400. Attendees have the chance to meet agents and editors, learn craft from authors, and uncover marketing secrets. Speakers have included J.A. Jance, Sheree Bykofsky, Kimberley Cameron, Jennie Dun-

ham, Donald Maass, Jandy Nelson, Chuck Sambuchino, Robert Dugoni, and Terry Brooks.

SALT CAY WRITERS RETREAT

Salt Cay Bahamas. (732)267-6449. **E-mail:** admin@saltcaywritersretreat.com. **Website:** www.saltcaywritersretreat.com. **Contact:** Karen Dionne and Christopher Graham. Five-day retreat held in the Bahamas in May. "The Salt Cay Writers Retreat is particularly suited for novelists (especially those writing literary, upmarket commercial fiction, or genre novelists wanting to write a breakout book), memoirists, and narrative nonfiction writers. However, any author (published or not-yet-published) who wishes to take their writing to the next level is welcome to apply." Speakers have included or will include editors Chuck Adams (Algonquin Books) and Amy Einhorn (Amy Einhorn Books); agents Jeff Kleinman, Michelle Brower, Erin Niumata, and Erin Harris (all of Folio Literary Management); and authors Robert Goolrick and Jacquelyn Mitchard.

COSTS $2,450 if you register on/before May 1; $2,950 after.

ACCOMMODATIONS Comfort Suites, Paradise Island, Nassau, Bahamas.

SAN DIEGO STATE UNIVERSITY WRITERS' CONFERENCE

SDSU College of Extended Studies, 5250 Campanile Dr., San Diego State University, San Diego CA 92182. (619)594-3946. **Fax:** (619)594-8566. **E-mail:** sdsuwritersconference@mail.sdsu.edu. **Website:** ces.sdsu.edu/writers. Estab. 1984. Annual conference held in January. Conference duration: 2.5 days. Average attendance: 350. Covers fiction, nonfiction, scriptwriting, and e-books. Held at the San Diego Marriott Mission Valley Hotel. Each year, the conference offers a variety of workshops for beginners and advanced writers. This conference allows the individual writer to choose which workshop best suits her needs. In addition to the workshops, editor reading appointments and agent/editor consultation appointments are provided so attendees may meet with editors and agents one-on-one to discuss specific questions. A reception is offered Saturday immediately following the workshops, offering attendees the opportunity to socialize with the faculty in a relaxed atmosphere.

COSTS Approximately $495-549. Extra costs for consultations.

ACCOMMODATIONS Attendees must make their own travel arrangements. A conference rate for attendees is available at the event hotel.

SAN FRANCISCO WRITERS CONFERENCE

1029 Jones St., San Francisco CA 94109. (415)673-0939. **E-mail:** barbara@sfwriters.org; sfwriterscon@aol.com.. **Website:** www.sfwriters.org. **Contact:** Barbara Santos, marketing director. Estab. 2003. 2016 dates: February 11-14. Annual conference held President's Day weekend in February. Average attendance: 700. More than 100 top authors, respected literary agents, and major publishing houses are at the event so attendees can make face-to-face contact with all the right people. Writers of nonfiction, fiction, poetry, and specialty writing (children's books, cookbooks, travel, etc.) will all benefit from the event. There are important sessions on marketing, self-publishing, technology, and trends in the publishing industry. Plus, there's an optional four-hour session called "Speed Dating for Agents" where attendees can meet with 20+ agents. Speakers have included Jennifer Crusie, R.L. Stine, Richard Paul Evans, Jamie Raab, Mary Roach, Jane Smiley, Debbie Macomber, Jane Friedman, Chuck Sambuchino, Clive Cussler, Guy Kawasaki, Lisa See, Steve Berry, and Jacquelyn Mitchard. More than 20 agents and editors participate each year, many of whom will be available for meetings with attendees."

COSTS Check the website for pricing. Pricing starts at $725 (as of the 2016 event) depending on when you signed up and early bird registration, etc.

ACCOMMODATIONS The Intercontinental Mark Hopkins Hotel is a historic landmark at the top of Nob Hill in San Francisco. The hotel is located so that everyone arriving at the Oakland or San Francisco airport can take BART to either the Embarcadero or Powell street exits, then walk or take a cable car or taxi directly to the hotel.

ADDITIONAL INFORMATION "Present yourself in a professional manner and the contacts you will make will be invaluable to your writing career. Fliers, details, and registration information are online."

SANTA BARBARA WRITERS CONFERENCE

27 W. Anapamu St., Suite 305, Santa Barbara CA 93101. (805)568-1516. **E-mail:** info@sbwriters.com. **Website:** www.sbwriters.com. Annual conference held in June. 2016 dates: June 5-10. Average attendance: 200. Covers fiction, nonfiction, journalism, memoir, poetry, playwriting, screenwriting, travel writing, young adult, children's literature, humor, and marketing. Speakers have included Ray Bradbury, William Styron, Eudora Welty, James Michener, Sue Grafton, Charles M. Schulz, Clive Cussler, Fannie Flagg, Elmore Leonard, and T.C. Boyle. Agents will appear on a panel; in addition, there will be an agents and editors day that allows writers to pitch their projects in one-on-one meetings. held at the Hyatt Santa Barbara.

COSTS Early conference registration is $575, and regular registration is $650.

ADDITIONAL INFORMATION Register online or contact for brochure and registration forms.

SCBWI; ANNUAL CONFERENCES ON WRITING AND ILLUSTRATING FOR CHILDREN

8271 Beverly Blvd., Los Angeles CA 90048. **E-mail:** scbwi@scbwi.org. **Website:** www.scbwi.org. **Contact:** Lin Oliver, conference director. The two events are writer and illustrator workshops geared toward all levels. **Open to students.** Covers all aspects of children's book and magazine publishing—the novel, illustration techniques, marketing, etc. Annual conferences held in the summer in Los Angeles and in New York in the winter. Cost of conference includes all 4 days and 1 banquet meal. Write for more information or visit website.

SCBWI—ALASKA; EVENTS

P.O. Box 84988, Fairbanks AK 99708-4988. (907)474-2138. **E-mail:** statalias@icloud.com. **Website:** alaska.scbwi.org. **Contact:** Cherie Stihler. SCBWI Alaska holds an annual conference every year. Visit website for details.

SCBWI—ARIZONA; EVENTS

P.O. Box 26384, Scottsdale AZ 85255-0123. **E-mail:** regionaladvisor@scbwi-az.org. **Website:** arizona.scbwi.org. **Contact:** Michelle Parker-Rock, regional advisor. SCBWI Arizona will offer a variety of workshops, retreats, intensives, conferences, meetings, and other craft- and industry-related events throughout the year. Open to members and nonmembers, published and nonpublished. Registration to major events is usually limited. Pre-registration always required. Visit website, write, or e-mail for more information.

❂ SCBWI—BRITISH ISLES: ILLUSTRATOR'S DAY (SPRING)/WRITER'S DAY (FALL)

Website: www.britishscbwi.org. (44)(208)249-9716. **E-mail:** ra@britishscbwi.org. **Website:** www.british-scbwi.org. **Regional Advisor:** Natascha Biebow. The group's SCBWI illustrator coordinator is Anne-Marie Perks. Writer and illustrator conference geared toward beginner, intermediate and advanced levels. Open to students. Cost of annual conference: £220 for SCBWI members/£250 for nonmembers; includes tuition and lunch.

SCBWI—CALIFORNIA (SAN FRANCISCO/SOUTH); GOLDEN GATE CONFERENCE AT ASILOMAR

Website: sfsouth.scbwi.org. **Contact:** Naomi Kinsman, regional advisor. Annual conference. 2016 dates: March 4-6. Welcomes published and not-yet-published writers and illustrators. Lectures and workshops are geared toward professionals and those striving to become professional. Program topics cover aspects of writing or illustrating from picture books to young adult novels. Past speakers include editors, agents, art directors, Newbery-Award-winning authors, and Caldecott-Award-winning illustrators. For more information, including exact costs and dates, visit the website.

❂ SCBWI—CANADA EAST

Canada. **E-mail:** canadaeast@scbwi.org; almafuller-ton@almafullerton.com. **Website:** www.canadaeast.scbwi.org. **Contact:** Alma Fullerton, regional advisor. Writer and illustrator events geared toward all levels. Usually offers 1 event in spring and another in the fall. Check website "Events" page for all updated information.

SCBWI—CAROLINAS; ANNUAL FALL CONFERENCE

P.O. Box 1216, Conover NC 28613. (919)967-2549. **Website:** http://carolinas.scbwi.org. **Website:** http://carolinas.scbwi.org. **E-mail:** scbwicarolinas@earthlink.net. **Regional Advisor:** Teresa Fannin. Annual Conference: The Power of Story. September 30-October 2, 2016 at the Crowne Plaza Hotel, Charlotte, NC. Past speakers included: Alvina Ling, senior editor, Little Brown Publishing; Liz Waniewski, editor, Dial Books for Young Readers; Alan Gratz, author, The Brooklyn Nine; Chris Richman, agent, Upstart Crow Literary Agency; Steve Watkins, 2009 SCBWI Golden Kite Winner, Down Sand Mountain, 2009 debut Author Fran Slayton, When the Whistle Blows. Friday afternoon manuscript and portfolio critiques, workshops focusing on the art and craft of writing and illustrating for children visit https://carolinas.scbwi.org for more information.

SCBWI CAROLINAS— SPRING RETREAT, THE ELEMENTS OF STORY

Website: carolinas.scbwi.org/events/from-picture-books-to-chapter-books. 2016 dates: April 4-10. Past speakers included Jennifer Rees, senior editor, Scholastic Books; Stacey Cantor, editor, Walker Books for Young Readers; Bruce Hale, author, The Chet Gecko series. Join us for a weekend of inspiring and informative talks on story in the peaceful seclusion of the center's woodland setting. For more information and registration, visit the website.

SCBWI—CENTRAL-COASTAL CALIFORNIA FALL CONFERENCE

P.O. Box 1500, Simi Valley CA 93062-1500. **E-mail:** cencal@scbwi.org. **Website:** cencal.scbwi.org. **Contact:** Mary Ann Fraser, regional advisor. Writers' and illustrators' events geared toward all levels. Annual. Speakers include editors, authors, illustrators, and agents. Fiction and nonfiction picture books, middle grade and YA novels, and magazine submissions addressed. There is an annual writing contest in all genres plus illustration display. Conference held in October. For fees and other information, e-mail or visit website.

SCBWI COLORADO/WYOMING (ROCKY MOUNTAIN); EVENTS

E-mail: lindsayeland@me.com, todd.tuell@rmcscbwi.org. **Website:** rmc.scbwi.org. **Contact:** Todd Tuell and Lindsay Eland, co-regional advisors. SCBWI Rocky Mountain chapter (CO/WY) offers special events, schmoozes, meetings, and conferences throughout the year. Major events: Fall Conference (annually, September); Summer Retreat, "Big Sur in the Rockies" (held 2-3 times each year). More info on website.

SCBWI EASTERN NEW YORK FALLING LEAVES MASTER CLASS RETREAT

E-mail: ntcastaldo@taconic.net. **Website:** eastern-ny.scbwi.org, scbwi-easternny.org. **Contact:** Nancy Castaldo, regional advisor. Annual master class retreat hosted by the SCBWI Eastern New York and held in Silver Bay on Lake George in November. Holds ms and portfolio critiques, Q&A and speaker sessions, intensives, and more, with respected authors and editors. Theme varies each year between picture books, novels, and nonfiction. Applications accepted June 15 through August 15. See website for more information.

SCBWI—EASTERN PENNSYLVANIA

E-mail: donnaboock@hotmail.com, easternpascbwi@yahoo.com. **Website:** epa.scbwi.org, easternpennpoints.wordpress.com. The Eastern Pennsylvania chapter of SCBWI plans conferences and local events that feature lessons on the craft of writing and illustrating books for children. Active members will have the opportunity to make connections to editors, agents, art directors, and authors, and have the pleasure of meeting others who also love writing and/or illustrating for children. 2016 events include a Pocono Retreat. 2016 dates: April 29–May 1.

SCBWI—FLORIDA: MID-YEAR WRITING WORKSHOP

12973 SW 112 Court, Miami FL 33186. (305)382-2677. **E-mail:** lindabernfeld@gmail.com; gabytriana@gmail.com. **Website:** florida.scbwi.org. **Contact:** Linda Bernfeld, co-regional advisor. Annual workshop held in June in Orlando. 2016 dates: June 10-11. Workshop is geared toward helping everyone hone their writing skills. Attendees choose one track and spend the day with industry leaders who share valuable information about that area of children's book writing. There are a minimum of 3 tracks: picture book, middle grade, and young adult. The 4th and 5th tracks are variable, covering subjects such as poetry, nonfiction, humor, or writing for magazines. E-mail for more information.

SCBWI—FLORIDA: REGIONAL CONFERENCE

12973 SW 112 Court, Miami FL 33186. (305)382-2677. **E-mail:** lindabernfeld@gmail.com; gabytriana@gmail.com. **Website:** florida.scbwi.org/events/2016_regional_conference. **Contact:** Linda Bernfeld, regional advisor. Annual conference held in January in Miami. 2016 dates: January 15-17. Past keynote speakers have included Linda Sue Park, Richard Peck, Bruce Coville, Bruce Hale, Arthur A. Levine, Judy Blume, Kate Dicamillo. The three-day conference will have workshops Friday afternoon and a field trip to Books and Books Friday evening.

SCBWI—ILLINOIS: PRAIRIE WRITERS DAY

E-mail: alicebmcginty@gmail.com. **Website:** illinois.scbwi.org. **Contact:** Alice McGinty, co-regional advisor. Full day of guest speakers, editors/agents TBD. Ms critiques available as well as break-out sessions on career and craft. See website for complete description. This event is usually held in the early summer.

SCBWI—IOWA CONFERENCES

E-mail: hecklit@aol.com. **Website:** iowa.scbwi.org. **Contact:** Connie Heckert, regional advisor. Writer and illustrator workshops in all genres of children writing. The Iowa region offers conferences of high quality events usually over a three-day period with registration options. Holds spring and fall events on a regional level, and network events across that state. Individual critiques and portfolio review offerings vary with the program and presenters. For more information, e-mail or visit website. Literary agents and editors are present at the events.

SCBWI—MIDATLANTIC; ANNUAL FALL CONFERENCE

P.O. Box 3215, Reston VA 20195. **E-mail:** scbwimidatlantic@gmail.com. **Website:** midatlantic.scbwi.org. For updates and details, visit website. Registration limited to 275. Conference fills quickly. Includes continental breakfast and boxed lunch. Optional craft-focused workshops and individual consultations with conference faculty are available for additional fees.

SCBWI—MIDSOUTH FALL CONFERENCE

P.O. Box 396, Cordova TN 38088. **E-mail:** ktubb@comcast.net. **Website:** midsouth.scbwi.org. **Contact:** Kristin Tubb, regional advisor. Annual conference for writers and illustrators of all levels. Usually held in the fall (September). In the past, workshops were offered on "Plotting Your Novel," "Understanding the Language of Editors," "Landing an Agent," "How to Prepare a Portfolio," "Negotiating a Contract," "The Basics for Beginners," and many others. Attendees are invited to bring a manuscript and/or art portfolio to share in the optional, no-charge critique group session. Illustrators are invited to bring color copies of their art (not originals) to be displayed in the illustrators' showcase. For an additional fee, attendees may schedule a 15-minute manuscript critique or portfo-

CONFERENCES & WORKSHOPS

lio critique by the editor, art director, or other expert consultant. Some agents and editors attend to meet with writers.

SCBWI—MISSOURI CHILDREN'S WRITER'S CONFERENCE

Website: missouri.scbwi.org. **Contact:** Kimberly Piddington, regional advisor. Open to students. Speakers include editors, writers, agents, and other professionals. Topics vary from year to year, but each conference offers sessions for both writers and illustrators as well as for newcomers and published writers. Previous topics included: "What Happens When Your Manuscript is Accepted" by Dawn Weinstock, editor; "Writing—Hobby or Vocation?" by Chris Kelleher; "Mother Time Gives Advice: Perspectives from a 25-Year Veteran" by Judith Mathews, editor; "Don't Be a Starving Writer" by Vicki Berger Erwin, author; and "Words and Pictures: History in the Making," by author-illustrator Cheryl Harness. Annual conference held in fall. For exact date(s), see the website.

SCBWI—NEW ENGLAND; ANNUAL CONFERENCE

Nashua NH 03063. **E-mail:** nescbwi2015@gmail.com. **Website:** newengland.scbwi.org. 2016 dates: April 29-May 1. Conference is for all levels of writers and illustrators. Open to students. Offers many workshops at each conference, and often there is a multi-day format. Examples of subjects addressed: manuscript development, revision, marketing your work, productive school visits, picture book dummy formatting, adding texture to your illustrations, etc. Annual conference held in spring. Registration limited to 450. Check website for updated pricing. Details (additional speakers, theme, number of workshop choices, etc.) will be posted to website as they become available. Registration doesn't start until March. Opportunities for one-on-one manuscript critiques and portfolio reviews will be available at the conference. Agents and editors in attendance to meet with writers.

SCBWI NEW ENGLAND WHISPERING PINES WRITER'S RETREAT

West Greenwich RI. **E-mail:** lyndamullalyhunt@yahoo.com, momeraths@verizon.net. **Website:** newengland.scbwi.org/whispering-pines. **Contact:** Lynda Mullaly Hunt, co-director; Mary Pierce, co-director. Three-day retreat (with stays overnight) that offers the opportunity to work intimately with professionals in

an idyllic setting. Attendees will work with others who are committed to quality children's literature in small groups and will benefit from a 30-minute one-on-one critique with a mentor. Also includes mentors' presentations and an intimate Q&A session, Team Kid Lit Jeopardy with prizes, and more. Retreat limited to 32 full-time participants. Held annually in mid-to-late March.

SCBWI—NEW JERSEY; ANNUAL SUMMER CONFERENCE

Website: newjersey.scbwi.org. **Contact:** Leeza Hernandez, regional advisor. This weekend conference is held in the summer. There are multiple one-on-one critiques, "how to" workshops for every level, first page sessions, agent pitches, and interaction with the faculty of editors, agents, art director, and authors. On Friday, attendees can sign up for writing intensives or register for illustrators' day with the art directors. Published authors attending the conference can sign up to participate in the bookfair to sell and autograph their books; illustrators have the opportunity to display their artwork. Attendees have the option to participate in group critiques after dinner on Saturday evening and attend a mix and mingle with the faculty on Friday night. Meals are included with the cost of admission. Conference is known for its high ratio of faculty to attendees and interaction opportunities.

SCBWI—NEW MEXICO CONFERENCE FOR CHILDREN'S WRITERS AND ILLUSTRATORS

PO Box 1084, Socorro NM. **E-mail:** carolinestarr@yahoo.com. **Website:** newmexico.scbwi.org. **Contact:** Linda Tripp, regional advisor; Caroline Starr, assistant advisor. Annual conference for beginner and intermediate writers and illustrators. Conference features editors, agents, art directors, illustrators, and authors. Offers intensive craft-based workshops and large-group presentations. See website for details. Monthly offerings include schmoozes, critique groups, and illustrator meetings.

SCBWI—NORTHERN OHIO ANNUAL CONFERENCE

225 N. Willow St., Kent OH 44240-2561. **E-mail:** vselvaggio@windstream.net. **Website:** ohionorth.scbwi.org. **Contact:** Victoria A. Selvaggio, regional advisor. Northern Ohio's conference is crafted for all levels of writers and illustrators of children's literature. An-

nual event held in the fall. "Our annual event will be held at the Sheraton Cleveland Airport Hotel. Conference costs will be posted on our website with registration information. SCBWI members receive a discount. Additional fees apply for late registration, critiques, or portfolio reviews. Cost includes the following: an optional Friday evening opening banquet from 6-10 p.m. with a keynote speaker; Saturday event from 8:30 a.m. to 5 p.m., which features a breakfast snack; the full-day conference with headliner presentations, general sessions, breakout workshops, lunch, panel discussion, bookstore, and an autograph session. The Illustrator Showcase is open to all attendees at no additional cost. Grand door prize, drawn at the end of the day Saturday, is free admission to the following year's conference. Further information, including headliner speakers will be posted on our website."

SCBWI—OREGON CONFERENCES

E-mail: suhligford@gmail.com, oregon@scbwi.org. **Website:** oregon.scbwi.org. **Contact:** Sue Ford, co-regional advisor; Judith Gardiner, co-regional advisor. Writer and illustrator workshops and presentations geared toward all levels. Invites editors, art directors, agents, attorneys, authors, illustrators, and others in the business of writing and illustrating for children. Faculty members offer craft presentations, workshops, first-page sessions, and individual critiques as well as informal networking opportunities. Critique group network opportunities for local group meetings and regional retreats; see website for details. Two main events per year: Writers and Illustrators Retreat held near Portland in October; Spring Conference held in the Portland area (two-day event in May). SCBWI Oregon is a regional chapter of the Society of Children's Book Writers and Illustrators. SCBWI Members receive a discount for all events. Oregon and South Washington members get preference.

SCBWI—SOUTHERN BREEZE; SPRINGMINGLE

P.O. Box 26282, Birmingham AL 35260. **Website:** southern-breeze.scbwi.org. **Contact:** Kathleen Bradshaw, co-regional advisor. Writer and illustrator conference geared toward intermediate, advanced, and professional levels. Speakers typically include agents, editors, authors, art directors, illustrators. Open to SCBWI members, non-members, and college students. Annual conference held in Atlanta, Georgia.

Usually held in late March. Registration limited. Manuscript critiques and portfolio reviews available for additional fee. Pre-registration is necessary. Visit website for more information.

SCBWI—SOUTHERN BREEZE; WRITING AND ILLUSTRATING FOR KIDS

P.O. Box 26282, Birmingham AL 35260. **E-mail:** klbradshaw@kathleenbradshaw.com. **Website:** southern-breeze.scbwi.org. **Contact:** Kathleen Bradshaw, co-regional advisor; Claudia Pearson, co-regional advisor. Fall event. Writer and illustrator workshops geared toward all levels. Open to SCBWI members, non-members and college students. All sessions pertain specifically to the production and support of quality children's literature. This one-day conference offers about 30 workshops on craft and the business of writing. Picture books, chapter books, and novels covered. Entry and professional level topics addressed by published writers and illustrators, editors, and agents. Annual fall conference is held in early October in the Birmingham metropolitan area. All workshops are limited to 30 or fewer people. Pre-registration is necessary. Some workshops fill quickly. Mss critiques and portfolio reviews are available for an additional fee; mss must be sent early. Registration is by mail ahead of time. Ms and portfolio reviews must be pre-paid and scheduled.

SCBWI—TAIWAN; EVENTS

E-mail: shunu2100@yahoo.com.tw. **Website:** taiwan.scbwi.org. **Regional Advisor:** Shu-Nu (Candy) Yen. Writer and illustrator workshops geared toward intermediate level. Open to students. Topics emphasized: "We regularly hold critiques for writers and for illustrators, and invite authors and illustrators visiting Taipei to give talks. See our website for more information."

SCBWI—WESTERN WASHINGTON STATE; CONFERENCE & RETREAT

E-mail: info@scbwi-washington.org, danajsullivan@comcast.net. **Website:** chinookupdate.blogspot.com, wwa.scbwi.org. **Contact:** Dana Arnim, co-regional advisor; Dana Sullivan, co-regional advisor. The Western Washington region of SCBWI hosts an annual conference in April, a retreat in November, and monthly meetings and events throughout the year. Visit the website for complete details.

SCIENCE FICTION WRITERS WORKSHOP

English Department/University of Kansas, Wesoce Hall, 1445 Jayhawk Blvd., Room 3001, Lawrence KS 66045-7590. (785)864-2508. **E-mail:** cmckit@ku.edu. **Website:** www.sfcenter.ku.edu/sfworkshop.htm. Estab. 1985. Annual workshop held in June. The workshop is "small, informal, and aimed at writers on the edge of publication or regular publication." This is an event for writing and marketing science fiction and fantasy. Workshop sessions operate informally in a university housing lounge on the University of Kansas campus where most participants also reside. Established in 1985 by James Gunn and currently led by Christopher McKitterick, with guest authors joining for the second week. Writer and editor instructors have included Lou Anders, Bradley Denton, James Gunn, Kij Johnson, John Ordover, Frederik Pohl, Pamela Sargent, and George Zebrowski. Each year the winners of the Campbell and Sturgeon Memorial awards participate in 1 or more days of the workshop.

COSTS $600, exclusive of meals and housing.

ACCOMMODATIONS Housing information is available online. Several airport shuttle services offer reasonable transportation from the Kansas City International Airport to Lawrence, Kansas.

ADDITIONAL INFORMATION Admission to the workshop is by submission of an acceptable story, usually by May. Two additional stories are submitted by the middle of June. These 3 stories are distributed to other participants for critiquing and are the basis for the first week of the workshop. One story is rewritten for the second week, when students also work with guest authors. See website for guidelines. This workshop is intended for writers who have just started to sell their work or need that extra bit of understanding or skill to become a published writer.

SEWANEE WRITERS' CONFERENCE

735 University Ave., 119 Gailor Hall, Stamler Center, Sewanee TN 37383-1000. (931)598-1654. **E-mail:** swc@sewanee.edu. **Website:** www.sewaneewriters.org. **Contact:** Adam Latham. Estab. 1990. Annual conference. 2016 dates: July 19-31. Average attendance: 150. "The University of the South will host the 27th session of the Sewanee Writers' Conference. Thanks to the generosity of the Walter E. Dakin Memorial Fund, supported by the estate of the late Tennessee Williams, the conference will gather a distinguished faculty to provide instruction and criticism through workshops and craft lectures in poetry, fiction, and playwriting. During an intense 12-day period, participants will read and critique workshop mss under the leadership of some of our country's finest fiction writers, poets, and playwrights. Faculty members and fellows give scheduled readings, senior faculty members offer craft lectures, and open-mic readings are available. Additional writers, along with a host of writing professionals, visit to give readings, participate in panel discussions, and answer questions from the audience. Receptions and mealtimes offer ample social opportunities. 2016 faculty included fiction writers Richard Bausch, John Casey, Tony Earley, Randall Kenan, Jill McCorkle, Alice McDermott, Erin McGraw, Christine Schutt, Allen Wier, and Steve Yarbrough. Attending poets included Daniel Anderson, B.H. Fairchild, Robert Hass, Mark Jarman, Maurice Manning, Marilyn Nelson, A.E. Stallings, and Sidney Wade. Naomi Iizuka and Dan O'Brien led the playwriting workshop. Charles Martin, A.E. Stallings, and N.S. Thompson offered a supplemental poetry translation workshop. Adrianne Harun, Andrew Hudgins, Charles Martin, and Wyatt Prunty will read from their work."

COSTS $1,100 for tuition; $800 for room, board, and activity costs.

ACCOMMODATIONS Participants are housed in single rooms in university dormitories. Bathrooms are shared by small groups.

SOUTH CAROLINA WRITERS WORKSHOP

4840 Forest Dr., Suite 6B, PMB 189, Columbia SC 29206. **E-mail:** scwwliaison@gmail.com, scww2013@gmail.com. **Website:** www.myscww.org. Estab. 1991. Conference in October held at the Metropolitan Conference Center in Columbia, South Carolina. Held almost every year. Conference duration: 3 days. The conference features critique sessions, open mic readings, presentations from agents and editors, and more. The conference features more than 50 different workshops for writers to choose from, dealing with all subjects of writing craft, writing business, getting an agent, and more. Agents will be in attendance.

SOUTHEASTERN WRITERS ASSOCIATION—ANNUAL WRITERS WORKSHOP

E-mail: purple@southeasternwriters.org. **Website:** www.southeasternwriters.org. Estab. 1975. Event is held at Epworth-by-the-Sea, St. Simons Island, Georgia. Annual four-day workshop—open to all writers. 2016 dates: June 18-21. There are 3 free evaluation conferences with instructors that are included with tuition (minimum two-day registration). The workshop has writing contests with cash prizes. Ms deadline: May 15 (contests), May 25 (evaluations).

COSTS $445 for 4 days; lower prices for daily tuition. See website for final pricing.

ACCOMMODATIONS Lodging at Epworth and throughout St. Simons Island. Visit website for more information.

SPACE COAST WRITERS GUILD ANNUAL CONFERENCE

E-mail: stilley@scwg.org. **Website:** www.scwg.org/conference.asp. Annual conference held the last weekend of January along the east coast of central Florida, though the event is not necessarily held every year. Conference duration: 2 days. Average attendance: 150+. This conference is hosted in Florida and features a variety of presenters on all writing topics. Critiques are available for a price, and agents in attendance will take pitches from writers. Previous presenters have included Debra Dixon, Davis Bunn (writer), Ellen Pepus (agent), Jennifer Crusie, Chuck Sambuchino, Madeline Smoot, Mike Resnick, Christina York, Ben Bova, and Elizabeth Sinclair. Check the website for up-to-date information and future dates.

ACCOMMODATIONS The conference is hosted on a beachside hotel, with special room rates available.

☉ SURREY INTERNATIONAL WRITERS' CONFERENCE

SiWC, 151-10090 152 St., Suite 544, Surrey BC V3R 8X8 Canada. **E-mail:** kathychung@siwc.ca. **Website:** www.siwc.ca. **Contact:** Kathy Chung, proposals contact and conference coordinator. Annual professional development writing conference outside Vancouver, Canada, held every fall. There are writing workshops geared toward beginner, intermediate, and advanced levels. The event has more than 70 workshops and panels, on all topics and genres, plus pre-conference master classes. Blue Pencil and agent/editor pitch sessions included. Different conference price packages available. Check the conference website for more information. This event has many literary agents in attendance taking pitches. Annual writing contest open to all.

TAOS SUMMER WRITERS' CONFERENCE

Department of English Language and Literature, MSC 03 2170, 1 University of New Mexico, Albuquer-que NM 87131. **E-mail:** swarner@unm.edu. **Website:** taosconf.unm.edu. **Contact:** Sharon Oard Warner. Estab. 1999. Annual conference held in July. 2016 dates: July 24-31. Offers workshops and master classes on topics such as the novel, short stories, poetry, creative nonfiction, memoir, prose style, screenwriting, humor writing, literary translation, book proposal, the query letter, and revision. Participants may also schedule a consultation with a visiting agent/editor.

COSTS Weeklong workshop registration $700; weekend workshop registration $400; master classes cost between $1,350 and $1,625; publishing consultations are $175.

TEXAS WRITING RETREAT

Grimes County TX **E-mail:** paultcuclis@gmail.com. **Website:** www.texaswritingretreat.com. **Contact:** Paul Cuclis, coordinator. Estab. 2013. The Texas Writing Retreat is an intimate event with a limited number of attendees. Held on a private residence ranch an hour outside of Houston, it has an agent and editor in attendance who both teaches and takes pitches. All attendees get to pitch the attending agent. Meals and excursions and amenities included. This is a unique event that combines craft sessions, business sessions, time for writing, relaxation, and more. The retreat is not held every year. It's best to check the website and see if there is a retreat in any given year.

COSTS Costs vary per event. There are different pricing options for those staying onsite vs. commuters.

ACCOMMODATIONS Private ranch residence in Texas.

TMCC WRITERS' CONFERENCE

Truckee Meadows Community College, 7000 Dandini Blvd., Reno NV 89512. (775)673-7111. **E-mail:** wdce@tmcc.edu. **Website:** wdce.tmcc.edu. Estab. 1991. Annual conference held in April. 2016 date: April 16. Average attendance: 150. Conference focuses on strengthening your fiction and nonfiction works, as well as how to pitch projects to agents and publishers. Site: Truckee Meadows Community College in Reno. "There is always an array of speakers and presenters with impressive literary credentials, including agents and editors." Speakers have included Chuck Sambuchino, Sheree Bykofsky, Andrea Brown, Dorothy Allison, Karen Joy Fowler, James D. Houston, James N. Frey, Gary Short, Jane Hirschfield, Dorianne Laux, and Kim Addonizio. Literary agents are onsite to take pitches from writers.

ACCOMMODATIONS Contact the conference manager to learn about accommodation discounts.

ADDITIONAL INFORMATION "The conference is open to all writers, regardless of their level of experience. Brochures are available online and mailed in January. Send inquiries via e-mail."

UNICORN WRITERS CONFERENCE

P.O. Box 176, Redding CT 06876. (203)938-7405. **E-mail:** unicornwritersconference@gmail.com. **Website:** www.unicornwritersconference.com. **Contact:** Jan L. Kardys, chairman. Estab. 2010. This writers conference draws upon its close proximity to New York City and pulls in over 35 literary agents and 15 major editors to pitch each year. There are ms review sessions (40 pages equals 30 minutes with an agent/editor), query/ms review sessions, and 5 different workshops every hour. $325 cost includes all workshops and 3 meals.

COSTS $325 includes all workshops (5 every hour to select on the day of the conference), a gift bag, and 3 meals. Additional cost for ms reviews: $60.

ACCOMMODATIONS Held at Reid Castle, Purchase, New York. Directions available on event website.

UNIVERSITY OF NORTH DAKOTA WRITERS CONFERENCE

Department of English, 110 Merrifield Hall, 276 Centennial Dr., Stop 7209, Grand Forks ND 58202. (701)777-2393. **Fax:** (701)777-2373. **E-mail:** crystal.alberts@e-mail.und.edu. **Website:** und.edu/orgs/writers-conference. **Contact:** Crystal Alberts, director. Estab. 1970. Annual event of 3-5 days. 2016 dates: April 6-8. Offers panels, readings, and films focused around a specific theme. Almost all events take place in the UND Memorial Union, which has a variety of small rooms and a 1,000-seat main hall. Past speakers include Art Spiegelman, Truman Capote, Sir Salman Rushdie, Allen Ginsberg, Alice Walker, and Louise Erdrich.

COSTS All events are free and open to the public. Donations accepted.

ACCOMMODATIONS Accommodations available at area hotels. Information on overnight accommodations available on website.

ADDITIONAL INFORMATION Schedule and other information available on website.

UNIVERSITY OF WISCONSIN AT MADISON WRITERS INSTITUTE

21 N. Park St., Madison WI 53715-1218. (608)265-3972. **E-mail:** laurie.scheer@wisc.edu. **Website:** https://uwwritersinstitute.wisc.edu. Estab. 1990. Annual conference. 2016 dates: April 15-17. Conference on fiction and nonfiction held at the University of Wisconsin at Madison. Guest speakers are published authors, editors, and agents.

COSTS $125-260, depending on discounts and if you attend 1 day or multiple days.

UW-MADISON WRITERS' INSTITUTE

21 N. Park St., Room 7312, Madison WI 53715. (608)265-3972. **Fax:** (608)265-2475. **E-mail:** laurie.scheer@wisc.edu. **Website:** www.uwwritersinstitute.org. **Contact:** Laurie Scheer. Estab. 1989. Annual conference usually held in the spring. Site: Madison Concourse Hotel, downtown Madison, Wisconsin. Average attendance: 600. Conference speakers provide workshops and consultations. For information, send e-mail, visit website, call, or fax. Accepts inquiries by SASE, e-mail, phone, fax. Agents and editors participate in conference.

COSTS $180-330.

ACCOMMODATIONS Provides a list of area hotels or lodging options.

ADDITIONAL INFORMATION Sponsors contest.

WESLEYAN WRITERS CONFERENCE

Wesleyan University, 294 High St., Room 207, Middletown CT 06459. (860)685-3604. **Fax:** (860)685-2441. **E-mail:** agreene@wesleyan.edu. **Website:** www.wesleyan.edu/writing/conference. Annual conference. 2016 dates: June 15-19. Average attendance: 100. Focuses on the novel, fiction techniques, short stories, poetry, screenwriting, nonfiction, literary journalism, memoir, mixed media work, and publishing. The conference is held on the campus of Wesleyan University, in the hills overlooking the Connecticut River. Features a faculty of award-winning writers, seminars, and readings of new fiction, poetry, nonfiction, and mixed media forms—as well as guest lectures on a range of topics including publishing. Both new and experienced writers are welcome. Participants may attend seminars in all genres. Speakers have included Esmond Harmsworth (Zachary Schuster Agency), Daniel Mandel (Sanford J. Greenburger Associates), Amy Williams (ICM and Collins McCormick), and many others. Agents will be speaking and available for meetings with attendees. Participants are often successful in finding agents and publishers for their mss. Wesleyan participants are also frequently featured in the anthology *Best New American Voices*. Meals are provided on campus. Lodging is available on campus or in town.

ADDITIONAL INFORMATION Ms critiques are available, but not required.

WESTERN RESERVE WRITERS & FREELANCE CONFERENCE

7700 Clocktower Dr., Kirtland OH 44094. (440)525-7812. **E-mail:** deencr@aol.com. **Website:** www.deannaadams.com. **Contact:** Deanna Adams, director and conference coordinator. Estab. 1983. Annual. Last conference held September 26, 2015. Conference duration: 1 day or half-day. Average attendance: 120. "The Western Reserve Writers Conference is designed for all writers, aspiring and professional, and offer presentations in all genres—nonfiction, fiction, poetry, essays, and creative nonfiction. There are sessions on the business of writing, including Web writing and successful freelance writing." Site: Located in the main building of Lakeland Community College, the conference is just off the I-90 freeway. Included throughout the day are one-on-one editing consults, a Q&A panel, and author signings.

ADDITIONAL INFORMATION Brochures for the conferences are available by January (for spring conference) and July (for the fall event). Also accepts inquiries by e-mail and phone. Editors always attend the conferences. Private editing consultations are available, as well.

WILLAMETTE WRITERS CONFERENCE

2108 Buck St., West Linn OR 97068. (503)305-6729. **Fax:** (503)344-6174. **Website:** www.willamettewriters.com/wwcon. Estab. 1981. Annual conference held in August. Conference duration: 3 days. Average attendance: 600. "Willamette Writers is open to all writers, and we plan our conference accordingly. We offer workshops on all aspects of fiction, nonfiction, marketing, the creative process, screenwriting, and more. Also, we invite top-notch inspirational speakers for keynote addresses. We always include at least 1 agent or editor panel and offer a variety of topics of interest to writers." Agents will be speaking and available for meetings with attendees.

COSTS Pricing schedule available online.

ACCOMMODATIONS If necessary, arrangements can be made on an individual basis through the conference hotel. Special rates may be available.

ADDITIONAL INFORMATION Brochure/guidelines are available for a catalog-sized SASE.

WOMEN WRITING THE WEST

8547 E. Araphoe Rd., Box J-541, Greenwood Village CO 80112-1436. **E-mail:** conference@womenwritingthewest.org, pamelanowak@hotmail.com. **Website:** www.womenwritingthewest.org. 2016 conference dates: October 13-16; location: Santa Fe, New Mexico. "Women Writing the West is a nonprofit association of writers, editors, publishers, agents, booksellers, and other professionals writing and promoting the women's West. As such, these women write their stories of the American West in a way that illuminates them authentically. In addition, the organization provides support, encouragement, and inspiration to all women writing about any facet of the American West. Membership is open to all interested persons worldwide. Open to students. Members actively exchange ideas on a list e-bulletin board. WWW membership also allows the choice of participation in our marketing marvel, and the annual WWW Catalog of Authors' Books. An annual conference is held every fall. Our blog, Facebook, and ListServ publish current WWW activities. We also share market research and articles of interest pertaining to American West literature and member news. Sponsors annual WILLA Literary Award, which is given in several categories for outstanding literature featuring women's stories, set in the West. The winner of a WILLA receives a cash award and a trophy at the annual conference. Contest open to nonmembers. Annual conference held the third weekend in October. Covers research, writing techniques, multiple genres, marketing/promotion, and more. Agents and editors will be speaking and available for one-on-one meetings with attendees. Conference location changes each year."

COSTS See website. Discounts available for members, and for specific days only.

ACCOMMODATIONS See website for location and accommodation details.

WORDS & MUSIC

Words & Music, A Literary Feast in New Orleans, The Pirate's Alley Faulkner Society, Inc., 624 Pirate's Alley, New Orleans LA 70116. (504)586-1609. **E-mail:**

faulkhouse@aol.com. **Website:** www.wordsand music.org. **Contact:** Rosemary James. Estab. 1997. Annual conference held in November. Conference duration: 5 days. Average attendance: 300. Presenters include authors, agents, editors, and publishers. Past speakers include agents Deborah Grosvenor, Judith Weber, Stuart Bernstein, Nat Sobel, Jeff Kleinman, Emma Sweeney, Liza Dawson, Brettne Bloom, Jennifer Weltz, and Michael Murphy; editors Sarah Crichton, Brenda Copeland, Andra Miller, Kristine Poupolo, Webster Younce, Ann Patty, Will Murphy, Jofie Ferrari-Adler, and Elizabeth Stein; critics Marie Arana, Jonathan Yardley, and Michael Dirda; fiction writers Adam Johnson, Julia Glass, Stewart O'Nan, Tom Franklin, Tom Piazza, Tea Obreht, Robert Goolrick, Oscar Hijuelos, Robert Olen Butler, Shirley Ann Grau, Mayra Montero, Ana Castillo, and Horacio Castellenos-Moya. Agents and editors critique mss in advance then meet with attendees one-on-one during the conference. A detailed schedule of master classes and workshops is available online.

COSTS See website for a costs and additional information on accommodations. Website will update closer to date of conference.

ACCOMMODATIONS Room block available at Hotel Monteleone and sister hotel, Bienville House in New Orleans.

ADDITIONAL INFORMATION Winners of 2016 William Faulkner Creative Writing Competition will be presented at Words & Music.

✪ WRITE CANADA

The Word Guild, Suite 226, 245 King George Rd., Brantford Onatrio N3R 7N7 Canada. **E-mail:** write canada@thewordguild.com. **Website:** thewordguild. com/events/write-canada. Conference duration: 3 days. Annual conference in Ontario for writers who are Christian of all types and at all stages. Offers solid instruction, stimulating interaction, exciting challenges, and worshipful community.

ADDITIONAL INFORMATION Write Canada is the nation's largest Christian writers' conference held annually. Each year hundreds of writers, editors, authors, journalists, columnists, bloggers, poets, and playwrights gather to hone their craft at the three-day conference. Over the past 3 decades, Write Canada has successfully equipped writers and editors, beginner to professional, from all across North America.

WRITE ON THE SOUND

City of Edmonds Arts Commission, Frances Anderson Center, 700 Main St., Edmonds WA 98020. (425)771-0228. **E-mail:** wots@edmondswa.gov. **Website:** www.writeonthesound.com. Estab. 1985. Intimate, affordable annual conference focused on the craft of writing. Held the first weekend in October. 2016 dates: September 30 through October 2. Conference duration: 2.5 days. Average attendance: 300. Features 30 presenters, a literary contest, ms critiques, roundtable discussions, book signing reception, on-site bookstore, and opportunity to network with faculty and attendees. Edmonds is located just north of Seattle on the Puget Sound.

COSTS See website for complete information.

ADDITIONAL INFORMATION Schedule posted on website mid-June. Registration open by late July.

WRITERS@WORK WRITING RETREAT

P.O. Box 711191, Salt Lake City UT 84171-1191. (801)996-3313. **E-mail:** jennifer@writersatwork. org. **Website:** www.writersatwork.org. Estab. 1985. Annual conference held in June. (The 2016 conference was June 15-19.) Conference duration: 4 days. Average attendance: 45. Workshop topics include a focus on novel, advanced fiction, generative fiction, nonfiction, poetry, and young adult fiction. Afternoon sessions will include craft lectures, discussions, and directed interviews with authors and editors. In addition to the traditional, one-on-one ms consultations, there will be many opportunities to mingle informally with visiting writers and editors. Held at the Alta Lodge in Alta Lodge, Utah. Speakers have included Steve Almond, Bret Lott, Shannon Hale, Emily Forland (Wendy Weil Agency), Julie Culver (Folio Literary Management), Chuck Adams (Algonquin Press), and Mark A. Taylor (Juniper Press).

COSTS $650-1,000, based on housing type and consultations.

ACCOMMODATIONS Onsite housing available. Additional lodging information is on the website.

WRITERS CONFERENCE AT OCEAN PARK

P.O. Box 172, Assonet ME 02702. (401)598-1424. **E-mail:** jbrosnan@jwu.edu. **Website:** www.oceanpark. org. Estab. 1941. Annual conference held in mid-August. Conference duration: 4 days. Average attendance: 50. "We try to present a balanced and eclectic conference. In addition to time and attention given to poetry, we also have children's literature, mystery writing, travel, fiction, nonfiction, journalism, and other issues of interest to writers. Our speakers are editors, writers, and other professionals. Our concentration is, by intention, a general view of writing to publish with supportive encouragement. We are located in Ocean Park, a small seashore village 14 miles south of Portland, Maine. Ours is a summer assembly center with many buildings from the Victorian age. The conference meets in Porter Hall, one of the assembly buildings which is listed in the National Register of Historic Places. Speakers have included Michael C. White (novelist/short story writer), Betsy Sholl (poet), Suzanne Strempek Shea (novelist), John Perrault (poet), Anita Shreve (novelist), Dawn Potter (poet), Bruce Pratt (fiction writer), Amy McDonald (children's author), Sandell Morse (memoirist), Kate Chadbourne (singer/songwriter), Wesley McNair (poet and Maine faculty member), and others. We usually have about 8 guest presenters each year." Writers/editors will be speaking, leading workshops, and available for meetings with attendees. Workshops start at 8:30 a.m. on Tuesday and continue through Friday. Opening event is Monday at 4 p.m.

COSTS $200. The fee does not include housing or meals, which must be arranged separately.

ACCOMMODATIONS "An accommodations list is available. We are in a summer resort area where motels, guest houses, and restaurants abound."

ADDITIONAL INFORMATION 2016 marks the conference's 76th anniversary.

WRITER'S DIGEST CONFERENCES

F+W: A Content and eCommerce Company, 10151 Carver Rd., Suite 200, Blue Ash OH 45242. (877)436-7764. **E-mail:** writersdigestconference@fwmedia.com. **Website:** www.writersdigestconference.com. **Contact:** Taylor Sferra. Estab. 1995. The Writer's Digest conferences feature an amazing lineup of speakers to help writers with the craft and business of writing. Each calendar year typically features multiple conferences around the country. In 2016, the New York conference will be August 12-14 at the New York Hilton Midtown. The most popular feature of the east coast conference is the agent pitch slam, in which potential authors are given the ability to pitch their books directly to agents. For more details, see

the website. There will be a 2016 west coast event in October 2016.

COSTS Cost varies by location and year. There are typically different pricing options for those who wish attend the pitch slam and those who just want to attend the conference education.

ACCOMMODATIONS A block of rooms at the event hotel are reserved for guests. See the travel page on the website for more information.

WRITERS IN PARADISE

Eckerd College, 4200 54th Ave. S, St. Petersburg FL 33711. (727)864-7994. **Fax:** (727)864-7575. **E-mail:** wip@eckerd.edu. **Website:** writersinparadise.eckerd.edu. Estab. 2005. Annual event held in January. Conference duration: 8 days. Average attendance: 84 maximum. Workshop. Offers college credit. "Writers in Paradise Conference offers workshop classes in fiction (novel and short story), poetry, and nonfiction. Working closely with our award-winning faculty, students will have stimulating opportunities to ask questions and learn valuable skills from fellow students and authors at the top of their form. Most importantly, the intimate size and secluded location of the Writers in Paradise experience allows you the time and opportunity to share your mss, critique one another's work, and discuss the craft of writing with experts and peers who can help guide you to the next level." Previous faculty includes Andre Dubus III (*House of Sand and Fog*), Michael Koryta (*So Cold the River*), Dennis Lehane (*The Given Day*), Laura Lippman (*I'd Know You Anywhere*), Seth Fishman (literary agent), Johnny Temple (Akashic Books), and more. Editors and agents attend the conference.

ADDITIONAL INFORMATION Application (December deadline) materials are required for prospective attendees.

WRITERS' LEAGUE OF TEXAS AGENTS & EDITORS CONFERENCE

Writers' League of Texas, 611 S. Congress Ave., Suite 200 A-3, Austin TX 78704. (512)499-8914. **E-mail:** conference@writersleague.org, jennifer@writersleague.org. **Website:** www.writersleague.org. **Contact:** Jennifer Ziegler, program director. Estab. 1982. Annual event held in June. For writers at every stage of their career, this standout conference includes panel discussions, genre-specific meetings, one-on-one consultations with top notch agents and editors, keynote speakers, and opportunities to network and connect.

COSTS Registration opens December 1 for members only at the early bird rate of $349. After January 5: $389 members / $449 nonmembers. After April 6: $429 members / $489 nonmembers. After June 5: $469 members / $509 nonmembers.

ADDITIONAL INFORMATION Contests and awards programs are offered separately. Brochures are available upon request.

WRITERS WEEKEND AT THE BEACH

P.O. Box 877, Ocean Park WA 98640. (360)665-4367. **E-mail:** director@opretreat.org. **Website:** www.opre treat.org/event/writers-weekend-at-the-beach. **Contact:** Brandon Scheer; Tracie Heskett. Estab. 1992. Annual conference held in March. Conference duration: 2 days. Average attendance: 45. A retreat for writers with an emphasis on poetry, fiction, and nonfiction. Held at the Ocean Park Methodist Retreat Center & Camp. Speakers have included Miralee Ferrell, Leslie Gould, Linda Clare, Birdie Etchison, Colette Tennant, Gail Denham, Patricia Rushford, and Marion Duckworth.

COSTS $200 for full registration before Feb. 15 and $215 after Feb. 15.

ACCOMMODATIONS Offers onsite overnight lodging.

WRITE-TO-PUBLISH CONFERENCE

WordPro Communication Services, 9118 W. Elmwood Dr., Suite 1G, Niles IL 60714-5820. (847)296-3964. **Fax:** (847)296-0754. **E-mail:** lin@writetopublish.com. **Website:** www.writetopublish.com. **Contact:** Lin Johnson, director. Estab. 1971. Annual. 2016 Conference dates: June 8-11. Average attendance: 200. Conference is focused for the Christian market and includes classes on writing for children. Writer workshops geared toward all levels. Open to students. Site: Wheaton College, Wheaton, IL (near Chicago).

COSTS Call or e-mail for more information.

ADDITIONAL INFORMATION Conference information available in January. For details, visit website, or e-mail brochure@writetopublish.com. Accepts inquiries by e-mail, fax, and phone.

WRITING AND ILLUSTRATING FOR YOUNG READERS CONFERENCE

1480 E. 9400 S, Sandy UT 84093. **E-mail:** staff@wifyr. com. **Website:** www.wifyr.com. Estab. 2000. Annual workshop. June 2016 dates: June 13-17. Conference duration: 5 days. Average attendance: 100+. Learn how to write, illustrate, and publish in the children's and young adult markets. Beginning and advanced writers and illustrators are tutored in a small-group workshop setting by published authors and artists and receive instruction from and network with editors, major publishing house representatives, and literary agents. Afternoon attendees get to hear practical writing and publishing tips from published authors, literary agents, and editors. Held at the Waterford School in Sandy, Utah. Speakers have included John Cusick, Stephen Fraser, Alyson Heller, and Ruth Katcher.

COSTS Costs available online.

ACCOMMODATIONS A block of rooms are available at the Best Western Cotton Tree Inn in Sandy, UT at a discounted rate. This rate is good as long as there are available rooms.

ADDITIONAL INFORMATION There is an online form to contact this event.

WYOMING WRITERS CONFERENCE

E-mail: president@wyowriters.org. **Website:** wyowriters.org. **Contact:** Chris Williams. This is a statewide writing conference for writers of Wyoming and neighboring states. 2016 conference dates: June 3-5, in Riverton, Wyoming. Each year, multiple published authors, editors, and literary agents are in attendance to meet with writers and take pitches. The location (city) of the conference varies from year to year.

CONTESTS, AWARDS, & GRANTS

JANE ADDAMS CHILDREN'S BOOK AWARDS

Jane Addams Peace Association, 777 United Nations Plaza, Sixth Floor, New York NY 10017. (212)652-8830. **E-mail:** info@janeaddamspeace.org. **Website:** www.janeaddamspeace.org. **Contact:** Heather Palmer, co-chair. The Jane Addams Children's Book Awards are given annually to the children's books published the preceding year that effectively promote the cause of peace, social justice, world community, and the equality of the sexes and all races as well as meeting conventional standards for excellence. Books eligible for this award may be fiction, poetry, or nonfiction. Books may be any length. Entries should be suitable for ages 2-12. See website for specific details on guidelines and required book themes. Deadline: December 31. Judged by a national committee of Women's International League for Peace and Freedom (WILPF) members concerned with children's books and their social values is responsible for making the changes each year.

✪ ALCUIN SOCIETY BOOK DESIGN AWARDS

P.O. Box 3216, Vancouver BC V6B 3X8, Canada. (604)732-5403. **E-mail:** awards@alcuinsociety.com; info@alcuinsociety.com. **Website:** alcuinsociety.com. **Contact:** Leah Gordon. The Alcuin Society Awards for Excellence in Book Design in Canada is the only national competition for book design in Canada. Winners are selected from books designed and published in Canada. Awards are presented annually at appropriate ceremonies held in each year. Winning books are exhibited nationally and internationally at the Tokyo, Frankfurt, and Leipzig Book Fairs, and are Canada's entries in the international competition in Leipzig, "Book Design From All Over the World" in the following spring. Submit previously published material from the year before the award's call for entries. Submissions made by the publisher, author, or designer (Canadian). Deadline: March 1. Prizes: 1st, 2nd, and 3rd in each category (at the discretion of the judges). Judged by professionals and those experienced in the field of book design.

AMERICAS AWARD

Website: http://claspprograms.org/americasaward. **Contact:** Denise Woltering. The Américas Award encourages and commends authors, illustrators, and publishers who produce quality children's and young adult books that portray Latin America, the Caribbean, or Latinos in the United States. Up to 2 awards (for primary and secondary reading levels) are given in recognition of US published works of fiction, poetry, folklore, or selected nonfiction (from picture books to works for young adults). The award winners and commended titles are selected for their (1) distinctive literary quality; (2) cultural contextualization; (3) exceptional integration of text, illustration, and design; and (4) potential for classroom use. To nominate a copyright title from the previous year, publishers are invited to submit review copies to the committee members listed on the website. Publishers should send 8 copies of the nominated book. Deadline: January 4. Prize: $500, plaque and a formal presentation at the Library of Congress, Washington DC.

AMERICA & ME ESSAY CONTEST

Farm Bureau Insurance, P.O. Box 30400, Lansing MI 48909. **E-mail:** lfedewa@fbinsmi.com. **Website:** www.farmbureauinsurance-mi.com. **Contact:** Lisa Fedewa. Focuses on encouraging students to write about their personal Michigan heroes: someone who lives in the state and who has encouraged them, taught them important lessons, and helped them pursue their dreams. Open to Michigan eighth graders. Contest rules and entry form available on website. Encourages Michigan youth to recognize the heroes in their communities and their state. Deadline: November 18. Prize: $1,000, plaque, and medallion for top 10 winners.

AMERICAN ASSOCIATION OF UNIVERSITY WOMEN AWARD IN JUVENILE LITERATURE

4610 Mail Service Center, Raleigh NC 27699-4610. (919)807-7290. **E-mail:** michael.hill@ncdcr.gov. **Website:** www.ncdcr.gov. **Contact:** Michael Hill, awards coordinator. Annual award. Book must be published during the year ending June 30. Submissions made by author, author's agent, or publisher. SASE for contest rules. Author must have maintained either legal residence or actual physical residence, or a combination of both, in the state of North Carolina for 3 years immediately preceding the close of the contest period. Only published work (books) eligible. Recognizes the year's best work of juvenile literature by a North Carolina resident. Deadline: July 15. Prize: Awards a cup to the winner and winner's name inscribed on a plaque displayed within the North Carolina Office of Archives and History. Judged by three-judge panel.
Competition receives 10-15 submissions per category.

HANS CHRISTIAN ANDERSEN AWARD

Nonnenweg 12, Postfach Basel CH-4009, Switzerland. **E-mail:** liz.page@ibby.org, ibby@ibby.org. **Website:** www.ibby.org. **Contact:** Liz Page, director. The Hans Christian Andersen Award, awarded every 2 years by the International Board on Books for Young People (IBBY), is the highest international recognition given

to an author and an illustrator of children's books. The Author's Award has been given since 1956, the Illustrator's Award since 1966. Her Majesty Queen Margrethe II of Denmark is the Patron of the Hans Christian Andersen Awards. The awards are presented at the biennial congresses of IBBY. Awarded to an author and to an illustrator, living at the time of the nomination, who by the outstanding value of their work are judged to have made a lasting contribution to literature for children and young people. The complete works of the author and of the illustrator will be taken into consideration in awarding the medal, which will be accompanied by a diploma. Candidates are nominated by National Sections of IBBY in good standing. Prize: Awards medals according to literary and artistic criteria. Judged by the Hans Christian Andersen Jury.

ATLANTIC WRITING COMPETITION FOR UNPUBLISHED MSS

Writers' Federation of Nova Scotia, 1113 Marginal Rd., Halifax NS B3H 4P7. (902)423-8116. **Fax:** (902)422-0881. **E-mail:** programs@writers.ns.ca. **Website:** www.writers.ns.ca. **Contact:** Robin Spittal, communications and development officer. Annual program designed to honor work by unpublished writers in all 4 Atlantic Provinces. Entry is open to writers unpublished in the category of writing they wish to enter. Prizes are presented in the fall of each year. Categories include: novel, writing for children, poetry, short story, juvenile/young adult novel, creative nonfiction, and play. Judges return written comments when competition is concluded. Page lengths and rules vary based on categories. See website for details. Any resident in the Atlantic Provinces since September 1 immediately prior to the deadline date is eligible to enter. Only one entry per category is allowed. Each entry requires its own entry form and registration fee. Deadline: January 7. Prizes vary based on categories. See website for details.

MARILYN BAILLIE PICTURE BOOK AWARD

The Canadian Children's Book Centre, 40 Orchard View Blvd., Suite 217, Toronto ON M4R 1B9, Canada. (416)975-0010, ext. 222. **Fax:** (416)975-8970. **E-mail:** meghan@bookcentre.ca. **Website:** bookcentre.ca. **Contact:** Meghan Howe. The Marilyn Baillie Picture Book Award honors excellence in the illustrated picture book format. To be eligible, the book must be an original work in English, aimed at children ages 3-8, written and illustrated by Canadians and first published in Canada. Eligible genres include fiction, nonfiction and poetry. Books must be published between January 1 and December 31 of the previous calendar year. New editions or re-issues of previously published books are not eligible for submission. Send 5 copies of title along with a completed submission form. Deadline: mid-December annually. Prize: $20,000.

MILDRED L. BATCHELDER AWARD

Website: www.ala.org/alsc/awardsgrants. The Batchelder Award is given to the most outstanding children's book originally published in a language other than English in a country other than the United States, and subsequently translated into English for publication in the US. Visit website for terms and criteria of award. The purpose of the award, a citation to an American publisher, is to encourage international exchange of quality children's books by recognizing US publishers of such books in translation. Deadline: December 31.

JOHN AND PATRICIA BEATTY AWARD

2471 Flores St., San Mateo CA 94403. (650)376-0886. **Fax:** (650)539-2341. **E-mail:** sarahmae.harper@gmail.com. **Website:** www.cla-net.org. **Contact:** Sarah Mae Harper, award chair. The California Library Association's John and Patricia Beatty Award, sponsored by Baker & Taylor, honors the author of a distinguished book for children or young adults that best promotes an awareness of California and its people. Must be a children's or young adult books published in the previous year, set in California, and highlight California's cultural heritage or future. Send title suggestiosn to the committee members. Deadline: January 31. Prize: $500 and an engraved plaque. Judged by a committee of CLA members, who select the winning title from books published in the United States during the preceding year.

♻ GEOFFREY BILSON AWARD FOR HISTORICAL FICTION FOR YOUNG PEOPLE

The Canadian Children's Book Centre, 40 Orchard View Blvd., Suite 217, Toronto ON M4R 1B9, Canada. (416)975-0010, ext. 222. **Fax:** (416)975-8970. **Website:** bookcentre.ca. **Contact:** Meghan Howe. Awarded annually to reward excellence in the writing of an outstanding work of historical fiction for young

readers, by a Canadian author, published in the previous calendar year. Open to Canadian citizens and residents of Canada for at least 2 years. Books must be published between January 1 and December 31 of the previous year. Books must be first foreign or first Canadian editions. Autobiographies are not eligible. Jury members will consider the following: historical setting and accuracy; strong character and plot development; well-told, original story; and stability of book for its intended age group. Send 5 copies of the title along with a completed submission form. Deadline: mid-December annually. Prize: $5,000.

THE IRMA S. AND JAMES H. BLACK AWARD

Bank Street College of Education, 610 W. 112th St., New York NY 10025-1898. (212)875-4458. **Fax:** (212)875-4558. **E-mail:** kfreda@bankstreet.edu. **Website:** www.bankstreet.edu/center-childrens-literature/irma-black-award. **Contact:** Kristin Freda. Award give to an outstanding book for young children—a book in which text and illustrations are inseparable, each enhancing and enlarging on the other to produce a singular whole. Entries must have been published during the previous calendar year. Publishers submit books. Submit only one copy of each book. Does not accept unpublished mss. Deadline: mid-December. Prize: A scroll with the recipient's name and a gold seal designed by Maurice Sendak. Judged by a committee of older children and children's literature professionals. Final judges are first-, second-, and third-grade classes at a number of cooperating schools.

BOSTON GLOBE-HORN BOOK AWARDS

The Boston Globe, Horn Book, Inc., 300 The Fenway, Palace Road Building, Suite P-311, Boston MA 02115. (617)278-0225. **Fax:** (617)278-6062. **E-mail:** info@hbook.com; khedeen@hbook.com. **Website:** www.hbook.com/boston-globe-horn-book-awards. **Contact:** Katrina Hedeen. Offered annually for excellence in literature for children and young adults (published June 1-May 31). Categories: picture book, fiction and poetry, nonfiction. Judges may also name up to 2 honor books in each category. Books must be published in the US, but may be written or illustrated by citizens of any country. *The Horn Book Magazine* publishes speeches given at awards ceremonies. Guidelines for SASE or online. Submit a book directly to each of the judges. See website for details on submitting, as well as contest guidelines. Deadline: May 15. Prize: $500 and an engraved silver bowl; honor book recipients receive an engraved silver plate. Judged by a panel of 3 judges selected each year.

ANN CONNOR BRIMER BOOK AWARD

(902)490-2742. **Website:** atlanticbookawards.ca. **Contact:** Laura Carter, Atlantic Book Awards Festival Coordinator. In 1990, the Nova Scotia Library Association established the Ann Connor Brimer Award for writers residing in Atlantic Canada who have made an outstanding contribution to writing for Atlantic Candian young people. Author must be alive and residing in Atlantic Canada at time of nomination. Book intended for youth up to the age of 15. Book in print and readily available. Fiction or nonfiction (except textbooks). Book must have been published within the previous year. Prize: $2,000.

BUCKEYE CHILDREN'S BOOK AWARD

Website: www.bcbookaward.info. **Contact:** Christine Watters, president. The Buckeye Childeren's Book Award Program is designed to encourage children to read literature critically, to promote teacher and librarian involvement in children's literature programs, and to commend authors of such literature, as well as to promote the use of libraries. Open to Ohio students. Award offered every year. Students may nominate only books published in the previous 2 years (for paperbacks, check the original hardcover publication date), and the book must be originally published in the United States. A book in a series that has previously won the award is not eligible for nonfiction. Deadline: March 10. Nominations for the following year's contest begins on March 15 and continues year-round.

RANDOLPH CALDECOTT MEDAL

50 E. Huron, Chicago IL 60611-2795. (312)944-7680. **Fax:** (312)440-9374. **E-mail:** alsc@ala.org; lschulte@ala.org. **Website:** www.ala.org. **Contact:** Laura Schulte-Cooper, program officer. The Caldecott Medal was named in honor of 19th-century English illustrator Randolph Caldecott. It is awarded annually by the Association for Library Service to Children, a division of the American Library Association, to the artist of the most distinguished American picture book for children. Illustrator must be a US citizen or resident. Must be published a year preceding award. SASE for award rules. Entries are not returned. Deadline: December 31.

CALIFORNIA YOUNG PLAYWRIGHTS CONTEST

Playwrights Project, 3675 Ruffin Rd., Suite 330, San Diego CA 92123-1870. (858)384-2970. **Fax:** (858)384-2974. **E-mail:** write@playwrightsproject.org. **Website:** www.playwrightsproject.org/programs/contest/. **Contact:** Cecelia Kouma, Executive director. Annual contest open to Californians under age 19. "Our organization and the contest is designed to nurture promising young writers. We hope to develop playwrights and audiences for live theater. We also teach playwriting." Submissions are required to be unpublished and not produced professionally. Submissions made by the author. SASE for contest rules and entry form. Scripts must be a minimum of 10 standard typewritten pages; send 2 copies. Scripts will *not* be returned. If requested, entrants receive detailed evaluation letter. Guidelines available online. Deadline: June 1. Prize: Scripts will be produced in spring at a professional theatre in San Diego. Judged by professionals in the theater community; changes somewhat each year.

CANADIAN TALES SHORT STORY WRITING CONTEST

Red Tuque Books, Unit #6, 477 Martin St., Penticton BC V2A 5L2, Canada. (778)476-5750. **Fax:** (778)476-5750. **E-mail:** dave@redtuquebooks.ca. **Website:** www.redtuquebooks.ca. **Contact:** David Korinetz, contest director. Offered annually for unpublished works. Check the guidelines on the website. Purpose of award is to promote Canada and Canadian publishing. Stories require a Canadian element. There are three ways to qualify: story can be written by a Canadian, written about Canadians, or take place somewhere in Canada. Deadline: December 31. Prize: first place: $500; second place: $150; third place: $100; and 10 prizes of $25 will be given to honorable mentions. All 13 winners will be published in an anthology. They will each receive a complimentary copy. Judged by Canadian authors/publishers in the appropriate genre. Acquires first print rights. Contest open to anyone. This contest switches genre every 3 years. 2016 is for fantasy and science fiction, 2017 is for mystery and horror, and 2018 is for romance, humor, and inspirational.

CASCADE WRITING CONTEST & AWARDS

Oregon Christian Writers, 1075 Willow Lake Rd. N., Keizer OR 97303. **E-mail:** cascade@oregonchristianwriters.org. **Website:** oregonchristianwriters. org. **Contact:** Marilyn Rhoads and Julie McDonald Zander. Annual multi-genre competition to encourage both published and emerging writers in the field of Christian writing. The Cascade Awards are presented at the annual Oregon Christian Writers Summer Conference (held at the Red Lion on the River in Portland, Oregon, each August) attended by national editors, agents, and professional authors. The contest is open for both published and unpublished works in the following categories: contemporary fiction book, historical fiction book, speculative fiction book, nonfiction book, memoir book, young adult/middle-grade fiction book, young adult/middle-grade nonfiction book, children's chapter book and picture book (fiction and nonfiction), poetry, devotional, article, column, story, or blog post. Two additional special Cascade Awards are presented each year: the Trailblazer Award, to a writer who has distinguished him/herself in the field of Christian writing; and a Writer of Promise Award, for a writer who demonstrates unusual promise in the field of Christian writing. For a full list of categories, guidelines, entry rules, and scoring elements, visit website. Entry forms will be available on the first day for entry. Deadline: March 31. Submissions period begins February 14. Prize: Award certificate and pin presented at the Cascade Awards ceremony during the Oregon Christian Writers Annual Summer Conference. Finalists are listed in the conference notebook and winners are listed online. Cascade Trophies are awarded to the recipients of the Trailblazer and Writer of Promise Awards. Judged by published authors, editors, librarians, and retail book store owners and employees. Final judging by editors, agents, and published authors from the Christian publishing industry.

CHILDREN'S AFRICANA BOOK AWARD

Outreach Council of the African Studies Association, c/o Rutgers University-Livingston Campus, 54 Joyce Kilmer Ave., Piscataway NJ 08854. (703)549-8208; (301)585-9136. **E-mail:** africaaccess@aol.com, harriet@africaaccessreview.org. **Website:** www.africaaccessreview.org. **Contact:** Brenda Randolph, chairperson. The Children's Africana Book Awards are presented annually to the authors and illustrators of the best books on Africa for children and young people published or distributed in the US. The awards were created by the Outreach Council of the African

Studies Association (ASA) to dispel stereotypes and encourage the publication and use of accurate, balanced children's materials about Africa. The awards are presented in 2 categories: Young Children and Older Readers. Entries must have been published in the calendar year previous to the award. Work submitted for awards must be suitable for children ages 4-18; a significant portion of books' content must be about Africa; must by copyrighted in the calendar year prior to award year; must be published or distributed in the US. Deadline: January 31 of the award year. Judged by African Studies and Children's Literature scholars. Nominated titles are read by committee members and reviewed by external African Studies scholars with specialized academic training.

CHILDREN'S BOOK GUILD AWARD FOR NONFICTION

E-mail: theguild@childrensbookguild.org. **Website:** www.childrensbookguild.org. Annual award. "One doesn't enter. One is selected. Our jury annually selects one author for the award." Honors an author or illustrator whose total work has contributed significantly to the quality of nonfiction for children. Prize: Cash and an engraved crystal paperweight. Judged by a jury of Children's Book Guild specialists, authors, and illustrators.

⟳ CHILDREN'S LITERATURE AWARD

Saskatchewan Book Awards, Inc., Box 20025, Regina SK S4P 4J7, Canada. (306)569-1585. **Fax:** (306)569-4187. **E-mail:** director@bookawards.sk.ca, info@bookawards.sk.ca. **Website:** www.bookawards.sk.ca. **Contact:** Courtney Bates-Hardy, executive director. Offered biennially. This award is presented to a Saskatchewan author or pair of authors, or to Saskatchewan author and a Saskatchewan illustrator, for the best book of children's literature, for ages 0-11, judged on the quality of the writing and illustration. Deadline: November 1. Prize: $2,000 (CAD).

CHRISTIAN BOOK AWARDS

Evangelical Christian Publishers Association, 9633 S. 48th St., Suite 140, Phoenix AZ 85044. (480)966-3998. **Fax:** (480)966-1944. **E-mail:** info@ecpa.org. **Website:** www.ecpa.org. **Contact:** Stan Jantz, ED. The Evangelical Christian Publishers Association (ECPA) recognizes quality and encourages excellence by presenting the ECPA Christian Book Awards® (formerly known as Gold Medallion) each year. Categories include fiction, nonfiction, children, inspiration, bibles, bible reference, and new author. All entries must be evangelical in nature and submitted through an ECPA member publisher. Books must have been published in the calendar year prior to the award. Publishing companies submitting entries must be ECPA members in good standing. See website for details. The Christian Book Awards® recognize the highest quality in Christian books and is among the oldest and most prestigious awards program in Christian publishing. Deadline: September 30. Submission period begins September 1. Judged by ECPA members, who are experts, authors, and retailers with years of experience in their field.

○   Book entries are submitted by ECPA member publishers according to criteria including date of publication and category.

○   CITY OF VANCOUVER BOOK AWARD

Cultural Services Dept., Woodward's Heritage Building, 111 W. Hastings St., Suite 501, Vancouver BC V6B 1H4, Canada. (604)829-2007. **Fax:** (604)871-6005. **E-mail:** marnie.rice@vancouver.ca; culture@vancouver.ca. **Website:** https://vancouver.ca/people-programs/city-of-vancouver-book-award.aspx. The annual City of Vancouver Book Award recognizes authors of excellence of any genre who contribute to the appreciation and understanding of Vancouver's history, unique character, or the achievements of its residents. The book must exhibit excellence in one or more of the following areas: content, illustration, design, format. The book must not be copyrighted prior to the previous year. Submit 4 copies of book. See website for details and guidelines. Deadline: May 18. Prize: $3,000. Judged by an independent jury.

○   CLA YOUNG ADULT BOOK AWARD

1150 Morrison Dr., Suite 400, Ottawa ON K2H 8S9, Canada. (613)232-9625. **Fax:** (613)563-9895. **E-mail:** cshea@cbvrsb.ca. **Website:** cla.ca. **Contact:** Carmelita Cechetto-Shea, chair. This award recognizes an author of an outstanding English language Canadian book that appeals to young adults between the ages of 13–18. To be eligible for consideration, the following must apply: it must be a work of fiction (novel, collection of short stories, or graphic novel), the title must be a Canadian publication in either hardcover or paperback, and the author must be a Canadian citizen or landed immigrant. The award is given annually, when

merited, at the Canadian Library Association's annual conference. Deadline: December 31. Prize: $1,000.

COLORADO BOOK AWARDS

(303)894-7951. **Fax:** (303)864-9361. **E-mail:** lansdown@coloradohumanities.org. **Website:** www.coloradohumanities.org. **Contact:** Marnie Lansdown. An annual program that celebrates the accomplishments of Colorado's outstanding authors, editors, illustrators, and photographers. Awards are presented in at least 10 categories including anthology/collection, biography, children's, creative nonfiction, fiction, history, nonfiction, pictorial, poetry, and young adult. To be eligible for a Colorado Book Award, a primary contributor to the book must be a Colorado writer, editor, illustrator, or photographer. Current Colorado residents are eligible, as are individuals engaged in ongoing literary work in the state and authors whose personal history, identity, or literary work reflect a strong Colorado influence. Authors not currently Colorado residents who feel their work is inspired by or connected to Colorado should submit a letter with his/her entry describing the connection. Deadline: January 8.

CRICKET LEAGUE

P.O. Box 300, Peru IL 61354. **E-mail:** cricket@cricketmedia.com. **Website:** www.cricketmagkids.com. Cricket League contests encourage creativity and give young people an opportunity to express themselves in writing, drawing, painting, or photography. There is a contest in each issue. Possible categories include story, poetry, art, or photography. Each contest relates to a specific theme described on each *Cricket* issue's Cricket League page and on the website. Signature verifying originality, age, and address of entrant and permission to publish required. Entries that do not relate to the current month's theme cannot be considered. Unpublished submissions only. Cricket League rules, contest theme, and submission deadline information can be found in the current issue of *Cricket* and via website. Deadline: The 25th of each month. Prize: Certificates. Judged by *Cricket* editors.

CWW ANNUAL WISCONSIN WRITERS AWARDS

Council for Wisconsin Writers, 6973 Heron Way, De Forest WI 53532. **E-mail:** karlahuston@gmail.com. **Website:** wiswriters.org/awards. **Contact:** Geoff Gilpin, president and annual awards co-chair; Karla Huston, secretary and annual awards co-chair; Jennifer

Morales, annual awards co-chair; Edward Schultz, annual awards co-chair. Offered annually for work published by Wisconsin writers during the previous calendar year. Nine awards: Major Achievement (presented in alternate years); short fiction; short nonfiction; nonfiction book; poetry book; fiction book; children's literature; Lorine Niedecker Poetry Award; Christopher Latham Sholes Award for Outstanding Service to Wisconsin Writers (presented in alternate years); Essay Award for Young Writers. Open to Wisconsin residents. Entries may be submitted via postal mail only. See website for guidelines and entry forms. Deadline: February 1. Submissions open on November 1. Prizes: First place: $500. Honorable mentions: $50.

MARGARET A. EDWARDS AWARD

50 East Huron St., Chicago IL 60611-2795. (312)280-4390. **Fax:** (312)280-5276. **E-mail:** yalsa@ala.org. **Website:** www.ala.org/yalsa/edwards. **Contact:** Nichole O'Connor. Annual award administered by the Young Adult Library Services Association (YALSA) of the American Library Association (ALA) and sponsored by *School Library Journal* magazine. Awarded to an author whose book or books, over a period of time, have been accepted by young adults as an authentic voice that continues to illuminate their experiences and emotions, giving insight into their lives. The book or books should enable them to understand themselves, the world in which they live, and their relationship with others and with society. The book or books must be in print at the time of the nomination. Submissions must be previously published no less than 5 years prior to the first meeting of the current Margaret A. Edwards Award Committee at Midwinter Meeting. Nomination form is available on the YALSA website. Deadline: December 1. Prize: $2,000. Judged by members of YALSA.

SHUBERT FENDRICH MEMORIAL PLAYWRITING CONTEST

Pioneer Drama Service, Inc., P.O. Box 4267, Englewood CO 80155. (303)779-4035. **Fax:** (303)779-4315. **E-mail:** editors@pioneerdrama.com, submissions@pioneerdrama.com. **Website:** www.pioneerdrama.com. **Contact:** Lori Conary, submissions editor. Annual competition that encourages the development of quality theatrical material for educational, community, and children's theatre markets. Previously unpublished submissions only. Considers only mss

with a running time between 20-90 minutes. Open to all writers not currently published by Pioneer Drama Service. Guidelines available online. No entry fee. Cover letter, SASE for return of ms, and proof of production or staged reading must accompany all submissions. Deadline: Ongoing contest; a winner is selected by June 1 each year from all submissions received the previous year. Prize: $1,000 royalty advance in addition to publication. Judged by editors.

DOROTHY CANFIELD FISHER CHILDREN'S BOOK AWARD

Midstate Library Service Center, 578 Paine Tunrpike. N., Berlin VT 05602. (802)828-6954. **E-mail:** grace.greene@state.vt.us. **Website:** www.dcfaward.org. **Contact:** Mary Linney, chair. Annual award to encourage Vermont children to become enthusiastic and discriminating readers by providing them with books of good quality by living American or Canadian authors published in the current year. E-mail for entry rules. Titles must be original work, published in the US, and be appropriate to children in grades 4-8. The book must be copyrighted in the current year. It must be written by an American author living in the US or Canada, or a Canadian author living in Canada or the US. Deadline: December of year book was published. Prize: Awards a scroll presented to the winning author at an award ceremony. Judged by children, grades 4-8, who vote for their favorite book.

☼ THE NORMA FLECK AWARD FOR CANADIAN CHILDREN'S NONFICTION

The Canadian Children's Book Centre, 40 Orchard View Blvd., Suite 217, Toronto ON M4R 1B9, Canada. (416)975-0010 ext. 222. **Fax:** (416)975-8970. **E-mail:** meghan@bookcentre.ca. **Website:** bookcentre.ca. **Contact:** Meghan Howe. The Norma Fleck Award was established by the Fleck Family Foundation to recognize and raise the profile of exceptional nonfiction books for children. Offered annually for books published between January 1 and December 31 of the previous calendar year. Open to Canadian citizens or landed immigrants. Books must be first foreign or first Canadian editions. Nonfiction books in the following categories are eligible: culture and the arts, science, biography, history, geography, reference, sports, activities, and pastimes. Deadline: mid-December annually. Prize: $10,000. The award will go to the author unless 40 percent or more of the text area is composed of original illustrations, in which case the award will be divided equally between author and illustrator.

FLICKER TALE CHILDREN'S BOOK AWARD

Morton Mandan Public Library, 609 W. Main St., Mandan ND 58554. **E-mail:** laustin@cdln.info. **Website:** ndla.info/flickertale. **Contact:** Linda Austin. Award gives children across the state of North Dakota a chance to vote for their book of choice from a nominated list of 16: 4 in the picture book category, 4 in the intermediate category, 4 in the juvenile category (for more advanced readers), and 4 in the upper-grade level nonfiction category. Also promotes awareness of quality literature for children. Previously published submissions only. Submissions nominated by librarians and teachers across the state of North Dakota. Deadline: April 1. Prize: A plaque from North Dakota Library Association and banquet dinner. Judged by children in North Dakota.

DON FREEMAN ILLUSTRATOR GRANTS

4727 Wilshire Blvd., Suite 301, Los Angeles CA 90010. (323)782-1010. **Fax:** (323)782-1892. **E-mail:** grants@scbwi.org; sarahbaker@scbwi.org. **Website:** www.scbwi.org. **Contact:** Sarah Baker. The grant-in-aid is available to both full and associate members of the SCBWI who, as artists, seriously intend to make picture books their chief contribution to the field of children's literature. Applications and prepared materials are available in October. Grant awarded and announced in August. SASE for award rules and entry forms. SASE for return of entries. Enables picture book artists to further their understanding, training, and work in the picture book genre. Deadline: March 31. Submission period begins March 1. Prize: Two grants of $1,000 each awarded annually. One grant to a published illustrator and one to a pre-published illustrator.

THEODOR SEUSS GEISEL AWARD

Association for Library Service to Children, Division of the American Library Association, 50 E. Huron, Chicago IL 60611. (800)545-2433. **E-mail:** alscawards@ala.org. **Website:** www.ala.org. The Theodor Seuss Geisel Award is given annually to the author(s) and illustrator(s) of the most distinguished American book for beginning readers published in English in the United States during the preceding year. The award is to recognize the author(s) and illustrator(s) who demonstrate great creativity and imagination in

his/her/their literary and artistic achievements to engage children in reading. Terms and criteria for the award are listed on the website. Entry will not be returned. Deadline: December 31. Prize: Medal given at awards ceremony during the ALA Annual Conference.

GOLDEN KITE AWARDS

Society of Children's Book Writers and Illustrators, SCBWI Golden Kite Awards, 8271 Beverly Blvd., Los Angeles CA 90048-4515. (323)782-1010. **Fax:** (323)782-1892. **E-mail:** sararutenberg@scbwi.org. **Website:** www.scbwi.org. Given annually to recognize excellence in children's literature in 4 categories: fiction, nonfiction, picture book text, and picture book illustration. Books submitted must be published in the previous calendar year. Both individuals and publishers may submit. Submit 4 copies of book. Submit to one category only, except in the case of picture books. Must be a current member of the SCBWI. Deadline: December 1. Prize: One Golden Kite Award Winner and one Honor Book will be chosen per category. Winners and honorees will receive a commemorative poster also sent to publishers, bookstores, libraries, and schools; a press release; an announcement on the SCBWI website and SCBWI Social Networks.

✪ GOVERNOR GENERAL'S LITERARY AWARDS

Canada Council for the Arts, 150 Elgin St., P.O. Box 1047, Ottawa ON K1P 5V8, Canada. (800)263-5588, ext. 5573. **Website:** canadacouncil.ca. The Canada Council for the Arts provides a wide range of grants and services to professional Canadian artists and art organizations in dance, media arts, music, theatre, writing, publishing, and the visual arts. Books must be first-edition literary trade books written, translated, or illustrated by Canadian citizens or permanent residents of Canada, and published in Canada or abroad in the previous year. In the case of translation, the original work must also be a Canadian-authored title. For complete eligibility criteria, deadlines, and submission procedures, please visit the website. The Governor General's Literary Awards are given annually for the best English-language and French-language work in each of 7 categories, including fiction, nonfiction, poetry, drama, children's literature (text), children's literature (illustrated books), and translation. Deadline: Depends on the book's publication date. See website for details. Prize: Each GG winner receives $25,000. Non-winning finalists receive $1,000. Publishers of the winning titles receive a $3,000 grant for promotional purposes. Evaluated by fellow authors, translators, and illustrators. For each category, a jury makes the final selection.

GUGGENHEIM FELLOWSHIPS

John Simon Guggenheim Memorial Foundation, 90 Park Ave., New York NY 10016. (212)687-4470. **E-mail:** fellowships@gf.org. **Website:** www.gf.org. Often characterized as "midcareer" awards, Guggenheim Fellowships are intended for men and women who have already demonstrated exceptional capacity for productive scholarship or exceptional creative ability in the arts. Fellowships are awarded through two annual competitions: one open to citizens and permanent residents of the United States and Canada, and the other open to citizens and permanent residents of Latin America and the Caribbean. Candidates must apply to the Guggenheim Foundation in order to be considered in either of these competitions. The Foundation receives between 3,500 and 4,000 applications each year. Although no one who applies is guaranteed success in the competition, there is no prescreening; all applications are reviewed. Approximately 200 Fellowships are awarded each year. Deadline: September 15.

HACKNEY LITERARY AWARDS

4650 Old Looney Mill Rd., Birmingham AL 35243. **E-mail:** info@hackneyliteraryawards.org. **Website:** hackneyliteraryawards.org. **Contact:** Myra Crawford, PhD, executive director. Offered annually for unpublished novels, short stories (maximum 5,000 words), and poetry (50 line limit). Guidelines on website. Deadline: September 30 (novels), November 30 (short stories and poetry). Prize: $5,000 in annual prizes for poetry and short fiction ($2,500 national and $2,500 state level). First place: $600; second place: $400; third Place: $250; plus $5,000 for an unpublished novel. Competition winners will be announced on the website each March.

COMPETITION FOR YOUTH THEATRE

P.O. Box 148, Beverly Hills CA 90213. **Website:** www.beverlyhillstheatreguild.com. **Contact:** Candace Coster, competition coordinator. The competition (Marilyn Hall Awards) consist sof 2 monetary prizes for plays suitable for grades 6-8 (middle school) or for plays suitable for grades 9-12 (high school). The 2 prizes will be awarded on the merits of the play scripts, which includes its suitability for the intended audience. The plays should be approximately 45-75 minutes. There is no production connected to any of the prizes, though a staged reading is optional at the discretion of the Beverly Hills Theatre Guild. Unpublished submissions only. Authors must be US citizens or legal residents and must sign entry form personally. Deadline: The last day of February. Submission period begins January 15. Prize: 1st prize: $700; 2nd prize: $300.

AURAND HARRIS MEMORIAL PLAYWRITING AWARD

The New England Theatre Conference, Inc., 215 Knob Hill Dr., Hamden CT 06518. **Fax:** (203)288-5938. **E-mail:** mail@netconline.org. **Website:** www.netconline.org. Offered annually for an unpublished full-length play for young audiences. Guidelines available online or for SASE. Open to all. Deadline: May 1. Prize: 1st place: $1,000; 2nd place: $500

HIGHLIGHTS FOR CHILDREN FICTION CONTEST

803 Church St., Honesdale PA 18431-1824. (570)253-1080. **Fax:** (570)251-7847. **E-mail:** eds@highlights-corp.com. **Website:** www.highlights.com. **Contact:** Christine French Cully, editor in chief. Unpublished submissions only. Open to any writer 16 years of age or older. Winners announced in May. Length up to 800 words. Stories for beginning readers should not exceed 500 words. Stories should be consistent with Highlights' editorial requirements. No violence, crime, or derogatory humor. Send SASE or visit website for guidelines and current theme. Stimulates interest in writing for children and rewards and recognizes excellence. Deadline: January 31. Submission period begins January 1. Prize: Three prizes of $1,000 or tuition for any Highlights Foundation Founders Workshop.

ERIC HOFFER BOOK AWARD

Hopewell Publications, LLC, P.O. Box 11, Titusville NJ 08560-0011. **Fax:** (609)964-1718. **E-mail:** info@hopepubs.com. **Website:** www.hofferaward.com. **Contact:** Christopher Klim, chair. Annual contest for previously published books. Recognizes excellence in independent publishing in many unique categories: art (titles capture the experience, execution, or demonstration of the arts); poetry (all styles); general fiction (nongenre-specific fiction); commercial fiction (genre-specific fiction); children (titles for young children); young adult (titles aimed at the juvenile and teen markets); culture (titles demonstrating the human or world experience); memoir (titles relating to personal experience); business (titles with application to today's business environment and emerging trends); reference (titles from traditional and emerging reference areas); home (titles with practical applications to home or home-related issues, including family); health (titles promoting physical, mental, and emotional well-being); self-help (titles involving new and emerging topics in self-help); spiritual (titles involving the mind and spirit, including relgion); legacy (titles over 2 years of age that hold particular relevance to any subject matter or form). Open to any writer of published work within the past 2 years, including categores for older books. This contest recognizes excellence in independent publishing in many unique categories. Also awards the Montaigne Medal for most thought-provoking book, the Da Vinci Eye for best cover, and the First Horizon Award for best new authors. Results published in the *US Review of Books*. Deadline: January 21. Prize: $2,000.

MARILYN HOLLINSHEAD VISITING SCHOLARS FELLOWSHIP

University of Minnesota, 113 Anderson Library, 222 21st Ave. S, Minneapolis MN 55455. **Website:** www.lib.umn.edu/clrc/awards-grants-and-fellowships. Marilyn Hollinshead Visiting Scholars Fund for Travel to the Kerlan Collection is available for research study. Applicants may request up to $1,500. Send a letter with the proposed purpose and plan to use specific research materials (mss and art), dates, and budget (including airfare and per diem). Travel and a written report on the project must be completed and submitted in the previous year. Deadline: June 1.

⊘ AMELIA FRANCES HOWARD-GIBBON ILLUSTRATOR'S AWARD

1150 Morrison Drive, Suite 400, Ottawa ON K 2H859, Canada. (613)232-9625. **Fax:** (613)563-9895. **Website:** cla.ca. **Contact:** Diana Cauthier. Annually awarded to an outstanding illustrator of a children's book published in Canada during the previous calendar year. The award is bestowed upon books that are suitable for children up to and including age 12. To be eligible for the award, an illustrator must be a Canadian citizen or a permanent resident of Canada, and the text of the book must be worthy of the book's illustrations. Deadline: November 30. Prize: A plaque and a check for $1,000 (CAD).

JULIA WARD HOWE AWARD

Boston Authors Club, 36 Sunhill Lane, Newton Center MA 02459. **E-mail:** bostonauthors@aol.com. **Website:** bostonauthorsclub.org. **Contact:** Alan Lawson. This annual award honors Julia Ward Howe and her literary friends who founded the Boston Authors Club in 1900. It also honors the membership over 110 years, consisting of novelists, biographers, historians, governors, senators, philosophers, poets, playwrights, and other luminaries. There are 2 categories: trade books and books for young readers (beginning with chapter books through young adult books). Authors must live or have lived (college counts) within a 100-mile radius of Boston within the past 5 years. Subsidized books, cookbooks, and picture books are not eligible. Deadline: January 15. Prize: $1,000. Judged by the members.

CAROL OTIS HURST CHILDREN'S BOOK PRIZE

Westfield Athenaeum, 6 Elm St., Westfield MA 01085. (413)568-7833. **Fax:** (413)568-0988. **Website:** www.westath.org. **Contact:** Pamela Weingart. The Carol Otis Hurst Children's Book Prize honors outstanding works of fiction and nonfiction, including biography and memoir, written for children and young adults through the age of 18 that exemplify the highest standards of research, analysis, and authorship in their portrayal of the New England Experience. The prize will be presented annually to an author whose book treats the region's history as broadly conceived to encompass one or more of the following elements: political experience, social development, fine and performing artistic expression, domestic life and arts, transportation and communication, changing technology, military experience at home and abroad, schooling, business and manufacturing, workers and the labor movement, agriculture and its transformation, racial and ethnic diversity, religious life and institutions, immigration and adjustment, sports at all levels, and the evolution of popular entertainment. The public presentation of the prize will be accompanied by a reading and/or talk by the recipient at a mutually agreed upon time during the spring immediately following the publication year. Books must have been copyrighted in their original format during the calendar year, January 1 to December 31, of the year preceding the year in which the prize is awarded. Any individual, publisher, or organization may nominate a book. See website for details and guidelines. Deadline: December 31. Prize: $500.

INSIGHT WRITING CONTEST

Insight Magazine, 55 W. Oak Ridge Dr., Hagerstown MD 21740-7390. **Fax:** (301)393-4055. **E-mail:** insight@rhpa.org. **Website:** www.insightmagazine.org. **Contact:** Omar Miranda, editor. Annual contest for writers in the categories of student short story, general short story, and student poetry. Unpublished submissions only. General category is open to all writers; student categories must be age 22 and younger. Deadline: July 31. Prizes: Student Short and General Short Story: 1st place: $250; 2nd place: $200; 3rd place: $150. Student poetry: 1st place: $100; 2nd place: $75; 3rd place: $50.

INTERNATIONAL LITERACY ASSOCIATION CHILDREN'S AND YOUNG ADULT'S BOOK AWARDS

P.O. Box 8139, 800 Barksdale Rd., Newark DE 19714-8139. (302)731-1600, ext. 221. **E-mail:** kbaughman@reading.org, committees@reading.org. **Website:** www.literacyworldwide.org. **Contact:** Kathy Baughman. The ILA Children's and Young Adults' Book Awards are intended for newly published authors who show unusual promise in the children's and young adults' book field. Awards are given for fiction and nonfiction in each of three categories: primary, intermediate, and young adult. Books from all countries and published in English for the first time during the previous calendar year will be considered. See website for eligibility and criteria information. Entry should be the author's first or second book. Deadline: January 15. Prize: $1,000.

✪ THE IODE JEAN THROOP BOOK AWARD

The Lillian H. Smith Children's Library, 239 College St., 4th St., Toronto ON M5T 1R5, Canada. (905)522-9537. **E-mail:** mcscott@torontopubliclibrary.ca; iodeontario@bellnet.ca. **Website:** www.iodeontario. ca. **Contact:** Martha Scott. Each year, the Municipal Chapter of Toronto IODE presents an award intended to encourage the publication of books for children between the ages of 6-12 years. The award-winner must be a Canadian citizen, resident in Toronto or the sur-

rounding area, and the book must be published in Canada. Deadline: December 31. Prize: Award and cash prize of $2,000. Judged by a selected committee.

ILA SHORT STORY AWARD

International Literacy Association, 800 Barksdale Rd., P.O. Box 8139, Newark DE 19714-8139. (302)731-1600. **Fax:** (302)731-1057. **E-mail:** committees@reading.org. **Website:** www.literacyworldwide.org. Offered to reward author of an original short story published for the first time in a periodical for children. (Periodicals should generally be aimed at readers around age 12.) Write for guidelines or download from website. Award is non-monetary. Both fiction and nonfiction stories are eligible; each will be rated according to the characteristics that are appropriate for the genre. The story should: create a believable world for the readers, be truthful and authentic in its presentation of information, serve as a reading and literary standard by which readers can measure other writing, and encourage young readers by providing them with an enjoyable reading experience. Deadline: November 15.

JEFFERSON CUP AWARDS

P.O. Box 56312, Virginia Beach VA 23456. (757)689-0594. **Website:** www.vla.org. **Contact:** Susan M. Catlett, current chairperson. The Jefferson Cup honors a distinguished biography, historical fiction, or American history book for young people. The Jefferson Cup Committee's goal is to promote reading about America's past; to encourage the quality writing of United States history, biography, and historical fiction for young people; and to recognize authors in these disciplines. Deadline: January 31.

EZRA JACK KEATS/KERLAN MEMORIAL FELLOWSHIP

University of Minnesota Libraries, 113 Elmer L. Andersen Library, 222 21st Ave. S, Minneapolis MN 55455. **E-mail:** asc-clrc@umn.edu. **Website:** www.lib. umn.edu/clrc/awards-grants-and-fellowships. This fellowship from the Ezra Jack Keats Foundation will provide $1,500 to a talented writer and/or illustrator of children's books who wishes to use the Kerlan Collection for the furtherance of his or her artistic development. Special consideration will be given to someone who would find it difficult to finance a visit to the Kerlan Collection. The Ezra Jack Keats Fellowship recipient will receive transportation costs and a per diem allotment. See website for application deadline and for digital application materials. Winner will be notified in February. Study and written report must be completed within the calendar year. Deadline: January 30.

EZRA JACK KEATS NEW WRITER AND NEW ILLUSTRATOR AWARDS

450 14th St., Brooklyn NY 11215-5702. **E-mail:** foundation@ezra-jack-keats.org. **Website:** www.ezra-jack-keats.org. Annual award to recognize and encourage new authors and illustrators starting out in the field of children's books. Many past winners of the Ezra Jack Keats Book Award have gone on to distinguished careers, creating books beloved by parents, children, librarians, and teachers around the world. Writers and illustrators must have had no more than 3 books previously published. Prize: $1,000 honorarium for each winner. Judged by a distinguished selection committee of early childhood education specialists, librarians, illustrators, and experts in children's literature.

THE KENTUCKY BLUEGRASS AWARD

Northern Kentucky University, 405 Steely Library, Nunn Drive, Highland Heights KY 41099. (859)572-6620. **E-mail:** smithjen@nku.edu. **Website:** kba.nku.edu. The Kentucky Bluegrass Award is a student choice program. The KBA promotes and encourages Kentucky students in kindergarten through grade 12 to read a variety of quality literature. Each year, a KBA committee for each grade category chooses the books for the four master lists (K-2, 3-5, 6-8, and 9-12). All Kentucky public and private schools, as well as public libraries, are welcome to participate in the program. To nominate a book, see the website for form and details. Deadline: March 1. Judged by students who read books and choose their favorite.

THE CORETTA SCOTT KING BOOK AWARDS

50 E. Huron St., Chicago IL 60611-2795. (800)545-2433. **E-mail:** olos@ala.org. **Website:** www.ala.org/csk. **Contact:** Office for Diversity, Literacy and Outreach Services. The Coretta Scott King Book Awards are given annually to outstanding African American authors and illustrators of books for children and young adults that demonstrate an appreciation of African American culture and universal human values. The award commemorates the life and work of Dr. Martin Luther King, Jr., and honors his wife, Mrs. Coretta Scott King, for her courage and determination to continue the work for peace and world brotherhood. Must be written for a youth audience in one of three categories: preschool-4th grade; 5th-8th grade; or 9th-12th grade. Book must be published in the year preceding the year the award is given, evidenced by the copyright date in the book. See website for full details, criteria, and eligibility concerns. Purpose is to encourage the artistic expression of the African American experience via literature and the graphic arts, including biographical, historical, and social history treatments by African American authors and illustrators. Deadline: December 1. Judged by The Coretta Scott King Book Awards Committee.

THE STEPHEN LEACOCK MEDAL FOR HUMOUR

149 Peter St. N., Orillia ON L3V 4Z4, Canada. (705)326-9286. **E-mail:** bettewalkerca@gmail.com. **Website:** leacock.ca. **Contact:** Bette Walker, award committee, Stephen Leacock Associates. The Leacock Associates awards the prestigious Leacock Medal for the best book of literary humor written by a Canadian and published in the current year. The winning author receives a cash prize of $15,000 thanks to the generous support of the TD Financial Group. 2 runners-up are each awarded a cash prize of $1,500. Entry fee: $200. Deadline: December 31.

LEAGUE OF UTAH WRITERS CONTEST

The League of Utah Writers, P.O. Box 64, Lewiston UT 84320. (435)755-7609. **E-mail:** luwcontest@gmail.com; luwriters@gmail.com. **Website:** luwriters.org. Open to any writer, the LUW Contest provides authors an opportunity to get their work read and critiqued. Multiple categories are offered; see website for details. Entries must be the original and unpublished work of the author. Winners are announced at the Annual Writers Round-Up in September. Those not present will be notified by e-mail. Deadline: June 15. Submissions period begins March 15. Prize: Cash prizes are awarded. Judged by professional authors and editors from outside the League.

MARSH AWARD FOR CHILDREN'S LITERATURE IN TRANSLATION

The English-Speaking Union, Dartmouth House, 37 Charles St., London England W1J 5ED, United Kingdom. 020 7529 1590. **E-mail:** emma.coffey@esu.org. **Website:** www.marshchristiantrust.org; www.esu.org. **Contact:** Emma Coffey, education officer. The Marsh

Award for Children's Literature in Translation, awarded biennially, was founded to celebrate the best translation of a children's book from a foreign language into English and published in the UK. It aims to spotlight the high quality and diversity of translated fiction for young readers. The Award is administered by the ESU on behalf of the Marsh Christian Trust. Submissions will be accepted from publishers for books produced for readers from 5-16 years of age. Guidelines and eligibility criteria available online.

MCKNIGHT ARTIST FELLOWSHIPS FOR WRITERS, LOFT AWARD(S) IN CHILDREN'S LITERATURE/CREATIVE PROSE/POETRY

The Loft Literary Center, 1011 Washington Ave. S., Suite 200, Open Book, Minneapolis MN 55415. (612)215-2575. **Fax:** (612)215-2576. **E-mail:** loft@loft.org. **Website:** www.loft.org. **Contact:** Bao Phi. "The Loft administers the McKnight Artists Fellowships for Writers. Five $25,000 awards are presented annually to accomplished Minnesota writers and spoken word artists. Four awards alternate annually between creative prose (fiction and creative nonfiction) and poetry/spoken word. The fifth award is presented in children's literature and alternates annually for writing for ages 8 and under and writing for children older than 8." The awards provide the writers the opportunity to focus on their craft for the course of the fellowship year. Prize: $25,000.

MCLAREN MEMORIAL COMEDY PLAYWRITING COMPETITION

Midland Community Theatre, 2000 W. Wadley, Midland TX 79705. (432)682-2544. **Fax:** (432)682-6136. **Website:** mctmidland.org. **Contact:** McLaren Chair. The McLaren Memorial Comedy Playwriting Competition was established to honor long-time MCT volunteer Mike McLaren who loved a good comedy, whether he was on stage or in the front row. Open to students. Annual contest. Unpublished submissions only. Submissions made by author. Rights to winning material acquired or purchased. First right of production or refusal is acquired by MCT. The contest is open to any playwright, but the play submitted must be unpublished and never produced in a for-profit setting. One previous production in a nonprofit theatre is acceptable. "Readings" do not count as productions. Deadline: January 31. Prize: $400. Judged by the audience present at the McLaren Festival when the staged readings are performed.

Full-length scripts only; no musicals or children's plays. Seeking comedies suitable for community theatre.

VICKY METCALF AWARD FOR LITERATURE FOR YOUNG PEOPLE

The Writers' Trust of Canada, 460 Richmond St. W., Suite 600, Toronto ON M5V 1Y1, Canada. (416)504-8222. **E-mail:** info@writerstrust.com. **Website:** www.writerstrust.com. **Contact:** Amanda Hopkins. The Vicky Metcalf Award is presented to a Canadian writer for a body of work in children's literature at The Writers' Trust Awards event held in Toronto each fall. Open to Canadian citizens and permanent residents only. Prize: $20,000.

MILKWEED PRIZE FOR CHILDREN'S LITERATURE

Milkweed Editions, 1011 Washington Ave. S., Suite 300, Minneapolis MN 55415. (612)332-3192. **Fax:** (612)215-2550. **E-mail:** editor@milkweed.org. **Website:** milkweed.org. Milkweed Editions will award the Milkweed Prize for Children's Literature to the best mss for young readers that Milkweed accepts for publication during the calendar year by a writer not previously published by Milkweed. All mss for young readers submitted for publication by Milkweed are automatically entered into the competition. Seeking full-length fiction between 90-200 pages. Does not consider picture books or poetry collections for young readers. Recognizes an outstanding literary novel for readers ages 8-13 and encourage writers to turn their attention to readers in this age group. Prize: $10,000 cash prize in addition to a publishing contract negotiated at the time of acceptance. Judged by the editors of Milkweed Editions.

MINNESOTA BOOK AWARDS

325 Cedar St., Suite 555, St. Paul MN 55101. (651)222-3242. **Fax:** (651)222-1988. **E-mail:** mnbookawards@thefriends.org; friends@thefriends.org; info@thefriends.org. **Website:** www.thefriends.org. A year-round program celebrating and honoring Minnesota's best books, culminating in an annual awards ceremony. Recognizes and honors achievement by members of Minnesota's book and book arts community. All books must be the work of a Minnesota author or primary artistic creator (current Minnesota resident who maintains a year-round residence in Minnesota). All books must be published within the calendar year

prior to the Awards presentation. Deadline: Nomination should be submitted by 5 p.m. on the first Friday in December.

NATIONAL BOOK AWARDS

National Book Foundation, 90 Broad St., Suite 604, New York NY 10004. (212)685-0261. **E-mail:** nationalbook@nationalbook.org; agall@nationalbook.org. **Website:** www.nationalbook.org. **Contact:** Amy Gall. The National Book Foundation and the National Book Awards celebrate the best of American literature, expand its audience, and enhance the cultural value of great writing in America. The contest offers prizes in 4 categories: fiction, nonfiction, poetry, and young people's literature. Books should be published between December 1 and November 30 of the past year. Submissions must be previously published and must be entered by the publisher. General guidelines available on website. Interested publishs should phone or e-mail the Foundation. Deadline: Submit entry form, payment, and a copy of the book by July 1. Prize: $10,000 in each category. Finalists will each receive a prize of $1,000. Judged by a category specific panel of 5 judges for each category.

NATIONAL OUTDOOR BOOK AWARDS

921 S. 8th Ave., Stop 8128, Pocatello ID 83209. (208)282-3912. **E-mail:** wattron@isu.edu. **Website:** www.noba-web.org. **Contact:** Ron Watters. Nine categories: History/biography, outdoor literature, instructional texts, outdoor adventure guides, nature guides, children's books, design/artistic merit, natural history literature, and nature and the environment. Additionally, a special award, the Outdoor Classic Award, is given annually to books that, over a period of time, have proven to be exceptionally valuable works in the outdoor field. Application forms and eligibility requirements are available online. Applications for the Awards program become available in early June. Deadline: August 25. Prize: Winning books are promoted nationally and are entitled to display the National Outdoor Book Award (NOBA) medallion.

NATIONAL WRITERS ASSOCIATION NONFICTION CONTEST

National Writers Association, 10940 S. Parker Rd., #508, Parker CO 80134. (303)841-0246. **E-mail:** natlwritersassn@hotmail.com. **Website:** www.nationalwriters.com. Only unpublished works may be submitted. Judging of entries will not begin until the contest ends. Nonfiction in the following areas will be accepted: articles—submission should include query letter, 1st page of ms, separate sheet citing 5 possible markets; essay—the complete essay and 5 possible markets on separate sheet; nonfiction book proposal including query letter, chapter-by-chapter outline, first chapter, bio, and market analysis. Those unsure of proper ms format should request Research Report #35. The purpose of the National Writers Association Nonfiction Contest is to encourage the writing of nonfiction and recognize those who excel in this field. Deadline: December 31. Prize: 1st-5th place awards. Other winners will be notified by March 31st. 1st place: $200 and Clearinghouse representation if winner is book proposal; 2nd place: $100; 3rd place: $50; 4th-10th places will receive a book. Honorable mentions receive a certificate. Judging will be based on originality, marketability, research, and reader interest. Copies of the judges evaluation sheets will be sent to entrants furnishing a SASE with their entry.

NATIONAL WRITERS ASSOCIATION SHORT STORY CONTEST

10940 S. Parker Rd., #508, Parker CO 80134. (303)841-0246. **E-mail:** natlwritersassn@hotmail.com. **Website:** www.nationalwriters.com. Any genre of short story ms may be entered. All entries must be postmarked by July 1. Contest opens April 1. Only unpublished works may be submitted. All mss must be typed, double-spaced, in the English language. Maximum length is 5,000 words. Those unsure of proper ms format should request Research Report #35. The entry must be accompanied by an entry form (photocopies are acceptable) and return SASE if you wish the material and rating sheets returned. Submissions will be destroyed, otherwise. Receipt of entry will not be acknowledged without a return postcard. Author's name and address must appear on the first page. Entries remain the property of the author and may be submitted during the contest as long as they are not published before the final notification of winners. Final prizes will be awarded in June. The purpose of the National Writers Association. Short Story Contest is to encourage the development of creative skills, recognize and reward outstanding ability in the area of short story writing. Prize: 1st place: $250; 2nd place: $100; 3rd place: $50; 4th-10th places will receive a book. 1st-3rd place winners may be asked to grant one-time rights for publication in *Authorship* magazine. Honorable Mentions receive a certificate. Judging will be based on originality, marketability, research, and reader interest. Copies of the judges evaluation sheets will be sent to entrants furnishing a SASE with their entry.

NATIONAL YOUNGARTS FOUNDATION

2100 Biscayne Blvd., Miami FL 33137. (305)377-1140. **Fax:** (305)377-1149. **E-mail:** info@nfaa.org; apply@youngarts.org. **Website:** www.youngarts.org. The National YoungArts Foundation (formerly known as the National Foundation for Advancement in the Arts) was established in 1981 by Lin and Ted Arison to identify and support the next generation of artists and to contribute to the cultural vitality of the nation by investing in the artistic development of talented young artists in the visual, literary, design and performing arts. Each year, there are approximately 11,000 applications submitted to YoungArts from 15-18-year-old (or grades 10-12) artists, and from these, approximately 700 winners are selected who are eligible to participate in programs in Miami, New York, Los Angeles, and Washington DC (with Chicago and other regions in the works). YoungArts provides these emerging artists with life-changing experiences and validation by renowned mentors, access to significant scholarships, national recognition, and other opportunities throughout their careers to help ensure that the nation's most outstanding emerging artists are encouraged to pursue careers in the arts. See website for details about applying. Prize: Cash awards up to $10,000.

JOHN NEWBERY MEDAL

Association for Library Service to Children, Division of the American Library Association, 50 E. Huron, Chicago IL 60611. (800)545-2433, ext. 2153. **Fax:** (312)280-5271. **E-mail:** alscawards@ala.org. **Website:** www.ala.org. The Newbery Medal is awarded annually by the American Library Association for the most distinguished contribution to American literature for children. Previously published submissions only; must be published prior to year award is given. SASE for award rules. Entries not returned. Medal awarded at Caldecott/Newbery banquet during ALA annual conference. Deadline: December 31. Judged by Newbery Award Selection Committee.

NEW ENGLAND BOOK AWARDS

1955 Massachusetts Ave., #2, Cambridge MA 02140. (617)547-3642. **Fax:** (617)547-3759. **E-mail:** nan@ neba.org. **Website:** www.newenglandbooks.org/BookAwards. **Contact:** Nan Sorenson, administrative coordinator. Annual award. Previously published submissions only. Submissions made by New England booksellers; publishers. Submit written nominations only; actual books should not be sent. Member bookstores receive materials to display winners' books. Award is given to a specific title, fiction, nonfiction, children's. The titles must be either about New England, set in New England, or by an author residing in the New England. The titles must be hardcover, paperback original, or reissue that was published between September 1 and August 31. Entries must be still in print and available. Deadline: June 10. Prize: Winners will receive $250 for literacy to a charity of their choice.

NEW VOICES AWARD

Website: www.leeandlow.com. Open to students. Annual award. Lee & Low Books is one of the few minority-owned publishing companies in the country and has published more than 100 first-time writers and illustrators. Winning titles include *The Blue Roses*, winner of a Patterson Prize for Books for Young People; *Janna and the Kings*, an IRA Children's Book Award Notable; and *Sixteen Years in Sixteen Seconds*, selected for the Texas Bluebonnet Award Masterlist. Submissions made by author. SASE for contest rules or visit website. Restrictions of media for illustrators: The author must be a writer of color who is a resident of the US and who has not previously published a children's picture book. For additional information, send SASE or visit Lee & Low's website. Encourages writers of color to enter the world of children's books. Deadline: September 30. Prize: $1,000 and standard publication contract (regardless of whether or not writer has an agent), along with an advance against royalties; New Voices Honor Award: $500 prize. Judged by Lee & Low editors.

NORTH AMERICAN INTERNATIONAL AUTO SHOW HIGH SCHOOL POSTER CONTEST

Detroit Auto Dealers Association, 1900 W. Big Beaver Rd., Troy MI 48084-3531. (248)643-0250. **Fax:** (248)283-5148. **E-mail:** sherp@dada.org. **Website:** naias.com. **Contact:** Sandy Herp. Open to students. Annual contest. Submissions made by the author and illustrator. Entrants must be Michigan high school students enrolled in grades 10-12. Winning posters may be displayed at the NAIAS and reproduced in the official NAIAS program, which is available to the public, international media, corporate executives, and automotive suppliers. Winning posters may also be displayed on the official NAIAS website at the sole discretion of the NAIAS. Contact Detroit Auto Dealers Association (DADA) for contest rules and entry forms or retrieve rules from website. Deadline: November. Prize: Chairman's Award: $1,000; State Farm Insurance Award: $1,000; Designer's Best of Show (Digital and Traditional): $500; Best Theme: $250; Best Use of Color: $250; Most Creative: $250. A winner will be chosen in each category from grades 10, 11 and 12. Prizes: 1st place in 10, 11, 12: $500; 2nd place: $250; 3rd place: $100. Judged by an independent panel of recognized representatives of the art community.

NORTHERN CALIFORNIA BOOK AWARDS

Northern California Book Reviewers Association, c/o Poetry Flash, 1450 Fourth St. #4, Berkeley CA 94710. (510)525-5476. **E-mail:** ncbr@poetryflash.org; editor@poetryflash.org. **Website:** www.poetryflash.org. **Contact:** Joyce Jenkins, executive director. Annual Northern California Book Award for outstanding book in literature, open to books published in the current calendar year by Northern California authors. NCBR presents annual awards to Bay Area (northern California) authors annually in fiction, nonfiction, poetry, and children's literature. Previously published books only. Must be published the calendar year prior to spring awards ceremony. Submissions nominated by publishers; author or agent could also nominate published work. Send 3 copies of the book to attention: NCBR. Encourages writers and stimulates interest in books and reading. Deadline: December 28. Prize: $100 honorarium and award certificate. Judging by voting members of the Northern California Book Reviewers.

OHIOANA BOOK AWARDS

Ohioana Library Association, 274 E. First Ave., Suite 300, Columbus OH 43201-3673. (614)466-3831. **Fax:** (614)728-6974. **E-mail:** ohioana@ohioana.org. **Website:** www.ohioana.org. **Contact:** David Weaver, executive director. Writers must have been born in Ohio or lived in Ohio for at least 5 years, but books about Ohio or an Ohioan need not be written by an Ohioan. Finalists announced in May and winners in July. Winners notified by mail in early summer. Offered annually to bring national attention to Ohio authors and

their books, published in the past year. (Books can only be considered once.) Categories: Fiction, nonfiction, juvenile, poetry, and books about Ohio or an Ohioan. Deadline: December 31. Prize: $1,000 cash prize, certificate, and glass sculpture. Judged by a jury selected by librarians, book reviewers, writers, and other knowledgeable people.

THE OKLAHOMA BOOK AWARDS

200 NE 18th St., Oklahoma City OK 73105. (405)521-2502. **Fax:** (405)525-7804. **E-mail:** connie.armstrong@libraries.ok.gov. **Website:** www.odl.state.ok.us/ocb. **Contact:** Connie Armstrong, executive director. This award honors Oklahoma writers and books about Oklahoma. Awards are presented to best books in fiction, nonfiction, children's, design and illustration, and poetry books about Oklahoma or books written by an author who was born, is living, or has lived in Oklahoma. SASE for award rules and entry forms. Winner will be announced at banquet in Oklahoma City. The Arrell Gibson Lifetime Achievement Award is also presented each year for a body of work. Previously published submissions only. Submissions made by the author, author's agent, or entered by a person or group of people, including the publisher. Must be published during the calendar year preceding the award. Deadline: January 10. Prize: Awards a medal. Judging by a panel of 5 people for each category, generally a librarian, a working writer in the genre, booksellers, editors, etc.

ORBIS PICTUS AWARD FOR OUTSTANDING NONFICTION FOR CHILDREN

1111 W. Kenyon Rd., Urbana IL 61801-1096. (217)328-3870. **Fax:** (217)328-0977. **E-mail:** elementary@ncte.org. **Website:** www.ncte.org/awards/orbispictus. The Orbis Pictus Award promotes and recognizes excellence in the writing of nonfiction for children. Orbis Pictus commemorates the work of Johannes Amos Comenius, *Orbis Pictus—The World in Pictures* (1657), considered to be the first book actually planned for children. Submissions should be made by an author, the author's agent, or by a person or group of people. Must be published in the calendar year of the competition. Deadline: November 1. Prize: A plaque given at the NCTE Elementary Section Luncheon at the NCTE Annual Convention in November. Up to 5 honor books awarded. Judged by members of the Orbis Pictus Committee.

OREGON BOOK AWARDS

925 SW Washington St., Portland OR 97205. (503)227-2583. **Fax:** (503)241-4256. **E-mail:** la@literary-arts.org. **Website:** www.literary-arts.org. **Contact:** Susan Denning, director of programs and events. The annual Oregon Book Awards celebrate Oregon authors in the areas of poetry, fiction, nonfiction, drama, and young readers' literature published between August 1 and July 31 of the previous calendar year. Awards are available for every category. See website for details. Entry fee determined by initial print run; see website for details. Entries must be previously published. Oregon residents only. Accepts inquiries by phone and e-mail. Finalists announced in January. Winners announced at an awards ceremony in November. List of winners available in April. Deadline: August 29. Prize: Grant of $2,500. (Grant money could vary.) Judged by writers who are selected from outside Oregon for their expertise in a genre. Past judges include Mark Doty, Colson Whitehead and Kim Barnes.

OREGON LITERARY FELLOWSHIPS

925 SW Washington, Portland OR 97205. (503)227-2583. **E-mail:** susan@literary-arts.org. **Website:** www.literary-arts.org. **Contact:** Susan Moore, director of programs and events. Oregon Literary Fellowships are intended to help Oregon writers initiate, develop, or complete literary projects in poetry, fiction, literary nonfiction, drama, and young readers literature. Writers in the early stages of their career are encouraged to apply. The awards are merit-based. Guidelines available in February for SASE. Accepts inquiries by e-mail, phone. Oregon residents only. Recipients announced in January. Deadline: Last Friday in June. Prize: $3,000 minimum award, for approximately 8 writers and 2 publishers. Judged by out-of-state writers

THE ORIGINAL ART

128 E. 63rd St., New York NY 10065. (212)838-2560. **Fax:** (212)838-2561. **E-mail:** kim@societyillustrators.org; info@societyillustrators.org. **Website:** www.societyillustrators.org. **Contact:** Kate Feirtag, exhibition director. The Original Art is an annual exhibit created to showcase illustrations from the year's best children's books published in the US. For editors and art directors, it's an inspiration and a treasure trove of talent to draw upon. Previously published submissions only. Request "call for entries" to receive contest rules and entry forms. Works will be displayed at the Society of Illustrators Museum of American Illustration in New York City October-November annually. Deadline: July 18. Judged by 7 professional artists and editors.

HELEN KEATING OTT AWARD FOR OUTSTANDING CONTRIBUTION TO CHILDREN'S LITERATURE

CSLA, 10157 SW Barbur Blvd., #102C, Portland OR 97219. (503)244-6919. **Fax:** (503)977-3734. **E-mail:** sharper1@kent.edu. **Website:** cslainfo.org. **Contact:** S. Meghan Harper, awards chair. Annual award given to a person or organization that has made a significant contribution to promoting high moral and ethical values through children's literature. Recipient is honored in July during the conference. Awards certificate of recognition, the awards banquet, and one-night's stay in the hotel. A nomination for an award may be made by anyone. An application form is available online. Elements of creativity and innovation will be given high priority by the judges.

PATERSON PRIZE FOR BOOKS FOR YOUNG PEOPLE

The Poetry Center at Passaic County Community College, One College Blvd., Paterson NJ 07505. (973)684-6555. **Fax:** (973)523-6085. **E-mail:** mgillan@pccc.edu. **Website:** www.poetrycenterpccc.com. **Contact:** Maria Mazziotti Gillan, executive director. Award for a book published in the previous year in each age category (Pre-K-Grade 3, Grades 4-6, Grades 7-12). Deadline: March 15. Prize: $500.

THE KATHERINE PATERSON PRIZE FOR YOUNG ADULT AND CHILDREN'S WRITING

Hunger Mountain, Vermont College of Fine Arts, 36 College St., Montpelier VT 05602. (802)828-8517. **E-mail:** hungermtn@vcfa.edu. **Website:** hungermtn.org. **Contact:** Samantha Kolber, managing editor. The annual Katherine Paterson Prize for Young Adult and Children's Writing honors the best in young adult and children's literature. Submit young adult or middle-grade mss, and writing for younger children, short stories, picture books, poetry, or novel excerpts, fewer than 10,000 words. Guidelines available on website. Deadline: March 1. Prize: $1,000 and publication for the first place winner; $100 each and publication for the three category winners. Judged by a guest judge every year. The 2016 judge was Rita Williams-Garcia, author of Newbery Honor-winning novel *One Crazy Summer*.

PENNSYLVANIA YOUNG READERS' CHOICE AWARDS PROGRAM

Website: www.psla.org. **Contact:** Alice L. Cyphers, co-coordinator. Submissions nominated by a person or group. Must be published within 5 years of the award—for example, books published in 2012 to present are eligible for the 2017-2018 award. Check the program wiki at pyrca.wikispaces.com for submission information. View information at the Pennsylvania School Librarians' website or the program wiki. Must be currently living in North America. The purpose of the Pennsylvania Young Reader's Choice Awards Program is to promote the reading of quality books by young people in the Commonwealth of Pennsylvania, to encourage teacher and librarian collaboration, and involvement in children's literature, and to honor authors whose works have been recognized by the students of Pennsylvania. Deadline: September 15. Prize: Framed certificate to winning authors. Four awards are given, one for each of the following grade level divisions: K-3, 3-6, 6-8, young adult. Judged by children of Pennsylvania (they vote).

PEN/PHYLLIS NAYLOR WORKING WRITER FELLOWSHIP

E-mail: awards@pen.org. **Website:** www.pen.org/awards. **Contact:** Arielle Anema, literary awards coordinator. Offered annually to an author of children's or young adult fiction. The Fellowship has been developed to help writers whose work is of high literary caliber but who have not yet attracted a broad readership. The Fellowship is designed to assist a writer at a crucial moment in his or her career to complete a book-length work-in-progress. Candidates have published at least 1 novel for children or young adults that has been received warmly by literary critics but has not generated sufficient income to support the author. Writers must be nominated by an editor or fellow author. See website for eligibility and nomination guidelines. Deadline: Submissions open during the summer of each year. Visit website for up-to-date information on deadlines. Prize: $5,000.

PLEASE TOUCH MUSEUM BOOK AWARD

Memorial Hall in Fairmount Park, 4231 Avenue of the Republic, Philadelphia PA 19131. (215)578-5153. **Fax:** (215)578-5171. **E-mail:** hboyd@pleasetouchmuseum.

org. **Website:** www.pleasetouchmuseum.org. **Contact:** Heather Boyd. This prestigious award has recognized and encouraged the publication of high-quality books. The award was exclusively created to recognize and encourage the writing of publications that help young children enjoy the process of learning through books, while reflecting PTM's philosophy of learning through play. The awards go to books that are imaginative, exceptionally illustrated, and help foster a child's life-long love of reading. To be eligible for consideration, a book must be distinguished in text, illustration, and ability to explore and clarify an idea for young children (ages 7 and under). Deadline: October 1. Books for each cycle must be published within previous calendar year (September-August). Judged by a panel of volunteer educators, artists, booksellers, children's authors, and librarians in conjunction with museum staff.

PNWA LITERARY CONTEST

Pacifc Northwest Writers Association, PMB 2717, 1420 NW Gilman Blvd., Suite 2, Issaquah WA 98027. (452)673-2665. **Fax:** (452)961-0768. **E-mail:** pnwa@pnwa.org. **Website:** www.pnwa.org. Annual literary contest with 12 different categories. See website for details and specific guidelines. Each entry receives 2 critiques. Winners announced at the PNWA Summer Conference, held annually in mid-July. Deadline: February 20. Prize: 1st place: $600; 2nd place: $300; 3rd place: $100. Judged by an agent or editor attending the conference.

POCKETS ANNUAL FICTION-WRITING CONTEST

P.O. Box 340004, Nashville TN 37203-0004. (615)340-7333. **Fax:** (615)340-7267. **E-mail:** pockets@upperroom.org. **Website:** pockets.upperroom.org. **Contact:** Lynn W. Gilliam, senior editor. Designed for 6- to 12-year-olds, *Pockets* magazine offers wholesome devotional readings that teach about God's love and presence in life. The content includes fiction, scripture stories, puzzles and games, poems, recipes, colorful pictures, activities, and scripture readings. Freelance submissions of stories, poems, recipes, puzzles and games, and activities are welcome. Stories should be 750-1,000 words. Multiple submissions are permitted. Past winners are ineligible. The primary purpose of *Pockets* is to help children grow in their relationship with God and to claim the good news of the gospel of Jesus Christ by applying it to their daily lives. *Pockets* espouses respect for all human beings and for God's creation. It regards a child's faith journey as an integral part of all of life and sees prayer as undergirding that journey. Deadline: August 15. Submission period begins March 15. Prize: $500 and publication in magazine.

THE EDGAR AWARDS

1140 Broadway, Suite 1507, New York NY 10001. (212)888-8171. **E-mail:** mwa@mysterywriters.org. **Website:** mysterywriters.org. Mystery Writers of America is the leading association for professional crime writers in the United States. Members of MWA include most major writers of crime fiction and nonfiction, as well as screenwriters, dramatists, editors, publishers, and other professionals in the field. Categories include: Best Novel, Best First Novel by an American Author, Best Paperback/E-Book Original, Best Fact Crime, Best Critical/Biographical, Best Short Story, Best Juvenile Mystery, Best Young Adult Mystery, Best Television Series Episode Teleplay, and Mary Higgins Clark Award. Purpose of the award: Honor authors of distinguished works in the mystery field. Previously published submissions only. Submissions should be made by the publisher. Work must be published/produced the year of the contest. Deadline: November 30. Prize: Awards ceramic bust of "Edgar" for winner; certificates for all nominees. Judged by active status members of Mystery Writers of America (writers).

MICHAEL L. PRINTZ AWARD

Young Adult Library Services Association, Division of the American Library Association, 50 E. Huron, Chicago IL 60611. (800)545-2433. **Fax:** (312)280-5276. **E-mail:** yalsa@ala.org. **Website:** www.ala.org/yalsa/printz. **Contact:** Nichole O'Connor, program officer for events and conferences. The Michael L. Printz Award annually honors the best book written for teens, based entirely on its literary merit, each year. In addition, the Printz Committee names up to 4 honor books, which also represent the best writing in young adult literature. The award-winning book can be fiction, nonfiction, poetry, or an anthology, and can be a work of joint authorship or editorship. The books must be published from January 1–December 31 of the preceding year and be designated by its publisher as being either a young adult book or published for the age range that YALSA defines as young adult,

e.g., ages 12-18. Deadline: December 1. Judged by an award committee.

THE PURPLE DRAGONFLY BOOK AWARDS

4696 W. Tyson St., Chandler AZ 85226-2903. (480)940-8182. **Fax:** (480)940-8787. **E-mail:** cristy@fivestarpublications.com; fivestarpublications@gmail.com. **Website:** www.purpledragonflybookawards.com; www.fivestarpublications.com; www.fivestar-bookawards.com. **Contact:** Cristy Bertini, contest coordinator. The Purple Dragonfly Book Awards are designed with children in mind. Awards are divided into 43 distinct subject categories, ranging from books on the environment and cooking to sports and family issues. The Purple Dragonfly Book Awards are geared toward stories that appeal to children of all ages. The awards are open to books published in any calendar year and in any country that are available for purchase. Books entered must be printed in English. Traditionally published, partnership published, and self-published books are permitted, as long as they fit the above criteria. Submit materials to: Cristy Bertini, Attn: Five Star Book Awards, 1271 Turkey St., Ware, MA 01082. Deadline: May 1. Prize: Grand-prize winner will receive a $300 cash prize, 100 foil award seals (more can be ordered for an extra charge), 1 hour of marketing consultation from Five Star Publications, and $100 worth of Five Star Publications' titles, as well as publicity on Five Star Publications' websites and inclusion in a winners' news release sent to a comprehensive list of media outlets. The Grand-prize winner will also be placed in the Five Star Dragonfly Book Awards virtual bookstore with a thumbnail of the book's cover, price, one-sentence description, and link to Amazon.com for purchasing purposes, if applicable. First place: All first-place winners of categories will be put into a drawing for a $100 prize. In addition, each first-place winner in each category receives a certificate commemorating their accomplishment, 25 foil award seals (more can be ordered for an extra charge), and mention on Five Star Publications' websites. Judged by industry experts with specific knowledge about the categories over which they preside.

QUILL AND SCROLL WRITING, PHOTO AND MULTIMEDIA CONTEST AND BLOGGING COMPETITION

School of Journalism, University of Iowa, 100 Adler Journalism Bldg., Iowa City IA 52242-2004. (319)335-3457. **Fax:** (319)335-3989. **E-mail:** quill-scroll@uiowa.

edu. **E-mail:** vanessa-shelton@uiowa.edu. **Website:** quillandscroll.org. **Contact:** Vanessa Shelton, contest director. Entries must have been published in a high school or profesional newspaper or website during the previous year, and must be the work of a currently enrolled high school student, when published. Open to students. Annual contest. Previously published submissions only. Submissions made by the author or school media adviser. Deadline: February 5. Prize: Winners will receive *Quill and Scroll*'s National Award Gold Key and, if seniors, are eligible to apply for one of the scholarships offered by *Quill and Scroll*. All winning entries are automatically eligible for the International Writing and Photo Sweepstakes Awards. Engraved plaque awarded to sweepstakes winners.

TOMÁS RIVERA MEXICAN AMERICAN CHILDREN'S BOOK AWARD

Texas State University, 601 University Dr., San Marcos TX 78666-4613. (512)245-2357. **E-mail:** riverabookaward@txstate.edu. **Website:** www.riverabookaward.org. **Contact:** Dr. Jesse Gainer, award director. Texas State University College of Education developed the Tomas Rivera Mexican American Children's Book Award to honor authors and illustrators who create literature that depicts the Mexican American experience. The award was established in 1995 and was named in honor of Dr. Tomas Rivera, a distinguished alumnus of Texas State University. The book will be written for younger children, grades K-5 (awarded in even years), or older children, grades 6-12 (awarded in odd years). The text and illustrations will be of highest quality. The portrayal/representations of Mexican Americans will be accurate and engaging, avoid stereotypes, and reflect rich characterization. The book may be fiction or nonfiction. See website for more details and directions. Deadline: November 1.

☼ ROCKY MOUNTAIN BOOK AWARD: ALBERTA CHILDREN'S CHOICE BOOK AWARD

Box 42, Lethbridge AB T1J 3Y3, Canada. (403)381-0855. **Website:** www.rmba.info. **Contact:** Michelle Dimnik, contest director. Annual contest open to Alberta students. No entry fee. Canadian authors and/or illustrators only. Submit entries to Richard Chase. Previously unpublished submissions only. Submissions made by author's agent or nominated by a person or group. Must be published within the 3 years prior to that year's award. Register before January 20th to take part in the Rocky Mountain Book Award. SASE for contest rules and entry forms. Purpose of contest: "Reading motivation for students, promotion of Canadian authors, illustrators and publishers." Prize: Gold medal and author tour of selected Alberta schools. Judging by students.

ROYAL DRAGONFLY BOOK AWARDS

Five Star Publications, Inc., 4696 W. Tyson St., Chandler AZ 85226. (480)940-8182. **Fax:** (480)940-8787. **E-mail:** cristy@fivestarpublications.com; fivestarpublications@gmail.com. **Website:** www.fivestarpublications.com; www.fivestarbookawards.com; www.royaldragonflybookawards.com. **Contact:** Cristy Bertini. Offered annually for any previously published work to honor authors for writing excellence of all types of literature—fiction and nonfiction—in 62 categories, appealing to a wide range of ages and comprehensive list of genres. Open to any title published in English. Entry forms are downloadable at www.royaldragonflybookawards.com. Guidelines available online. Send submissions to Cristy Bertini, Attn.: Five Star Book Awards, 1271 Turkey St., Ware, MA 01082. Deadline: October 1. Prize: Grand-prize winner receives $300, while another entrant will be the lucky winner of a $100 drawing. All first-place winners receive foil award seals and are included in a publicity campaign announcing winners. All first- and second-place winners and honorable mentions receive certificates.

✪ SASKATCHEWAN BOOK AWARDS

315-1102 Eighth Ave., Regina SK S4R 1C9, Canada. (306)569-1585. **E-mail:** director@bookawards.sk.ca. **Website:** www.bookawards.sk.ca. **Contact:** Courtney Bates-Hardy, administrative director. Saskatchewan Book Awards celebrates, promotes, and rewards Saskatchewan authors and publishers worthy of recognition through 14 awards, granted on an annual or semiannual basis. Awards: fiction, nonfiction, poetry, scholarly, first book, *Prix du Livre Français*, Regina, Saskatoon, Aboriginal Peoples' Writing, Aboriginal Peoples' Publishing, Publishing in Education, Publishing, Children's Literature/Young Adult Literature, Book of the Year. Deadline: Early November. Prize: $2,000 (CAD) for all awards except Book of the Year, which is $3,000 (CAD). Juries are made up of writing and publishing professionals from outside of Saskatchewan.

☼   Saskatchewan Book Awards is the only provincially focused book award program in Saskatchewan and a principal ambassador for Saskatchewan's literary community. Its solid reputation for celebrating artistic excellence in style is recognized nationally.

SCBWI MAGAZINE MERIT AWARDS

4727 Wilshire Blvd., Suite 301, Los Angeles CA 90010. (323)782-1010. **Fax:** (323)782-1892. **E-mail:** grants@scbwi.org. **Website:** www.scbwi.org. **Contact:** Stephanie Gordon, award coordinator. The SCBWI is a professional organization of writers, illustrators, and others interested in children's literature. Membership is open to the general public at large. All magazine work for young people by an SCBWI member—writer, artist, or photographer—is eligible during the year of original publication. In the case of co-authored work, both authors must be SCBWI members. Members must submit their own work. Requirements for entrants: 4 copies each of the published work and proof of publication (may be contents page) showing the name of the magazine and the date of issue. Previously published submissions only. For rules and procedures, see website. Recognizes outstanding original magazine work for young people published during that year, and having been written or illustrated by members of SCBWI. Deadline: December 15 of the year of publication. Submission period begins January 1. Prize: Awards plaques and honor certificates for each of 4 categories (fiction, nonfiction, illustration and poetry). Judged by a magazine editor and two "full" SCBWI members.

SCBWI WORK-IN-PROGRESS GRANTS

8271 Beverly Blvd., Los Angeles CA 90048. (323)782-1010. **Fax:** (323)782-1892. **E-mail:** grants@scbwi.org, wipgrant@scbwi.org. **Website:** www.scbwi.org. The SCBWI Work-in-Progress Grants have been established to assist children's book writers in the completion of a specific project. Five categories: picture book text, chapter books/early readers, middle-grade, young adult fiction, nonfiction, and multicultural fiction or nonfiction. SASE for applications for grants. The grants are available to both full and associate members of the SCBWI. They are not available for projects on which there are already contracts. Previous recipients not eligible to apply. Deadline: March 31. Submission period begins March 1.

HELEN SHEEHAN YOUNG ADULT BOOK

PRIZE

Elephant Rock Books, P.O. Box 119, Ashford CT 06278. **E-mail:** elephantrockbooksya@gmail.com. **Website:** elephantrockbooks.com/ya.html. **Contact:** Jotham Burrello and Amanda Hurley. Elephant Rock is a small independent publisher. Their first young adult book, *The Carnival at Bray* by Jessie Ann Foley was a Morris Award Finalist and Printz Honor Book. Runs contest every other year. Check website for details. Guidelines are available online: www.elephantrockbooks.com/about.html#submissions. "Elephant Rock Books' teen imprint is looking for a great story to follow our critically acclaimed novel *The Carnival at Bray*. We're after quality stories with heart, guts, and a clear voice. We're especially interested in the quirky, the hopeful, and the real. We are not particularly interested in genre fiction and prefer standalone novels, unless you've got the next *Hunger Games*. We seek writers who believe in the transformative power of a great story, so show us what you've got." Deadline: July 1. Prize: $1,000 as an advance. Judges vary year to year.

SKIPPING STONES BOOK AWARDS

E-mail: editor@skippingstones.org. **Website:** www.skippingstones.org. **Contact:** Arun N. Toke', executive editor. Open to published books, publications/magazines, educational videos, and DVDs. Annual awards. Submissions made by the author or publishers and/or producers. Send request for contest rules and entry forms or visit website. Many educational publications announce the winners of our book awards. The winning books and educational videos/DVDs are announced in the July-September issue of *Skipping Stones* and also on the website. In addition to announcements on social media pages, the reviews of winning titles are posted on website. *Skipping Stones* multicultural magazine has been published for more than 25 years. Recognizes exceptional, literary, and artistic contributions to juvenile/children's literature, as well as teaching resources and educational audio/video resources in the areas of multicultural awareness, nature and ecology, social issues, peace, and nonviolence. Deadline: February 28. Prize: Winners receive gold honor award seals, attractive honor certificates, and publicity via multiple outlets. Judged by a multicultural selection committee of editors, students, parents, teachers, and librarians.

SKIPPING STONES YOUTH HONOR AWARDS

P.O. Box 3939, Eugene OR 97403-0939. (541)342-4956. **E-mail:** editor@skippingstones.org. **Website:** www.skippingstones.org. Now celebrating its 28th year, *Skipping Stones* is a winner of N.A.M.E.EDPRESS, Newsstand Resources, Writer and Parent's Choice Awards. Open to students. Annual awards. Submissions made by the author. The winners are published in the October-December issue of *Skipping Stones*. Everyone who enters the contest receives the Autumn issue featuring Youth Awards. SASE for contest rules or download from website. Entries must include certificate of originality by a parent and/or teacher and a cover letter that included cultural background information on the author. Submissions can either be mailed or e-mailed. Up to 10 awards are given in three categories: (1) Compositions (essays, poems, short stories, songs, travelogues, etc.): Entries should be typed (double-spaced) or neatly handwritten. Fiction or nonfiction should be limited to 1,000 words; poems to 30 lines. Non-English writings are also welcome. (2) Artwork (drawings, cartoons, paintings, or photo essays with captions): Entries should have the artist's name, age, and address on the back of each page. Send the originals with SASE. Black and white photos are especially welcome. Limit: 8 pieces. (3) Youth Organizations: Describe how your club or group works to: (a) preserve the nature and ecology in your area, (b) enhance the quality of life for low-income, minority, or disabled, or (c) improve racial or cultural harmony in your school or community. Use the same format as for compositions. Recognizes youth, 7-17, for their contributions to multicultural awareness, nature and ecology, social issues, peace, and nonviolence. Also promotes creativity, self-esteem, and writing skills and to recognize important work being done by youth organizations. Deadline: June 25. Judged by *Skipping Stones* staff.

KAY SNOW WRITING CONTEST

Willamette Writers, 2108 Buck St., West Linn OR 97068. (503)305-6729. **Fax:** (503)344-6174. **E-mail:** reg@willamettewriters.com. **Website:** willamettewriters.org. Willamette Writers is the largest writers' organization in Oregon and one of the largest writers' organizations in the United States. It is a non-profit, tax-exempt Oregon corporation led by volunteers. Elected officials and directors administer an active program of monthly meetings, special seminars, workshops, and an annual writing conference. Continuing with established programs and starting new ones is only made possible by strong volunteer support. See website for specific details and rules. There are six different categories writers can enter: Adult Fiction, Adult Nonfiction, Poetry, Juvenile Short Story, Screenwriting, and Student Writer. The purpose of this annual writing contest, named in honor of Willamette Writer's founder, Kay Snow, is to help writers reach professional goals in writing in a broad array of categories and to encourage student writers. Deadline: April 23. Submission deadline begins January 15. Prize: One first prize of $300, one second place prize of $150, and a third place prize of $50 per winning entry in each of the six categories. Student first prize is $50, $20 for second place, $10 for third.

SOCIETY OF MIDLAND AUTHORS AWARD

Society of Midland Authors, P.O. Box 10419, Chicago IL 60610-0419. **E-mail:** marlenetbrill@comcast.net. **Website:** www.midlandauthors.com. **Contact:** Marlene Targ Brill, awards chair. Since 1957, the Society has presented annual awards for the best books written by Midwestern authors. The contest is open to any title published within the year prior to the contest year. Open to adult and children's authors/poets who reside in, were born in, or have strong ties to a Midland state, which includes Illinois, Indiana, Iowa, Kansas, Michigan, Minnesota, Missouri, Nebraska, North Dakota, South Dakota, Ohio, and Wisconsin. The Society of Midland Authors (SMA) Award is presented to one title in each of six categories: adult nonfiction, adult fiction, adult biography and memoir, children's nonfiction, children's fiction, and poetry. Books and entry forms must be mailed to the 3 judges in each category; for a list of judges and the entry form, visit the website. Do not mail books to the society's P.O. box. The fee can be sent to the SMA P.O. box or paid via Paypal. Deadline: January 7. Prize: $500 and a plaque that is awarded at the SMA banquet in May in Chicago. Honorary winners receive a plaque.

SYDNEY TAYLOR BOOK AWARD

Association of Jewish Libraries, P.O. Box 1118, Teaneck NJ 07666. (212)725-5359. **E-mail:** chair@sydneytaylorbookaward.org; Ellen.tilman@gmail.com. **Website:** jewishlibraries.org. **Contact:** Ellen Tilman, chair. The Sydney Taylor Book Award is presented annually to outstanding books for children and teens that authentically portray the Jewish experience. Deadline: November 30. Cannot guarantee that books received after November 30 will be considered. Prize: Gold medals are presented in 3 categories: younger readers, older readers, and teen readers. Honor books are awarded in silver medals, and notable books are named in each category.

SYDNEY TAYLOR MS COMPETITION

Association of Jewish Libraries, 204 Park St., Montclair NJ 07042-2903. **E-mail:** stmacajl@aol.com. **Website:** jewishlibraries.org. **Contact:** Aileen Grossberg. This competition is for unpublished writers of fiction. Material should be for readers ages 8-13, with universal appeal that will serve to deepen the understanding of Judaism for all children, revealing positive aspects of Jewish life. Download rules and forms from website. Must be an unpublished fiction writer or a student; also, books must range from 64-200 pages. "AJL assumes no responsibility for publication, but hopes this cash incentive will serve to encourage new writers of children's stories with Jewish themes for all children." Deadline: September 30. Prize: $1,000. Judging by qualified judges from within the Association of Jewish Libraries.

☺ TD CANADIAN CHILDREN'S LITERATURE AWARD

The Canadian Children's Book Centre, 40 Orchard View Blvd., Suite 217, Toronto ON M4R 1B9, Canada. (416)975-0010, ext. 222. **Fax:** (416)975-8970. **E-mail:** meghan@bookcentre.ca. **Website:** bookcentre. ca. **Contact:** Meghan Howe. The TD Canadian Children's Literature Award is for the most distinguished book of the year. All books, in any genre, written and illustrated by Canadians and for children ages 1-12 are eligible. Only books first published in Canada are eligible for submission. Books must be published between January 1 and December 31 of the previous calendar year. Open to Canadian citizens and/or permanent residents of Canada. Deadline: mid-December. Prizes: Two prizes of $30,000, 1 for English, 1 for French. $20,000 will be divided among the Honour Book English titles and Honour Book French titles, to a maximum of 4; $2,500 shall go to each of the publishers of the English and French grand-prize winning books for promotion and publicity.

☺ TORONTO BOOK AWARDS

City of Toronto c/o Toronto Arts & Culture, Cultural Partnerships, City Hall, 9E, 100 Queen St. W., Toronto ON M5H 2N2, Canada. **E-mail:** shan@toronto.ca. **Website:** www.toronto.ca/book_awards. The Toronto Book Awards honor authors of books of literary or artistic merit that are evocative of Toronto. There are no separate categories; all books are judged together. Any fiction or nonfiction book published in English for adults and/or children that are evocative of Toronto are eligible. To be eligible, books must be published between January 1 and December 31 of previous year. Deadline: April 30. Prize: Each finalist receives $1,000, and the winning author receives the remaining prize money ($14,000 total in prize money available).

VEGETARIAN ESSAY CONTEST

The Vegetarian Resource Group, P.O. Box 1463, Baltimore MD 21203. (410)366-VEGE. **Fax:** (410)366-8804. **E-mail:** vrg@vrg.org. **Website:** www.vrg.org. Write an essay of 2-3 pages on any aspect of vegetarianism. Entrants should base their paper on interviewing, research, and/or personal opinion. You need not be a vegetarian to enter. Three different entry categories: age 14-18; age 9-13; and age 8 and under. Prize: $50.

VFW VOICE OF DEMOCRACY

Veterans of Foreign Wars of the U.S., National Headquarters, 406 W. 34th St., Kansas City MO 64111. (816)968-1117. **E-mail:** kharmer@vfw.org. **Website:** www.vfw.org/community/voice-of-democracy. The Voice of Democracy Program is open to students in grades 9-12 (on the November 1 deadline), who are enrolled in a public, private, or parochial high school or home study program in the United States and its territories. Contact your local VFW Post to enter (entry must not be mailed to the VFW National Headquarters, only to a local, participating VFW Post). Purpose is to give high school students the opportunity to voice their opinions about their responsibility to our country and to convey those opinions via the broadcast media to all of America. Deadline: November 1. Prize: Winners receive awards ranging from $1,000-30,000.

☻ WESTERN AUSTRALIAN PREMIER'S BOOK AWARDS

State Library of Western Australia, Perth Cultural Centre, 25 Francis St., Perth WA 6000, Australia. (61)(8)9427-3151. **E-mail:** premiersbookawards@ slwa.wa.gov.au. **Website:** pba.slwa.wa.gov.au. **Contact:** Karen de San Miguel. Annual competition for Australian citizens or permanent residents of Australia, or writers whose work has Australia as its primary focus. Categories: children's books, digital narrative, fiction, nonfiction, poetry, scripts, writing for young adults, West Australian history, and Western Australian emerging writers. Submit 5 original copies of the work to be considered for the awards. All works must have been published between January 1 and December 31 of the prior year. See website for details and rules of entry. Deadline: January 31. Prize: Awards $25,000 for Premier's Prize; awards $15,000 each for the Children's Books, Digital Narrative, Fiction, and Nonfiction categories; awards $10,000 each for the Poetry, Scripts, Western Australian History, Western Australian Emerging Writers, and Writing for Young Adults; awards $5,000 for People's Choice Award.

WESTERN HERITAGE AWARDS

National Cowboy & Western Heritage Museum, 1700 NE 63rd St., Oklahoma City OK 73111-7997. (405)478-2250. **Fax:** (405)478-4714. **Website:** nationalcowboymuseum.org. **Contact:** Jessica Limestall. The National Cowboy & Western Heritage Museum Western Heritage Awards were established to honor and encourage the legacy of those whose works in literature, music, film, and television reflect the significant stories of the American West. Accepted categories for literary entries: western novel, nonfiction book, art book, photography book, juvenile book, magazine article, or poetry book. Previously published submissions only; must be published the calendar year before the awards are presented. Requirements for entrants: The material must pertain to the development or preservation of the West, either from a historical or contemporary viewpoint. Literary entries must have been published between December 1 and November 30 of calendar year. Five copies of each published work must be furnished for judging with each entry, along with the completed entry form. Works recognized during special awards ceremonies held annually at the museum. There is an autograph party preceding the awards. Awards ceremonies are sometimes broadcast. The WHA are presented annually to encourage the accurate and artistic telling of great stories of the West through 16 categories of western literature, television, film and music; including fiction, nonfiction, children's books and poetry. See website for details and category definitions. Deadline: November 30. Prize:

Awards a Wrangler bronze sculpture designed by famed western artist, John Free. Judged by a panel of judges selected each year with distinction in various fields of western art and heritage.

WESTERN WRITERS OF AMERICA

271CR 219, Encampment WY 82325. (307)329-8942. **Fax:** (307)327-5465 (call first). **E-mail:** wwa.moulton@gmail.com. **Website:** westernwriters.org. **Contact:** Candy Moulton, executive director. Seventeen Spur Award categories in various aspects of the American West. Send entry form with your published work. Accepts multiple submissions, each with its own entry form. The nonprofit Western Writers of America has promoted and honored the best in Western literature with the annual Spur Awards, selected by panels of judges. Awards, for material published last year, are given for works whose inspirations, image, and literary excellence best represent the reality and spirit of the American West.

JACKIE WHITE MEMORIAL NATIONAL CHILDREN'S PLAY WRITING CONTEST

1800 Nelwood Dr., Columbia MO 65202-1447. (573)874-5628. **E-mail:** jwmcontest@cectheatre.org. **Website:** www.cectheatre.org. **Contact:** Tom Phillips. Annual contest that encourages playwrights to write quality plays for family audiences. Previously unpublished submissions only. Submissions made by author. Play may be performed during the following season. All submissions will be read by at least 3 readers. Author will receive a written evaluation of the script. Guidelines available online. Deadline: June 1. Prize: $500 with production possible. Judging by current and past board members of CEC and by non-board members who direct plays at CEC.

LAURA INGALLS WILDER AWARD

50 E. Huron, Chicago IL 60611. (800)545-2433. **E-mail:** alscawards@ala.org. **Website:** www.ala.org/alsc/awardsgrants/bookmedia/wildermedal. Award offered every 2 years. The Wilder Award honors an author or illustrator whose books, published in the US, have made, over a period of years, a substantial and lasting contribution to literature for children. The candidates must be nominated by ALSC members. Medal presented at Newbery/Caldecott banquet during annual conference. Judging by Wilder Award Selection Committee.

WILLA LITERARY AWARD

E-mail: Anneschroederauthor@gmail.com. **Website:** www.womenwritingthewest.org. **Contact:** Anne Schroeder. The WILLA Literary Award honors the year's best in published literature featuring women's or girls' stories set in the West. Women Writing the West (WWW), a nonprofit association of writers and other professionals writing and promoting the Women's West, underwrites and presents the nationally recognized award annually (for work published between January 1 and December 31). The award is named in honor of Pulitzer Prize winner Willa Cather, one of the country's foremost novelists. The award is given in 7 categories: historical fiction, contemporary fiction, original softcover fiction, creative nonfiction, scholarly nonfiction, poetry, and children's/young adult fiction/nonfiction. Entry forms available on the website. Deadline: November 1–February 1. Prize: $100 and a trophy. Finalist receives a plaque. Both receive digital and sticker award emblems for book covers. Notice of winning and finalist titles mailed to more than 4,000 booksellers, libraries, and others. Award announcement is in early August, and awards are presented to the winners and finalists at the annual WWW Fall Conference. Judged by professional librarians not affiliated with WWW.

RITA WILLIAMS YOUNG ADULT PROSE PRIZE CATEGORY

Soul-Making Keats Literary Competition, The Webhallow House, 1544 Sweetwood Dr., Broadmoor Village CA 94015-2029. **E-mail:** SoulKeats@mail.com. **Website:** www.soulmakingcontest.us. **Contact:** Eileen Malone. For writers in grades 9-12 or equivalent age. Up to 3,000 words in prose form of choice. Complete rules and guidelines available online. Deadline: November 30 (postmarked). Prize: $100 for first place; $50 for second place; $25 for third place. Judged (and sponsored) by Rita Wiliams, an Emmy-award winning investigative reporter with KTVU-TV in Oakland, California.

PAUL A. WITTY OUTSTANDING LITERATURE AWARD

P.O. Box 8139, Newark DE 19714-8139. (800)336-7323. **Fax:** (302)731-1057. **Website:** www.literacyworldwide.org. **Contact:** Marcie Craig Post, executive director. This award recognizes excellence in original poetry or prose written by students. Elementary and secondary students whose work is selected will receive an award. Deadline: February 2. Prize: Not less than $25 and a citation of merit.

WORK-IN-PROGRESS GRANT

Society of Children's Book Writers and Illustrators (SCBWI), 8271 Beverly Blvd., Los Angeles CA 90048. (323)782-1010. **E-mail:** grants@scbwi.org; wipgrant@scbwi.org. **Website:** www.scbwi.org. Four grants—1 designated specifically for a contemporary novel for young people, 1 for nonfiction, 1 for an unpublished writer, 1 general fiction—to assist SCBWI members in the completion of a specific project. Open to SCBWI members only. Deadline: March 31. Open to submissions on March 1.

WRITE NOW

Indiana Repertory Theatre, 140 W. Washington St., Indianapolis IN 46204. (480)921-5770. **E-mail:** info@writenow.co. **Website:** www.writenow.co. The purpose of this biennial workshop is to encourage writers to create strikingly original scripts for young audiences. It provides a forum through which each playwright receives constructive criticism and the support of a development team consisting of a professional director and dramaturg. Finalists will spend approximately 1 week in workshop with their development team. At the end of the week, each play will be read as a part of the Write Now convening. Guidelines available online. Deadline: July 31.

WRITER'S DIGEST SELF-PUBLISHED BOOK AWARDS

Writer's Digest, 10151 Carver Rd., Suite #200, Blue Ash OH 45242. (715)445-4612, ext. 13430. **E-mail:** WritersDigestSelfPublishingCompetition@fwmedia.com. **Website:** www.writersdigest.com. **Contact:** Nicole Howard. Contest open to all English-language, self-published books for which the authors have paid the full cost of publication, or the cost of printing has been paid for by a grant or as part of a prize. Categories include: mainstream/literary fiction, genre fiction, nonfiction, inspirational (spiritual/new age), life Stories (biographies/autobiographies/family histories/memoirs), children's books, reference books (directories/encyclopedias/guide books), poetry, and middle-grade/young adult Books. Judges reserve the right to re-categorize entries. Judges reserve the right to withhold prizes in any category. All winners will be notified in October. Entrants must send a printed and bound book. Entries will be evaluated on content, writing quality, and overall quality of production and appearance. No handwritten books are accepted. Books must have been published within the past 5 years from the competition deadline. Books that have previously won awards from *Writer's Digest* are not eligible. Early bird deadline: April 1; Deadline: May 2. Prize: Grand orize: $8,000, a trip to the Writer's Digest Conference, promotion in *Writer's Digest*, 10 copies of the book will be sent to major review houses, and a guaranteed review in *Midwest Book Review*; 1st place (9 winners): $1,000 and promotion in *Writer's Digest*; Honorable mentions: $50 worth of Writer's Digest Books and promotion on www.writersdigest.com. All entrants will receive a brief commentary from one of the judges.

WRITER'S DIGEST SELF-PUBLISHED E-BOOK AWARDS

Writer's Digest, 10151 Carver Rd., Suite #200, Blue Ash OH 45242. (715)445-4612, ext. 13430. **E-mail:** WritersDigestSelfPublishingCompetition@fwmedia.com. **Website:** www.writersdigest.com. **Contact:** Nicole Howard. Contest open to all English-language, self-published e-books for which the authors have paid the full cost of publication, or the cost of publication has been paid for by a grant or as part of a prize. Categories include: mainstream/literary fiction, genre fiction, nonfiction (includes reference books), inspirational (spiritual/new age), life stories (biographies/autobiographies/family histories/memoirs), children's books, poetry, and middle-grade/young adult books. Judges reserve the right to re-categorize entries. Judges reserve the right to withhold prizes in any category. All winners will be notified by December 31. Entrants must enter online. Entrants may provide a file of the book or submit entry by the Amazon gifting process. Acceptable file types include: .epub, .mobi, .ipa. Word processing documents will not be accepted. Entries will be evaluated on content, writing quality, and overall quality of production and appearance. Books must have been published within the past 5 years from the competition deadline. Books that have previously won awards from *Writer's Digest* are not eligible. Early bird deadline: August 1; Deadline: September 19. Prizes: Grand prize: $3,000, promotion in *Writer's Digest*, a full 250-word (minimum) editorial review, $200 worth of Writer's Digest Books, and more; 1st place (9 winners): $1,000 and promotion

in *Writer's Digest*; Honorable mentions: $50 worth of Writer's Digest Books and promotion on www.writersdigest.com. All entrants will receive a brief commentary from one of the judges.

WRITERS-EDITORS NETWORK INTERNATIONAL WRITING COMPETITION

CNW Publishing, P.O. Box A, North Stratford NH 03590-0167. **E-mail:** contestentry@writers-editors.com, info@writers-editors.com. **Website:** www.writers-editors.com. **Contact:** Dana K. Cassell, executive director. Annual award to recognize publishable talent. New categories and awards as of 2016: nonfiction (unpublished or self-published; may be an article, blog post, essay/opinion piece, column, nonfiction book chapter, children's article, or book chapter); fiction (unpublished or self-published; may be a short story, novel chapter, young adult, or children's story or book chapter); poetry (unpublished or self-published; may be traditional or free verse poetry or children's verse). Guidelines available online. Open to any writer. Maximum length: 4,000 words. Accepts inquiries by e-mail, phone, and mail. Entry form online. Results announced May 31. Winners notified by mail and posted on website. Results available for SASE or visit website. Deadline: March 15. Prize: 1st place: $150 plus one year Writers-Editors membership; 2nd place: $100; 3rd place: $75. All winners and honorable mentions will receive certificates as warranted. Most Promising entry in each category will receive a free critique by a contest judge. Judged by editors, librarians, and writers.

○ WRITERS' GUILD OF ALBERTA AWARDS

Writers' Guild of Alberta, Percy Page Centre, 11759 Groat Rd., Edmonton AB T5M 3K6, Canada. (780)422-8174. **Fax:** (780)422-2663. **E-mail:** mail@writersguild.ca. **Website:** writersguild.ca. **Contact:** Executive Director. Offers the following awards: Wilfrid Eggleston Award for Nonfiction; Georges Bugnet Award for Fiction; Howard O'Hagan Award for Short Story; Stephan G. Stephansson Award for Poetry; R. Ross Annett Award for Children's Literature; Gwen Pharis Ringwood Award for Drama; Jon Whyte Memorial Essay Award; James H. Gray Award for Short Nonfiction. Eligible entries will have been published anywhere in the world between January 1 and December 31 of the current year. The authors must have been residents of Alberta for at least 12 of the 18 months prior to December 31. Unpublished mss, except in the drama and essay categories, are not eligible. Anthologies are not eligible. Works may be submitted by authors, publishers, or any interested parties. Deadline: December 31. Prize: Winning authors receive $1,500; short piece prize winners receive $700.

WRITERS' LEAGUE OF TEXAS BOOK AWARDS

Writers' League of Texas, 611 S. Congress Ave., Suite 200A-3, Austin TX 78704. (512)499-8914. **Fax:** (512)499-0441. **E-mail:** sara@writersleague.org. **Website:** www.writersleague.org. Open to Texas authors of books published the previous year. Authors are required to show proof of Texas residency (current or past), but are not required to be members of the Writers' League of Texas. Deadline: Open to submissions from October 1 to January 15. Prize: $1,000 and a commemorative award.

WRITING CONFERENCE WRITING CONTESTS

P.O. Box 664, Ottawa KS 66067-0664. (785)242-2947. **Fax:** (785)242-2473. **E-mail:** jbushman@writingconference.com, support@studentq.com. **Website:** www.writingconference.com. **Contact:** John H. Bushman, contest director. Unpublished submissions only. Submissions made by the author or teacher. Purpose of contest: To further writing by students with awards for narration, exposition, and poetry at the elementary, middle school, and high school levels. Deadline: January 8. Prize: Awards plaque and publication of winning entry online, April issue. Judged by a panel of teachers.

YEARBOOK EXCELLENCE CONTEST

100 Adler Journalism Building, Iowa City IA 52242-2004. (319)335-3457. **Fax:** (319)335-3989. **E-mail:** quill-scroll@uiowa.edu. **Website:** www.quilland-scroll.org. **Contact:** Vanessa Shelton, executive director. High school students who are contributors to or staff members of a student yearbook at any public or private high school are invited to enter the competition. Awards will be made in each of the 18 divisions. There are two enrollment categories: Class A: more than 750 students; Class B: 749 or fewer. Winners will receive Quill and Scroll's National Award Gold Key and, if seniors, are eligible to apply for one of the Edward J. Nell Memorial or George and Ophelia Gallup scholarships. Open to students whose schools have Quill and Scroll charters. Previously published submissions only. Submissions made by the author or school yearbook adviser. Must be published in the 12-month span prior to contest deadline. Visit website for list of current and previous winners. Purpose is to recognize and reward student journalists for their work in yearbooks and to provide student winners an opportunity to apply for a scholarship to be used freshman year in college for students planning to major in journalism. Deadline: November 1.

YOUNG READER'S CHOICE AWARD

E-mail: hbray@missoula.lib.mt.us. **Website:** www.pnla.org. **Contact:** Honore Bray, president. The Pacific Northwest Library Association's Young Reader's Choice Award is the oldest children's choice award in the US and Canada. Nominations are taken only from children, teachers, parents, and librarians in the Pacific Northwest: Alaska, Alberta, British Columbia, Idaho, Montana, and Washington. Nominations will not be accepted from publishers. Nominations may include fiction, nonfiction, graphic novels, anime, and manga. Nominated titles are those published 3 years prior to the award year. Deadline: February 1. Books will be judged on popularity with readers. Age appropriateness will be considered when choosing which of the three divisions a book is placed. Other considerations may include reading enjoyment; reading level; interest level; genre representation; gender representation; racial diversity; diversity of social, political, economic, or religions viewpoints; regional consideration; effectiveness of expression; and imagination. The Pacific Northwest Library Association is committed to intellectual freedom and diversity of ideas. No title will be excluded because of race, nationality, religion, gender, sexual orientation, political, or social view of either the author or the material.

THE YOUTH HONOR AWARDS

Skipping Stones Youth Honor Awards, Skipping Stones Magazine, *Skipping Stones Magazine*, P.O. Box 3939, Eugene OR 97403. (541)342-4956. **E-mail:** info@skippingstones.org, editor@skippingstones.org. **Website:** www.skippingstones.org. **Contact:** Arun N. Toke, editor and publisher. *Skipping Stones* is an international, literary, and multicultural children's magazine that encourages cooperation, creativity, and celebration of cultural and linguistic diversity. It explores stewardship of the ecological and social webs that nurture us. It offers a forum for communication among children from different lands and backgrounds. *Skipping Stones* expands horizons in a playful, creative way. This is a non-commercial, non-profit magazine with no advertisements. In its 28th year. Original writing and art from youth, ages 7-17, should be typed or neatly handwritten. The entries should be appropriate for ages 7-17. Prose fewer than 1,000 words; poems fewer than 30 lines. Non-English and bilingual writings are welcome. To promote multicultural, international and nature awareness. Deadline: June 25. Prize: An Honor Award Certificate, a subscription to *Skipping Stones* and 5 nature and/or multicultural books. They are also invited to join the Student Review Board. Everyone who enters the contest receives the autumn issue featuring the 10 winners and other noteworthy entries. Judged by editors and interns at the *Skipping Stones* magazine.

Youth awards are for children only; you must be under 18 years of age to qualify.

ANNA ZORNIO MEMORIAL CHILDREN'S THEATRE PLAYWRITING COMPETITION

University of New Hampshire, Department of Theatre and Dance, PCAC, 30 Academic Way, Durham NH 03824. (603)862-3038. **Fax:** (603)862-0298. **E-mail:** mike.wood@unh.edu. **Website:** cola.unh.edu/theatre-dance/progra/anna-zornio-childrens-theatre-playwriting-award. **Contact:** Michael Wood. Offered every 4 years for unpublished well-written plays or musicals appropriate for young audiences with a maximum length of 60 minutes. May submit more than 1 play, but not more than 3. Honors the late Anna Zornio, an alumna of The University of New Hampshire, for dedication to and inspiration of playwriting for young people, grades K-12. Deadline: March. Prize: $500.

SUBJECT INDEX

ARTS/CRAFTS

BIOGRAPHY

CAREERS

HISTORY NONFICTION

HOBBIES

MULTICULTURAL NONFICTION

MUSIC/DANCE

NATURE/ENVIRONMENT

NATURE/ENVIRONMENT NONFICTION

POETRY

EDITOR & AGENT NAMES INDEX

Agency) 286

Edgecombe, Lindsay (Levine Greenberg Rostan Literary Agency, Inc.) 276

Egan-Miller, Danielle (Browne & Miller Literary Associates, LLC) 243

Einstein, Susanna (Einstein Literary Management) 256

Eisenman, Leigh (HSG Agency) 270

Elblonk, Matthew (DeFiore & Co. Literary Management, Inc.) 251

Elkstrom, Rachel (Irene Goodman Literary Agency) 265

Ellison, Nicholas (Sanford J. Greenbuger Associates, Inc.) 267

Ellenberg, Ethan (Ethan Ellenberg Literary Agency) 256

Endrulat, Harry (The Rights Factory) 289

Epstein, Linda (Emerald City Literary Agency) 258

Evans, Mary (Mary Evans Inc.) 257

Evans, Stephanie (Fineprint Literary Management) 258

Faderin, Kemi (Dystel & Goderich Literary Management) 255

Fargis, Alison (Stonesong) 295

Farstad, Colin (DeFiore & Co. Literary Management, Inc.) 251

Faust, Katherine (Curtis Brown, Ltd.) 241

Faust, Jessica (Bookends Literary Agency) 238

Fehr, Don (Trident Media Group) 300

Ferrara, Moe (Bookends Literary Agency) 238

Filina, Olga (The Rights Factory) 289

Finch, Diana (Diana Finch Literary Agency) 257

Fine, Celeste (Sterling Lord Literistic, Inc.) 278

Finkelstein, Jesse (Transatlantic Literary Agency) 298

Fitzhenry, Sharon (Fitzhenry & Whiteside, Ltd.) 203

Flaherty, Heather (The Bent Agency) 237

Flannery, Jennifer (Flannery Literary) 258

Flashman, Melissa (Trident Media Group) 300

Flum, Caitie (Liza Dawson Associates) 249

Flynn, Jacqueline (Joelle Delbourgo Associates, Inc.) 252

Forland, Emily (Brandt & Hochman Literary Agents, Inc.) 240

Forrer, David (Inkwell Management, LLC) 271

Forrie, Allan (Thistledown Press Ltd.) 210

Foster, Roz (Sandra Dijkstra Literary Agency) 253

Fox, Diana (Fox Literary) 261

Fraser-Bub, MacKenzie (Fraser-Bub Literary, LLC) 261

Fraser, Stephen (The Jennifer De Chiara Literary Agency) 251

Frederick, Holly (Curtis Brown, Ltd.) 241

Freet, Roger (Foundry Literary + Media) 260

Fretwell-Hill, Stephanie (Red Fox Literary) 287

Freymann, Sarah Jane (Sarah Jane Freymann Literary Agency) 261

Fried, Rachael (Sanford J. Greenbuger Associates, Inc.) 267

Friedman, Phil (Scholastic Library Publishing) 186

Friedman, Rebecca (Rebcca Friedman Literary Agency) 262

Friedstein, Adam (Anderson Literary Management, LLC) 236

Froman, Craig (Master Books) 170

Fugate, David (Launchbooks Literary Agency) 275

Fury, Louise (The Bent Agency) 237

Galit, Lauren (LKG Agency) 277

Gallagher, Lisa (DeFiore & Co. Literary Management, Inc.) 251

Gallt, Nancy (Nancy Gallt Literary Agency) 264

Gaule, mary (Mary Evans Inc.) 257

Gayle, Nadeen (Serendipity Literary Agency, LLC) 292

Gelbman, Leslie (Berkley/NAL) 145

Gelfman, Jane (Gelfman Schneider/ICM Partners) 264

Gendell, Yfat Reiss (Foundry Literary + Media) 260

Getzler, Josh (HSG Agency) 270

Gerety, Emily (Pants on Fire Press) 176

Ghahremani, Taylor (Full Circle Literary, LLC) 263

Ginsberg, Peter (Curtis Brown, Ltd.) 241

Ginsberg, Susan (Writers House) 304

Giovinazzo, Elena (Pippin Properties, Inc.) 286

Glick, Stacy Kendall (Dystel & Goderich Literary Management) 255

Goderich, Miriam (Dystel & Goderich Literary

Hogrebe, Christina (Jane Rotrosen Agency, LLC) 290

Horrmann, Markus (Regal Hoffman & Associates, LLC) 288

Holland, Joyce (D4eo Literary Agency) 248

Hoogland, Michael (Dystel & Goderich Literary Management) 255

Hosier, Erin (Dunow, Carlson, & Lerner Agency) 254

Hovemann, Glenn (Dawn Publications) 153

Howard, Marilyn (Creative Freelancers, Inc.) 305

Howell, Pam (D4eo Literary Agency) 248

Howland, Carrie (Donadio & Olson, Inc.) 253

Hubbard, Mandy (Emerald City Literary Agency) 258

Hughes, Amy (Dunow, Carlson, & Lerner Agency) 254

Hunter, Kristy (The Knight Agency) 273

Hurley, Alexis (Inkwell Management, LLC) 271

Hwang, Annie (Folio Literary Management, LLC) 258

Jacks, Nathaniel (Inkwell Management, LLC) 271

Jackson, Eleanor (Dunow, Carlson, & Lerner Agency) 254

Jackson, Heather (David Black Literary Agency) 238

Jain, Amanda (Inklings Literary Agency) 271

Jaffa, Molly (Folio Literary Management, LLC) 258

James, Nicole (Chalberg & Sussman) 245

Jeglinski, Melissa (The Knight Agency) 273

Johns, Chelcee (Serendipity Literary Agency, LLC) 292

Johnson, Brianne (Writers House) 304

Johnson, Michelle (Inklings Literary Agency) 271

Johnson-Blalock, Jennifer (Liza Dawson Associates) 249

Kahan, Alex (Nomad Press) 174

Kahn, Jody (Brandt & Hochman Literary Agents, Inc.) 240

Kaiser, Cecily (Phaidon Press) 179

Kaplan, Deborah (Razorbill) 183

Kardon, Julia (Mary Evans Inc.) 257

Karmatz-Rudy, Caryn (DeFiore & Co. Literary Management, Inc.) 251

Kasdin, Steve (Curtis Brown, Ltd.) 241

Kenny, Julia (Dunow, Carlson, & Lerner Agency) 254

Kenshole, Fiona (Transatlantic Literary Agency) 298

Kepner, Chris (Victoria Sanders & Associates) 292

Keyes, Emily S. (Fuse Literary) 263

Kietlinski, Teresa (Bookmark Literary) 239

Kim, Emily Sylvan (Prospect Agency) 286

Kimber, Natalie (The Rights Factory) 289

Kirschbaum, Larry (Waxman Leavell Literary Agency, Inc.) 301

Kirtland, Kim-Mei (Howard Morhaim Literary Agency) 283

Kleinman, Jeff (Folio Literary Management, LLC) 258

Klinger, Harvey (Harvey Klinger, Inc.) 273

Knapp, Peter (New Leaf Literary & Media, Inc.) 285

Knight, Deidre (The Knight Agency) 273

Knowlton, Ginger (Curtis Brown, Ltd.) 241

Knowlton, Timothy (Curtis Brown, Ltd.) 241

Kong, Kelvin (The Rights Factory) 289

Kotchman, Katie (Don Congdon Associates Inc.) 246

Kracht, Elizabeth (Kimberly Cameron & Associates) 244

Kreit, Eileen Bishop (Puffin Books) 182

Krienke, Mary (Sterling Lord Literistic, Inc.) 278

Kriss, Miriam (Irene Goodman Literary Agency) 265

Kroll, Edite (Edite Kroll Literary Agency, Inc.) 275

Krysan, Alan E. (Windward Publishing) 195

Kukla, Lauren (Mighty Media Press) 171

Kye-Casella, Maura (Don Congdon Associates Inc.) 246

Lakosil, Natalie (Bradford Literary Agency) 239

Lamba, Marie (The Jennifer De Chiara Literary Agency) 251

Lange, Heide (Sanford J. Greenbuger Associates, Inc.) 267

Larson, Ellen (The Poisoned Pencil) 181

LaPolla, Sarah (Bradford Literary Agency) 239

Latshaw, Katherine (Folio Literary Management, LLC) 258

Laughran, Jennifer (Andrea Brown literary Agency, Inc.) 243

AGE-LEVEL INDEX

YOUNG ADULT

AGE-LEVEL INDEX

PHOTOGRAPHY INDEX

ILLUSTRATION INDEX

MAGAZINES

GENERAL INDEX